CW01647942

Machiavelli's Broken World

Machiavelli's Broken World

JOHN M. NAJEMY

OXFORD
UNIVERSITY PRESS

OXFORD
UNIVERSITY PRESS

Great Clarendon Street, Oxford, OX2 6DP,
United Kingdom

Oxford University Press is a department of the University of Oxford.
It furthers the University's objective of excellence in research, scholarship,
and education by publishing worldwide. Oxford is a registered trade mark of
Oxford University Press in the UK and in certain other countries

© John M. Najemy 2022

The moral rights of the author have been asserted

First Edition published in 2022

Impression: 1

All rights reserved. No part of this publication may be reproduced, stored in
a retrieval system, or transmitted, in any form or by any means, without the
prior permission in writing of Oxford University Press, or as expressly permitted
by law, by licence or under terms agreed with the appropriate reprographics
rights organization. Enquiries concerning reproduction outside the scope of the
above should be sent to the Rights Department, Oxford University Press, at the
address above

You must not circulate this work in any other form
and you must impose this same condition on any acquirer

Published in the United States of America by Oxford University Press
198 Madison Avenue, New York, NY 10016, United States of America

British Library Cataloguing in Publication Data
Data available

Library of Congress Control Number: 2021948088

ISBN 978–0–19–958092–7

DOI: 10.1093/oso/9780199580927.001.0001

Printed and bound in Great Britain by
Clays Ltd, Elcograf S.p.A.

Links to third party websites are provided by Oxford in good faith and
for information only. Oxford disclaims any responsibility for the materials
contained in any third party website referenced in this work.

To Amy

Preface

In the almost thirty years since I published a study of how Machiavelli's epistolary dialogue with Francesco Vettori shaped the intellectual context in which he wrote *The Prince*, much new scholarship and critical reflection have significantly expanded and enriched the landscape of Machiavelli studies. Continuing unabated, this rich outpouring of original and stimulating work is eloquent testimony to the enduring fascination and importance of Machiavelli. Now, after years devoted to the history of Florence, I return to Machiavelli and to an aspect of his thought that has received less attention than I believe it merits: the centrality of history, and particularly of Italian history, in his political theory. Machiavelli was acutely aware of living through a time of crisis and calamity in Italy's history, and his works are suffused with expressions of both anguish and accusation over its suffering. But he also sought to understand and explain the causes of Italy's agonies. What I offer here is an inquiry into his assessment of the origins and authors of the crises that afflicted his Italy. The role of antiquity in his thought is universally recognized: Machiavelli repeatedly affirms Greek and Roman history as a touchstone of political judgment. Less studied is his critical analysis of Italy's modern history, which, far from a repository of examples to support his theories and hypotheses, was the ground on which he built them.

Machiavelli points unhesitatingly to the failures of Italy's princes, popes, and condottieri, condemning their irresponsibility and corruption. Indeed, if we ask what Italian prince, prelate, republican leader, or professional soldier of his time or of the fifteenth century he unambiguously admired, it is difficult to find one: not Cosimo or Lorenzo de' Medici or Francesco Sforza or Julius II or even, as I will try to persuade skeptical readers, Cesare Borgia. I can think of only one: Antonio Giacomini, who is little known except to specialists (on him see Chapter 1). But Machiavelli went beyond assessing the failures of individuals. His more profound contribution was to expose the flawed social and institutional contexts that produced these failures. He identified the interests and ambitions motivating the collective actors who contributed to Italy's calamities, focusing in particular on the role of the elite and noble classes which produced Italy's political, military, and ecclesiastical leaders. Not least among the claims for Machiavelli's originality is his tight linkage of the social and the political, his insistence on making the social the framework for comprehending the political and asking how social structures and competing collective interests conditioned politics, power, and government. The centrality of these social divisions in Machiavelli's reading of Roman history is widely acknowledged, less so in his understanding of Italian history.

This study is grounded in the conviction that Machiavelli can be understood only in his own terms and language. It is no less true for being a truism that translations distort (and betray, as one says in Italian), some, of course, more than others. Machiavelli's words often meant quite different things from what the same or similar-looking words mean in modern Italian, to say nothing of their faux amis in English, in part because only with difficulty can translations account for Machiavelli's tendency to invest terms with technical value or meaning, as Fredi Chiappelli showed long ago in his *Studi sul linguaggio del Machiavelli* (Florence: Felice le Monnier, 1952), and in part because words mean different things depending on the company they keep with other words. We who write about Machiavelli in other languages must translate his texts as best we can, and in these pages the translations are my own. But I also frequently include next to the translations the words he wrote, sometimes with brief explanations of how meanings vary according to context for terms such as *stato*, *autorità*, *rispetti*, *generosità*, *abietto*, *accidenti*, *scandalo*, *onesto*, *prudenzia*, *imperio*, and of course the family of *ordini*, *ordinario*, *ordinato*, *straordinario*, and many others. In requesting the patience of benevolent readers confronted with many interpolated bits of Machiavelli's texts, I also offer them the chance to assess and critique my readings. Whatever the judgment, I believe it essential, as far as possible, to focus on how Machiavelli said things in his own language.

I have finished this book in the dreadful pandemic of 2020–1. Before it descended upon us, I had already selected its title, which translates "questo guasto mondo" from the introductory chapter of book five of the *Florentine Histories*, an expression, among many others, of Machiavelli's anguish over the wreckage of broken institutions, corruption, and lost liberty in his Italy—anguish that, sadly, now seems applicable to our own breaking world, and not only because of the pandemic. Yet, amid so much loss, the pleasure of fellowship within the shared enterprise of Machiavelli studies remains vibrant. I happily acknowledge the friendship and intellectual companionship (alas, for now only remote) of Jérémie Barthas, Erica Benner, Robert Black, Alison Brown, Andrea Guidi, Anthony Molho, and Gabriele Pedullà. I thank former OUP editor Christopher Wheeler for the invitation to undertake the project, Oxford University Press and editor Cathryn Steele for patiently awaiting and graciously accepting a long overdue manuscript, two outside readers for their thoughtful comments and critiques, and Timothy Beck for his patience and good cheer in the copyediting process. Last and best, I dedicate this book with love, admiration, and gratitude to my wife, Amy Bloch, whose moral support and steady encouragement sustain me and whose sage advice over the years and astute scrutiny of the manuscript have helped me see things more clearly.

JN

Guilderland, New York
August 2021

Contents

Abbreviations of Frequently Cited Works of Machiavelli

A	"Ambizione," in *Capitoli. Introduzione, testo critico e commentario*, ed. Giorgio Inglese (Rome: Bulzoni, 1981), pp. 143–9.
AG	*Arte della guerra*, ed. Denis Fachard and Giorgio Masi, in Machiavelli *L'Arte della guerra. Scritti politici minori*, ed. Jean-Jacques Marchand, Denis Fachard, and Giorgio Masi (Rome: Salerno Editrice, 2001).
D^1	*Decennale primo*, ed. Antonio Corsaro, in *SPP*, pp. 13–51.
D^2	*Decennale secondo*, ed. Antonio Corsaro, in *SPP*, pp. 52–65.
Discursus	*Discursus florentinarum rerum post mortem iunioris Laurentii Medices*, ed. Jean-Jacques Marchand, in *SPM*, pp. 621–41.
DL	*Discorsi sopra la prima deca di Tito Livio*, ed. Giorgio Inglese (Milan: Rizzoli, 1984).
	Discorsi sopra la prima deca di Tito Livio, ed. Francesco Bausi, 2 vols. (Rome: Salerno Editrice, 2001).
IF	*Istorie fiorentine*, ed. Alessandro Montevecchi and Carlo Varotti, 2 vols., in *OS* (Rome: Salerno Editrice, 2010).
LCSG	*Legazioni. Commissarie, Scritti di governo*, 7 vols. (Rome: Salerno Editrice, 2002–11). Editors of individual volumes are identified in the first citation of each volume.
Lettere	*Opere di Niccolò Machiavelli*, vol. 3, ed. Franco Gaeta (Turin: UTET, 1984).
OS	*Opere storiche*, ed. Alessandro Montevecchi, Carlo Varotti, and Gian Mario Anselmi, 2 vols. (Rome: Salerno Editrice, 2010).
P	*Il principe*, ed. Giorgio Inglese (Turin: Einaudi, 1995).
SPM	*Scritti politici minori*, ed. Jean-Jacques Marchand, in *L'Arte della guerra. Scritti politici minori*, ed. Jean-Jacques Marchand, Denis Fachard, and Giorgio Masi (Rome: Salerno Editrice, 2001).
SPP	*Scritti in poesia e in prosa*, ed. A. Corsaro, P. Cosentino, E. Cutinelli-Rèndina, F. Grazzini, N. Marcelli, F. Bausi (Rome: Salerno Editrice, 2012).

1

The Travails of Italy Viewed from the Chancery

From his earliest writings during the chancery years through all his major works, Machiavelli displayed an unsparing critique of Italy's leaders and elites—a critique that ranged between searching analysis and emotional condemnation. He perceived Italy as victimized as much by its own princes, governments, Church, and military leaders as by foreign armies, and, consequently, as mired in a crisis from which there was no escape without a radical rethinking of the structures of politics and social organization. Italy's misfortunes at the hands of its own elites were always foremost in his thinking. It will be useful to recall some of the famous passages in which the scars left by the deep anguish Machiavelli felt over Italy's suffering are plainly visible.

In chapter 12 of *The Prince* he bemoans Italy's degradation by foreign armies in harrowingly emotional language, describing the peninsula as "overrun by Charles, despoiled by Louis, violated by Ferdinand, and humiliated by the Swiss [corsa da Carlo, predata da Luigi, sforzata da Ferrando e vituperata da' Svizzeri]." In the same chapter, he expresses agreement with the unnamed critic—probably the Dominican Girolamo Savonarola, whose apocalyptic preaching deeply influenced the Florentines in the 1490s—"who said our sins were the cause" of the disaster. He "spoke the truth," Machiavelli comments, but only in part, he adds, because the sins were not the ones he had supposed; they were instead the "sins of princes," who "have suffered the punishment for them" (*P* 12.9, 31).[1] "Princes" here stands for governments and governors of all kinds, from the republics of Venice and Florence to the dukes of Milan, the de facto signori of cities (particularly in the States of the Church), the kings of Naples, and of course the popes. Although Machiavelli also criticizes the European monarchs, especially Louis XII of France, whose errors cost him his Italian conquests and Florence its republic, it is the Italian "princes" who bear the chief responsibility for an Italy "overrun," "despoiled," "violated," and "humiliated." In chapter 24 he assigns the responsibility for this unforgiveable catastrophe to "these princes of ours," whom he excoriates for accusing fortune, instead of their own indolence ("ignavia," a moral deficiency), for the loss of their states (*P* 24.8). In chapter 26, the "Exhortation to Take Hold of

[1] Passages from *The Prince* are cited in the text with the abbreviation *P* followed by chapter number and sentence number(s) from the edition by Giorgio Inglese (see list of abbreviations).

Machiavelli's Broken World. John M. Najemy, Oxford University Press. © John M. Najemy 2022.
DOI: 10.1093/oso/9780199580927.003.0001

Italy and Restore Her in Liberty from the Barbarians," he famously decries Italy's subjection to a slavery worse than that of the biblical Hebrews in Egypt: a land "without leadership, without order, beaten, despoiled, lacerated, overrun," exposed to "every sort of ruin," almost "lifeless," covered with "wounds" and "long-festering sores" (*P* 26.3–5). At the end of the "Exhortation," Machiavelli quotes the stirring lines of Petrarch's "Italia mia" that foresee the victory of valor ("virtú") over wild fury ("furore") and express confidence in the "ancient valor of Italian hearts [l'antico valore nelli italici cor]" that "is not yet extinguished." Petrarch's poem begins, however, with a lament that his "speech"—his poetry—is helpless to heal the "mortal wounds [piaghe mortali]" that he sees on the "fair body" of his Italy. Machiavelli may have had these verses in mind in picturing Italy as "beaten, despoiled, lacerated, overrun," and disfigured by "wounds" and "long-festering sores."[2]

In the proem to book 2 of the *Discourses on Livy*, pondering how one can determine whether antiquity was superior to the modern age (as many humanists had asserted), Machiavelli ventures the theory that collective virtú had been transmitted from one ancient empire to another until all the world's virtú became concentrated in Rome. After Rome's fall, however, virtú fragmented and dispersed among many nations, including the kingdom of the Franks, the kingdom of the Turks, that of the "Soldano" (the Mameluke kingdom of Egypt), the people of Germany, and, "earlier," the "Saracen sect" (the first wave of Muslim expansion), which "did such great things and occupied so much of the world after destroying the eastern Roman Empire." All these countries and peoples possessed, and some still possess, a share of this virtú, and the peoples of those nations would be wrong to praise past times over the present. But Italy and Greece, Machiavelli says, received no part of Rome's virtú, and their inhabitants have every "right to condemn their own times and praise ancient times, because those ancient times had many things that make them marvelous and admirable," whereas in these modern times "there is nothing that redeems their extreme misery, infamy, and shame, in which there is no observance of religion, or law, or military duty; they are instead stained with every sort of filth." Machiavelli's theoretical ruminations on world history now yield to savage denunciation of Italy's governing classes. "And these vices are all the more detestable insofar as they are found in those who occupy seats of judgment, who exercise command over everyone and expect to be worshipped [in coloro che seggono *pro tribunali*, comandano a ciascuno e vogliono essere adorati]" (*DL* 2.proemio.12–17),[3] in other words, in princes and governors, military captains, judges, and, as the desire to be "worshipped" suggests, priests

[2] Francesco Bausi explores the echoes of Petrarch in *Prince* 26 in "Petrarca, Machiavelli, Il *Principe*," in *Niccolò Machiavelli politico storico letterato*, ed. Jean-Jacques Marchand (Rome: Salerno Editrice, 1996), pp. 41–58.

[3] Passages from the *Discourses on Livy* are cited in the text with the abbreviation *DL* followed by book number, chapter number (or proem), and sentence number(s) from the editions by Giorgio Inglese and Francesco Bausi (see list of abbreviations).

and popes. Here again is Machiavelli's barely controlled anger over the failures of Italy's governing classes that he had expressed in chapters 12, 24, and 26 of *The Prince*. At the end of the proem of book 2, claiming "not to know whether, in praising the times of the ancient Romans and condemning our own," he "deserves to be included among those who deceive themselves," Machiavelli sets aside the theory of the migration of virtú and declares: "In truth, if the virtú that reigned [in antiquity] and the vice that now reigns were not clearer than the sun, I would be more restrained in my assertions.... But because the matter is so evident that everyone sees it, I will be bold in openly saying what I understand of those times and of these, so that the spirits of the young who will read these writings of mine can escape these [present] times and prepare themselves to imitate those ancient times, whenever fortune might give them the opportunity" (*DL* 2.proemio.22–4).

A similar condemnation of Italy's leaders appears in the opening chapter of book 5 of the *Florentine Histories*, where Machiavelli revisits the question with a different set of historical assumptions but arrives at the same conclusion. In some of the cities that emerged after the collapse of the Roman Empire, he says, there arose "so much virtú" that, although none was strong enough to dominate the others, they were, nonetheless, sufficiently united and well organized that they succeeded in "liberating and defending" Italy from the "barbarians." This alludes to the resistance of the medieval city-states against the attempts of the Hohenstaufen Holy Roman Emperors to impose imperial hegemony in the twelfth and thirteenth centuries. Although the "virtú" of these new states failed to produce an era of durable peace—because none was able to dominate the others—neither was it a time of dangerous or savage wars. Machiavelli here indulges, as he often does, his overstated critique of Italian warfare as not worthy even of the name, because "they cannot be called wars if combatants are not killed, cities not sacked, and states not destroyed. Those wars sank into such weakness that they were begun without fear, conducted without danger, and concluded without harm." To be sure, fifteenth-century wars in Italy were, for the most part, nowhere near as violent and destructive as those that began with the French invasion of 1494. But Machiavelli's exaggeration of the feebleness of pre-1494 Italian warfare allowed him, once again, to denounce the failures of Italy's princes and military captains. Whereas elsewhere virtú was destroyed by long periods of peace, in Italy, by contrast, it was "extinguished by the cowardice" of these wars. Machiavelli forewarns his readers—as they commence the second half of the *Histories*—that this debility of Italian arms will become clear from his narrative of events between 1434 (the year Cosimo de' Medici and his faction took the reins of power in Florence) and 1494 (the year of the first French invasion and the expulsion of the Medici). Readers will see, he says, how at the end of this period "the way was again opened to the barbarians and Italy was placed in bondage to them"; they will see also, "to their great astonishment, how many noble peoples were shackled [tenuti in freno] by such weak and badly administered arms." The implication is that Italy's rulers not only failed to protect the peninsula from foreign invaders but also robbed their own peoples of liberty and arms. Italy's dysfunctional military organization had political causes and consequences, and knowledge of these failures, Machiavelli insists, is as valuable as stories of ancient valor and greatness. He concludes the chapter by emphasizing the utility of learning the history of this political and military malpractice: "If, in the description of the events of this broken world [questo guasto mondo], there are no tales of soldiers' bravery or military commanders' skill or citizens' love of country," readers will instead "see with what deceptions, cunning, and artifice princes, soldiers, and leaders of republics conducted themselves in order to maintain reputations they did not deserve. This is, perhaps, no less useful than learning about ancient deeds; for if the latter can inspire noble-minded spirits to emulation," an account of the deficiencies of the broken modern world will inspire them "to shun and extinguish" its failings (*IF* 5.1.8–14).[4]

Still another expression of Machiavelli's anguish over Italy's calamitous recent history and his anger against its ruling elites appears in the conclusion of the *Art of War*. Machiavelli has the dialogue's main speaker, the famed mercenary captain Fabrizio Colonna, deliver an impassioned castigation of Italy's princes. Explaining why Italian soldiers are inferior to the Swiss and Spaniards, Fabrizio lays the blame at the feet of Italy's princes. The Italians, he says, lack good military organization ("ordine") because they do not have "wise princes." That they are the "disgrace of the world [il vituperio del mondo]" is not the fault of the people, "but of their princes, who" (as Machiavelli says in *Prince* 12) "have been punished for it." For their "ignoranza" (ignorance, neglect, lack of awareness) they have suffered "just retribution in losing their states ignominiously." As confirmation of their failure, Fabrizio invites his interlocutors to consider the wars that have occurred in Italy since the arrival of the French in 1494. War, he says, usually makes men bellicose and brings them renown; yet, the greater and fiercer the recent wars of this time, the more they diminished the reputation of both soldiers and leaders (*AG* 7.229–32).[5] The princes' "ignoranza" lured them into a fool's paradise. With bitter sarcasm, Fabrizio—but surely we have Machiavelli's voice here—indicts Italy's princes for devoting themselves exclusively to the appurtenances, privileges, and frivolities of their princely status while "ignoring" the duty to defend their states. Before "our Italian princes tasted the blows of war" from the north, Machiavelli has Fabrizio say, "they believed it was sufficient to be able to think up a clever riposte in their studies; to write an elegant letter; to display wit and

[4] Passages from the *Florentine Histories* are cited in the text with the abbreviation *IF* followed by book number, chapter, and sentence number(s) from the edition by Alessandro Montevecchi and Carlo Varotti (see list of abbreviations).

[5] Passages from *The Art of War* are cited in the text with the abbreviation *AG* followed by book number and sentence number(s) from the edition by Denis Fachard and Giorgio Masi (see list of abbreviations).

quickness in speech; to know how to concoct a scam; to adorn oneself with precious stones and gold; to slumber and dine in greater luxury than anyone else; to keep plentiful lascivious pleasures at hand; to treat one's subjects with avarice and arrogance; to become enfeebled in indolence; to award military promotions in return for favors; to display contempt if anyone showed some praiseworthy way [of doing things differently]; and to want their words to be accepted as the responses of oracles" and hence never to be questioned. This long, angry list of the deficiencies of Italy's princes is a ferocious condemnation of the style and culture of the fifteenth-century princely courts and perhaps also of the leaders of the republics. Fabrizio makes this multitude of failings the enabling cause of the disaster that began in 1494, because "the wretches did not realize that they were readying themselves to be the prey of whoever attacked them. From this came, in 1494, the overwhelming panic, the sudden flights, and the astonishing collapses. Thus were three very powerful states that existed in Italy repeatedly sacked and laid waste" (Naples by the French in 1494 and later by the Spaniards; Milan by the French in 1499 and again in 1515; and Venice in 1509 by French and imperial armies in an alliance supported by Pope Julius II). "Worse yet," says Fabrizio, is that the princes who still survive in Italy continue on the same erroneous path and live in the same "disorder" as their heedless fifteenth-century predecessors (*AG* 7.236–8). Italy's tragedy was both historical and current. The last sentence of the *Florentine Histories* laments the inability of Italy's princes to either satisfy or curb the "ambition" of Milan's Ludovico Sforza, from which "came the evil seeds that ruined, and are still ruining, Italy" (*IF* 8.36.24–5).

Machiavelli wrote these major works (and his plays and much poetry) in an astonishingly productive thirteen-year period following the collapse of the Florentine republic in 1512 and his dismissal from the chancery posts from which he had witnessed, and reported on, the disasters first-hand. In the chancery years (1498–1512) his close encounters with the major players of Italian and European politics, his role in negotiations with foreign governments, and his proximity to decision-making in his own republic, in other Italian states, France, the Holy Roman Empire, and the papacy gave Machiavelli a view of things permitted to few political thinkers of his time. He himself emphasized this direct experience as one of the two sources of his knowledge of politics, the other being his life-long reading of ancient (and modern) history (and poetry). The dedicatory letter of *The Prince* famously identifies the foundation of his "knowledge of the actions of powerful men" in the combination of his "lunga esperienza" of modern things and "constant reading [lezione] of ancient things" (*P* Ded.2). In the dedicatory letter of the *Discourses* he similarly declares that the book contains what he had learned from "long experience [pratica] and constant reading of the things of the world" (*DL* Ded.2). The "constant reading of ancient things" alludes to Machiavelli's humanist education and his deep (if not professionally polished) immersion in ancient literature and history. The combination of political experience and humanist culture was by no means unique to Machiavelli. In addition to numerous fifteenth-century examples, many of his contemporaries, including Francesco Guicciardini, Baldesar Castiglione, and Francesco Vettori (whose famous two-year correspondence with Machiavelli in 1513–15 surrounded and conditioned the composition of *The Prince*), could have claimed the same twin sources as the soil in which their understanding of the political world grew. In Machiavelli's case, however, the end of his "lunga esperienza" of contemporary events gave his writing career an altogether different character from those of these three contemporaries. Relegated to the status of persona non grata by the Medici regime that replaced the republic in 1512, he lost the direct connection to politics and power that he had enjoyed for almost fifteen years. For a time the Medici mistrusted him, no doubt because of his prominence in the republican government. His attempts to win their favor in 1513 failed; few sought his advice or opinions; and, to his chagrin, no one (excepting, at the outset, Vettori and, later, the circle that met in the Rucellai gardens, the Orti Oricellari) paid much attention to him until his partial reacceptance into the good graces of the regime provided important contacts, a few commissions, and the contract, approved by Cardinal Giulio de' Medici in 1520, to write the *Florentine Histories*.

From the end of 1512 to 1519, however, Machiavelli was largely ignored. In these years he belonged to no faction or political group. Because of his loyal collaboration with Piero Soderini, the lifetime standard-bearer of justice of the republic that kept the Medici in exile for eighteen years, he was suspect to their regime, so much so that, on the flimsiest bit of (non)evidence, he was accused of involvement in a plot against them and suffered arrest, imprisonment, and torture. Once released in March 1513, he was forbidden to leave the Florentine dominion or, except once when summoned, to enter the palace of the Signoria that had been his workplace for fifteen years. Thereafter, as he began to write, he had to be—and was, for the most part—cautious. As Cardinal Giovanni de' Medici, who became Pope Leo X that same month, his brother Giuliano, and their nephew Lorenzo consolidated their control, they gradually had less reason to be suspicious of him. He was free to write, provided he avoided, as he did, open polemics (camouflaged ones were another matter) and kept his distance from conspiracies against the regime. These were years of relative isolation in which he was beholden to no one—in the service of no government or powerful patron. Hence, they were also years of a considerable degree of intellectual freedom that allowed him to interrogate the political world and assess its dilemmas in his own terms, in ways that were not available to Guicciardini, Castiglione, or Vettori, who all had more or less uninterrupted careers in the service of princes and Medici popes. In the *proemio* of the *Dialogo del Reggimento di Firenze*, written in the early 1520s, Guicciardini acknowledged "the very great and extraordinary debts" he had with the Medici family, and especially its two popes, having been "employed and exceedingly honored by them as one in whom they have had…supreme trust."[6] Castiglione's whole life was devoted to service, as courtier and ambassador, in the courts of Mantua and Urbino and the papacy of Clement VII (Giulio de' Medici). The difficulty of speaking truth to princes is a prominent theme in the conversations of *Il Cortegiano*. In book 4 Ottaviano Fregoso, asked what instruction he would give a prince whose favor and trust he enjoys, laughs and says: "If I had the favor of some princes I know and freely told them my opinion, I would, I fear, soon lose that favor."[7] Francesco Vettori made a smooth transition from the republic to the restored Medici, becoming Florentine ambassador to the papal court in early 1513, just as Cardinal Giovanni ascended the throne, and two years later one of the younger Lorenzo's chief advisers. For Machiavelli, however, his former close association with Piero Soderini and the fallen republic made any similar soft landing impossible. But the isolation he endured, and the independence he gained in return, allowed him, as Guicciardini put it in a 1521 letter commenting on Machiavelli's unorthodox ideas about religion, to challenge conventional beliefs with his "contraria professione." Machiavelli did not disagree; in his reply, he confirmed Guicciardini's judgment and even expanded the range of his habitual rejection of common opinion from religion to "many other things": "True it is, and I know it, that I am opposed [contrario], as in many other things, to the opinions of my fellow citizens."[8]

After his ordeal in the winter of 1512–13, Machiavelli wrote all or most of *The Prince* within the next year or so, first "addressing" it to Giuliano and then "dedicating" it to the younger Lorenzo, in the (fruitless) hope of gaining their attention and favor. He was one of several Florentines who offered advice to Florence's new rulers, although none wrote anything as substantial or memorable or innovative as his *Prince*. Francesco Vettori's brother Paolo penned a memorandum ("Ricordi") to Cardinal Giovanni[9] (it has been intriguingly suggested that Machiavelli may have co-authored it),[10] Similar memoranda came to the Medici

[6] Francesco Guicciardini, *Dialogo del Reggimento di Firenze*, in Guicciardini, *Opere*, ed. Emanuela Lugnani Scarano (Turin: UTET, 1970), vol. 1, pp. 301–2.

[7] Baldesar Castiglione, *Il Cortegiano*, ed. Bruno Maier (Turin: UTET, 1955), p. 479. On this theme in *The Courtier*, see my "Arms and Letters: The Crisis of Courtly Culture in the Wars of Italy," in *Italy and the European Powers: The Impact of War, 1500–1530*, ed. Christine Shaw (Leiden: Brill, 2006), pp. 207–38.

[8] *Lettere*, pp. 519–20. On the 1521 correspondence with Guicciardini, see my "Amici: Machiavelli e Guicciardini nelle guerre d'Italia," in *Atlante della letteratura italiana*, ed. Sergio Luzzatto and Gabriele Pedullà, vol. 1, *Dalle Origini al Rinascimento*, ed. Amedeo de Vincentiis (Turin: Einaudi, 2010), pp. 774–80.

[9] "Ricordi di Paolo Vettori al cardinale de' Medici sopra le cose di Firenze," in Rudolf von Albertini, *Firenze dalla repubblica al principato. Storia e coscienza politica* (Turin: Einaudi, 1970), pp. 22–4, 357–9.

[10] Mikael Hörnqvist, "Approaching the Medici: Machiavelli as Co-author of Paolo Vettori's *Ricordi* of 1512?," in *Florence and Beyond: Culture, Society and Politics in Renaissance Italy*, ed. David S. Peterson with Daniel E. Bornstein (Toronto: Centre for Reformation and Renaissance Studies, 2008), pp. 399–417.

over the next few years from Francesco Guicciardini,[11] his nephew Niccolò,[12] and Lodovico Alamanni.[13] They were all, in the parlance of the time, "friends" of the Medici and members of the elite class of ottimati who accepted, in some cases welcomed, and were admitted into the new order of things. Machiavelli's circumstances, by contrast, were more delicate. The Medici shunned him and he remained in official disfavor. For this reason, he declined Francesco Vettori's invitation to visit him in Rome, fearing that, if he called upon the exiled Soderini who was then living there, as loyalty and decorum would have required, he might face arrest upon his return to Florence.[14] Machiavelli's awkward situation made prudence imperative in any writings he wanted the Medici to see, first and foremost *The Prince*. Unflattering or critical judgments of persons who were, or had been, allies of the Medici, not to speak of course of the Medici themselves, required a degree of dissimulation. The need for caution was particularly acute given that, beyond the formal dedication, it was from Pope Leo that Machiavelli hoped his words would find a favorable reception. It was in this awkward mix of freedom and restraint that, in the years after 1512, he addressed the calamity that had befallen Italy.

Machiavelli's situation had of course been very different during the years of government service, when frequent negotiations with the major protagonists of Italian and European politics and daily involvement in the dilemmas and crises of Florence's territorial dominion gave him a view of contemporary history unparalleled in his time. From the beginning of his service in 1498, he held two positions. As head of the second chancery, he conveyed instructions from the magistracy of the Ten, who managed the republic's military and security policies, to the civilian commissioners who supervised the military captains and condottieri, to the officials who represented Florentine authority in the towns and cities of the dominion, and to the inhabitants of the same. Machiavelli thus coordinated the functions of all the above in the dominion's security arrangements. In his other major role, as secretary to the Ten, he was sent as an envoy or emissary (*mandatario*) on missions, called legations (*legazioni*), to the governments of other Italian states, including the papacy, and to the courts of France and the Holy Roman Empire. Machiavelli never held the rank of ambassador (*oratore*), but his role as *mandatario*, less ceremonial and lacking the authority to sign treaties, was actually of greater significance in conducting confidential negotiations, conveying his government's intentions, gathering intelligence, often in secret, identifying useful sources, interpreting the objectives of both allies and enemies, and reporting, in frequent and lengthy dispatches back to the Ten, what he learned from the rulers and secretaries, ministers, and various agents with whom he spoke.

[11] In *Dialogo e discorsi del reggimento di Firenze*, ed. Roberto Palmarocchi (Bari: Laterza, 1932), pp. 267–81.

[12] Albertini, *Firenze dalla repubblica*, pp. 365–75.

[13] Albertini, *Firenze dalla repubblica*, pp. 376–84.

[14] *Lettere*, p. 427.

As head of the second chancery, Machiavelli came face to face with the vulnerabilities of Florence's territorial state, its precarious hold on the subject territories, and its inadequate military resources. In 1498 he sent a stream of memoranda and exhortations to commissioners, condottieri, and dominion towns as Florence confronted the incursion by a coalition of enemies seeking to restore Piero de' Medici to power. In 1501 Cesare Borgia invaded Florentine territory and, while promising no harm, allowed his condottiere Vitellozzo Vitelli to conduct damaging raids. In 1502 the same Vitellozzo Vitelli invaded the southeastern sector of the dominion, occupying the city of Arezzo and the Valdichiana to the south. Only the intervention of troops sent by King Louis XII of France compelled Vitelli's withdrawal. This was a particularly dangerous crisis because Vitelli brought with him the exiled Piero de' Medici, who attempted to rouse the population in support of a restoration of Medici rule. Machiavelli was closely involved in arranging Vitelli's expulsion by French forces, handling a rogue French captain, and coordinating the restoration of Florentine authority over the territories with commissioners who included Piero Soderini (just before his election as lifetime standard-bearer). His duties sometimes took him into the dominion, as, for example, in 1500, when he served as secretary to commissioners overseeing military operations against Pisa, which had broken away from Florentine rule when the French invaded in 1494. In 1501 the government sent him several times to Pistoia to investigate factional conflicts that were endangering the dominion's northern border. Florence's vulnerability to foreign invasion and to raids and incursions by the likes of Borgia, Vitelli, and their allies impressed upon Machiavelli the need for stronger, homegrown military forces. His growing awareness of the need to "provide for arms" matured into the plan for the militia that he urged on Piero Soderini in 1504–5 and which, over the objections of ottimati who feared putting arms in the hands of either the city's working class or the inhabitants of the dominion, he succeeded in getting approved in 1506. His chancery experience here led to a major, and controversial, institutional innovation that became a pillar of his political theory.[15]

As envoy of the Ten, in little over fourteen years Machiavelli was sent on some forty missions during which he experienced the instability of the Italian states, ravaged by foreign invaders and occupiers, victimized by each other's rapacity and treachery, and betrayed by their own princes' inability and incompetence to protect them. His first years in the chancery were dominated by the momentous convulsions caused by the 1499 invasion by Louis XII. Louis's irruption into what had been a precarious balance among the major states of Italy—Milan, Venice, Florence, the States of the Church, and the kingdom of Naples—changed

[15] Jérémie Barthas, "'Altra volta ne ragionai a lungo': A Reinterpretation of Niccolò Machiavelli's Cryptic Clause in *The Prince*," in *The Art and Language of Power in Renaissance Florence: Essays for Alison Brown*, ed. Amy R. Bloch, Carolyn James, and Camilla Russell (Toronto: Centre for Reformation and Renaissance Studies, 2019), pp. 155–86.

everything in more, and more profound, ways than the invasion of his predecessor Charles VIII in 1494. Louis subjected the duchy of Milan to French rule, and the Venetian republic, which had vied over more than a century with the Visconti and Sforza dukes of Milan for dominance in the great plain that stretches across northern Italy, joined the French king's campaign to share in the territorial spoils of the division of the Milanese state. Machiavelli spent most of the second half of 1500 at Louis's court in central France seeking assurances for Florence's security and assistance in recovering Pisa. Louis's other objective was the kingdom of Naples. In 1500 he agreed to divide the southern kingdom with Spain, which already controlled Sicily. By the next year, the independent kingdom of Naples was no more, and within three years the Spaniards pushed the French completely out of the South. Louis also allied with the Borgia pope, Alexander VI, whose grandiose ambition to impose his family's power throughout central Italy centered on the creation of a Borgia principality in the volatile Romagna region, a project entrusted to his son Cesare to whom Louis promised support and arms. Borgia ambitions threatened Florence most of all, and Machiavelli was twice sent as envoy to Cesare to assess his aims and strength. In a series of lightning attacks in 1500–2 Borgia seized most of the cities in the Romagna and on the central Adriatic coast, took Urbino, and chased Duke Guidobaldo, son of the legendary Federico da Montefeltro, into exile. Cesare's chief military captains, among them Vitellozzo Vitelli and members of the Roman baronial family of the Orsini, began to fear his expanding power and in 1502 conspired to liquidate him. Feigning reconciliation, Cesare lured them into a trap and had them all killed. Machiavelli was with Borgia when this occurred, and the suddenness and brutality of the event made a deep impression on him that he recorded in *The Prince*. But the death of Pope Alexander in 1503 quickly brought about the collapse of the ephemeral Borgia principality. Machiavelli was sent to Rome to observe and report on Cesare's futile attempt to salvage his house of cards and also to gauge the intentions and temperament of the new pope, Giuliano della Rovere, who took the portentous name of Julius II. Aiming to extend papal power over the whole of the patchwork construct of the States of the Church, Julius launched a campaign in 1506 to remove, or at least disempower, the lords of Perugia and Bologna and regain control of the Romagna cities that Cesare Borgia had seized five and six years earlier. The Ten sent Machiavelli to accompany Julius and observe this undertaking that threatened to destabilize the entire peninsula, chiefly because Julius's territorial objectives brought him into conflict with Venice, which regarded the Romagna as being in its own sphere of influence. The explosive pope enlisted King Louis in an alliance to punish Venice, and the ensuing war in 1509 temporarily, but devastatingly, destroyed Venetian power on the Italian mainland. Julius then turned his ire against France, and the Florentines, fearful of being caught between Julius and Louis, sent Machiavelli to France again, in 1510, to urge the French to desist from demanding that Florence join France in the war that everyone knew was coming. Julius, now enraged at both Louis and Florence, the latter for not allying with him to "liberate" Italy, as he famously said, from the "barbarians," brought Venice, Spain, and the Swiss into an alliance that drove the French from Italy in 1512. This left Florence exposed to Julius's revenge, which came in the form of a Spanish army that descended on Tuscany, sacked the city of Prato, and supported the anti-Soderini ottimati in dismantling the republic and restoring the Medici to power. Within two months, the new Medici regime terminated Machiavelli's positions in the chancery. In his official capacity Machiavelli had witnessed and often been directly at the scene of many of the critical events of this continuous twelve-year series of cataclysms that utterly disfigured Italy.

"FORTUNE HAS NOT PUT AN END TO ITALY'S STRIFE"

Chancery custom did not permit Machiavelli to comment directly or extensively on the republic's dominion or foreign policies, and certainly not on its domestic politics. He was a civil servant who held his posts at the pleasure of the committees and councils of Florentine government. As such, and especially in the opinion of those ottimati who were antagonistic to the republic and, after 1502, to its leader Piero Soderini, Machiavelli was not to express judgments or critique the views of the republic's governors. But he found it difficult to adhere to these restrictions and occasionally expressed opinions in his dispatches that irritated members of the political leadership. On one occasion that we know of—no doubt there were others—he had to be warned to adhere to the discretion expected of chancery officials. In October 1502, during his three-month legation to Cesare Borgia, his chancery colleague Biagio Buonaccorsi—than whom Machiavelli had no more loyal or devoted friend—wrote to say that, in his view (and presumably that of others), Machiavelli had "made too bold a conclusion" in assessing that Borgia's forces were such that the conspirators who were plotting against him could no longer harm him. "It seems to me—not that, as far as I know, you've received any criticism for this," Buonaccorsi wrote, "—that you can't make such a definitive judgment [che voi non ne possiate fare iudicio così resoluto]," because, writing from Borgia's camp, Machiavelli could not have had reliable information about his enemies' forces. Therefore, Buonaccorsi concluded, "once you have prudently and meticulously discussed what you observe, leave the judgment of things to others [del iudicio rimetetevene a altri]."[16]

Yet Machiavelli found opportunities to express judgments, assessments, and criticisms of what he saw as the errors or misguided aims of Italy's governments, his own included. His humanist education provided the literary skills, historical

[16] *Lettere*, pp. 137–8.

knowledge, and cultural perspectives for such critiques. His early absorption of the humanist reverence for antiquity, particularly the conviction that the moderns should look to the ancients for lessons to help them govern and defend their polities, always remained with him. But it was not without ambivalence. Writing after the invasions and the occupation of much of Italy by foreigners—the "barbarous domination that stinks in everyone's nostrils," as he puts it in *Prince* 26.28—he found it impossible to recycle the celebratory rhetoric of fifteenth-century humanism. Emulating the ancients was now more problematic: he believed that modern Italians had failed to do so wisely and profitably. Italy's new reality shattered illusions about an easy, far less an already accomplished, revival of ancient virtues, especially Roman political virtues. Yet his emotional declaration that "the ancient valor in Italian hearts is not yet dead"—part conviction, part wish—demonstrates that, even in his darkest hours Machiavelli did not relinquish the hope of the recovery, nurtured by attention to the experience of the ancients, of a strong and self-reliant Italy. Aware of the yawning abyss between antiquity—especially the idealized antiquity of Renaissance imagination that seemed ever more remote—and a modern world that failed to make profitable use of ancient history, he experienced the yearning for that glorious past simultaneously as both inspiration and frustration. The promise of what antiquity could teach the moderns never lost its seductive power for him, even as he developed critical approaches to knowing the past and writing history.

Works of ancient history provided the material for comparisons and interpretations. Although Machiavelli was primarily focused on pressing issues of administration and diplomacy during the years of government service, bits of evidence attest to his strong, almost reflexive, turn to ancient history for comparisons that could shed light on contemporary events. In October 1502, while he was at Cesare Borgia's camp in Imola, he wrote to Biagio Buonaccorsi asking for a copy of Plutarch's *Lives* (which had received various, sometimes partial, translations into Latin in the fifteenth century as well as a vernacular translation printed in 1482). Machiavelli's request is lost, but in his reply Buonaccorsi wrote: "We've tried searching for some copies of the *Lives* of Plutarch, and we find none for sale in Florence. Be patient: we'll have to write to Venice."[17] That this was not Machiavelli's only request for books while he was away is suggested by Buonaccorsi's jocular complaint: "But damn you, really, for asking for so many things."[18]

From his literary culture, especially his immersion in ancient Latin and vernacular Tuscan poetry, Machiavelli acquired a finely honed capacity for figurative

[17] According to Corrado Vivanti (Machiavelli, *Opere*, 3 vols., ed. C. Vivanti, [Turin: Einaudi-Gallimard, 1999], vol. 2, p. 1477), there were no printed copies of the *Lives* in Florence in the fifteenth century, but several in Venice. On the 1482 vernacular translation, see Virgilio Costa, "Sulle prime traduzioni italiane a stampa delle opere di Plutarco (secc. XV–XVI)," in *Volgarizzare e tradurre dall'Umanesimo all'età contemporanea*, ed. Maria Accame (Tivoli: Edizioni TORED, 2012), pp. 83–107, esp. 84–8.

[18] *Lettere*, p. 129.

language, equivocality, allegory, and irony, all of which made poetry a fertile genre for political critique and also gave a poetic quality to much of his prose. We have recently learned much about the echoes in his writings of Lucretius, whose *De rerum natura* he copied in its entirety sometime before entering the chancery.[19] Letters to Machiavelli from chancery colleagues occasionally give glimpses of the classical literary culture they shared. Particularly revealing are the letters of Agostino Vespucci, Machiavelli's outspoken chancery assistant ("coadiutore"), who sometimes wrote all or parts of his private letters to Machiavelli in Latin, lacing them with classical allusions and quotations. From Rome in July 1501, he treated Machiavelli to gossip about the wine-fueled parties of their mutual friends and a mocking diatribe against Pope Alexander. Rumors of a Turkish invasion, Vespucci wrote, were causing the pope to sigh and say, seemingly in desperation, "Heu quae me tellus, que me equora possunt accipere? [Alas, what land, what seas can accept me now?]"—a quotation from the speech in Virgil's *Aeneid* (2.69–70) in which the Greek spy Sinon tricks the Trojans into believing he had been persecuted and banished by the Greeks and that the wooden horse was an offering to the gods. Vespucci does not identify the source or context of the quotation, evidently assuming Machiavelli would understand that it associated Alexander with fraud and deceit. With a quotation from Cicero (*Letters to Atticus* 9.10.6) whose source Vespucci similarly does not specify, he accuses the pope of "playing the part of Sulla"—the Roman warlord who led the army of the senatorial party in the civil war—"proscribing more people every day [sullaturit et proscripturit]," confiscating possessions, sentencing enemies to death or forced labor, and encouraging his "barons and friends" to commit similar outrages. Turning the pope's reported fear of a Turkish invasion into the only hope of eradicating the Borgia plague, Vespucci concludes the diatribe by asserting that, "since Christians aren't lifting a finger, the Turks will, it seems, have to remove this scum from human company: all right-thinking persons say so unanimously."[20] Through classical literary allusions, Vespucci conveyed a scathing denunciation of Alexander that he knew Machiavelli understood and shared.

Machiavelli's poetic compositions from the chancery years include the first *Decennale* ("Decade") and the *Capitoli*, the poems on "fortune," "ingratitude," and "ambition." The *Decennale*, written in late 1504, became his first published work in 1506. It consists of 550 verses that narrate Italy's vicissitudes in the ten years following the French invasion of 1494. Although written in the rhymed tercets (*terza rima*) of Dante's *Commedia*, its opening lines echo the solemn beginning of Virgil's great epic, the *Aeneid*, the story of Aeneas's predestined but stormy journey from ruined Troy to Italy. Virgil "sings" of "arms and of the man" who first

[19] Alison Brown, *The Return of Lucretius to Renaissance Florence* (Cambridge, Mass.: Harvard University Press, 2010), pp. 68–87.

[20] *Lettere*, p. 106.

came from Troy to Italian shores, "an exile by fate…much buffeted by violence from above," but who successfully pursues and fulfills his heroic duty to found Rome. The *Decennale* can be read as a dystopic converse of the *Aeneid*. Machiavelli "will sing of the travails of Italy [io canterò l'italice fatiche] / that occurred in the past decade under stars inimical to her well-being" (*D*^{1} 1–3),[21] an allusion to the invasions and wars that demolished several Italian states and inflicted a level of violence previously unknown in Italy. Despite evoking the *Aeneid*'s somber opening lines, Machiavelli quickly reveals the very different outcome of his story: whereas Aeneas' struggles with fate and the gods culminate in his reaching Italy and preparing the foundation of mighty Rome, the *Decennale* narrates the "mountainous and swampy warpaths full of blood and the dead" and the "discord" that opened the way for the invaders and permitted "barbaric hordes to overrun" Italy (D^1 4–5, 16–18). There are no heroes in the *Decennale* (with one possible exception: see below, pp. 36–37), no redemption of a suffering Italy. Nor is the mournful account of the decade's events subsumed under impersonal forces of history or attributed to either nature or the times. Machiavelli identifies the chief protagonists—individuals, families (sometimes with plays on their names), republics, princes, popes, and military captains—and leaves no doubt about who did what to bring Italy to its lamentable state. He is, for obvious reasons, rather harsher on deceased protagonists than on living ones, but no one (again, with one exception) escapes some degree of censure.

Beginning with the French invasion of 1494, the narrative underscores the consequences for Florence: "All Tuscany was thrown into confusion, and you"—Machiavelli apostrophizes the Florentines—"lost Pisa and the territories the Medici family gave" to the French, a reference to Piero de' Medici's hasty and unauthorized surrender to Charles VIII of key fortresses in the western part of the dominion. This reckless action triggered the uprising in Florence that exiled Piero and his brothers. Yet, because these losses "broke apart your territorial dominion [el vostro stato guasto] and you saw your city in great danger, you were unable to rejoice, as you should have, at being freed of the burden [basto: the yoke of the Medici regime] that kept you oppressed for sixty years" (*D*^{1} 22–9). Piero makes one more appearance in the poem, as Florence's "great rebel," instigated by Venice to attempt (in 1497) to overthrow the Florentine republic and restore the Medici regime by force of arms—a shocking episode, the poem says with mordant irony, that "gave birth to…the burial [ne nacque…la sepoltura] of five citizens" (*D*^{1} 151–3) convicted and executed for conspiring with Piero.

Florence itself earns mixed judgments. On the one hand, its display of "unity in defense of its freedom" (in 1494) persuaded the French to leave the city (*D*^{1} 34–9).

[21] Numbered verses of the *Decennale*, abbreviated as *D*^{1} (see list of abbreviations), are cited from the edition by Antonio Corsaro in *SPP*, pp. 16–51. Another edition with useful notes is in Machiavelli, *Opere*, ed. Vivanti, vol. 1, pp. 93–107, 814–26.

With their "new constitution [nuovi ordin]" created after the expulsion of the Medici—above all the Great Council—the Florentines "founded" a "stato popular [popular government]" (D^1 70–2). Machiavelli does not mention here (as he will in *The Prince* and the *Discourses on Livy*) Savonarola's crucial role in urging the Florentines to reform their government. In fact, his comment on the influential preacher, inserted later in the poem after the episode of Piero de' Medici's attempted coup, is one of scathing irony. "What offended many [citizens] even more"—more, presumably, than Piero's assault—"and caused disunity amongst you was that faction [scola: school] under whose banner your city lay. I speak of the great Savonarola, who, inspired by divine power [virtú], kept you bound with his words [parola: preaching]. But because many feared to see their patria ruined little by little under his prophetic teaching, no way of restoring unity amongst you could be found unless his divine light either became brighter or was extinguished by a greater fire [spento…con maggior foco]" (D^1 154–65), "maggior foco" referring to the friar's fiery end at the stake. Machiavelli implies that Savonarola caused intolerable division in the city with preaching so powerful that it seemed inspired by the Almighty and that the only escape from this discord was either for Savonarola's power to increase or for the Florentines to eliminate him, as they did. Machiavelli thus suggests that there was something dangerously destabilizing about the way Savonarola combined religious prophecy with politics. The poem goes on to assert that Florence's acceptance of French protection and assistance against Pisa "made you obsequious and abject" and "your government [stato] unable to make firm decisions" (D^1 280–8). "You were without arms," living "a caso"—without firm direction—"and were always fearful of being undefended if danger threatened" (D^1 319–24). Florence, Machiavelli continues, had to call upon the French to end the rebellion of Arezzo and the Valdichiana, incited and led by Vitellozzo Vitelli with the Borgias behind him (and accompanied by Piero de' Medici). This "grievous wound" (D^1 331–9) was preceded and followed by many failed attempts to regain Pisa, even with French support (D^1 370–2)—until five years after the composition of the *Decennale*.

As he does in the *Florentine Histories*, so also in the *Decennale* Machiavelli identifies Ludovico Sforza of Milan ("il Moro") as the "principal agent [primo motor] of your affliction" ("your" here presumably indicating all Italy) for having invited Charles VIII to pursue his claim to the Neapolitan throne. Seeing the magnitude and ease of French conquests, Ludovico realized "his obvious foolishness [stultizia certa]" and "feared falling into the very ditch he himself had dug with so much sweat" (D^1 49–54). Knowing he could not resist the French himself, he assembled a coalition of the pope, the emperor, and (chiefly) Venice (D^1 55–7) to engage the French at Fornovo (July 1495). But the "vigorous and ferocious" French "attacked the Italians with such virtú that they routed them [sopra 'l ventre suo oltre passaro: literally, overran their belly]. The river [Taro] appeared full of blood, men, weapons and horses fallen to the French sword" (D^1 82–90). Machiavelli will include this battle ("il Taro") in *The Prince* (26.19) among others in which wholly Italian armies made a "mala pruova [poor showing]." Actually, there was no clear victor, as both sides suffered heavy losses and the French left Italy. So Ludovico survived his folly, but only for the moment. Four years later, Louis XII made the invasion of Italy and conquest of Milan his first order of business. This time, "with the crown of France at his very gates," Ludovico "fled to save his skin." The French occupied Milan and the western part of the duchy, and Venice "planted its banners without any obstacle" as far as the Adda river and Cremona (D^1 232–7). "As soon as [Louis] returned to France, Milan recalled Ludovico," but the French quickly rushed back and defeated "the Moor, devoid of help." Ludovico "went off, a wretched prisoner, to France" (D^1 250–64). Having ignited the disaster in 1494, Ludovico found no supporters in his hour of need.

The *Decennale* portrays the Venetians as relentlessly seizing territory from other Italian states and expanding their power throughout the peninsula. Before recounting their occupation, in league with the French, of a large chunk of the Milanese duchy (in 1499–1500), Machiavelli notes that, after the French withdrew from Naples (in 1495), King Ferdinand II "handed over to [the Venetians] more than half of Apulia" (including five port cities they had already occupied) in return for their support against the French, "and made them its lord," i.e. transferred formal possession (D^1 100–2). It was the Venetians, in whom "Ambizion had surged" (D^1 142–3), who "led your great rebel [Piero de' Medici, in 1497] to the walls of the city" (D^1 151–3) and sent forces (in 1498) to assist Pisa, "advancing their standard against you [Florentines]." To draw Florentine forces away from Pisa, "la gente Marchesca" (troops of Venice whose patron saint was Mark) invaded the Florentine dominion, "first at Marradi [from the Romagna] and then in the Casentino," north of Arezzo. Florentine forces repulsed them and their allies, "the Orso [Bear: the Orsini] and [the duke of] Urbino," but "after Mark was beaten back in this way, / he made an agreement with [King] Louis in France / to avenge the blow he had suffered." Machiavelli does not specify against whom Venice sought vengeance, but a few lines further on he reveals that "they secretly divided Lombardy with the great Christian king [Louis]." Fear of a Turkish assault finally forced Venice to make peace with Florence and withdraw its forces from Pisa (D^1 181–216).

The *Decennale* devotes much attention to the famous mercenaries of the decade—the Vitelli brothers Paolo and Vitellozzo and, most of all, Cesare Borgia—professional soldiers who were also signori of cities (the Vitelli in Città di Castello, just beyond Florence's eastern border) or, in Borgia's case, duke of the Romagna. Florence hired Paolo Vitelli in 1498 as commander of its forces against Pisa, with high hopes for a quick victory: "because you believed you were fierce, powerful, and sturdy / with the strength of these arms" (D^1 187–8), "you wanted to be seen on the walls of Pisa with the Vitelli standard" (D^1 191–2). Vitelli never gave Florence the desired victory, but he did drive the Venetians from the Casentino

(D^1 196–202), after which Florence sent him back to resume the siege of Pisa. But a month was wasted "sanz'alcun frutto [with no success]," because, the poem says, "Fortune cruelly opposed the promising start." But Machiavelli immediately clarifies that it was Vitelli's treachery, not Fortune, that sabotaged the campaign: "Long would it take to recount all the wrongs, all the acts of treachery [l'inganni] that occurred in that siege," in addition to the deadly "fever that killed so many citizens." Convinced that Vitelli had betrayed them, the Florentines withdrew their army, arrested him, and "took revenge, sentencing him to death / for the great harm he caused" (D^1 219–31). But they paid dearly for this swift punishment, when (in 1502) "you were without arms, and stood in great fear of the Calf's one remaining horn [pel corno ch'al Vitel era rimaso]," namely, Paolo's brother Vitellozzo, who, "full of hatred for you / because of his brother's bitter torment, sparked the rebellion of Arezzo / through betrayal, and the entire Valdichiana / and the other cities snatched from you in an instant" (D^1 319–36). To heal the "grievous wound" and "free you from so savage an assault, you called in the French" (D^1 337–42) to force Vitellozzo out of Arezzo (D^1 349–54). Machiavelli omits to mention what all contemporaries knew, namely that Piero de' Medici accompanied Vitellozzo into Arezzo and the Valdichiana, magnifying the dilemma Florence faced from maintaining control of the dominion territories to preserving the republic itself. Immediately following Vitellozzo's occupation of Arezzo, the situation became even more dire as Cesare Borgia "seized the duchy of Urbino in a single leap," leaving the Florentines "with their hearts and souls in suspense," fearful that Borgia might join his forces with Vitellozzo's "and with him descend upon you to do you harm" (D^1 343–8).

The first mention of Borgia in the *Decennale* occurs in connection with Charles VIII's campaign to seize the Neapolitan kingdom and claim it for the French crown. In the first of the poem's reproaches against the Borgias, Machiavelli says that Charles, despite his alliance with Pope Alexander, did not trust him and insisted on taking Cesare with him—in effect, as a hostage—to ensure his father's support in the campaign. Although Alexander initially encouraged King Alfonso to resist the French, he now sided with the invaders and, as Machiavelli bluntly puts it, "did not trouble himself with the shame" of having betrayed Alfonso (D^1 40–5). As the French were returning north after their easy victory, Cesare "fled" from the French army, angering the king (D^1 63). When Louis XII ascended the throne, Alexander, knowing "that on his own he could not / accomplish any great thing [cosa magna], / sought the new king's favor / approved his divorce" (from Jeanne, daughter of Louis XI and sister of Charles VIII, which allowed him to marry Charles's widow, Anne of Brittany) "and gave him Brittany." Machiavelli omits the detail that it was Cesare who personally delivered to Louis the bull announcing the divorce, but he does say that, "in return, the king promised [Alexander] the lordship [signoria] / and territories [stati] of the Romagna." The "signoria" of the Romagna was not, of course, the king's to give, but the essence of the deal was military support for Cesare's ambitions. "Alexander, bereft / of one to hold his standard high [avendo Alessandro carestia / di chi tenessi la suo 'nsegna eretta]"—because his eldest son, Juan Borgia, was dead—"turned to the son who belonged to the coterie / of the exalted clerics [la setta / de' gran chercuti: the College of Cardinals] and removed him from them, / swapping his cardinal's hat [berretta] for a military cap [cappello]" (D^1 169–80) and making him standard-bearer of the armies of the Church. Cesare had been made a cardinal by his father in 1492, but with Juan gone Alexander's extravagant plans for expanding Borgia power rested instead with the son he had destined for the Church. Did Machiavelli intend a sardonic, mocking sneer at the image of the aged Alexander needing someone to hold his standard "eretta"? And, in light of the Florentine ritual of snatching hats from the heads of boys to extort sexual favors, one wonders if Machiavelli intended a joke at Cesare's expense in picturing Alexander swapping Cesare's "berretta" for a "cappello" to symbolize his new role.[22]

The poem returns to Cesare when King Louis gives him the promised soldiers (1499–1500) for the campaign to "make himself lord of Imola and Forlì / under the banner of the three lilies" of the crown of France (D^1 238–43). Machiavelli thus underscores the dependence on French military assistance of both Cesare and Alexander. In the next campaign (1501), Borgia and his soldiers are said to have accomplished "astonishing feats [mirabil opra], / seizing Faenza in a short time / and turning Romagna upside down." There must be a tinge of irony here, because, as Machiavelli well knew, Faenza actually withstood Borgia's attack for five months;[23] the "astonishing feats," moreover, did not extend to Bologna, where Bentivoglio forces held off "the violent attack of [Cesare's] soldiers" (D^1 289–97). Unable to take Bologna, Borgia invaded the Florentine dominion trying to pressure the Florentines into concessions: "having left [Bologna], he came into Tuscany / re-clothing [or re-covering] himself with your *spoglie*, as he set his *campo* above yours" (D^1 298–300).[24] "Campo" can mean either camp or army, and Machiavelli could be saying that, when Borgia arrived in the Arno valley, he stationed his army near Florence's forces (actually near the town of Campi, suggesting a possible play on words). More ambiguous and intriguing is the preceding verse. "Spoglie" can signify the spoils or booty looted in war, in which case the verse may allude to the plundering of a number of villages and much of the

[22] On hat snatching in Florence, see Michael Rocke, *Forbidden Friendships: Homosexuality and Male Culture in Renaissance Florence* (New York and Oxford: Oxford University Press, 1996), p. 155. On the comic undertones of these verses, see Anna Maria Cabrini, "Intorno al primo 'Decennale'," *Rinascimento* 33 (1993): 69–89 (at 81–2); and Giorgio Bárberi Squarotti, *Machiavelli o la scelta della letteratura* (Rome: Bulzoni, 1987), pp. 97–105.

[23] Gabriele Pepe, *La politica dei Borgia* (Naples: Riccardo Ricciardi Editore, 1945), pp. 170–5.

[24] Corsaro's edition has "ricoprendo," whereas Inglese has "rivestendo"; see Inglese's "Contributo al testo critico dei 'Decennali' di Niccolò Machiavelli," *Annali dell'Istituto Italiano per gli Studi Storici* 8 (1983–4): 115–73.

countryside by Borgia's troops, who, according to the chronicler Piero Parenti,[25] stole 420 pairs of oxen, 80 buffalo, and between 800 and 1,000 mules loaded with cloth, implements, and tools. But "spoglie" also means garments, or clothes, and, figuratively, the verse might be a metaphor for Borgia's changing tactics and comportment, specifically, his oscillation between threats and entreaties. He insisted he was entering the dominion as an ally (which was technically correct, given that he and Florence were both allies of King Louis) and wanted both a formal alliance with Florence and appointment as its captain-general (see Chapter 3). In this reading, Borgia "re-clothed himself" as a Florentine ally, despite the predations suggested by the other meaning of "spoglie." And this suggests yet another possibility. The phrase "rivestirsi delle spoglie altrui" is akin to the familiar locution "ricoprirsi del mantello di altri" ("to cover oneself with the cloak of another"), whose meaning is to excuse oneself by shifting the blame onto others—an act of deception and dishonesty. As we shall see, when Machiavelli met Borgia in 1502, the latter denied, falsely, that his troops had had any part in the acts of plunder in May 1501, which, he claimed, were perpetrated by Vitellozzo Vitelli's soldiers. The verse could indeed encompass all these meanings: simultaneously engaging in plunder while denying that he was responsible for it, Borgia covered himself with the metaphorical cloak of blaming Vitellozzo for seizing the "spoglie" that he, Borgia, and his troops carried off, all the while professing friendship and the desire for alliance with Florence. The next tercet says his tactic of intimidation worked, at least in compelling the Florentines to accept his demands: "in order to escape such afflictions, / unable to do otherwise / you acceded in some part to his wishes" (D^1 301–3), granting the appointment as captain-general and promising a large sum of money. They did so to be rid of him, and neither agreement was ever fulfilled: the appointment remained a dead letter, much to Borgia's chagrin, and the promised sum was never paid.

After asserting that Borgia presented himself to Louis XII to "justify [iustificar] himself" (D^1 353–4) and that he "cleared himself [purgato s'ebbe]" (D^1 382) of his role in Vitelli's occupation of Arezzo and the Valdichiana, the *Decennale* says Borgia wanted to try again to take Bologna. But his own condottieri, chiefly Vitelli and Paolo Orsini, refused to join him. Here, the poem implies, was the origin of the conspiracy hatched against Borgia at Magione (in 1502) by his condottieri. Having until this point referred to some of the poem's protagonists as the animals suggested by their names ("Orso" for Orsini, "Vitel" for Vitelli, "Galli" for the Gauls/French), Machiavelli now introduces animal metaphors to convey the hatred between Borgia and the conspirators: "turned against themselves, these serpents / full of poison began to tear each other / and with their claws and teeth to lacerate one another." Again Machiavelli underscores Borgia's dependence on

[25] Piero di Marco Parenti, *Storia fiorentina II 1496–1502*, ed. Andrea Matucci (Florence: Olschki, 2005), pp. 448–50.

France: "Because it was difficult for him to flee, / to escape the danger he had to / cover himself again with the shield of France [con lo scudo di Francia ricoprirsi]" (D^1 382–93). Here Machiavelli may have been recalling Cesare's elation, expressed to Machiavelli himself in October 1502, upon receiving King Louis's promise of military support for an assault on Bologna: "Imagine," he told Machiavelli, "what kind of reply I shall receive [from the king] for my defense against [the conspirators]."[26] As it happened, the French played no part in the denouement of the drama. With promises of reconciliation and peace, Borgia lured the conspirators into the famous trap at Senigallia: "To snare his enemies with birdlime, / and to draw them into his lair, / this basilisk [bavalischio] sweetly whistled." The basilisk is a mythological reptile whose breath and glance are reputed fatal, and here the sweetness of its whistle suffices easily to lure its victims to their deaths. Oliverotto da Fermo and Vitellozzo Vitelli, "with those Orsini who had been such friends to him, / rushed headlong into his net [rete], / where the Orso lost more than one paw / and the Vitel had the other horn lopped off." Alluding to Borgia's expulsion of two other conspirators from their cities, Giampaolo Baglioni, signore of Perugia, and Pandolfo Petrucci, signore of Siena, Machiavelli adds that "Perugia and Siena also felt the Hydra's flames." Borgia is now likened to another imaginary and hideous creature, the many-headed monster slain by Hercules. Nor was Cardinal Orsini (killed in Rome) "able to escape the miseries of his pitiable family" (D^1 394–408).

But these images of fearsome and grotesque power are undercut by Cesare's ignominious collapse following Alexander's death (August 1503) and the election of Pope Julius II. Because they failed to support the French (in 1503) in the war with Spain over Naples, Alexander—characterized as "mascagno [wily, malicious]" (D^1 425)—and Cesare searched for a new ally who "could give them other territories as prey [altri stati in preda]." Addressing the Florentines, Machiavelli says that, "in order not to be their prey, / as you had daily been, / and so that [Cesare] not take possession of Marzocco [Florence], / you hired" a French nobleman and his lances to ensure the city's security and assist in operations against Pisa (D^1 424–38). As relations between Alexander and King Louis deteriorated into "vicious anger [collera maligna]," Cesare and Alexander both became ill, and the latter died (August 1503). Machiavelli mixes irony and devastating sarcasm in recording Alexander's exit from earthly life: "the spirit of the glorious Alexander, / to find its repose, / was taken up among the blessed souls; / his three dear, devoted handmaidens / Lust, Simony, and Cruelty / followed his holy footsteps" (D^1 439–47). The consequences of the pope's death for Cesare were disastrous: "As soon as

[26] Niccolò Machiavelli, *Legazioni. Commissarie. Scritti di governo*, vol. 2, ed. Denis Fachard and Emanuele Cutinelli-Rèndina (Rome: Salerno Editrice, 2003), p. 346. The volumes of the *Legazioni* will be cited with the abbreviation *LCSG*, followed by the volume, document, and sentence number(s).

Alexander was slain by heaven [dal ciel ucciso]"—suggesting that the Almighty himself decided to expunge this embodiment of lust, simony, and cruelty—"the stato [the territorial dominion] of his duke of Valentinois [Cesare] / was broken and divided into many parts. / The Baglioni, Vitelli, Orsini, and the offspring / of Montefeltro [Duke Guidobaldo] returned to their cities, / and Mark [Venice] took Rimini and Faenza. / The Baglioni and Orsini chased [Cesare] back to Rome / to torment him / and re-clothed themselves with his *spoglie*," which, in this case, presumably refers to the wealth and power they deprived him of. At first, the new pope, Julius II, "greatly nourished his hopes,"—deceitfully, as we shall see—and Cesare "believed he would find in others / [namely, Julius] the compassion he never felt within himself" (a paraphrase, as we shall see, of a passage from one of Machiavelli's dispatches from Rome as he witnessed Borgia's downfall). Julius prevented him from escaping and kept him under watch (D^1 463–77). Following him to his final humiliation, the *Decennale* recounts that Julius handed him over to the Spanish viceroy of Naples, "who imposed the penalty [i.e. imprisonment] / merited by a rebel against Christ [un rebellante a Cristo]. / And to abase such great arrogance, / he sent off to Spain, bound and vanquished / the man who formerly made you [Florentines] tremble and Rome cry" (510–16).

Machiavelli was cautious in characterizing the new pope in the *Decennale*, no doubt because Florence hoped for good relations at this early moment of his pontificate. Nonetheless, there are hints of what he must have perceived, during the legation of late 1503 (see Chapter 4), as the perils that would emerge from the combination of the pontiff's choleric temperament and fervid ambition. He "was made gatekeeper [portinar] of Paradise / to alleviate the world's miseries" (D^1 460–2), Machiavelli writes. Disposing of Cesare Borgia could be seen in that light, although Machiavelli makes it clear that Julius did so with treachery and bad faith (D^1 472–4). Near the end of the poem, Machiavelli writes that "the kingdoms and powers are not united, / nor can they be, because the pope [Julius] wants / to heal the Church's wounds" (D^1 526–8)—an early intimation, perhaps, of Julius's role in fomenting division in Italy and Europe, and of the disasters he would inflict on Italy in the pursuit of his ambitions.

The *Decennale*'s most debated verses are about the 1502 Arezzo crisis and its aftermath. The rebellion was one of Florence's "four mortal wounds," the other three being the simultaneous loss of the Valdichiana, the ongoing rebellion of Pisa, and factional mayhem in Pistoia (although it is also possible that the four wounds included the "confusïon [disorientation]" (D^1 362) of the Florentines, with Arezzo and the Valdichiana counted as a single *ferita*). Machiavelli lauds an unnamed Florentine, referred to as "colui," who then "governava el vostro stato" and whose "industria [determination and skill]" secured the arrival "in time" of the indispensable French assistance needed to expel Vitellozzo from Arezzo, and who "healed three of the four wounds," the exception being Pisa. Most critics have agreed with Gennaro Sasso that "colui" is Alamanno Salviati,[27] the influential ottimate who was among the priors of July–August 1502 and, according to Francesco Guicciardini's laudatory account in the *Storie fiorentine*, enjoyed "so much trust and influence [tanta fede ed autorità]" in the Signoria "that one could say he managed everything [governassi ogni cosa]" and brought the Arezzo crisis to a successful conclusion. Even if we discount that Guicciardini married Salviati's daughter in 1508 and began writing the *Storie* that same year or the next, it is curious that no other contemporary source confirms Guicciardini's account or even mentions Salviati's role in the resolution of the crisis. Moreover, verse 357 (left untranslated above) does not necessarily mean that "colui" was "governing" the "state." Despite the great influence Guicciardini attributes to Salviati, no single member of the nine-man Signoria could or would ever have been said to "govern" the republic or the state. Moreover, "stato," in Machiavelli's lexicon, especially at this time, more often refers to Florence's territorial dominion than to the government or "state" (as we use the term). There are, in fact, good reasons for believing that "colui" is actually Piero Soderini. It was Soderini who, as envoy to King Louis, arranged for the military assistance to arrive "in time [a tempo]" (D^1 355); who, as a member of the magistracy of the Ten, contributed to formulating policy concerning both foreign relations and the security of the territorial "stato"; and who, as appointed commissioner, coordinated the operations of the military commanders, oversaw the restoration of the occupied territories, and implemented policy toward Arezzo after its recovery. Soderini was also deeply involved in the pacification of Pistoia from early in 1501. For these reasons, the possibility that these verses are about Piero Soderini should not be dismissed.[28]

What follows these verses, moreover, is clearly about Soderini. In August, as the Arezzo crisis was winding down, the Florentine councils debated and approved a monumental constitutional innovation, adding life tenure to the office of standard-bearer of justice, the first among equals in the Signoria. The election was entrusted to the Great Council, and in September Piero Soderini emerged the winner. The *Decennale* associates Soderini's election with hopes for better times: "The peaceful day having come / when your people, made bold, / created the bearer of their standard, / two horns of its deer" (the image on the Soderini family coat of arms) "were so capable / that on their solid rock" (on their "soda petra," a play on Piero Soderini's name) "you were able to build your peace." But, as Machiavelli knew better than anyone, Soderini soon attracted the hostility of powerful ottimati, including Alamanno Salviati, for not countenancing the more restrictive constitutional reforms they wanted. The final tercet of this section almost certainly reprimands

[27] Gennaro Sasso, "Per alcuni versi del primo «Decennale»," in Sasso, *Machiavelli e gli antichi e altri saggi*, 4 vols. (Milan and Naples: Riccardo Ricciardi, 1987–97), vol. 2, pp. 165–95.

[28] I examine this hypothesis in greater detail in "Machiavelli and Arezzo," in *Renaissance Politics and Culture: Essays in Honour of Robert Black*, ed. Jonathan Davies and John Monfasani (Leiden and Boston: Brill, 2021), pp. 107–38.

Salviati as one who "retreated" from his initial support of the institution of the lifetime gonfaloniership and began opposing Soderini: "And if anyone retreats from this institution [da tal ordine] / for any reason, he cannot be / a good surveyor of this world" (D^1 355–81).

Unlike the *Aeneid*, written when Rome's civil wars finally ended in the Augustan peace, the *Decennale* foresees the continuation of Italy's pain: "Fortune is not yet satisfied / and has not put an end to Italy's strife [italiche lite], / nor has the cause of so many evils been extinguished. The kingdoms and powers are not united, / nor can they be." Machiavelli points to several sources of instability, including, as already noted, Pope Julius's determination to "heal the wounds of the Church"; Venice, characterized as "full of both fear and thirst, / wavering between peace and war; / and you [Florentines]," who "have a just desire" to regain Pisa. The emperor-elect wants to be crowned by the pope, the king of France is smarting from the blow he suffered (in the South), and the king of Spain (now also of Naples) sets snares and traps for his neighbors. "So one can easily see / that if a new fire is lit among them, / the flame will reach to the heavens" (D^1 523–40). The flame of Italy's predictable disaster already burns in Machiavelli: "So my spirit likewise is all aflame, / burdened now with hope and now with fear, / so much so that, bit by bit, it is consumed" (D^1 541–3). Florence's fate remains precarious in the face of Italy's instability and the danger of further conflagrations. The *Decennale* repeatedly castigates the Florentines for the inadequacy of their arms and dependence on the arms of others. It concludes in uncertainty about the future. Addressing the Florentines, Machiavelli says he "desires to know where, freighted / with so many burdens or in what harbor, / your ship must go with these winds" of war. "Yet we have faith in the expert helmsman"—Piero Soderini—"and in the oars, the sails, and the cordage. / But the voyage would be easy and brief / if you reopened the temple of Mars" (D^1 544–50). This famous last line alludes to the militia Machiavelli promoted and was in the process of organizing, recruiting, and training in early 1506 when the *Decennale* received its first authorized printing. The safe "harbor" of the Florentine ship of state is the public militia that, so Machiavelli believed, would allow the Florentines to embrace the military valor the Romans associated with Mars, father of Romulus and the Roman people.

"TWO FURIES SENT TO DEPRIVE US OF PEACE"

Machiavelli's perception of the underlying cause of Italy's troubles is poetically prefigured in the "Capitolo dell'Ambizione,"[29] dedicated to Luigi Guicciardini

[29] "Ambizione" (abbreviated as *A*) is cited by the numbered verses in Giorgio Inglese's edition of the *Capitoli* (see list of abbreviations); another excellent edition, by Nicoletta Marcelli with emendations based on a newly discovered manuscript, is in *SPP*, pp. 106–19 (text) and 517–18 (emendations).

(Francesco's brother) and written while Machiavelli was in Verona, in Venetian territory, between the end of November and the middle of December 1509. The Ten sent him first to Mantua to execute a payment to Emperor Maximilian, and then to Verona to assess the ongoing conflict between Venice and the emperor in the aftermath of Venice's defeat earlier that year (see Chapter 2).[30] The poem addresses the etiology of conflict and the destructive power of war by personifying "Ambizione" and "Avarizia" (the latter in the sense of greed) as two "furies" sent into the world by a "hidden power" (*A* 10–30), accompanied by Envy, Sloth, Hatred, Cruelty, Arrogance, and Deceit, to cast out Concord, Tranquility, Peace, and Love ("Carità") (*A* 37–45). They arrived when humanity still lived simple lives and knew neither "poverty nor riches" (*A* 52–4). The "evil seed" of Ambition filled Cain with its poison and caused the world's "first violent death" (*A* 46–8, 58–60); it then grew, "multiplying the causes of evil" and giving men "no reason to repent of evildoing." In the absence of law or binding compacts ("sanza legge o patto"), the varying fortunes of men led to the constant "fluctuation of every human condition [el varïar d'ogni stato mortale]" (*A* 61–6). This might allude to the general instability of human affairs, but what follows points to Ambition's devastating political effects. "This" (i.e. "varïar") has "many times drawn the kings of France [Questo ha di Francia el re piú volte tratto]": an ambiguous verse that could mean "drawn the kings *from* France [into Italy?]" or led them to desires and actions that damaged their kingdom.[31] The probability of the latter reading is perhaps enhanced by the next two verses: "this has undone the stato of King Alfonso [of Naples], of Lodovico [Sforza], and San Marco," i.e. Venice (*A* 67–9).

The poem changes direction when it raises three questions: "why one people commands and another mourns, even as Ambition reigns everywhere; why France is always victorious" (a verse obviously written after France's victory over Venice in 1509 and before the Swiss defeated the French in 1512) "and, by contrast, all Italy is shattered by a turbulent sea of torments; and why to these lands [Italy, or the Venetian dominion?] has come the suffering [penitenzia] caused by the wicked seed that Ambition and Avarice generate" (*A* 82–90). Machiavelli here emphasizes that different conditions produce different results in different places and that the evil influences of the furies are not inevitably the same or equally distributed. Ambition's grievous power can be tempered either by individual valor—by "a courageous heart and prowess in arms [un cor feroce, una virtute armata]"—or by a people who, having once lived an "unbridled [effrenata] life" (another manuscript has "savage [efferata]") "is educated and organized with good laws and institutions [di buone leggi instrutta et ordinata]" (*A* 91–6). Without such laws and discipline, a people that is both "ambitious and cowardly"

[30] Machiavelli's instructions and dispatches are in *Legazioni. Commissarie. Scritti di governo*, vol. 6, ed. Denis Fachard and Emanuele Cutinelli-Rèndina (Rome: Salerno Editrice, 2011), pp. 371–405.
[31] See Marcelli's observations in *SPP*, p. 111, n. 67.

becomes "servile" and suffers all manner of disaster and ruin: "If cowardice [Viltà] and defective institutions [Tristo ordin] sit aside Ambition, every disaster, every calamity, and every other evil—all will come quickly" (*A* 103–8). The "ordin" of "Tristo ordin" is a collective noun denoting the "ordini," a polity's institutions and norms; it also echoes the Ordinanza, the official name of the public militia Machiavelli organized from the population of Florence's dominion. The critical role of "ordini" in politics, civil society, and military organization would later emerge as the conceptual center of Machiavelli's political thought.

In "Ambizione" Machiavelli rejects explanations from "nature" of Italy's decline: "if someone lays to nature the blame that in Italy, so afflicted and exhausted, men are not born so fierce and rugged, I say this does not excuse or exonerate this Italy[32] of ours, because *educazion* can compensate for what nature lacks" (*A* 109–14). "Educazione" in Machiavelli's lexicon is upbringing as shaped by training, customs, and religion, as well as education in our sense of the term: in sum, socialization in civic norms and duties. "Formerly"—in the ancient past—*educazione* "made Italy flourish and conquer the entire world; rugged [fiera] *educazion* gave it courage" (*A* 115–17). (Ancient Italy, not Rome alone, was the paragon of "fiera educazione.") Although in the 1506 *Ghiribizzi* to Giovanbattista Soderini (see Chapter 4), in the "Capitolo di Fortuna," and in chapter 25 of *The Prince*, Machiavelli asserts that each person's "nature" precludes the ability to adjust to changing times, he never accepted the notion that a people or a political community possesses a similarly unchanging nature that determines, much less pre-determines, historical outcomes. Occasionally, in frustration or anger, he lashed out at the weakness or deficiencies of Florentines or Italians or, in this case, Venice, scolding "Saint Mark" for "learning too late, perhaps in vain, and at great cost to himself, how necessary it is to have a sword, and not a book, in hand" (*A* 166–8). But what Machiavelli castigates is a contingent disposition, a collective weakness caused by the loss, or careless abandonment, of what "educazione" should have firmly instilled in a people. Such failures are, in his understanding, products of history. This is what happened to Italy, which "now lives, if it is life to live in tears, under the ruinous fate that its indolence [ozio] has for so long merited." The "wounds" that have drained the life out of Italy's regions are cowardice ("Viltà") and an ambiguous "one [quello]" (*A* 118–23), which could be the "ozio" of the preceding verse or the "Tristo ordin," which in verse 106 he also pairs with "Viltà." In either case, the poem historicizes Italy's wretched condition and loss of "fiera educazione," refuting explanations from nature or historical inevitability or the influences of heavenly bodies. He presents the fate of Venice, its territorial state ripped apart in the war of 1509, as a "wretched example [l'esemplo tristo]" (*A* 162) that should serve as a lesson to the rest of Italy. Machiavelli fills thirty lines of the poem (*A* 130–59) with

[32] Marcelli reads "viltà" in the newly discovered manuscript, whereas Inglese reads "Italia" in other manuscripts. But it is clear that Machiavelli means the "viltà" of Italy.

images of the death, pain, cruelty, and trauma suffered by the civilian population of the Veneto in this war: survivors weeping for dead fathers or husbands; men, beaten and naked, driven in sorrow from their homes; fathers holding their sons tightly, both killed by a single thrust of a soldier's sword; families leaving their homes in grief; children "born" from their mothers' wombs cut open by soldiers; mothers consoling their daughters over "unhappy marriages" and "cruel husbands"; trenches and rivers filled with blood, severed heads, legs, arms, and other mangled body parts; birds of prey, wild animals, and dogs becoming their horrid "burial places"; dark, terrified faces of people stunned by new blows and fears; the earth soaked with tears and blood; the air filled with screams, sobbing, and sighing. These horrifying images refer specifically to the atrocities of the 1509 war against Venice, but they also evoke the suffering and death inflicted on Italy since 1494 that Machiavelli will again lament, in passionate language, in *The Prince*.

At the poem's conclusion, Machiavelli fears that "Ambition, with her horde" of companions, "is flying over the mountains of Tuscany" and has "already sown so many sparks among those [in Florence] bloated with hostility [invidia, in the sense of antagonism, animosity]" that it will cause a conflagration, unless "miglior ordin"—better institutions of government, better laws, and better arms—"extinguishes" the sparks (*A* 181–7). It has plausibly been speculated that these last verses allude to the growing internal opposition to Soderini from his ottimati enemies.[33] Machiavelli clearly had premonitions—which came nightmarishly true in 1512—of the danger Florence would face if Ambition overwhelmed the ordini.

"GO DIE WITH ALL YOUR MONEY, SINCE YOU DID NOT WANT TO LIVE WITHOUT IT"

Other vehicles available to Machiavelli for expressing his convictions in the chancery years were the reports written at the conclusion of diplomatic missions or in defense of his controversial project for the militia, and speeches drafted for his political superiors to deliver, in which the voice of a designated speaker thinly disguises his own, thus revealing his criticisms of the failings of the government or the political class on specific issues. The piece commonly titled "Parole da dirle sopra la provvisione del danaio [Words to be Spoken on the Proposed Law for Appropriating Funds]"[34] supports the levying of a tax to strengthen Florence's defenses. Some believe Machiavelli wrote it years later for inclusion in a projected

[33] Inglese ed., *Capitoli*, pp. 98–102.
[34] Passages cited by numbered sentences in *SPM*, pp. 446–52.

history of these years,[35] while others maintain that it was written in "March 1503" (as Machiavelli wrote on the autograph) or shortly thereafter.[36] "Words to be Spoken" is a plea to the Florentines for greater sacrifice for the republic's defense in the aftermath of Cesare Borgia's stunning elimination of his faithless former allies at the end of 1502 when he was at the height of his power. It begins with the kind of theoretical maxim Machiavelli liked: "All cities that in any time have been ruled by an absolute prince [principe soluto], by oligarchies [ottimati], or by the people, as this city is, have had, for their defense, force [le forze] mixed with prudence; for prudence alone is not enough, and force cannot achieve a conclusion, or, if it does, cannot preserve what it achieves. These two things, therefore, are the sinews [nervo] of all the governments [signorie] that have ever existed or will exist in the world." From this premise concerning the life and strength of governments, the speaker declares that the consequences of a failure to provide for both force and prudence are the "overthrow of kingdoms" and the "destruction of countries and cities." "Two months earlier," he says, he had been hopeful, but he is now dumbfounded and dismayed by the obstinacy of the councils in refusing to approve the appropriation of funds for defense ("Parole" 1–6).[37] The speaker's strategy to persuade the council members to change course consists of two alternating modes of argument. On the one hand, he employs maxims like the one at the beginning of the speech: "every city and state must consider as enemies all those who have any hope of occupying its territory and against whom they have no defense"; and "men cannot and must not be loyal servants of a government [signore] by which they can be neither defended nor punished [corretti]" ("Parole" 13–15). The loyalty of the population, in other words, rests on the government's ability to defend it. On the other hand, the speaker paints a dire picture of the risks Florence faces as a consequence of both the dysfunctional nature of its territorial state and the wider geopolitical situation in Italy, risks made more vivid by the example of a city—the imperial capital of Constantinople—recently overrun and occupied (in 1453) because its citizens refused to pay for defense. The maxims, which, on their own, might have assumed an abstract dimension, acquire weight and force from the demonstration of Florence's vulnerability in the concrete realities of Italy's recent history and the specific situation at the beginning of 1503, and it is to the latter that the speech devotes more space. Cities that lack strong military forces come to ruin, says the speaker, through either physical destruction or enslavement: "you have come close to both this year and you will

[35] Robert Black, *Machiavelli* (London and New York: Routledge, 2013), pp. 58–9 and 320, nn. 49–56, for relevant bibliography.

[36] Jean-Jacques Marchand, *SPM*, p. 445; Giorgio Inglese, *Per Machiavelli. L'arte dello stato, la cognizione delle storie* (Rome: Carocci Editore, 2006), pp. 13–14; Anna Maria Cabrini, "‹Le forze mescolate con la prudenza›," in *Machiavelli senza i Medici (1498–1512) Scrittura del potere / Potere della scrittura* (Rome: Salerno Editrice, 2006), pp. 333–4.

[37] Piero Parenti recounts the opposition to the legislation; *Storia fiorentina III (1502–1518)*, ed. Andrea Matucci (Pisa: Edizioni della [Scuola] Normale, 2018), p. 96.

be there again unless you change your views" ("Parole" 10), as the rest of the speech intends to demonstrate.

The speaker recalls the loss and recovery of Arezzo as the event that spurred the Florentines to adopt, in 1502, the constitutional innovation of a lifetime standard-bearer of justice as head of government—the office to which Piero Soderini was elected. The speaker asks his listeners to "examine our internal situation" and "to look squarely at ourselves [guardarci in seno]: you will see yourselves unarmed, you will see your subjects [in the territories] lacking in loyalty, as you experienced just months ago"—a reference to the apparent willingness of some substantial portion of the population of Arezzo and the Valdichiana to welcome a return of the Medici. At this point, Machiavelli inserts the maxim that "men cannot and must not be loyal servants of a government by which they can be neither defended nor punished." Condemning the policy that resulted in Pistoia, the Romagna, and Barga "becoming nests and hideouts for all manner of thieves," the speaker comments with sarcastic irony that "everyone knows how well you have been able to restrain them. All those places that have been assaulted [by Borgia or Vitelli or Pisa] know well how you have been able to defend them.... You cannot call them your subjects, but rather the subjects of whoever is the first to attack them" ("Parole" 15–19). This indictment of the myopic policies of Florence's ruling class with regard to the defense of the dominion would remain one of Machiavelli's major concerns. It lies at the heart of his proposal over the next few years for the institution of a militia recruited from those territories.

Turning to the political scene beyond Florence, the speaker's critique reflects Machiavelli's experience as envoy and negotiator. "You Florentines," he warns, "find yourselves surrounded by two or three cities"—the allusion is to Siena, Lucca, and Pisa—"who desire your death more than their own life. Go further, beyond Tuscany, and consider all of Italy; you see it under the king of France [who was occupying Milan], Venice, the pope, and Valentino [Cesare Borgia]" ("Parole" 20–1). The Florentines, he warns, need to consider the risks of their dependence on France for protection. He deems it a "reckless [temeraria] opinion" to suppose that, "being under the king's protection, with our enemies eliminated, and Valentino having no reason to attack us," Florence does not need its own military forces ("Parole" 13). The "reckless opinion" reflects the situation of early 1503, after Borgia's sensational entrapment and murder of Vitellozzo Vitelli, Oliverotto da Fermo, and two of the Orsini, all of whom had conspired against him. This was the brief period after Florence's "enemies"—Vitelli and the Orsini—had indeed been eradicated, and before Cesare's own downfall. The complacency of those who thought that Florence no longer faced any threats was dangerously mistaken. The Florentines should take no comfort, the speaker says, in Vitelli's having been expelled from Arezzo by Louis XII and then killed by Borgia. The king will assist Florence only if the city possesses enough military strength to make it necessary for him to "keep you in serious consideration in every deliberation of his." Only by having their own arms will the Florentines "not tempt any other power to ask the king to give you up, disarmed as you are, as prey" ("Parole" 22–4). This is a reference to Cesare Borgia, whose expansionist ambitions had been made possible by the alliance between Alexander and Louis. After a disparaging comment on Venice, whose "ambition everyone is aware of," the speech focuses on the real danger: "on the pope and his duke [al papa e al duca suo]," with the possessive "suo" suggesting a dismissive view of Cesare as the pope's child, or creature, who could do, or be, little or nothing without papal backing. The contempt extends to both: "Everyone knows what their nature and appetite are, how they operate, and what trust one can give or expect from them" ("Parole" 27–8). As we shall see in Chapter 3, for two years Borgia had been asking the Florentines to appoint him as their military captain, something they had no intention of doing even as they always let him think some agreement might be possible. Machiavelli's speaker alludes to this when he says that, if an agreement were reached, the fact remains that only "those princes who cannot attack you will be your friends," which will be the case only if Florence strengthens its own forces. He then offers another general rule: "among men in private life [fra gli uomini privati], laws and written agreements ensure the observance of trust, but among princes only arms do so." Nor will the French king always be of a mind to defend Florence. Not being able in every moment to "put their hand on another's sword," the Florentines would do well to "have their own sword at their side and to gird themselves with it when the enemy is still distant" ("Parole" 30–1).

Machiavelli then introduces the historical example, "which many of you must remember" (although it occurred fifty years earlier), of the refusal of the inhabitants of Constantinople to make financial contributions to the defense of their city against the Ottoman Turks in 1453. Machiavelli's speaker summarizes the story as follows. The emperor (Constantine XI Palaiologos), knowing the attack was imminent and that regular revenues were insufficient, summoned the citizens and explained the danger and the need for additional contributions. "They mocked him [se ne feciono beffe]." But when they heard the artillery barrage against the city walls, they rushed backed crying and carrying armloads of money. It was too late, and the emperor sent them away, saying: "Go die with all your money, since you did not want to live without it" ("Parole" 32–4). The story has about it the air of an oft-repeated apocryphal tale, but it is possible that Machiavelli adapted it from one of the chronicle sources of the siege and capture of Constantinople. An addendum by the Venetian Marco Barbaro to the *Giornale dell'assedio di Costantinopoli* of his kinsman Niccolò Barbaro recounts a story with a similar beginning but rather different ending. In this version the emperor, "being very poor, asked for loans from his barons, who all pleaded that they had no money at all." But the Turks discovered that the barons had a great deal of money. "It is said" that one Greek baron sent his two daughters to the Turks, each with a plate full of money, in order to ingratiate himself with the city's new masters. "The Turk" paid him great honor for this tribute, whereupon other Greek nobles likewise came forward with whatever amounts of cash they could assemble. "The Turk" accepted the gifts and honored their bearers. But when the money stopped coming, he had them all decapitated, saying "they were all dogs for not wanting to give this money to their lord [the emperor] and for thus letting the city be lost."[38]

Even if he knew this gruesome version, Machiavelli could not have used it in a speech meant to persuade rich Florentines to pay more taxes for defense, although, as we shall see, draconian punishments of the wealthy and selfish upper classes were often tempting fantasies for him. In any event, Machiavelli's speaker likens the blindness of the citizens of Constantinople to that of the Florentines. Returning to the Borgia menace, he recalls that, when the duke left Rome with his soldiers in September 1500, Florence lived in fear, unarmed and not knowing whether he intended to move into Tuscany or go east and then north into the Romagna. "Everyone prayed that God might give us time" to prepare defenses. When Borgia went east toward Pesaro and the danger no longer seemed imminent, the Florentines let themselves fall into "reckless complacency [confidenzia temeraria]" that made it impossible to persuade them to approve any proposal for defense spending, despite many warnings of looming threats. But the dangers, "which you stubbornly did not believe," soon reappeared, and, "in this very place [the council hall], assembled on 26 April, 1501, you heard" the news that Borgia had seized Faenza (and, as the speaker did not need to remind them, marched on Bologna, the gateway to Florence through the Apennines). "You saw the tears of your gonfaloniere"—Piero Soderini, then serving a regular two-month term in the office—"who cried over your incredulity and stubbornness." Machiavelli has the speaker say that, if the councils had approved appropriations six months earlier, some good would have come of it; doing so only six days before [Borgia's invasion] could accomplish little for the city's safety. "When, on the 4th of May [1501], you were informed that the enemy army was in Firenzuola" (midway between Bologna and Florence), the city "was in an uproar and you began to see the rewards of your obstinacy: you saw your houses burned, your possessions seized as booty, your subjects [in the dominion] slain and taken prisoner, your women violated, and your properties given to ruin [dare il guasto], and you were unable to take any countermeasures." Alluding to the inhabitants of Constantinople who refused to make financial sacrifices for the defense of their city, the speaker says that Florentines who initially balked at contributing "20 ducats"—these are symbolic numbers—"now had 200 taken from them and paid the 20 as well." He strongly hints at domestic political discord over taxes and the city's policy toward Borgia. "When you should have blamed your own incredulity and obstinacy, you blamed the wickedness of the citizens and the ambition of the ottimati, like those

[38] Nicolò Barbaro, *Giornale dell'assedio di Costantinopoli, 1453*, ed. Enrico Cornet (Vienna: Libreria Tendler, 1856), pp. 65–6.

who, constantly in error, think they've never made an error and, seeing the sun, believe it will never rain, as is happening now" ("Parole" 36–40). The non-elite (the popolo) who constituted the majority of the Great Council in which tax bills were voted on, did in fact accuse the ottimati of having collaborated with Borgia and having conspired to allow him to invade the dominion in a plot to bring down the popular government.[39] This allusion to internal political controversies suggests that the speech, whether or not it was ever delivered, was meant for the Great Council, not the Council of Eighty in which the ottimati were more heavily represented.

The speaker berates the Florentines for not having believed that Borgia and his army could be on Florentine territory in eight days, the Venetians in two days, or that King Louis might be prevented by other concerns from rescuing Florence. "You do not see the weakness of your present condition, nor the unpredictability [variazione] of fortune." "I tell you that fortune does not change its opinion where there is no change in [your] way of doing things [dove non si muta ordine], nor are the heavens able or willing to preserve a thing [i.e. a city] bent on its own ruin." No doubt realizing, however, that ending on such a pessimistic note would not strengthen the council's resolve, Machiavelli has the speaker conclude with a paean to Florence's love of liberty: "I cannot believe this will be the case, because I see that you are free Florentines and in your hands lies your liberty, for which I believe you will have the regard of those who are born free and desire to live free" ("Parole" 41–5). Despite this gesture to Florentine traditions of love of liberty, the core of the speech is a stern indictment of the political class for its failure to recognize dangers and pay for adequate military forces. That he speaks here generically of "forces" and not of a homegrown militia does not mean Machiavelli was not already thinking in this direction. But if the speech was to have any chance of persuading the council to appropriate more funds for arms, it was best not to inject the controversial question of putting those arms in the hands of either the citizens of Florence or the inhabitants of its subject territories.

Machiavelli addressed the problems of Florence's regional state in another early text, a short, unfinished piece known as "Del modo di trattare i popoli della Valdichiana ribellati [On How to Manage the Towns of the Valdichiana that Rebelled]."[40] Here, too, opinions differ over whether Machiavelli wrote it in 1503 or some years later. Even if written later, however, it expresses many of Machiavelli's known concerns about Florentine policy toward the sometimes less than loyal dominion subjects in the 1502 rebellion of Arezzo and the Valdichiana and about the dangers to which their disloyalty exposed Florence given the designs of both

[39] Parenti, *Storia fiorentina*, ed. Matucci, vol. 2, p. 439; Piero Vaglienti, *Storia dei suoi tempi, 1492–1514*, ed. Giuliana Berti, Michele Luzzati, and Ezio Tongiorgi (Pisa: Nistri-Lischi and Pacini Editori, 1982), p. 131; Francesco Guicciardini, *Storie fiorentine*, ed. Alessandro Montevecchi (Milan: Biblioteca Universale Rizzoli, 1998), ch. 21, pp. 342–3.

[40] Passages cited by numbered sentences in *SPM*, pp. 458–65.

Cesare Borgia and the Medici.[41] Like "Parole da dirle," "Del modo" reads like a speech. It also begins with a loose translation of the speech that, according to Livy (8.13.11–18), Lucius Furius Camillus pronounced in the Roman senate after he had quelled the rebellion of the cities of Latium. Camillus warns the senate that it must decide whether it wishes to treat the defeated cities with forgiveness or punishing cruelty. In Livy's text Camillus asserts that "certainly that dominion is by far the strongest in which subjects willingly obey [Certe id firmissimum longe imperium est quo oboedientes gaudent]." Machiavelli embellishes this to say: "that dominion is most strong that has loyal subjects bound to their prince by ties of affection [quello imperio essere fermissimo che ha i sudditi suoi fedeli e al suo principe affezionati]"—"principe" here in the sense of sovereign rule whatever the constitutional form—in this case a republic—not in the narrow sense of a monarch. Following Livy, Machiavelli says the senate praised Camillus' speech and decided that, since no single policy would be appropriate for all the formerly rebellious cities, the Romans would need to treat each city according to its particular circumstances. Somewhat oversimplifying the variety of policies Livy says the senate adopted, Machiavelli states that in each case the Romans chose one of two starkly opposing approaches. "Judging every other middle course [via di mezzo] to be damaging," they sought to regain the loyalty of certain cities with gestures of kindness, while they inflicted such brutal penalties on others as to deprive them of all possibility of further rebellion (or reconciliation) ("Del modo" 7–14).

"If it is true," Machiavelli's narrator says, "that works of history [le istorie] are the guide [maestra] to our actions, especially those of political leaders [principi]," and that men have always had the same desires ("passioni"), the comparable experiences of Florence and ancient Rome with rebellious cities show that "it was not wrong for those entrusted with judging and punishing the towns of the Valdichiana to follow the example of [the Romans] who were once masters of the world" ("Del modo" 18–20). The Florentines were correct, he says, to respect existing agreements and attempt to win back with favors the cities of Cortona, Castiglione (now Castiglion Fiorentino), Il Borgo (now Sansepolcro), and Foiano, but they should not have been so lenient with Arezzo, for "the Romans believed that rebellious cities should either be favored or crushed [o beneficare o spegnere]." "To me," the speaker says, "it seems you have done neither of these things with the Aretines," for "one cannot characterize as favors [benefizio] making them come to Florence [as hostages], depriving them of offices, selling their possessions, denouncing them publicly, and billeting soldiers in their homes." Nor can it be called establishing security over them to leave the city walls intact, allow five-sixths of the population to remain, not introduce new inhabitants to keep them

[41] Luca Vannini, *Firenze, i Medici e le città soggette: le rivolte al dominio fiorentino tra '400 e '500. I casi di Volterra, Pistoia e Arezzo*, tesi di Dottorato di Ricerca in Storia, Università degli Studi, Florence, 2012/2014; see pp. 36–46, 70–83, 220–73 for Arezzo and the Valdichiana.

under control, and not arrange matters so that "you would not have to spend more holding Arezzo than fighting an external enemy" ("Del modo" 18–27). Instead, by enacting a mix of punitive and conciliatory measures, Florence increased both its vulnerability and defense costs. "Del modo" then leaves aside these theoretical considerations and recalls that the need to protect its power in Arezzo had caused Florence to ask the duke of Milan for military assistance in 1498 and to divert their captain, Paolo Vitelli, and his forces from the Pisan campaign into the Casentino. So fraught is the relationship between Florence and Arezzo, says the speaker, that he predicts that, "if Florence were attacked—may God preserve us from it—Arezzo would either rebel or give you so much trouble guarding it that it becomes an intolerable expense" ("Del modo" 28–30).

The final section of "Del modo" turns to the likelihood of Florence being attacked and "whether there is anyone who has designs on Arezzo," a topic, says the speaker, that "I have heard people discuss and therefore do not want to omit." Whatever foreign dangers lurk from ultramontane princes, "let us now speak of the fear that is closer by." He means, of course, Cesare Borgia. "Those who have observed the duke" (as no one more than Machiavelli had) "see that, with regard to maintaining control of his territories, he has never planned to rely on Italian alliances [amicizie], having always thought little of Venice and less of you [Florentines]." "If this is true, he must be planning to build such a large territorial state" ("tanto stato," which can also mean "such power and reputation") in Italy that he can be secure on his own and make other powers desire *his* friendship. "If this is his intention, and if he seeks rule over Tuscany [aspiri allo imperio di Toscana] as the closest and most suitable territory in which to construct a monarchical state [regno] together with the other territories he holds…it remains to be seen whether this is the right moment for him to act on these aims of his." That these were indeed Borgia's aims the speaker considers certain, given the duke's mistrust of Italian alliances, "his ambition," and the fact that he has kept "you dangling about any agreement and has never wanted to come to an understanding with you" ("Del modo" 31–4). The curious thing is that (as we shall see in Chapter 3), throughout 1501 and 1502, it was Borgia who, with a mixture of cajolery, threats, and promises, sought an agreement with Florence for appointment as captain-general, and the Florentines who resisted, hesitated, and kept *him* dangling, ultimately never agreeing to any such thing. Machiavelli creates a semi-fictional scenario in which Borgia refuses the Florentines' desire for an alliance, rather than the reverse.

Machiavelli has his speaker use an intriguing metaphor in wondering "whether this is the right moment for Borgia to realize these objectives of his [colorire questi suoi disegni]." "Colorire" here means to put into practice, carry out, or accomplish,[42] and it suggests another meaning of "disegni," namely, "drawings,"

[42] See the *Grande dizionario della lingua italiana*, ed. S. Battaglia, vol. 3, p. 317.

perhaps hinting that Borgia's plans were still largely, as it were, on paper. But "colorire" also means to give a decent and honorable appearance to something dishonest or devious, as Machiavelli uses it in the 1498 letter to Ricciardo Becchi to characterize Savonarola's oratorical duplicity.[43] Whether or not Machiavelli meant to conflate the two meanings in "Del modo," his speaker recalls having heard Cardinal Francesco Soderini, brother of Piero, say that, among the other things for which one might praise Pope Alexander and Cesare as great men is that "they expertly recognize the opportunity and know well how to use it [che siano conoscitori della occasione e che la sappiano usare benissimo]." If the implication is that, in the cardinal's judgment, the present moment was indeed the propitious opportunity for Borgia to "seek rule over Tuscany" as the best way to consolidate his territories, the intriguing thing is that the speaker in "Del modo" does not agree. "If one were to debate whether this is the opportune and secure moment for [Borgia] to bring matters to a head" ("stringervi": move ahead, press on), "I would say no. However, considering that the duke cannot wait for a complete victory, because he hasn't much time on account of what little life remains for the pope, he must use the first opportunity [occasione] that presents itself and must entrust a good part of his cause to fortune." The truncated text ends in the middle of a sentence that is about to explain two ways in which the opportunity to defeat "you [Florentines]" could present itself to Borgia ("Del modo" 34–7). Either Machiavelli stopped there, for whatever reason, or what he wrote next is lost. But these last lines of "Del modo" undercut the idea, attributed to Cardinal Soderini, that Cesare was an expert evaluator of the "occasione" and ready to realize his aim of seizing Tuscany and building a large state. In the moment imagined in the speech, Cesare appears to have missed the "occasione," because his father's impending death precluded waiting for the right moment to act. He is here, as he is in the legations and in *The Prince*, the plaything of fortune, dependent on the arms of others and on circumstances over which he never established adequate control. In Machiavelli's judgment, despite his boastful claims and inflated self-congratulatory rhetoric, Borgia failed to consolidate his territories and devote himself to the arduous process of building a state or even achieving military self-sufficiency.

"WHAT WILL BECOME OF THE OTHERS IF JUSTICE, STRENGTH, AND UNITY WERE OF NO AVAIL TO SO GREAT AN EMPIRE?"

Machiavelli may have contemplated a longer historical work during his years in the chancery. Agostino Vespucci, who arranged for the printing of the *Decennale*

[43] *Lettere*, p. 70: "viene secondando e tempi, e le sue bugie colorendo."

in 1506, penned a dedicatory letter "to the men of Florence" in which he declared that the poem was but a "pledge," or promise, of a work "being forged more extensively and with greater exertion in [Machiavelli's] workshop."[44] In a comment inserted in the margin of a manuscript in 1503, hence prior to the *Decennale*, Vespucci noted that Machiavelli was "writing a history of these times."[45] No such work has been found, although it has been speculated that the notes he compiled on events of the years 1494 to 1498[46] may have been preparation for such a history. Still, it is difficult to see where Machiavelli would have found the leisure to write a substantial book in the years of his chancery and diplomatic service. The history he eventually wrote—not of his own times but of Florence, and in part of Italy, to 1492—would have to wait until the 1520s.

He did, however, plan and partially complete a second *Decennale*,[47] meant to be, as the opening tercet states, a verse chronicle of the decade following that of the first *Decennale*. But the text we have goes no further than 1509. It is generally assumed that Machiavelli wrote it in or shortly after 1514, on the assumption that he would not have begun a work with the stated intention of covering the ten years from 1504 to 1514 before they were all behind him. He may have left it unfinished because of the awkwardness he would have confronted narrating the events of 1512–13: the sudden departure of the French in the summer of 1512, chased from Italy by the Swiss, leaving Florence at the mercy of Pope Julius and Spain; the savage attack against Prato by Spanish troops in August 1512, carried out with the approval and support of Pope Julius and Cardinal Giovanni de' Medici, which emboldened Soderini's ottimati enemies to force him out of both his office and the city; and the return in September of the Medici, who dismantled the institutions of the popular republic, ended Machiavelli's career in government in November, and, in early 1513, subjected him to arrest, incarceration, and torture. By 1513, the Medici controlled both Florence and, with Cardinal Giovanni's election as Pope Leo X, Rome and the papacy as well. In 1514 it would not have been prudent to express sorrow, much less criticism or anger, over these events. Still, we must wonder why, if Machiavelli began the work in 1514, he did so knowing he would somehow have to deal with the disasters of 1512–13, or be impossibly silent about them, or interrupt the project and leave it unfinished, as apparently happened. Near the beginning of the poem, he alludes to the devastation he felt, but without specifying its source: "I will sing, and I shall be resolute [ardito] / in singing through copious tears [fra molto pianto], even as / I have become almost dumbstruck by grief [pel dolor divenuto smarrito]" (D^2 7–9).

44 *SPP*, pp. 14–15.

45 Francesca Klein, *Scritture e governo dello stato a Firenze nel Rinascimento. Cancellieri, ufficiali, archivi* (Florence: Edifir, 2013), p. 274.

46 *OS* (see list of abbreviations), vol. 2, pp. 915–52.

47 Abbreviated as D^2, ed. A. Corsaro, in *SPP*, pp. 52–65; passages cited by numbered verses.

The truncated second *Decennale* continues Machiavelli's polemic against the fecklessness of the Italian states, particularly Florence and Venice. But it also contains a lavish encomium of the civilian commissioner-general Antonio Giacomini, Machiavelli's colleague in the military administration of the dominion and, of all Florentines, perhaps the one he most admired. The poem recounts a lost opportunity in 1505 to bring to a conclusion the long war for the recovery of Pisa. A victory achieved "through the virtú of your Giacomino" (D^2 31–3) was negated by the mismanagement of the follow-up encounter. Although some blamed Giacomini as much for the defeat as for the earlier victory, Machiavelli is unstinting in his praise for him, in part because he was, in Machiavelli's eyes, the ideal citizen-soldier. Emphasizing that he was neither a military professional nor a hired foreigner, he writes that "through his virtú, his calling [destino], / he reached as much glory and fame / as ever did any other private citizen [privato cittadino]. / He endured much for his patria, / and upheld the dignity of your military forces / with great justice for a long time, / avid for honor, generous with money; / he lived full of such great virtú / that merits much more than the honor I give him" (D^2 34–42). Machiavelli's esteem for Giacomini remained high through the years. In the sketch of his life in the *Nature di uomini fiorentini*,[48] he describes him as "far beyond all other citizens of Florence, the most skilled in matters of war." In a particularly striking phrase, he says Giacomini was "unbending in his loyalty [severo nel servare] to the sovereignty of the republic [maestà publica]." He reinforces the concept asserting that, "privato,"—as a private citizen—"he was without attachment to a faction [sanza parte] and without ambition of any sort" (ambition, of course, in the very negative sense of the "Capitolo dell'Ambizione"), and that, "quando publico"—when holding official positions—"he desired only the glory and praise of the city." The title of chapter 16 of book 3 of the *Discourses on Livy* asserts that "in difficult times men of genuine virtú are sought, whereas in peaceful times men who enjoy more favor because of their wealth or family connections are sought, not men of virtú." In this same chapter, Machiavelli says that, in the "many wars since 1494," Florence's citizens (presumably those who enjoyed wealth and family connections) "made a poor showing" until the city chanced to find "one who showed how armies are to be commanded, and this was Antonio Giacomini." Whenever dangerous wars were being fought and a commissioner-general had to be appointed, Giacomini had no competition. But if an easy victory was anticipated, as in 1509 when Pisa was ready to surrender, he was passed over in favor of others who, in Machiavelli's opinion, bungled the operations and accepted easier terms for the Pisans. Giacomini's "indignation" at being slighted on this occasion was exceedingly strong (*DL* 3.16.14–18). The *Second Decennale* describes Giacomini "now"—presumably in 1514, and in any case after 1509—as

48 *OS*, vol. 2, pp. 74–5.

"disregarded and defamed.... So much do they who do well displease fortune" (D^2 43–5). In lauding Giacomini and lamenting how he was shunted aside, Machiavelli aimed his ire at the ottimati.

Pope Julius figures prominently in the *Second Decennale*. "Unable to restrain his fierce spirit [feroce animo]...and full of inborn anger and fury [furor: madness]," Julius "spewed out his first poison [primo veleno]" against those who were "occupying his cities" in the papal states. To unseat all these "tyrants," he left Rome threatening war against the Baglioni of Perugia and the Bentivoglio of Bologna (D^2 85–96). The characterization of the 1506 campaign as Julius's "first poison" alludes to the even greater poison he "spewed" in the vicious war against Venice in 1509 and the bloody 1512 war of his Holy League that expelled the French from Italy. In Chapter 4 we will explore in depth Machiavelli's observations of, and reactions to, Julius during the 1506 campaign and the 1510 legation to France when he negotiated with King Louis and his ministers in an effort to forestall more of Julius's "furor."

Further entangling the dangerous web of animosities and ambitions that Italy faced from foreign powers was the expedition in 1508 of the emperor-elect Maximilian, initially to counter French power in Italy. The *Second Decennale* recounts his address to a diet of barons in Constance in which he bemoans the "wrongs" perpetrated by the French and orders his troops into Italy. "France and Mark," Machiavelli writes, united their forces to impede Maximilian's advance (although in reality it was the Venetians who stopped him). Seeking to exploit this victory, "Mark did not remain content with defense" and went on the offensive, seizing Gorizia and Trieste and forcing the emperor to sue for peace (D^2 115–32). Machiavelli says Venice went too far: this was "the meal, / the inauspicious bite, the poisonous food / that sickened St. Mark's stomach" and caused the pope, Spain, France, and Maximilian to band together in the League of Cambrai to punish Venice, with each member of the coalition free to pursue his own objectives (D^2 133–44). Machiavelli's critique of what he considered Venice's ill-conceived expansion—biting off too much without adequate means of defending what it took—will be among the reasons why, in the major works, he judges ancient Rome superior to Venice, despite the latter's longer history. The unfinished *Second Decennale* culminates in the papal-French-Spanish-imperial war against Venice in 1509, whose terrible consequences for the civilian population Machiavelli had lamented in the "Capitolo dell'Ambizione."

The League's assault on Venice ironically created the opportunity for Florence's conquest, at long last, of Pisa. With the attention of Ferdinand, Louis, and Maximilian focused on assembling their firepower on Venice, "Pisa was left alone," and the Florentines immediately tightened the siege of the city, preventing the import of foodstuffs. "For four months, you [Florence] surrounded [Pisa] / amid many difficulties and much exertion, / and at great expense [con assia dispendio] you starved them" into submission. "Despite being a tenacious enemy, / compelled and vanquished by necessity, / [Pisa] returned in tears to her former chains." After Venice's defeat, the poem continues, "Julius rushed up" from Rome with soldiers and chose as his first target Faenza—whose occupation by Venice since the fall of Cesare Borgia had been a constant thorn in his side. "In the end, Mark lay prone on the ground…fallen from such exalted heights" (D^2 157–77).

The sudden collapse of Venetian power and the loss, albeit temporary, of so much of its terraferma possessions prompted Machiavelli to ponder the shocking outcome as an ominous warning, or foretaste, of Italy's fate. He had of course already witnessed (and experienced) the tragic sequel in 1512–13. Paraphrasing a tercet from Petrarch's *Triumph of Death*,[49] he asks: "What will become of [the other states of Italy] if this one"—namely Venice, reputed to be the strongest—"burned and froze in just a few days, and if to so great an empire"—alluding perhaps both to Venice's maritime empire and its more recent expansion in Italy—"justice, strength, and unity were of no avail?" And, paraphrasing verses from both Petrarch and Dante that apostrophize the arrogant,[50] Machiavelli excoriates the Venetians and the ruling classes of all Italy: "Go ahead, you arrogant men, with ever haughty countenance, / you who hold the scepters and crowns, / and know not any truth of the future! / So much does your present thirst blind you / that it holds a heavy veil over your eyes / and you do not see things from afar. / This is why the whirling of the heavens / buffets your dominions [stati] this way and that, / more often than it changes summer into winter; / for if your prudence were addressed / to recognizing the malady and finding a remedy, / the heavens would be deprived of such power" (D^2 178–92). Although written perhaps five years after Venice's defeat, these lines, like the tercets of "Ambition," convey the fears and foreboding Machiavelli felt in 1509.

[49] Petrarch, *Triumphus Mortis*, 127–8: "Che fia de l'altre, se questa arse et alse / in poche notti e sì cangiò piú volte?" Noted by Corsaro, *SPP*, p. 62.

[50] Petrarch, *Triumphus Fame*, 2.142: "Gite, superbi, o miseri cristiani"; Dante, *Purgatorio* 12.70: "Or superbite, e via col viso altero, / figliuoli d'Eva." Also noted by Corsaro, *SPP*, p. 63.

2
Sins of Princes

In contemplating Italy's troubled history, Machiavelli inquired into both the who and the why. He asked, first, who was accountable for Italy's catastrophe? What decisions, policies, actions, or inactions contributed to the crisis? Machiavelli was not hesitant to apportion blame. As the speaker who introduces *Mandragola* says in the prologue (vv. 67–72), the author is quite skilled in "dir male"—in speaking ill, finding fault. In fact, it was, he says, "his first art." The second question seeks the deeper causes of Italy's calamity. What were the elements of structural weakness and institutional deficiency—the systemic disorders—that made possible the erroneous decisions and actions of individuals and governments? This is where Machiavelli's originality lies, for his approach to this question goes beyond the traditional focus on the virtues and vices of princes. He did not deny the importance or effects of the qualities and attributes, positive and negative, of princes and republican ruling classes. But he did not stop there. His inquiry into the more profound causes of Italy's dysfunctional politics broke new ground in the history of political thought. Machiavelli directed blame for Italy's woes at three broad categories of leaders: princes and governors of republics; mercenaries; and popes and the Church. This chapter provides an overview of his critique of the princes and republics.

VENICE

Like most of his contemporaries, Machiavelli held Ludovico Sforza of Milan responsible for opening the door to the foreign invasions by encouraging King Charles VIII of France to invade Italy in 1494 in pursuit of dynastic claims to the kingdom of Naples. But for the second French invasion, in 1499, whose consequences were far greater and more lasting, he blamed Venice.[1] Italy's subjugation to foreign domination really began with King Louis XII's conquest of Milan in 1499–1500 and the coordinated Franco-Spanish attack on Naples in 1501, which initiated the long series of wars between France and Spain for control of the peninsula. Machiavelli does not mince words about Venice's responsibility for the 1499 invasion. In *The Prince* he flatly states that "King Louis was brought into Italy

[1] On Machiavelli's views on Venice, see Sasso, *Machiavelli e gli antichi*, vol. 3, pp. 3–46; and Innocenzo Cervelli, *Machiavelli e la crisi dello Stato veneziano* (Naples: Guida, 1974).

Machiavelli's Broken World. John M. Najemy, Oxford University Press. © John M. Najemy 2022.
DOI: 10.1093/oso/9780199580927.003.0002

by the ambition of the Venetians," who supported his objectives because they "wanted to acquire half of Lombardy" as their reward for cooperating with France. Machiavelli says he "will not criticize [Louis's] decision" to ally with Venice, given that, owing to the "conduct [portamenti]" of Charles VIII five years earlier, he had no "friends" in Italy and needed to find support wherever he could. His judgment of Venice is different. As soon as Louis took Lombardy, most of the states of north-central Italy flocked to his side. Machiavelli lists them—Genoa, Florence, the marquis of Mantua, the duke of Ferrara, the Bentivoglio (of Bologna), the Madonna of Forlí (Caterina Sforza Riario), and the lords of Faenza, Rimini, Pesaro, Camerino, Piombino, Lucca, Pisa, and Siena—and comments derisively that the Venetians, seeing this rush to win the king's favor, "could now ponder the recklessness [temerità] of their decision." Trivializing Venice's gains (which were greater than he implies) and exaggerating France's, Machiavelli mocks the Venetians saying that, "in order to acquire two cities in Lombardy, they made the king signore of two-thirds of Italy" (*P* 3.32–5).

The Borgia pope, Alexander VI, was the third member of the fateful alliance of 1499. Looking for allies, Machiavelli says, to support the ambitions he harbored for his son Cesare, he found a willing accomplice in Venice. In the *Prince*'s chapter on "ecclesiastical principalities" he says that, of the five principal states of Italy, the ones considered most likely to disrupt the precarious balance formalized among them in the Lega Italica of 1455 were the papacy and Venice (*P* 11.7–8). His explanation of Alexander's alliance with Venice is that, to achieve his territorial ambitions, "it was necessary [for Alexander] to upset existing arrangements [ordini] and disrupt [disordinare] the states of Italy." This was "easy for him," Machiavelli says, because he found the Venetians, for reasons of their own, willing to facilitate the arrival of the French in Italy. "The king thus entered Italy with the help of the Venetians and the agreement of Alexander" (*P* 7.10–15). Later in *The Prince*, he comments that Venice's alliance with France, which "could have been avoided," was instead the "cause of its ruin" (*P* 21.22).

Machiavelli had little use for the already established and widely shared idealization of Venice as a perfect republic whose mixed constitution of the one, the few, and the many guaranteed its internal peace and legendary durability—notions that had taken hold not only in Venice but also among many Florentine ottimati as well. Introducing Venice in chapters 28 and 29 of the first book of the *Florentine Histories* (his summary of Italy's history from the fall of Rome to the early fifteenth century), he alludes to this "myth of Venice" in foreseeing that, to some, "it might seem incongruous" that he "has waited so long to discuss the Venetians, given that theirs is a republic which, for its organization [ordine] and power, must be celebrated over every other polity [principato] in Italy." This is not Machiavelli's opinion; it is the assumption behind the expected disapproval of those who might think he delayed too long in bringing Venice into his narrative. In fact, he wants "to dispel any surprise about his having waited to discuss Venice and clarify the reason for it." To this end, he will reach back in time to explain Venice's origins and why the Venetians themselves got involved so late in the political affairs of Italy (*IF* 1.28.10). He quickly summarizes the story of Venice's founding by inhabitants of the mainland who, fleeing the invading Huns, took refuge on the barren islands and swamps of the lagoon and built a city that, over the centuries, grew enormously in population, wealth, and power from maritime commerce as they acquired "the ports of Greece and Syria" and dominated the Adriatic, the Aegean, and the eastern shore of the Mediterranean. For "many years" (actually centuries), the only "dominion" the Venetians aspired to was that which "facilitated the transport of the goods" they traded. In return for making their ships available to the French for their voyages to "Asia" (in the fourth Crusade), they "received the island of Crete." For as long as they continued on this path, Machiavelli writes, "their reputation on the seas was terrifying [terribile] and in Italy greatly esteemed [venerando]" (*IF* 1.29.11–12). In *The Prince* he writes that, in the centuries of their maritime prowess, before turning their ambitions to the Italian mainland, the Venetians fought their wars "gloriously" and "virtuosissimamente," with the participation of both their nobles ("gentili uomini") and "armed plebs" (*P* 12.23).

Machiavelli's negative judgment of Venice emerges in connection with its expansion onto the Italian mainland (in the fourteenth and especially the fifteenth century). The Venetians, he says in strikingly blunt terms, were "driven by a lust for domination [cacciati dalla cupidità del dominare] and were considered so powerful that not only Italian princes but also the kings of Europe were terrified of them" (*IF* 1.29.13). For as long as they were successful, Machiavelli cuttingly remarks in the *Discourses*, they believed they earned their good fortune "with the virtú they did not have, and became so insolent that they called the king of France the little child [figliuolo] of San Marco, had no respect for the Church, thought Italy was not big enough for them, and persuaded themselves that they were going to create a *monarchia*"—an empire—"like that of the Romans" (*DL* 3.31.14). But the great flaw of their expansion into mainland Italy was their dependence on mercenaries. "When they began to fight on land," the Venetians no longer fought wars themselves and instead "followed the customs of Italian warfare" by employing mercenaries. At the outset, with not much territory to defend, they had little to fear from their hired captains; as their terraferma state grew, however, so did their dependence on powerful captains who became more difficult to control (*P* 12.24–6). When "their luck ran out" (with the military catastrophe of 1509), they lost their entire "stato" (their territorial dominion in Italy) as their subject cities rebelled and surrendered to the invading French and Germans. They ceded other territories to the pope (in the Romagna) and to the king of Spain (the Adriatic ports) "out of cowardice and self-abasement [per viltà e abiezione d'animo]," even offering to become tributaries of the emperor and sending letters to Pope Julius "full of despair and obsequiousness [sommissione], trying to move him to compassion."

This disaster happened, Machiavelli says scornfully, in just four days with only half the army having been defeated: what he calls a "mezza rotta," erroneously faulting a Venetian official, a "provveditore" (equivalent to Florence's commissioners), for leaving the field of battle with "more than 25,000 soldiers between infantry and cavalry" (*DL* 3.31.15–16), when it was actually the mercenary captain Niccolò Orsini who led these forces away from the fighting—a strange error for Machiavelli, who was always eager to highlight mercenary malfeasance.

The "viltà" that caused the Venetians to lose both their "stato" and their courage ("l'animo"), resulted, Machiavelli believes, from defective military institutions ("ordini non buoni nelle cose della guerra") (*DL* 3.31.18). At the core of Venice's flawed military "ordini" was the failure to build sufficient forces to secure the cities and territories it occupied and the consequent dependence on mercenaries. In fact, Machiavelli knew—and says so through the voice of Fabrizio Colonna in the *Art of War* (*AG* 7.242)—that the Venetians made, but abandoned, efforts to recruit a fighting force from their Italian territories. Machiavelli's understanding of the problems of fighting with mercenaries will be examined in the next chapter, but here it may be noted that, among the consequences he saw of employing, but not fully trusting, mercenaries, was the reluctance to give hired commanders full authority to make battlefield decisions. The governors of Venice and Florence, Machiavelli asserts, insisted on "being informed and expressing their views each time their captains or civilian commissioners wanted to position a piece of artillery." Such practices, he laments, "have reduced the two republics to the conditions in which they now find themselves" (*DL* 2.33.12–13). Noting that the Venetians increasingly employed mercenaries because they did not want "to obey one of their own citizens" in war (*AG* 1.159), Machiavelli has Fabrizio Colonna say that "if the Venetians had been wise in this as they were in all their other ordini," they would have created "una nuova monarchia nel mondo" (the same characterization of their ambition that Machiavelli attributes to the Venetians themselves in the *Discourses*). Fabrizio argues that they were certainly wrong to refuse to entrust command of their armies to their own citizens if they doubted their sea captains could fight effectively on land. If their reluctance was motivated by the fear that a citizen commander could make himself a tyrant, they were misguided in this too. If, previously, no citizen with command of arms on the seas had ever made himself a tyrant, there was even less chance that a commander on land would have been able to do so. Fabrizio concludes by asserting that not arms in the hands of citizens but "defective institutions of governance [malvagi ordini del governo]" bring about tyranny in a city. Because the Venetians had "buono governo," they should have had nothing to fear from citizens commanding their arms (*AG* 1.178–86).

Machiavelli had another explanation for Venetian reluctance to create an army from its territories, namely, the practice of literally buying alliances and security. As the title of chapter 30 of book 2 of the *Discourses* asserts—"Truly powerful republics and princes do not buy alliances with money, but with the virtú and renown of their military forces"—Machiavelli had a low opinion of states that substituted cash for good arms. His criticism is directed at both Florence and Venice. "It would be a lengthy task to recount how many times...the Florentines and Venetians paid their way out of a war...and how many cities the Florentines and Venetians purchased" (rather than conquered). When Florence's reputation was at its height, he says, with some exaggeration, there wasn't a single petty lord in the Romagna who was not on the Florentine payroll. But "what they acquired with gold"—with money—"they are unable to defend with steel"—with arms (*DL* 2.30.8–14). Summarizing Venice's constitutional development in chapter 6 of book 1 of the *Discourses*, Machiavelli emphasizes the role of money in the republic's expansion, claiming that most of its territorial gains in Italy had been achieved not with war, "but with money and cunning [con danari e con astuzia]," and linking this practice to Venice's inability to defend what it acquired. For republics that depend on money, he insists that expansion is a "poison" to be avoided (*DL* 1.6.26–8). In the famous chapter in which he denies that money is the sinews of war, he asserts that "the Venetians, a few years ago"—the reference is to the defeat at Agnadello—"despite their treasury being full of money, lost their whole territorial state and were unable to be defended by it" (*DL* 2.10.17). Machiavelli praises states that expand and grow but insists that this is beneficial only when expansion is accompanied by increased military strength. A state that "acquires territory [imperio] but not simultaneously military strength [forze] must come to ruin," and a state "that impoverishes itself in war cannot acquire such strength even if it is victorious," as is also the case with states that "spend more on territorial acquisitions than they gain from them." Both the Venetians and Florentines were guilty of this, and as a consequence "were much weaker when Venice had Lombardy and Florence had Tuscany than they had been when Venice was content with the sea"—satisfied with its maritime empire—"and Florence was content with six miles" between its northern and southern borders (*DL* 2.19.22–3), this last passage echoing Cacciaguida's nostalgia for the earlier, smaller, and more peaceful city of Dante's imagination with boundaries "al Galluzzo e a Trespiano" (*Paradiso* 16.52–4). In the case of Venice, the combination of these weaknesses made it easier for its adversaries to launch the massive attack of 1509. In 1506 Pope Julius, whose patchwork armies of mercenaries and auxiliaries should have been no match for Venice's larger army, persuaded the Venetians to remain neutral and out of the way as he marched into the Romagna and toward Bologna (*DL* 3.44.6–8). In *The Prince* Machiavelli says the Venetians were held back by fear (*P* 25.21). Three years later, "the Church"—Pope Julius—"deprived Venice of its power with the help of France" (*DL* 1.12.20).

In *Discourses* 1.6 Machiavelli locates the underlying cause of Venice's military weakness in its social organization, which rigidly separated nobles, called "gentili uomini," who sat in the Great Council, from "popolani." The ruling nobles "kept the others in check [chi reggeva gli teneva a freno]" and "did not use them in matters in which they could gain power [e non gli adoperava in cose dove ei potessono pigliare autorità]," which, Machiavelli explains, meant "not using the plebs in war." This policy, combined with denying a political role to newcomers, keeps a state "disarmato," unable to defend its territorial gains, and "so weak" that it "becomes the prey" of whoever attacks it (*DL* 1.6.7–11, 17–21). His legation to Mantua and Verona in November–December 1509 must have given him an inkling of Venice's misspent possibilities in this regard. He became aware of the contrasting attitudes of the "gentili uomini" and the peasants in the terraferma in the struggle between Venice and the League of Cambrai. Two days after he arrived in Mantua, he reported that Vicenza had rebelled against its imperial occupiers and welcomed a return to Venetian control. The League feared Verona might do likewise (*LCSG* 6.201.9–12): "it is believed that the Veronese have a great desire to imitate the Vicentines," and, despite the presence of French forces, "the people [e' popoli] sometimes want to satisfy a desire [si vogliono cavare una voglia] without thinking what could come of it" (*LCSG* 6.202.8–9). From Verona he told the Ten that the city's "gentili uomini" were not "marcheschi"—not loyal to Venice—but that the "infima plebe" is "all Venetian [tutta viniziana]." The Venetians, encamped five miles to the east with 5,000 "paid infantry" and "a very great number of angry peasants [villani arrabbiati]," were "feeling out the mood of the people [tastare el popolo]"—presumably the "infima plebe" that was "all for Venice"—to see if some uprising [tumulto] could get them into the city" (*LCSG* 6.204.6, 11–13). Conversely, because "the king of France has a great longing for [Verona]," the "gentili uomini fervently want him to have it" (*LCSG* 6.206.5). League forces were readying an assault to sack and pillage Vicenza "to purge the city of its sins" in having welcomed the return of the Venetians. But "one sees and hears the most extraordinary things," Machiavelli says: "the peasants [contadini], whose spirits have conceived a wish to die and take vengeance [for Venice], have become more stubborn and enraged against the enemies of the Venetians than the Jews were against the Romans. Every day one of them, taken prisoner, prefers death to renouncing the name of Venice [si lascia ammazzare per non negare el nome viniziano]. Just yesterday evening, one, brought before the [imperial governor of Verona], said he was *marchescho* [loyal to Venice] and wanted to die *marchescho*, and had no wish to live otherwise. The [governor] had him hanged, and no offer to spare him or anything else could make him relinquish this conviction. So, considering everything, it is impossible for these kings [Louis and Maximilian] to hold on to these lands as long as these peasants are alive" (*LCSG* 6.207.4–6).[2]

[2] Edward Muir elucidates the passage in "Was There Republicanism in the Renaissance Republics? Venice after Agnadello," in *Venice Reconsidered: The History and Civilization of an Italian City-State, 1297–1797*, ed. John Martin and Dennis Romano (Baltimore: The Johns Hopkins University Press, 2000), pp. 137–67 (at 150).

Machiavelli was clearly very impressed by the steadfast loyalty to Venice displayed by both the city "plebe" and, especially, the peasants of the countryside. He makes no mention of this in the major works, but one wonders if, when excoriating the Venetians in the *Discourses* for not "using the plebs in war," he thought back to those peasants willing to die for Venice.

A few days later, Machiavelli commented that, the longer the League lets the war drag on, "the more the peasants' desire to return to their former masters [primi padroni] will grow" (*LCSG* 6. 208.9–10). Meanwhile, the "gentili uomini" of Verona, fearful of the vacillation of the League powers and seeing the Venetians on the offensive with the countryside their ally ("el paese loro partigiano"), were taking their possessions and families to Mantua for safety (*LCSG* 6.216.12). Aware that the Venetians were retaking cities they had lost (although Verona was not recaptured until some years later) and that in those cities they were painting images of St. Mark with a sword, rather than a book, Machiavelli comments: "it seems they have realized at their own expense that studies and books are not enough to hold on to stati [territories]" (*LCSG* 6.212.15–16), as he accuses them of believing in "Ambizione." One wonders if he reflected on what the Venetian territorial state might have been if Venice's aristocracy had been willing to harness the fervor of the peasants in support of their "stato di terra."[3]

FLORENCE

Machiavelli's assessment of Florence's domestic political history, as presented in the *Florentine Histories*, will be examined in the second half of this study. Here the focus will be his comments on Florence's relations with other Italian states and, for the Medici period, its part in the increasing precariousness of the so-called balance of power. As the smallest and militarily weakest of the major states in the second half of the fifteenth century, Florence rarely sent its forces outside Tuscany. By contrast, the kings of Naples, the Venetians, the dukes of Milan, and the papacy were frequently engaged in hostilities beyond their borders, often attempting to expand their territorial dominions. In both the *Florentine Histories* and the *Discourses* Machiavelli calls attention to Florence's frequent dependence on princely states both in and beyond Italy for security and to the problems this entailed. Twice, he notes, the Florentines formally submitted to the Angevin king Robert of Naples to gain his help: in 1313 when, unable to secure his protection "as allies [amici]," they "gave him the city for five years so that he would defend

[3] Cervelli analyzes the relevance of these dispatches to Machiavelli's critique of Venice's "stato" in *Machiavelli e la crisi dello stato veneziano*, pp. 331–62. See also E. Igor Mineo, "Lo stato veneziano attraverso Machiavelli (a proposito di *Machiavelli e la crisi dello stato veneziano*)," *Studi storici* 60 (2019), pp. 559–71; and Romain Descendre, "Venezia" in the *Enciclopedia machiavelliana*, ed. Gennaro Sasso and Giorgio Inglese, vol. 2 (Rome: Istituto della Enciclopedia Italiana, 2014), pp. 654–8.

them as his men [come suoi uomini]"—his subjects—against Emperor Henry VII (*IF* 2.24.4); and in 1325, when, faced with the even more dangerous threat from Castruccio Castracani, the lord of Lucca, they turned once more to Robert, who again required them to accept his assistance as "sudditi [subjects]," not "amici" (*DL* 2.9.14). "In order to be defended, they had to give themselves [gli ebbero a darsi] to King Robert" (*DL* 2.12.21–2) and "were forced to accept as their signore" his son Charles, duke of Calabria, because the Angevins of Naples, Machiavelli says, "being accustomed to exercising lordship [signoreggiare] over Florence, wanted its obedience rather than its friendship." Unable to go immediately to Florence, Charles sent as his "vicario" the French/Neapolitan nobleman Walter of Brienne, whose "mild demeanor" on that occasion (*IF* 2.30.2–5) prompted the Florentines to request his help in the fiscal and military crisis of 1342–3. (Machiavelli's account of the latter episode is discussed in Chapter 6). The Angevins were always inclined to reprise the "lordship" in Florence that Robert's grandfather, Charles of Anjou, had established in the 1260s after obliterating Hohenstaufen rule in central and southern Italy.

Further instances noted by Machiavelli of Florentine appeals to powerful foreigners include their willingness to pay the emperor-elect Rupert of Bavaria the huge sum of 200,000 florins for military assistance (in 1401) in the war against Giangaleazzo Visconti of Milan. To emphasize the futility of such appeals, Machiavelli claims that, as soon as Rupert arrived in Italy and collected the money, he turned around and went back to Germany, whereas in fact he did engage Visconti forces, albeit with no success (*DL* 3.43.9–12). In 1479, when Pope Sixtus IV and King Ferrante of Naples declared war after the Pazzi conspiracy failed to kill Lorenzo, the Florentines, "being allies [amici] of the king of France, received from that alliance 'more fine words than defense' [magis nomen quam praesidium, paraphrasing Livy 7.29]" (*DL* 2.11.3). And Machiavelli was keenly aware of the on-and-off military assistance promised by Louis XII for the recovery of Pisa. His general point is that reliance on foreign protectors more often than not resulted in either no real help or in a weakening or loss of the city's independence.

Machiavelli saw differences of opinion within the political leadership as sometimes damaging to the republic's standing vis-à-vis other states. In the *Discourses* he recalls that when Louis XII was preparing his 1499 invasion of Italy he sought an agreement with Florence (like those he secured with both Venice and Pope Alexander). Florence's ambassadors offered neutrality in return for the king's protection and preservation of its government, and Louis gave the Florentines one month to ratify the ambassadors' offer. But "the ratification was delayed by those who ill-advisedly [per poca prudenza] took the side of Ludovico [Sforza]," whose removal from power in Milan was Louis's first objective in Italy. Once the king was on the verge of victory, the Florentines hurriedly sought to ratify the agreement, but Louis refused to accept it "because he knew the Florentines, now compelled to offer it, were not doing so willingly. This cost the city of Florence great sums of money," Machiavelli says, and "almost cost them the loss of their stato" (which here could mean either the territorial dominion or the republican government, or both). The split between those who preferred to stay with Ludovico and those who thought it more prudent to ally with Louis resulted in a dangerous impasse. In Machiavelli's opinion, the failure to ratify in time did not help Ludovico, who, even if he had successfully resisted the French, would have shown much more antagonism to Florence than Louis did (*DL* 2.15.18–22).

Machiavelli alludes in this same passage to a later episode, without identifying it, in which the Florentines did lose their "stato" for "a similar reason." The reference is no doubt to the republic's attempt to remain neutral between France and Pope Julius in 1510–12 (see Chapter 4). Although, elsewhere in the *Discourses*, Machiavelli ascribes the fall of the republic in 1512 to its steadfast adherence to the French alliance (*DL* 1.59.12), in another chapter he claims that certain (unnamed) "citizens" brought the Spanish army into Florentine territory "to repatriate the Medici" and "extort money from the city." These citizens told the Spaniards they would take up arms to support them as soon as they arrived, but when the promised uprising failed to materialize the Spaniards, being short on provisions, sought to resolve the standoff though a negotiated agreement. Machiavelli says the popolo—the non-elite members of the Great Council—refused to negotiate and that their refusal led to the sack of Prato and the collapse of the republic. He scolds the "arrogant popolo" for rejecting all the demands of the Spaniards, who wanted three things: the overthrow of the republic ("mutare lo stato"); repudiation of the French alliance; and money. The popolo should have been willing, says Machiavelli, to accept an agreement to preserve the republic, without objecting to the payment the Spaniards demanded or to the return of the Medici as private citizens. By stubbornly resisting all three demands, they lost everything, the republic included (*DL* 2.27.13–18). Machiavelli here highlights the divergent views of the elite ottimati and the non-elite members of the Council, who refused to countenance the repatriation of the Medici in any capacity. Elsewhere, as we shall see, he blames the ottimati.

Florence's relations with its neighbors were tense, controversial, and sometimes confrontational, including during Machiavelli's years in government. Of those that became subject cities, at least two—Arezzo and Pisa—escaped Florentine rule and had to be forced back into the dominion. As second chancellor whose responsibilities included coordinating security and military affairs, Machiavelli was at the center of these complex problems. He was often critical of Florence's dealings, past and contemporary, with its Tuscan neighbors, but not always consistent in the direction of his criticism. On the one hand, he praised a policy of friendly engagement to welcome neighboring cities into alliance with Florence. "Everyone knows," he writes in *Discourses* 2.21, "how, long ago, the city of Pistoia voluntarily came under Florentine rule [sotto lo imperio fiorentino]." This happened because the Florentines treated the people of Pistoia "like brothers," Machiavelli asserts (overlooking some less than fraternal episodes). On the other hand, "everyone knows how much enmity [inimicizia] there has been between the Florentines" and the cities of Pisa, Lucca, and Siena, "which have made every possible effort" to avoid subjection to their more powerful neighbor. Machiavelli did not have to remind his readers that Florence was never able to force Lucca into its dominion, despite two costly wars launched for that purpose, and that Pisa, conquered by siege and starvation in 1406, reclaimed its freedom when the French arrived in 1494 and resisted another siege over fifteen years before succumbing in 1509. Machiavelli speculates that "if the Florentines, either through leagues or alliances[4] had placated [dimesticati] and not embittered [insalvatichiti: literally, made wild] their neighbors, by now they would without doubt be lords [signori] of Tuscany," to which he adds a note of caution and realism: "I don't conclude on these grounds that arms and force are not to be used, only that they should be kept in reserve as a last resort" (*DL* 2.21.16–20). Elsewhere, he confirms his approval of friendly engagement, asserting that the Florentines succeeded in bringing Pistoia, wracked by warring internal factions, into the dominion "by alternately favoring one faction over the other but eliminating neither, to the point where, exhausted by its turbulent politics, [Pistoia] spontaneously threw itself into the arms of Florence" (*DL* 2.25.11).

In the *Florentine Histories*, after recounting the revolt against Walter of Brienne in 1343, Machiavelli inserts a short chapter on the rebellion of the subject cities of Arezzo, Castiglion (Fiorentino), Pistoia, Volterra, Colle (Val d'Elsa), and San Gimignano. Florence's expulsion of Brienne, he writes, "emboldened all the subject cities to recover their liberty." "In an instant Florence shed its tyrant and lost its dominion; in regaining its own liberty it taught its subjects how to regain theirs." The Florentine government "judged it preferable to mollify its subjects with peace rather than turn them into enemies with war; so they showed them that they were as pleased with their liberty as they were with their own." Florence sent ambassadors to Arezzo to relinquish its rule ("renunziare allo imperio") over the city and conclude an agreement, by which the Florentines could gain the benefit of friendship with the Aretines as allies that they were unable to have when they were subjects. They did the same with the other cities. "This policy, wisely adopted," Machiavelli concludes, "had a happy outcome, because not too many years later Arezzo returned to Florentine rule"—the implication is that they did so willingly—as did "the other cities in just a few months." Machiavelli was exaggerating here—Florence regained Arezzo forty years later—and a comparison of his

[4] Machiavelli writes "aiuti" here, which I translate as alliances because the same word appears in the next chapter where he says the new French king, Francis I, seeking to regain the duchy of Milan, "wanted *aiuti* in Italy who could smooth the way for his expedition, and, besides the Venetians...sounded out the Florentines and Pope Leo X" (*DL* 2.22.7).

account with those of his sources (Giovanni Villani, Marchionne di Coppo Stefani, and Leonardo Bruni) reveals some inaccuracies in the passage.[5] But the lesson he draws from this is that "often one obtains things sooner and with fewer risks and expense by sidestepping them [fuggirle]"—by letting them go—"than by pursuing them with all of one's power and persistence" (*IF* 2.38). Machiavelli turns an episode that garnered relatively minor attention in his sources into a moral for his own times and, perhaps, a rebuke of Florence's relentless pursuit of domination over Pisa.

Implicit in these no doubt overly cheerful stories of how Florence won the loyal friendship of neighbors whom they treated "like brothers" and whose regained liberty from Florentine domination they allegedly welcomed is a thinly veiled critique of what was in most cases Florence's severe treatment of neighbors who fought strenuously to escape its control. As we have already seen, in the "Words to be Spoken" of 1503 Machiavelli begins his survey of the dangers confronting Florence by observing that "you find yourselves amidst two or three cities"—Pisa, Lucca, and Siena—"that desire your death more than their own life." He was fully aware, from first-hand involvement, of the intense hatred the Pisans harbored for Florence on account of the several sieges, the repeated destruction of crops in efforts to starve them into submission, and the (failed) attempt to divert the course of the Arno away from Pisa. When Pisa finally surrendered, in 1509, Machiavelli was congratulated by friends for a great victory.[6] But he did not share in the triumphalism of the moment, and, in this connection, it is remarkable and revealing that in the *Florentine Histories* there is only a glancing mention of the earlier conquest of Pisa in 1406, whose cruelty troubled the consciences of many Florentines at the time. He says only that, after Giangaleazzo Visconti died in 1402, Florence, lacking powerful enemies, "carried out the Pisan campaign and gloriously achieved victory" and that the regime of 1382–1434 conducted "many wars with much glory and added to the city's dominion Arezzo, Pisa, Cortona, Livorno, and Montepulciano" (*IF* 3.29.2–8). That is all Machiavelli has to say about what was perhaps the most significant addition to Florence's territorial state, the conquest that made the republic one of Italy's major powers. Did the long and brutal war against Pisa in his own day cause Machiavelli to avert his mind's eye from the horrors of the first conquest? He does not similarly shy away from the ferocious suppression of the rebellion of the subject city of Volterra in 1472, into which Lorenzo de' Medici sent Federico da Montefeltro and his army, causing the "destruction and sack of the city, which for an entire day was plundered and raided, with neither women nor religious sites being spared." Nor does

[5] See Anna Maria Cabrini, *Per una valutazione delle "Istorie fiorentine" del Machiavelli. Note sulle fonti del Secondo Libro* (Florence: La Nuova Italia Editrice, 1985), pp. 324–9.

[6] See the letters of Agostino Vespucci (8 June 1509) and Filippo Casavecchia (17 June 1509), in *Lettere*, pp. 306–10.

Machiavelli hesitate to assert that "it was entirely Lorenzo de' Medici's operation [impresa]" (*IF* 7.30.10–13; on which, see Chapter 9).

Machiavelli faults the Florentines for a variety of errors in the administration of the territorial state. In his analysis of the general uselessness of fortresses, he says that the ones Florence built (before 1494) in the western portion of the dominion were inadequate, preventing neither the French army from invading nor the Pisans from declaring their independence after the French seized them. The Florentines, says Machiavelli, should have adopted the Roman policy of either making the conquered city an ally ("compagna") or destroying it. "If the fortresses had not been there, the Florentines would not have depended on them to hold Pisa, and the king [Charles] would not have been able to deprive the Florentines of Pisa in that way" (*DL* 2.24.36–8). In other words, because the Florentines were unable to defend the fortresses, they had to cede them to Charles, which made it easier for the Pisans to break away. Subsequent French promises to assist in the recovery of Pisa cost Florence a great deal of treasure and sparked one crisis after another. Here too Florence made mistakes. For example, Machiavelli recalls that in 1500, as the forces of the French captain Beaumont were preparing to lay siege, Pisan envoys came to him offering to surrender the city under the condition that the French not hand Pisa over to Florence for four months. The Florentines "absolutely refused the offer," Machiavelli says, because "they had unwisely" (from "debolezza di consiglio") "placed themselves in the king's hands, despite not trusting him" and consequently failed to understand that it would have been better to let the Pisans surrender to the French and then accept the city from the king, rather than "buy the king's promises" that he would one day restore to Florence a Pisa he did not as yet control (*DL* 1.38.13–16).

Despite his praise for Florence's "brotherly" treatment of Pistoia, elsewhere he cites Pistoia as an example of the mistaken and failed Florentine policy of taking the "middle way [via del mezzo]." Of the three ways of pacifying a city rent by factional divisions—killing the factional leaders, banishing them, and urging them to make peace—the Florentines always chose the third way, which, Machiavelli says, is the "most damaging, least certain, and most useless" of the three. Ever greater violence and discord followed each attempt to reconcile the factions, until, worn out by these repeated failures, (in early 1502) the Florentines tried the second method of exiling some of the factional leaders and imprisoning others, which brought some stability. Machiavelli was closely involved with the resolution of the Pistoia crisis, having been sent there three times in 1501, but, despite the partial success of the second method, he insists that the first—killing the leaders—would have been safer. He regrets that weak republics—among which he counts Florence—are unable carry out actions that have about them "il grande e il generoso." In Machiavelli and other writers of the time, "generoso" often means noble and suggests the related qualities of altruism, courage, and sacrifice; hence actions that have in them "il grande e il generoso" can be understood as ones that are exceptional, courageous, and motivated by concern for the common good. (Needless to say, "generous," without extensive qualification, would be a misleading translation.) But "the weakness of modern men, caused by their weak upbringing [debole educazione]" and "poor knowledge of things" (or history: "poca notizia delle cose") causes them to assess "the judgments of the ancients" as "in part inhumane and in part impossible" (*DL* 3.27.2–13).

Weak defenses and inadequate cohesion within the dominion, especially after 1494, Machiavelli contends, made Florence's territorial state an easy target for enemies aiming to undermine the republican government. Venice, he recalls, sent troops to support Pisa and, in 1498, invaded the dominion in collusion with the exiled Medici (*DL* 3.18.14–19). The two episodes that most impressed upon Machiavelli the need for stronger defenses—a conviction that ultimately led to the militia he promoted, planned, and created in 1506—were Cesare Borgia's invasion in 1501 and Vitellozzo Vitelli's occupation of Arezzo and the Valdichiana in 1502. Having seized Faenza (but not Bologna), Borgia wanted his army to return to Rome through Tuscany and sent an envoy to ask the Florentines for a safe-conduct ("passo"). (He also demanded that the Florentines convert their government into an oligarchy of twenty or twenty-five citizens.)[7] According to Machiavelli, in the advisory session convened by Florence's Signoria to discuss the city's response, no one was in favor of allowing Borgia to traverse Florentine territory. Actually, this was not so: some did advise granting Borgia the permission he sought because Florence did not have the forces to stop him.[8] Biagio Buonaccorsi relates that Florence sent three ambassadors, Piero Soderini, Alamanno Salviati, and Iacopo de' Nerli, to offer Borgia a rapid passage through the dominion on three conditions: that his troops not enter any walled town, that he not bring with him Orsini and Vitelli troops, and that he take the road farthest from the city of Florence.[9] The conditions were not observed: the troops of Orsini and Vitelli, who detested Florence, invaded the dominion and inflicted much damage; and Borgia himself, as we have seen, brought his troops to within a few miles of the city. Machiavelli mentions none of this and instead accuses the Florentines of "not following the Roman procedure, for, with [Borgia] very well armed and the Florentines so poorly armed that they could not prevent him from passing through" Florentine territory, "it would have been more to their honor if it seemed he was traversing the dominion with their permission than forcing his way through" (*DL* 1.38.7–11). The criticism is slightly off the mark, given that Borgia did enter the dominion with the negotiated permission of the Florentines. Machiavelli was certainly aware of the facts, and what vexed him and caused him

[7] Parenti, *Storia fiorentina*, ed. Matucci, vol. 2, p. 437.

[8] *Consulte e pratiche della Repubblica fiorentina 1498–1505*, 2 vols., ed. Denis Fachard (Geneva: Droz, 1993), vol. 2, pp. 628–39. See also note 25 in *DL*, ed. Bausi, 1.38, p. 188.

[9] Biagio Buonaccorsi, *Diario dall'anno 1498 all'anno 1512 e altri scritti*, ed. Enrico Niccolini (Rome: Istituto Storico Italiano per il Medio Evo, 1999), p. 105.

to recall the episode as he did may have been Florence's inability to oppose any resistance, either to prevent Borgia and the others from invading or to stop them, especially Vitelli, from plundering towns and farms.

The other major instance, which certainly frustrated Machiavelli, of Florence's weakness vis-à-vis malign external actors was the Arezzo crisis of June 1502, when Vitellozzo Vitelli and his troops occupied the southeastern portion of the dominion, with the unacknowledged support of Cesare Borgia and, behind him, Pope Alexander. Vitelli was accompanied by Piero de' Medici, who tried to find support for restoring his family to power. Echoing his memorandum on how to deal with the towns that had rebelled ("Del modo di trattare"), in the *Discourses* Machiavelli takes the Florentines to task for adopting the "via del mezzo"—the half-way solution that the Romans "always fled"—in dealing with disloyal towns. Had the Florentines implemented the Roman policy of favoring the less culpable towns with privileges and grants of citizenship and destroying the more resolutely defiant ones, especially Arezzo, and resettling their inhabitants so that they "could no longer do harm," "they would have secured the dominion, made Florence more powerful," and acquired the lands they needed for agricultural production. "Instead they adopted the via del mezzo," neither fully pardoning and rewarding the Aretines nor sufficiently punishing them or destroying the city. "To anyone advising that Arezzo be destroyed, those who considered themselves wiser said it would not be to the republic's honor to demolish it, because it would seem that Florence lacked the strength to hold it." Such arguments, Machiavelli avers, might seem valid, but "honor consists in being able, and knowing how, to punish [a rebellious town], not in being able to hold it in the face of a thousand dangers" (*DL* 2.23.7–19).

Machiavelli returns to the Arezzo rebellion in *Discourses* 3.27, the same chapter in which he gives a more critical view of Florence's policy toward Pistoia. He recalls that the French commander, Antoine de Torote Langres (Machiavelli calls him Lanc), sent by King Louis to ratify the restoration of the occupied territories to Florence, visited each of the towns. In each, some inhabitants approached him to proclaim their loyalty to the "parte [faction]" of the Marzocco, the image of a lion supporting a shield depicted with a lily, that was the symbol of the Florentine republic. Instead of welcoming these declarations, Langres denounced "this division" between implied pro-Florentine and anti-Florentine subjects. In France, he told them, anyone who said he belongs to the "parte" of the king would be punished for suggesting the existence of a "parte" opposed to the king. Machiavelli of course knew, but does not mention here, that in the towns Piero de' Medici entered during the rebellion many inhabitants also pledged fealty to the Marzocco shouting the Medici cry "Palle, palle." They apparently assumed that Florentine sovereignty inhered as much in the Medici as in the republic that displaced them. The memory of Langres' scolding of those who thought it necessary, when the crisis was over, to affirm their allegiance to the republic strengthened Machiavelli's awareness of the danger of divided loyalties in the dominion. For Machiavelli, the episode underscored the importance, for a state, of commanding the loyalty and obedience of all its citizens and subjects. The source, he says, of the erroneous opinion that it is possible to control a city by exploiting its internal differences is the "weakness of those who govern [di chi è signore], who, aware of their inability to hold territories [stati] by force and with virtú, turn to such methods, which are sometimes useful in quiet times, but which in difficult times reveal how fallacious they are" (*DL* 3.27.22–3). The danger of wavering loyalties in the dominion remained a constant concern for Machiavelli and one of his chief criticisms of Florence's administration of the territorial state.

Florence's most consequential impact on the geopolitical configuration of Italy in the fifteenth century was Cosimo de' Medici's alliance with Francesco Sforza. Florence under the Medici did not have the military strength to indulge expansionist ambitions (as it had in the late fourteenth and early fifteenth centuries). But it was the wealthiest of the Italian states, and both the pre-Medici republic and the Medici regime used their considerable financial resources to assert influence and assist allies. Sforza was receiving subsidies from Cosimo while still a free-lance mercenary, and in the struggle for Milan in the late 1440s Cosimo's financial and diplomatic support was crucial to Sforza's success. In addition to the private assistance he gave Sforza, Cosimo used his influence to persuade the Florentine government to make public funds available to him.

In chapter 23 of book 6 of the *Histories*, Machiavelli assesses Cosimo's alliance with Sforza while highlighting the controversy it generated in Florence. Filippo Maria Visconti's death in 1447 without male heirs opened a triangular struggle pitting the Ambrosian Republic, established by the Milanese, against both Venice and Sforza, who simultaneously fought each other as both sought to abolish the republic. No one in Florence wanted Venice to seize control of the whole of Italy north of the Po (what was then called Lombardy), but opinions were divided over whether to support the fledgling republic or Sforza. Machiavelli dramatizes the opposition to the alliance with Sforza in a debate (perhaps invented, perhaps partially embellished, and, in any case, situated in 1449) in which Neri Capponi, the war hero who defeated the Milanese forces at Anghiari in 1440, argues that Sforza would be too dangerous as duke of Milan and that Lombardy should be divided between the Ambrosian and Venetian republics. Machiavelli has Cosimo's "friends" reject Capponi's views and accuse him of not wanting Sforza to become duke of Milan because he did not want Cosimo to become more powerful in Florence. Machiavelli thus uses the debate to emphasize that Florence's foreign policy was being driven by Cosimo's aims and interests and that the disagreements about Sforza turned on whether Cosimo should be allowed to enhance his power with a strategic foreign alliance. He has Cosimo oppose Capponi's views and assert that assisting Sforza would be beneficial to Florence and Italy. Machiavelli's Cosimo also affirms that "it is an unwise opinion to believe that the

Milanese can keep themselves free." Milan will inevitably fall, says Cosimo, to either Sforza or Venice, because "the characteristics [qualità] of its citizenry, their way of life, and their entrenched factional divisions [le sette antiquate] are inimical to any form of republican governance [civile governo]." This echoes the assessment of Milan in *Discourses* 1.17.10–11 as a city whose advanced state of corruption makes liberty unsustainable. Machiavelli has Cosimo reject Capponi's warning that the Milanese might submit to Venice in order to escape Sforza's clutches: they would not do so, says Cosimo, because Sforza, unlike the Venetians, has his "parte" in Milan, i.e. his faction of supporters. "These differences of opinion kept the city in high suspense," but Cosimo's view of course prevailed (*IF* 6.23.5–12).[10] The Venetians, Machiavelli adds, seeing Florence's old fear of Visconti Milan transferred to themselves, became hostile to their former Florentine allies, and the result was the diplomatic rearrangement in which Florence and Milan became allied against Venice and Naples (*IF* 6.25.3–4). When the Venetian ambassador in Florence expressed his government's dismay at Cosimo's abandonment of their long-standing alliance, the Signoria entrusted the reply to Cosimo, who, Machiavelli writes, delivered "a long and wise oration," emphasizing how much Venice had benefitted from its thirty-year alliance with Florence, especially "how much *imperio* [territorial aggrandizement] it had acquired with Florentine money, soldiers, and counsel." Machiavelli then has Cosimo say, somewhat ominously, that, seeing no merit in the Venetians' grievances, "he fears they contain some hidden poison not immediately recognizable. If so, the Florentines would make clear to everyone that, as beneficial as their friendship had been, in the same measure would their enmity be damaging." Ostensibly offering solace for the alliance switch, Machiavelli's Cosimo alludes to potential future conflicts between the two republics (*IF* 6.25.8–10).

Cosimo's realignment of peninsular alliances is often seen as a masterstroke of diplomatic engineering that strengthened the equilibrium—the balance of power—among the Italian states and, with it, the peace of Italy. But in the rest of the *Histories* Machiavelli shows how often Venice subsequently created problems for both Italy and Florence. As we shall see, in 1467, the Venetians allowed their chief condottiere to lead an army to the Romagna borderlands in support of anti-Medici Florentine exiles, where they burned down a town and damaged the countryside (*IF* 7.20); in 1482, they attacked Ferrara and drew much of the rest of Italy into a war no one else wanted (*IF* 8.24); and, as we have seen, in 1496 they sent troops to support Pisa against Florence and in 1498 expanded their hostile actions to the Tuscan-Romagnol mountains and the Casentino, these latter incursions posing the added threat of the presence, among the invaders, of the exiled Medici brothers, Piero and Giuliano. Although the Florentines expelled the intruders,

[10] See Chapter 8 for the domestic implications of this debate.

Machiavelli claims in the *Decennale* that, stung by this defeat, the Venetians "avenged the blow they suffered" by forming the fateful alliance in 1499 with King Louis (D^1 181–204), thus suggesting that at least part of Venice's motivation in inviting the French into Italy was revenge against Florence. More than once he attributes to the Venetians a "lust for power [cupidità del dominare]" (*IF* 1.29.13; 6.26.12), emphasizing their never satiated desire for expansion. Little wonder, then, that in *The Prince* (11.6–8) he says Venice was thought to be one of the two most likely sources of aggressive actions capable of upsetting the equilibrium of the Italian states. He had more than enough reason to conclude that Cosimo's diplomatic revolution, motivated by the calculus that Francesco Sforza would be a reliable protector of the Medici family and regime, brought more problems than benefits, for both Florence and Italy.

MILAN

However much the Sforza dynasty provided security for the Medici regime, Machiavelli saw its role in the wider theater of peninsular politics as destabilizing. As we have seen, he traces the disasters that "have devastated and are still devastating Italy" to the "evil seeds" of Ludovico Sforza's "ambition" (*IF* 8.36.25), declaring him the "cause" (*IF* 8.18.7) and "primo motor" (D^1 51) of Italy's ruin. But Machiavelli's critique of Milan's ruling families reaches further back to the succession crises and divided inheritances of the fourteenth century and their consequences for both the Milanese "stato" and Italy. In the *Histories* he recounts the victory of Matteo Visconti (in 1311) over the rival Della Torre family and summarizes, with some inaccuracies, the various successions down to the joint succession (in 1354) of the brothers Bernabò and Galeazzo. When Galeazzo died (in 1378), his son, Giangaleazzo, "divided the stato with [his uncle] Bernabò," but seven years later treacherously ("con inganno") murdered him and became sole ruler of the Visconti dominions (*IF* 1.27.5–13; the murder is also recalled, emphasizing the "fraude," in *DL* 2.13.7). When Giangaleazzo died (in 1402), another joint succession ensued, between his sons Giovanni Maria and Filippo Maria: "the stato was divided into many parts, and in the troubles that followed Giovanni Maria was killed," according to Machiavelli by the "popolo di Milano" (*IF* 1.27.14), "and Filippo Maria was imprisoned" (*IF* 1.34.4). The dissolution of the Visconti "stato" and the young ages of Giangaleazzo's sons allowed the condottiere Facino Cane, who had for a time been in Giangaleazzo's service, to seize control of large swaths of the dominions. Facino died without male heirs (in 1412) and bequeathed "his stati [territories]" to his wife Beatrice (di Tenda, known to modernity as the tragic heroine of the eponymous opera by Vincenzo Bellini). The deaths of both Facino and Giovanni Maria paved the way for Filippo Maria's reconstitution of his father's "stato." According to Machiavelli, Facino "arranged with his friends for

Beatrice to be married to Filippo Maria, and, as a result of this marriage," Machiavelli writes, "Filippo became powerful and regained Milan and the whole stato of Lombardy," adding, with cutting sarcasm, that, "grateful for these great favors, as all princes almost always are," he "accused his wife of adultery and had her executed" (*IF* 1.37). Machiavelli's emphasis on the importance of the marriage for Filippo Maria's assertion of control over Milan and Lombardy anticipates a central theme in his narrative of the rise to power a generation later of Francesco Sforza, whose single-minded pursuit of marriage to Filippo Maria's daughter, Bianca Maria, governed his every action for a decade. Bringing full circle the deadly sacrifice of women in Milan's ducal dynasties, Machiavelli later relates (*IF* 7.33.8) the rumor that Francesco's son and heir, Galeazzo Maria, had Bianca Maria, his own mother, killed soon after taking power.

Machiavelli's best-known utterance about Francesco Sforza may be the brief comment in *The Prince* (7.6) that "from a private station [as a condottiere] he became duke of Milan with the appropriate means [debiti mezzi] and with his great virtú," an assessment Machiavelli contrasts in the same chapter with Cesare Borgia's rise to power through the "fortuna" of his papal father. Machiavelli says no more about Sforza in chapter 7, but, from the lengthy account in the *Florentine Histories* of Sforza's career as a condottiere and his conquest of the duchy, it is difficult to see how the "debiti mezzi" he allegedly employed had much to do with virtú in any of its meanings. In Machiavelli's telling, his methods included betrayal and broken promises, the frequent abandonment of one employer for another, playing the states of Italy off against each other, and, most of all, the pursuit of marriage to Bianca Maria, a prospect that Duke Filippo Maria held out as early as the mid-1430s in an effort—largely futile—to control his ambitious captain. Sforza left the service of Filippo Maria to become captain of the Venetian-Florentine-papal league and consequently fought against Filippo Maria. But when he took his forces into Lombardy to confront the Milanese army, he refused to cross the Po "because he did not wish to deprive himself of the hopes he had for the marriage alliance," which "had a strong hold on him [moveva forte il conte]." "Because the duke [Filippo Maria] had no male heirs, [Sforza] hoped through the marriage to make himself signore of Milan, which is why he always suspended military planning with the Florentines" (*IF* 5.13.5, 14). Venice wanted to sever ties with him, convinced of the "necessity of curbing his insolence once and for all and not letting it grow to the point of becoming incorrigible" (*IF* 5.14.2–5). Without breaking his contract with Florence, Sforza returned to the service of Filippo Maria, who tried to keep him loyal by several times making preparations for the wedding, only to postpone it, and by giving him ample supplies of cash (presumably to counteract the financial backing Sforza received from Cosimo de' Medici). The Florentines wanted him to return to Tuscany, but Sforza's "desire that the marriage alliance be concluded kept him undecided [sospeso]" (*IF* 5.18.7–10). Feeling "mocked [sbeffato]" by Filippo Maria and nursing "great hatred" for him, Sforza signed a new agreement with Florence and Venice (*IF* 5.19.9) and began military operations *against* Visconti in Lombardy (*IF* 5.22–5). The duke sought a reconciliation in vain, and hostilities resumed. When Sforza suffered a major defeat at the hands of Visconti's chief condottiere, Niccolò Piccinino, it seemed, Machiavelli writes, a "clear victory" for Filippo Maria and "definitive ruin" for Sforza. But Sforza escaped disaster when Piccinino so angered Visconti by demanding the city of Piacenza as his reward that the duke immediately offered Sforza a truce and prompt marriage to his daughter. Sforza agreed and the wedding took place (1441). Rephrasing his Milanese source, Giovanni Simonetta, Machiavelli attributes the sudden turn of events, so unexpectedly favorable for Sforza, to "fortune, who never lacks for ways to favor friends and foil enemies" (*IF* 6.4.5). Far from rising to power by means of his own virtú, as Machiavelli claims in *The Prince*, in the *Histories* Sforza becomes another creature of fortune.

Visconti and Sforza continued to quarrel, but when Venetian forces defeated Filippo Maria's army and occupied territories up to the city of Milan itself, the duke begged Sforza for help. Machiavelli says both Visconti and Venice now needed Sforza, and each offered him complete command of their respective armies, the Venetians adding Milan itself as inducement. Sforza took Visconti's offer, preferring not to be under the thumb of Venice and knowing that the duke's death was not far off (*IF* 6.12). Filippo Maria died in 1447 and, once again, the Visconti state disintegrated. Machiavelli says the people of the city of Milan were divided between those who "wanted to live free" and those who preferred to live under a "principe," among the latter some favoring Sforza and others King Alfonso of Naples. But those "who loved liberty were more united" and proclaimed a republic. Many cities of the former duchy, however, refused to recognize the authority of Milan's republic, thinking that they could, like Milan itself, "enjoy their own liberty." Pavia and Parma declared their independence. Of the cities not inclined to go that route, Lodi and Piacenza "gave themselves to the Venetians" (IF 6.13.6–8). The citizens of Pavia, realizing at a certain point that they lacked the military force to defend their independence, offered the city to Sforza under the condition that he not subject them to the "rule [imperio] of Milan." Sforza feared Milanese anger if he took possession of Pavia but decided to accept it, reminding the Milanese that Pavia would otherwise no doubt seek Venice's protection. Although dismayed by what they saw as Sforza's betrayal, the Milanese, having indeed nowhere else to turn except to the dreaded Venetians, concluded that they could not sever their contract with Sforza (*IF* 6.17.2–7). Machiavelli's account calls attention to the incomplete integration of these formerly independent cities (still partly autonomous in their internal affairs), which the Visconti had brought under their personal lordship but never forged into a cohesive state—a failure that interested Machiavelli no doubt because of the similar problems in the Florentine dominion. The separate directions taken by the cities of Lombardy after Filippo Maria's death must have reminded Machiavelli of Pisa's revolt in 1494 and the rebellion of Arezzo in 1502.

Following Simonetta's account, Machiavelli describes Sforza at the moment of Filippo Maria's death as unprepared (his troops not "ad ordine"), fearful of Venetian retribution, mistrustful of the other Italian powers, and resigned "to show his face to fortune" and "let himself be counseled by whatever events [accidenti] fortune might bring." He at first welcomed the proclamation of the Ambrosian Republic, but only because he assumed the Milanese could "turn to no other arms but his" for defense against Venetian ambitions to occupy the whole of the former Visconti dominion (*IF* 6.13.1–4). Sforza defeated the Venetians in several engagements, but when the Milanese discovered Sforza's "ambition and the goal" to which he aspired—lordship over Milan—they "were deeply perturbed" (*IF* 6.17.6). Sforza soon betrayed the republic and signed an agreement (in 1448) with Venice: in return for the financial resources he needed to subdue Milan and dissolve the republic, he would restore territories he had seized from Venice and even hand over parts of the Visconti dominion (*IF* 6.19.5–8). The doomed Ambrosian Republic sent ambassadors to Sforza to express dismay and aggrieved submission. Machiavelli transforms the speech he found in Simonetta from a cringing supplication for mercy into an angry and indignant denunciation of Sforza's "cruelty, ambition, and arrogance." "How miserable," he has them say, "are cities that must defend their liberty against the ambition of those who desire to suppress it. Unhappier still are those compelled to defend themselves with faithless mercenary arms like yours." Prophesying the calamities that awaited the Sforza, the ambassadors warn him that the "rule [regno]" he has begun "with deceit and infamy will end in disgrace and disaster" (*IF* 6.20.13–17)—allusions to the assassination of Sforza's son and heir, Duke Galeazzo Maria (in 1476), the expulsion of Ludovico il Moro (in 1499–1500) who ended his life in a French prison, and the seizure of the duchy by the French, the Swiss, the French again, and eventually Spain in the 1520s.

Elsewhere, in his own voice, Machiavelli has unflattering things to say about Sforza. In the *Ritratto di cose di Francia*,[11] written in 1511–12, explaining the marriage connection between the Visconti and the house of Orléans, he says that the "stato di Milano" was "usurped by the Sforzeschi, illegitimately, as they say, because it should have passed to the heirs of Valentina," the daughter of Giangaleazzo who married a duke of Orléans and became the grandmother of Louis XII. In *The Prince*, giving examples of mercenaries who aspire to their own "glory [grandezza]" and are therefore dangerous to the states that employ them, Machiavelli says that, although the Milanese hired Sforza to defend them against the Venetians, he instead "joined with [the Venetians] to crush them" (*P* 12.10–16). He criticizes

[11] *SPM*, pp. 541–66 (at 564).

Sforza for building the Castello (Sforzesco) in Milan, claiming it "has done and will do more damage to the House of Sforza than any other defect [disordine] of that stato" (*P* 20.28), thus hinting at other unspecified *disordini*. Machiavelli's most damning denunciation of the founder of the Sforza dynasty is in the first book of the *Art of War*, where he has Fabrizio Colonna enunciate the principle that war must never be the profession of private individuals, that only governments, whether republics or princes, should engage in war and should never let any citizen or subject exercise it as "his private profession [sua particolare arte]." Private citizens or subjects, Fabrizio says, cannot make war their full-time profession without being "rapacious, fraudulent, and violent." The aim of "supporting oneself at all times" in the profession of war results in "plunder and violence and killings that such soldiers inflict on friends and enemies alike." Mercenaries, Fabrizio says, want wars to last as long as possible, and if peace comes they routinely resort to pillaging. He recalls the free-lance "companies" that extorted money from cities and sometimes sacked them. And he implicates Sforza: "In the age of our fathers, Francesco Sforza, in order to live ostentatiously [onorevolmente] in times of peace, not only deceived the Milanese people whose hired soldier he was but also robbed them of their liberty and made himself their prince" (*AG* 1.51–6). If they have large enough armies, Fabrizio adds, again adducing Sforza as his example, mercenaries can do "serious damage" (*AG* 1.100–1). He cites Sforza yet another time in emphasizing how much cities should fear hired foreign soldiers (*AG* 1.175).

It is not only in Sforza's career as a mercenary and his suppression of the liberty of the Milanese people that Machiavelli reveals his darker side. In the *Florentine Histories*, he recounts a spine-chilling episode of Sforza's brutality. Sforza and King Ferdinand of Naples (called Ferrando by Machiavelli and Ferrante by most modern historians) were allies in the mid-1460s, and each planned, with the other's complicity, to rid himself of the chief threat to his power and thus enhance the prospects of a smooth succession for their heirs. Ferrante's threat came from the kingdom's barons, and Machiavelli says he dealt with it by "expunging" them. Sforza saw the threat in Iacopo Piccinino, the son of Niccolò who had become the "primo capitano"—the leading mercenary—of Italy. Because Iacopo had no "stato" (ruled no territory), says Machiavelli, "anyone who did have a stato had to fear him, especially [Sforza], who, troubled by his own example" in having risen from professional mercenary to duke of Milan, "feared he would be unable to keep his stato and securely bequeath it to his sons as long as Iacopo was alive." Machiavelli here puts his finger on a major weakness of many of Italy's princely states, namely, the insecurity of princes who rose from a "private station" to lordship and therefore lacked the legitimacy of generations of hereditary succession behind them. He recounts the sordid story over two chapters. Iacopo Piccinino, he says, was frightened by what Ferrante's assault on the barons might portend for him and so decided to reconcile with Sforza and "put himself in the duke's hands" by returning to Milan (*IF* 7.7.4–9). Iacopo had loyally served both Filippo Maria and the

Ambrosian Republic, in the process acquiring many friends and much good will in Milan. But his popularity proved to be his undoing. Whereas Sforza's power had engendered some envy among the Milanese, Iacopo's absence from the city made the people long to see him. Large crowds enthusiastically welcomed him and sang his name—a display of affection that hastened his demise, Machiavelli says, because "the greater the duke's fear of him, the more he desired to eliminate him." The scheme began with Sforza allowing his daughter Drusiana's long-promised marriage to Iacopo to take place. Ferrante then invited Iacopo into his service, and the newlyweds traveled to Naples where they were warmly welcomed and fêted, after which Ferrante completed the betrayal by imprisoning and killing Iacopo. Machiavelli's comment on the episode is a savage denunciation of "our Italian princes," who "feared and extinguished in others the virtú that was lacking in themselves, so that, with no one possessing any virtú, they exposed [Italy] to the ruin that, a short while later, destroyed and tormented it" (*IF* 7.8).

Commenting in *The Prince* (14.3) on the importance of arms to a prince's success, Machiavelli says that "because Francesco Sforza was armed, he became duke of Milan from a private station [di privato]," whereas "his sons, because they shunned the discomforts [disagi] of arms, fell from the status of dukes to a private station [di duchi diventorono privati]." This was Ludovico's fate. It did not happen to Galeazzo Maria, but several times in the *Florentine Histories* Machiavelli notes the contemporary perception of his ineptitude in military matters. One such moment occurred after Francesco died in 1466 in the midst of the struggle in Florence, following Cosimo de' Medici's death two years earlier, over the continuation of Medici control (see Chapter 9). Opponents of the Medici regime sought to prevent the confirmation, requested by Galeazzo Maria, of his father's agreement with Florence and to annul Florence's alleged obligation to pay an annual subvention. They argued that the agreement made with Francesco had lapsed with his death; nor, they added, was there any reason to renew the accord or the payments, "because, since Galeazzo does not have the same virtú [military expertise] Francesco had, they could not expect any advantage [utile]" from renewing the agreement (*IF* 7.12.6–8). Piero de' Medici emerged victorious over his rivals and confirmed the pact. The next year, when the condottiere Bartolomeo Colleoni and a group of other captains, supported by Venice, threatened Florentine territory, Florence joined King Ferrante and Galeazzo Maria in a defensive alliance. With neither army showing much inclination to engage in serious combat, Florentine officials complained that they were spending a great deal of money for no purpose and blamed their own civilian commissioners. But the commissioners protested that the "cause" of the inaction, as Machiavelli says, "was entirely Duke Galeazzo, who, because he had much power [autorità] but little experience, was unable to make useful decisions and did not trust those who could. No *virtuosa* or useful operation could possibly be carried out as long as [Galeazzo] remained with the army," Machiavelli has them insist. The solution was to trick him into going home. The Florentines told him that, although "it was of great benefit that he had come in person to assist them," nonetheless "they valued his and his state's security [salute] over their own interests. If his state was secure, they could hope for fortunate outcomes in all matters; otherwise, they feared every sort of adversity. Hence they believed it was not safe for him to remain absent from Milan for very long. Because he had recently come to power [sendo nuovo nello stato] and had neighbors [the Venetians] who were both powerful and fearful of him, anyone seeking to conspire against him could easily do so." What Machiavelli reports (or, more likely, invents) here was a ruse, and he says Galeazzo fell for it. He "liked their advice and returned to Milan without giving it another thought." Without this "impediment," the commissioners showed they were correct in attributing the sluggish pace of military operations to Galeazzo's incompetence and moved quickly to engage the enemy (*IF* 7.20.5–12). Machiavelli evidently enjoyed this story.

The account of Galeazzo Maria's state visit to Florence (in 1471) is an indictment of both Lorenzo's Florence and the culture of the ducal court. In a city already straying from its sober traditions of decorum and moderation in dress and speech (the consequences of peace, Machiavelli explains), the duke and his courtiers displayed an even greater disrespect for custom by eating meat throughout the Lenten season. When the church of Santo Spirito went up in flames during a religious play, many believed the Almighty was "outraged at us and wanted to show his anger." "If, therefore," Machiavelli comments, "the duke found the city of Florence full of courtly frivolities and customs contrary to any well-ordered polity [cortigiane delicatezze e costumi a ogni bene ordinata civilità contrari], he left it even more so" (*IF* 7.28). In the *Histories* Machiavelli portrays Galeazzo in terms similar to those he has Fabrizio use at the end of the *Art of War* to excoriate dissolute princes more interested in opulence and pleasure than in governance or defense of their states. The corruption displayed by the ducal court sets the stage for Machiavelli's account of Galeazzo's assassination (in 1476), which he says, alluding to the Pazzi conspiracy sixteen months later, was "a portent of greater evils." Surpassing the court's licentiousness in Florence, the duke's depravity at home knew no bounds. Machiavelli describes him, partly in the accusations of the conspirators and partly in his own narrative voice, as "lecherous [libidinoso] and cruel," a violator of "noble ladies" who "took pleasure in publicizing" his conquests, had men killed with great cruelty, and lived with the monstrous rumor that he had his own mother killed in order to seize the dowry—the city of Cremona—she had brought to her marriage to Francesco Sforza. Three young nobles, two of them "dishonored" by the duke's liberties with women of their families, fortified these personal motives with a detestation of all princes imbibed from their humanist teacher Cola da Montano, who spurred them to action (*IF* 7.33.1–10). The murder took place in the church of Santo Stefano on December 26, 1476. The conspirators had hoped, even assumed, that the attack would find favor with the people and spark a popular uprising, but none of this happened. Although the conspiracy, planned in secret and courageously executed, succeeded in killing Galeazzo, the failure of the larger purpose of freeing the patria from tyranny was sealed when those whom the conspirators hoped would follow and defend them did neither. Machiavelli comments that "princes should therefore learn to live in such a manner, and make themselves so revered and loved, that no one plotting to kill them could have any hope of saving himself" (*IF* 7.34.21–6).

By the time the narrative reaches Ludovico il Moro, the dysfunctions of the Sforza dynasty no longer occasion surprise. Machiavelli recounts yet another succession crisis, triggered by the assassination of Galeazzo, whose only son, Giangaleazzo, was a child. Officially, the boy was the new duke, but in reality whoever had custody of him controlled the duchy. The struggle pitted, on one side, his mother, the duchess Bona di Savoia, and the powerful secretary Cicco Simonetta who had been administering the state for some years, and, on the other side, the brothers of Galeazzo Maria, chief among them Ludovico. Initially, the duchess, supported by Simonetta, had the stronger hand and exiled Ludovico and his brothers who made several unsuccessful attempts to force their way back to Milan (*IF* 8.13.1–4). They finally succeeded (in 1479–80) as a result of a bizarre episode of palace intrigue that Machiavelli adapted from Bernardino Corio's *Storia di Milano*.[12] When Ludovico entered the Milanese dominion with a contingent of troops, "Milan and the entire stato," says Machiavelli, "were up in arms." Several Sforza friends advised the duchess to allow Ludovico's return "in order to put an end to the disputes" that were roiling the city. The leading voice among those urging her to readmit Ludovico was a certain Antonio Tassino, described by Machiavelli as a native of Ferrara "of humble origins" who had entered the service of Duke Galeazzo Maria as Bona's personal attendant ("cameriere"). Machiavelli hints, tongue-in-cheek, at the amorous relationship between Bona and Tassino that most historians accept as fact when he says that "either because he was handsome [bello di corpo] or because of some other secret ability [segreta virtú], after the duke's death he rose to such influence with the duchess that he practically governed the stato." This deeply offended Cicco Simonetta, whom Machiavelli lauds as "most distinguished for his wisdom [prudenzia] and long experience [lunga pratica]." He had served the Sforza and the duchess for many years but was now doing everything possible to diminish the upstart Tassino's influence with the duchess. Tassino's motivation, Machiavelli says, in advising Bona to repatriate Ludovico was his need for protection against Simonetta. She rashly acted on Tassino's advice without consulting Simonetta, who, foreseeing his own doom and her inevitable loss of power, told her: "You have made a decision that will cost me

[12] Bernardino Corio, *Storia di Milano*, 2 vols., ed. Anna Morisi Guerra (Turin: UTET, 1978), vol. 2, pp. 1422–3. Marcello Simonetta perceptively analyzes Machiavelli's adaptation of Corio in *Rinascimento segreto. Il mondo del Segretario da Petrarca a Machiavelli* (Milan: FrancoAngeli, 2004), pp. 161–3.

my life and you the stato." Ludovico had Simonetta executed and Tassino exiled. The angry and disconsolate duchess left the city, conceding custody of her young son to Ludovico. Machiavelli concludes the story saying, "And so Ludovico was now sole ruler of the duchy of Milan and became, as will be shown, the cause of Italy's ruin" (*IF* 8.18.1–7). Implied in this non sequitur is that Italy's fate depended on a family whose erratic and unstable character was once again on display in this ludicrous contest for power.

THE "MINOR PRINCES"

Neither a state—many statelets of various types perhaps, but not a unitary state—nor, in any effective sense, governed by the papacy,[13] the so-called States of the Church, from Bologna and the Romagna in the north, south through the Marche and Umbria, and west to Lazio and Rome, were the powder keg of Machiavelli's Italy: a disparate patchwork of cities and towns whose instability and weakness invited frequent attempts by neighboring states to seize bits of territory or establish unofficial control over one or more cities, and whose ambitious princes, many of whom moonlighted as mercenaries, often created friction and hostilities among their more powerful neighbors. Machiavelli was aware that this unwieldy and ungovernable oddity was an accident of history. Naming the "stati" of Italy in the tenth century, he says Tuscany and the Romagna were governed by a representative of the Ottonian emperors (*IF* 1.13.1). Although he gets the names wrong, he presents the struggle between Pope Gregory VII and Emperor Henry IV in the eleventh century as a turning point for Italy, with some cities supporting the pope and others the emperor: this, he says, "was the seed of the Guelf and Ghibelline factions," which guaranteed that, even when the "barbarian floods" receded, "Italy would be lacerated by internal wars" (*IF* 1.15.4). Listing the major cities of the (Lombard) League that resisted the twelfth-century emperor Frederick Barbarossa, Machiavelli says they included "most of the cities of the Romagna" but that "some cities of Lombardy, the Romagna, and the Marche at times favored one side and at other times, whenever necessary, the other side" (*IF* 1.21.3). Nine chapters later, he explains how the Romagna and the Marche attained the political configuration that endured until the convulsions of the early sixteenth century. Following Biondo Flavio's account in the *Decades*, he says the Avignonese Pope Benedict XII (1334–42) was wary of Emperor Ludwig of Bavaria's ambition to increase his power in the parts of Italy nominally subject to the empire. To prevent Ludwig from making himself "signore" of Italy, Benedict "sought alliances with all those who had unlawfully seized [usurpato] cities that once obeyed the emperor,"

[13] For the popes as "princes" of the papal states, see Chapter 4.

granting formal titles (vicariates) to these "tyrants of Lombardy," thus securing their legal right ("giusto titolo") to possess the cities they ruled and binding them "to the defense of Italy." In retaliation, the emperor "seeing with how much liberality the pope had given away the cities of the empire, and so as not to be less liberal with the possessions of others than the pope had been, awarded the cities of the Church to their tyrants," thus legitimating their possession of them with "imperial authority." In effect, the papacy legitimated the rule by local lords of nominally imperial cities, as the emperor legitimated the rule by local lords of cities nominally subject to the Church, each subverting the authority of the other. Machiavelli names the ruling families of the major cities within the papal states: the Malatesta in Rimini, Pesaro, and Fano; the Montefeltro in Urbino; the Da Varano in Camerino; the Da Polenta in Ravenna; the Ordelaffi in Forlì and Cesena; the Manfredi in Faenza; and the Alidosi in Imola. Beyond these "were many others in many other cities, so that few cities subject to the Church were left without a principe." This, he writes, "kept the Church weak down to the time of Alexander VI, who, in our own time, restored the Church's authority" by overthrowing these petty dynasties (*IF* 1.30.1–4).

Much of this, borrowed uncritically from Biondo Flavio, was wrong in details, but the wider picture—the establishment of a myriad of local dynasties and the consequent weakening of the Church's influence in cities and territories nominally subject to it—was largely accurate. For Machiavelli, it serves as an introduction to his summary assessment of the dysfunctions of Italy's military and political leadership in the thirty-ninth and last chapter of the first book of the *Histories*. This overview of Italy's "princes and arms" in the first half of the fifteenth century begins with the "principal states." About Naples he says only that Joanna II "held the kingdom." Some of the cities of the "Marche, the Patrimony [of St. Peter—more or less modern Lazio], and the Romagna" were subject to the Church; others were held by their "vicari" or "tyrants," such as, Machiavelli says—reprising information from chapter 30—Ferrara, Modena, and Reggio by the Este; Faenza by the Manfredi; Imola by the Alidosi; Forlì by the Ordelaffi; Rimini and Pesaro by the Malatesta; and Camerino by the Da Varano. One part of "Lombardy," he says, was subject to Duke Filippo (Visconti), the other part to the Venetians. With the exception of the Gonzaga of Mantua, he points out, all the cities of "Lombardy" that were once ruled by family dynasties had been absorbed into either the Milanese or Venetian dominions. Florence ruled "most of Tuscany"; only Lucca, under the Guinigi family, and "free" Siena were independent of Florence. The Genoese were sometimes independent and sometimes ruled by France or Milan and were now numbered among the "minor powers [minori potentati]" (*IF* 1.39.1–5).

Machiavelli then comes to the most important aspect of all the "principal powers," namely, that they were "unarmed," lacking their own (as opposed to mercenary) arms. This negligence extended to the princes' and governors' lack of interest in military matters. Duke Filippo Maria Visconti "stayed out of sight in his ducal chambers" and let his commissioners administer his wars. When the Venetians turned to expansion in Italy, they abandoned the arms that had made them "glorious" in maritime warfare and followed the customs of the "other Italians" in putting their armies under the governance of "others" (mercenaries). The popes, because it was inappropriate for men of religion to bear arms, and Queen Joanna, as a woman, both did out of necessity what the others had done through a "bad choice [mala elezione]." The Florentines, having suppressed their "nobility" over the course of many internal conflicts and "left the republic in the hands of men raised in commerce [nutricati nella mercanzia]" (merchants), likewise "followed the practices and the fortune of the others." The consequence of this general disinclination of the "principal states" to provide their own military forces was that "the arms of Italy were in the hands of either the lesser princes [minori principi]"—rulers of de facto autonomous cities, mainly in the papal dominions—"or men without territory or states [uomini senza stato]." This, for Machiavelli, was the fundamental problem. The "minori principi," he says, embraced the profession of arms to enhance their security and wealth. The "uomini senza stato," having been "raised [nutricati] from boyhood" in a culture of arms, "knowing no other profession [arte], sought, through arms, the honor that comes from wealth or power [con avere o con potenza onorarsi]" (*IF* 1.39.6–7). This blurred differentiation of the motives of the two groups—both seeking wealth, security, power, and prestige—underscores the difficulty of distinguishing them: many stateless mercenaries became or aspired to become rulers of states, and many "minor princes" hired themselves out as mercenaries. Machiavelli will illustrate throughout the *Histories* the outsized power of military captains from both groups and the ways in which they influenced and distorted relations among the "stati principali," among other reasons because of the ease with which they changed employers and, in the case of the "uomini senza stato," because of their desire to acquire lordship in some city. Their role was a constant source of instability in Italian inter-state relations and, consequently, a major cause of the strategic weakness of the larger states that employed them.

Machiavelli illustrates the destabilizing effects of military power in the hands of the "minori principi" in the *Histories* beginning in book 5 as he turns from the predominant focus on Florence in books 2–4 to the broader Italian picture. To prevent Florence from conquering Lucca—the year is 1437—Duke Filippo Maria planned to send troops into Tuscany. To keep the duke occupied in Lombardy, Florence urged Venice to attack Milanese positions. But Venice's chief captain, Gianfrancesco Gonzaga, the marquis of Mantua, decided at this moment not to renew his contract with Venice and, even worse, agreed to fight for Visconti. The "frightened" Venetians replied to the Florentine request that, far from widening the war, they were unable even to continue it unless Florence allowed Francesco Sforza, then in Florence's service, to move his forces into Lombardy and he was willing to cross the Po (as he had previously refused to do to protect the prospects of marrying Filippo Maria's daughter). "Without a captain," the Venetians said, they could not fight a war, and their only hope was to get Sforza into Lombardy. For Florence it was essential to shift hostilities away from Tuscany, even though without Sforza there was no hope of success against Lucca (*IF* 5.13.1–4). In this case, the marquis's sudden decision to "abandon" the Venetians, as Machiavelli puts it, and fight for their Milanese enemy created a predicament that Sforza, a stateless mercenary with great ambitions, compounded. Commenting on the disintegration of Venice's military situation (in 1438 and 1439), Machiavelli again blames the marquis "who for many years had been the condottiere of their republic [and who], beyond anything they could have believed, had abandoned them and sided with the duke" of Milan. Consequently, "what pride [superbia] prevented [the Venetians] from doing at the beginning of the war"—namely, seeking assistance from Florence or Francesco Sforza—"fear now compelled them to do" (*IF* 5.19.1–3). The result was an alliance between Florence and Venice (February 1439) to defend Sforza's "stati" (his family's feudal possessions) in the Marche—a joint effort of two great republics to protect the territories of a mercenary captain. Joining this "league" were also the signore of Faenza, Guidantonio Manfredi, the sons of Pandolfo Malatesta of Rimini, and Pietro Giampaolo Orsini, a freelance captain of the powerful Roman family who was frequently in the service of Florence. "With great promises," but without success, they tried to lure Gianfrancesco Gonzaga away from his new contract with Duke Filippo Maria. To make matters worse, Guidantonio Manfredi broke his agreement and, "finding better terms," also went over to the Duke of Milan, "which deprived the league of the hope it had" of quickly pushing Filippo Maria out of the Romagna and establishing control over the region. Despite the formidable alliance of Florence, Venice, Sforza, the rulers of Rimini and, as they had assumed, the signore of Faenza—Rimini and Faenza being critical to managing the Romagna—the defection of the last of these scuttled one of the league's main objectives (*IF* 5.19.10–11). Soon thereafter, the sons of Pandolfo Malatesta also deserted Venice and allied with Visconti, which "displeased" the Venetians but frightened the Florentines because their captain, Pietro Giampaolo Orsini, was in Malatesta territory and in danger of losing his forces (*IF* 5.29.1–2). Such was the ability of "minor princes" to confound the aims of the larger states.

Sigismondo Malatesta, signore of Rimini, was another of Machiavelli's powerful "minor princes." He introduces him in the context of an angry rift between Visconti and Sforza (in 1444). Sigismondo had married a daughter of Sforza, hoping the family connection would persuade Sforza to give him the lordship ("signoria") of Pesaro, then occupied by Sforza (purchased, in fact, from a cousin of Sigismondo). Instead, Sforza gave it to his own brother, infuriating Sigismondo, whose anger increased when his "enemy" Federico da Montefeltro acquired the lordship of Urbino through Sforza's "favors." So Sigismondo transferred his allegiance from Sforza to Filippo Maria and urged the pope (Eugenius IV) and the king of Naples (now Alfonso of Aragon: see below) to strike Sforza. But before that could happen, Sforza attacked Sigismondo "to give him a taste of the war he desired." "Immediately," Machiavelli writes, "clashes were everywhere in the Romagna and the Marche," as the duke of Milan, the pope, and the king sent troops to support Sigismondo, while the Florentines and Venetians sent financial help to Sforza. Filippo Maria thought this a good opportunity to seize some of the cities Sforza had occupied in Lombardy, but Florence and Venice defended them (on behalf of Sforza). Now war broke out in Lombardy as well. The Venetians won several battles, seized big chunks of the Visconti state, and crossed the Adda to raid territories "as far as Milan." Filippo Maria appealed for help to his ally Alfonso, thus igniting a peninsular-wide war (*IF* 6.11). Machiavelli's summary of these events shows how all the major states of Italy were drawn into a war that started because the signore of Rimini was angry that a powerful mercenary—Sforza—did not give him the town of Pesaro.

When next we encounter Sigismondo in Machiavelli's narrative, he is one of two captains—the other being Federico da Montefeltro—leading Florentine troops against King Alfonso's incursion into Tuscany (in 1447). A short time before, Sigismondo had been Alfonso's ally. There was "discordia" between Sigismondo and Federico, but the Florentine civilian commissioners were able to smooth things over, allowing them to work together successfully (*IF* 6.15.7). Two years later, at the time of the Ambrosian Republic, Sigismondo was fighting for Venice against Sforza's attempt to seize Milan. Encamped at the Adda, the Venetians debated whether to attack Sforza in order to relieve the besieged city of Milan. Sigismondo argued against the plan, because he knew the ability ("virtú") of Sforza and his army and, moreover, knowing that Sforza's army was dangerously short of grain and hay, "believed it possible to achieve a secure victory without fighting." So he advised that Venetian forces stay put. The Venetians agreed, hoping the Milanese would accept to be governed by them ("sotto il loro imperio") and assuming they would never yield to Sforza after all the wrongs he had inflicted on them. It did not turn out as Sigismondo predicted. In their dire need, the Milanese turned to Sforza and accepted him as their "principe" (*IF* 6.24.5–8, 18–21). Machiavelli does not directly blame Sigismondo, but the narrative clearly implies that whatever hope Venice had of bringing Milan under its "imperio" was thwarted by his faulty judgment. Sigismondo then turns up as co-captain, with Astorre Manfredi, the signore of Faenza, of Florence's forces in its war (1452) with Alfonso (*IF* 6.28.11–12). But when the principal states of Italy agreed to a general peace and formed the Lega Italica (1455), Alfonso refused to ratify his kingdom's participation unless he were given license to make war on Sigismondo and Astorre (and also Genoa). He did this, Machiavelli comments sardonically, "so that the seeds of war in Italy might remain" (*IF* 6.32.11). Machiavelli notes that Alfonso had his condottiere Iacopo Piccinino attack Sigismondo in 1456, without, however, achieving any worthwhile result (*IF* 6.35.1–3). When Alfonso's successor,

Ferrante, decided to end hostilities with Sigismondo and sign a formal agreement, Piccinino was so angry that he abandoned Ferrante and joined the rival Angevin contender for the Neapolitan throne, who, together with Piccinino and the Neapolitan barons, conquered most of the kingdom, except the capital, seemingly spelling the end of Aragonese rule in the kingdom. But it was only temporary. Piccinino switched sides again, returning to Ferrante and helping him regain the kingdom and remain in power (*IF* 6.37.9–14). Such are the repercussions, in Machiavelli's narrative, of the ambitions and animosities of Sigismondo Malatesta.

Federico da Montefeltro is the most famous of the mercenary captains among the fifteenth-century "minori principi." Machiavelli first mentions him as gaining the "signoria" of Urbino (1444) as a young client-ally of Francesco Sforza when the latter, although still a free-lance mercenary, was the most powerful lord in the Marche (*IF* 6.11.6). Shortly thereafter (1447–8), Federico is in the service of Florence against the invading army of King Alfonso of Naples (*IF* 6.15.7), but five years later he is commanding Alfonso's army of 12,000 soldiers *against* Florence (*IF* 6.28.2). In the war between Ferrante of Naples and the Angevin contender in the late 1450s Machiavelli says Ferrante "sent money to Federico," who raised troops and, despite an initial setback, helped the king preserve his rule (*IF* 6.37.11). The Florentines and their allies, Ferrante and Galeazzo Maria Sforza, hired Federico as captain of the forces defending Florence against the attack (1467) by Venice's captain Bartolomeo Colleoni and Ercole d'Este of Ferrara (*IF* 7.20.4). Federico was again in the employ of Florence, or rather of Lorenzo de' Medici, as commander of the army of 10,000 infantry and 2,000 cavalry that sacked the defenseless city of Volterra (in 1472) (*IF* 7.30.7–12). But in the very next chapter, introducing him, as if he had not properly done so previously, as "principe of Urbino, then considered most excellent in arms," Machiavelli explains how Federico switched sides. Italy was at the time, he explains, divided into two leagues, one consisting of Florence, Venice, and Milan, the other of King Ferrante of Naples and Pope Sixtus IV. Seeking to win him over to the papal-Neapolitan camp, Ferrante invited Federico to Naples. He "obeyed, to the astonishment [ammirazione] and displeasure of the Florentines," who thought Federico might fall into the same trap into which Ferrante and Francesco Sforza had lured Iacopo Piccinino. "But the opposite happened, for Federico returned from Naples and Rome highly honored and as captain of their league" (*IF* 7.31.10–13). Machiavelli does not mention Federico's important role, which we now know he had, together with Ferrante, Pope Sixtus, and the Pazzi family, in the 1478 plot against the Medici. But he does highlight Federico's prominent military role in the ensuing war in which papal and Neapolitan forces invaded Tuscany and nearly brought down the Medici regime: the enemy armies, he says, were "under the command" of Federico (*IF* 8.12.2). Machiavelli mentions him one more time, when the Italian states formed two coalitions to fight the so-called War of Ferrara (1482–4), with Venice and Sixtus seeking to punish Ferrara and take some of its territory, and

Ferrante, Milan, and Florence loosely cooperating to defend the Este state. Each participant needed a captain to lead its forces: Milan hired Federico (*IF* 8.23.1), and the Venetians secured the services of Roberto da Sanseverino (*IF* 8.22.15). Early in the war Federico became ill and died (*IF* 8.24.1). No further discussion, much less judgment, of him appears in the *Histories*. But there is a brief and revealing comment in the *Spogli*, Machiavelli's notes on events between 1464 and 1501. Sometime after Federico died, Machiavelli writes, "letters of the Duke of Urbino [Federico] were found showing that he was negotiating [teneva pratiche] with signor Ruberto," at the time when they were meant to be fighting against each other on behalf of the states that employed them. This sentence is preceded by a brief one in Latin: "Nulla fides apud mercennarios milites"—"There can be no trust in mercenary captains."[14] This is the judgment of Federico that Machiavelli declined to include in his account of the Pazzi conspiracy.

Girolamo Riario was one of several nephews Sixtus IV promoted to positions of power. His and his uncle's aim was to create a state in the Romagna that would have included cities stretching from Imola down the Via Aemilia. Machiavelli implies that the first step was Sixtus's concession of Forlì to his nephew and the removal of the long-time ruling family of the Ordelaffi. He also says that Duke Galeazzo Maria Sforza was so impressed by Sixtus's "ambitious methods [modo di procedere ambizioso]" that he betrothed his (illegitimate) daughter Caterina to Riario and gave him Imola, seized from the Alidosi, as her dowry (*IF* 7.22.6–8). There are factual errors here: in reality, the Alidosi had been pushed out much earlier by the Visconti and replaced by the Manfredi; as for Forlì, Riario gained possession of it later (in 1480). But Machiavelli's point is that Forlì and Imola were two key cities in any plan to carve out a Romagnol state and that Riario's ambition in this region was the seed from which the Pazzi conspiracy grew. Sixtus and Ferrante, he says, claimed that the cause of their "hatred" for Florence was its alliance with Venice, because Sixtus "did not believe the Church could maintain its prestige [reputazione] or that Count Girolamo [Riario] could maintain his territories [stati] in the Romagna as long as the Florentines and Venetians remained allies" (*IF* 7.31.16). Faenza was another piece of the Romagna puzzle, and Riario was claiming the rights to certain towns that he accused the signore of Faenza, Carlo Manfredi, of having seized (*IF* 8.4.1–2).

Riario was deeply involved in organizing the Pazzi conspiracy. He and Francesco Pazzi, who lived in Rome because he too hated the Medici, plotted together to overthrow their regime ("mutare lo stato"). Success, as they knew, depended on killing both Lorenzo and his brother Giuliano (*IF* 8.3.2–10). In the event, they assassinated only Giuliano, and Riario escaped Lorenzo's retribution for a decade. A few years later, he was again (or still) pursuing his ambitions in the

[14] *OS*, vol. 2, p. 961.

Romagna. As the coalitions were forming in advance of the War of Ferrara, Riario made a splashy visit to Venice to cement the alliance between the republic and Pope Sixtus. The Venetians showered him with great honor and awarded him citizenship and membership in the Venetian nobility (*IF* 8.22.14). In the *Spogli*, Machiavelli says "Count Girolamo went to Venice to keep his foot in two stirrups [per tenere il piè in dua staffe],"[15] in other words, to play both sides and keep relations open with each. Only later in the *Histories* does Machiavelli tell the reader in what Riario's duplicity consisted. Representatives of the states allied against Venice held a conference (a "dieta," in 1482) at Cremona to plan the defense of Ferrara. Machiavelli lists the participants: the duke of Calabria (King Ferrante's son), Ludovico il Moro, Lorenzo de' Medici, "many other Italian princes," the pope's legate (Cardinal Francesco Gonzaga)—and "il conte Girolamo" Riario (*IF* 8.25.2), thus revealing that Sixtus and Riario were about to abandon Venice. All Italy soon became embroiled in the hostilities. In the first phase, Venice, Sixtus, and Riario faced Naples, Milan, Florence, Mantua, and the Duke of Urbino. After Sixtus and Riario switched sides, the Venetians faced, as Machiavelli puts it, "Italia tutta unita loro contro" (*IF* 8.25.7). Venice escaped this predicament and lost no territory, thanks to a separate peace in 1484 that the republic was able to extract from Ludovico il Moro (*IF* 8.26.6). Although the war cannot entirely be attributed to Girolamo Riario's ambitions and deceptions, Machiavelli uses the episode to show how even a "minor prince" could unsettle alliances and push Italy into destabilizing hostilities.

Among the families of the "minori principi" who had a substantial military role and thus significant impact on Italian politics was the Este dynasty of Ferrara. In chapter 2 of *The Prince*, Machiavelli cites the Este duchy as an "example" (his only Italian example) of how much easier it is to preserve hereditary, as opposed to new, principalities, owing to the people's long familiarity with the ruling family: provided their princes do not violate long-established customs and institutions, or commit injustices or grave offenses against their subjects, they will keep the people's love. The Este dynasty's long, uninterrupted rule in Ferrara, which stretched back to the thirteenth century, is the reason why, according to Machiavelli, Duke Ercole was able to survive the attacks by the Venetians in 1484 and by Pope Julius in 1510. In the *Florentine Histories*, he has more to say about both Ercole and Borso, his brother and predecessor. Borso first appears as an ally of the anti-Medici group that sought to remove Piero de' Medici from power and restore traditional constitutional government in 1466. Contemplating a show of force, they "engaged [soldare] the marquis of Ferrara" (*IF* 7.13.10), and, after some debate, asked him "to bring his troops toward the city" (*IF* 7.15.3). For his part, Piero did not lack for potential military aid from the outside: he renewed the old

[15] *OS*, vol. 2, p. 959.

agreement with Milan as requested by Duke Galeazzo, and after the Medici prevailed over their opponents he entered into a formal alliance with Galeazzo and King Ferrante. When the Venetians sent (or allowed) their mercenary captain Colleoni to attack Florentine territory in support of the exiles who had lost their struggle with Piero, Borso sent Ercole to join Colleoni. Together they entered the Florentine dominion, "burned the town of Dovadola and did some damage in the surrounding area" (*IF* 7.20.2–4).

Despite Ercole d'Este's participation in hostilities against Florence in 1467, ten years later, in the war following the Pazzi conspiracy, the Florentines hired him as captain of their forces against the armies of Ferrante and Sixtus led by Federico of Urbino. Machiavelli says the Florentine army gave the enemy "so many problems" that Federico requested a three-day truce, which, once granted, "put the Florentines at such a disadvantage that those who requested it were astonished at having obtained it, for without it Federico's forces would have had to withdraw in shame." Machiavelli does not say who granted the truce, but it can only have been Ercole. Given the opportunity to reorganize, Federico's army went on the offensive, and Duke Ercole, "having achieved little for himself and less for others," i.e. the Florentines, "returned to his stato" (*IF* 8.12.4–10). The next year, however, in addition to hiring Federico Gonzaga, the marquis of Mantua, the Florentines "recalled" Duke Ercole (*IF* 8.14.8), and, once again, Machiavelli makes it clear that they regretted doing so. Welcome news of a victory near Lake Trasimeno (which, however, Machiavelli attributes to the civilian commissioner Iacopo Guicciardini and the condottiere Roberto Malatesta) was received in Florence "with praise from the leaders and the pleasure of all." But the praise and pleasure were short-lived. The victory would have brought "honor and benefit" to the Florentines, Machiavelli writes, if the "disturbances [disordini] that broke out in the army had not upset everything." What happened was that the two captains—Ercole d'Este and Federico Gonzaga—quarreled over the division of the spoils with such vehemence that their armies assaulted each other in deadly combat. The Florentines decided they could not keep both captains, and it was agreed that Ercole and his troops should return home (*IF* 8.15.9–11). So, for the second time, Ercole undermined what promised to be a Florentine victory.

Machiavelli also comments on Ercole's part in igniting the War of Ferrara. The Venetians, he says, believed they had "reasonable justification [cagione ragionevole]" to seize Ferrara because of Ercole's refusal to fulfill the duchy's obligations to accept the presence in the city of the Venetian official known as the "visdomine" and to continue buying specified quantities of salt from Venice. Ercole claimed that, according to the original agreement, both obligations lapsed after seventy years, whereas the Venetians insisted that, for as long as the Este occupied the contested territory of the Polesine (between the Po and the Adige: roughly the area of the modern province of Rovigo), the obligations remained in force. "Because [Ercole] refused to acquiesce, the Venetians believed they had just cause to resort to arms" (*IF* 8.22.10–13). Ercole was no more responsible for the ensuing war than the Venetians, indeed perhaps less, but Machiavelli saw this as another instance of the ambition of a "minor prince" intersecting with the interests of a major power and destabilizing relations among the Italian states to the point of igniting a war that involved all the major powers. Predictably, the conflict went badly for Ercole and Ferrara, until Sixtus, realizing that Venetian "power [grandezza]" spelled disaster for the Church and Italy, switched sides and joined with the other powers to stop Venice's war on Ferrara (*IF* 8.24.1–4). When Venice refused to withdraw, the league sent both Neapolitan and Florentine forces to defend Ferrara (*IF* 8.25.1) and push back the Venetians. Machiavelli thinks Venice could have lost the whole of its "stato" in Lombardy and was saved only by dissension between Naples and Milan and the separate peace achieved with Ludovico il Moro in 1484 (*IF* 8.26).

Of all the "minor princes" whose ambitions convulsed Italy, the most notorious were Cesare Borgia, who straddled the grey area between "minor princes" and "uomini senza stato," and Vitellozzo Vitelli, the condottiere who assisted in Cesare Borgia's conquests but then conspired against him and paid for the treachery with his life. Borgia's importance in Machiavelli's chancery career and political thought warrants a full treatment in the next chapter. As for Vitellozzo, he does not of course appear in the *Histories* because the most notable episodes of his career took place after 1492, where the narrative concludes. In *The Prince* he is mentioned among Borgia's condottieri (*P* 7.40, 13.11), as one of the doomed conspirators against him (*P* 8.21), and, together with his brother Paolo, as having given Oliverotto da Fermo his military training (*P* 8.14). But there is no mention in *The Prince* of the most threatening (to the Florentines) of Vitellozzo's exploits, his occupation of Arezzo and the Valdichiana in 1502, the most likely reason being the fact that Piero de' Medici entered Florentine territory with Vitellozzo to rally Medici loyalists for a restoration of the regime, which made Piero, and not for the first time, not only an enemy but a traitor to the republic. It was obviously prudent to refrain from discussing the episode in a book Machiavelli hoped would gain the attention of Piero's brother, Pope Leo. However, as we saw in the first *Decennale*, Vitellozzo and his family loom large in Machiavelli's perception of the vulnerability of both Florence and Italy to soldier/princes of his ilk. The Vitelli were signori of Città di Castello, a town in papal territory very near to the Florentine dominion. In the *Histories*, Machiavelli calls Vitellozzo's father, Niccolò, "principe" of the city and notes the "great friendship" he had with Lorenzo de' Medici. When (in 1474) Pope Sixtus IV, "wanting to keep the cities of the Church obedient" to their papal overlord, besieged Città di Castello, Lorenzo gave Niccolò assistance, which, as Machiavelli puts it, "was not enough to defend Niccolò, but was indeed sufficient to sow the first seeds of the hostility [inimicizia] between Sixtus and the Medici, which produced the evil fruit" of the Pazzi conspiracy four years later (*IF* 7.31.1–3). In the ensuing war, the Florentines tried, again unsuccessfully, to restore Niccolò to power (*IF* 8.15.5–6), and tried again in the War of

Ferrara, this time with success (*IF* 8.23.4), only to see Sixtus besiege Città di Castello a second time (in 1484) and send Niccolò once more into exile (*IF* 8.27.1). In the "Frammenti storici," Machiavelli's notes summarizing events from 1494 to 1498, he recounts how, in 1497, Vitellozzo's forces defeated those of Pope Alexander for control of the town of Citerna, just outside Città di Castello.[16] Machiavelli's attention to the twists and turns of Vitelli fortunes (above all, of course, the execution of Paolo in 1499 by the Florentines and Vitellozzo's fate in 1502) underscores his awareness of how the ambitions of "minor princes" caused friction and conflict in the overlapping spheres of influence of larger powers.

Machiavelli also denounces the negligent governance of "minor princes" in their own principalities. In *Discourses* 3.29, he holds princes responsible for their subjects' "sins [peccati]," but in this context crimes, which they commit because of the princes' negligence or because princes themselves are stained by the same crimes. "If one examines the populations thought to be most inclined to robberies and similar sins, one sees it all comes about because those who governed them were of similar character [natura]." As an example of "the most evil way of life [sceleratissima vita]," Machiavelli cites the petty principalities of the Romagna. The homicides and thefts that occurred so frequently there for the slightest pretext were the result, he says, of the "wickedness [tristizia] of those princes, not the wicked nature of the people, as the princes claimed." His explanation for this lies in the meager financial resources of the signori. Because they were "poor" but "wanted to live as the wealthy do, they were forced to engage often in theft in a variety of ways." Among the "dishonest things they did was to make laws prohibiting some act and then allow the same laws not to be obeyed. Nor did they punish those who violated the law until many people had done so. Only then did they inflict punishments, not out of zeal for the law, but out of a greedy desire to collect the monetary penalties." Many problems resulted from this, Machiavelli claims: people became impoverished, but their behavior did not improve, because, as princes victimized those forced to pay the fines, the latter in turn preyed upon those still weaker (*DL* 3.29.2–8). The chapter ends with a (slightly inexact) quotation from Lorenzo de' Medici's *Rappresentazione di san Giovanni e Paolo*: "E quel che fa 'l signor fanno poi molti, / Ché nel signor son tutti gli occhi vòlti [What the prince does many then do / for the eyes of all are turned to their lord]."

THE KINGDOM OF NAPLES

In 1505 Piero Soderini tried, unsuccessfully, to send Machiavelli to Naples in an effort to persuade the Spanish viceroy Gonzalo Fernández de Córdoba (called Consalvo in Italy) not to send troops to support Pisa in its war with Florence.

[16] *OS*, vol. 2, pp. 940–1.

Soderini's ottimati opponents blocked Machiavelli's appointment and succeeded in having one of their own, Roberto Acciaiuoli, sent in his place.[17] As far as we know, Machiavelli never went to Naples during the chancery years, but it has recently been discovered that he may have briefly visited in 1516 on behalf of Paolo Vettori, a Medici ally, in connection with the preparation of the papal fleet to fight the Barbary pirates.[18] If it occurred, it was at most a short visit that did not allow time or opportunity for inquiries about political conditions. The independent Aragonese dynasty that had ruled Naples since 1442 was dissolved in 1501, when the kingdom was divided between Spain and France. Two years later, the French were defeated and permanently expelled from the South as the former kingdom of Naples was joined to the kingdom of Sicily ruled by the Spanish king Ferdinand of Aragon, whose grandson, Charles Habsburg, succeeded him in 1516 as king of Spain and Naples.

Despite little or no personal experience of the South, Machiavelli was acutely aware of the central role the kings and barons of Naples played in fifteenth-century Italy's fractured history.[19] In *The Prince* (24.5) he names, first, the king of Naples, then the duke of Milan "and others," among the "signori" who "have lost their states in our times." The kingdom's loss of independence and incorporation into the Spanish empire were among the calamitous results of the crisis that erupted in 1494. But Machiavelli also recognized the former kingdom's interventionist role in peninsular politics and warfare as a recurrent and often aggressively destabilizing force that went back centuries. In the first book of the *Florentine Histories*, he summarizes the thirteenth-century emperor Frederick II's near total conquest of Italy, including the Lombard communes and Tuscany, where he "incited so much conflict that it brought about the ruination of all Italy" with the proliferation of the pro-imperial Ghibelline and pro-papal Guelf parties (*IF* 1.21.5–7). At the beginning of book 7 of the *Histories*, justifying the attention devoted in the preceding book to Lombardy and Naples in a history of Florence, Machiavelli asserts that most of the wars in which Florence became involved originated in the "actions of other Italian peoples and princes." He cites the war, discussed at the end of book 6, between the Aragonese king of Naples, Ferrante, and the Angevin claimant, Jean d'Anjou. In fact, as Machiavelli points out, the

[17] Roberto Ridolfi, *Vita di Niccolò Machiavelli*, 7th edn. (Florence: Sansoni, 1978), pp. 135 and 466 n. 27, citing Guicciardini: see *Storie fiorentine*, ed. Montevecchi, ch. 25, p. 418. Support for Machiavelli's appointment was voiced in a *pratica* of May 23, 1505; *Consulte e pratiche 1505–1512*, ed. Denis Fachard (Geneva: Droz, 1988), p. 4.

[18] Andrea Guidi and Marcello Simonetta, "Machiavelli, Paolo Vettori e la caccia ai pirati nel Mediterraneo: ancora sui 'negozi' di Niccolò nell''ozio' di Sant'Andrea," in *Niccolò Machiavelli. Dai 'castellucci' di San Casciano alla comunicazione politica contemporanea*, ed. Andrea Guidi (Rome: Vecchiarelli Editore, 2019), pp. 19–33.

[19] For an overview of Machiavelli's treatment of Neapolitan history, see Carlo De Frede, "Machiavelli e il Regno di Napoli," in De Frede, *La crisi del Regno di Napoli nella riflessione politica di Machiavelli e Guicciardini* (Naples: Liguori, 2006), pp. 5–59.

Florentines actually stayed out of that war, but their refusal to assist Ferrante, which nearly cost him his kingdom, filled him with "indignation," "hatred, and deep enmity" for the Florentines and gave rise to "grandissimi mali" (*IF* 7.1.1–3)—an allusion to the Pazzi conspiracy against the Medici of which Ferrante was one of the chief authors.

Dynastic conflicts and internal political instability created the conditions in which, according to Machiavelli, Naples often exported its turmoil to the rest of Italy and even beyond. Recounting in *Histories* 1.38 Queen Joanna II's accession to the throne at the death of her brother Ladislas in 1414, Machiavelli writes that "in addition to the kingdom, he left her a great army whose captains were the chief condottieri of Italy; among the most prominent was [Muzio Attendolo] Sforza da Cotignuola" (father of Francesco Sforza). Joanna's French husband, himself "of royal blood," declared himself king, and he and Joanna fought over the throne, each alternately gaining the upper hand, until she won. But Sforza abandoned her (in 1420), hoping she would beg him to return and, presumably, pay him more. (Machiavelli scathingly recalls this betrayal and manipulation in the *Art of War* 1.58.) Joanna turned instead for help to the king of Aragon and Sicily, Alfonso V, whom she adopted (as heir to the throne), and also to Braccio da Montone, Sforza's great rival among Italy's freelance condottieri. Alfonso pursued his own ambitions and began seizing the kingdom's fortresses, creating fear in Joanna and suspicion between them that led to armed confrontation in which she, with the help of Sforza, who had returned to her employ, defeated Alfonso, drove him from Naples, and revoked the adoption (1423). When Sforza died, Joanna was again bereft of arms and would have lost her kingdom, Machiavelli says, if Filippo Visconti, the duke of Milan, had not come to her aid and, as Machiavelli asserts, expelled Alfonso from Italy. Braccio took Alfonso's side and continued fighting against Joanna, whereupon the pope (Martin V) engaged Sforza's son, Francesco, to hunt down and kill Braccio (*IF* 1.38). Machiavelli will later tell his readers that hostilities between the Bracceschi and the Sforzeschi continued for a long time thereafter (*IF* 5.2). Joanna emerged victorious and reigned until her death in 1435, but the bungled succession, complicated by her unwise marriage and untrustworthy military captain, came at the cost not only of armed clashes but also and more ominously of introducing the king of Aragon as a rival claimant and the duke of Milan as a kingmaker into the struggle for the kingdom.

Having initially, and disastrously, selected Alfonso as her heir, Joanna subsequently decided, in her 1434 will and testament, to keep the kingdom in the house of Anjou, designating as her successor, as Machiavelli recounts in book 5 of the *Histories*, her distant relative René of Anjou. But others too had their eyes on the prize. Machiavelli says Alfonso intended to "seize the kingdom" in alliance with "many barons," whereas the "Neapolitans," also "with many barons," favored René. The pope (Eugenius IV) wanted to install his own governor (under the assumption that Joanna's death ended the Angevin dynasty and that the kingdom therefore reverted to its feudal overlord, the pope). Three foreigners (i.e. non-Neapolitans: Alfonso, René, and Eugenius) now contended for the kingdom. Alfonso, welcomed by his group of barons and "intending to bend the Neapolitans to his will," sent his fleet to besiege the coastal city and port of Gaeta. The Neapolitans appealed for help to Filippo Maria Visconti, who induced the Genoese—Genoa being under Visconti rule at the time—to send warships against Alfonso, "not only to please the duke, their prince, but also to safeguard the *mercanzie*"—the business interests and assets—"they had in Naples and Gaeta." The fleets met in a battle (August 1434) in which the Aragonese were defeated and Alfonso and many "principi [barons]" were taken prisoner. The Genoese handed Alfonso over to Visconti. "This victory frightened all the princes [principi: rulers] of Italy who feared the power of Filippo [Visconti]." Machiavelli recounts the story of how Alfonso persuaded Filippo Maria that it would be to his advantage to be allied with a king of Naples who posed no threat to him, namely himself, rather than one whose close ties to the royal house of France (René was a cousin of King Charles VII) could result in Visconti facing threats from both France and Naples. "These words made such a powerful impression on the duke that he changed his mind, freed Alfonso, and sent him with full honors" back to the kingdom (*IF* 5.5).

In 1442, Alfonso besieged Naples, defeated René, and took control of the kingdom. Machiavelli makes a point of noting that his victory gave Alfonso the opportunity to seize Francesco Sforza's territories in the kingdom, including Benevento. This proved easy as long as Sforza was occupied in wars in Lombardy, but, when these paused, Alfonso feared Sforza would come south to recover his lands and support René's cause. So he asked Visconti, for the sake of the "friendship" forged during the king's captivity, to keep Sforza occupied with campaigns in the north. Just as Visconti had earlier turned to a third party, the Genoese, to aid René and the Neapolitans in the succession crisis of 1434–5, this time he encouraged Pope Eugenius to retake the territories in the papal states seized by Sforza, even offering the services of his captain Niccolò Piccinino. The pope "avidly [cupidamente]" accepted this counsel, out of "hatred" for Sforza and a desire to recover "what was his." While Piccinino's and Eugenius's troops fought against Sforza, Alfonso took Naples, René left the kingdom and, after a short stay in Florence, returned to France. In the meantime, Sforza, losing city after city to Piccinino, begged the Florentines and Venetians for assistance, ominously warning that, if Eugenius and Alfonso were not stopped, they would ally with Visconti and "divide up Italy." Machiavelli wants his readers to be aware of the consequences that spilled over from the war of the Neapolitan succession into the rest of Italy. But there was more. Florence and Venice were reluctant to send help to Sforza because they did not want to make enemies of Alfonso and the pope and also because they had promised to help the Bentivoglio signore of Bologna free his city from Visconti control. Before deciding, as they ultimately did, to assist Sforza, they reaffirmed their alliance with Visconti. Having favored war against Sforza for as long as René challenged Alfonso, now that René had departed Italy Visconti no longer wanted to see Sforza lose his territories. He therefore not only agreed that Florence and Venice could support Sforza; he also told Alfonso to "return to his kingdom and cease making war" on Sforza. Although he was reluctant to end this campaign, Alfonso agreed, because of his "debts to the duke [Visconti]," to withdraw his troops from the papal territories where he had been fighting Sforza (*IF* 6.5). All this flowed from the dispute between Aragonese and Angevin claimants to the Neapolitan crown.

Alfonso owed his victory in large part to the support of Filippo Maria Visconti. When Visconti suffered a major defeat by the Venetians (in 1446) and was in danger of losing the duchy, he appealed to Alfonso for help (*IF* 6.11.11–12). Visconti died the next year, and, as already noted, Machiavelli says both Sforza and Alfonso had supporters among those who wanted a "prince" to rule Milan (*IF* 6.13.6–7). Alfonso's promise to help Filippo Maria had apparently included an agreement that he would attack the Florentines; so in 1447, Alfonso, "wanting to continue the campaign in Tuscany, according to what had been decided with Filippo," and "wanting a foothold in the Florentine dominion [stato]," occupied the town of Cennina (west of Arezzo). The Florentines, "disturbed by this unexpected event," hired soldiers and prepared for war. Unable to proceed from this direction, Alfonso moved toward Volterra where he captured several fortified towns and then invaded Pisan territory. The next year he seized the port city of Piombino and settled in for a "long war" against Florence (*IF* 6.15). Because of the insalubrious conditions, his forces suffered many casualties, and the Florentines too had difficulties provisioning their soldiers. They were about to agree to the king's offer to withdraw in exchange for 50,000 florins, when Neri Capponi persuaded the Florentines not to accept it. An agreement between Florence and the lord of Piombino finally persuaded Alfonso to leave, even as he continued to threaten more war (*IF* 6.16.1–9). After Sforza took Milan in early 1450, a radically reorganized system of alliances emerged among the states of Italy. As we have seen, Machiavelli emphasizes (*IF* 6.23) Cosimo de' Medici's role in steering the Florentines—many of them quite reluctant—away from their traditional ties to Venice into a new alliance with Sforza's Milan. Venice and Alfonso likewise formed an alliance, promising to strike their new enemies simultaneously (*IF* 6.25.3–4). Alfonso expelled Florentine merchants from Naples, "without any hesitancy" about violating the peace signed the year before (for his withdrawal from Piombino) "and without a pretext, let alone a just cause [sanza averne, non che giusta, ma colorita cagione]" (*IF* 6.26.1–4). He then launched a full-scale invasion of Tuscany (in 1452). Machiavelli says Alfonso sent his son Ferrante with an army of 12,000 soldiers, captained by Federico of Urbino, who entered Florentine territory through the Valdichiana and into the Chianti region, but without achieving any significant victory or territorial gain. Alfonso also sent a fleet to besiege the coastal town of Vada (south of Livorno), but Florentine forces kept the invaders hemmed in against the coast (*IF* 6.28). Machiavelli says Florence easily recovered the towns occupied by the Aragonese who resorted to raids, depredations, and disruptions (*IF* 6.30.1–5).

In the aftermath of the Ottoman conquest of Constantinople in 1453, Pope Nicholas V summoned the major Italian states to a peace conference. Machiavelli says they all sent representatives but quickly encountered "difficulties," the first of which, in his account, was Alfonso's demand that the Florentines compensate him for the expenses he incurred in the recently concluded war. Florence turned the same demand back on him. Venice and Sforza argued over cities in the Po valley, but they broke the deadlock by announcing on April 9, 1454—Machiavelli gives the exact date—that they had reached a settlement (the Peace of Lodi). The other states were given a month to ratify and join the agreement. Florence, Pope Nicholas, and some of the lesser powers did so before the end of April, and Florence, Sforza, and Venice also signed a twenty-five-year peace (in early 1455, thus creating the Lega Italica). Only Alfonso, Machiavelli pointedly observes, was reluctant to ratify the Peace of Lodi, complaining that it was beneath his dignity to subscribe a treaty not as a "principale" (one who decides), but as an "aderente" (who agrees to what others decide). It took some persuasion by the other parties to get him to sign, and even when he did he insisted, "in order that the seeds of war should persist in Italy," as already noted, that he be given license to make war on Genoa, on Sigismondo Malatesta, and on Astorre Manfredi, lord of Faenza, even without any provocation on their part" (*IF* 6.32.1–11). And, in fact, as Machiavelli notes, in 1456 Alfonso, "unhappy with the peace" to which he and the other states had agreed, attacked Genoa "by sea and by land." But this gave him and his kingdom "more war than he would have wanted." The Genoese, knowing they could not resist an attack on their own, offered the lordship ("imperio") of the city to King Charles VII of France, who accepted and sent Jean d'Anjou, son of René, to take possession of Genoa (*IF* 6.35).

Alfonso's impulsive actions resulted in reigniting the war for the Neapolitan throne between the Aragonese and the Angevins. Genoa's decision to become a French protectorate "displeased Alfonso," as he realized he had brought down on his head a "too important enemy," leaving his heir, Ferrante, in unexpected and unnecessary danger when he succeeded his father a few months later. "Full of fear [sospetto]" facing "such a powerful enemy in Italy," namely France, Ferrante was also "apprehensive about the loyalty [dubitando della fede] of many of his barons," who, "in their thirst for change might side with the French." Even the new pope (Calixtus III Borgia) tried to take advantage of Ferrante's precarious situation to reclaim the kingdom as a papal fief and install his own nephew (Pietro Lodovico Borgia) as governor. Only Calixtus's death (1458) and the election of Alfonso's ally Enea Silvio Piccolomini as Pius II removed this threat (*IF* 6.36). But Alfonso's reckless attack against Genoa produced still more problems for Ferrante. Dissension between the Fregoso, one of the two most powerful Genoese families, and the city's new overlord, Jean d'Anjou, sparked "greater and more important wars than the past ones." Pleased at this rupture between the Fregoso and the Angevin governor, Ferrante sent soldiers and money to the former. But in a decisive clash Jean's forces killed or captured all the Fregoso troops supported by Ferrante, and "this victory gave Jean courage to undertake the campaign for the kingdom [of Naples]." Alfonso's blunder in attacking Genoa now resulted in an invasion of the kingdom of Naples itself and a war involving several Italian states. In October 1459, Jean accompanied a "powerful fleet" to Baiae, west of Naples near Pozzuoli, where he was welcomed by one of the kingdom's most influential barons, the duke of Sessa. Jean quickly gained the support of the prince of Taranto, other barons, and many important cities, including L'Aquila. "The kingdom was almost entirely demolished [in rovina]," Machiavelli comments. Ferrante's hold on it rapidly disintegrated, and he requested and received help from Pope Pius and Duke Francesco Sforza. Florence and Venice remained neutral (a decision, as already noted, that would have serious consequences for Florence two decades later). Iacopo Piccinino, Ferrante's captain general, was so angered by the king's agreement to employ Sigismondo Malatesta, Piccinino's old enemy, that he switched sides and fought for Jean d'Anjou. Even the arrival of a sizeable army recruited by Federico da Montefeltro could not prevent Ferrante's disastrous defeat and the capture of many of his captains by the Angevins at the Sarno river (July 1460). Most of the kingdom now declared loyalty to Jean. Naples, a few other cities, and some of the lesser barons were the only pieces of the kingdom that stayed with Ferrante. Piccinino urged Jean to seize Naples, where Ferrante had taken refuge; had he done so, Machiavelli claims, it might have ended the Aragonese monarchy in Naples. But Jean preferred first to occupy the rest of the realm thinking this would make the capture of Naples easier. His decision, says Machiavelli, deprived his successful military campaign of its victory, because Jean did not know that "the members follow the head more easily than the head follows the members" (*IF* 6.37). Ferrante appealed again to Pius and Sforza for help and began recovering some of the cities captured by Jean's army. But it was events in Genoa that turned the war in Ferrante's favor. The Genoese, "provoked by the avaricious and haughty French" and aided by the Milanese, rose in rebellion against their new overlord. Jean's father, René, arrived with a fleet, intending to protect his son's crumbling power, but his forces were routed even as they were disembarking, causing René to return "humiliated [svergognato]" to Provence. Although frightened by the news of his father's defeat, Jean continued fighting, "assisted by those barons who, because they had revolted against Ferrante, believed there was no hope of reconciliation with him." Machiavelli says the war came to an end in 1463 (actually it was 1462), when Jean d'Anjou was decisively defeated at Troia, near Foggia (*IF* 6.38).

The polemical subtext of Machiavelli's narrative of Alfonso's reign emerges against the background of the humanist adulation of the king. Machiavelli's contemporaries knew that Alfonso had become the object of encomiastic tributes and biographies by humanists and literati grateful for his patronage and admiring of his dedication to learning. They portrayed him as a heroic figure who dominated Italian politics with courage and magnanimity (he was dubbed "the Magnanimous"). Among the early representations of Alfonso in these terms, particularly important was Bartolomeo Facio's *De rebus gestis ab Alphonso primo Neapolitanorum rege*, completed by 1455.[20] Following Facio, court historians and humanists continued to extol the king. It is therefore telling that, in Machiavelli's account, there is not a trace of this image of Alfonso. From beginning to end, the portrait of Alfonso in the *Histories* highlights his follies and errors. As Machiavelli saw him, the precariousness of Alfonso's claim to the throne caused him to involve Italy's other powers, chiefly the Visconti and the Sforza, in protecting it. Even when his power seemed secure, Machiavelli implies, overweening ambition pushed him into foolish military campaigns that repeatedly convulsed Italy. One cause of this behavior, Machiavelli suggests, was Alfonso's insecure claim to the throne; another was the always latent and sometimes active disloyalty of the barons, the "principi" of the Neapolitan kingdom who never ceased hungering for a royal regime that would let them govern their fiefdoms and pursue their interests as they wished and who sometimes cooperated with other powers in and beyond Italy to achieve this objective. The combination of precarious legitimacy and a restive nobility made the kingdom a source of instability for all Italy. The legacy of Alfonso's last folly exploded in the first years of Ferrante's reign into a war that lasted, as Machiavelli notes, for four years and whose repercussions reverberated long afterwards.

Machiavelli highlights the constant threat to the monarchy from the "baroni," or "principi." Shortly after the victory over the Angevins in 1462/3, Ferrante and Francesco Sforza judged this the moment to free themselves from certain threats, in Sforza's case, the dangerous popularity among the Milanese of Iacopo Piccinino; in Ferrante's case, the need for security against the barons who had allied with Jean d'Anjou. Machiavelli says Ferrante "sought an agreement with the barons with all the ingenuity [con ogni industria]" he could muster and "employed every skill in securing himself against them. He says Ferrante "succeeded in this most fortunately [felicemente]," because the barons "saw that, if they remained at war with the king, their destruction was assured; if they came to an agreement and trusted him, they would be in constant fear of him [ne stavano dubii]." But because, as Machiavelli theorizes, "men always flee more willingly from the evil that is certain," which in this case was their inevitable destruction if they continued fighting Ferrante, they decided instead to "trust in the peace offered by the king." Yet, "once they put themselves in the king's hands, they were crushed

[20] Jerry H. Bentley, *Politics and Culture in Renaissance Naples* (Princeton: Princeton University Press, 1987), pp. 228–32.

[spenti] by him in various ways and under various pretexts" (*IF* 7.7.4–8). This does not mean they were physically eliminated; in fact, they continued to be a thorn in Ferrante's side, for example, in the rebellion of 1485–6. But Machiavelli does not specify what he believes Ferrante did in the 1460s to suppress or neutralize the barons, at least for a time.

Ferrante played a central role in the Pazzi conspiracy and subsequent war. As already noted, Machiavelli attributes the king's animosity toward the Medici to their failure to assist him in his war against Jean d'Anjou in the early 1460s. Ferrante's anger—his "sdegno"—"caused the greatest evils," Machiavelli writes, "as our narrative will show" (*IF* 7.1.2–3). By the mid-1470s, he says, the major states of Italy were divided into two groups: Venice, Florence, and Milan in one camp, Pope Sixtus and Ferrante in the other (*IF* 7.31.8–9). To explain Ferrante's willingness to join the murderous conspiracy and the war he and Sixtus launched after the plotters failed to kill both Medici brothers, Machiavelli offers no more than the king's "sdegno" from fifteen years earlier. Whereas Sixtus had "reasons to justify" his decision to attack Lorenzo (*IF* 8.11.5), Machiavelli presents no such rationale for Ferrante. When the Pazzi and Riario conspirators decided on a plan to kill Lorenzo and Giuliano, "they thought the pope and the king would quickly agree to it, provided it were shown to them how easy it would be" (*IF* 8.3.7). Once the plot was hatched in Rome, Ferrante promised whatever help might be needed (*IF* 8.4.14). When it failed and the "overthrow of the regime [mutazione dello stato] that the pope and the king wanted" did not occur, "they decided that what they were unable to obtain by means of conspiracies they would get by war" (*IF* 8.10.1). In mid-1478, three months after the bloody attack in Florence Cathedral, Neapolitan and papal troops invaded Florentine territory, led by Ferrante's son Alfonso and Federico da Montefeltro (*IF* 8.12.1–2). Machiavelli focuses on the machinations involving Genoa and Milan that were part of Ferrante's strategy, as they had been for his father. Aware that Venice was refusing to help Florence, whose only ally in the war was Milan, Ferrante schemed to deprive the Florentines of even the little assistance they were receiving from that source by getting the Adorno faction in Genoa to ignite a rebellion against Milanese rule, which, he assumed, would prevent the duchess, Bona (widow of Galeazzo Maria), from assisting Florence. But she engineered her own coup in Genoa, installing the Fregoso in power and driving out the Adorno. Sixtus and Ferrante then sent the Adorno exiles into Tuscany, led by the condottiere Roberto da Sanseverino, forcing the Florentines to deploy troops in the northwest against the Genoese invaders, even as they were fighting the Neapolitan army on their southern border. In the summer of 1479, Sanseverino's marauders sacked several towns and plundered the Pisan countryside up to the walls of the city (*IF* 8.13.5–10). Some six months later, a member of the Fregoso clan conspired with a group from Sarzana (purchased by Florence in 1468) to seize the town and imprison the resident Florentine official. This, Machiavelli says, "greatly upset the leading members of the regime [a' principi dello stato] in Florence, as they were persuaded it had all happened on the orders of King Ferrante." Alfonso, who was with the army near Siena, denied any involvement on his or his father's part (*IF* 8.18.8–10), but Machiavelli implies that the Florentines did not believe these denials. Twice in the first year and a half of the war, Ferrante, or those acting on his behalf, meddled in Genoese politics for the purpose of creating even more difficulties for Florence.

In the second year of the war, Machiavelli writes, many Florentines, increasingly anxious over military setbacks and high taxes, conveyed to the regime's leaders their wish for a resolution of the conflict. Seeing no other solution, Lorenzo went to Naples seeking a separate peace with Ferrante (*IF* 8.17.3–9). Because of rumors that some in Florence were open to a change in the regime's leadership and would have liked Ferrante to keep Lorenzo in Naples, perhaps even deal with him as he had with Iacopo Piccinino, the king delayed Lorenzo's return hoping for a "tumulto" in Florence. Ferrante was still trying, by other means, to overthrow the Medici regime. There was no "tumulto," and Lorenzo returned home in March 1480, bringing with him a peace agreement that satisfied the city's desire for an end to the war but displeased not only the pope and Venice but also many Florentines when they learned that the restitution of territories occupied by Neapolitan forces was left to Ferrante's discretion ("arbitrio"). Moreover, despite the peace agreement, Alfonso and his army were not withdrawing. Alfonso claimed his presence in Siena was needed because he had been made the "arbiter" of numerous disputes among the citizens. He fined many, imprisoned and exiled others, and even sentenced some to death. This, Machiavelli says, made both the Sienese and the Florentines fear that he wanted to make himself "principe" of Siena. Machiavelli thus implies that the ambition of the Aragonese rulers of Naples to expand their power to the center and north of Italy had not abated. Everyone in Florence, he says, both the people and the regime's leaders, believed that the city "had never been in greater danger of losing its liberty" (*IF* 8.19.9–16). The danger subsided when the Ottomans attacked Otranto (August 1480), causing Ferrante to recall Alfonso and the army back to the kingdom (*IF* 8.20) and to restore the occupied territories to Florence (*IF* 8.22.1–3). The delight of the Florentines at being released from the Aragonese stranglehold was enhanced, Machiavelli adds, by Alfonso's laments as he left Siena, "accusing fortune of depriving him of the *imperio* of Tuscany through such an unexpected and improbable event [insperato e non ragionevole accidente]" (*IF* 8.21.2)—"non ragionevole" in the sense of coming, as it were, out of nowhere. That Alfonso thought he had been cheated of the "imperio di Toscana" strengthens Machiavelli's implied accusation that the ambition of the Aragonese monarchy to extend its power into Tuscany was pretentious, destabilizing, and, in its own way, "non ragionevole"—not justified by any legal, dynastic, or historical claim. In the War of Ferrara, Ferrante sent Alfonso north once again, this time to fight papal forces led by Roberto Malatesta. Machiavelli twice mentions Alfonso's depredations around Rome, where he did "much damage" and "every day raided and plundered" up to the walls of the city (*IF* 8.23.4–8). But when Malatesta drew him into a full-scale battle—which Machiavelli says was "fought with more virtú than any in the preceding fifty years in Italy" and resulted in a thousand fatalities (August 1482)—his infantry attacked the Neapolitan cavalry so forcefully that Alfonso turned tail and ran. Machiavelli, who always tenaciously insisted on the superiority of infantry, may have felt vindicated by the victory of Malatesta's infantry over Alfonso's cavalry. Adding his own mockery to the humiliating defeat, he says Alfonso would have been taken prisoner had he not been rescued by Turkish soldiers from the same force that had attacked Otranto (*IF* 8.23.12).

Just when it seemed that the Venetians, with "all Italy united against them" (*IF* 8.25.7) might lose "all the territories [tutto lo stato] they held in Lombardy," Machiavelli introduces the dispute between Alfonso and Ludovico Sforza that saved Venice from defeat. Giangaleazzo Sforza, son of the assassinated Galeazzo Maria, had by now reached the age at which he could have assumed the responsibilities of the ducal office that his uncle Ludovico had usurped. Giangaleazzo was married to a daughter, Isabella, of Alfonso, who wanted his son-in-law, not Ludovico, to rule the duchy, perhaps expecting that through Isabella he, Alfonso, would control the Milanese state. The Venetians foiled the plan by secretly negotiating a separate peace with Ludovico in August 1484 that quickly ended the war. When Milan withdrew from the league, the other powers, tired of a war they had almost won and then did not, agreed to a peace that kept Ludovico in power and allowed Venice to regain the territories occupied by the league's army (*IF* 8.26). Alfonso's attempt to interfere in Sforza family politics deprived the league of victory.

The last significant appearance of either Ferrante or Alfonso in Machiavelli's *Histories* occurs in the account of the barons' rebellion of 1485–6. Once again, it is Alfonso who sets the trouble in motion. "With the pretext [sotto colore]" of wanting to resolve quarrels among the countryside population in the region around the important city of L'Aquila, and with the intention of bringing the city, which until then enjoyed virtual independence in the kingdom, under stricter obedience to the king, Alfonso summoned to a meeting the count of Montorio, a baron who enjoyed much prestige in L'Aquila. The invitation was a trap: Alfonso took the count prisoner and sent him to Naples. Machiavelli focuses more on the reaction in L'Aquila than among the barons. A popular revolt erupted, as angry Aquilani took up arms and killed the king's commissioner and several citizens known to be partisans of the king. L'Aquila is near what was then the boundary between the kingdom of Naples and the papal states, and the enraged populace raised the banners of the Church and sent ambassadors to Pope Innocent VIII (Giovanbattista Cybo) to offer him the city and beg for help against "the royal tyranny." Innocent was a Genoese who shared his countrymen's old animosity toward the house of Aragon, and Machiavelli says he took up the defense of the Aquilani "as one who for reasons both private and public hated the king." It was Innocent, Machiavelli asserts, who implored many of the barons to rebel, including the princes of Altamura, Salerno, and Bisignano. The Florentines, involved in military operations elsewhere (against Genoa, to regain Sarzana) were reluctant to intervene. Yet, Machiavelli says, bound by treaty to Ferrante, they "put loyalty before self-interest [preposono la fede alle commodità]" and sent troops to assist the king. Ferrante was now fighting one war against papal forces near Rome and another against the barons within the kingdom. Machiavelli does not recount the events, saying only that Ferrante emerged victorious "everywhere," signed a peace treaty with Innocent in 1486, and reconciled with the rebel barons. According to Machiavelli, just two persons, only one of them a noble, were executed—the count of Sarno (Ferrante's personal adviser) and the king's secretary, both for the crime of "revealing the king's secrets to the pope" (*IF* 8.32). In fact, Ferrante neither observed the terms of the treaty nor made any genuine effort at reconciliation with the barons. The executions were more numerous than Machiavelli implies, and many barons, their estates confiscated, were imprisoned and spent years in Ferrante's dreaded dungeon.[21] Machiavelli's omission of the details of the rebellion, its suppression, and the sentences carried out against the barons is curious in light of his insistence, as we shall see, on the damaging role of noble ambition in the Italian states.

Stopping short of the French invasion, the *Florentine Histories* lack an assessment of Alfonso's role in the calamity that opened in 1494 and led to the collapse of the Aragonese monarchy in Naples. In *Discourses* 2.12.12–13, Machiavelli briefly mentions what he considered Alfonso's fatal mistake in confronting the French invasion. "Everyone knows," he writes, that "Ferrante, king of Naples, was considered a most wise prince in his time." Two years before he died in January 1494, knowing the attack was coming, "on his deathbed he advised his son Alfonso, among other admonitions, to await the enemy from within the kingdom and under no circumstances send his forces outside the stato; he should instead wait inside its borders *tutto intero*," i.e. with all his forces gathered together. Alfonso ignored this advice and sent "an army into the Romagna" and, "without fighting, lost both the army and the stato." Machiavelli does not provide enough context in this passage to permit readers without knowledge of the events to understand why this action caused Alfonso to lose both his army and his kingdom. In the summer of 1494,[22] Alfonso sent one part of his army by sea to confront the French in Genoa and another, commanded by his son Ferdinand (called Ferrandino), north to confront Ludovico Sforza, at this moment an enemy of

[21] Bentley, *Politics and Culture in Renaissance Naples*, pp. 31–3.

[22] For what follows, see Cecil H. Clough, "The Romagna Campaign of 1494: A Significant Military Encounter," in *The French Descent into Renaissance Italy, 1494–95: Antecedents and Effects*, ed. David Abulafia (Aldershot: Ashgate Variorum, 1995), pp. 191–215.

Naples and nervous ally of the French. Hoping to steer the French away from Milan toward Naples, Ludovico sent a combined French-Milanese force into the Romagna to halt the progress of Ferrandino's army, which lacked the strength to break through toward Milan. Both armies shied away from open confrontation, and this is presumably what Machiavelli refers to when he says the Neapolitans lost "without fighting [senza combattere]." But what he means saying that Alfonso and Ferrandino "lost the army" is less clear. This could allude to Alfonso's division of the Neapolitan forces between Genoa and the Romagna, a decision that weakened the kingdom's defenses. Alfonso did not, in short, keep his army "tutto intero." But there is another possible interpretation. Ferrandino's army and the French-Milanese army approached one another in late October north of Imola, where, even without a direct confrontation, the French carried out the first of the great massacres of the Italian wars, killing most of the inhabitants of the town of Mordano while Ferrandino's army stood by, just seven miles away. This shocking event frightened and demoralized the Neapolitan force. Several condottieri abandoned the army, as did the Florentine contingent, and soon thereafter what was left of the army withdrew and returned south. Nothing now prevented Charles VIII from slicing through Italy and occupying Naples, thus initiating the sequence of events by which the Aragonese dynasty, buffeted by both France and Spain, "perdé" the "stato" of Naples.

What did Machiavelli think of Alfonso's part in this debacle? In the first of the "Frammenti storici,"[23] he translated portions of Bernardo Rucellai's Latin *De bello italico* that provide an indirect answer. On Alfonso's ambition: "Some believed that neither love of his daughter nor hatred of Ludovico [il Moro] motivated Alfonso, but rather the ambition to seize, by right of inheritance, the stato of Lombardy, which Filippo Visconti, who had no male progeny, bequeathed to his grandfather Alfonso for him to defend against the Venetians who coveted it after [Filippo's] death" (4). Alfonso "made an agreement with the Florentines, ostensibly to unite for the good of the city, but actually to detach them from friendship with Ludovico," (5) who, unable to persuade Piero de' Medici to renew their former alliance, sent ambassadors to Charles VIII to implore him to undertake the expedition to Italy (7–8). In this version, Alfonso shares blame with Piero and Ludovico for the botched diplomacy that unleashed the French invasion. When the feared invasion materialized, "Alfonso secluded himself in grief, such that it was rumored he had gone mad [impazzato]. Having recovered his senses [riavuti gli spiriti], he decided to confront fortune" and send the army with Ferrandino into Lombardy, "hoping to seize the stato from Ludovico" (18–19). The army went to Ravenna near the [French-Milanese] camp but dithered for a while "because

[23] *OS*, vol. 2, pp. 915–17 (passages cited by numbered sentences).

Ferrandino lacked the authority [from Alfonso] to commence hostilities" (21).[24] Machiavelli's translation of Rucellai's scathing assessment of Alfonso suggests his agreement and supports his condemnation, in *Prince* 24, of the king of Naples, among other signori of Italy, who, wrongly blaming fortune, "lost their states" because of their own "ignavia [sloth]" and reckless ambition.

[24] For the original passages, see Bernardo Rucellai, *De bello italico. La guerra d'Italia*, ed. Donatella Coppini (Florence: Firenze University Press, 2011), pp. 50–3, 56–7, 72–3, 76–7.

3
Mercenaries and Cesare Borgia

"NO MAN CAN LIVE HONORABLY BY THIS *ARTE*"

In the last chapter of book 1 of the *Florentine Histories* Machiavelli underscores the conjoint responsibility of princes and mercenary captains for Italy's sorry state. Because all the "principal powers were without arms of their own," "Italian arms were in the hands of the lesser princes [minori principi] or men without territories [uomini senza stato]," the latter being mercenaries who did not govern, but aspired to gain and rule, their own states. A thirst for profit and security motivated the rulers of smaller principalities to acquire arms, but the "uomini senza stato" were "raised from infancy in [a culture of] arms and, knowing no other profession [arte], sought by means of arms to make themselves honored with wealth and power." Machiavelli lists in this chapter the "most renowned" mercenary captains only of the early fifteenth century (because the first book of the *Histories* stops there), saving discussion of many others for the later books. This early roster includes Carmagnola (Francesco Bussone, count of Carmagnola), who fought for Filippo Maria Visconti, then for Venice, and was executed by the Venetians when suspected of subverting battlefield operations; Francesco Sforza, who fought for every major power in Italy and became duke of Milan after betraying the Ambrosian Republic; Niccolò Piccinino, originally from Perugia, one of Filippo Maria's leading captains and a chief architect of the Visconti territorial state until he angered the duke demanding Piacenza for himself; Agnolo della Pergola, employed by the Church and then Visconti; the brothers Lorenzo and Micheletto Attenduli, the first of whom fought for all the Italian powers, the second mostly for Venice against Francesco Sforza; Tartaglia (Angelo Lavello), who fought with both Muzio Attendolo Sforza and Braccio da Montone; Iacopaccio (Giacomo Caldora), who fought with Braccio da Montone and for both the papacy and Queen Joanna II of Naples; Ceccolino (Michelotti) da Perugia, employed by Visconti; Niccolò da Tolentino, whose employers included the Church, Visconti, Joanna II, and Florence; Guido Torello, who was mostly in the service of Visconti; Antonio (Gambacorta) da Pontedera, who fought with the Colonna of Rome; and "many others similar to these." Of these, only Francesco Sforza acquired a state, which allows Machiavelli to differentiate these "uomini senza stato" from the "signori of which I have spoken above," namely, the captains who rose from the ranks of professional soldiers to become rulers of principalities. Machiavelli adds a third group, namely, the "baroni of Rome, the Orsini and Colonna, together

Machiavelli's Broken World. John M. Najemy, Oxford University Press. © John M. Najemy 2022.
DOI: 10.1093/oso/9780199580927.003.0003

with other signori and gentili uomini of the kingdom [of Naples] and of Lombardy." All these professional soldiers created "a kind of association and secret pact [come una lega e intelligenza insieme]" and made [war] their "arte [profession]." The purpose of their "pact," according to Machiavelli, was to "temporize" and avoid pitched battles, "and in the end they reduced war to such a level of debasement [viltà] that any average commander in whom there was a shadow of reborn ancient virtú would have humiliated them, to the astonishment of all Italy which, in its lack of wisdom, had honored them. My history," Machiavelli angrily declares, "will be full of these slothful princes and cowardly arms" (*IF* 1.39.6–10).

In *Prince* 12 Machiavelli asserts that the "ruina di Italia" was the result of its long-term dependence on "mercenary arms" and affirms the principle that arms "must be administered either by a prince or by a republic," in other words, by government and not by private or non-state actors. He cites Rome, Sparta, and the modern Swiss as examples of states "very well armed and very free" and contrasts them with states that entrusted arms to mercenaries to whom, more often than not, they lost their liberty. Mercenaries hired by the Carthaginians revolted and nearly defeated their employers in a long war. The Thebans lost their independence to their mercenary captain, Philip of Macedon. Among modern examples, Machiavelli cites the Milanese, who hired Francesco Sforza to defend them against Venice, only to see him switch sides and subjugate his employers; and Queen Joanna of Naples, who—suddenly abandoned and left defenseless by her hired captain, Sforza's father (Muzio Attendolo)—was forced to "throw herself into the arms" of the king of Aragon. In all these cases (or nearly so in the case of Carthage), states that depended on mercenaries or foreign arms were swallowed up by them (*P* 12.8–17).

Turning to Venice and Florence, Machiavelli acknowledges that both republics employed mercenaries who defended them and increased their territorial dominions without seizing power and making themselves their "principi." The Florentines, he says, were simply lucky—"favored by chance [da la sorte]"—because, among their valorous [virtuosi] captains from whom they might have had to fear such a fate, some "did not win" the wars they fought, others had rivals who constrained their political ambitions, and still others turned their ambitions elsewhere. As an example of "capitani virtuosi" who "did not win," Machiavelli cites the legendary John Hawkwood. He assumes his readers know that Hawkwood was the renowned fourteenth-century English mercenary who, after fighting for Milan and the papacy, entered Florentine service during the War of the Eight Saints (1375–8) against the papacy and spent most of the rest of his career with Florence. Because Hawkwood "did not win," Machiavelli says, his loyalty was never tested, but "everyone" agrees that, "had he won," Florence would have been "at his mercy [a sua discrezione]." The argument is somewhat forced. Machiavelli neglects to mention that, if Hawkwood did not win, neither did he lose. The two major wars in which he commanded troops for Florence—the papal war and the conflict with Milan in

1390–2—both ended in standoffs. In the latter conflict, he skillfully executed a necessary retreat. Perhaps this is what Machiavelli had in mind claiming that he achieved no victory. He also omits the fact that, after his death in 1394, Florence honored Hawkwood with a frescoed equestrian portrait in the cathedral.[1] Machiavelli's example of a Florentine mercenary captain whose political ambitions were thwarted by a rival is Muzio Attendolo Sforza. Muzio fought for the Florentines at Casalecchio, near Bologna, in 1402, where the victory of Giangaleazzo's army seemed to open the way for an attack on Florence, which, however, failed to materialize only because the duke died a few months later. But Muzio also took part in the successful siege of Pisa in 1406. Machiavelli implies, rather implausibly and without explanation, that Florence narrowly escaped losing its liberty because Muzio was so preoccupied with his adversary Braccio. The evident exaggeration of the threat posed by Muzio alludes to his son Francesco's betrayal of Milan's Ambrosian Republic, which Machiavelli mentions a few sentences earlier and refers to again in the next sentence on mercenary commanders who steered their ambitions "elsewhere," his first example being "Francesco," who "turned his ambition to Lombardy" (*P* 12.17–21).

Machiavelli then addresses the problematic episode of Paolo Vitelli, hired by Florence (in 1498) as captain general in the war against Pisa. He praises Vitelli as a "very prudent" commander who rose from "privata fortuna" to "great fame." "If," Machiavelli affirms, "he had captured Pisa, no one would deny that the Florentines would have had to stay with him"—"stare seco," keep him in their employ—"because, if he had become the hired soldier of their enemies, [the Florentines] would have had no remedy"—no hope of avoiding defeat or worse. "And if they kept him in their employ, they would have had to obey him," be forced, in effect, to accept him as lord of the city (*P* 12.22). Machiavelli cautiously omits here what every Florentine knew: a year after hiring Vitelli, the Florentines accused him of sabotaging the campaign against Pisa, disobeying the civilian commissioners, and negotiating with Florence's enemies. He was arrested and quickly executed for treason on October 1, 1499. Machiavelli mentions Vitelli's death in chapter 8, where he notes that Oliverotto da Fermo served a military apprenticeship with Vitelli and fought with him until he, Vitelli, was "morto," killed (*P* 8.13–14)—how or by whom Machiavelli does not say. In *The Prince* Machiavelli says not a word about Vitelli's highly controversial execution, even though, just days after the event, responding to the aspersions of an official of Lucca, he defended his government's action.[2] As the chronicler Piero Parenti explains, Vitelli conspired with Pope Alexander, Venice, and the Pisans to return the exiled Piero de' Medici to

[1] See William Caferro, *John Hawkwood: An English Mercenary in Fourteenth-Century Italy* (Baltimore: Johns Hopkins University Press, 2006).

[2] *Lettere*, pp. 84–6.

power, even negotiating with Piero himself.[3] Until his death in 1503, Piero was among the republic's most dangerous enemies, as shown by his attempted coup in 1497 and his complicity in the occupation of Arezzo by Vitelli's brother Vitellozzo. What made Paolo's betrayal and execution sensitive topics in Florence after the return of the Medici in 1512 is that Paolo and Piero were brothers-in-law, Vitelli having married a sister, Girolama, of Piero's wife, Alfonsina Orsini. Machiavelli no doubt thought it prudent not to rehearse the full story of Vitelli's employment by Florence in a book meant for Medici eyes. But he is nonetheless Machiavelli's best example of the danger to Florence of its mercenary captains.

Machiavelli tells the same story in *Prince* 12 about Venice's experience with mercenaries that he outlines in *Histories* 1.39. For as long as Venice's expansion took place far from the Italian mainland, the republic's nobles ("gentili uomini") and armed plebs ("plebe armata") fought "securely," "gloriously," and "virtuosissimamente," but when they began fighting to expand their terraferma dominion they "abandoned this virtú and adopted the customs of war in Italy" by hiring mercenaries. At first, they made only moderate gains and had little to fear from the captains they employed. But when (in the 1420s) they expanded their presence in Italy, "which happened under Carmagnola," "they got a taste of their error." Previously in the service of Filippo Maria Visconti, Carmagnola won a major victory over his former employer (in May 1427) in which, Machiavelli says, he showed himself to be "virtuosissimo." But he suddenly became reluctant to fight, and the Venetians concluded they could no longer gain military victories "with him." Unable to release him for fear of losing what they had acquired, "in order to protect themselves" they were "forced" to kill him (in 1432) (*P* 12.23–5). The Venetians found themselves in a situation quite similar to what the Florentines experienced with Paolo Vitelli sixty-seven years later: fearful both of keeping him and of letting him go. Here, too, Machiavelli does not tell the full story. In addition to disputes over how much of the year he was expected to keep his forces ready and in the field,[4] Carmagnola's inactivity after the 1427 victory generated suspicions and then charges of collusion with the Milanese.[5] It is more difficult to understand Machiavelli's silence in this case than in that of Vitelli and Florence. The Venetians continued to employ mercenary captains (he names "Bartolomeo da Bergomo," known as Bartolomeo Colleoni, and Roberto da Sanseverino), but with them they feared losses, not further gains. Machiavelli blames mercenaries for the Venetians' sudden defeat in 1509 at Agnadello, "where in one day they lost what in eight hundred years they had acquired with so much effort." He concludes

[3] Parenti, *Storia fiorentina*, ed. Matucci, vol. 2, pp. 290–1, 303, 305, 307.

[4] Michael Mallett, *Mercenaries and their Masters: Warfare in Renaissance Italy* (Totowa, New Jersey: Rowman and Littlefield, 1974), pp. 96–100.

[5] Geoffrey Trease, *The Condottieri: Soldiers of Fortune* (New York: Holt, Rinehart and Winston, 1971), pp. 242–58.

this survey with the judgment that mercenary arms produce "only slow, laborious, weak gains and sudden, bewildering losses" (*P* 12.26).

Still in *Prince* 12, Machiavelli provides a brief history of the rise of mercenaries. Having "come, with these examples, to Italy, which for many years has been dominated [governata] by mercenary arms," he proposes to discuss their "origin and development" from a longer historical perspective ("piú da alto") "so that we will be better able to reform them. You should know, therefore, that in these recent times, as soon as the [Holy Roman] Empire began to be pushed out of Italy and the popes acquired more prestige in the temporal sphere, Italy was divided into several states." The events, not exactly "recent," to which Machiavelli refers here are the struggles of the Italian cities against the campaigns of the Hohenstaufen emperors Frederick Barbarossa, Henry VI, and Frederick II between the mid-twelfth and the mid-thirteenth century to bring northern and central Italy (and, in the case of Frederick II, the whole of Italy) under imperial rule. In resisting and ultimately defeating these efforts, the cities emerged as de facto self-governing entities. In an observation whose full significance Machiavelli will elucidate in the *Discourses on Livy*, he notes that "many of the large cities took up arms against their own nobles, who, supported by the emperors, had previously kept the cities oppressed." In many instances, "their own citizens became the rulers [principi]." This might refer to the emergence of strongmen, de facto lords (signori), but also to the city-republics, or communes, in which the leading citizens ("principi" in the Roman sense of first citizens) governed. Machiavelli introduces the papacy too into this brief historical sketch, affirming that, "in order to enhance its temporal power," the Church allied with the cities to repel the emperors. Although he does not explicitly state that the Church, in so doing, extended its own territorial dominions (as in fact it did), he does say that "almost all of Italy" (evidently excluding the South) "came into the hands of the Church and a number of republics [qualche republica]." And, because "the priests and those other citizens"—the merchant and professional classes—"were unaccustomed to wielding arms, they began hiring foreigners" to fight their wars. Mercenaries became necessary because the merchant and professional classes that came to power in the struggle against the emperors were disinclined to assume the military role previously fulfilled by the powerful families—Machiavelli calls them "nobles"—that had constituted the warrior elements of urban society. Many of these newly liberated cities had even "taken up arms" against the nobles, disarming and disenfranchising them (*P* 12.27–9). He was, of course, acutely aware, from his experience in promoting Florence's militia, of how stubbornly Italy's merchant elites refused either to bear arms or to arm the lower classes of their cities, preferring instead to employ mercenaries.

Machiavelli identifies Alberico da Barbiano (calling him Alberico di Cunio because he was from the family of the counts of Cunio in the Romagna) as the "first captain to bring renown to mercenary armies," but without mentioning that

Alberico was a disciple of Hawkwood and created the first freelance company composed entirely of Italians. In the *Florentine Histories* 1.34.1–2, Machiavelli says many foreign soldiers—English, Germans, and Bretons—were in Italy in the fourteenth century, some brought in by foreign princes, others by the Avignonese popes, and that "all Italian princes" of the time employed these foreigners in their wars until Alberico (whom he erroneously calls Lodovico here) founded a company of Italian soldiers, called San Giorgio, whose "virtú" and "disciplina" "in a short time reduced the reputation of foreign arms and gave it to the Italians. Italian princes thereafter fought their wars with Italian soldiers."[6] In *The Prince*, however, Machiavelli does not praise Alberico's employment of Italians, no doubt because it would have been incompatible with his overall excoriation of mercenaries. But he does credit Alberico with having instilled "disciplina" in his troops and having imparted this "disciplina" to Braccio da Montone and Muzio Attendolo Sforza, who "in their time were the arbiters [arbitri] of Italy." Ultimately, however, their legacy was noxious: "after these came all the others who, down to our own time, have commanded these [mercenary] arms, and the result of their virtú"—here savagely ironic—"is that Italy has been overrun by Charles, despoiled by Louis, violated by Ferdinand, and humiliated by the Swiss" (*P* 12.30–1)—Machiavelli's angriest indictment and bitterest condemnation of the *false* "virtú" of mercenaries.

Particularly troubling for Machiavelli was the mercenaries' devaluation of infantry. This happened, he says, because mercenaries were "sanza stato"—without territorial lordship—and relied exclusively on their skill ("industria") as soldiers. Implied in this cryptic formulation is that only sufficiently large territories have the population resources from which princes and republics can recruit soldiers in the quantities needed for an infantry force. Not only did these captains lack territories, and hence population; they also lacked the financial wherewithal to pay large numbers of infantrymen, and the relatively small infantry forces they could afford gave them little benefit or prestige. Hence, they favored cavalry over infantry. This critique underpins Machiavelli's insistence on the superiority of infantry. By scorning infantry, mercenaries (and their employers) kept the people unarmed and Italy militarily weak. He accuses them of bringing still more shame to Italy in their cowardly approach to combat and their attempts to spare themselves and their soldiers anxiety ("paura") and effort ("fatica") by limiting casualties, taking and releasing prisoners without ransom, foregoing nighttime attacks, and not fighting in winter. Although partly exaggerated, these accusations reflect to a degree common practices among all armies of the time. "All these things were allowed by their military procedures [ordini] and devised by them to avoid, as has been said, exertion and danger. And the result is

[6] On Alberico, see Trease, *The Condottieri*, 169–84.

that they have dragged Italy down to slavery and humiliation [hanno condotta la Italia stiava e vituperata]" (*P* 12.32–4).

In *Discourses* 2.18 Machiavelli expands his explanation of why mercenary captains neglected infantry. After evaluating the evidence from ancient and especially Roman history for the superiority of infantry over cavalry, he offers another look at the emergence and development of mercenary armies in Italy. The ultimate responsibility lies with the "Italian princes who have made Italy a slave to foreigners." Among their "sins," he writes (echoing the accusation in *Prince* 12.9), "none is greater than their having had little regard" for infantry and "having devoted all their concern" to cavalry. This happened "because of the wickedness [malignità] of the heads [of the mercenary companies] and the ignorance of those who were governing states." In a sentence that has caused some puzzlement, Machiavelli says that "because, prior to the last twenty-five years [da venticinque anni indietro] the practice of warfare in Italy was restricted to men who did not rule states and were in effect soldiers of fortune, they pondered how they could maintain their power being armed themselves and keeping the princes unarmed." There is here at least the suggestion that mercenary captains strategically enhanced their own power by keeping their employers unarmed; if so, it would explain why Machiavelli accuses them of "malignità." Whereas in *Prince* 12 mercenary captains could not afford to pay large numbers of infantrymen and hence turned to cavalry, in *Discourses* 2.18 it is the princes who are unable to sustain such expense. "Because [mercenary captains] could not be paid enough [by their employer princes] to maintain a permanent infantry force and did not have subjects they could make use of, and because a small number of infantry gave them no renown, they turned to keeping cavalry. Two or three hundred cavalry paid [by the prince/employer] were sufficient for a condottiere to maintain his reputation, and the cost was not so great that it could not be met by those who governed states." Machiavelli reinforces the suggestion that mercenary captains did this deliberately to enhance their own power when he says that, "in order for this to happen more easily, and to enhance their reputation, they deprived infantry of all respect and honor and transferred it to their cavalry." They so persisted in this error that infantry was a minimal part of even large armies, and this "weakened Italian military forces so much that the country has easily been overrun by the northerners" (*DL* 2.18.12–17). Machiavelli here makes the mercenaries responsible not only for Italy's inability to withstand the invaders but also for having weakened its princes and governors.

Machiavelli's critique of the military malfeasance of Italy's princes continues with his condemnation, in *Prince* 13, of auxiliaries—troops of another power—as "the other [type of] useless arms." He cites Pope Julius's decision, after the "poor showing of his mercenaries" in an attempt to seize Ferrara in 1510, to ally with Ferdinand of Spain and employ Spanish auxiliaries, thus "throwing himself entirely into the hands of a foreigner"—a "decision that could not have been more ill-advised." Auxiliaries "are almost always harmful," Machiavelli says, because "if they lose, you suffer defeat; if they are victorious, you are their prisoner." Julius evaded the first of these outcomes only by his "good fortune." After the French routed his Spanish auxiliaries at Ravenna in April 1512, the Swiss rescued Julius from the consequences of his "bad choice [mala elezione]" when, in the summer of that year, they entered the war and drove the French from Italy, "beyond his and everyone else's expectation [fuora di ogni opinione e sua e d'altri]" (*P* 13.1–4). Although Julius escaped becoming a "prisoner" of the French and emerged victorious on the backs of the Swiss, this fortuitous outcome does not cause Machiavelli to hesitate in faulting Julius for depending on auxiliaries. If in chapter 25 he attributes Julius's long string of successes to his "good fortune," in chapter 13 he makes it clear that this "good fortune" masked serious errors. A second example of the uselessness and even danger of auxiliaries comes from Machiavelli's own Florence. The decision in 1500 to entrust the war to recover Pisa to 10,000 French soldiers, he says, "exposed [the Florentines] to greater danger than anything they had ever faced in other troubles." As in the case of Paolo Vitelli, Machiavelli expected his readers to know what happened. By delaying action against the Pisans, the French seemed to be taking their side, and when Florence withheld payments the French made threatening noises against Florence itself. Machiavelli then turns to a foreign example: the decision of the Byzantine emperor (John VI Kantakouzenos, who reigned in the mid-fourteenth century) to invite a contingent of Ottoman Turks (Machiavelli again says 10,000) to assist him against neighboring rivals. The Turks never left and this "was the beginning of Greece's submission to the infidels" (*P* 13.5–6).

Machiavelli's other Italian example in chapter 13 is Cesare Borgia. This passage begins with the affirmation that "I will never hesitate to cite Cesare Borgia and his actions." In fact, however, Machiavelli proceeds to criticize most of the actions he attributes to him: his conquest of the Romagna with French auxiliaries; and, after realizing their unreliability, his decision to hire Vitelli and Orsini mercenaries. Only after seeing how untrustworthy and dangerous mercenaries were did he determine to dismiss them and obtain "his own" arms. The problem—just as in *Prince* 7 (see below in this chapter)—is that Machiavelli provides no particulars of the arms Borgia allegedly made "his own." The difference between employing auxiliaries or mercenaries and having one's own arms can "easily be seen," Machiavelli writes, in the contrast between Borgia's reputation when he fought with French troops or Orsini and Vitelli mercenaries and the reputation he gained once he had only his own troops and depended on no one. "One finds that his reputation always grew, and never was he more esteemed than when everyone saw that he possessed completely his own arms" (*P* 13.11–12). Yet Machiavelli does not say when or how this happened and never cites any "actions" in support of the assertion that Borgia acquired his own arms. In fact, as we shall see, Borgia never raised an army from the territories he briefly held. This passage should be read as an exhortation to the Medici to do what Cesare Borgia did *not* do. The known facts—known to Machiavelli, as we shall see, and to us—are that Borgia's arms were French auxiliaries and Italian and Spanish mercenaries.

The positive examples of chapter 13—of princes who fought with their own arms and thereby demonstrated the greater wisdom of doing so—are ancient, foreign, or literary figures. Except for the phantom Borgia, there are no modern Italian examples. Hiero of Syracuse eliminated the mercenaries he found when he took command of the Syracusan armies. David refused Saul's offer of his arms—protective armor and a sword—and preferred to fight with his own sling and (as Machiavelli has it) a knife. More pertinent but from outside Italy is the fifteenth-century French king Charles VII, who created a militia of both cavalry and infantry and liberated France from the English. Machiavelli calls Charles's militia an "ordinanza"—the same official name of his Florentine militia. But Charles's successor, Louis XI, dismantled this homegrown force and hired Swiss mercenaries, thus sowing the seeds, says Machiavelli, of the "dangers" France was "now" experiencing (a silent reference to the defeats inflicted on the French by the Swiss in 1512 and again in 1513 at Novara). Engaging Swiss auxiliaries caused the French to become dependent on them, Machiavelli contends, and weakened French morale and fighting spirit, just as happened, he adds, to the Romans when they employed Goths as mercenaries (in the fourth century CE). Machiavelli's conclusion directly links the lack of one's own arms to dependence on fortune: "without one's own arms, no principato [no state of any kind] is secure; indeed, it is completely indebted [obligato] to fortune" (*P* 13.13–26).

Only at the end of the chapter, perhaps realizing he has so far said nothing about what having "one's own arms" entails in practice and about where and how to obtain them, does Machiavelli add that "arme proprie" consist "either of your subjects or your citizens or your subordinates [creati tua]." About how to organize them, he says only that "this will be easy to discover if one examines the methods of the four I have named above, and if one sees how Philip, father of Alexander the Great, and many republics and princes have armed themselves." Opinions differ as to whether the "four" to whom Machiavelli refers are those discussed in this chapter (Cesare Borgia, Hiero of Syracuse, David, and Charles VII) or the four founders of chapter 6 (Moses, Cyrus, Theseus, and Romulus). In either case, Machiavelli does not say, even in general terms, how any of them, Philip of Macedon included, created their own arms. Of all nine examples, only the "ordinanza" of France's Charles VII could possibly have provided a model capable of yielding practical lessons. It may seem odd that Machiavelli, who had designed, recruited, and planned every detail of the Florentine militia, has so little to say here about the specifics of raising "one's own arms." The lack of attention to the practicalities and modalities of the issue may indicate that the chief purpose of this chapter, as of much of *The Prince*, was less to teach the Medici or anyone else what to do than what *not* to do—to castigate the manifold errors of Italy's modern princes who too often did what they should not have done. Machiavelli may also have presumed that the Medici, who dismantled his militia upon their return to power in 1512, would not—at that moment—have welcomed instructions about how to build a new one.

Mercenary captains, in Machiavelli's perception, may have lacked courage in avoiding excessive exertions on the battlefield, but he saw no deficit of ambition in them. Because they, more than the princes, controlled Italian arms, they often determined when wars were fought and for what purpose. In the *Histories* he writes that, by the early fifteenth century, "whenever peace came through an agreement among princes, it was soon thereafter disrupted by those who possessed the arms." Professional soldiers were now strong enough to impose their own aims and decide the fate of states for which they—in theory—worked. He recounts how, after Duke Filippo Maria Visconti signed a peace treaty with Florence and Venice in 1433, "the mercenaries [soldati: paid troops] wanted to continue the war and turned against the Church," eventually seizing considerable chunks of its territories and bringing them under their personal control. Machiavelli introduces here the two competing mercenary alliances (he calls them "sette di armi"—military factions): the "braccesca," whose leaders ("principe") were Niccolò Piccinino and Niccolò Fortebraccio; and the "sforzesca," whose "capo" was "Count Francesco, son of [Muzio Attendolo] Sforza." "Almost all the other arms in Italy were allied with [one or the other of] these factions." Private armies, only loosely tied to their employer/princes, now controlled the military, and much of the political, fortunes of Italy. Machiavelli says Sforza's faction was held in higher regard, both because of his "virtú" and because the duke of Milan had promised him his daughter in marriage (*IF* 5.2.1–4). As we have already seen, books 5 and 6 of the *Histories* follow the twists and turns of Sforza's relentless ambition, his changing alliances and eventual conquest, through deceit and betrayal, of the Milanese duchy. He is Machiavelli's prime example of the dysfunctional relationship between freelance mercenary commanders and Italy's princes.

In the *Art of War* Machiavelli entrusts, with evident irony, his most sustained excoriation of mercenaries to a fictional speaker with the name of the age's most renowned mercenary captain, Fabrizio Colonna.[7] The "arte" of the book's title is not "art," as it is usually translated, but rather "profession" or "occupation," and the essence of the critique Machiavelli has Fabrizio speak is that war should never be an "arte," a full-time profession. Men who practice war as an "arte" "cannot live honorably [onestamente] from it." Only "a republic or a kingdom"—governments—should practice war as an "arte." No "well-ordered" republic or kingdom has ever allowed its

[7] I explore the puzzle in "Fabrizio Colonna and Machiavelli's *Art of War*" in *Warfare and Politics: Cities and Government in Renaissance Tuscany and Venice*, ed. Humfrey Butters and Gabriele Neher (Amsterdam: Amsterdam University Press, 2019), pp. 143–60.

citizens or subjects to engage in it as a profession. To attempt to make a living or derive profit ("utilità") from it at all times, in peace as well as in war, one must be "rapacious, fraudulent, and violent." Those who practice war as a profession have no choice but to do so constantly, because "this profession cannot sustain them [non gli nutrisce] in times of peace." They are therefore compelled either to engage in "robberies, acts of violence, and killings" against friends and enemies alike in order to "nourish" themselves in peacetime, or else deceive their employers into prolonging wars. But if peace does come, it often happens that mercenary captains, having lost their stipends, turn their forces into freelance companies ("rizzano una bandiera di ventura") and mercilessly plunder whole territories (*AG* 1.51–3).

Fabrizio cites Francesco Sforza as a prime example, not of virtú, as Machiavelli characterizes him in *Prince* 7, but of the "evil deeds" commonly perpetrated by mercenaries. He asks his interlocutors in the dialogue: "Do you not recall from your history how, when wars ended, with many mercenaries [soldati] in Italy lacking stipends [sanza soldo], several brigades gathered together in what were called Companies, which went around extorting money from cities and plundering the countryside, against which no protection was possible?" After an ancient example, Fabrizio introduces Sforza. "In the time of our fathers, Francesco Sforza, in order to live in high style [onorevolmente] in peacetime, not only deceived the Milanese whose paid soldier [soldato] he was, but also robbed them of their liberty and became their prince. All the other mercenary soldiers in Italy have been like him in that they pursued warfare as their personal profession [particolare arte]; and if they did not become dukes of Milan through their evil deeds [malignitadi], all the more do they deserve censure, because, if we examine their careers, without gaining [what Sforza did] they all share the same culpability." Fabrizio adduces, as further examples of faithless and dangerous mercenaries, Muzio Attendolo, Sforza's father, and Braccio da Montone, both of whom betrayed Queen Joanna of Naples trying to "seize the kingdom from her." Fabrizio concludes that the causes of "such disorders"—"disordini" in Machiavelli's lexicon signifying illegalities that damage or destroy laws and institutions—are "men who utilized the mercenary trade as their private profession [lo esercizio del soldo per loro propria arte]" (*AG* 1.54–60).

Fabrizio's interlocutor in book 1, Cosimo Rucellai, is puzzled by this harsh criticism of such renowned captains. He says he used to think of the professional military (the "arte del soldo," literally the "money trade") as "the most excellent and honorable" of all professions. Now, having heard Fabrizio's denunciation of them, he cannot understand why Caesar, Pompey, Scipio, Marcellus, and other Roman generals are held in such esteem and honored as gods (*AG* 1.63). Fabrizio grounds his answer in the two principles he has already enunciated: that "a good man" cannot make the military his "arte"; and that "no well-ordered republic or kingdom has ever permitted its citizens or subjects to make it their arte." On these grounds, he answers Cosimo's query about the Roman generals, distinguishing between, on the one hand, "Caesar, Pompey, and almost all the other generals who came after the last Carthaginian war and who gained fame as valorous [valenti] men, but not as good men," and, on the other hand, "those who lived before them" (Scipio and Marcellus, heroes of the struggle against Carthage) "who won glory as both good and valorous men," precisely because "they did not make war their full-time profession," as "did those I mentioned first" (Caesar and Pompey). Fabrizio asserts that, for as long as the Roman republic was unstained by corruption (whose meaning he is about to make clear), Roman nobles did not exploit the military profession in peacetime to acquire power by violating the laws, despoiling the provinces, or "usurping tyrannical powers over their country [usurpando e tiranneggiando la patria]." Nor did members of the non-noble classes "make themselves the clients of private citizens [aderirsi agli uomini privati]" or participate in any "tyrannical assault [tirannico insulto]" against the republic in order to make a full-time living "in the profession of war [con l'arte della guerra]." In that early time, generals and soldiers alike were more than happy, at war's end, to return to "vita privata," each "to his [civilian] profession [all'arte sua]." No one attempted to live from the spoils of war (*AG* 1.64–8). A "well-ordered city," as Machiavelli believes Rome was before the middle of the second century BCE, should allow only the "publico"—the state—to make war its "arte" (*AG* 1.75).

Cosimo accepts Fabrizio's reasoning in the case of republics but asks if kings should not want to surround themselves with men who make war a full-time profession. No, Fabrizio replies, a "well-ordered" kingdom should flee from such men (he calls them "artefici": practitioners of an "arte"), because they "are, in and of themselves, the corruption [corruttela] of their king and in every way agents of tyranny [ministri della tirannide]." Kingdoms that tolerate them cannot be considered "bene ordinati," and permanent armies that make war their "arte" are dangerous to kings (*AG* 1.77–84). For centuries, Fabrizio explains, the Romans avoided this danger by rotating the army's units. Later, however, "first Octavian and then Tiberius, thinking more of their own power than of the public good [all'utile publico], began to disarm the Roman people in order to rule them more easily." To the same end, they created the Praetorian Guard, which became a permanent force whose members exercised "la milizia per loro arte" and soon aimed its "insolence" against the emperors themselves, creating, removing, and even killing them at whim. From this ancient example, Fabrizio concludes that, when wars end, rulers who wish to live securely should not only want their infantry to return home to their civilian professions, but "must also want [debbe volere]" their noble captains ("principi") to return "to governing their own populations" and the "gentili uomini" to return to the cultivation of their lands (*AG* 1.85–93). Fabrizio's juxtaposition of "principi" and "gentili uomini" echoes an important passage—to be examined in due course—from the *Discourses on Livy* (1.55) where Machiavelli discusses two categories of warrior nobles: "gentiluomini" who live on income from landed wealth, and "signori di castella," who rule fortified towns ("castella") and have territories of their own and subjects who obey them. From their ranks—and the Colonna are a prime example—came many of the mercenary captains who made war their full-time profession.

In emphasizing the danger to the security of a prince or republic of powerful warrior nobles who command private armies, refuse to go home when wars end, and demand stipends in peacetime, Machiavelli's Fabrizio describes dysfunctions of the military system of his time that come uncomfortably close to the historical Fabrizio. The Colonna were both "gentiluomini" and "signori di castella" with vast landed estates and jurisdiction over territories and populations, and they produced many professional captains. According to his own principles, Fabrizio is among those who should have returned to governing their "subjects" in peacetime. But he is slow to apply the principle to himself, provoking Cosimo to press the point, albeit indirectly. While praising Fabrizio's "ragionamento" and claiming never to have thought of these matters in this way, he asks about the many "signori" and "gentili uomini" who "support themselves in peacetime through military activities, as do your peers [i pari vostri] who take regular stipends [provisioni] from princes and cities" (*AG* 1.94–5). Fabrizio acknowledges that keeping cavalry ("genti d'arme") permanently employed is a "corrupt system [modo corrotto] and not good," because "these men who make war their profession... would give rise to a thousand problems" every day in states that employ them if they had large enough contingents of soldiers. Because most companies are relatively small and unable to constitute real armies, he thinks they "cannot often do serious damage. Nonetheless, they have done so many times, as I told you happened with Francesco Sforza and his father and with Braccio [da Montone] of Perugia. So I do not approve of this custom of keeping cavalry full time; it is corrupt and can cause great problems" (*AG* 1.99–102). This is the second damning characterization of Francesco Sforza in the first book of the *Art of War* as a type of ambitious mercenary whose private interests undermine states, both republics and kingdoms, and weaken their defenses.

Fabrizio does finally admit that he too is complicit in this "most corrupt system [ordine corrottissimo]" because he accepts the peacetime "stipends reserved for me and other captains." Instead of hiring professionals, wise republics and kings should have their own citizens serve as commanders and should want them to return home, each to his "arte," after the conclusion of a war. But the fictional Fabrizio quickly retreats from this admission of complicity by denying, in a surprising reversal, that he has *ever* practiced war as a profession, a denial that patently contradicts the reality of the historical Fabrizio Colonna. Acknowledging that he is one of the nobles who govern territories and have subjects who obey them, he insists that his "arte" is to "govern his subjects and defend them and, in order to be able to do so, to love peace and know how to make [saper fare] war." "My king," he says, "rewards and esteems me not so much for my understanding of war as for my ability to advise him in peace." The suggestion of his complicity in the corruption he describes evidently puts Fabrizio uneasily on the defensive, as he declares he shall have no more to say on the subject (*AG* 1.106–11). His claim of having "subjects" to "govern and defend" alludes to the historical Fabrizio Colonna's social and political status as a noble who possessed extensive territories and considerable political power and who, according to the ideas spoken by his fictional counterpart, should have returned home to govern and defend his subjects—but generally did not. Instead of governing and defending "their" populations, these full-time professional captains too often became "rapacious, fraudulent, and violent" threats to the states they claimed to serve while at the same time making impossible the Roman-like citizen armies Fabrizio claims to admire. In the seventh and last book of the *Art of War*, he bitterly denounces the laziness and immorality of his troops and their lack of discipline, obedience, and loyalty to him, presenting these failings as ineradicable deficiencies in the soldiers themselves—the human "materia" over which he has no control (*AG* 7.212–24). It does not occur to him that such behaviors were inherent in a system of mercenary arms with intermittent periods of activity and irregular pay. The Fabrizio of the dialogue represents the inability of Italy's warrior nobles to acknowledge their own precarious loyalties, their search for private advantage, and their complicity in Italy's subjugation to foreigners.

"BEGINNING TO BE ACCUSTOMED TO RESTRAINING HIS DESIRES"

Cesare Borgia a mercenary? Of course. He began his dramatic career on the stage of Italian politics as a warrior "senza stato," soldier for hire, and French client. With funds from his father, Pope Alexander, and arms from King Louis, he briefly brought several cities and territories under his control attempting to piece together a "stato," and just as quickly lost it all when his father died and he found himself at the mercy of a pope, Julius II, who detested the Borgias. Machiavelli found him intriguing—above all as a bombastic failure and prime example of the dysfunction of Italian arms entrusted to the wrong hands. In Borgia's case, the arms were never enough to accomplish the goal of creating a state, which, had he succeeded, would have been a protectorate of the papacy or at war with the next pope. Far from being a model "new prince" representing any hope for a suffering Italy, Borgia was to Machiavelli a product and symptom of everything that was wrong about the relationship in Italy between the political and the military. The following pages examine Machiavelli's evolving perception of Borgia through a deep dive into the legations in which he carefully observed him. The chapter concludes with a hypothesis concerning the way Machiavelli represents and interprets this experience in chapter 7 of *The Prince*.

Cesare was the bearer and instrument of his father's ambition to establish a Borgia principality in the Romagna, the tumultuous region of the papal states that popes rarely had under effective control. Cesare first appears in Machiavelli's chancery papers on January 7, 1499, in a letter to commissioner Piero Corsini with the news that Borgia, having been made duke of Valentinois (in southeastern France on the Rhône) by King Louis, for which he was often thereafter called Valentino and sometimes Valentinese by the Italians, had arrived at the royal court at Chinon "with such pomp and ostentatious display [tanta pompa e apparato] that it was considered an astonishing thing [cosa mirabile]" ("mirabile" in the sense of stupefying, not necessarily conveying a favorable impression). "According to what our ambassadors tell us about him," Machiavelli added, "he will greatly favor our cause."[8] The ambassadors were wrong. Later that year, Borgia began seizing the cities of the Romagna, and, by mid-1500, when the Florentine government sent Machiavelli and Francesco Della Casa as envoys to France to ascertain the king's willingness to help Florence regain Pisa, Borgia's ambitions seemed more threatening. In a dispatch of August 12 from the peripatetic royal court, then at Montargis in the Loiret, the envoys reported the rumor that Pope Alexander was pressuring Louis to assist Cesare in the conquest of Faenza. The pope wanted Faenza added to the already captured cities of Forlì and Imola, as Machiavelli puts it, "per il suo [for his] Valentinese," the same dismissive way of referring to Cesare he would use in "Words to be Spoken." Louis, however, was said to be reluctant because "it seemed to him he had already done [Cesare] many favors." Machiavelli and Della Casa also reported that a representative of Vitellozzo Vitelli was openly declaring at the court what harm Vitellozzo would inflict on the Florentines "if the pope or someone else" launched a war against them. The "someone else" was of course Cesare. According to Vitelli's emissary, Alexander "would be even more inclined" to take up arms against Florence than against Faenza if a quarrel between Florence and Louis provoked the king to give the green light for an assault (*LCSG* 1.270.22–4).

In September, Della Casa became ill and left the court (*LCSG* 1.286.3). While waiting for a new and fully accredited ambassador to arrive, Machiavelli negotiated with the French on his own. By October, the Florentine Signoria was sufficiently worried about Borgia to instruct Machiavelli to ask Louis for assurances against the growing peril. Despite the risk of putting into writing their concerns about aggression from Borgia, the "grave dangers" brewing in Italy persuaded the Signoria not to wait until their new ambassador arrived at the court. On October 11 they reported to Machiavelli that Alexander had "assembled an army under the command of Cesare" and his chief lieutenants, including Vitellozzo Vitelli, "with the aim [disegno], so they say," of seizing Rimini, Pesaro, and Faenza. But the real objective of the Borgias, as the Signoria learned from "reliable sources," was to

[8] *Legazioni. Commissarie. Scritti di governo*, vol. 1, ed. Jean-Jacques Marchand (Rome: Salerno Editrice, 2002), pp. 182–3. Passages are cited in the text with the abbreviation *LCSG*, followed by volume number, document number, and numbered subsections; e.g. in this case (*LCSG* 1.111.9).

raise disturbances in certain cities of the Florentine dominion and restore the Medici to power in Florence. "The pope has been made to understand that doing so is necessary if he wishes...to hold on to whatever territory [stato] he might acquire, and that this objective would best be met by having a government [stato] in Florence installed by him rather than by anyone else."[9] The Signoria instructed Machiavelli to tell Louis that Florentine "liberty" was at stake and to ask the king for his help; specifically, they wanted Louis to warn Alexander to "remove these suspicions" of any intention to invade Florentine territory (*LCSG* 1.290.3–8). Ten days later the Signoria told Machiavelli that Borgia's troops had not entered the dominion as had been feared and now seemed headed for Faenza. Machiavelli was nonetheless to explain the risks Florence faced, but "moderating his words and not presenting the matter so urgently, and to discuss with [the king] the dangers we face from the arrival of [Borgia's] troops in the Romagna" (*LCSG* 1.292.7–11).

Writing from Nantes on October 25, Machiavelli explained Louis's reluctance to stop Borgia from taking Faenza. "With regard to what might happen in Italy, His Majesty holds the pope in higher consideration [fa piú stima] than any other Italian power, both because he is more poised for military action, less worn down by war, beset by fewer obstacles, and also because he is the head of our religion [capo della religione]." The consensus at the court, Machiavelli wrote, was that Louis had allowed Cesare to seize much of the Romagna and might let him take Bologna because he knows "the pope's appetite is insatiable" (*LCSG* 1.293.13–16). On November 4 Machiavelli wrote that, knowing the Signoria's fear of the "hostile intentions [malo animo]" of Valentino's army, he decided to raise the issue with both the king and Georges d'Amboise, the cardinal of Rouen and the king's powerful first minister. Rouen did not believe Alexander would attempt any undertaking in Italy without Louis's permission; he assured Machiavelli that the king had given none and that, if the pope went ahead on his own, Louis would come to Florence's aid. The Florentines, Rouen warned rather ominously, should "remain the king's allies," as the help of others will not be enough if they "should lose his good graces" (*LCSG* 1.295.3–6). The next day, having received another letter from the Signoria expressing worries about Valentino's intentions, Machiavelli again sought out Rouen to explain Florence's fears. Once Faenza was taken (which then seemed imminent, although it did not happen until the following April of 1501), it would be only too easy for Borgia's forces to march into Florentine territory and, with "one of the rebels" (Giuliano de' Medici) in their train, to "attempt something damaging to [Florentine] liberty." Machiavelli told Rouen that such an attack against Louis's devoted Florentine allies would dishonor the king and that it was therefore urgent that Louis warn both the pope and Borgia that he would consider any hostile action against Florence as an attack against himself.

[9] An instance in which "stato" means two different things in the same sentence.

Machiavelli describes how Rouen took him by the hand ("mi prese per mano") and led him into the presence of two of the king's other high officials, who lectured Machiavelli on honor and dishonor, insisting that it was "the king who had been dishonored for your sake" because Florence had "broken the agreements by withholding payments" it owed the king (for troops he had sent to Tuscany). "Now," Rouen continued, "because you fear the pope, you seek the king's favors, which His Majesty is not about to give until he understands clearly whether you are or are not his friends." Machiavelli, never at a loss for words no matter how intimidating the situation, replied that he "believed there was no reason [for the French] to doubt the friendship of the Florentines," especially considering the loyalty they—and they alone in Italy—had shown Louis and his predecessor when the French faced adversities; for these, said Machiavelli, are the times "when the loyalty of friends is usually tested [si suole sperimentare la fede delli amici]." The Florentines, he added, did not deserve to be treated like this, "nor should the Most Christian King permit it." A disgruntled Rouen signaled that he had had enough of the envoy's presumption by replying "only" that Florence's new ambassador should come quickly or send instructions. Machiavelli reminded Rouen of the emissary Alexander sent to Pisa (in an effort to win the Pisans to the Borgia cause), but Rouen replied, angrily ("alterato"), "that it meant nothing [che non era *rien*]" (*LCSG* 1.295.8–13).

Such an exchange in the presence of the king's ministers must have made for an uncomfortable and tense encounter.[10] But the next day, Florimond Robertet, the king's secretary and member of the royal council, sought out Machiavelli to say he had specific instructions from Louis and Rouen to tell the king's lieutenant in Milan and his ambassador in Rome to make it clear to Alexander and Cesare how much it displeases the king to hear of talk in Cesare's army about hostile actions against Florence, with or without the Medici rebels. The king would in no way tolerate this and ordered Robertet to write "as urgently as possible" in support of Florence (*LCSG* 1.295.14). On November 21 Robertet reiterated these assurances and offered some advice that Machiavelli relayed to the Ten. The king, he said, would do no harm ("villania") to the Florentines and would permit no one else to do so, "unless the Florentines did it to themselves through their lack of unity [per essere disunite] and because some in the city do not love its liberty [chi ama poco la libertà di quella]." Robertet advised "your Signorie to be careful" about this. Machiavelli added to the dispatch, in his own voice, that it was urgent "to remove from the opinions of the French any perception of Florentine disunity, which would cause as much harm here [at the court], were it to be believed, as the reality of disunity would do in Florence" (*LCSG* 1.301.27–8). Machiavelli did not have to

[10] In *The Prince* (3.48) Machiavelli famously recalls an exchange in Nantes in which, to Rouen's aspersion that the Italians do not understand war, Machiavelli countered that the French do not understand the "stato." Is he referring to the meeting recounted in the dispatch of November 4, 1500?

spell out the meaning of this warning: the Florentines who allegedly "do not love [the city's] liberty" were the ottimati who opposed the popular republic established in 1494 and were suspected of conspiring with Borgia to reinstate the Medici—suspicions that became direct accusations when Cesare invaded Florentine territory in May 1501 and demanded, unsuccessfully, the institution of an oligarchic government along the lines promoted by the intransigent ottimati.

In this same dispatch of November 21, Machiavelli, now in Tours with the court, reported that an unnamed "friend" told him that Louis's ambassador in Venice, urged on by the papal ambassador, reported to the Venetian senate that rumors were circulating of a secret alliance of Florence, Bologna, Ferrara, and Mantua to drive the French from Italy (*LCSG* 1.301.15). Alexander had instructed his ambassador at the French court to persuade Louis of the truth of these rumors and to recommend that he could break up the alleged conspiracy by putting Piero de' Medici back in Florence, "in this way securing the government [stato] of the city to his purposes." The papal ambassador also reported that Cardinal de' Medici—Giovanni, Piero's brother—had appealed to the pope to be allowed to return to "casa sua" and that Alexander felt compelled to accede to the cardinal's "just entreaties" because Giovanni was a "man of the Church." If Louis agreed not to object to the cardinal's request, it would signal that he had abandoned his alliance with Florence. Alexander was, evidently, plotting to undermine Florence's alliance with France, bring down the Florentine republic, and restore the Medici to power. In connection with this plot, so Machiavelli's informant claimed, "they" (papal agents?) "had got Piero de' Medici out of France and brought him to Pisa" (*LCSG* 1.301.16–19). With Pisa fighting to preserve its independence, Florence's adversaries often tried to get a foothold in Pisan affairs. With ample irony and sarcasm, Machiavelli considered the alleged conspiracy a "disegno"—a scheme or plot—"worthy of His Holiness" and lamented to Rouen "the malice [malignità] of [Florence's] enemies." He dissected the absurdity of the rumored plot, suggesting that the king "keep clear of those who were seeking the destruction of his friends for the sole purpose of making themselves more powerful and making it easier for them to wrest Italy from his hands." Still speaking to Rouen, Machiavelli offered some advice for the king: that he "should follow the method [ordine] of those who in the past have wanted to take hold of a foreign country, which is to weaken the powerful [diminuire e' potenti], indulge [vezzeggiare] the subjects, support one's friends, and stay clear of allies [compagni] who want equal power in the country" (*LCSG* 1.301.20–3). Machiavelli was here beginning to sketch out the analysis he would offer in chapter 3 of *The Prince* of the errors that cost Louis his Italian conquests.

Machiavelli had one more meeting with Louis, reported to the Signoria in a dispatch of November 24 from Tours. Armed with a list of grievances, including Cesare's seizure of the Val di Lamone (which extends south from Faenza into Tuscany) and his menacing designs on Faenza, Machiavelli says he "decided to go again" to His Majesty and explain the reason for Florence's failure fully to pay the monies it owed the French crown. The city faced enormous expenses, he explained, especially with "Valentino victorious at its borders [in the Romagna], not only with his own forces"—and here was the core of Florence's complaint—"but also with those of His Majesty" (*LCSG* 1.302.6–7). Louis had in fact sent a contingent of 100 lances to assist Cesare, chiefly in order to maintain good relations with Alexander. The king assured Machiavelli, however, that if Borgia moved against Florence or Bologna, the French cavalry would stop him: "so on this score you [Florentines] can rest easy." Louis countered the other Florentine complaints with what Machiavelli calls "his usual gripes [sue querimonie usitate]," insisting that it was the Florentines who had broken the agreements by not paying their debts. Machiavelli pressed the Florentine case, but "no matter what I said to him—and I said so much that I feared I had abused his patience—I was unable to get any other response from him" (*LCSG* 1.302.8–10). Taking his leave of the king, Machiavelli went to Robertet, who again offered the assurance that "Valentino's successes have irritated the king" and that, unless the Florentines sabotaged their own interests, all would turn out well for them (*LCSG* 1.302.11–13). The mission was finished and Machiavelli returned to Florence. In April 1501, the French lances sent by Louis fought side by side with Borgia's troops to take Faenza. Bologna eluded Borgia, but in May he invaded Florentine territory, making demands and terrorizing the countryside. Machiavelli no doubt recalled with some chagrin all the promises and assurances offered to him in France.

From his post in the chancery, Machiavelli conveyed instructions from the Signoria and the Ten to officials in the dominion on how to respond to the crisis of Borgia's invasion. Diplomatic etiquette required that he not openly describe Cesare as an enemy, because of Florence's relative military weakness, its commercial interests in Rome, and the long common border with the papal states, all of which meant that Florence had to maintain formally correct relations with Alexander VI. Moreover, Alexander and Cesare were allies of King Louis, as was Florence. Without French protection, Florence would have been at the mercy of Cesare and his condottieri, above all Vitellozzo Vitelli, who thirsted for revenge for the execution of his brother Paolo. Machiavelli's instructions from the chancery were therefore careful to distinguish Borgia's actions and intentions from those of Vitelli and other captains in Borgia's army. In certain passages, nonetheless, it is clear that Machiavelli—and, obviously, his superiors as well—knew that Borgia was playing a double game, professing friendship and the desire for alliance with Florence while letting his condottieri engage in predatory violence as they sliced through the dominion. On May 1, 1501, Machiavelli told the commissioners in Prato and Pistoia to be watchful because, "according to reliable reports," Borgia had "decided on a move against one or another of our towns" in preparation for coming south toward Florence; "knowing the [anti-Florentine] feelings [umori] in Valentino's army, we are of the opinion that this could happen." He reminded the commissioner in Prato to recruit one man per household from the population and ready them for action (*LCSG* 2.47.6)—an example of the ad hoc contado mobilization that preceded Machiavelli's militia. To the commissioner in Firenzuola (near the road Borgia was about to take south from Bologna), Machiavelli wrote on May 5 that "we will do the utmost to provide security and not abandon these subjects of ours" in the hill towns vulnerable to attack. The commissioner was to do his best to alleviate the understandable anxiety of the inhabitants by telling them the truth ("faccendoli capaci della verità") about Florentine defensive maneuvers. He should "encourage these subjects of ours to come out of the woods and return to their homes, because the pope is not about to declare war against us"—an acknowledgment that behind Cesare's actions lay Alexander's strategic command. Moreover, beholden as they were to King Louis, Borgia and his condottieri could only act with the king's "wishes and consent," which made it all the more urgent (as the French had warned Machiavelli) to maintain the king's favorable disposition toward Florence (*LCSG* 2.48.3–5, 9).

On May 7 Machiavelli tried to calm the frightened Florentine official in Scarperia (in the Mugello valley), whose letters to the chancery were "full of consternation and fear" that would have been excessive, Machiavelli averred, even if Borgia's troops were besieging the town and destroying its walls. In fact, his army was some distance to the east, and "we have good relations [buona amicizia] with the duke and the pope." Scarperia was in no danger, and "hence it is not necessary to frighten our subjects in this way: encourage them instead to be watchful and keep their eyes on the mountain passes." Urging him not to believe every rumor, Machiavelli wrote: "we have wanted to tell you this so you can reassure both yourself and our subjects [in Scarperia], because we're not going to abandon them, provided you and they do your duty." Here we see Machiavelli in another role, as he attempts, in the face of undeniable dangers, to instill confidence in the Florentine officials of the dominion and in its population. Yet, in the same letter he did not hide the peril represented by the presence in Borgia's army of the Orsini (traditional allies of the Medici and hence antagonistic to the republic) and the Vitelli: "because they are our enemies, we believe they could surprise us with some aggressive action. But we don't think we'll be attacked by others" (*LCSG* 2.49.3–7), he added, referring to Borgia. On May 8 Machiavelli informed Florence's civilian commissioners in the Romagna and the Mugello that Piero Soderini, Alamanno Salviati, and Iacopo Nerli had been sent as ambassadors to Borgia's camp. If their mission did not produce the desired result, the commissioners should make every effort to determine what they needed to do "for the security of our towns and contado" (*LCSG* 2.52.5–7). On the 10th he informed the commissioner in Cascina and the resident Florentine official in San Miniato in the lower Arno valley that Borgia was passing through the dominion with his army "as an ally [amico], because this is what has been agreed with us." But some of his troops were heading to Ponte a Signa, only eight miles from Florence, and Machiavelli warned that, "although [Borgia] was traversing Florentine territory as an ally/friend and without attempting anything," the towns of the area must "take precautions against him and his army as enemies [si guardino da lui e da sue genti come nimico] and not allow him or his troops into the cities" (*LCSG* 2.53.5–7). The next day, he told the commissioners in Castrocaro (in the Florentine Romagna) and the Casentino that, "although [Borgia's] words and actions have until now been those of a friend, nonetheless many other signs make us fearful [ci fanno dubitare]." They should therefore assemble all infantry under their jurisdiction, have them well armed and adequately supplied for at least ten days, lead them to Scarperia, and keep the chancery informed of their number and whereabouts at every stage (*LCSG* 2.56.3). Two days later Machiavelli informed the official in Cascina that the Ten were unable at the moment to provide him with more troops, supplies, and munitions "because we are deeply involved in grave matters of supreme importance in which our liberty is very nearly hanging in the balance [per disputarsi quasi che della libertà nostra]." The official should "do his duty as a devoted citizen" with the troops he has, "for every person is obligated to his country [ciascuno è tenuto verso la patria sua]" (*LCSG* 2.59.4–7). A similar message went to the commissioner in Livorno: meeting the emergency of Borgia's incursion was the government's highest priority, and while his army "is for the moment conducting itself as a friendly force," "we hope in God and justice [ragione] that no violence will be done to us" (*LCSG* 2.60.5–7). Just two days later, however, this hope was shown to be in vain, as Machiavelli informed the three ambassadors sent to Borgia that his troops had caused "infinite destruction of livestock and everything else throughout our dominion." They were also "hurting the city in a most important way that could not do greater damage to the citizens [of Florence itself], namely, by stealing wool from our subjects" (presumably from spinners or weavers who worked in their homes) and sending it to Bologna. The notice concluded with the pious hope that the great harm this did "displeases" Borgia, "as we trust he will satisfactorily demonstrate given our long-standing friendship" (*LCSG* 2.62.3–4).

With his troops menacingly close to Florence, Borgia issued a series of demands to the Florentine ambassadors. According to Parenti, he wanted three things: the Medici readmitted to Florence, the government restricted to twenty or twenty-five leading citizens, and a mutual defense agreement with himself as the city's paid captain. The ambassadors replied that any notion of "overturning the government [mutare qui stato e governo] was impossible" and that "every citizen would sooner prefer death and the destruction of the city [prima s'accetterebbe per qualunque cittadino la morte e la desolazione della città]" to readmitting Piero de' Medici or changing the government. With regard to the third demand, they said they would discuss it with the Signoria. After much debate and over considerable opposition, the Council of Eighty approved a two-year agreement that gave Borgia command of 300 cavalry.[11] On May 16 Machiavelli announced the news of the "lega e confederazione" with Borgia to the captain and commissioner of Arezzo and the captains of Borgo Sansepolcro, Empoli, Colle Valdelsa, San Gimignano, and Volterra. He specified that the forces under Borgia's command were to be employed "in whatever need might arise in our stato" (*LCSG* 2.63.4), implying that they were not to be integrated into Borgia's army for campaigns outside the dominion. Since Borgia quickly left Florentine territory and never returned, the contract ("condotta") for his services was not implemented. Florence also agreed to pay Borgia 36,000 ducats,[12] but never made the payment. "This duke is our friend and ally," Machiavelli wrote to the Florentine captain in Volterra, "but you will nonetheless not relax your guard" (*LCSG* 2.64.5). Even when Borgia's troops raided and destroyed peasant properties in the Valdera, Machiavelli reassured the Florentine podestà of the district that, because the "lega e amicizia" precluded any hostile action by Borgia, the raids must be attributed to the "insolence" of his condottieri (*LCSG* 2.68.3–5). But to the visiting French envoy the Florentines did not mince words: Machiavelli says they told him that the previous year's poor harvest would not of itself have created insuperable difficulties "were it not for Valentino's army, which, with its innumerable dishonorable actions [disonestà], has tormented and starved half our dominion" (*LCSG* 2.72.5).

Borgia took his troops out of Florentine territory in early June 1501 and turned his attention south, joining the French in their war against Spain for control of the Neapolitan kingdom, as his alliance with Louis required him to do. He took part in the savage massacre at Capua in July (Machiavelli includes it in the dolorous list of Italian defeats in *Prince* 26.19). The threat of aggression from Borgia diminished for a time as he spent most of the second half of 1501 and the first half of 1502 in Rome. But new dangers appeared in June 1502, when rebellion erupted in Arezzo and Borgia's condottiere Vitellozzo Vitelli, accompanied by Piero de' Medici, invaded and spread the rebellion from Arezzo into the Valdichiana and the Casentino. Florentines feared a conspiracy involving Cesare, Alexander, and Vitelli, aimed, once again, at undermining the republic and restoring the Medici. Borgia insisted, unconvincingly to most, that he had no part in Vitelli's actions. Then, on June 20, Borgia stunned Florence and Italy by seizing the duchy of Urbino and chasing Duke Guidobaldo da Montefeltro into exile. Borgia now controlled the Romagna to the northeast and Urbino to the east of Florence, with Vitelli occupying the southeastern portion of the dominion. Feeling confident enough to pressure the Florentines, he demanded that they send an ambassador to hear what he wanted.

The Signoria and the Ten sent Francesco Soderini, brother of Piero and bishop of Volterra, with Machiavelli as his secretary. Before Machiavelli was recalled at

[11] Parenti, *Storia fiorentina*, ed. Matucci, vol. 2, pp. 437–42.
[12] Bartolomeo Cerretani, *Storia fiorentina*, ed. G. Berti (Florence: Olschki, 1994), p. 289.

the end of June, they dispatched two letters, both signed by Soderini, who of course approved their contents, but written by Machiavelli, who may also have composed parts of them. On June 22, while still on the road, they wrote to inform the Signoria that they learned of the seizure of Urbino from an envoy of Borgia who was carrying the duke's demand that the Florentines hand over Guidobaldo da Montefeltro, who, Borgia believed, had fled into Florentine territory. According to the envoy, Borgia was of "good disposition" toward Florence and expressed "unhappiness with the actions of those attacking you," a reference to Vitelli's occupation of Arezzo. The dispatch ends with a short paragraph about Borgia's seizure of Urbino. The "way" he achieved the surprise victory was "entirely grounded" in the duke's "prudenzia" (here meaning cleverness and intelligence): while feigning a move against the small principality of Camerino, he suddenly and in secret moved north to Urbino and took it without a fight. "Your Lordships should take note of this stratagem and such speed, combined with exceptional good fortune [coniunta con una estrema felicità]" (*LCSG* 2.175).

Four days later, Francesco Soderini and/or Machiavelli wrote a longer report of their meetings with Borgia and with Giulio and Paolo Orsini, two of his chief condottieri. Although Soderini no doubt shaped the report's overall content (he refers to himself once in the first person, recalling his diplomatic mission to France some months earlier [*LCSG* 2.180.40]), there are signs of Machiavelli's language[13] and judgments. Borgia summoned Machiavelli and Soderini as soon as they arrived. He thanked them for their congratulations on his "new acquisition" of Urbino but then groused over Florence's failure to provide the financial and military assistance promised a year earlier (*LCSG* 2.180.6–8). He wanted now to make a final effort ("ultima prova") at an alliance, warning, however, that if the Florentines did not reciprocate he would do what was necessary for the security of his territories in view of the long border they shared. He "carried on at length," claiming, with considerable exaggeration, that "the year before" (when he invaded Florentine territory) it was "in his power not only to restore the [Medici] exiles" but also to impose a government of his choosing. "We replied" that it was not the Florentines who failed to respect the agreements; it was rather the "malicious actions [sinistri modi]" (the pillaging by the troops) that conveyed little regard for Florence (*LCSG* 2.180.10–12). "Without beating around the bush [sanza molto circuito di parole]," Borgia said: "'First, I want to know with whom I am negotiating this agreement'" because "'I know all too well that your city is not favorably disposed toward me; indeed, it maligns me as an assassin and tries to incriminate

[13] An example: "he carried on at length—si distese assai" (*LCSG* 2.180.10)—is a locution Machiavelli employs elsewhere. In September 1500, he reported that Rouen, speaking in anger, "si distese con assai parole" (*LCSG* 1.285.10). In 1503, describing the agitated Borgia's rants against the Florentines, he says: "e qui si distese con parole piene di veleno e di passione [words full of poison and anger]" (*LCSG* 3.231.13). The expression also appears in two dispatches of the 1505 legation to Siena (*LCSG* 4.510.13; *LCSG* 4.512.8).

me before the pope and the king of France.'" "'I do not like this government [of yours] and cannot trust it; you must change it [bisogna lo mutiate] and provide guarantees that you will carry out what you promise; otherwise you will quickly understand that I cannot continue like this; and if you will not have me as an ally [amico], you will discover what it is to have me as an enemy [inimico]'" (*LCSG* 2.180.14–16). Soderini must have spoken the response to this outrageous demand that Florence change its government to serve Borgia's interests, but the way it is recorded in the dispatch suggests the economy and trenchancy of Machiavelli's prose: "We answered that the city has the best government it is able to devise, and, being itself satisfied with it, its friends can likewise be satisfied." "Should your Excellency [Borgia] decide once and for all to be the good friend he claims to be, he would find firm reciprocity [in us]" (*LCSG* 2.180.17–18).

Borgia "always returned" to the same arguments, and nothing the Florentine envoys said changed his hard line. They protested that neither they nor their city had expected such treatment. Borgia asked what they thought he wanted from them aside from justifying himself. They replied that, if Florence's friendship was useful to him, they expected some significant favors they knew were in his power to give, "especially since Vitellozzo is his man." In so saying, they made it clear that the Florentines knew Borgia was behind Vitelli's seizure of Arezzo and could bring it to an end. But Borgia replied that they should expect no favors at all: "'not only do you not deserve any; you have forfeited even [the right to ask]. It is true,'" he acknowledged, "'that Vitelli is my man, but I swear I knew nothing about the Arezzo conspiracy. Yet I was not unhappy over what you [Florentines] lost and indeed took pleasure from it and will continue to do so if [you suffer more losses].'" He issued an ultimatum: "'Come to a decision quickly,'" for "'between you [Florentines] and me there can be no middle way: you must be either my friends or my enemies.'" This, Soderini and Machiavelli wrote, "was what we got from all the discussions, which were very long." Borgia expressed contempt for Florence's military weakness, "lack of unity, and poor governance," which enabled "Vitelli by himself," i.e. without Borgia's troops, to inflict a punishing blow against the republic. In response to the envoys' counterarguments and especially their assertion that Florence had the protection of French cavalry and that King Louis was offended by Borgia's actions against Florence, he insisted he knew the French as well as any man in Italy and that in the end the Florentines, not he, would be duped. (He was of course wrong in this arrogantly stated assumption.) Aware that Borgia was not about to soften his stance, and wanting to give the Signoria time to consider his demand for an alliance, the envoys asked him to think things over until the next day. He assured them, however, that he would not change his mind (*LCSG* 2.180.19–29). The next day Borgia had them meet with Giulio and Paolo Orsini, who repeated the demands for a reform of Florence's government, asserting that Louis had consented to Orsini and Borgia designs on Florentine territory, and threatening an imminent invasion and occupation (*LCSG* 2.180.34–43). Two more visitors, an envoy from Vitellozzo and another from Pandolfo Petrucci of Siena, tried to impress upon Soderini and Machiavelli the size of Borgia's army, claiming that he had between 20,000 and 25,000 men. The two Florentines thought this exaggerated and estimated his force at 16,000 (2.180.44, 50).

The most famous passage of the dispatch is the rhetorically embellished portrait of Borgia: "Questo Signore è molto splendido e magnifico" and "so bold [animoso] in military matters that there is no task so great that does not seem small to him. For glory and acquiring territory [stato] he never rests, nor does he acknowledge fatigue or danger. He arrives in one place before his departure from another is known. He makes himself well liked by his hired soldiers and has recruited the best men in Italy. All this, in addition to constant good fortune [una perpetua fortuna], renders him victorious and fearsome." Although the letter is signed by Soderini, the impression shared by many that these are Machiavelli's words is understandable. The characterization of Borgia as "tanto animoso" and the beneficiary of "perpetual good fortune" will reappear in Machiavelli's dispatch of October 27, 1502, where he describes him as "uomo animoso, fortunato e pieno di speranza" (*LCSG* 2.272.16). The notion that no task is so great that it does not seem small to him is echoed in a dispatch of January 8, 1503, a week after Borgia eliminated his faithless former condottieri at Senigallia, in which he attributes to him "unheard of good fortune, an audacity and a more than human hope that he can achieve his every desire [una fortuna inaudita, uno animo e una speranza piú che umana di potere conseguire ogni suo desiderio]" (*LCSG* 2.336.13). But the laudatory judgments in the dispatch of June 1502 actually convey Borgia's own perception of himself and his self-confidence—not an objective observation by Machiavelli (and/or Soderini). It is Borgia himself who never acknowledges fatigue or danger; the description of him as "splendido e magnifico" refers to his bearing, dress, and self-presentation and echoes Machiavelli's sardonic report of Borgia's arrival in France in 1499 "with such pomp and ostentatious display that it was considered an astonishing thing." "Splendido," moreover, is a word Machiavelli often uses ironically to mock excess, pretentiousness, and immoderate display.[14] Finally, although Borgia's "perpetual [good] fortune" certainly underscores his many successes to that point, in the light of Machiavelli's evolving notion of fortune it also hints at the duke's chronic dependence on others—his papal father, the king of France, and the mercenary soldiers in his service. Like everything Machiavelli wrote about Cesare, including the seventh chapter of *The Prince*, this

[14] Three examples: in the *Vita di Castruccio Castracani*, the rich and ostentatious man whose house was so full of precious furnishings that Castruccio decided to expectorate into the man's face because he did not know where it would offend him less is described as "ricchissimo e splendidissimo" (*OS*, vol. 1, p. 60). The ninth-century parish priests of Rome "began to call themselves cardinals to adorn their power" with a "splendido titolo" (*IF* 1.11.8). Walter of Brienne organized the "plebe" and "popolo minuto" of Florence into festive companies to which, honored with "splendidi tituli," he gave banners and money (*IF* 2.36.7).

portrait simultaneously extols the duke's projection of power and success while hinting at its hollowness. Shortly after Machiavelli's return to Florence, he received a letter from Francesco Soderini, who, still in Urbino, confirmed that Borgia's military strength had been exaggerated. Soderini's assessment of the duke's forces was such that, as Machiavelli puts it, "if true, would make us more secure and make the recovery of our territories easier" (*LCSG* 2.181.5). Borgia's bravado rarely matched the reality of things.

By September 1502, the Arezzo crisis was resolved, owing largely to the intervention of the French. With the occupied territories regained and Vitellozzo expelled, Borgia was once again the focus of Florentine worries. Florence's ambassador at the French court (in Genoa), reported that Cesare enjoyed "the greatest favor" with the king and that "one can therefore believe he will return [to central Italy] more powerful than ever" (*LCSG* 2.227.5). On September 14 Machiavelli told Florence's civilian commissioner in Castiglion Fiorentino that Borgia was expected to try again to take Bologna and had Louis's permission to do so (*LCSG* 2.234.6). In October word came that the king was prepared to give Cesare 100 or 200 lances for a new attempt on Bologna (*LCSG* 2.241.16). On October 4, writing to Antonio Giacomini, Machiavelli underscored the importance of the secret meeting at Magione, to which Giacomini had alerted the Ten (*LCSG* 2.244.5), in which Borgia's condottieri hatched the conspiracy against him. The same day, Machiavelli gave the commissioner in Cortona the names of most of the conspirators: Vitellozzo Vitelli; Giampaolo Baglioni, signore of Perugia; the Orsini; Giovanni Bentivoglio, lord of Bologna; and Pandolfo Petrucci, political boss of Siena, the last two represented by proxies (*LCSG* 2.245.4). Missing in Machiavelli's list are Oliverotto Euffreducci, signore of Fermo, and Guidobaldo da Montefeltro, whom Borgia had expelled from Urbino in June. Machiavelli told Giacomini that the Ten immediately sent word of the conspiracy to the French court and within the next day or two would send a courier post-haste to Borgia himself. He asked Giacomini to learn what he could of the conspirators' movements and of Piero de' Medici's possible involvement (*LCSG* 2.244.6–7). To the commissioner in Cortona he wrote that, "because such a gathering might not bode well for us," he too should keep an eye on it "to discern the decisions and movements" of the participants. "Above all else," he added, "make every effort to learn if Piero de' Medici appears in the town" (*LCSG* 2.245.5–6). The Florentines had good reason to be worried about the conspirators, recalling their predations in the dominion in May 1501 and Vitellozzo's invasion of Arezzo and the Valdichiana in June 1502, which opened the gates to Piero.

On October 5 the Signoria sent Machiavelli as emissary to Borgia's camp at Imola in the Romagna to observe his side of this potentially explosive conflict and to assess the duke's intentions toward Florence. Machiavelli was well aware that Borgia, facing great danger, wanted Florence's support. The constant refrain of their meetings over the three months of the legation was Borgia's desire—actually his urgent need, often expressed as a demand—for alliance with Florence and the implementation of his appointment as captain, agreed to (under duress) the previous year. He wanted Florence as a contractually bound ally, both because he no longer trusted his condottieri and, despite his boast that he knew King Louis better than anyone in Italy, because the French were actually less committed to him than he believed (or wanted others to believe). Borgia never succeeded in persuading the Florentines to grant the formal alliance he sought, partly because he needed them more than they needed him—if they needed him at all. The major objectives of Machiavelli's mission were to put Borgia off, by assuring him he would convey his wishes to his superiors, and to assess his military strength. The Florentines believed Borgia lacked adequate arms and political support to achieve his objectives without their help. And they were not at all unhappy to see him threatened by faithless former lieutenants or, as it happened, to learn of his spectacular success in destroying them.

Machiavelli's initial commission was to assure Borgia that Florence considered the betrayal perpetrated against him by the conspirators as having been inflicted against their common ally and protector, King Louis, and that the Florentines intended to remain his and his father's "buoni amici" (*LCSG* 2.250.2). As soon as Machiavelli arrived in Imola on October 7, he went to Borgia, who greeted him "amorevolmente." Reiterating his wish for "alliance/friendship" with Florence, Borgia immediately sought to exonerate himself from any responsibility for the violence that had occurred during his incursion into Florentine territory in May 1501. It was Vitelli and the Orsini who begged him—Vitellozzo allegedly crying at the duke's feet—to let them cross through Florence's dominion on their way back to Rome. Borgia claimed that he agreed, but only provided they did no damage and there was no talk of reinstating the Medici. The depredations carried out by Vitelli and Orsini troops were, he said, an attempt to subvert his plan to "fare amicizia" with the Florentines (*LCSG* 2.251.5–8). He assured Machiavelli that the invasion of Arezzo a year later occurred without his foreknowledge and that his effort to get Vitelli to withdraw was the origin of the ill will that gave rise to the Magione conspiracy (*LCSG* 2.251.12–13). On every count, Borgia portrayed his conduct as blameless. Yet, once again, as in the June meeting in Urbino, protestations of friendship were accompanied by warnings that the Florentines must choose—this time between him and the conspirators—and that to remain neutral would leave Florence vulnerable no matter the outcome (*LCSG* 2.251.17).

Borgia also sought to pressure the Florentines with confident boasts that he had Louis's unquestioning military and political support. Two days later, he showed Machiavelli a letter he received from the papal ambassador at the French court who claimed that the king and Cardinal Rouen were well disposed to do Borgia favors and that, as soon as they learned that he wanted troops to assault Bologna, they had instructed the king's lieutenant in Milan to send him 300 lances. The ambassador included with the letter a copy of the instruction Louis sent to Milan, which Borgia read aloud in its entirety to Machiavelli, even inviting him to look at the ambassador's signature, which Machiavelli said he recognized, having seen it in France. "So you see, Secretary," Borgia crowed, "what a strong [letter] this is," adding (as already noted) "Imagine what kind of reply I shall receive [from the king] for my defense against" the conspirators, "most of whom His Majesty considers dangerous enemies because they have constantly sought to move pieces on the Italian chessboard [muovere qualche scacco in Italia] against his interests." Borgia predicted the conspiracy would conclude, not only in his favor, but indeed to his advantage. He told Machiavelli to inform his government that "I am not about to give up nor will I lack for friends, among whom," he added, reiterating his desire for an alliance, "I want to include Their Lordships [the governors of Florence]" (*LCSG* 2.253.5–9). He urged him to warn his superiors that remaining neutral would in any event cost them, but that by aligning themselves with one of the parties to the conflict—Borgia obviously meant himself—they too could come out as winners. Machiavelli told the Ten he "could not express in writing with what a display of affection" for Florence Borgia spoke and "with how much self-justification for past events." Borgia, he added, was not likely to wait long for Florence's answer (*LCSG* 2.253.16–19).

Cesare's insistent wish for alliance with Florence was further pressed on Machiavelli, as he reported on October 13, by a secretary of Ercole d'Este, the duke of Ferrara, and by Borgia's secretary, messer Agapito Gerardini, who warned that Florence was losing a "bella occasione" to ally with "this glorious and most fortunate lord who is accustomed to winning and whose power, since the condotta was agreed to [in 1501], has increased while yours has diminished" (*LCSG* 2.256.6–9). Machiavelli told the Ten that Borgia had "his gaze fixed [gli occhi volti]" on the condotta (*LCSG* 2.256.12). On October 16 Borgia said he wanted Florence to send troops toward Città di Castello to block the movement of Vitellozzo's forces. (Machiavelli added a suggestion of his own to the Ten, namely, that, since Borgia would have no way of verifying the numbers, "it would be possible to send two and tell him four" [2.260.5–10].) The next day, another of Borgia's chief advisers told Machiavelli that Cesare lamented Florence's reluctance to sign a formal agreement, which should have been an easy decision in view of their common enemies. According to this unnamed advisor, Borgia complained: "Why do the [Florentine] Signori hesitate to come to a decision? Nothing makes me suspicious of them except their unwillingness to declare themselves. And the only reason I want a proposal [for a formal alliance] to come first from them is to enhance the stability of an agreement" (*LCSG* 2.262.12–15)—as if Borgia had not all along been advancing proposals and ultimatums. Machiavelli concluded his dispatch of October 17 by offering an opinion that was not warmly received back in Florence: "If Your Lordships [the Ten] were to ask me what I believe about these movements [involving the conspirators and the duke], I would answer, if I may be forgiven for doing so, that Borgia will not be lacking in the good fortune he has had up to now, as long as the pope is alive and the alliance with the king continues. For those who have given cause to be suspected of being his enemies no longer have the opportunity to do him much damage, and even less will they have that opportunity tomorrow than today" (*LCSG* 2.262.27). In response to this unsolicited assessment (repeated on October 23) of Borgia's strength and the diminished prospects of the conspirators, Machiavelli's chancery colleague Biagio Buonaccorsi cautioned him that, although his presence at the duke's camp in Imola allowed him to observe the extent of Borgia's forces, it did not give him direct or reliable knowledge of the arms or movements of the conspirators. Machiavelli's assertion of the conspirators' inability to harm him was therefore seen in Florence as "troppo gagliarda"—too forceful, too bold—because other reports indicated that the conspirators had considerable strength. This was the occasion on which, conveying a criticism that obviously originated among certain political leaders, Biagio advised Machiavelli to report in detail everything he observed but to "leave judgments to others."[15]

Yet he was also becoming aware of Borgia's vulnerabilities. The obsessive requests for an alliance with Florence more than hinted at desperation on Borgia's part. "Tell your Signori," the duke reiterated on October 20, "that I am prepared to establish a firm and indissoluble alliance with them, in which they will gain as much benefit as they could wish from my assistance and my *fortuna*" (*LCSG* 2.264.7). In another dispatch on the same day, Machiavelli relayed the news that the conspirators' troops had defeated the combined forces of three of Borgia's lieutenants, don Michele (Miguel de Corella), don Ugo (de Moncada), and messer Ramiro (de Lorqua), and forced them to retreat. "Since I've been here"—just two weeks—he reported, Borgia "has spent on messengers and emissaries as much as other governments spend in two years," evidently in search of allies and military support (*LCSG* 2.265.11, 16). On October 23, while awaiting the arrival of French cavalry, Borgia confidently predicted he would defeat the conspirators but admitted to Machiavelli that, "when you first arrived, I did not speak to you so openly because my stato was in poor condition [assai cattivo grado]. Urbino had rebelled, and I did not know what support [fondamento] I had. I was in confusion [disordine] everywhere with these new territories [stati nuovi]; I did not want your Signori to think I was making big promises out of great fear. But now that I fear less, I can promise more; and when the time comes that I no longer fear at all, actions will be added to my promises" (*LCSG* 2.269.15–16). He told Machiavelli that Antonio da Venafro, secretary of Siena's Pandolfo Petrucci who had joined the conspiracy, had presented a proposal on behalf of the Orsini to overthrow the government [mutare stato] in Florence. Borgia said he replied that "the stato of Florence was an ally of the king of France, whose loyal servant [servitore] I am," and that the

[15] *Lettere*, pp. 137–8.

Florentines "have never injured me; on the contrary, and better still, I was prepared to sign an alliance with them." The Sienese emissary asked Borgia not to sign anything until he conferred with the other conspirators and could return with further ideas for "something good," to which Borgia replied that the negotiations had advanced too far to halt the alliance with Florence (which was, of course, not true). He assured Machiavelli that, although he was willing to listen to the conspirators' proposals, he would "never agree to anything against Florence's government, unless," he added rather ominously, "it gives me reason [occasione] to do so" (*LCSG* 2.269.18–22)—"occasione" here suggesting provocation.

Still in the same dispatch of October 23, Machiavelli addressed the Ten: "Your Lordships understand the words this Signore uses, and I've not written the half of it. Consider the person who is speaking and judge him according to your usual wisdom." To what was Machiavelli referring? To the scarcely credible pledge—after all the threats to upend the republic and reinstate the Medici—that he would never do anything against Florence's government? To the frank admission that his dominions were in disorder and that, although beset by "great fear," he anticipated the day, soon to come, when his fears would dissipate and actions would be joined to words? Or was Machiavelli suggesting—without overtly offering an opinion that might be seen as "troppo gagliarda"—that Borgia's main weapon in the face of his political and military deficiencies was a combination of feigned friendship, contrived candor, bluster, and threats? Machiavelli's next sentences point to these weaknesses: "Since I have been here, this Signore's stato [his standing or status? or his territorial dominion?] has rested solely on his good fortune, the cause of which is the firmly held opinion [opinione certa] that the king of France will supply him with troops and the pope will provide the funds, and something else that has been of no less use to him, namely, the slowness of his enemies to close in on him [strignerlo]." He repeats his already expressed view that Borgia's enemies "are no longer able to do him much harm, because he has supplied all the important cities with infantry and equipped the fortresses very well" (*LCSG* 2.269.24–6). Yet Borgia's ability to confront the military threat still depended on securing French help: "he continues to solicit the resources to engage [his enemies] in battle [uscire in campagna], which consist solely in the arrival of the French" (*LCSG* 2.269.31).

Without fully theorizing the distinction, which a decade later became the conceptual foundation of chapter 7 of *The Prince*, between precarious states founded on fortune and stable states founded on virtú, Machiavelli presents it here in nuce: the judgment that Borgia's "stato" rested "solely" on his "good fortune," which in turn rested on the somewhat oxymoronic "opinione certa" that he would get arms from the French and financial backing from his father, reveals his fundamental weakness: his dependence and consequent lack of autonomy. Borgia could build nothing on his own. He depended on the French (whose soldiers, as we shall see, came and quickly left), on his aging papal father (who died the next year), on the Florentines (who knew that he needed them more than they needed him), and on mercenaries who betrayed him and upon whom he wreaked murderous vengeance. None of these hoped-for sources of support provided sufficient arms, and he never created his own.[16] The view of Borgia as a would-be "prince" who too confidently believed his own bluster—a perception Machiavelli would dramatize in *The Prince*—has already taken shape.

On October 27 Machiavelli informed the Ten that Vitelli's forces had seized the fortress of Fossombrone from Borgia. But the alliance among the conspirators was already disintegrating, for, as he reported, Paolo Orsini was in Imola seeking a separate agreement with Borgia (*LCSG* 2.272.3–4, 15). Assessing the difficulties and, in his view, the unlikelihood of an accord, Machiavelli wrote that "anyone who examines the circumstances of both parties knows that this signore [Borgia] is bold [animoso], fortunate, and full of hope, supported by a pope and a king, and that he has been wronged [iniuriato] not only in a stato he wanted to take"—Bologna, denied to him by the French—"but also in one he had already taken"—Urbino, which rebelled against him. The conspirators were "fearful for their own stati." They were "intimidated by his power [grandezza] before they inflicted these injuries, and are now even more so. Nor does one see how he can forgive them for the offense or how they can relinquish their fears." "People say [Ragionasi] reconciliation is possible only if both unite against a third party," which, Machiavelli says, could only be either Venice or Florence: attacking Florence would be easier, but King Louis would oppose it; the reverse was true of Venice. Machiavelli was evaluating hypotheses here—"it isn't believed that either will occur, it's only being discussed as something possible" (*LCSG* 2.272.16–19). He conveyed this speculation to his superiors because he still perceived Borgia as a potential threat to Florence. Even after rumors of an agreement between Borgia and the conspirators circulated on October 29, Machiavelli remained skeptical because he saw Borgia spending huge sums to ready himself for war ("spendere in grosso per ordinarsi alla guerra") and heard his insiders denouncing the Orsini as traitors and referring to the "agreement" as merely a way of buying time. Machiavelli found it difficult to believe the Orsini were not aware of this and confessed that he was perplexed ("sí che io mi confundo"). But he was also worried that the secrecy surrounding the alleged agreement might bode ill for Florence, especially because someone in Borgia's inner circle "said certain things to me I didn't like, asserting that Your Lordships had had plenty of time to come to an agreement with the duke, but that the time for that had passed" (*LCSG* 2.275.4–11). The next day Borgia gave assurances that the terms of reconciliation with the conspirators said nothing about Florence, but Machiavelli thought it too early to tell and said he would try to get a copy of the agreement (*LCSG* 2.276.6–10). Machiavelli's skepticism proved well founded when, on November 1, Borgia's secretary Agapito

[16] I examine Machiavelli's assessment of Borgia's military deficiencies in "Machiavelli and Cesare Borgia: A Reconsideration of Chapter 7 of *The Prince*," *The Review of Politics* 75 (2013): 539–56.

Gerardini revealed that the accord was not in fact settled and important issues still divided the two sides. Gerardini considered the proposed treaty "laughable," because it was being imposed on Borgia to his detriment and danger (*LCSG* 2.278.4–8).

Machiavelli still believed the resolution would be a violent one. On November 3 he wrote: "if the words and negotiations suggest an agreement, the orders given and the preparations being made point to war." Five companies of French cavalry had arrived in Borgia's camp, and Machiavelli paid visits to no fewer than seven of their commanders: "they recognized me from our previous meetings; all greeted me warmly [lietamente] and offered their assistance; as far as I could determine, they are your allies [partigiani] and highly praise Your Lordships" (*LCSG* 2.280.6–8). Also arriving was the apostolic protonotary of Bologna, Antongaleazzo Bentivoglio, son of Giovanni. Because of Borgia's constant designs on Bologna, which nearly resulted in an attack early in 1501, Giovanni Bentivoglio had joined the Magione conspiracy. Yet now he was offering a separate peace. From the duke's inner circle, Machiavelli learned that, if Bentivoglio was willing to support him against Vitelli and the Orsini, Borgia was ready to sign a fully guaranteed peace accord. According to Machiavelli's informant, Borgia "very much wanted this, for it had been demonstrated to him that his dominions would enjoy greater stability by keeping messer Giovanni in power and making him an ally than by expelling him and seizing a city [Bologna] he [Borgia] could not hold and which, in time, would be the source of his ruin" (*LCSG* 2.280.10–12). This hinted at differences of opinion between Borgia and some of his advisers who were apparently trying to rein in his overweening ambition and belligerence. It made an impression on Machiavelli, who, ten days later, restated to the Ten this "demonstration" to Borgia of his unrealistic desires and the precariousness of his dominions. On November 13, commenting on Cesare's reluctance to abandon his designs on Bologna, he wrote: "If anyone objects that the duke would find it distressing not to satisfy his desire to take Bologna [che al Duca parrà grave non si cavare la voglia di Bologna]," which the agreement required him to forgo, "the answer is what I have written several times before—that it has been demonstrated to him that it is better to make an alliance that will endure than to seize a city that cannot be held. Moreover, the Orsini and Vitelli have given him a lesson that should make him wise, if he is not already. They have shown him that he needs to think more about maintaining what he has acquired [mantenere lo acquistato] than about acquiring more, and the way to maintain [what he has] is to be armed with his own arms, pamper [vezzeggiare] his subjects, and make allies of his neighbors. And this is his plan" (*LCSG* 2.287.18–20). The comment about the lesson that "should make [Borgia] wise, if he is not already," suggests that Machiavelli agreed with those who were trying to persuade Borgia of the wisdom of accepting limits.

On November 8 Machiavelli wrote two letters to the Ten. In the first, he reported that Borgia asked if the marquis of Mantua, Francesco Gonzaga (who had commanded the forces against the retreating French at Fornovo in 1495), had accepted the condotta Florence offered him in early October. (In fact, Florence subsequently withdrew the offer because of objections from King Louis.) Borgia then wanted to know: "What condotta will your Signori give *me*?" Machiavelli replied that he did not know the Ten's intentions, but that "until now" he had assumed Borgia "was more inclined to employ others [than to be employed by other powers]." Borgia complained that Florence's reluctance to offer a condotta failed to respect his honor "as a professional soldier [professione di soldato] and an ally" of Florence, warning that a failure to come to an agreement might generate "some resentment [sdegno]" between them (*LCSG* 2.283.7–10, 15). Borgia's position was becoming weaker. In the same dispatch, Machiavelli reported that another piece of his hastily assembled territories had fallen away with the surrender to Orsini troops of the fortress of Pergola, south of Fossombrone. Borgia was still waiting for Swiss and French auxiliaries to arrive. One of his secretaries told Machiavelli the duke had ordered a part of the French contingent to proceed no farther than Parma. "Doesn't the duke want to protect himself against his enemies?" asked a puzzled Machiavelli, assuming Borgia would have wanted all the French troops to arrive quickly. The secretary replied, cryptically: "You [Florentines] are the reason for this: you did not know the right moment [non avete saputo conoscere el tempo] to ensure the duke's and your own security," to which Machiavelli retorted, equally ambiguously, that "we were not shown the way to do it" (*LCSG* 2.283.18–23).

The same day, November 8, Machiavelli penned a second dispatch in which he claims to report what an unnamed "friend" and confidant told him concerning Borgia's plans. It has been plausibly speculated that the "friend" was one of the duke's inner circle, possibly messer Agapito Gerardini, and not, as many have assumed, a rhetorical device for Machiavelli to express his own views.[17] If this is so, and especially because it is unlikely that one of Borgia's advisers would have spoken to Machiavelli in such detail without permission, this remarkable text is all the more valuable as a window into both Borgia's thinking and Machiavelli's understanding of his situation. Although filled with expressions of Borgia's confident foresight and trust in ultimate success, the detachment from reality evinced by the plans strongly suggests desperation behind the bravado. Reiterating Borgia's disappointment over Florence's disinclination to enter into a formal alliance, the "friend" warns that Borgia might turn elsewhere for allies. The duke knows, he says, that "the pope could die any day" and that he must therefore find some other "fondamento" for maintaining his territories: his first foundation is the king of France; the second "his own arms [armi proprie]." Machiavelli could

[17] Paul Larivaille, "Confidenti machiavelliani—nominati ed innominati—tra i «primi ministri» di Cesare Borgia," in *Machiavelli senza i Medici (1498–1512)*, ed. Marchand, pp. 195–219.

not have failed to reflect that the French "foundation" was nothing new, given that Cesare and Alexander had been Louis's allies since 1499, and that, after three years and more of conquering (and sometimes losing) territories, Borgia was only now organizing "his own arms." The "friend" points to the recent formation of a contingent of 500 men-at-arms and the same number of light horse, which "will be [ready] in a few days." Because "in time, these two foundations might not suffice," Borgia "is thinking of making allies of his neighbors and of those who must defend him in order to defend themselves, namely, the Florentines, Bolognese, Mantua, and Ferrara." Cesare considers the alliance with Ferrara already achieved because of the marriage of his sister (Lucrezia to Alfonso d'Este) and because of the favor he, Borgia, has shown to "the cardinal" (Ippolito). He similarly expects cooperation from the Gonzaga of Mantua in return for promoting the marquis's brother (Sigismondo) to a cardinalate (which, as it happened, not Borgia, but his mortal enemy Julius II did in 1505) and for betrothing his daughter Luisa to the marquis's heir, Federico (which never took place). Cesare even expects that the marquis and his brother would pay 40,000 ducats for the cardinalate and that this sum would cover the dowry for his daughter. The "friend" predicts that all this "was going to happen in any case and that debts of this kind maintain alliances [amicizia]." Negotiations for a separate peace with Bologna were still ongoing, and the "friend" foresees success because Cesare wants the treaty and because it would also benefit the Bentivoglio. Moreover, the duke "was never as desirous of possessing Bologna as he was of seeing himself secure on that front, and as long as he has that security he will be satisfied." This was a scarcely credible assertion in view of Borgia's endless attempts to get King Louis's permission to seize Bologna. Nor does Machiavelli himself seem to believe it, to judge from his comment five days later about Borgia's difficulty in relinquishing his desire for Bologna. "These four states, if they are united," the "friend" concludes, "will command respect," because they border on one another and because Louis will be able to rely on them and will increase their power (*LCSG* 2.284.4–12).

Borgia's plan presupposed Florence's willingness to join this completely imaginary confederation. Only now does the "friend" address Borgia's relations with Florence: "Less than three days ago I heard the duke discussing your Florentine Signori, saying that he wanted them to use his territories freely and him to use theirs, since they and he are both allies of France." Borgia, he says, would do nothing against Florence, even in the absence of a formal alliance. Should an alliance be concluded, however, the Florentines would see what difference there is between his friendship and that of others. Keeping relations on an informal basis, the "friend" adds, will prove more troublesome for Florence than for the duke, because he has on his side both France and the "aforementioned states" with which he is confident of forging alliances, whereas Florence, he claims, has only France. He therefore predicts that "your Signori will come to have more need of the duke than he of them," but that he would not for this reason be disinclined to help the Florentines. However, if they need assistance and are not bound by a formal treaty, he might or might not provide it. The "friend" asks if it would not be a great boon to Florence if Borgia helped the city regain Pisa and eliminate Vitellozzo, "two wounds [piaghe]" (the same metaphor Machiavelli will employ in the *Decennale*), "which, if not healed, will cause you to be ill and perhaps perish." The Florentines need only respect the "old condotta" promised in 1501, which the duke "prizes more than riches and every other thing." Anticipating the objection that Borgia was then negotiating with Vitellozzo and the Orsini, the "friend" notes that nothing was as yet agreed to and that Borgia would trade the best city under his control for an agreement *not* to be reached with them. Moreover, he "must save some of the Orsini, because, when his father dies, he will need friends in Rome"—another acknowledgment of the looming precariousness of his situation. As for Vitellozzo, Borgia considers him "a poisonous snake [serpente avvelenato] and the fuse [fuoco] of Tuscany and Italy." This was all by way of assuring Machiavelli and the Florentines that, despite ongoing efforts at reconciliation with the conspirators, Borgia was and always would be willing to enter into an alliance with Florence. Substituting the stick of threats for the carrot of proffered friendship, the "friend" asks Machiavelli to remind the gonfaloniere (Piero Soderini had been installed in office a few days before) or the Ten "that the king of France could easily order your Signori to honor the condotta promised to the duke, forcing them against their will to put some of their troops in his service" (*LCSG* 2.284.13–22). The message was clear: better to do it now, voluntarily.

Machiavelli's reply can be misunderstood if not read in context. Borgia was wise to seek both arms and allies, he averred, and the Florentines did indeed want to reacquire Pisa and protect themselves against Vitellozzo, although "they no longer took him too seriously" and, such was the implication, did not need Borgia's help on that front. Claiming that he had spoken on his own ("parlando sempre come da me") about the condotta, Machiavelli told the "friend" that, "in view of the stato he holds, the duke should not be judged as are other signori, who have only *la carrozza*," literally a carriage, signifying the trappings of rule; "he should instead be spoken of as a new power [nuovo potentato] in Italy with whom it is more appropriate to enter into a treaty and an alliance [una lega e un'amicizia] rather than a condotta." One of Machiavelli's objectives in this legation was to put off any consideration of activating the condotta, the contract mercenaries and their employers signed. Speaking to Borgia through the "friend," he was flattering him, encouraging him to think of himself as the ruler of an Italian state (a "potentato"), not as a hired captain, but he was doing so in order to deflect further talk of a condotta, which was the last thing Florence wanted. Moreover, he continued, "because alliances among rulers [amicizie fra i Signori] are secured with arms, and arms alone cause such alliances to be honored," Machiavelli added that the Ten "for their part would not see what security they would have if three-quarters or three-fifths of their arms were in the duke's hands." This was a blunt rejection of Borgia's insistent demand that Florence implement the condotta. Far from seeing any security in such an arrangement, the Florentines saw only danger. Telling Borgia's confidant that the duke should think of himself as a "nuovo potentato in Italia" was part of the rhetorical strategy Machiavelli employed to convey the message that the Florentines did not need him. He concluded the dispatch acknowledging that he could not say how much of what the "friend" said came from him and how much from Borgia. "I can say only that he is one of the most important of the duke's men and that, if this was his own speculation [fantasia], he could be deceiving himself" (*LCSG* 2.284.25–8, 34–5).

Having received Machiavelli's dispatches of November 8 and 13, the Ten told Machiavelli they now "understand more accurately the duke's thinking and his aims concerning Florence, and how our policy toward him has been interpreted with little memory of the past and even less regard about what might ensue: in sum, he bases everything on the hope that he will be able to arrange and manage his future affairs and give them whatever name he wants, considering that, on the one hand, he seeks an alliance and a formal treaty, but when it comes to details he mentions only those that redound to his own benefit." "The alliance he wants with us is all for himself," "unstable" and "lacking the basic foundation necessary for all states, namely the security, benefit, utility, and honor of each party. We see that he wants only the condotta, which is unacceptable to us because of the expense; nor would it be regarded as being to our benefit, because it is not appropriate to entrust the entire stato"—the security of the dominion—"to one man, as you wisely replied to that friend." The Ten instructed Machiavelli to insist that Florence certainly wanted "amicizia"—meaning informal friendship—but that there was to be no further thought of a condotta (*LCSG* 2.290.4, 7, 9–11).

When Machiavelli next spoke with Borgia, on November 19, he did not mince words in conveying his government's firm decision not to offer a condotta. The Ten, he said, had expressed some anger and irritation ("alterazione e dispiacere") over Borgia's demand, both because granting a contract was "impossible" and because he was more concerned with his own "particulare"—his own benefit—than with their mutual interests. If, Machiavelli told Borgia, he were willing to put aside his demand for a condotta, the Florentines would be open to any other type of alliance. Borgia rejected this half-hearted proposal "with no sign of anger," asserting that any alliance without a condotta "would negate the first principles of an alliance." Machiavelli countered that alliances without condotte were made every day and that "durable alliances are those that serve the needs of both parties." If that was where the Florentines intended to leave matters, Borgia said, it was fine with him. Yet he left the door open, "speaking many loving words" and reiterating his intentions in the event the Florentines changed their minds. He tried to curry favor by revealing to Machiavelli the double-dealing of Giampaolo Baglioni, who, while feigning friendship with Florence, told Borgia that during Vitellozzo's occupation of Arezzo he had wanted to join him in restoring the

Medici to power. In a meeting that same day with the "friend" who had presented to Machiavelli Cesare's plans, Machiavelli again ruled out a condotta. Not even to consider it was not to respect the duke's honor, said the "friend," who suggested—another sign of desperation—that, instead of a condotta, Florence could give him a "provisione"—a stipend. Machiavelli retorted that changing the name would not change the substance and that, in any case, before he could forward such a proposal to his government, he would need to know what immediate and clear benefit it would bring to Florence. The "friend" said he would think about it (*LCSG* 2.294.5–17, 24, 30–1), but when he broached the subject again, on December 9, while still expressing surprise that Florence had not offered a condotta, he said Borgia would agree to any arrangement that "satisfied his honor" (*LCSG* 2.310.7).

On November 20 Machiavelli reported that the rest of the French lances had arrived, bringing the total in Borgia's camp to 450. There was still no sign of the Swiss. Everyone, he says, was waiting anxiously to see the extent of Cesare's military preparations (*LCSG* 2.294.33–8). On November 26 there was much speculation about why Borgia was delaying his departure from Imola: some guessed he was out of funds and waiting for money from Rome; others thought he was waiting for the Swiss troops to arrive—confirmations, both, of his dependence on others. Machiavelli also reported that, according to the duke's financial officer, Alessandro Spannocchi, Borgia had spent no less than 60,000 ducats since the beginning of October. Yet his cavalry had not been paid since they arrived in camp, and at Fossombrone they were driven off by Vitellozzo's infantry without putting up a fight. This revelation prompted Machiavelli to comment to the Ten: "I have gladly written this to Your Lordships, so that you may see that when others are in disarray [in disordine] they do not spend less than you do, nor are they better served by mercenaries [soldati] than you are. Conversely, he who is well armed, with his own arms, attains the same [good] results whichever way he turns" (*LCSG* 2.297.10, 22–3). Clearly, Machiavelli did not consider that Borgia was "well armed with his own arms." On the 28th Machiavelli learned from the Ten that French troops were being readied for a campaign in the South against the Spaniards but would first assist Borgia in recovering Urbino and Camerino. He would then be obligated to send his forces wherever King Louis intended to engage the Spaniards—another indication of Borgia's subservience to the French (*LCSG* 2.298.7). Meanwhile, the Swiss—Machiavelli calls them "questi benedetti Svizzeri"—had still not appeared (*LCSG* 2.299.27). Borgia was now unwilling to leave Imola until he knew the plans for retaking Urbino (*LCSG* 2.300.5), which depended on the French.

On December 2 Machiavelli reported that the agreement between Borgia and Giovanni Bentivoglio of Bologna had been finalized and ratified. He thought this a potentially favorable turn of events for Florence. "In addition to the other benefits [Florence] can hope to gain from this, I see one that should not be underestimated, which is that the duke is beginning to be accustomed to restraining his desires [si cominci avvezzare a tenersi delle voglie] and to learning that fortune will not grant him all his wishes [come la fortuna non liene dà tutte vinte]. This will make it easier to pull him in whatever direction Your Lordships might wish" (*LCSG* 2.302.4–5). Increasingly aware of Cesare's growing vulnerability and gradual retreat from his grandiose ambitions, Machiavelli implies that Florence now had the upper hand. On December 6, in their first meeting in ten days, Borgia told Machiavelli that of the 600 French lances that had arrived—more than the 450 he had expected—he would keep only 200 or 250 once matters were resolved, "because their troops are intolerable destroyers of the country" who plunder and steal from the inhabitants (*LCSG* 2.305.22).

On December 10 Borgia finally departed Imola for Forlì and then Cesena. Machiavelli was ill for several days and waited a day to rejoin the duke's camp (*LCSG* 2.305.27; *LCSG* 2.311.9). On the 14th, he commented on the depredations of Borgia's army, especially the French troops, who took what they wanted wherever they encamped: "Your Lordships can imagine how things are here and how they were in Imola, where the court resided for three months and the whole army for two months and consumed everything down to the pebbles." "I tell Your Lordships this so you will understand that the French and all the other hired soldiers are no different in Romagna from what they were in Tuscany" (*LCSG* 2.314.9). A further sign of the deteriorating condition of Borgia's territories was that, as the Ten wrote to Machiavelli on December 17, many inhabitants were leaving with their possessions and seeking refuge in Bagno (di Romagna, in Florentine territory), where Florence's capitano was instructed to give them safe haven, and in towns near Florence's border with the duchy of Urbino, which Borgia had just recaptured. Fearing that he might try to force them back, the Ten asked Machiavelli to do his best to prevent any incursion of his troops into Florentine territory (*LCSG* 2.315.5–6). On December 14 Machiavelli reported that observers were waiting apprehensively ("stanno sospesi") for Cesare's next move. They were certain that, despite the announced reconciliation with the conspirators, Borgia had no choice but to "secure himself against those who have perpetrated this vile deed [villania] and come within a hair's breadth [ad un pelo] of taking his stato." Machiavelli agreed with this assessment. The Venetians worried he might seize Ravenna, or possibly Cervia, from their dominions. Others speculated he might go to Naples with the French, and within his entourage many thought he would return to Rome at Christmas to deal with his enemies from there. Machiavelli advised his government to send an ambassador to come to an agreement with Borgia and begged the Ten to let him return home (*LCSG* 2.314.10–20). Had they acceded to his request, he would have missed the dramatic events—the murder of Ramiro de Lorqua and the entrapment and murder of the conspirators—that loom so large in his recollections of Borgia in *The Prince*.

On December 18 Borgia repeated his wish for Florence's "amicizia"—the closer the alliance, he said, the more valuable it would be as a "very great foundation for his state/power [fondamento grandissimo allo stato suo]." Borgia was still looking for "fondamenti" to buttress his precarious dominions. Reprising the unrealistic idea first suggested to Machiavelli by the "friend" in early November, the duke proposed a hypothetical alliance of Florence, Ferrara, Mantua, Bologna, and himself. He said (again) that he had promised little when he was unable to do much, but now, with Urbino and Camerino recaptured and having 10,000 cavalry without the Vitelli and Orsini, he was able to offer Florence much assistance. Indeed, he promised that, if Florence were attacked, he would come immediately to its aid without waiting for an invitation. A declaration of readiness to come uninvited to Florence's rescue with 10,000 cavalry must have seemed more a threat than an offer of help. There is a tone of bemused irony in Machiavelli's comment to the Ten about Cesare's double-edged grandiloquence in this meeting: "I fear Your Lordships will think I've put words in [Borgia's] mouth, because I myself can scarcely believe the words I heard him speak and the gestures that accompanied them" (*LCSG* 2.316.4–8). As we shall see, this is precisely what Machiavelli would do in *The Prince*—represent in both direct and indirect discourse Borgia's exaggerated and bombastic rhetoric. Just the claim of 10,000 cavalry must have elicited silent laughter from Machiavelli, given that his estimate in early October of the duke's cavalry was no more than 650, now supplemented by a possibly equal number (according to Borgia) of French lances. But most of the latter were just about to abandon him.

On December 20 Machiavelli reported seeing all the French captains—they "seemed angry," as he interpreted their gestures—going to meet Borgia. Surmising that something important was happening, Machiavelli sought out the Baron de Berry, pretending that the Ten had instructed him to do so. Berry told him they had received orders to return to Milan and within two days would all be gone, but he did not know why. This unexpected turn of events "plunged the thinking of the court into confusion [ha mandato el cervello sottosopra a questa Corte]." Machiavelli too found it inexplicable, telling the Ten he could not assess its significance. Berry also told him that the French captains had decided, for reasons of security, that they would never again march without infantry; they had suffered some "iniuria" inflicted by the local peasantry and had been unable to retaliate. The implication is that only infantry could have established control over the population, and Machiavelli, who valued infantry over cavalry, remarked that the baron's words were worthy of note: "parendomi parole da notarle" (*LCSG* 2.319.2–13).

When the French left for Bologna on December 22, Machiavelli was still searching for an explanation: "this decision, so sudden and unexpected, has everyone talking and engaging in fanciful speculations [ogni uomo fa sua castellucci]. From trustworthy sources one gets nothing that seems reasonable to anyone." Among the "trustworthy sources" Machiavelli consulted were the French commanders, Berry and Jacques de Clermont ("Montison"), Louis's governor in Lodi, who confirmed that the French were departing out of "compassione" for the local population, which had suffered constant raids by French troops, but also for Borgia himself, "because he no longer needed them" and because the region, "oppressed [aggravato] by so many soldiers, was becoming hostile [inimico] to him." According to Borgia's inner circle, "he could no longer tolerate" the French and said that "the arms of his allies gave him more trouble than those of his enemies"—hardly compatible with Borgia's proud affirmation of the solidity of French support. Machiavelli was still in search of an explanation for their sudden departure, and, with Borgia for the moment unwilling to meet him, he could only relay the hypotheses he heard, most of which speculated that Louis needed the troops in Lombardy or was angry with the pope. Machiavelli assessed Cesare's remaining military strength as including 600 infantry from the Val di Lamone and 1,500 Swiss, Germans, and Gascons. The long-awaited contingent of 1,000 Swiss was still in Faenza. The bottom line, as Machiavelli put it, was that Borgia "had lost more than half of his forces and two-thirds of his reputation. Nor is it believed he can do many of the things he predicted earlier." Guidobaldo da Montefeltro had recovered the fortress of San Leo; the other fortresses of the duchy of Urbino were destroyed; and Camerino, which Borgia had confidently asserted just days before was safely under his control, was now refusing to obey him. Machiavelli's perception of Borgia's drastically weakened position prompted him to warn the Ten to consider whether the "straits [necessità]" in which Borgia was about to enter "could cause him to throw himself into the lap of your inveterate enemies [fare gittarsi in grembo a chi è naturale inimico vostro]"—Vitelli and the Orsini (*LCSG* 2.322.5–20).

In this instance, however, Machiavelli's intuition missed the mark. Far from reconciling with the conspirators, Borgia eliminated them. First, Cesare had his governor general in the Romagna, the condottiere Ramiro de Lorqua, imprisoned and spectacularly executed in Cesena. In the dispatch of December 23 Machiavelli reported that Ramiro had been imprisoned and was expected to be "sacrificed" to "questi populi" of the Romagna, "who greatly desire it" (*LCSG* 2.322.23). On the 26th he sent the famous dispatch with the news that Ramiro "was found this morning in two pieces in the piazza, where he still is; the whole population [of Cesena] has been able to see it. No one knows why he was killed, except that so it has pleased the prince,[18] who shows he knows how to make and destroy men as he wishes, according to their merits" (*LCSG* 2.323.13). A decade later in *The Prince* (7.25), Machiavelli attributed to Ramiro the merit of having brought peace and unity to the previously lawless and violent region. But in 1502 he knew that Ramiro's administration of the Romagna had actually generated fierce hatred among the local population. Moreover, according to Venice's ambassador at the

[18] "che li è piaciuto cosí al Principe" echoes "Quod principi placuit, legis habet vigorem [what pleases the prince has the force of law]" from Justinian's *Institutes* 1.2.6, in which the "princeps" is of course the emperor.

papal court, Alexander claimed that Ramiro was plotting with Vitelli and the Orsini against Cesare.[19] If true, Ramiro's murder was the first step in the elimination of the conspirators.

Machiavelli was now scurrying to keep up with Borgia as he headed south. Not knowing where he was going, he told the Ten that "this lord is very secretive; I don't believe anyone except himself knows what he is about to do; his closest ministers have several times told me that he never announces anything until he does it, and he does it only when necessity compels him and not otherwise" (*LCSG* 2.323.10). He followed Borgia from Cesena to Pesaro to Fano to Senigallia, where, on December 31, he penned the brief dispatch announcing that Borgia's men had seized and imprisoned Vitellozzo Vitelli and the Orsini: "In my opinion they won't be alive tomorrow" (*LCSG* 2.326.5–8). Intent on seizing the conspirators' home cities, Borgia immediately left Senigallia and moved a dozen miles west to Corinaldo. Machiavelli followed and, on January 1, 1503, he briefly summarized the dramatic events of the previous day: the seizure of Paolo Orsini and his cousin Francesco, duke of Gravina, and the execution of Vitellozzo and Oliverotto. A more detailed account, written on December 31 and mentioned in the dispatch of January 1, has not survived (*LCSG* 2.327.3–6). Two weeks later, he began, but never finished, an overview of the events. Now aware that his letters since the end of December, which "would have provided a good understanding" of events, had not reached Florence, Machiavelli proposes "to write in this letter every detail of what happened, having now the opportunity to do so," because the new ambassador, Iacopo Salviati, had taken over the mission. "I think you will welcome it on account of the "exceptional [rara] and memorable nature" of what he had witnessed. Cesare is described as fully aware of the conspiracy and of the pretext of attacking Senigallia as an opportunity to assassinate him. Machiavelli describes how he lured them into the trap by separating his forces into small groups, hiding them along the road, thus deceiving his adversaries into believing he had fewer troops than he actually had and persuading them to leave their soldiers outside the city. As Borgia approached, the conspirators emerged from Senigallia to greet him, one by one, "randomly, compelled by necessity and shame." Only Vitellozzo Vitelli is individually described: riding on a mule, unarmed, wearing a black threadbare cloak and a black winter coat over it, "his face pale and stunned, clearly signaling to everyone his coming death" (*LCSG* 2.340.2–15, 18–21). Aside from Borgia's tactical positioning of his troops, however, the letter says very little about his objectives or state of mind. Nor does Machiavelli characterize Borgia's success as exemplary or worthy of imitation.[20]

[19] *Dispacci di Antonio Giustinian, ambasciatore veneto in Roma dal 1502 al 1505*, ed. Pasquale Villari, 3 vols. (Florence, 1876), vol. 1, p. 304.

[20] Rinaldo Rinaldi provides valuable commentary on the letter in his edition of the *Discorsi sopra la prima deca di Tito Livio*, 2 vols. (Turin: UTET, 2006), vol. 2, pp. 1644–50.

Machiavelli incorporated some parts of this incomplete letter into the piece variously titled as the "Descrittione," "Tradimento," or "Il modo" of how Duke Valentino killed Vitellozzo, Oliverotto da Fermo, Paolo Orsini, and the duke of Gravina Francesco Orsini. Exactly how the two texts are related, however, is obscured by uncertainty about when Machiavelli wrote the "Description," some assigning it to 1503, others preferring 1514–17.[21] The "Description" places the murders in a wider context, including Borgia's return to Imola (in September 1502), after visiting King Louis in Lombardy to "justify himself" against Florence's accusations that he had orchestrated the Arezzo rebellion, his plan to wrest Bologna from the Bentivoglio (which did not happen), and the formation of the conspiracy by the Vitelli, Orsini, and others who believed it necessary to "restrain his ambition [frenare l'appetito suo]" to prevent their own ruin (1–3). News of the Magione conspiracy spread "throughout all Italy," and cities "unhappy under the duke's rule hoped they could change things." Machiavelli says the conspirators asked Florence to join them in "extinguishing the fire" that threatened them all and that the Florentines refused out of "hatred" for Vitelli and the Orsini: "not only did they not ally with them, they also sent their secretary Niccolò Machiavegli [sic], to offer the duke [Borgia] refuge and aid against these new enemies of his" (4–12). (As we know, the Ten authorized Machiavelli to assure Borgia of Florence's "friendship," but to rebuff his requests for activation of the condotta.) The claim that Florence offered him "refuge and aid" underscores Borgia's vulnerability, insufficient arms, and need for help. Most strikingly, Machiavelli describes Borgia as "full of fear [pieno di paura] in Imola, because, suddenly and unexpectedly, his hired captains having become his enemies, he faced an imminent war without arms [disarmato]" (13). This is starkly at odds with the image of himself as a confident and well-armed prince that Borgia regularly conveyed to Machiavelli. The "Description" says he took courage from the Florentines' "offer," and "delayed going to war with the few soldiers he had," while negotiating an accord with the conspirators and strengthening his forces by "asking the king of France for troops and hiring all the cavalrymen he could find" (14–16). Here too Machiavelli emphasizes Borgia's lack of arms and dependence on mercenaries and the French. The defeat of his troops at Fossombrone (in late October 1502) made him feign an attempt at reconciliation: "Being a great dissembler [grandissimo simulatore]," he promised his former condottieri that his conquests would be theirs: "it was enough for him to have the title of prince but he wanted the principality to be theirs" (17–18). Fortified by the arrival of 500 French lances, he reconfirmed the conspirators' condotte, promised them large sums of money, and agreed not to

[21] See Brian Richardson, "Per la datazione del 'Tradimento del duca Valentino' del Machiavelli," *La Bibliofilía* 81 (1979): 75–85; and Giorgio Inglese, *La vita di Castruccio Castracani e altri scritti* (Milan: Rizzoli, 1991), pp. 22–7 (analysis) and 95–106 (text). Marchand also discusses the issue in *SPM*, pp. 594–6, and publishes the text, pp. 597–606 (citations from the numbered subdivisions of this edition).

attack the Bentivoglio. In return, they restored Urbino to him and agreed to assist his campaigns and not undertake military actions without his permission (22–4).

The "Description" claims that the conspirators proposed an attack on Florence that Borgia rejected because the Florentines were his "friends." He and they agreed instead to join forces against the small city of Senigallia. To Borgia this was the "occasione buona" that would raise no suspicions because the conspirators themselves had suggested it. "To reassure them even more" that he was coming to Senigallia in peace, he "dismissed all his French troops" (27–31) and persuaded Vitellozzo and the Orsini to wait for him in Senigallia while he approached from Fano. Machiavelli says Vitelli acquiesced in this arrangement only with great reluctance "because the death of his brother [Paolo] had taught him that one must never offend a prince and then put one's trust in him" (32–3). Vitellozzo is described as "completely distraught [tutto aflitto], as if aware of his approaching death." His appearance provoked "astonishment [ammirazione] in those who knew the man's virtú [military ability] and past good fortune (46–7). Borgia's men quickly seized the conspirators as they entered Senigallia (52–3). That same night Vitellozzo and Oliverotto were killed: "Neither of them spoke words worthy of their past life": Vitellozzo asked for a plenary indulgence from the pope; and Oliverotto tearfully protested that Vitellozzo was responsible for all the offenses against Borgia. The text ends abruptly after noting that, on January 18 (1503), Borgia had the two Orsini strangled in Castello della Pieve (57–9). The image of Cesare Borgia in the "Description" is not laudatory, as often claimed. Machiavelli does not present him as worthy of imitation; there are no expressions of praise, much less idealization. If anything, the narrative emphasizes the insufficiency of his arms, his reliance on the French, and his inability to cajole or threaten the Florentines into assisting him. That he was saved, on this occasion, by stealth and (as Machiavelli puts it in the dispatch of January 8) "unheard-of good fortune" did not, given fortune's capriciousness, bode well for his future.

In his dispatch of January 1, 1503, from Corinaldo, Machiavelli recounts a conversation he had with Borgia in the early evening of the 31st, after the four conspirators had been taken prisoner. The duke was in "the best of moods [colla migliore cera del mondo]," expressing his delight over the sudden elimination of his enemies and, once again, his great affection for Florence. He said again why he desired an alliance, provided, of course, the Florentines reciprocated. Machiavelli was "astonished [ammirato]" at this display. Assuming he now had a strong hand to play, Borgia wanted Machiavelli to convey congratulations to the Florentines for the elimination of their, his, and King Louis's mortal enemies and for the removal of "the seeds of division and discord that were about to destroy Italy." Florence's Signori, he said, should consider themselves in his debt. He wanted them to proclaim "far and loud that they are his friends/allies [mostrare a tutto el mondo essere sua amiche]" and, as a demonstration of that friendship, to send cavalry and infantry to Sansepolcro to join his troops and prepare to strike either

Città di Castello (home of the Vitelli) or Perugia (Baglioni's city). The Florentines, said the duke, no longer had any reason to be fearful of the Vitelli or the other conspirators because he, Borgia, was "well armed" and "your enemies have been taken prisoner." Lastly, he wanted the Florentines to hand over Duke Guidobaldo da Montefeltro, if he had taken refuge in Florentine territory. Up to this point Machiavelli listened quietly to all of Borgia's demands, but, hearing this last one, he broke in sharply to say that it would be inconsistent with the "dignity" of Florence to deliver Guidobaldo to Borgia: the Florentines "would never do it." Borgia backed off, saying it would be sufficient if they detained him. "Many men, friends who know our city," Machiavelli told the Ten, "have impressed upon me" that this is a "grande occasione" for the Florentines to form an alliance with Borgia and that they should not delay in sending one of their "leading citizens as ambassador." "This was urged on me again and again by persons who have the interests of our city at heart." Machiavelli said he was relaying this out of the sense of duty with which he had always served the Ten, possibly implying some skepticism about the idea. He also reported that Borgia planned to move quickly to Perugia and Città di Castello and, "one fears," even to Siena (for retribution against Pandolfo Petrucci). His final objective would be to destroy Orsini strongholds in and around Rome (*LCSG* 2.327.7–16).

Machiavelli learned from one of Borgia's closest advisers on January 2 that, for the moment, he was keeping the Orsini cousins alive in the expectation of a trial in Rome that might include other family members. He intended "to liberate all the cities of the Church [the papal states] from their factions and tyrants and return them to papal rule, keeping only the Romagna for himself." Any future pontiff, so said this adviser, would be in Borgia's debt "because he would no longer be a *servo* of the Orsini and the Colonna, as popes had always been." "For a long time," the adviser asserted, Borgia "has had no other thought except for how he could pacify [quietare] the Romagna and Tuscany," which he believes he has accomplished by removing the source of the troubles. "What's left is a fire that can be extinguished with a drop of water." He too urged the Florentines to send an ambassador to sign a formal agreement, to make "every display of friendship" toward the duke, and to set aside all delaying tactics and hesitations (*LCSG* 2.329.6–9). Machiavelli apparently made no reply to the assertion that Borgia was planning "to pacify" the Romagna *and* Tuscany. That Borgia thought himself able, or authorized, to "quietare" Tuscany anticipates his fantastical ambition, related by Machiavelli in *Prince* 7.33–4, of becoming "signore di Toscana" in order to acquire enough "imperio" to survive his father's death.

Machiavelli accompanied Borgia and his troops to Sassoferrato on January 3 and then to Gualdo Tadino (northeast of Perugia) two days later (*LCSG* 2.332.4). On January 4 the Ten wrote to both Machiavelli and Giovanvittorio Soderini in Rome to say they had received conflicting reports concerning the events in Senigallia, some of which claimed that all four of Borgia's former lieutenants had been killed, others that they were still the duke's prisoners. Knowing that, either way, Borgia had neutralized the conspirators, they told Machiavelli to congratulate him, "but with moderation nonetheless [con modestia nondimeno], and to show that we presume these actions were taken because they were necessary and because [the conspirators] had given cause for them, so that it will not seem that we congratulate him unduly or believe that what happened was done without concern for trust and honor." He was to make clear all the reasons for which "we are pleased, including for our own interests, which are chiefly two: the destruction of our enemies and the love we bear His Holiness the pope and His Excellency the duke" (*LCSG* 2.333). The Ten were asking Machiavelli to walk a fine line between expressing gratitude and keeping the necessary distance.

On January 6 Machiavelli wrote that Borgia intended to move south to Assisi and then on to Siena "to install a government in that city to his liking" (*LCSG* 2.335.10). Two days later, he reported that Sienese ambassadors were in Borgia's camp asking why he planned to attack their city. His only target, he replied, was Pandolfo Petrucci: if the Sienese were willing to give him up, he had no further quarrel with them. The ambassadors broke off negotiations; "matters remain ambiguous and no one dares predict the outcome." The looming confrontation prompted Machiavelli to sketch an intriguing comparison of Borgia and Petrucci.[22] In Borgia, "one sees an unheard of [good] fortune, a boldness [uno animo] and a more than human hope of being able to realize his every desire [una speranza piú che umana di potere conseguire ogni suo desiderio]." Behind the apparent praise, the reiterated suggestion of exceptionality—"unheard of" successes and the "more than human hope of realizing his every desire"—places Borgia on precarious heights. Petrucci, by contrast, is described as "a man of much *prudenzia*" (perhaps meaning both prudence and wisdom here) in a stato he holds with great prestige [con grande reputazione] and without enemies of much importance," because he had either killed them or reconciled with them (*LCSG* 2.336.10–13). Does Machiavelli praise Borgia more highly than Petrucci here? Next to Petrucci's prudence and renown, Borgia's profile veers toward that of a reckless adventurer who fails to assess things realistically and who, even now, depends on the arms of others, as suggested by Machiavelli's prediction that he will ask Florence to attack Siena. He tells the Ten that, "concerning his intentions toward Your Lordships, his words have always been and still are as good as I have written, spoken reasonably [con ragione] and so animatedly [vivamente] that, if he believed them to be true as he speaks them, we could rest easy about him." Implied here is that Borgia does not believe what he says. "Nonetheless, the experience of others must make us cautious. Nor should we underestimate his tactics when we negotiated the agreement with him [in 1501], because, once he

[22] On Petrucci, see Christine Shaw, *L'ascesa al potere di Pandolfo Petrucci il magnifico, Signore di Siena (1487–1500)* (Siena: Il Leccio, 2001).

made known his desire for the condotta and lost any hope of getting it, he always steered clear and made light of it, saying a general alliance was enough for him, as one does who sees he is unable to compel you and wants to wait for a time when he can. He thought he could temporize successfully, because it was clear Your Lordships were not about to harm him given [Florence's alliance with] France, the circumstances of his enemies, and your [military] weakness. So he saw benefit in deferring the matter. I do not wish to infer anything more from this except to remind Your Lordships that, once he has succeeded in this campaign against Siena, which is coming soon, the opportunity [occasione] he has waited and planned for will have come" (*LCSG* 2.336.15–18)—a warning that Borgia had not abandoned his designs on Florence and Tuscany.

From Torgiano, a few miles southeast of Perugia, Machiavelli reported on a long and remarkable meeting with Borgia on January 10 in which the duke made yet another appeal for an alliance with Florence and now also for military assistance in removing Petrucci from Siena. "You know how much affection I have for Your Signori, whom I consider among the principal foundations of my power [de' primi fondamenti allo stato mio] in Italy," he told Machiavelli. Eliminating Petrucci "would be the last stage of our campaign for the security of both our states." Borgia considered Petrucci a danger because of his cleverness and ample financial resources: "he is a spark from which great conflagrations are to be feared." He had assured the Sienese ambassadors that he "did not want their liberty," only the expulsion of Petrucci. But if they refused, he would bring artillery to the walls of Siena and use all necessary force to achieve his purpose, with no intention, however, of occupying Siena; "in any case, the master of the shop [el maestro della bottega], who is the king of France, would not be happy if I took Siena for myself, and I am not so rash as to convince myself" to do so. This was all leading to another attempt to persuade the Florentines to agree to an alliance and provide him with military assistance. Again he argued that he had done the Florentines a great service for which they should reward him: "if a year ago anyone had promised to eliminate Vitellozzo and Oliverotto, destroy the Orsini, and expel Giampaolo [Baglioni] and Pandolfo and had asked for 100,000 ducats in return, your Signoria would have come running to give the money. Now that this has happened without any cost or effort or burden [for Florence], although the debt is not in writing, it is tacitly understood; and therefore it is well to begin paying it so that your city will not seem ungrateful to me or others, contrary to its custom and nature." Florence, Borgia insisted, had no justification for not willingly taking part in expelling Petrucci, which would be in its interest and the king's interest. With Petrucci gone, "your Signori and I would both be free of all fear for our stati," and "we"—did Cesare mean to include Florence in this next hypothetical scenario?—"could hasten with our troops to the kingdom [of Naples] and to Lombardy wherever His Majesty requires." His appeal for Florence's help is not motivated, he says, by any "fear that I cannot accomplish the task [of expelling Petrucci] myself, but because I want all Italy to be certain of our *amicizia*." Machiavelli does not say in the dispatch that he made any reply to this long speech, only that, as Borgia asked, he would relay his requests to the Ten and ask for an "immediate answer" (*LCSG* 2.338.6–18).

As noted, Machiavelli's dispatches, from even before Senigallia, had not been reaching Florence. He suspected as much because he was not receiving the Ten's letters. From Assisi on January 8 he wrote that "everyone here is beginning to be astonished that Your Lordships have not written or sent any word to this prince to congratulate him for what he recently accomplished to your benefit, for which he thinks your entire city is beholden to him." In another expression of aggrieved under-appreciation, Borgia said: "it would have cost your city 200,000 ducats to eliminate Vitellozzo and destroy the Orsini" on its own, and even so "you would not have succeeded as efficiently [sí netto]" as he did (*LCSG* 2.336.5). On January 12 Machiavelli was in Città della Pieve (then called Castello della Pieve). On the way a letter finally reached him from the Ten, written on the 5th, that upset him greatly ("mi dette passione assai") because from it he learned that none of his recent letters had reached Florence. He was further dismayed by another letter, of the 9th, informing him that only his letters of January 1 and 2 had arrived: "it seems my work has vanished when it was most needed and for which I should have received greater appreciation. Wise men, as Your Lordships are, nonetheless know it is not enough to do one's duty—one must also have good luck." So he sat down and summarized all the letters he had written since Senigallia (*LCSG* 2.339.4–19). He also recounted another meeting with Borgia in which he informed him of the pleasure with which the Florentines learned of his elimination of the conspirators. Borgia was pleased by the appointment of Iacopo Salviati as ambassador: "the stature of the man selected delighted him, and he awaits him with great anticipation." They talked again of Borgia's determination to expel Petrucci from Siena. Borgia had sent an emissary to Rome, for the purpose, as Machiavelli gathered from a "trustworthy source," to "discuss this undertaking with the pope and hear his opinion about whether, if an acceptable agreement could be reached with Pandolfo, they should accept it. For it seemed to [Cesare] that having to deal with Siena and the Orsini at the same time would be biting off more than he could chew [parendogli avere troppe cose da masticare]"—another instance, this one recognized by Borgia himself, of overreaching and the need for restraint. Machiavelli thought the reassessment made sense ("la cosa non è sproporzionata"), "even if totally contrary" to the duke's earlier insistence that Petrucci had to be removed (*LCSG* 2.339.20–3). When he wrote his last dispatch of the long legation in Castiglione Fiorentino on January 21, he reported that an agreement had been reached for Petrucci's departure from Siena without military action and that Borgia was headed to Orvieto (*LCSG* 2.341.3). After three and a half months of almost daily contact, Machiavelli took his leave of Cesare, rode home, and, within a week, resumed his duties in the chancery.

"THE POPE WOULD LIKE IT BETTER IF YOU GAVE HIM THE FINAL PUSH"

The Florentines worried less about Borgia in 1503, not only after Alexander VI's death in August but in the first half of the year as well. At the end of January Petrucci left Siena (*LCSG* 2.346.6)—just when Borgia ran out of money and could not pay his troops (*LCSG* 2.345.5–6). His absence from the Romagna weakened his hold on the region. In early February, Venetian forces gathered at Ravenna for an attack on cities Borgia had controlled (*LCSG* 2.350.7; *LCSG* 2.353.3; *LCSG* 2.356.3). By April Petrucci was back in Siena. In the contested triangle of Arezzo, Sansepolcro, and Città di Castello the situation was still tense. Although Arezzo was again under Florentine rule, its anti-Florentine exiles remained a threat. Sansepolcro (Machiavelli calls "il Borgo") was still in Florentine hands but likewise vulnerable to the machinations of Aretine exiles. Alexander VI appointed an Aretine rebel as podestà of Città di Castello (in papal territory), and Machiavelli speculated that it would become a gathering-place for anti-Florentine exiles (*LCSG* 2.368.3). Cesare was engaged in a protracted siege of Ceri, an Orsini stronghold northwest of Rome. In early April Machiavelli informed the commissioner in Sansepolcro that Borgia had completed the operation and was sending cavalry back toward Perugia (*LCSG* 2.379.12). Until then, his absence from the borderlands gave Florence the opportunity, as Machiavelli wrote on April 4 to Giovanni Ridolfi, captain and commissioner in Arezzo, to oust some of the Aretine rebels with the help of the local population. This, he said, would bring "great security" to Arezzo and Sansepolcro (*LCSG* 2.376.5).

At the end of April the Ten sent Machiavelli to Siena to inform Petrucci that Alexander and Cesare were again asking for "amicizia" and a "lega" with Florence, indeed "with greater urgency and insistence," allegedly "for the common defense of the states in Italy" (*LCSG* 2.395.3–6). On May 1 Machiavelli reported to Florence's commissioner in Sansepolcro on Cesare's declining military strength: "The duke has dismissed all his Italian infantry and much of his ultramontane infantry as well, such that, compared to what he had three months ago, he hardly has a thousand left. He has also dismissed all the Bolognese cavalry, and we understand that some of his French cavalry will either return to Lombardy or go to the kingdom" to join the war against Spain. About the arrival of Borgia's forces in the triangle, Machiavelli commented that it certainly merited attention and "must make us vigilant." Surmising that the purpose was "to divert us from other operations," he concluded that "we must therefore be concerned about [Sansepolcro] and not be lacking in prudence or diligence or fortitude." "Nonetheless," he continued, "because [Borgia] has so thinned out his forces [lo essersi lui alleggerito di genti]," "it does not seem reasonable to us that the duke is about to do us any harm against the wishes of His Majesty. Nor do we have the slightest indication that His Majesty would allow him to." Moreover, Machiavelli thought Borgia's still precarious hold over key cities just across the border in papal territory limited his freedom of action: "Nor does the arrival of his troops in Perugia and [Città di] Castello conflict with this assessment of ours, because they are new territories [stati nuovi: new to Borgia's dominions], with powerful rebels beyond their walls." Cesare "must try to establish secure control over them with his forces," which, as Machiavelli explains at the beginning of this letter, were seriously depleted (*LCSG* 3.1.4–5).[23] Just four months after Borgia's stunning annihilation of the conspirators at Senigallia, Machiavelli saw him as militarily weaker and beset by problems that diminished whatever threat he had previously posed to Florence.

On May 14 Machiavelli informed Giovanni Ridolfi in Arezzo of rumors that Cesare's troops in Perugia and Città di Castello had come to "unsettle our territorial dominion [molestare lo stato nostro]" (*LCSG* 3.21.3–5). In a memorandum the same day to the commissioner in Sansepolcro, he speculated that Borgia's purpose in bringing troops to Perugia was perhaps to draw the Florentines away from their planned destruction of crops in Pisan territory. This, Machiavelli opined, the duke would have a "great desire" to do, if Florence were his only concern. But "our spirits are somewhat uplifted [alquanto sollevati con lo animo] about this, because Cesare and Alexander are so dependent on the king [obbligati ad el Re]" that "they must feel, we won't say reverence for him, but great hesitation [respetti grandi]. If [Cesare] engaged in some rash or reckless action [qualche temerità], the king would chastise him. Although we know the duke is willful, young, and full of self-assurance [volonteroso, giovane e pieno di confidenzia], nonetheless we don't judge him to be completely reckless [al tutto temerario] and about to launch an undertaking that would cause his ruin." Machiavelli admits he and the Ten could be wrong: "we don't hold this opinion obstinately; on the contrary, we think we could easily be deceived. We will not, therefore, leave [Sansepolcro] completely unprotected" (*LCSG* 3.22.4–12). At the end of May, he informed the commissioners that most of Borgia's troops were returning to Rome (*LCSG* 3.44.10; 3.49.12). In mid-June some of his cavalry units abandoned him in Città di Castello and were seen going north on their way "home" (*LCSG* 3.77.4–5).

As the Florentines watched, with considerable trepidation, troop movements that presaged war between Spain and France, they never lost sight of Cesare. There were reports in July that he was rebuilding his cavalry (*LCSG* 3.109.9). But his actions were now circumscribed by this much larger conflict in the South, and "we do not know if he is a Spaniard or a Frenchman" (*LCSG* 3.118.10), whether, in other words, Borgia intended to enter the fray on the side of Spain or France. The Florentines were confident he could not harm them because French cavalry were on their way from Lombardy, and "within a few days we ourselves will have more than a thousand cavalry in the Valdichiana" (*LCSG* 3.128.3). From Arezzo, close to where Borgia's troops had arrived, Giovanni Ridolfi expressed, in a now lost letter

[23] *Legazioni. Commissarie. Scritti di governo*, vol. 3, ed. Jean-Jacques Marchand and Matteo Melera-Morettini (Rome: Salerno Editrice, 2005).

to the Ten or Machiavelli or both, his view that Borgia was about to strike Florence directly, because, as he thought, the Spaniards would defeat the French at Gaeta (north of Naples), and a French defeat would remove the major constraint on Borgia. On August 4 Machiavelli replied, rejecting Ridolfi's prediction, in an unusual letter (*LCSG* 3.133) whose dialogical character is quite unlike the usual conveyance of instructions and information in chancery memoranda. Written in the first-person plural, the letter conveys the official view of the Ten, who probably left it to Machiavelli to put it in his own words. "We cannot deny that the forces Valentino has brought to the region give us cause for concern, because having such forces so close by...warrants serious consideration and adequate preparations to thwart the plans of those plotting against us. As we have written to you on other occasions, we believe we can be hurt in one of two ways: either through subterfuge [inganno] by provoking the rebellion of some of these cities, or by direct, open attack [per via di una guerra ordinata e *aperto Marte*]." Subterfuge seemed more likely than an attack. "First, let us establish this premise [fondamento], namely, that the duke cannot reasonably launch a war and openly move against us given the strength of the king of France and his large army in Lombardy, which any day now is about to pass through here." Machiavelli tells Ridolfi that Gaeta was not about to fall, "as you believe"; in fact, the "Spanish force encamped outside Gaeta had pulled back four miles. If for eight days the Spaniards had not dared" to assault Gaeta, it "seems reasonable" that they would not do so now that 7,000 additional French infantry were on the way. So "the assumption you make that, because Gaeta is about to fall, Valentino will soon make a military move, is groundless; on the contrary, the situation confirms us in our opinion." "Therefore, your further premise, that, for fear of the Venetians, the French will not leave Lombardy [to go south and engage the Spaniards], proves hollow." "We do not see, given these circumstances, how the duke can begin a war and openly destabilize the situation in Tuscany, because it is possible in a thousand ways, even with only half these favorable conditions, to light fires even under his bed [possendo in mille modi esserli, con la metà di questi favori, messo fuoco infino sotto el letto]." The striking metaphor highlights Borgia's vulnerability in his own territories—even before his father's fatal illness, which was only days away. He could try to foment rebellion in one of the Florentine cities, but "we can reasonably feel secure in those areas, assuming the situation does not change" (*LCSG* 3.133.3–12). Such was the cautious optimism of the Florentines two weeks before the event that changed everything.

On August 18 word came from Rome that Alexander and Cesare were both ill, and the next day that Alexander was dead (*LCSG* 3.145–6). On the 24th Machiavelli wrote to Giovanni Ridolfi that the French and Spaniards were positioning themselves to influence the conclave that would elect a new pope. Borgia, he added, "isn't yet dead, but is gravely ill" (*LCSG* 3.148.5–6). The following day, despite reports that Cesare was recovering (*LCSG* 3.153.4), Machiavelli informed

Giovanni Gonzaga, one of Florence's condottieri, that "the whole territory [stato] of Urbino has already risen in rebellion and reaffirmed its loyalty to Duke Guidobaldo" (*LCSG* 3.150.3). Armed uprisings also broke out in Città di Castello (*LCSG* 3.153.12), and the signore of Camerino, Gianmaria da Varano, whom Borgia had expelled, returned to his "stato" (*LCSG* 3.158.15). Borgia's dominion was quickly crumbling, as was his influence in Rome where foreign armies and the ever-powerful Colonna and Orsini were creating turmoil in the tense interregnum. The French were showing some ill will toward Borgia, insisting on the reinstatement of all the local lords he had expelled. Worried about Spanish influence over Borgia, the French declared that either "God will give the Church a good and just pontiff" or "there will be schism" and that they would ensure an election free of threats of violence and according to the laws of the Church, as befits the true Christian way [ordinariamente come si conviene al vero vivere cristiano]: "if others want to use force, they [the French] will prevent it" (*LCSG* 3.158.3–9). On August 31 Machiavelli told Giovanni Ridolfi that Prospero Colonna had arrived in Rome with "perhaps two thousand persons" and met with Borgia, raising suspicions of an alliance between them (*LCSG* 3.162.10). In early September, Machiavelli conveyed to Giovanbattista Ridolfi, commissioner in Castrocaro (not to be confused with his kinsman Giovanni Ridolfi), the Ten's opinion that, if Borgia "exaggerates his strength [magnifica le cose sue]," he is compelled to do so "by the fear of losing his dominions [stati]. Nor is it true, as [Borgia] writes, that he has been made Gonfaloniere of the Church [captain of the papal forces], and many other things he claims in his favor are also not true. But it is indeed true that he has lost Piombino, together with the fortresses and everything else, and also Urbino, and all his other troubles [disordini], which are well known to you, should become greater by the day, assuming that the future pope will be of the same mind and purpose as past popes have always been" (*LCSG* 3.164.6–8) (presumably to reassert papal control over the Romagna). This perception of Borgia in his time of difficulty—that he was "magnifying" his strength, making claims that were untrue, and engaging in delusions out of desperation—will be reflected in Machiavelli's account of his rise and fall in chapter 7 of *The Prince*.

Machiavelli wrote to Giovanbattista Ridolfi on September 4 that Cesare had left Rome for the Borgia stronghold at Nepi, north of Rome, with 400 cavalry, 400 light horse, 3,000 infantry and "all his treasure, which, they say, between cash and valuables amounts to 600,000 ducats." He joined his forces with the French army "and threw himself completely into the arms of the king [in tutto si è gittato nelle braccia del Re]. They say he is seriously ill, his legs swollen up beyond his thighs, and has himself carried about on a stretcher. It is believed he is dying; yet the French will make use of him to make Rouen [Cardinal Georges d'Amboise] pope" (*LCSG* 3.166.10–12), which, of course, did not happen. As Borgia's power declined and concerns grew over Venetian designs on his territories, Florentine policy in the Romagna took a new turn. On September 7 Machiavelli told Giovanbattista Ridolfi that, for the moment, the Ten considered it unlikely that the Venetians, being aware that King Louis "is today the arbiter of the affairs of Italy," would initiate any aggressive actions (*LCSG* 3.167.6). A few days later, he informed Ridolfi that Borgia had formally aligned with France (literally, "declared himself French: si è dichiarato franzese"), but that his agreement with the king seemed a "very weak thing." He was, moreover, "gravely ill," his troops were "not very numerous," and his artillery had been confiscated by (oddly enough) the College of Cardinals. Giampaolo Baglioni had just retaken Perugia, which, as Machiavelli observed, seriously diminished Borgia's "stati" and "partigiani." "If the French don't rescue him [literally, pull him up by the hair] once again, he'll have nothing left. The towns [in the Romagna] that have already rebelled against him completely block his path for aiding the cities he still has" (*LCSG* 3.171.5–9). With Borgia in this weakened condition, Florence now preferred to leave under his nominal control the cities that had not rebelled rather than let them fall under Venetian control, "as you yourself," he told Giovanbattista Ridolfi, "wisely reason" (*LCSG* 3.172.3–10). The Ten, Machiavelli wrote, modified the strategy somewhat, telling Ridolfi to promise Florence's support to whichever of the three claimants to the Romagna cities—Cesare, the Church, or their exiled former rulers—had in each case the most local support (*LCSG* 3.174.9–11).

On September 23 Machiavelli informed Giovanbattista Ridolfi that letters from the Ferrarese ambassador in Rome announced the election of Francesco Todeschini Piccolomini, Cardinal of Siena, as Pope Pius III. (Curiously, the letters reported that he took the name of Clement VIII, *LCSG* 3.186.4.) Although he lived less than a month in the papal office, Pius played an important role in Borgia's downfall. On September 29 Machiavelli informed Ridolfi that Borgia had recovered from his illness and was in Nepi with an estimated 200 cavalry, 300 light horse, and 1,000 infantry—considerably less than what he was said to have at the beginning of September. He had a safe-conduct from the French to take his forces through the territories of the "king's friends"—chiefly Florence—and into the Romagna (*LCSG* 3.190.4). In mid-October he assembled his forces for the journey, but before they left Rome his infantry stopped in their tracks in the piazza San Pietro and refused to proceed until they were paid. Facing this mutiny, Borgia went to Pius, presumably to request the funds he needed. Instead, the pope ordered him taken to the Castel Sant'Angelo. As Machiavelli told the new Florentine commissioner in the Romagna, Pierfrancesco Tosinghi, Borgia "was seen going into the Castello; some say the pope put him there to protect him; others say he was taken there as a prisoner. His cavalry and infantry have disintegrated, some units taken by the Orsini, others by the College of Cardinals." At this moment, the elderly pope fell ill and was close to death. "So you see," Machiavelli told Tosinghi, "in what a situation the duke finds himself." To forestall Venetian designs on the Romagna cities, the Ten decided not to publicize Borgia's predicament. Machiavelli instructed Tosinghi not to "let it be known that Borgia had been taken prisoner in the Castello but to say he had been put there for his own safety" and "will be able to leave Rome securely" (*LCSG* 3.206.3–11). Borgia never returned to the Romagna.

Pius III died on October 18. Another conclave was about to convene, and the Ten sent Machiavelli to observe both the conclave and Borgia's efforts to survive what everyone predicted would be the elevation of his and his father's old enemy, Cardinal Giuliano della Rovere. In his first dispatch from Rome, on October 28, Machiavelli reported that, although Borgia was still in the Castel Sant'Angelo, "he was more hopeful than ever of doing great things, assuming the election of a pope according to the wishes of his friends." The betting in Rome, Machiavelli said, gave Della Rovere a 32 percent chance of election and his nearest rival 22 percent (*LCSG* 3.216.16–21). On October 30 Machiavelli wrote that Cesare's influence among the Spanish cardinals was so great that he was much sought after by contenders for the papal office. Every day several cardinals visited him in the Castello, and "it is believed that whoever becomes pope will be in his debt [arà obbligo seco]. He lives with this hope of being favored by the new pontiff." But in a postscript Machiavelli expressed skepticism: "It remains to be seen whether the duke will succeed in being favored by the new pope" (*LCSG* 3.218.12, 26). The next night he reported that Della Rovere was now being given a 90 percent chance of being elected because two obstacles had been removed. Those very same Spanish cardinals, "amici del Duca," on whose support Borgia had based his hopes, now "all threw their support" to Della Rovere. According to Machiavelli, one could "easily speculate" why this happened: "the duke needs to be revived [risu[s]citato]," implying that Borgia considered Della Rovere—of all people—his only hope of recovering from recent setbacks and therefore told the Spanish cardinals to vote for him. And they were only too willing to do so because "they want to line their pockets [essere arricchiti]," presumably with the bribes and lucrative benefices that Della Rovere was liberally promising. With the Spanish cardinals won over, Rouen's chances disintegrated, and in the early morning of November 1, 1503, Giuliano della Rovere was elected as Julius II (*LCSG* 3.220.4–8; 3.221).

On November 4, with the election concluded, Machiavelli wrote at length about the difficulties Julius would face in keeping the many promises he had made to gain support in the conclave, particularly to Cesare Borgia, who was of "greater use" to him in getting elected "than anyone else. People say [the pope] has promised to restore all his dominions in the Romagna" and has given him Ostia "for his security." Released from the Castello, Cesare was now "in the papal palace in a place called the Stanze Nuove" with forty of his closest assistants ("primi servidori"). "It is not known if he will stay [in Rome] or leave." Some were saying he would go to Genoa, where he allegedly had 200,000 ducats deposited, and from there via Lombardy back to the Romagna. Others speculated he would stay in Rome until Julius's coronation, expecting to be made "Gonfaloniere di Santa

Chiesa, as was promised him, and to regain his territories with the prestige" of this title. Still others, whom Machiavelli characterizes as "not among the least wise," and with whom he therefore presumably agreed, thought that, because Julius had depended on Borgia's support and made him "great promises," he needed to keep him close at hand and maintain good relations ("intrattenerlo"), but that, if Cesare did not leave when he could, he would find himself trapped in Rome, because "the deep-seated hatred [naturale odio] that His Holiness has always had for him is well known, and [Julius] cannot have so quickly forgotten the exile he endured for ten years." The likelihood that this is indeed Machiavelli's opinion is enhanced by his assertion that Borgia "is letting himself get carried away [si lascia traportare] by that bold self-confidence of his [da quella sua animosa confidenzia], believing that the words of others are more trustworthy than his own have been." This openly critical judgment sets the tone for Machiavelli's observation of Borgia throughout the legation. Although he implies that Cesare is already trapped in a struggle with Julius from which he cannot escape, for the moment he cautiously acknowledges that he cannot foresee the outcome and that "it is necessary to wait for time, the father of truth," to reveal it (*LCSG* 3.227.6–13).

On November 5 Machiavelli met with Borgia, apparently for the first time since the January days following the events of Senigallia ten months before. The underlying purpose of the visit, as Machiavelli puts it, was "to see better where he stood and what could be hoped or feared from him." When he showed him the Ten's letters concerning Venice's plan to seize control of the Romagna cities, Borgia "became exceedingly agitated [si turbò sopra a modo] and began to bemoan Your Lordships acrimoniously, saying that you had always been his enemies and that you, not the Venetians, are the cause of his grief." He complained that "with a mere hundred soldiers you could have secured his possession of the territories and did not want to do it. He will make every effort to ensure that you are the first to repent of it." Moreover, "because Imola is now lost [to him], he no longer wishes to recruit troops and lose the rest [of his territories] trying to regain what he has lost. He no longer wants to be deceived by you and intends to yield to the Venetians what remains of his dominions; he believes he will soon see your dominions [stato] destroyed and will laugh over it." "And here he carried on [si distese] with words full of poison and fury." Machiavelli depicts an unhinged Borgia willing to surrender all his conquests to Venice to gain revenge against Florence, which he now imagines as the author of all his ills. To the Ten Machiavelli expressed exasperation and contempt for what he considered a pathetic display of wildness: "I did not lack for arguments with which to respond, nor would I have lacked the words, but I decided to calm him down and took my leave of him as nimbly as I could, although it seemed to take a thousand years" (*LCSG* 3.231.13–14). In the next day's dispatch, he reported Cardinal Soderini's account of Borgia's irrational and contradictory outbursts. Beyond his "usual numerous grievances" against the French and everyone else, Soderini said Borgia hoped to retake his territories and expected to secure appointment as Gonfaloniere of the Church. Soderini cautioned him that it was "useless to despair," which only makes things worse. That Borgia was now in a state in which he could be manipulated is suggested by Machiavelli's request to the Ten for instructions about how "I should deal with [maneggiare] the duke and if and how we should keep on good terms [intrattenere] with him" (*LCSG* 3.232.5–10). The portrait of Borgia that Machiavelli created a decade later in *The Prince* owes as much, perhaps more, to what he saw and heard of Borgia's bizarre behavior in November 1503 as it does to what Machiavelli had witnessed a year earlier.

Machiavelli met with Cardinals Soderini and Rouen, who were waiting to hear Borgia's response concerning Venetian designs in the Romagna. Rouen was angry about how Borgia spoke with Machiavelli, declaring that "God has never left any sin unpunished and won't leave these unpunished either." Machiavelli further reported that Borgia, contradicting what he had said the day before, was scraping together some soldiers. His advisers, "whom I know, tell me he wants to return to the Romagna in any event with as many troops as possible." But Machiavelli was again skeptical: Borgia had lost the fortress of Imola, and "after his angry outburst I don't know if he'll change his mind." Rouen and other (unnamed) cardinals "who keep a close watch on Italian affairs" were of the opinion that the Romagna would come under the control of either Pope Julius or King Louis: in other words, that Borgia would soon be out of the picture (*LCSG* 3.231.14–18). Fear of Venetian expansion, however, pushed both Florence and Julius to consider the possibility of using Borgia as a buffer and encouraging him—up to a point—in his wish to return. Machiavelli was meeting with Cardinal Soderini on November 10 when a messenger arrived from Borgia with a request for safe passage through Florentine territory (*LCSG* 3.236.4–5). He wanted the Ten informed that he would send a representative to Florence to receive a safe-conduct issued according to his specifications. Borgia was reportedly "in good spirits" and optimistic about quickly wresting the Romagna cities from the Venetians, "provided that Your Lordships do not give up all hope" (*LCSG* 3.237.3–5).

On November 11 Machiavelli addressed the crux of Borgia's dilemma: "It is believed that Julius is not genuinely well disposed toward him. Nonetheless, he strings him along [lo intrattiene] for two reasons: first, to keep faith with him" because of his "debt [obligo] to him, recognizing as he must that he owes the papacy in large part to him"; and second, because, lacking his own military forces, Julius "thinks Borgia can mount greater resistance against Venice than anyone else." For this reason, Machiavelli continues, the pope "urges him to depart and has written letters on his behalf to Your Lordships for transit [through Florentine territory] and safe-conduct" (*LCSG* 3.239.21). Borgia summoned Machiavelli to a meeting and seemed quite changed from five days before when he had spewed fury and frustration against the Florentines. He said he no longer wanted to dwell on the past—presumably, Florence's refusal to support him in the Romagna—and preferred to focus on the "bene commune," the concern he shared with Florence in preventing Venetian domination of the region. Confident of Julius's help, he told Machiavelli about the letters the pope had written on his behalf and advised that the Florentines too should think about assisting him. Later that same day Machiavelli had a long talk with Alessandro Spannocchi, Borgia's financial manager from whom he had learned a year earlier how much the duke fruitlessly spent in hiring mercenaries. According to Spannocchi, Borgia was uncertain about how to reach the Romagna, whether to travel overland with his approximately 400 horse and same number of infantrymen or to send the troops overland while he sailed to Livorno—in Florentine territory—to join his troops "in sul dominio vostro," where he "could speak with certain citizens and settle his affairs with you [Florentines]. But he wants no delays and expects to find the terms of the agreement already drawn up and needing only his signature." Spannocchi added that Borgia wanted "to be received" in Livorno, presumably meaning a formal welcome by Florentine officials. Machiavelli said he would write all this to the Ten and "gave [Spannocchi] good hope" (*LCSG* 3.239.24–9). Two days later, he wrote that Borgia was waiting for a decision from Florence and added that he, too, was waiting, being unable to continue negotiating until the Ten announced their wishes in the matter (*LCSG* 3.241.4).

On November 14 Machiavelli reported on a meeting of the pope, Cardinals Rouen, Volterra (Soderini), Ferrara (Ippolito d'Este), an unspecified number of Spanish cardinals, and Borgia himself, convened "to reach a conclusion concerning the duke's departure." They decided he should go by sea, not to Livorno, but to either Portovenere or La Spezia in Genoese territory (then under French control), and from there east through the mountains of the Garfagnana to Ferrara, where, according to Cardinal d'Este, Duke Ercole was willing to assist Borgia (perhaps because of the marriage of Cesare's sister, Lucrezia, to Ercole's son and heir Alfonso). Cesare would then travel south to Imola to rejoin his troops who, in this never realized plan, would have come overland through Florentine territory. Julius would provide him with as many letters credential ("brevi e patenti") as Borgia needed—but nothing more.

Particularly noteworthy in this dispatch is Machiavelli's report of Cardinal Soderini's skepticism about the wisdom, from Florence's point of view, of assisting Borgia's return to the Romagna. He was "astonished" that the Ten had not yet communicated their instructions on the matter. In the meeting with the pope and cardinals, he had consequently been able to say only that the Ten would do everything possible to prevent the Romagna from succumbing to Venice and that, if they thought the best way to achieve this was to support Borgia, he was certain they would. Soderini had apparently shared his doubts privately with Machiavelli, as indicated by their being shrouded in code: "What makes him hesitant about this matter of the duke is that he is himself uncertain about whether it is advantageous to have the duke nearby as signore of three or four of the [Romagnol] cities." If it were possible to trust him, it would be "most useful; but, knowing [Borgia's] dangerous nature, [Soderini] greatly fears that [the Florentines] would not be able to restrain him" and would face problems no different from what they would have if the Venetians controlled the region. Because "the people of the Romagnol cities have become Borgia's declared enemies [scoperti inimici]," Soderini feared that supporting him might hasten a Venetian takeover. The pope and cardinals wanted Borgia to leave immediately, but Soderini was not at all certain he would go, "because the duke appears to him to be unstable, vacillating, and fearful [vario, irresoluto e sospettoso], unable to hold firm to any decision, whether he is so by nature or whether these blows of fortune have stunned him [lo abbino stupefatto] and, being unaccustomed to receiving them, he is losing his way [vi si aggiri drento]." Another cardinal conveyed a similar judgment: "the duke seems to be out of his mind [pareva uscito del cervello]" and "so confused and indecisive [avviluppato e irresoluto] that he himself does not know what he wants to do" (*LCSG* 3.243.4–18).

On the same day, the 14th, although Machiavelli would not learn of it until the 18th, the Ten denied Borgia's request for safe passage through Florentine territory. They instructed Machiavelli to tell Julius and Rouen that "such a thing in no way pleases us, nor would it be tolerated by the people [dallo universale] of this city," because it would "revive the memory of his other passage [in May 1501] and cause everyone to relive the fear of his actions at that time" (*LCSG* 3.244.4–5). In a private letter to Machiavelli, Biagio Buonaccorsi wrote, in code, that Borgia's very name was an object of such hatred in Florence that, when the question of the safe-conduct was put to a vote in the Council of Eighty (which included more than eighty citizens, hence the higher vote totals), "around ninety" voted against it and "approximately twenty" in favor.[24] Machiavelli was to explain that the Ten's reason for denying Borgia the safe-conduct was to avoid any risky action that could "cause the peoples of the Romagna to throw themselves, out of sheer desperation, into the arms of the Venetians," and to inform Julius, privately, of Borgia's "nature" (or temperament: "qual sia la natura sua"), "about which you are well informed." Telling the pope what Borgia had blurted out a few days earlier about wanting the Romagna towns to be taken by the Venetians would demonstrate why Florence could not possibly want to have "una tal natura" nearby, unable as it would be to rely on him for very long. Machiavelli was also to tell Julius what Borgia's "intentions toward us have always been" (*LCSG* 3.244.6–10) and persuade him that, because sending Borgia to the Romagna as a bulwark against Venice was not a workable plan, the pope and Rouen should seek "some other safer solution" (*LCSG* 3.245.8–9). The Ten wanted Julius and Rouen to know that, by "evading the burden" of stopping the Venetians, they were allowing them to engage in operations

[24] *Lettere*, p. 175. The actual count was eighty-seven against: *Consulte e pratiche della Repubblica fiorentina, 1498–1505*, vol. 2, pp. 981–2.

"that will lead to their domination of Italy" ("che li conduce alla monarchia di Italia": the striking phrase, here used by the Ten, that Machiavelli would repeat in both the *Discourses* and the *Art of War*). Consequently, the Ten added, "we will focus on our own concerns and make the decisions that seem best to us. We now understand, given the sluggish and slow actions [of Julius and the French], that they have no desire to prevent this" (*LCSG* 3.246.5). Two days later, the Ten expressed more frustration and exasperation over papal and French inaction. Having learned of Borgia's "persistence in the same designs" and "the listless countermeasures" taken by the pope and France, the Ten were ever more of the opinion that nothing could stop the Venetians. They took solace in the conviction that they had done all they could to protect the Church's rights in the Romagna but declared they would no longer devote financial resources or exert themselves in the effort, especially as both Faenza and Forlì would soon be taken by Venice. Borgia, they concluded, "would not have arrived in time to recover the cities, even if he had flown [etiam se fussi volato], and as soon as they learned of his departure [from Rome] all those cities would have fallen to the Venetians" because "the inclination of their inhabitants to do what we predicted has continuously grown"—namely, to reject Borgia and take refuge under Venetian protection. Nor could the pope act in time to save Faenza unless he "immediately" sent a high-ranking prelate with a great deal of money to raise troops to resist the besieging Venetian army (*LCSG* 3.248.3–9). In Rome, according to Machiavelli, people continued to believe Borgia would depart within a matter of days. "All over Rome it is said he is going [to Florence] because he is your captain." Knowing this was not true, Machiavelli wryly commented that "every day his situation gives rise to fictions like this [simili novelle]" (*LCSG* 3.247.18).

Machiavelli told the Ten that Julius happily accepted Florence's denial of the safe-conduct ("la andava bene cosí"), which showed that "what previously was in doubt is now clear," namely, that to Julius "it seemed to take a thousand years to be rid of him [li paressi mill'anni di levarsilo d'inanzi]"—the last words in code, and the same expression Machiavelli had used in describing his own eagerness to get away from Borgia two weeks earlier. The pope was pleased because Florence's decision meant he did not have to rescind promises he made to Borgia, who therefore had no grounds to complain that Julius did not "keep faith" with him. Julius was pleased also that the possibility of using Borgia in the Romagna, if needed, was not entirely foreclosed. In any case, "it was of no concern to him [non se ne cura] what you [Florentines] or others might do against the duke." Julius predicted that, when Borgia realized he had been "abandoned" by Florence, he would have to hand over to the Church what little territory he still held, and the rest of the Romagna would easily fall back under papal rule. Expressing his gratitude to Florence for its opposition to Venetian ambitions, Julius acknowledged that he urged Borgia to return there "in order to push him away [from Rome]." "It was clear," Machiavelli concluded, "that the pope wants him to go" (*LCSG* 3.249.9–15).

On the same day Borgia summoned Machiavelli and subjected him to another tirade. Although aggrieved that Florence had not conceded the safe-conduct, he still hoped it would be waiting for him. He had already sent his cavalry toward Tuscany assuming they would be respectfully received by the Florentines. Claiming not to have anticipated this refusal, he said he found it difficult to understand why, given Florence's fear of Venetian ambitions in the Romagna, it rejected the assistance he was offering to hinder them. He threatened to accept Venice's offer to share control of the Romagna with him, which, he said, would inflict a mortal wound on Florence, literally "strike at your heart [vi offenderà infino al cuore]." Faced again with the task of deflecting Borgia's anger, Machiavelli replied that Florence had not actually denied the safe-conduct but wanted first to clarify its terms and conditions. He urged Borgia to send an envoy to Florence and assured him that "something good" would be worked out. Borgia was "partly satisfied." But he suspected the Ten were dithering, perhaps trying to trick him; if so, "he would ally with the Venetians and the devil and head to Pisa" (to disrupt Florentine operations there) "and would spend all the funds and deploy all the forces and alliances at his disposal to hurt you [Florentines]." Machiavelli assured the Ten that what he told Borgia about negotiating terms and working something out was "only to give him a little hope so he would not delay any longer and so that the pope would not have to ask you to give him the safe-conduct." The Ten could deal with Borgia's envoy as they wished, he suggested, even break off talks, and they should locate the duke's troops and disarm them (*LCSG* 3.249.16–27). Borgia left for the port of Ostia on November 19, "to the satisfaction of everyone in this city," intending to proceed to La Spezia and from there to the Romagna. Machiavelli feared he might be sufficiently angry at the Florentines to disembark at Pisa, "as he suggested to me the last time I spoke with him" (*LCSG* 3.251.3–7). The next day, he told the Ten that Borgia had sent 700 cavalry overland toward Tuscany and was also dispatching an envoy who carried Machiavelli's letter and another from Cardinal Soderini. In code, Machiavelli explained that the cardinal's letter was for show ("to satisfy," or placate, "him and for no other purpose"), "because the pope and Rouen would take it badly, to say the least, if the duke were given the safe-conduct" (*LCSG* 3.252.4–6). Borgia, however, got only as far as Ostia. On November 20 two of his closest collaborators decided not to join him there "so as not to partake of his ill fortune." Machiavelli believed that all the favors Borgia received from Julius and the French had as their main objective that "he go with God, the sooner the better." The Florentines, he added, were now free to deal with him in whatever way they deemed best. They could, if they thought it useful, assist him, "although the pope would like it better if you gave him the final push"—"se li dia la pinta," the *spinta* given by the executioner to one condemned to death by hanging.[25] While he

[25] The phrase is explained in *LCSG*, vol. 3, p. 383, n. 15. See also the entry for "pinta" in the *Grande dizionario della lingua italiana*, vol. 13, p. 501.

waited for the weather to clear for sailing, Borgia sent his troops toward Tuscany without guarantees of security from Florence or Siena or the Baglioni of Perugia, and "everyone here laughs at his situation [si ride de' casi sua]" (*LCSG* 3.253.14–20). The Ten confirmed that Borgia's return to the Romagna was not in Florence's interest, "now much less than before" (*LCSG* 3.254.12).

Julius's vacillations then took a new turn. Events in Faenza and the Romagna had kept him awake the previous night, he told Cardinal Soderini, and, "thinking it would be better to have the duke rather than the Venetians" in the Romagna, he now pondered the possibility of cooperating with Borgia to keep the Venetians away from the region's key fortresses. He asked Soderini to go to Ostia to work out the arrangements. Borgia agreed to the plan, but Julius then changed his mind and decided against it, only to re-embrace it ("if he doesn't change his mind again," Machiavelli commented with more than a hint of exasperation), believing it the most effective way of dealing with Venice. Machiavelli's account of these reversals highlights Julius's confusion and incoherence. Later in the dispatch he told the Ten "they should not hope that Julius or the French will stand up to Venice with either troops or financial resources," advising that Florence "should build its foundations on anything but the money and troops of others" (*LCSG* 3.256.10–14, 23). On November 23 he reported a rumor circulating in Rome, allegedly from a reliable source, according to which Borgia refused the part of the plan that required him to hand over the Romagna fortresses to the pope and that Julius, "angered" by this, ordered Borgia's arrest and detention "as his prisoner" (*LCSG* 3.263.16). The next day Machiavelli confirmed that Borgia had indeed been arrested and was on a French ship. "It is not believed [Julius] will do him further harm for now, nor is it known for certain that the pope has ordered Borgia's soldiers to be disarmed, but it is assumed [it will happen] in the nature of things, because"—and this in code—"they are heading [to Tuscany] without a safe-conduct" (*LCSG* 3.264.20–1). Referring to his dispatches of the preceding days, on November 26 Machiavelli wrote: "I told you that the duke had already played out all his roles [aveva fatto oggimai tutti gli atti suoi]" (reading "atti" as the acts of a play, as if to say: the comedy is finished). He was now at the pope's mercy. There was even a rumor—false as it turned out—that Julius had him thrown into the Tiber: "I cannot confirm or refute it, [but] I believe that, if it isn't true, it will be." Machiavelli offers here his famous cutting judgment of Julius: "one sees that the pope is beginning to repay his debts most honorably by cancelling them with the cotton of his inkwell [li cancella con la bambagia del calamaio]." The debts are the promises he had made to anyone and everyone with influence in Rome, Borgia included, in order to secure his election. Cotton removes ink from paper, and the image of Julius erasing the ink from documents conveys Machiavelli's sense of the ease with which the pope made promises and debts disappear. As for Borgia, "whether he is dead or alive, now that he has been captured there is no longer any need to think about his affairs" (*LCSG* 3.268.4–7).

At the end of November, Julius was searching for a way to seize control of the Romagna fortresses. Borgia was reputed to have support in Imola, and his castellan in Forlì was determined to remain loyal for as long as he knew the duke was alive (*LCSG* 3.271.11). The Ten, who still had no confirmation of Borgia's arrest, met with his envoy, who offered "justifications for past things" (as Borgia himself had done in October 1502 in Imola) and conveyed the duke's "firm wish for an alliance with this city," a condotta as "captain" of Florence's armies, and safe-conduct for his troops. The Ten explained to Machiavelli that they negotiated with the envoy only to put him off until they had confirmation of Borgia's arrest which would render even the pretense of further negotiation pointless. Upon learning that Borgia's troops had been disarmed and neutralized, the Ten wrote that "we could not be more pleased at the direction events in the Romagna are beginning to take" (*LCSG* 3.270.3–7). No doubt they were even more pleased when Machiavelli's dispatch of the 28th brought word that Julius had ordered the papal guard to bring Borgia back to Rome from Ostia. It was now clear, Machiavelli said, that the pope intended to deal with Borgia "a ferri puliti"—swords drawn, figuratively, without camouflaging his intention to neutralize him. Machiavelli added, using religious language rather unusual for him, that Borgia's "sins have step by step brought him to *penitenza*"—which here hovers between penance for sins and punishment for crimes. "May God let matters be resolved for the best" (*LCSG* 3.271.4–8). The next day Machiavelli reported that the pope's guard returned from Ostia with Borgia under arrest. Remnants of his infantry limped back to Rome, and his "gentiluomini will have to return to their homes" (*LCSG* 3.274.8–10). "Since I've been here, the duke's situation has undergone a thousand changes," Machiavelli wrote on November 30, "always for the worse [sono sempre ite alla ingiú]" (*LCSG* 3.275.14). Three days later he wrote: "thus it seems that, little by little, the duke is slipping into his tomb [a poco a poco sdruccioli nello avello]" (*LCSG* 3.281.6–8). In the custody of the pope's guard Borgia was treated with formal courtesy, although one rumor had it that Julius would soon have him confined in the Castel Sant'Angelo (*LCSG* 3.284.21–2; *LCSG* 3.289.7–8). At the end of December, the Spanish army commanded by the viceroy Consalvo inflicted the historic defeat on the French at the Garigliano river that sealed Spain's conquest of Naples and the South. Spanish influence in Rome consequently increased and permitted Borgia's release in April 1504, after the Romagna fortresses had been secured by papal forces. Borgia went to Naples expecting Consalvo to help him recover his lost dominions, but King Ferdinand of Spain, who saw Borgia as an obstacle to his alliance with Julius, ordered his arrest and had him deported to Spain, where he died in 1507.

The troops Borgia sent into Tuscany, led by the notorious don Michele, entered Florentine territory near Cortona at the end of November and were quickly set upon and disarmed by the local inhabitants; don Michele was handed over to the Florentine podestà in Castiglion Fiorentino (*LCSG* 3.276.4–5). Julius, who wanted him sent to Rome, expressed great pleasure that his capture would provide the "opportunity to reveal all the cruelties committed against God and men over the past eleven years [of the Borgia pontificate], the robberies, murders, sacrilegious acts, and infinite other evils" (*LCSG* 3.277.13–16). "Smiling," he said "he wanted to talk to [don Michele] to learn some things from him about how better to govern the Church" (*LCSG* 3.281.4). One imagines he knew that Machiavelli appreciated the joke. Julius and his court were in high spirits on December 6, as he and "tutta Roma" were waiting "con una grandissima festa" for don Michele; "they would like him to be here on Sunday to parade him before the triumph [per poterlo menare innanzi al trionfo]; but they'll take him at any time and he'll be welcome whenever" he arrives (*LCSG* 3.284.10). The "triumph" was the procession to San Paolo fuori le mura, scheduled for the Sunday following the *possesso* of the basilica of San Giovanni in Laterano (*LCSG* 3.282.8; *LCSG* 3.284.7–8). Had he arrived in time, don Michele would have been paraded as a prisoner and living symbol of Julius's triumph over the Borgias, much as captured prisoners of war were forced to march in ancient Roman triumphal processions. On December 8 the Ten told Machiavelli they could not make a decision about surrendering don Michele because their six-month term of office was about to expire and they had not yet interrogated him to their satisfaction (*LCSG* 3.288.5–6). Machiavelli gently chided them "con reverenzia," urging them to reply to Julius and "conclude this matter in a way that confirms the Pontiff still more in good will" toward Florence (*LCSG* 3.290.8–9). The Ten quickly reversed course and sent don Michele to Rome. Julius was "extraordinarily pleased," as Machiavelli informed the Ten on December 16 (*LCSG* 3.294.9), the last day of the legation.

PRINCE 7: "E LUI MI DISSE"

Endlessly repeated opinions to the contrary notwithstanding, Machiavelli's direct experience of Cesare Borgia persuaded him that he was failure—a self-destructive and, in the end, pathetic failure. In Machiavelli's judgment, Borgia's attempt to create a state in central Italy was fatally flawed by the lack of his own arms, a destructive relationship with untrustworthy mercenaries (much like himself), overweening ambition, and debilitating dependence on two powerful masters, his papal father and the king of France. Close attention to Machiavelli's observations of Borgia and the menace he represented render highly problematic readings that profess to see an admiring portrait in chapter 7 of *The Prince*.[26] To claim that Machiavelli saw him as the model of the "principe nuovo" called for in the work's last chapter

[26] There are exceptions: a good one is by Erica Benner, *Machiavelli's* Prince: *A New Reading* (Oxford: Oxford University Press, 2013), pp. 89–110, which perceptively interprets the portrait of Borgia as saturated with irony.

one must ignore what he had seen and knew of Borgia. Yet chapter 7 seems to say some positive things about him: that he did everything a "prudente e virtuoso" man "had to do to put down roots [barbe] in territories [stati] that the arms and fortune of others had given him" and, in so doing, "established strong foundations [grandi fondamenti] for his future power" (*P* 7.7). Machiavelli thinks it "not superfluous" to discuss these foundations because he "would not know what better precepts to give a new prince than the example of [Borgia's] deeds" (*P* 7.9). The problem is that Borgia never did put down those "roots" or establish those solid "foundations," as should be clear from the stunning and irreversible suddenness with which he lost his "stati" and his power evaporated after Alexander died. At first, Machiavelli acknowledges this failure only tangentially with a curious euphemism of inadequate benefit or profit: "and if his methods did not benefit him [e se gli ordini sua non gli profittorno], it was not his fault because it resulted from an inordinate and exceptional malice of fortune [una estraordinaria ed estrema malignità di fortuna]" (*P* 7.9). Although this appears to exculpate Borgia, chapter 7 demonstrates that he never acquired adequate arms and never escaped reliance on papal and French power. His failure is here attributed to the "malice of fortune," but the rest of the chapter amply illustrates more concrete weaknesses.

Machiavelli's analysis of Borgia's failure begins by noting that Alexander's ambition to make his "young son [figliuolo]" the "signore" of "some territory [alcuno stato]" was hampered by many obstacles ("assai difficultà"). First, the undertaking was possible only within the papal states of which Alexander was nominal sovereign. But both Milan and Venice were strongly opposed to it because parts of these papal territories were either under their "protection" or within their spheres of influence. Another problem was that "Italian arms, especially those of which [Borgia] could avail himself," were in the hands of those who feared any expansion of papal power—arms Borgia "could therefore not trust"—specifically the Roman baronial families, the Orsini, Colonna, "and their allies [complici]" (*P* 7.10–12). "Complici" might refer either to followers of the Orsini and Colonna or to local warrior lords who had de facto control of cities within the papal states, like the Baglioni of Perugia and the Vitelli of Città di Castello. Either way, Borgia started with this weakness: with no arms of his own, he depended on soldiers for hire, mostly from within the papal states, who had no interest in the prospect of a more powerful pope whose son wanted to oust and replace them. "It was therefore necessary to disrupt these arrangements [ordini] and unsettle the states of Italy [some manuscripts have "di coloro"—the baronial families] in order to gain secure control over some [parte] of them" (*P* 7.13). Whether Machiavelli meant control over the Orsini and Colonna or over parts of the Milanese and Venetian states is unclear.

The opportunity came with Louis XII's invasion in 1499, supported by both Alexander and Venice, the former seeking military assistance for his son's ambitions in the Romagna, the latter hoping, as Machiavelli says in the chapter on

Louis's Italian policy, to acquire half of "Lombardy" with the collapse of the Sforza duchy (*P* 3.32). In return for Alexander's support, Louis gave Cesare the troops he needed (*P* 7.15). With the Romagna "acquired" and the "Colonna defeated" (Machiavelli does not say how or where the Colonna were "sbattuti"), Borgia wanted to "proceed further." But "two things stood in his way": first, his military forces, especially the Orsini, did not "seem loyal"; second, Louis had his own ambitions in Italy: either could threaten Borgia's conquests or prevent further expansion. Orsini disloyalty was confirmed when, after seizing Faenza (in early 1501) and advancing on Bologna, he saw them "go cold." When he "attacked Tuscany"—Machiavelli assumes Borgia was the originator of Vitellozzo Vitelli's 1502 occupation of Arezzo and the Valdichiana—Louis forced him to withdraw (*P* 7.16–17). These rebuffs made Borgia "decide no longer to depend on the arms and fortune of others." In Machiavelli's narrative, Borgia comes to this realization fully three years after launching his campaigns. He "weakened the Orsini and Colonna factions in Rome" by luring away all their "aderenti [allies, followers] who were gentili uomini [nobles], making them his own gentili uomini" and giving them stipends and contracts ("condotte") (*P* 7.18). Machiavelli says Borgia wanted to destroy the Orsini leadership, and the opportunity came when they and his other condottieri formed the Magione conspiracy, "from which resulted the rebellion of Urbino [against Borgia], tumults in the Romagna, and countless dangers for the duke, all of which he overcame with the help of the French" (*P* 7.19–20). The reader may ask where—and if—in all this Borgia ceased to be "dependent on the arms and fortune of others." In any event, "because he no longer trusted France or other outside forces, he resorted to deceit [inganni]" (*P* 7.21), tricking the Orsini into a sham reconciliation and letting their naiveté ("simplicità") lead them to their doom in Senigallia.

By eliminating the conspirators and making their "complici" his allies, Machiavelli writes, Borgia "had laid very good foundations for his power, possessing the whole of the Romagna and the duchy of Urbino, and above all because it seemed to him [parendoli] that he had made the Romagna friendly to himself and won over its people because they began to enjoy their well-being." Commenting that this "is worthy of note and imitation by others," Machiavelli moves back in time and says that, when Borgia conquered the region, "he found it ruled by incompetent lords who despoiled their subjects more than they disciplined [corretti] them and gave them cause for discord rather than unity, such that the entire region was full of thievery, conflicts, and every sort of arrogance [insolenzia]." So "he decided it was necessary, in order to make the region peaceful and obedient to his supreme power [al braccio regio], to give it good government. He therefore appointed messer Ramiro de Lorqua, a cruel and inflexible man, and gave him full powers. In a short time [Ramiro] pacified and united the region," Machiavelli adds, "to great acclaim" (*P* 7.22–5), presumably for Borgia, although this seems difficult to reconcile with what follows.

The only way Machiavelli could have known of Borgia's assessment of conditions in the Romagna when it came under his control, and therefore the rationale behind his appointment of Ramiro, is from having heard these things from Borgia himself. Machiavelli echoes Borgia's own account of the motivations behind the appointment. This is an important turning point in the chapter, which, to this point (aside from the alleged "decision no longer to depend on the arms and fortune of others"), recounts events known to contemporaries. But from here on, it is Borgia's voice that we hear through Machiavelli's words—his own justifications of his actions, his strategies for the future, and his explanations for why it all failed. The assertion that Ramiro pacified and united the Romagna can only be, again, Borgia's opinion, which is, moreover, contradicted by Borgia's "judgment" in the next sentence "that such excessive power [autorità] was not necessary because he feared it would become hateful" (itself a non sequitur). We now learn that the alleged attempt to pacify and unify the region brought hatred rather than acclaim. To counter this hatred, Machiavelli writes, Borgia instituted a civil court "in which every city would have a representative" (*P* 7.26). As Machiavelli knew, the Ruota, instituted in October 1502, began functioning only in June 1503. If, as must be the case, Borgia said these things to Machiavelli during the legation, hence no later than January 1503, he can only have been expressing a hope or expectation that the new court would deflect the hatred aroused by Ramiro's "excessive power." In the meantime, "recognizing that [Ramiro's] brutal measures had generated some hatred against himself," Borgia implemented a second remedy: "to purge the minds of the people [of this hatred] and completely win them over, he wanted to show that, if there had been any cruelty, it came not from him but from the merciless nature of his minister" and therefore had him killed. Borgia's account of Ramiro's role contains an underlying incoherence: he pacified and unified the region to "great acclaim" but also generated hatred against Borgia through his severities. Borgia hoped that the "savageness [ferocità]" of the spectacle of Ramiro's body laid out in two pieces in the piazza of Cesena would leave the people feeling "both satisfied and stunned" (*P* 7.27–8). But did the people believe the Romagna had actually been pacified and unified? Where and how, amidst Ramiro's cruelties, did they "taste" any "well-being"? Did the duke's "ferocità" cancel the minister's "crudeltà"? The passage reproduces the contradictory rationalizations of a political actor unsure of how to justify his actions.[27]

Machiavelli puts aside the loose threads and unresolved questions of Borgia's Romagna policy and announces a "return to where we started"—to before the discussion of how Borgia allegedly brought "good government" to the Romagna. He "was very powerful and partly protected against present dangers, because he

[27] Michael McCanles similarly sees Machiavelli reproducing Cesare's own "discourse," including "his rationalization of his downfall," in *The Discourse of* Il Principe (Malibu: Undena Publications: 1983), pp. 70–85 (at 74).

had armed himself in his own way [a suo modo] and mostly eliminated the arms [of the conspirators] that could have attacked him." But we are not told which arms—what kind or how many—Borgia now had "a suo modo" that he had not previously had. Machiavelli knew he often exaggerated his strength and displayed an arrogant self-confidence that masked insecurity. His remaining concern, Machiavelli says, was the king of France, who, Borgia "knew," now realized his "error" in having supported him and would not allow him to seize more territory. So the duke began to "seek new alliances" and to "waver [vacillare] with the French" in his obligation to join them "in their advance toward Naples against the Spaniards."[28] He wanted to secure himself against the French (we are not told how), and "would have quickly succeeded if Alexander had still been alive" (*P* 7.29–30).

Machiavelli now separates what Borgia did "with regard to present matters" from how he intended to manage "future things" (*P* 7.31–2). Because Machiavelli was writing a decade after these events, this curious division between "present" and "future" things only makes sense if the assumed vantage point from which Borgia's career is being viewed is just after the murders of Ramiro and the conspirators, presumably January, 1503, when Machiavelli had many long conversations with Cesare who was, seemingly, at the height of his power. The "now" of chapter 7, the division between "present/past" and "future," is situated in the moment in which Borgia, having destroyed the conspiracy, made bold plans for the "future"—plans he never succeeded in implementing.

With regard to "future things," Machiavelli says Borgia had to confront a "first worry," namely, the possibility that his father's successor "might not be his ally [amico] and might try to deprive him of what Alexander had given him." Borgia sought to protect himself against this eventuality in four ways, Machiavelli says, here again, and more directly, echoing what Borgia told him. His four plans were, first, to "eliminate" the families of the "signori" he had ousted to prevent a future pope from reinstating them; second, to win over all the "gentili uomini" of Rome in order to restrain the new pope; third, to gain as much influence as he could in the College of Cardinals (to make it "as much his as he could"); and fourth, to acquire a large enough territorial state ("acquistare tanto imperio") before Alexander died so as to be able, on his own, to repulse any attack (*P* 7.33). The next sentence—"When Alexander died, [Cesare] had achieved three of these things and nearly accomplished the fourth"—can only be Borgia's own and exaggerated assessment, because Machiavelli well knew that, neither by January nor by August 1503, when Alexander died, had Borgia achieved the first or third aim,

[28] This may refer to a plan attributed to Borgia in the *Diario* of Biagio Buonaccorsi, ed. Niccolini, pp. 133–5 and 280, according to which, in the summer of 1503, he intended to lag behind the French army as it passed through Tuscany on its way south, thus putting himself beyond the reach of the French and having a free hand to attack Florence. Inglese quotes the passage in his edition of *Il principe*, pp. 47–8. As discussed above (pp. 135–6), Machiavelli and the Ten evidently did not take the threat seriously.

and that the claim of having nearly accomplished the fourth was a complete fantasy. About the first, Machiavelli says Borgia "killed as many of the dispossessed signori as he could get his hands on" (*P* 7.34). He may have said this, but only two were killed, the others escaped, and most of these returned to their cities after his downfall. As for the second objective, he had already lured many of Rome's "gentili uomini" into his camp (*P* 7.18), who then, however, abandoned him when he most needed them in late 1503. About the third aim, although the Spanish cardinals were his allies at the outset, he had no choice but to release them to vote for his mortal enemy, Giuliano della Rovere.

But it is especially the allegedly "nearly accomplished" fourth goal—becoming "lord of Tuscany"—that Machiavelli knew was not only not "nearly accomplished" but also delusional: "With regard to new acquisitions, he aimed [aveva disegnato] to become signore of Tuscany; he already possessed Perugia and Piombino and had taken Pisa under his protection (*P* 7.34). Perugia, which Borgia had seized from Giampaolo Baglioni (one of the conspirators), was in the papal states, not Tuscany. Borgia took Piombino, an independent principality on the Tuscan coast, from the ruling family of the Appiani in 1501. The Pisans, tenaciously fighting to preserve their independence, made a formal agreement to submit to Pope Alexander just before he died, but it was never implemented and Borgia had no realistic way of putting significant forces into Pisan territory. As already noted, Machiavelli and the Ten had calmly rejected the concern in early August 1503 that Borgia might attack the Florentine dominion. The notion of becoming "signore di Toscana" emerged from the rantings of an overly ambitious, inadequately armed, and increasingly desperate warlord who had lost the support of the French and alternated between threatening Florence and begging for an alliance. Machiavelli represents this fantasy as follows: "as soon as he no longer had to be concerned about France—which he did not have to be because the French had already been deprived of the kingdom [of Naples] by the Spaniards, such that both [France and Spain] were forced to buy his friendship—he was about to jump into Pisa." In fact, neither France nor Spain had any intention or need to "buy" his friendship. The fantasy continues: "After that, Lucca and Siena would immediately yield, partly from hatred [invidia] of the Florentines, partly from fear [of Borgia]. And the Florentines would have no escape [rimedio]. And if he had succeeded [in becoming signore of Tuscany]—which he was about to do in the very year Alexander died—he would have gained enough strength and prestige to stand on his own and would no longer have depended [per sé stesso si sarebbe retto e non sarebbe piú dependuto] on the fortune and arms of others, but on his own power and virtú" (*P* 7.35–7). Only after all these imagined "future" victories and conquests, Machiavelli writes, would Borgia have acquired the "strength and prestige to stand on his own." But with whose arms would he have been able to seize (or "pacify") Tuscany if he did not yet have his own arms?

Of course the grand plan failed, because it was a fantasy, not a plan. Machiavelli says it failed because—but this is surely Borgia's plaintive voice—his father died too soon, leaving him "with only the stato of Romagna stabilized [assolidato]" (in view of the uprisings immediately after Alexander's death, Machiavelli knew, as we do, that the Romagna was in no way "stabilized"), "with all the other [territories] shaky [in aria], between two very powerful and hostile armies" (of Spain and France), and he himself "deathly ill" (*P* 7.38)—although he recovered very quickly. The rationalizations continue: Borgia's "fearlessness [ferocità] and virtú" were so great and his "foundations so strong" that, "if he had not had those armies [of France and Spain] arrayed against him or if he had been well, he would have overcome every difficulty." But were we not just told that he no longer had to worry about France and Spain, both allegedly trying to "buy" his friendship? As evidence of his "strong foundations," Machiavelli says "the Romagna waited for him more than a month" (*P* 7.38–40). The claim that a month is evidence of loyalty must be sardonic. Borgia no doubt wanted to believe that they "waited for him," but many cities did not wait even a month. As early as mid-September, some towns were asking to come under Florentine protection (see above, p. 124). The chronicler Bartolomeo Cerretani confirms this, recounting that, in late September, when the Florentines sent Giovanbattista Ridolfi to Faenza, "he found not only the people of Faenza, but the whole of the Romagna prepared to throw themselves into the lap of our rule [voltta al gittarssi in grembbo alla nostra signoria]" and become part of the Florentine dominion.[29] The Florentines helped the Ordelaffi regain Forlì, and in quick succession Guidobaldo da Montefeltro was back in Urbino, the Vitelli in Città di Castello, the Appiani in Piombino, and the Baglioni in Perugia. Uprisings against Borgia's rule spread throughout the Romagna and the Marche, and by the end of October only the fortresses of Cesena and Imola were still under the control of his castellans. However much Cesare was inclined to "magnificare le cose sue," as Machiavelli wrote in early September, his "foundations" were actually very weak.

Borgia's voice—which now fully occupies this part of chapter 7—makes more claims for "solid foundations," declaring that he "remained secure in Rome" and that, "although he could not arrange the election of the pope he wanted, he was at least able to prevent the election of one he did not want." This too was clearly not so. Julius destroyed him within a month, but even Pius III had already denied him the funds he needed and detained him in Castel Sant'Angelo. At this point Machiavelli directly introduces Borgia's voice: "and if he had been well during Alexander's fatal illness, everything would have been easy for him. And he told me—*e lui mi disse*—that in the days when Julius was elected, he had thought of everything that could happen at his father's death and for everything had found a solution, except that he never thought that, as his father was dying, he too would

[29] Cerretani, *Storia fiorentina*, ed. Berti, p. 325.

be at death's door" (*P* 7.40–1). The problem with blaming his illness is that, by the time of Julius's election on November 1, Borgia had long since recovered. Alexander's death removed the foundation of his power; Cesare's illness was not the cause of his downfall. Machiavelli's representation of what Borgia told him suggests how, in his agitated state in early November, he grasped desperately for an explanation that concealed his own shortcomings.

At the end of the chapter, Machiavelli returns to fulsome praise of Borgia, or seems to: "Considering all his deeds, I would not know how to reproach him; on the contrary, I think it appropriate to propose him as one to be imitated by all who rise to power through fortune and the arms of others." *Through fortune and the arms of others*: Machiavelli here underscores the foundational flaw of Borgia's attempt to create a new state—the lack of his own arms and unceasing dependence on others. In a double-edged characterization, he says Borgia "could not have acted differently," because of his "animo grande" and "intenzione alta" (*P* 7.42). This can perhaps be read positively as denoting great courage and noble intentions. But these characterizations echo Sallust's portrait of Catiline whose "vastus animus"—insatiable ambition—"always lusted after the extravagant, the unbelievable, things out of reach [inmoderata incredibilia nimis alta]," and whose "animus ferox"—untamable spirit (echoed in Borgia's "ferocità" at 7.39)—became "more agitated every day" (*Catilina* 5.5–7).

Machiavelli then itemizes the tasks necessary for a "principato nuovo" and claims that one "cannot find more accessible [freschi: ripe, ready] examples than Borgia's deeds." Here is the list (*P* 7.43), with brief notes on what Borgia actually accomplished with regard to each task:

- "Gain security against enemies and win friends." He was never secure against the enmity of Pope Julius or the signori he dispossessed. His security vis-à-vis the conspirators in 1502 was achieved by murdering some of them, but those who survived had the last laugh. As for winning friends, he never succeeded in persuading Florence to ally with him.
- "Conquer either by force or fraud." The force behind his early conquests was supplied by others. He took Urbino by stealth and deceived the conspirators into the trap in Senigallia. Neither fraud nor force worked against Florence and he himself fell victim to Julius's "fraude."
- "Make oneself loved and feared by the populations [of acquired territories]." Despite his wishful thinking about having won the friendship of the Romagnol people, Borgia made himself, his rule, and especially his all-powerful minister Ramiro de Lorqua hated.
- "Make oneself followed and respected by hired soldiers [soldati]." His condottieri feared and conspired against him; later his hired troops refused to fight because they saw his power crumbling.

- "Eliminate those who can, or must, do you harm." He eliminated four of the conspirators, but not all the Orsini or the families of the signori he dispossessed. He was helpless against Julius.
- "Renovate old institutions with new ones." The civic tribunal (Ruota) was his only institutional innovation, and it was too little, too late. He never raised a reliable militia.
- "Be severe and well-liked, magnanimous and generous [liberale]." Borgia let messer Ramiro practice severity, then killed him to escape its consequences. Are there any instances of magnanimity and generosity?
- "Disband disloyal military units and create new ones." Borgia eliminated his disloyal condottieri, but he continued to rely on mercenaries and auxiliaries as much as any ruler or state in Italy, possibly more.
- "Maintain the friendship of kings and princes so they will gladly do you favors and only reluctantly do you harm." Borgia's actions caused Louis to rein him in on several occasions, and neither Louis nor Ferdinand of Spain rescued him when his power collapsed.

Borgia failed to accomplish adequately any of these objectives, and in the end the reader wonders of what, precisely, Borgia is an example worthy of imitation. Not of success, evidently. Is he an example of the most that can be achieved by one who relies on fortune and the arms of others? Or, more likely, of the ineluctable failure of those who attempt to gain and govern states without adequate arms of their own? The "only" thing, Machiavelli concludes, for which one can blame Borgia was the "bad choice [mala elezione]" he made in the election of Pope Julius:[30] "If he could not make a pope of his own liking, he could have prevented the election of one not to his liking; and he should never have allowed the election of any cardinal he had offended or who might have reason to fear him if elected." Machiavelli mentions some of those he had offended, and at the top of the list is Giuliano della Rovere. "He should first of all have had a Spaniard elected, or, if this was not possible, he should have agreed to [the election of] Rouen," not Della Rovere, because "he deceives himself who believes that recent favors make powerful figures [personaggi grandi] forget old injuries. So the duke erred in this choice, and that was the cause of his final ruin" (*P* 7.45–9). But Machiavelli knew Borgia could have done none of these things, because he himself made the deal with Julius to swing the support of the Spanish cardinals to him in return for promises Julius never kept. Did Borgia know he could no more have prevented Julius's election than he could have arranged the election of a Spanish cardinal? He lacked the strength and influence to effect such choices, because, as Machiavelli knew but Borgia failed ever to acknowledge, he was utterly dependent on the

[30] On the election: Christine Shaw, *Julius II: The Warrior Pope* (Oxford: Blackwell, 1993), pp. 117–25.

arms—and the votes—of others and, hence, on fortune. Once elected, Julius cancelled his promises and quickly pushed Borgia to oblivion. Machiavelli gives two, only apparently divergent, explanations of Borgia's downfall—the "malice of fortune" and the "bad choice" of "allowing" Julius's elevation to the papacy, which in reality was not his choice. The two interpretations are not contradictory: they converge on the same fatal condition of dependence that Cesare never seriously sought to overcome by building, with his own arms, a state with genuinely strong foundations. He is an example of the failure to escape the lack of autonomy that Machiavelli calls fortune.

4
The Papacy and Julius II

"FOR OUR LACK OF UNITY WE ITALIANS ARE INDEBTED TO THE CHURCH"

Machiavelli's discussions of the Church—the Roman papacy and cardinals—mostly concern its role as one of Italy's five "powers," its governance of the States of the Church in central Italy, and the baneful influence of the popes and their families on Italian politics. He commented often, if sporadically, on these topics in dispatches from the legations to Cesare Borgia, in the *Decennali*, occasional memoranda, and, as we shall see in this chapter, in dispatches from the legations to Julius II in 1503 and 1506 and to the French court in 1510, when Julius was the central issue of Machiavelli's negotiations with King Louis and his ministers. Machiavelli's first analytical treatment of the Church, in chapter 11 of *The Prince*, reveals the heavy weight of these experiences. The "ecclesiastical principalities" analyzed in this chapter—actually just one such principality—are the last in the taxonomy of princely states discussed in *The Prince*. The chapter opens with the ironic observation that ecclesiastical principalities, although "acquired either by virtú or by fortune, are maintained by neither the one nor the other," but rather by the "venerable institutions [ordini antiquati] of religion, which have been so strong that they keep their rulers [principi: the popes] secure in their power no matter how they live or conduct themselves." Hence, "they alone have territories [stati] and do not defend them; they have subjects and do not govern them. Their territories, though undefended, are not taken from them; their subjects, though not governed, are not troubled by it; they neither think about breaking free, nor are they able to." For all these reasons "only these principalities are secure and happy" (*P* 11.1–4). Except for the notion that religious traditions and the prestige of the papacy helped to keep the popes in power and preserve the papal states (at least on paper), none of this was true, as Machiavelli well knew. The "venerable institutions of religion" did not prevent rebellions (in the *Florentines Histories*, 6.29, Machiavelli discusses the 1453 conspiracy of Stefano Porcari against Nicholas V), attempted assassinations, or the violence of the baronial families, Orsini and Colonna, that often drove the popes from Rome to seek refuge elsewhere. Some popes did defend their territories or tried to, usually with military forces not their own and with very mixed results. And, although they never established unitary governance over their disparate territories, they did—precisely in the years in which Machiavelli observed it up close—establish tighter

Machiavelli's Broken World. John M. Najemy, Oxford University Press. © John M. Najemy 2022.
DOI: 10.1093/oso/9780199580927.003.0004

control over major cities within their dominions that had long enjoyed de facto self-government. The opening sentences of chapter 11 express Machiavelli's underlying contempt for the Church as a governing and political entity, a contempt whose deeper reasons he will elaborate in the *Discourses on Livy* and the *Florentine Histories.* The alleged immunity of ecclesiastical principalities to the forces of history and the vagaries of power derives, he says, from their being "sustained by superior causes inaccessible to the human mind"; "because they are created and maintained by God, it would be the act of a presumptuous and reckless man to discuss them." This is Machiavelli's usual (one is tempted to say ritual) gesture of respect for the mysteries of religion, by which he takes his distance from theological and supernatural explanations. Yet he immediately asserts that there are other causes of the Church's power that can indeed be analyzed and discussed. He imagines a reader asking how it happened that the Church, which, before the pontificate of Alexander VI, was little esteemed not only by Italy's major powers ("potentati") but even by minor barons and signori, came to such "power [grandezza]" in temporal matters that it now makes "a king of France tremble and is able to expel him from Italy and destroy the Venetians" (*P* 11.4–5). This recent and dramatic reversal in the Church's stature, Machiavelli implies, needs to be understood in history, as the product of ambition, power, and corruption.

Before the French invaded Italy, Machiavelli writes, Italy was "under the power [imperio] of the pope, the Venetians, the king of Naples, the duke of Milan, and the Florentines"—the five major states that, as he assumes his readers know, had created the Lega Italica of 1455. These "potentati" had two chief concerns: keeping foreign armies out of Italy, and preventing any one of them from occupying more territory ("piú stato"). The two that gave most cause for concern—the states that, according to Machiavelli, the others thought most likely to contravene these agreements and throw the system into crisis—were Venice and the papacy. Venetian expansion on the Italian mainland had been steady throughout the fifteenth century, and the rest of Italy feared its continuation. Containing Venice, Machiavelli says, required the concerted effort of the other states, as happened, he adds, in the War of Ferrara (of 1482–4; see Chapter 2). To hold the papacy in check, on the other hand, the other states relied on the "barons of Rome," who, divided as they were into the factions of the Orsini and Colonna families, created constant strife and, being well armed, kept the popes "weak and vulnerable." Occasionally, a bold ("animoso") pope ascended the throne: Machiavelli cites Sixtus IV (Francesco della Rovere, r. 1471–84), who, as he did not need to remind his readers, had orchestrated the Pazzi conspiracy against the Medici and promoted the political aspirations of several nephews, one of whom, Giuliano della Rovere, became Pope Julius II. In the *Florentine Histories* (7.31.1–3) Machiavelli recalls that (in 1474) Sixtus, wishing to subject all the cities of the States of the Church to papal authority, punished two of them for rebelling against their papal overlord. He had Spoleto sacked and Città di Castello besieged (in both cases by nephew Giuliano, although Machiavelli does not mention this). Yet, as Machiavelli says in *Prince* 11, neither fortune nor cleverness ("il sapere") could free the papacy from the constraints imposed by the short duration of papal reigns, which lasted "on average ten years." Consequently, there was no consistent policy toward the factions: if a pope weakened one faction, his successor might favor that faction and weaken the other. "Hence the temporal power of the papacy was scarcely respected in Italy" (*P* 11.6–11). The warring Roman noble families and the absence of continuity from one pontificate to the next prevented the papacy from constructing a stable state, or even keeping Rome peaceful.

This all changed, Machiavelli claims, with the papacy of Alexander VI (Rodrigo Borgia), "who, of all the pontiffs" in the Church's long history, "showed how much a pope could enhance his power with money and military forces." Through his son Cesare, whom Machiavelli here dubs the pope's "instrumento" (his agent or tool), and with the "opportunity" provided by the French invasion (of 1499), Alexander "accomplished all the things I discuss above [in chapter 7] concerning the actions of the duke. And, although Alexander's intention was to make the duke [Cesare] powerful, not the Church, what he did redounded nonetheless to the power [grandezza] of the Church, which, after his death, and once the duke was eliminated [spento il duca], was the heir to [Alexander's] labors" (*P* 11.12–13).

"Then came Pope Julius." Machiavelli omits to say that Alexander and Julius were mortal enemies. Because of his emphasis on the expanding power of the Church, he makes it, not Julius, the "heir" to Alexander's efforts. But the transfer of this legacy depended on Cesare's elimination, and this, as Machiavelli knew from having witnessed it (see Chapter 3), was Julius's accomplishment. Alexander prepared the way for Julius, who found the Church powerful ("grande"), Machiavelli writes, because of two factors: first, "all the Romagna" had come under its control (an assertion that overlooks Venice's occupation of several of the Romagna cities for a number of years after Cesare's removal); and second, Alexander had destroyed ("spenti") the "baroni di Roma" and "reduced to nothing their factions." Again, not quite so. Alexander had indeed been hostile to both the Colonna and the Orsini, particularly the latter, several of whom he and Cesare had had killed and dispossessed of vast properties. But Julius restored the Orsini lands, married his daughter, Felice, to Gian Giordano Orsini,[1] and established good relations with the Colonna, especially Fabrizio, who commanded a unit in the papal army and later, in 1511, became governor-general of the army of the Holy League that Julius assembled to drive France from Italy. Machiavelli may have had in mind the diminished ability of these families and their factions to disrupt papal policies or Rome itself during Julius's pontificate, but the "baroni di Roma" were by no means "extinguished" under, or by, Julius. What really linked the two pontificates was the

[1] Caroline P. Murphy, *The Pope's Daughter: The Extraordinary Life of Felice della Rovere* (Oxford: Oxford University Press, 2005), pp. 79–86.

system of amassing financial resources: Julius "found the way open for a method of accumulating funds that had never been used before Alexander." Without naming or describing this "method"—there was good reason not to—Machiavelli was alluding to simony, the sale of Church offices. Although previous popes had engaged in this practice, Machiavelli's exaggerated claim that it had "never been used before Alexander" calls attention to the greater scale of such traffic during these two pontificates and thus places a cloud over the methods they employed to make the Church "great." By expanding this practice, Julius was able to launch his campaigns to "take Bologna, extinguish [spegnere] the Venetians, and drive the French out of Italy" (*P* 11.14–17). Highlighting the methods and means that allowed Julius to pursue these ambitions and make the Church powerful in the short run leaves open the possibility of deleterious consequences for Italy in the longer term.

Machiavelli viewed the growth of the Church's temporal power under Alexander and Julius as a major turning point in the modern history of both Italy and the Church. But this was not a favorable judgment. Elsewhere, he presents Alexander and Julius as the fateful proximate initiators of Italy's disasters. In *The Prince* he steers clear of harmful consequences of the expansion of the Church's power, as he obviously had to in a book intended for the Medici and in a chapter that concludes with a rhetorical gesture of obeisance to the new Medici pope, Leo X, elected earlier in the year Machiavelli wrote *The Prince*. The chapter's last sentence asserts that "His Holiness Pope Leo, therefore, found the papacy very powerful [potentissimo], and one may hope that, just as [Alexander and Julius] made it powerful [grande] with arms, [Leo] will, with his goodness and countless other virtues, make it very powerful [grandissimo] and revered" (*P* 11.18). Although the passage contrasts the "arms" of Alexander and Julius with the "goodness" and "virtues" of Leo, it nonetheless makes Leo the heir to predecessors who increased the papacy's power with arms and money. Indeed, Leo too would make ample use of both. Because of the close ties between Julius and Leo, however, any mention of the negative aspects of Julius's pontificate would have been ill-advised in a work addressed to the Medici family and their recently elected pope.

Machiavelli briefly summarizes Julius's triumphs in taking Bologna (from Giovanni Bentivoglio in 1506), devastating the Venetians (in 1509), keeping the factions of the Colonna and the Orsini in the weakened condition "in which he found them," and expelling the French from Italy (in 1512). He succeeded in all these endeavors, Machiavelli claims, "and did so with all the more praise because he accomplished these things to increase the power of the Church and not that of any private person [alcuno privato]" (*P* 11.15), a statement that, although it overlooks Julius's efforts to ensure the succession of his nephew Francesco Maria della Rovere to the duchy of Urbino and the promotion of other nephews within the Church, points with some justification to the greater moderation of Julius's nepotism when compared with Alexander's. This resumé of successes, however, neglects to mention that Bologna, never a secure conquest, rebelled against Julius a few years later and welcomed the return of the Bentivoglio protected by French arms (but reverted to papal rule shortly thereafter); that Venice quickly recovered its terraferma dominion after the 1509 defeat; and that in 1512 the French actually defeated the papal-Spanish army at Ravenna, seemingly wrecking Julius's ambitions, until he was rescued by his Swiss allies who swarmed into Lombardy, attacked French strongholds, and caused Louis to cut his losses and retreat to France. Machiavelli prudently neglects to mention any of this in *Prince* 11, no doubt assuming that even indirect or implied criticism of Julius would have irritated Leo, who had been Julius's ally and trusted collaborator. In addition to Leo's long friendship with Julius's daughter,[2] whose husband was from Leo's mother's family, the Orsini, he, as Cardinal Giovanni de' Medici, had been Julius's legate in Bologna, then in the Romagna in 1511, and yet again in the papal-Spanish army that was defeated at Ravenna, where he was briefly taken prisoner by the French. Once the Swiss drove the French from Italy, Julius seized on Florence's isolation to send a Spanish army into Tuscany to expel Piero Soderini and restore the Medici to power after eighteen years of exile. Cardinal Giovanni accompanied the Spanish forces to Florence, waited outside the walls while they sacked Prato massacring hundreds, perhaps thousands, and gave his blessing to the coup d'état. The Medici were the direct beneficiaries of the (fortuitous) outcome of Julius's war against France, never more clearly so than when Giovanni was elected to succeed Julius in early 1513. Having outlined the Church's rise to unprecedented power, culminating in the elevation of Cardinal Giovanni to the papacy (which would not have happened without the return of his family to power in Florence), Machiavelli was obviously not about to dwell—not in this context (he would do so elsewhere)—on how Julius, and Alexander before him, had colluded with ultramontane powers to subjugate and humiliate Italy. Nor would he have hinted at Cardinal Giovanni's complicity in this larger outcome of Julius's policies.

Although Machiavelli usually separates his critiques of the Church and Christianity, in *Discourses* 1.12 he links them as causal agents of Italy's crisis. Chapter 11 opens his extended discussion of Roman religion as founded by Numa and the important part it played in "commanding the armies, animating [animire][3] the plebs, keeping men good and bad men ashamed." From Numa's religion came good laws, good fortune, and great success (*DL* 1.11.8, 17). In chapter 12 he contrasts these beneficial results of Roman religion with the negative effects of Christianity on modern states. All princes and leaders of republics, Machiavelli says, if they wish their states to remain uncorrupted, must maintain the ceremonies of their religion uncorrupted and hold them in reverence; they must protect its "foundations" and support and enhance "all the things that occur in its

[2] Murphy, *The Pope's Daughter*, pp. 95–6.

[3] Some manuscripts have *riunire* rather than *animire*; see Machiavelli, *Discorsi*, ed. Inglese, p. 219, and Machiavelli, *Discorsi* ed. Bausi, vol. 2, p. 889.

favor, even if they think them false." In ancient Rome this meant defending and supporting the prognostications of oracles, diviners, and augurs. "Wise" leaders support the belief in miracles, which even "false religions celebrate," Machiavelli avers (somewhat blurring the line between "true" and "false" religions), and use their authority to strengthen the people's acceptance of, and devotion to, their religion. Machiavelli cites the story in Livy in which Roman soldiers attacking the city of Veii entered the temple of Juno "tutti devoti e pieni di religione [all devout and full of reverence]" and asked the statue of the goddess if she wanted to come to Rome. Some thought they saw the statue nod in reply; others thought they heard it say "yes" (*DL* 1.12.2–11). In Livy (5.22) Camillus, who commanded the army that conquered Veii, says nothing about the apparent miracle and only later has a temple built in Rome in honor of Juno. Machiavelli embellishes the story: "Camillus and the other leading citizens completely confirmed the [soldiers'] opinion and encouraged their credulity." In the next sentence he writes: "If this *religione* had been preserved in the beginnings[4] of the Christian commonwealth as its giver instituted it [La quale religione, se ne' princìpi della republica cristiana si fusse mantenuta secondo che dal datore d'essa ne fu ordinato], Christian states and republics would be more united and much happier than they are." The usual reading of this passage assumes that "religione" refers to the Christian religion and that its "datore" is Christ. But the meaning of "religione" in this sentence is obviously conditioned by what Machiavelli has just written about the Roman soldiers' credulity—their willingness to believe—as a function of their being "pieni di religione," which in the Roman context denotes reverence and piety. It seems more likely, therefore, that Machiavelli is lamenting the loss or absence in Christianity of the kind of piety, expressed as reverence for mysteries, miracles, and ceremonies, displayed by Rome's soldiers. If the "religione" referred to here is this reverential piety—not Christianity—its "datore" is Numa, not Christ. Machiavelli uses "religione" in two distinct senses in this chapter and plays on the distinction: "religione" as piety allows him to assert that "there is no better measure of its decline than to see how the peoples who are closest to the Roman Church, which is the head of our *religione*, have the least *religione*" (*DL* 1.12.12–13). "Our religione" is Christianity, but the "religione" that the peoples nearest the Roman Church have too little of is the piety of the ancient Romans. The "Roman Church" is of course the papacy and ecclesiastical hierarchy, and "the peoples who are closest to the Roman Church" are the Italians. Machiavelli's point in this passage is that Christendom would have been happier and more united if it had preserved the piety and reverence for things sacred characteristic of the religion Numa

[4] See the arguments for accepting "princìpi" (beginnings) instead of "prìncipi" (princes) in the perceptive reading by Emanuele Cutinelli-Rèndina, *Chiesa e religione in Machiavelli* (Pisa-Rome: Istituti Editoriali e Poligrafici Internazionali, 1998), pp. 179–84.

persuaded the Romans to accept. Yet we shall see that in Machiavelli's reading there is a darker side to Roman piety.

First, though, Machiavelli focuses on the noxious consequences of Christianity. The effect of the Roman Church's lack of *religione*/piety on the peoples of Italy leads him to a scathing denunciation, still in chapter 12, of the papacy as a major cause of Italy's woes. To refute the opinion held by many that the "well-being [bene essere]" of the cities of Italy is owing to the Roman Church," he offers two considerations. The first is that, "because of the wicked behavior of the curia [corte]"—the pope and College of Cardinals—Italy "has lost all devotion and piety [ogni divozione e ogni religione]." This has caused "innumerable problems and *disordini*," because where there is "religione" one assumes the presence of "everything good," and "where it is lacking one assumes the contrary." To see proof of this, Machiavelli comments with stinging humor, one would have to send the Roman court, "with the authority it has in Italy, to the cities of the Swiss, who are the only people who live according to the *religione* and military practices of the ancients. One would see that, in a short time, the evil customs of the [Roman] court would cause greater *disordine*" than anything else ever could.[5] The humor becomes bitter irony when Machiavelli declares that "we [Italians], therefore, have this first debt to the Church and the priests in having become without piety [sanza religione] and wicked [cattivi]" (*DL* 1.12.15–18).

Machiavelli's second reason for rejecting the opinion that the Church has benefited Italy is more straightforwardly political. "We have an even greater debt" to the Church, and this is "the second cause of our ruin," namely, that "the Church has kept and still keeps this country divided." Here—and not in the last chapter of *The Prince*, as so often claimed—is where Machiavelli laments Italy's lack of political unity. His premise is that "no country [provincia] is ever united or happy unless it comes entirely under obedience to one republic or one prince, as has happened in France and Spain." The reason Italy has not done so is the Church's temporal power—its governance of territories in central Italy. The Church "has never been powerful enough or possessed enough virtú to establish its own absolute power [occupare la tirannide][6] and make itself ruler [principe] of Italy." Nor, "on the other hand, has it been so weak that, from fear of losing its temporal possessions, it could not call upon someone powerful enough to defend it" against a rival in Italy. Machiavelli cites Charlemagne's defense of the papacy against the Lombards and, "in our time," the Church's alliance with France to defeat Venice (in 1509) and its alliance with the Swiss to expel the French (in 1512). These are the momentous events that changed the political face of Italy by driving out the

[5] I follow the reorganization of the text of chapter 12 suggested by Mario Martelli in "La logica provvidenzialistica e il capitolo XXVI del *Principe*," *Interpres* (1981–2): 375–8, and implemented by Bausi in his edition of the *Discorsi*, vol. 2, pp. 87, 818.

[6] Or "occupare il rimanente d'Italia," as Inglese prefers in his edition, pp. 96, 222.

French, installing the Swiss over a puppet Sforza duke in Milan, consolidating Spanish hegemony in the South, and bringing down the republic of the Great Council in Florence. Although Machiavelli does not mention him in this chapter, the prime mover of all this was Pope Julius. Being unable to extend its power over all of Italy while still able to prevent anyone else from doing so, the Church, Machiavelli believes, is the reason why Italy is divided among a plethora of princes and governments and has never come under a single political authority. "From this situation such disunity and weakness have resulted that Italy has become prey, not only to powerful barbarians, but to anyone who attacks it. For this we Italians are indebted to the Church, and to no one else" (*DL* 1.12.18–21).

Machiavelli sketches the historical origins of this development early in the *Florentine Histories*. Until the eighth century, the "influence [autorità]" of the popes rested on the "holiness of their lives and their miracles," not on political power. Even after the emperors left Rome, papal "autorità" depended exclusively on reverence for their "demeanor [costumi]" and theological "teachings [dottrina]." When Theodoric established his capital in Ravenna (at the end of the fifth century), Rome was left "sanza principe"—without an acknowledged political leader—and the Roman people increasingly "gave their obedience" to the popes. Yet this did not increase their "autorità" (here meaning power) very much. Only with the arrival of the Lombards and the division of Italy between them and the eastern Roman Empire did the popes assume a more active political role ("farsi piú vivo"), enhancing their "prestige [dignità]" and security in alliances with both of these powers. But after the decline of the "Impero orientale," the popes could no longer depend on it for protection against the Lombards and, needing support from other quarters, they turned (in the eighth century) to the kings of France. This, according to Machiavelli, was the great turning point in the history of the papacy, with lasting consequences for Italy: "From that time forward, of all the wars waged by the barbarians in Italy, the popes were the cause of most of them, and, of all the barbarians who flooded into Italy, most were summoned by the popes. This practice has lasted down to our own times and has kept and still keeps Italy divided and weak [disunita e inferma]." As the eastern empire fades from the narrative, the papacy becomes central to Italy's "disunity" and "infirmity": "It will be seen how the popes, at first with excommunications, subsequently with both excommunications and arms combined with indulgences, became feared and revered; and how, because they used both [spiritual weapons and arms] badly, they have completely lost the first [the effectiveness of spiritual weapons], and, as regards the second [arms], are dependent on others" (*IF* 1.9)—an allusion to Alexander VI's (and Cesare Borgia's) dependence on France and Julius's dependence first on France and then on Spain and the Swiss, which allowed these foreign powers to invade and dominate much of Italy.

Machiavelli's account of the origins of the papacy's dependence on foreign arms underscores the constant danger of its always precarious temporal power for all of Italy. He reprises the issue in *Histories* 1.23, discussing the growing enmity in the 1270s between the popes and Charles of Anjou. A decade earlier, the popes had invited Charles to Italy to counter the Hohenstaufen and their Ghibelline allies. But after Charles brought most of southern and central Italy under his control, "Pope Adrian V" (r. 1276),[7] Machiavelli writes, "could not tolerate [Charles's] power and urged Emperor Rudolph (Habsburg) to enter Italy against Charles." Machiavelli emphasizes the irony of the papacy's appeal to the German Rudolph to neutralize the French Charles whom the popes themselves had brought into Italy to obliterate the German-Sicilian Hohenstaufen. He caustically comments: "in this way the pontiffs, sometimes for love of religion, sometimes for their own ambition, never ceased introducing into Italy new discords [omori] and stirring up new wars. After making one prince powerful, they regretted doing so and tried to destroy him. Nor did they allow anyone else to control the country they themselves were too weak to control. Princes feared the popes, because they always emerged victorious either by fighting or by fleeing" (*IF* 1.23.3–4).

Inviting foreign princes to Italy to support papal political objectives was not the only way the popes caused long-term damage to Italy, according to Machiavelli. In this same chapter he criticizes their use of the office, beginning with Nicholas III (r. 1277–80), "di casa Orsina,"—Giovanni Gaetano Orsini—to advance the ambitions of family members. Describing Nicholas as "audace [bold]" and "ambizioso," Machiavelli summarizes his consequential achievements: despite the brevity of his pontificate, he pressured Charles of Anjou to loosen his grip on Tuscany, deprived him of the office of senator in Rome, and initiated the negotiations that resulted, shortly after his death, in the great rebellion of the Sicilian Vespers against Charles and the Angevins. Nicholas appointed "uno suo nipote cardinale" as apostolic legate over wide territories in northern and central Italy. He persuaded Rudolph to cede to the papacy the Romagna and the city of Bologna, designating Bertoldo Orsini (another nephew) as duke. He died before he could realize his grandiose last objective of making two other family members kings in Lombardy and Tuscany "to defend the Church against the Germans if they came to Italy and against the French [the Angevins] in the kingdom [of Naples]." Dante (*Inferno* 19) and the chronicler Giovanni Villani (8.54)[8] had already made Pope Nicholas notorious for his simony and nepotism, and Machiavelli identifies these aspects of his pontificate as especially damaging for the future of the Church and Italy: "He was the first of the popes who openly displayed his own ambition and who schemed, under the pretext of making the Church powerful, to honor and favor his family members." Before Nicholas, Machiavelli writes, no mention was

[7] Machiavelli may have confused Adrian V, who was pope for a month in 1276, with Gregory X (r. 1271–6), who invited Rudolph to intervene. Rudolph was King of the Romans, crowned in Aachen but never in Rome, and did not enter Italy.

[8] Giovanni Villani, *Nuova Cronica*, 3 vols., ed. G. Porta (Parma: Guanda Editore, 1990–1), vol. 1, pp. 494–6; passages cited in the text by book and chapter numbers.

ever made of popes' nephews or relatives, but "from this moment on my history will be full of them, so much so that we will even hear of popes' sons"—an allusion to Alexander VI's promotion of his son. "Now there is nothing left for popes to attempt, having up to our own times arranged for their sons to become princes, except to bequeath to them a hereditary papacy." That scandalous thought leads Machiavelli to reflect on the meager chances of success of any such attempt to highjack the papacy as a dynastic inheritance. Princedoms created by popes (for their relatives) have been short-lived, he says, and, because of the brevity of their pontificates, "for the most part popes either do not finish planting their seedlings [piantare le piante loro] or, if they do, they leave them with so few and such weak roots [con sí poche e deboli barbe] that, once the virtú that nourishes them is gone, the first puff of wind causes them to shrivel" (*IF* 1.23.11–13). Machiavelli had used "barbe" as a metaphor for weak foundations in *The Prince*'s chapter on Cesare Borgia, discussing the precariousness of states quickly created and dependent on external support and hence on fortune. "Like all things in nature that grow quickly," they cannot put down "roots [barbe]," and consequently "the first bad weather kills them." Although in *The Prince* he entertains the theoretical possibility that outstanding virtú could help the "weak roots" survive and grow (*P* 7.4), in the *Histories* he concludes that even this hypothetical virtú cannot last long and the "barbe" have no chance of developing stronger roots.

Machiavelli also indicts Christianity as a major contributor to Italy's crisis. In *Discourses* 2.2 he describes ancient Italy as a land of free peoples—in two senses: self-governing and independent of foreign rulers—and asks why the ancients loved freedom more than modern peoples do. "In these modern times there is only one land which can be said to have free cities within it"—he means Germany, or, more specifically, the Swiss—"but in ancient times in all lands there were many very free peoples." In ancient Italy, "from the mountains that divide Tuscany from Lombardy to the southernmost point of Italy, they were all free peoples, such as the Etruscans, Romans, and Samnites and many others who lived in the rest of Italy" (*DL* 2.2.2–6). After enumerating at length the benefits of liberty, the harm inflicted by the tyrannical rule of a monarch, the love of liberty exhibited by ancient peoples, and the vengeance they exacted against those who deprived them of their liberty, Machiavelli says he believes the greater love of freedom manifested by ancient peoples "resulted from the same cause that now makes men less strong, which is, I believe, the difference between our *educazione* and that of the ancients, grounded in the difference between our religion and that of the ancients" (*DL* 2.2.26). As noted in Chapter 1, "educazione," for Machiavelli, is a broader concept than education in English usage: it includes upbringing and acculturation, the absorption by individuals of the sum of customs, mores, principles, and modes of behavior that constitute a society's culture, the process by which people internalize and share the values of their society. Yet he did not think of "educazione" as beyond the reach of personal agency and choice. In the "Capitolo dell'Ambizione" he denies that modern Italy's weakness is attributable to "nature," insisting that "*educazion* can compensate for what nature lacks." In antiquity, "*educazione* made Italy flourish and conquer the entire world; rugged *educazion* gave [Italy] courage [La fiera educazion li dette ardire]" (*A* 109–17).

Machiavelli locates the difference between ancient and modern *educazione* in what distinguishes "ancient religion" from Christianity. Because "our religion has shown us the truth and the true way [la verità e la vera via]," echoing John 14:6 where Jesus says "Ego sum via et veritas et vita," it "makes us esteem less the honor of the world." The ancients, by contrast, because they held worldly honor in great esteem as the highest good, were "fiercer in their actions." This, Machiavelli says, is evident in their rituals, in the difference between the "magnificence of their sacrifices and the humbleness of ours, in which there is some elegance, more refined than magnificent, but no fierce or strong action." The "terrifying" spectacle of ancient animal sacrifices, "full of blood and ferocity," in which "many animals were slaughtered," had the effect, he claims, of making men similarly fierce. Ancient religion "beatified only men teeming with worldly glory, such as generals of armies and rulers of states [principi di republiche]." By contrast, "our religion has glorified humble and contemplative men more than men of action. It has placed the highest good in humility, self-mortification, and contempt for things human," whereas ancient religion placed it in "greatness of spirit, bodily strength, and all the other things likely to make men exceedingly strong." Christianity requires acceptance of suffering, not vigorous action. "If our religion requires you to have any fortitude [fortezza], it wants you to be prepared to suffer more than to perform any arduous deed" (*DL* 2.2.27–33).

Machiavelli asserts that the radically different ethos of the *educazione* inculcated by Christianity had enormous political consequences. "This way of living, then, seems to have made the world weak and given it up as prey to evil men [uomini scelerati], who can securely control it because they see that most people [l'università degli uomini], in order to reach paradise, think more of enduring their injuries [le sue battiture] than of avenging them." There is an intriguing ambiguity in this sentence. Depending on whether "sue" in "le sue battiture" refers to the "università degli uomini" or to the "uomini scelerati," the "battiture" that Christians willingly endure in order to gain entrance into paradise could be either the misfortunes and afflictions that befall them from the random vicissitudes of life—their own *battiture*—or the cruelties inflicted by the "uomini scelerati." Both readings are possible.[9] But the latter would make Christianity the enabling cause of oppression, abuse, and violence perpetrated by overbearingly powerful "uomini scelerati." Either way, however, under Christianity, the "università degli uomini" become victims of an evil few, because acceptance of suffering for a higher goal

[9] See the note in *Discorsi*, ed. Bausi, vol. 1, p. 318, n. 87.

leaves the realm of human action and power to men evil both in their inner selves and in their actions and behavior: a *uomo scelerato* is not just bad; he is also guilty of crimes and cruelties. Machiavelli faults the "viltà"—cowardice, abjection—of "those who have interpreted our religion according to sloth [or lethargy: secondo l'ozio], and not according to virtú": if "they" (curiously, not *we*) "were to consider how Christianity allows us to exalt and defend our country, they would see how it wants us to love and honor it and prepare ourselves to be such as can defend it." Machiavelli here proposes a malleable Christianity, capable of being interpreted and applied to various ends. Characterizing as "false" the interpretations of Christianity whose "educazioni" (in the plural, in the sense of teachings) allow unquestioned authority to "uomini scelerati," he claims that these "false interpretations" account for the smaller number of republics and the diminished love of liberty among the moderns, presumably by turning men away from the vigorous defense of their countries. Yet he complicates the assignment of blame to Christianity by adding that it was the Roman Empire, "with its arms and great power," that snuffed out "all the republics and free communities [viveri civili]" (*DL* 2.2.34–8). This nebulous double causation of the declining love of freedom, and hence of the reduced number of republics—attributed on the one hand to the "false interpretations" of Christianity and on the other to the suffocating power of the Roman Empire—appears again near the end of book 2 of the *Art of War*, where Fabrizio Colonna says (*AG* 2.303–305) that the Roman Empire "extinguished" all the republics and principalities of Europe and Africa and most of those in Asia, leaving no place for virtú except in Rome itself. And when the empire collapsed, its corrupted virtú could not be reborn because "today's way of living, as a consequence of the Christian religion, does not impose the same necessity of defending [one's country] that existed in antiquity." Machiavelli advances a two-stage explanation for the weakened love of liberty: first, the overwhelming power of Rome; then, after its fall, the distorted teachings of Christianity.

A more pointed assignment of responsibility to the Christian faith for the political debilitation of Italy occurs in the opening chapter of the third book of the *Discourses*, where Machiavelli theorizes the necessity for religions and republics to return often to their origins and animating principles if they are to enjoy long life. In the case of Christianity, he says that "if saints Francis and Dominic had not drawn our religion back to its beginnings" by reviving "poverty and the example of Christ's life," Christianity would have disappeared, because these foundational precepts no longer had any purchase on the minds of men. At first glance, this seems to be praise for the thirteenth-century reformers who revived the ideals of the imitation of Christ and made the sanctification of everyday life the centerpiece of Christian life, bringing religion out of the cloister and convent and into the cities, families, and workplaces of the laity. But Machiavelli turns quickly to an ironic conclusion. The "ordini" of the Franciscans and Dominicans ("ordini" signifying both the mendicant orders they created and the principles and practices that structured the life in society of the friars and their lay followers) "were so potent that they are the reason why the dishonorableness [disonestà] of the prelates and heads of the religion did not destroy" Christianity. By practicing poverty and winning the trust of the people through confessions and sermons, Machiavelli says, the mendicant orders "persuaded the people that it is evil to speak evil of evil and better to live in obedience [to the prelates] and leave it to God to punish their errors. Thus they [the leaders of the Church] do the worst they can, because they have no fear of punishments they neither see nor believe." Machiavelli's conclusion that "this renewal [rinnovazione] therefore preserved and continues to preserve this religion" quietly overlooks the scathingly ironic paradox that the price of preserving the ideals of primitive Christianity was the protection of the evil actions of its prelates and the immunity they gained to "do the worst they can" (*DL* 3.1.32–4).

This critique of Christianity as an *instrumentum regni* easily manipulable in the service of the powerful has a parallel in Machiavelli's ambivalent assessment of Roman religion. On the one hand, as we have seen, he says (in *DL* 1.11) that the religion introduced by Numa created in Rome a "civilità"—a city of laws and a law-abiding population. Machiavelli repeats the legend he knew from Livy, Ovid, and Plutarch according to which, in order to persuade the Romans to accept his new religious "ordini," Numa successfully deceived them into believing that he had received instructions from the semi-divine Egeria. Rome, Machiavelli thinks, was more indebted to Numa than even to Romulus for its greatness, because its "religione" (here again meaning piety) made its arms formidable. He sums up this apparently laudable view of Roman religion by saying that, "All things considered, it was among the chief causes of [Rome's] felicità," its good fortune and success, "because [Numa's religione] produced good ordini, good ordini in turn bring good fortune, and from good fortune came all the successful outcomes of [Rome's] endeavors. As divine worship [culto divino] is the cause of the greatness of republics, so contempt for religion is the cause of their ruin" (*DL* 1.11.17–18).

That is one side of Machiavelli's view of Roman religion. The other is the persistent attention to its role in reducing the people, or plebs, to obedience and conformity through fear of both God and the breaking of oaths. Rome's plebeians, Machiavelli writes, "were more fearful of breaking oaths than of breaking the laws, because they more greatly revered the power of God than that of men." (The oath sworn by Roman soldiers was the *sacramentum*, a solemn obligation and "sacred bond" with "religious implications," "transforming a citizen into a warrior and sealing a pact between him and the gods of his mother city, the state, his commander and his fellow soldiers.")[10] Machiavelli foregrounds the nobility's success in exploiting to its own advantage this fear among the plebs. After citing the

[10] Claude Nicolet, *The World of the Citizen in Republican Rome*, tr. P. S. Falla (Berkeley and Los Angeles: University of California Press, 1980), pp. 102–4.

episode in which Scipio Africanus forces his soldiers, demoralized after the catastrophic defeat at Cannae, to swear an oath not to abandon the patria, thus reviving their will to fight—an example of the beneficial effect of Numa's religion—Machiavelli recalls from Livy (7.4–5) a very different example of the potency of oaths. When the tribune Marcus Pomponius accused the patrician Lucius Manlius of wrongdoing, Lucius' son Titus, by threatening to kill the tribune, forced him to swear an oath to rescind the accusation against his father. The tribune swore the oath and withdrew the accusation "out of fear," compelled *not* to render justice by his sacred commitment sworn before the gods (*DL* 1.11.4–6).

In *Discourses* 1.13 Machiavelli summarizes three episodes from Livy that illustrate how the Romans "made use of religion." After ten years of besieging Veii, Rome's exasperated and exhausted soldiers wanted to return home, but the army's patrician commanders took advantage of the plebs' superstitious beliefs by invoking an old prophecy according to which Veii would be taken in the year that Lake Albano was drained. The lake was rising at the time and would soon be drained (so the commanders told the soldiers, who, because the lake is southeast of Rome and Veii north of the city, could not see it for themselves). Here again, as in the example of Scipio Africanus, the commanders "made use of religion [si valevano della religione]" to give the soldiers courage and hope to continue the siege (*DL* 1.13.4–5; cf. Livy 5.15–16). It brought Rome a military victory, and Machiavelli calls it a case of "religion well used." But it was no less an example of the use of religion to influence the plebs. In the other two episodes of chapter 13, religion is unambiguously used to trick the plebeians into complying with the wishes of the nobles. After the plebs succeeded in electing a majority of plebeians to the office of the military tribunes with consular power (in 400 BCE), the nobles frightened the plebs into revoking the election and restricting the office to patricians by claiming that the pestilence, famine, and strange occurrences of that year were all signs that the gods were angry over Rome's misuse of its sovereign power ("male usato la maiestà del suo imperio") and that the only way to placate them was to resume electing only nobles as military tribunes. The plebs, "terrified by religious scruple [sbigottita da questa religione]," did exactly that (*DL* 1.13.2–3; cf. Livy 5.13–14). The third example is the episode of the tribune (Gaius) Terentilius's effort to limit the powers of the consuls. Only later, in chapter 39 of book 1, does Machiavelli explain that Terentilius proposed the creation of a committee of five to "review" and "limit" consular authority (*DL* 1.39.8–13). In chapter 13 he recounts the reaction of the nobility, who turned to "religione" to thwart the plan. They did so, says Machiavelli, in two ways. The first was to have the prophetic Sybilline Books consulted and "have the response given" that the city was in danger of losing its liberty because of civil discord. The tribunes exposed the ploy, but the ominous response of the Sybilline Books "put such terror in the breasts of the plebs that it made them less willing to listen to the tribunes." Here too religious scruple and fear weakened the tribunes' constitutional power. The second method adopted by the patricians was to invent an external threat by the hostile Aequi and Volsci. The tribunes recognized this as a subterfuge, but when one of the patrician consuls warned of threatening dangers to the city and "forced the plebs to swear [an oath] not to deviate from" his orders, the frightened populace obeyed. Soon thereafter, this consul died and his replacement, "in order to prevent the plebs from thinking about the Terentilian law," ordered them out of Rome to confront the Volsci, claiming that the oath they had sworn obligated them to obey him. The tribunes objected that the oath had been given to the deceased consul and was no longer operative. Yet the plebs, "from fear of religious scruple [per paura della religione], preferred to obey the consul instead of the tribunes." Quoting Livy (3.20), Machiavelli has the plebs justify their decision as a defense of the "antica religione" in which "not yet was there the neglect of the gods that now possesses the world, nor did each man interpret oaths and laws to suit himself [nec interpretando sibi quisque iusiurandum et leges aptas faciebat]." Seeing the determination of the plebs to obey the patrician consul, the tribunes, "fearing to lose their dignity entirely," agreed to follow the consul's command and not to raise Terentilius's proposal for a year. "Thus," Machiavelli concludes, "did religion allow the senate to overcome difficulties it would never have resolved without it" (*DL* 1.13.6–13; cf. Livy 3.10, 15–21).

If the plebs believed they were upholding the purity of the "antica religione" by rejecting personal and adaptable "interpretations" of oaths and laws, Rome's patricians, as Machiavelli reveals in the next chapter, suffered no such delusion. The title of chapter 14 states that "the Romans interpreted [interpretavano] the auspices according to necessity and wisely made a show of observing religion [e con la prudenza mostravano di osservare la religione] when they were forced not to observe it; and if anyone rashly belittled [religion], they punished him." The episode recounted here underscores the importance among the Romans of the auguries, which Machiavelli calls the "foundation" of their religion and the "cause" of the republic's well-being. Never undertaking any "important action" without consulting the "diviners [auspici]," they included in their armies the *pullarii* (chicken-handlers), who took the auspices before any military engagement and informed the commanders whether the chickens had eaten. If they had, it was a good omen that confirmed the Romans in the knowledge that they enjoyed the gods' favor and would be victorious. But if "reason [ragione] showed them that a thing ought to be done" even if the chickens had not eaten and the auspices were unfavorable, they went ahead and did it anyway, "turning things around so shrewdly with various methods and schemes [rivoltavanla con termini e modi tanto attamente] that it did not seem they did so with any disrespect for religion" (*DL* 1.14.2–5). The army's commanders "interpreted the auspices according to necessity," manipulating adverse auspices to conform to their plans.

To illustrate this, Machiavelli summarizes (from Livy 10.40) the story of the consul Lucius Papirius who, confident of "certain victory" in the war against the

Samnites (293 BCE), ordered the *pullarii* to take the auspices. The chickens did not eat, but the chief of the *pullarii*, knowing that the commanders, expecting victory, were eager for battle, and not wanting to deprive them of the opportunity, lied and told Papirius that the chickens had eaten. As the consul was preparing his legions, he learned that the chickens had in fact not eaten but said that, "as far as he and the army were concerned, the auspices were good and that, if the chicken-handlers had told lies, those lies would redound to their harm [in pregiudizio suo]." Papirius was determined to proceed to battle, but he had to avert the potential scandal that would erupt among the soldiers if they learned that he had ignored the unfavorable auspices and sent them into the fray nonetheless. So he ordered the *pullarii* into the front rank of the Roman battle formation. Machiavelli comments—and this is not in Livy—that Papirius did this "so that the outcome would correspond to the prophecy [perché lo effetto corrispondesse al pronostico]," perhaps both to the consul's prediction that those who lied about the auspices would come to a bad end, and also to the "pronostico," albeit false, of Roman victory. Predictably, the chief chicken-handler was "by chance [a caso]" struck and killed by a javelin from a Roman soldier. When the consul learned what had happened, Machiavelli says, he announced that everything "was proceeding well and with the favor of the gods, because, with the death of that liar, the army was cleansed of all blame and liberated from any wrath [the gods] might have conceived against him" (or the army). Machiavelli inserts another judgment of his own: "by knowing well how to fit his plans [col sapere bene accomodare i disegni suoi] to the auspices," Papirius led his troops into battle "without the army being aware that he had in any way neglected the ordini of their religion" (*DL* 1.14.6–10). Here again, the patricians deceived the plebeian soldiers by taking advantage of their religious scruples and their fear of offending the gods to get them to do what they, the patricians, wanted. In Machiavelli's reading Roman religion served the interests of the patricians more than those of the plebs.[11]

When Machiavelli wrote in *Discourses* 3.1 that, by reviving Christianity's original principles, Saints Francis and Dominic "persuaded the people that it is evil to speak evil of evil and good to live in obedience" to the prelates, he might also have been thinking of Girolamo Savonarola, the Dominican friar who, with charisma and prophetic oratory, sought to return the Florentines to the virtuous simplicity, as he imagined it, of original Christianity and, in so doing, profoundly influenced Florence's political life in the 1490s, both before and after the expulsion of the Medici. Unlike Francis and Dominic, the success of whose new mendicant orders led to their canonization, when the Florentines tired of Savonarola's puritanical reforms and denunciations of immorality, he was martyred by the same community that had avidly embraced and encouraged his prophetic vision.

[11] Further explored in my "Papirius and the Chickens, or Machiavelli on the Necessity of Interpreting Religion," *Journal of the History of Ideas* 60 (1999): 659–81.

In subjecting him to a harrowing death the Florentines yielded to the most powerful of his menacing antagonists, Pope Alexander VI, and Machiavelli might well have reflected that, for all his moral purity, great learning, and contributions to the new republic of the Great Council, in the end Savonarola's legacy was, ironically, acceptance by many Florentines that "it is evil to speak evil of evil and good to live in obedience" to prelates who "do the worst they can because they have no fear of punishment" (*DL* 3.1.32–4). This might help us understand Machiavelli's persistent ambivalence about Savonarola. On the one hand, he admired the eloquent oratory of "quel gran Savonerola," inspired by "virtú divina," who kept the Florentines "spellbound with his words" (D^1 157–9) and gave them new political "ordini" (*P* 6.23). With some oversimplification, Machiavelli attributed to the friar the institutional structure and civic ethos of the post-Medici republic. Despite the furious controversies that led to his execution in 1498, the "ordini"—especially the Great Council—that he endorsed survived him and remained in place until the Medici coup of 1512. This is why Machiavelli places him, in chapter 6 of *The Prince*, in, or near, the company of the legendary lawgivers Moses, Cyrus, Romulus, and Theseus. In the *Discourses* he compares Savonarola to Numa, who, in order to persuade the Romans to accept his new religious "ordini," claimed to have received them from a semi-divine source. No "ordinatore," Machiavelli says, has ever succeeded in having new and unusual laws accepted by the people without "recourse to God." It may be easier to introduce new things to less refined and less educated people, he continues, but "Savonarola persuaded the Florentines, who do not think themselves ignorant or unrefined, that he spoke with God." Adopting a tone of respectful distance, Machiavelli declines to say whether he believes this was true or not, "because of so great a man one must speak with reverence." One could suspect insincerity in these words, but not in what comes next: "but I do say that countless people believed him without having seen any exceptional thing to make them believe, because his life, his learning, and the substance of what he said to them were enough to gain their trust" (*DL* 1.11.10–12, 24–5). Whereas, following Livy, Machiavelli says Numa "pretended [simulò]" to have been intimate with the nymph he claimed as the source of the religion he invented, in Savonarola's case he says it was his virtuous life and his learning that persuaded the people to trust and believe him.[12]

But Savonarola does not escape criticism, especially in connection with his political role. Summarizing two of Savonarola's last sermons (March 1498) in a letter to Florence's ambassador to the papal court, Ricciardo Becchi, Machiavelli describes the skill with which Savonarola altered his interpretation of the chosen

[12] Two good readings of Machiavelli's view of Savonarola as favorable: Mario Martelli, "Machiavelli e Savonarola," in *Savonarola: democrazia tirannide profezia*, ed. Gian Carlo Garfagnini (Florence: SISMEL Edizioni del Galluzzo, 1998), pp. 67–89; and Mark Jurdjevic, *A Great and Wretched City: Promise and Failure in Machiavelli's Florentine Political Thought* (Cambridge, Mass.: Harvard University Press, 2014), pp. 16–52.

biblical passage, thereby modifying his message, after learning that the newly elected Signoria did not consist of the opponents he feared would be selected. But Machiavelli's reaction is critical: the friar, he wrote, "has changed his cloak [mutato mantello]" and "in this way, in my judgment, he conforms to [viene secondando] the times and camouflages his lies."[13] Already in the first *Decennale* he presents Savonarola as the leader of a political faction that "kept you [Florentines] divided" and caused many to fear the ruin of their patria "under his prophetic teaching," unless his "divine light"—his prophetic power—"either grew or was snuffed out by a greater fire [maggior foco]" (D^1 154–65)—an allusion to his burning at the stake suggesting that only his death could quell the discord he helped create. In *The Prince*, while implying that he aspired to the high purposes of Moses, Cyrus, Romulus, and Theseus, who all succeeded in founding states, Savonarola is said to have "perished amidst his new ordini," because "all armed prophets are victorious, but all unarmed ones have come to ruin" (*P* 6.21–3). On the one hand, therefore, Machiavelli acclaims Savonarola's role in shaping the new institutions of the post-Medici republic; on the other hand, he reproves the would-be lawgiver for lacking the means or ability to keep the people steadfast in their devotion to the new constitution whose creation and acceptance by the people he powerfully supported. A similar criticism appears in *Discourses* 3.30 where Machiavelli asserts the "necessity" for one who wishes to do something beneficial to his city of ridding himself, one way or another, of those who impede him out of resentment ("invidia"). Moses, he says, accomplished this by "killing countless men" in order for his "laws and ordini to be accepted" and implemented. Savonarola "recognized very well the same necessity" but did not have the "autorità" (the legal authority and political power) to act on it. Savonarola's downfall, he concludes, was caused by his not knowing how, or not being able, to overcome the hostility of his enemies (*DL* 3.30.15–20).

Machiavelli takes Savonarola to task in *Discourses* 1.45 for a specific and grievous political error. Although he again acknowledges that Florence's government was reformed in 1494 "with the help of Brother Girolamo Savonarola, whose writings display the learning, wisdom and virtú of his spirit [animo]," he faults him for failing to insist, in an explosively controversial case, on the enforcement of the law guaranteeing the right of appeal against convictions for crimes against the state ("casi di stato"), a law whose acceptance Savonarola himself had strongly promoted in 1495 in his quest for amnesty for, and reconciliation with, the Mediceans. According to the law, any citizen convicted of crimes against the state and sentenced to capital punishment had the right to appeal the conviction to the Great Council.[14] In 1497 five prominent citizens (Bernardo del Nero, Niccolò Ridolfi, Lorenzo Tornabuoni, Giannozzo Pucci, and Giovanni Cambi) were found guilty

[13] *Lettere*, pp. 69–70.

[14] For the background and text of the law, see *Provvisioni concernenti l'ordinamento della Repubblica Fiorentina, 1494–1512*, ed. Giorgio Cadoni (Rome: Istituto Storico Italiano per il Medio Evo, 1994), vol. 1, pp. 108–18.

of such a crime. (Machiavelli omits here the crucial fact that they had conspired with the exiled Piero de' Medici to overthrow the republic and restore him to power by force of arms.) Anger at the five ran so high that many Florentines—especially in the faction affiliated with Savonarola and led by Francesco Valori—wanted to deny the appeal and proceed immediately to their execution.[15] Remaining silent, Savonarola left it to Valori and his faction to justify denying the appeal. Machiavelli emphasizes that Savonarola himself had promoted the law establishing the right of appeal "to protect citizens" (from malicious or hurried prosecution), and that the law had been approved "con difficultà grandissima." He considers the friar's silence an egregious error: denying the appeal and failing to observe the law "diminished Savonarola's reputation more than any other event. If the right of appeal was useful, he should have insisted on allowing it to the five; if it was not, he should not have had it approved." The event was "all the more notorious because, in the many sermons Savonarola gave after the law was disregarded [literally, broken: rotta], he never once either denounced or justified those who broke it: he refused to denounce [the violation] because it served his interests" in removing dangerous enemies; "nor could he justify" the violation of the law, as it would have contradicted his own fervent efforts in favor of its passage and opened him to charges of hypocrisy.[16] Machiavelli delivers a brutal judgment: "This matter, in revealing his ambitious and factional [ambizioso e partigiano] spirit ruined his reputation and brought down on him much opprobrium" (*DL* 1.45.9–12). Attributing to "ambition" and "factional spirit" Savonarola's failure to uphold the law implies that, despite his frequently announced aim of reconciling the parties and preventing vindictive recrimination, he himself fell victim to the thirst for partisan advantage and revenge. Savonarola's "writings" may have "displayed the learning, wisdom, and virtú of his *animo*," but his betrayal through silence of a principle he had embraced revealed a quite different "animo," fired by ambition and partisan rancor.

"HIS PROUD AND CHOLERIC NATURE"

Of the popes of Machiavelli's lifetime, Julius II was the one he observed most closely and who had the most consequential impact on Italy and Florence (with the possible exception, late in Machiavelli's life, of the calamitous Clement VII [r. 1523–34] whose criminal incompetence led to the Sack of Rome just weeks

[15] Alison Brown lucidly examines the episode in *Piero di Lorenzo de' Medici and the Crisis of Renaissance Italy* (Cambridge: Cambridge University Press, 2020), pp. 254–70. See also Guicciardini, *Storie fiorentine*, ed. Montevecchi, ch. 15, pp. 254–64.

[16] John P. McCormick illuminates the theoretical dilemmas these events posed for Machiavelli in *Machiavellian Democracy* (Cambridge: Cambridge University Press, 2011), pp. 129–33.

before Machiavelli died in 1527 and, three years later, to the horrific siege of Florence and suppression of the Last Republic). In the *Storia d'Italia* Guicciardini, recounting Julius's role, when he was still Cardinal Della Rovere, in urging Charles VIII to bring his army across the Alps, called him the "*fatale* [fateful, or fatal] instrument, then, before, and afterwards, of the evils that befell Italy [de' mali d'Italia]."[17] It was Julius who destroyed Cesare Borgia; who led armies against the signori of the two most important cities, Perugia and Bologna, of the papal states; who promoted the huge coalition (the League of Cambrai) against Venice that inflicted the defeat in 1509 that temporarily cost the republic its terraferma dominion; who organized the Holy League to drive the French, his former allies against Venice, out of Italy; who enabled Spain's power in Italy to grow beyond the Neapolitan Regno; who injected the Swiss as major players in Italian politics; and who engaged a Spanish army to oust the Florentine republic of 1494–1512 and restore the Medici to power. Julius kept Italy in crisis after crisis for a decade.[18] Machiavelli witnessed much of this in person as Florence's envoy to the papal court during two legations and, whether in person or from the chancery, always had his eye on this astonishing and scandalous pope. Like Chapter 3 on Cesare Borgia, this chapter includes a deep dive into Machiavelli's dispatches and chancery memoranda to assess how he experienced, and reacted to, Julius II.

Machiavelli's first opportunity to observe Julius in action was the legation to Rome in late 1503. On November 1, writing to the Ten, he characterized as "straordinaria" both Julius's "creazione" (election) and its "pubblicazione," because "they have elected this pope in open conclave [a conclavi aperto]" (there were occasional open conclaves until Gregory XV instituted closure and secret ballots in 1621). "Pubblicazione" might refer to the opening of the ballots, known in canon law as the *publicatio*, and the recording of the names of cardinals who received votes. Machiavelli may also, or instead, have meant the announcement of the election to the public, for he writes that, "no sooner had [the cardinals] gathered together, which was around midnight" (between October 31 and November 1) "than they released it and made it publicly known [lo mandorno fuora a pubblicare]." He had written earlier dispatches (*LCSG* 3.220 and 221) "on [the basis of] those public announcements." Machiavelli then says: "we are now at the 15th hour [*c.*9 a.m. on November 1] and the prescribed formalities [cirimonie ordinarie] have still not been carried out" (*LCSG* 3.222.5). A "straordinaria" election, "open conclave," a hurried announcement in the middle of the night, and the absence of the "cirimonie ordinarie" all imply a rushed election, possibly not in conformity with canon law. Machiavelli may not have meant to cast doubt on the election's legitimacy, but he was certainly calling attention to Julius's lack of

[17] Francesco Guicciardini, *Storia d'Italia*, book 1, ch. 9, in *Opere*, ed. Lugnani Scarano, vol. 2, p. 155.
[18] See the excellent biography by Shaw, *Julius II*.

concern for protocol and tradition and to his urgency about getting the news out as quickly as possible. Was the rush a reflection of Julius's worry that some of those who supported his election might change their minds? "One who reflects carefully on the support Julius has received will judge it miraculous," because, in the end, everyone—Machiavelli lists them: all the factions within the College of Cardinals, the kings of Spain and France, the rival factions of Roman barons, and Borgia himself—favored his election (*LCSG* 3.222.6). Although the Florentine community in Rome was "tutta rallegrata," Cardinal Soderini was more cautious. He told Machiavelli "he believes it's been many years since [Florence] has been able to hope for so much from a pope as it can from this one, provided," he added, "they know how to *temporeggiarlo*," by which, in light of Julius's explosive career as a cardinal, Soderini presumably meant knowing how to keep Julius under control by taking things slowly and thus moderating his often impulsive and angry reactions. Machiavelli predicted that Julius would have his hands full keeping the promises he made to win the support of so many people and factions for his election, "because," he explained, many of those promises "are contradictory" (*LCSG* 3.223.6–9).

Five days after the election, Machiavelli "presented himself at the feet of the pontiff" to convey Florence's congratulations and offer "all the strength [potere] of this republic in his honor and benefit." On the same day, Cardinals Soderini and Rouen urged Machiavelli to show Julius the letters he had just received from the Ten expressing concern about Venetian encroachment in the Romagna. Julius seemed unconcerned, Machiavelli reports, convinced as he was that the local lords of the Romagna would act in accordance with his interests, not those of the Venetians, as soon as they learned of his election. Machiavelli then met with Cardinals Ascanio Sforza, Rafaello Riario, and Federico Sanseverino, to whom he spoke forcefully of the danger of Venetian expansion, reminding them that at stake was not the "libertà" of Tuscany but of the Church itself, and that if Venice got any stronger "the pope would become the chaplain [cappellano] of the Venetians"—a rather audacious thing to say to a group of cardinals. Machiavelli thought they understood the gravity of the situation, and they promised to do whatever they could (*LCSG* 3.231.5–12).

The Ten wrote again to Machiavelli about the worsening situation in the Romagna: if, just days before, there seemed to be an "ounce" of danger, now there was a "pound." They urged him to go again to Julius and emphasize the seriousness of Venetian ambitions in what were, after all, territories of the Church and ask him to intervene. "If it seems appropriate, you could remind" Julius that Borgia "would not be a bad way to stabilize matters in the Romagna" (*LCSG* 3.233). Fear of Venetian expansion was pushing both Florence and Julius to ponder the possibility of using Borgia to halt it. Several cardinals, including Francesco Soderini, spoke to Julius and found him strongly inclined not to allow the Venetians to gain the upper hand in the Romagna. Julius reportedly said to them: "I have always been a friend to the Venetians and will continue to be, provided their aims do not exceed what is honorable. But if they intend to take what belongs to the Church, I will use all possible force to prevent them from succeeding." Issuing a threat that anticipated what he would do in 1509, he added, "I will incite all the princes of Christendom against them" (*LCSG* 3.235.10). According to Soderini, who showed the pope the latest letters from the Ten, Julius was "greatly disturbed" by Venice's actions. But Machiavelli commented that, although the pope said he was determined to halt the Venetian advance, he had not decided which of the signori of the Romagna cities he should support. Machiavelli thought Julius "confuso" about what to do, in part because his thoughts were on the "bella festa" he was planning for his coronation and "not worrying overmuch about extraneous problems" (*LCSG* 3.236.6–9). On November 11 Machiavelli reported that Julius was aware that, lacking sufficient military force, he could not expel Venice from the Romagna; all he could do was send an envoy to negotiate (*LCSG* 3.239.3–4).

Despite Julius's "confusion" and military weakness, Machiavelli nonetheless saw him as the focal point, or hinge, of all the most important conflicts in Italy. He provided the Ten with a wide-ranging analysis of the pope's dilemmas and possible courses of action, "in order that Your Lordships may be better able to discern how the pope can maneuver or what help can be expected from him against Venetian intentions." Here in Rome, Machiavelli begins, "is where all the most important [political] issues are dealt with." "The first and most important" is the struggle between France and Spain; the second is the Romagna; "then there are the factions of the [Roman] barons, and Duke Valentino [Cesare Borgia]. The pope is at the center of all these conflicts [umori]." But he is unable to do much about them: "because he has been in the papal office for so short a time, lacks soldiers and money, and is indebted to everyone for his election," he "cannot undertake any military action and must on the contrary navigate among these conflicts" until more favorable circumstances allow him to align himself in each case one way or the other. Although he is considered pro-French by "inner inclination [affezione naturale], he nevertheless conducts himself with Spain in such a way as to give no cause for complaint; nor does he lean so far toward Spain as to cause France to take offense." Venetian moves in the Romagna weigh heavily on him, and "you" (Florentines) complain to him about them. "It stands to reason that the situation in the Romagna deeply offends him because he is a bold [animoso] man who wants the [States of the] Church to expand, not diminish, during his time in office." Nonetheless, "on the one hand he accepts the explanations of the Venetians, giving the impression of believing they have acted from hatred of Borgia and not against the Church; on the other hand, he displays his unhappiness to you" over Venetian occupation of Church territory. Machiavelli says he has written this "discorso" to satisfy the Ten's request "that he profile the pope's mind [che si ritraessi la mente del Papa], what he wants to do or can do and what he wants you to do"—but also so that the Ten will not "hope for more from here," in other words, not to expect Julius to intervene militarily against Venice. "You should think of other means" of holding Venice off, "either by supporting [Borgia] or in some other way if there is one." The Ten should assume, for the moment, that Julius "will have to be satisfied with any possible outcome" in the Romagna as long as "matters there do not slip from the Church's control" (*LCSG* 3.239.14–23). Central to this portrait of the pope's "mind" is Machiavelli's perception that Julius was trapped by the contingencies of the moment, unable to take decisive action, forced to compromise with everyone and bide his time—a portrait starkly at odds with the "impetuous" Julius that Machiavelli would depict a decade later in chapter 25 of *The Prince*.

On November 16 Machiavelli reported that Julius had convened a meeting of some ten or eleven cardinals, "from amongst those who hold the honor and liberty" of the Church "piú a cuore," to discuss the situation in the Romagna. They decided to send the bishop of Tivoli, Angelo Leonini, to Venice to demand a cessation of its military operations and the transfer to papal authority of the territories it was occupying, and Cardinal Soderini to the Romagna to quell the uprisings and turn the situation there as best he could to the advantage of the Church. This, Machiavelli claims, showed the pontiff's determination to rescue these territories for the Church, as did his tough and menacing interview with the Venetian ambassador in which he said "he would never have believed that [the Venetians] so little appreciated the favors he has always bestowed on Venice as to seek to dishonor and dismember the [States of the] Church during his pontificate. Should they persist in such behavior, he was ready to sever all ties of friendship and destroy everything before letting the Church be dishonored and dismembered and indeed would summon the whole world against them" (*LCSG* 3.247.4–7, 11)—another anticipation of what the vengeful Julius did eventually do.

Four days later, Machiavelli had an audience with Julius in which he read to him the newest letters from the Ten. "His Holiness demonstrated great displeasure" over Venice's aggressive actions "and said he would stop at nothing to protect the honor of the Church. He had sent envoys to the Romagna, and would send others of even greater prestige [autorità]." To Florence's laments over papal inaction, Julius explained that "he had wanted to wait for a reply from Venice before proceeding further, so that he could act with greater justification and clarity concerning Venetian intentions." Now these reports from Florence persuaded him to put more pressure on Venice by appealing "to the princes" (of Italy? or also of France and Spain?) and their ambassadors in Rome. He intended to stop treating the Venetians with respectful formalities ("uscire di cirimonie") and asked Machiavelli to assure the Ten he would do everything he could to protect the Church's "liberty" and the security of its friends. But he asked for their understanding if, in these early days of his pontificate, he was not taking more forceful action. Not to do so was "against his nature," but, "lacking soldiers and funds, he was constrained by necessity." This, Machiavelli concluded, was as much of a commitment as he could get from Julius with regard to Venice; for the moment, Florence could not hope for more. Pondering Julius's comment about inaction being "against his nature," Machiavelli opined that "one thing does give cause for hope," namely, Julius's "proud and choleric nature [nella natura sua onorevole e collerica]," "onorevole" here meaning easily offended in matters affecting his honor. The ease with which Julius takes offense, Machiavelli adds, will "inflame him [lo accenderà]," and his quickness to anger "will impel him to take action against those who seek to dishonor the Church." However, having just written that his "proud and choleric nature" was cause for hope, Machiavelli then implies that Julius's temperament made him vulnerable to manipulation by the Venetians, who, "knowing his nature, will try to mollify him [addormentarlo]," literally, to lull him to sleep, and "placate this nature of his [satisfare a questa sua natura]," by "showing him that they wish to be his good sons and want not only the Romagna but all their dominions to be obedient to him." As evidence of this, Machiavelli notes that Venice sent no fewer than eight ambassadors to his coronation—something, he says, they had never previously done. The ambassadors put on a fancy show ("se ne fanno belli") and spoke everywhere in the papal court of the great joy in Venice over Julius's election and how they wished to honor him and wanted him as their "father, protector, and defender." Machiavelli thinks it was a clever ruse: "they are counting on these methods to be able to lull him to sleep and incline him to their purposes, and they won't be ashamed to present themselves as the servants of this pontiff in order to be able subsequently to rule over everyone." Seeing how Julius's "choleric nature" made him vulnerable to Venetian trickery, Machiavelli advised the Ten that it would be well "not to be outdone in [demonstrations of] humility and ceremony, since you cannot keep pace [with the Venetians] in power and good fortune" (*LCSG* 3.253.4–13). This is the beginning of Machiavelli's assessment of Julius's "natura," to which he would return, sometimes mystified and fascinated, sometimes fearful or disgusted, in the *Ghiribizzi* of 1506, in subsequent legations, in *The Prince*, and in the *Discourses*. In *The Prince* he would convert the quickness with which Julius took offense and let anger spur him to action into the "impetuosity" that he declares preferable to circumspection or caution. But in 1503 Machiavelli saw his "proud and choleric nature" as a source of weakness that exposed him to manipulation.

Faenza's surrender to the Venetians angered him, but Julius hesitated to take stern measures. Cardinal Soderini advised him to summon the ambassadors "di tutte le nazioni," including Venice, and in their presence to protest the "iniurie"—the wrongs, injustices, and injuries—inflicted on the Church by the Venetians. Soderini reminded Julius that his uncle, Pope Sixtus IV, brought "all of Italy" into an alliance against Venice (in the War of Ferrara of 1482–4). One imagines Julius did not need to be reminded of this, but he decided it was best not "to irritate the Venetians so soon." Soderini could not persuade him to adopt a harder line and told Machiavelli that "he sees the pope on the one hand unhappy and of a mind to resolve matters [with Venice] when the time seemed right, but on the other hand more hesitant" ("piú respettivo"—the very term Machiavelli would contrast with "impetuoso" in *Prince* 25)—"and more diffident [piú freddo] about taking the necessary measures" (*LCSG* 3.256.5–9). In *The Prince* Machiavelli would declare that Julius "acted *impetuosamente* in every matter," but in 1503 he saw him, in part through Cardinal Soderini's eyes, as more vacillating and even pusillanimous than *impetuoso*. So mystifyingly timid did Julius's inaction seem that some in Florence speculated, as the Ten told Machiavelli, that Venice's moves in the Romagna must have had "the agreement and permission of the pontiff. And perhaps this is not wrong, given what little concern [the Venetians] have shown for the Church and the pope in the agreements" they entered into with the cities of the Romagna (*LCSG* 3.257.15). In his dispatch of November 23 Machiavelli blamed the pope's failure to take the necessary actions against Venice on "the malice of the times and the misfortune of the weak [la malignità de' tempi e la cattiva sorta delli impotenti]" (*LCSG* 3.263.13)—a phrase that strikingly anticipates "the malignità di fortuna" stemming from the condition of dependence that Machiavelli offers in *Prince* 7 as one explanation of Cesare Borgia's failure.

When Machiavelli shared with Cardinal Soderini the Ten's suspicions that Julius and Venice were colluding, Soderini said he and Rouen had feared the same thing and discussed it several times, especially in view of Julius's slowness to act, but that, having subsequently spoken with the pope and seen how angry he was about Venetian operations, they could not believe it. Rouen likewise expressed great anger at the Venetians, "using grievous and extremely poisonous words," and suggested that their aggressive moves in the Romagna "could easily spell their ruin." According to Machiavelli, "in truth, one sees here a universal hatred of the Venetians," and "everyone cries out against them." "In sum, the general opinion is that the Venetians' seizure of Faenza will either open the door to all Italy for them or will be their ruin." In another meeting with the pope Machiavelli heard Julius say "he would ally with France and the emperor and would think of nothing but the destruction" of Venice (*LCSG* 3.264.4–16).

Although he was determined to regain control of the Romagna fortresses and halt the encroachments of the Venetians, for the moment the only weapons Julius had, Machiavelli wrote, were "warnings and threats," adding, with irony, "Your Lordships see how effective these are." He reminded the Ten that Cardinals Soderini and Rouen had rejected the suspicion that Julius was colluding with Venice, because they judged the pope to be "not two-faced, but instead impulsive and impetuous [non lo avendo per uomo doppio ma piú tosto rotto e impetuoso]." Soderini told Machiavelli that Rouen once even put the question of collusion squarely to Julius, who became hot with anger ("riscaldato e alterato") and solemnly swore that he was fiercely opposed to Venice's actions and that his words could not more decisively show his displeasure. Machiavelli nonetheless alluded to doubts among other well-informed observers who speculated that, among the many promises Cardinal Della Rovere had made to become pope, he might have promised some part of the Romagna to Venice (*LCSG* 3.268.18–21). Julius was becoming an intriguing puzzle for Machiavelli. On December 1, echoing what Francesco Soderini had told him, he wrote: "those familiar with the pope do not fear that he has consented to this undertaking by the Venetians, nor can it be thought that he is playing a double game [che vadi doppio], given that until now he has not been known to be such." They think of him instead as a "uomo rotto e sanza rispetti"—impulsive, reckless, and lacking caution and prudence (*LCSG* 3.277.9). The assumption behind this judgment was, evidently, that to engage in the deception of a "double game" required studied caution, calculation, and awareness of the attendant pitfalls and risks—a frame of mind summarized in the "rispetti" that Julius lacked. The image of a reckless Julius stayed with Machiavelli, famously in the *Ghiribizzi*, in which he wrote that "This pope, who has neither scales nor a measuring rule at home, achieves by chance, and unarmed, what with planning and arms should have been difficult to accomplish." And in 1513 Machiavelli told Francesco Vettori that King Ferdinand of Spain could not have trusted Julius, because he, Julius, was "instabile, rotto, furioso e misero"[19]—unstable, reckless, crazed, and tightfisted. The characterization of Julius as "furioso," written just after his death and in the aftermath of the catastrophic wars he had unleashed, extends his recklessness to the edge of madness. Such was Machiavelli's view of Julius just months before he penned the memorable portrait of him in *Prince* 25.

"FORCES SO GREAT AS TO MAKE ITALY TREMBLE"

Throughout 1504, Julius was trying to recover the cities and fortresses occupied by Venice. In June Machiavelli received a report in the chancery from Giovanni Ridolfi, commissioner in Castrocaro, that Julius was preparing to seize the fortress of Forlì, whose castellan, although holding it in Borgia's name, had become "more docile [piú umile]" since the duke's imprisonment. "We are pleased to know this," Machiavelli commented, "and we believe that, if the castellan's hopes were based on Borgia, they will slip through his fingers more each day as it becomes known that Consalvo is keeping him locked up" (*LCSG* 4.14.3–4).[20] In July Machiavelli told Ridolfi that the Ten were entrusting him with making Florentine artillery available to the duke of Urbino, who was leading papal troops as they closed in on Forlì. Julius was worried that the artillery would not be ready for the final assault (*LCSG* 4.32.4), but in August, again to Ridolfi, Machiavelli reported the "great

[19] *Lettere*, pp. 242–3 (*Ghiribizzi*), 383 (letter of April 29, 1513).

[20] *Legazioni. Commissarie. Scritti di governo*, vol. 4, ed. Denis Fachard and Emanuele Cutinelli-Rèndina (Rome: Salerno Editrice, 2006).

pleasure" of the Ten upon learning of the pope's recovery of the fortress of Forlì. The Ten asked Ridolfi to extend their warmest congratulations to Duke Guidobaldo and the hope that this victory would ensure the "liberty of the Church" (*LCSG* 4.65.9–11). Throughout 1504 official pronouncements from Florence, as relayed by Machiavelli, supported Julius's aims in the Romagna, no doubt because his success there provided a bulwark against Venetian expansionism.

By mid-1505, however, relations with Julius were changing. On May 29 an advisory *pratica*, redacted by Machiavelli himself, discussed Florence's options for the selection of a new military captain. Francesco Pepi, who belonged to the faction of ottimati hostile to Piero Soderini, said that, if Florence wanted someone of great reputation, they could turn to the Colonna family. But if they turned to that family's most famous captain, Fabrizio—as, in fact, Soderini wanted to do—Pepi foresaw "difficulties" and "negative consequences" stemming from the pope's changed attitude toward Florence. Julius, he said, "seems patently more hostile this year than he was a year ago." Pepi speculated that the reason was that he wanted his nephew Francesco Maria della Rovere to succeed to the duchy of Urbino when Guidobaldo died and feared that Fabrizio, who was married to a daughter of Federico da Montefeltro, Guidobaldo's father, might press the claims of his son to the duchy. The pope, said Pepi, "does not want the Colonna to become powerful and has therefore allied with the Orsini" (long-time rivals of the Colonna and related by marriage to the exiled Medici). Julius wanted Florence as well to ally with the Orsini, but, Pepi continued, "because Florence is at present opposed to the Orsini, Julius has become hostile to Florence and will continue to be until it turns toward the Orsini." Hence, Pepi opposed offering a contract to Fabrizio (*LCSG* 4.432.4–14).[21] These and other objections dissuaded Soderini from pursuing Fabrizio. Machiavelli no doubt realized from this episode that Julius's hardening attitude toward Florence and the Soderini government was rooted in the politics of family ambition, rivalries, and alliances. In July 1505 Pandolfo Petrucci of Siena told Machiavelli he feared Julius was seeking to create disturbances in Tuscany and predicted that he "might one day become another [Pope] Alexander," to which Machiavelli replied: "it is all the more necessary to extinguish these sparks" (*LCSG* 4.513.14–15).

In the summer of 1506 Julius was planning his expedition to Perugia and Bologna to reassert papal control over these two most important cities of the States of the Church. On June 12 Machiavelli wrote a private letter to Giovanni Ridolfi, now general commissioner on the Pisan front, to report that Julius was attempting to hire Swiss infantry and also asking the French for cavalry units to support the expedition. The French were willing to accede to Julius's request if he hired a small number of Swiss, but would oppose him if he hired a larger

[21] The *pratica* is also in *Consulte e pratiche, 1505–1512*, p. 13.

contingent, which, they surmised, would suggest that his ambitions extended beyond Perugia and Bologna.[22] At the end of June Machiavelli conveyed to the new Florentine captain in Castrocaro the Ten's permission to allow the papal governor of Forlì to recruit infantry into the service of the Church from nearby Florentine territories. This was to be done, however, with "as little publicity as possible [con meno demostrazione si può]." The Ten consented "because the pope had always allowed us to recruit troops within the Church's dominions," and "we would be ungrateful not to give His Holiness the same right [autorità]" (*LCSG* 5.389.9).[23] One wonders what Machiavelli, who had spent the previous winter raising and training troops for Florence's militia, thought of his government's decision to let Church officials recruit inhabitants of Florentine territories into the papal army. Late in July, when a Florentine official reported that the pope's condottiere Paolo Ramazzotto was seeking as many as 500 infantry around Marradi, the Ten had Machiavelli tell their commissioner in the area to investigate the matter and find out whether Ramazzotto was actually enlisting these troops on behalf of the pope or for someone else or some other purpose (*LCSG* 5.445.3–4; *LCSG* 5.446.5–8).

Julius announced his expedition on August 17, 1506, and nine days later left Rome with much of the papal court and guard.[24] The Signoria quickly sent Machiavelli as envoy, with instructions "to find His Holiness" and convey their response to Julius's plans for the "impresa [campaign] di Bologna" and particularly to the pope's request that Florence make available to him the services of the condottiere Marcantonio Colonna, Fabrizio's cousin, who had been employed by Florence since 1504. Machiavelli was to "praise the good and holy decision" to carry out the "impresa," but also to tell Julius that the request for "our condottiere and his troops came to us suddenly and unexpectedly and has therefore left us in considerable uncertainty [alquanto sospesi]." He was to inform Julius that, since March, Florence had terminated the contracts of several of its condottieri and could not afford to lend Marcantonio to the pope without incurring excessive risks in its war with Pisa. Machiavelli was, in effect, to buy time by promising that Florence would accede to the pope's request, but only after operations against Pisa closed down for the winter and Julius's campaign against Bologna had begun (*LCSG* 5.457.3–9). The Florentines knew, of course, that Julius could not let his campaign drag on into the winter.

[22] *Lettere*, p. 224.

[23] *Legazioni. Commissarie. Scritti di governo*, vol. 5, ed. Jean-Jacques Marchand, Andrea Guidi, and Matteo Melera-Morettini (Rome: Salerno Editrice, 2008).

[24] Emanuele Cutinelli-Rèndina provides an excellent analysis of Machiavelli's dispatches from this legation in *Chiesa e religione*, pp. 37–57, coming to somewhat different conclusions from mine concerning Machiavelli's judgment of Julius. Christine Shaw surveys the expedition from Julius's perspective in *Julius II*, pp. 150–61.

Machiavelli reached the papal court on August 27, 1506, in Nepi, some thirty miles north of Rome. The next day, from nearby Civita Castellana, he wrote a first and lengthy dispatch after having met with Julius, Cardinal Soderini, Cardinal Francesco Alidosi, and the papal protonotary.[25] To the pope he conveyed the undying devotion of the Ten and their approval of the "holy" expedition on which he had embarked. But Machiavelli also explained why the Ten had been slow to respond to Julius's request for the services of Marcantonio Colonna, namely, the expected arrival in Tuscany of Ferdinand of Spain, the rumors that the emperor (Maximilian) was amassing troops at the border of Venice's dominion, and Florence's ongoing struggle with Pisa. In these circumstances, he said, Florence could not allow Marcantonio to leave his command and join Julius's march to Bologna. Machiavelli also told Julius—begging the pontiff's forgiveness ("e di questo mi perdoni vostra Beatitudine") as he did so—that the Ten did not think "the affairs of the Church were being managed [si maneggino] the way those of princes are [in conformità di quelle de' principi]." In this surprisingly audacious critique of Julius's governance of the States of the Church Machiavelli specifically mentions the lax controls over exiles from papal cities and the absence of any sign of French support for the expedition, which "diminishes confidence [toglie fede]" in what Julius had been publicly asserting. The Florentines would not of course fail to provide assistance, he assured him—just as soon as the promised French support materialized, implying, in effect, that, to secure Florence's support, Julius was disingenuously pretending that French military help was already guaranteed. Machiavelli may have mused that, in this respect at least, Julius was not so different from Cesare Borgia. Both lacked sufficient arms for their grandiose projects, both claimed to have the full backing of the French king, and both sought alliances with, and military assistance from, Florence. Machiavelli concluded his presentation saying that nothing could better express the wishes of his government or more fully confirm the truth of what he had been saying than the text itself of his instructions (the "commissione"), which he pulled from his pocket and read to Julius, "de verbo ad verbum" (*LCSG* 5.459.3–11).

Julius listened "attentively and happily [lietamente]" and, "after carefully considering what he had heard," replied that the Florentines "feared three things": first, that French support was not coming; second, that he was "conducting the expedition tepidly [la governassi fredda]"; and third, that he might come to an agreement with Giovanni Bentivoglio, signore of Bologna, to let him remain in control of the city. On the first point, Julius showed Machiavelli King Louis's signature on the instructions brought by his representative (the bishop of Aix-en-Provence, Pierre Le Filleul, called Monsignore d'Ais in Machiavelli's

[25] On this dispatch, see the intriguing essay by Jean-Jacques Marchand, "Teatralità nel primo Machiavelli. Il dispaccio ai Dieci di Balía del 28 agosto 1506," in *Il Teatro di Machiavelli*, ed. Gennaro Barbarisi and Anna Maria Cabrini (Milan: Cisalpino, 2005), pp. 45–66.

dispatches). Just as Machiavelli had read aloud to Julius his "commissione" from the Ten, the pope similarly read aloud from the document the passages in which Louis approved the "impresa di Bologna," offered to give the pope 400 to 500 lances, and encouraged him to conclude the matter "presto presto." He then read two letters in which the king instructed his governor in Milan (Charles d'Amboise, Cardinal Rouen's brother) to send the lances whenever they were requested on the pope's behalf. As for the alleged lethargy of the enterprise, Julius replied that he was already on his way to Bologna and could not conduct the matter more spiritedly ("piú calda") than by leading it in person as he was. Nor did he intend to let Giovanni Bentivoglio remain in Bologna: he did not want him to stay in any official capacity, and Bentivoglio "would be crazy to stay as a private citizen" (*LCSG* 5.459.12–17).

King Louis's intentions were not as clear as Julius claimed. On the same day Monsignore d'Ais took Machiavelli aside to explain "the difficulties he had had in getting the king to agree" to assist Julius. Louis initially did not believe Julius would actually carry out the announced campaign, but now, "seeing him on the move, the king's inclination to assist him will redouble." Machiavelli replied that the Florentines were astonished that an envoy of the king's governor in Milan had gone to Bologna to assure Bentivoglio that Louis would not fail him. Machiavelli should not be so surprised, Ais said: either the governor did this on his own, or, if with the king's consent, it was because Louis "sees that matters in Rome never reach any conclusion or get properly launched [non sortire effetto, né darsi principio a cosa veruna]." Ais said that, when Louis and Julius reached their agreement, he heard the king loudly announce to the Bolognese ambassador that the people of Bologna should be of good cheer and have no fear, because Julius was asking for French support only for Perugia, and, "if he sought help for anything else, [Louis] would refuse" (*LCSG* 5.459.20–2). The ambiguity no doubt fed Florentine skepticism about Julius's real intentions and capabilities.

Still on the same day, during a visit to the fortress in nearby Civita Castellana (rebuilt by Antonio da Sangallo under Alexander VI: Machiavelli calls it "cosa rara [exceptional, splendid]"), Julius took Machiavelli aside and repeated all the same assurances he had given him that morning. To reassure the Florentines that he had the necessary military strength, he said he had 400 "well paid" cavalry in addition to those coming from France and, so he hoped, from Florence. He also expected a hundred or more "stradiotti" (light horse) from Naples and Giampaolo Baglioni's cavalry, claiming also to have an abundance of infantry whose sources and number he did not specify. Julius prodded the Florentines to join this (still unassembled) army: when "all these forces" are together, "yours," he said, "will not want to be the last" to arrive. Machiavelli told the Ten he made no commitments ("Io stetti sempre largo"), replying in generalities and steering clear of Julius's not so subtle pressure on Florence to join the expedition. This conversation persuaded Machiavelli that "not many days will pass before Julius asks you to let our forces" join his, "despite the fact that the king's troops have not moved" (*LCSG* 5.459.23–6). Machiavelli knew Julius had still not created the army he would need to expel Bentivoglio from Bologna. At the end of this long dispatch, he gave a quick summary of where the pope intended to go over the next few weeks: to Viterbo, Orvieto, Piegaro, and Perugia, where, he noted, "he might stay for a short or a long time, for no one knows what his intentions are with regard to arranging things there or how he wishes to deal with Giampaolo." After Perugia, Julius would proceed to Urbino, where, as Machiavelli notes without comment, "he wants to hire 4,000 infantry" (*LCSG* 5.459.29–30), which was rather at odds with the boast, earlier that day, that he already had a "bag full of infantry."

From Viterbo, on August 31, Machiavelli reported that the marquis of Mantua, Francesco Gonzaga, had sent word that, on orders from King Louis, he would not meet Julius as promised. This prompted speculation that Louis had decided not to support the expedition after all. Machiavelli assessed Julius's strength: "the pope is riding in person and going forward according to preset stages of his route. He is not yet recruiting infantry and has no plans for other men-at-arms [cavalry] beyond those I have already indicated to Your Lordships." Machiavelli enumerated Julius's forces, existing and hoped for: 200 cavalry from the duke of Urbino and 100 from Francesco Maria della Rovere (Julius's nephew), both contingents already near Perugia; 75 cavalry in the Romagna under orders to join the pope; and 50 mounted crossbowmen "who, being equivalent to 25 men-at-arms, complete the number of 400" men-at-arms of which Julius had boasted. These, Machiavelli wrote, were Julius's "own and present forces [presenti e sue proprie]." Giampaolo Baglioni's cavalry and the Neapolitan *stradiotti* would be in addition to these. Expressing doubts about Julius's military preparations, Machiavelli comments that "one hears of no other provision for this undertaking, neither infantry nor anything else," but he repeats the rumor ("dicesi") that Julius will recruit infantry at Urbino (*LCSG* 5.461.6–14). Francesco Gonzaga's defection upset the pope, as Machiavelli wrote on September 1, for Julius now realized he needed "greater and better organized forces [maggiore fondamento e piú ordinato]," in other words, the French. Without assurance that French troops were on the way, Julius decided he would not go beyond Perugia or, at most, Urbino. Whereas three days earlier he had said he would make use of French forces only if necessary, he made their involvement the sine qua non of the entire enterprise. Nonetheless, he sent an envoy to Bologna to announce his intention to enter the city, demanding preparations for his arrival and for billeting 500 French lances in the Bolognese contado (*LCSG* 5.462.3–7). He would bide his time between Viterbo and Urbino, neither recruiting troops nor spending money until he had word that French forces had begun to move from Milan to Bologna. So much did Julius seem hampered by dependence on France that, as Machiavelli wrote, the Bentivoglio envoy in the papal court took great comfort from the delay and from the belief that the Bolognese had secure promises of protection from Louis (*LCSG* 5.464.7).

The Venetians complicated matters by offering to help Julius take Bologna and expel the Bentivoglio—if he ceded Faenza and Rimini to them. Julius "scoffed at the idea [si fa beffe]," Machiavelli reported, "and wouldn't hear of it." Yet there was some concern that, if the French failed to assist him, he might accept Venice's offer. Because of already signed agreements with France, Julius would not have doubted the French if it were not for the marquis of Mantua's sudden decision, imposed by Louis, not to join the expedition. This "keeps everyone in anxious suspense [fa stare li animi sospesi]." Machiavelli told the Ten that Julius would "perhaps" go to Montefiascone the next day but then cautioned: "I say 'perhaps' in order not to be in error." He advised the Ten not to be astonished at Julius's reversals and shifts—his "variazioni," a term that will play a key role in the discussion of Julius in *The Prince*—"because in these matters he has made and will make many changes; those who know the pope say that nothing fixed in one place can be found there the next day" (*LCSG* 5.464.5–15).

By September 5 the papal court was in Orvieto, where Machiavelli again wrote that Julius considered French support essential to the campaign and that without it he would return to Rome, "unless he turns to help from others"—alluding presumably to Venice's offer—"which people don't think will happen." Being close to Perugia, and with the Bologna project temporarily on hold, Julius turned his attention to Giampaolo Baglioni. He wanted control of the city's fortresses and towers, and the Perugian envoys, speaking on behalf of the communal authorities, "freely" consented. It was not clear, Machiavelli wrote, what sort of agreement Julius sought with Baglioni, "because until now he has wanted Giampaolo out of Perugia or at least for him to stay as a private citizen with no soldiers" under his command. "He could perhaps change his mind, partly out of necessity and partly as a result of persuasion from [Baglioni's] numerous supporters" in the papal court. The "necessity" to which Machiavelli alludes was that, to secure Bologna, Julius might need Giampaolo's cavalry and infantry, which "makes it difficult" to expel him. "Once this difficulty has been demonstrated to the pope, he will easily be persuaded" that it is preferable to enlist Giampaolo in the march on Bologna than to try to banish him, that "once Bologna is taken care of, [Julius] will not lack the means to secure Perugia, and that it is better to undertake one such enterprise [at a time], not two, because one could ruin the other. For these reasons it is thought that, for now, Giampaolo could easily escape "questa fortuna"—the *mis*fortune of exile (*LCSG* 5.466.4–10).

Machiavelli continued to portray Julius as indecisive and easily swayed by the opinions of others and changing circumstances, as an impulsive actor who needed to be kept in check by his handlers. On September 6 he reported the arrival in Orvieto of Guidobaldo da Montefeltro and the papal legate of Perugia,[26] who "are

[26] The papal legate of Perugia was not Cardinal Giovanni de' Medici (as asserted in *LCSG*, p. 449, n. 3, and elsewhere in the volume). According to the *Saggio di memorie storiche civili ed ecclesiastiche*

steering matters toward the hoped-for objective, namely, to save [salvare] Giampaolo. They have persuaded Julius to be satisfied with making use of him and his troops in the Bologna campaign, but not to hire him as a condottiere or otherwise offer him a contract. [Julius] will give [Giampaolo] and his troops an honorable subvention for this undertaking and [Giampaolo] will come here [to Orvieto] in person to pay homage to the pope. He could arrive at any hour." Machiavelli added that "it is believed the pope will not change his mind because he has around him those who keep him under control [chi li tiene le mani addosso: keep their hands on him] and will not let him deviate [variare] in those things that are in their interest" (*LCSG* 5.468.4). The Ten expressed their puzzlement: "we don't know what to say or what judgment to make of this undertaking of the pope, given his difficulties in obtaining the support he had planned on"—the Ten had learned that Julius's agreement with Louis was never securely settled—"and we strongly fear that, given his nature [attesa la natura sua] and despairing of the support [he expected], he might try something different and come to an agreement with the Venetians" (*LCSG* 5.469.4–5).

Baglioni arrived in Orvieto on September 8 (*LCSG* 5.470.9) and was "ceremoniously" received by Julius. The next day they both departed: Julius to Città della Pieve and then to Castiglione del Lago; Baglioni home to Perugia. They agreed that Baglioni would yield command of Perugia's fortresses and gates to Julius and entrust one or two of his sons to the custody of the duke of Urbino as pledges; that Julius would station 500 infantry in Perugia's main piazza and 50 at each of the gates; and that Baglioni and his cavalry would be at the pope's service in the Bologna campaign (*LCSG* 5.471.5–8). Machiavelli reported that Julius said "he wanted to completely humiliate [al tutto abbassare]" Giampaolo, who, like his sons, was consigned to the duke of Urbino. Julius did not intend to "take his life" for past offenses but from this point forward would punish him for the least misstep (*LCSG* 5.475.12). Meanwhile, word came that Francesco Gonzaga had reversed his earlier decision and was coming to meet Julius. With Baglioni neutralized, everyone now assumed, as Machiavelli informed the Ten, that the Bologna campaign seemed much "easier" and Bentivoglio's prospects much grimmer. Gonzaga's imminent arrival was seen as evidence that the French would keep their promises to Julius and that the expedition would proceed unimpeded (*LCSG* 5.471.11–12). The Ten asked Machiavelli to make Julius aware of how much it would damage his honor if, out of desperation, he agreed to a deal with Venice (*LCSG* 5.469.4). Machiavelli assured them the pope was being told this every day, "but if Louis

della città di Perugia by Annibale Mariotti (Perugia, 1806), the legate was Antonio Feltreo della Rovere. I thank Andrea Guidi for alerting me to this source. According to the entry on him by Raffaella Cascioli in the *Dizionario biografico degli Italiani*, vol. 46, 1996 (consulted online: https://www.treccani.it/enciclopedia/antonio-ferreri_(Dizionario-Biografico)/), his original name was Antonio Ferreri. While not actually related to Julius, he had entered the service of the della Rovere, who gave him the privilege of using their name.

plays a duplicitous game with him [se Francia farà seco a mal gioco]," he added, Julius might prefer harm to the Church and risk to others (i.e. Florence) "to his own shame, which would indeed be great if he returned to Rome without undertaking any of the things for which he set out. Those who know his nature fear this, as do Your Lordships, but they see no solution for him except to do what he thinks would be harmful to let others [the Venetians] do." Julius's fear of humiliation, in other words, would drive him on to Bologna (*LCSG* 5.475.7–8).

On September 13 Julius entered Perugia "solennemente." But just at this moment of his show of strength, word arrived (through Rouen's nephew) that Louis was now discouraging Julius from going on to Bologna and, given the tenuous French hold on Milan, would give him no military assistance. "The pope is exceedingly angry [alterato assai] over this; nonetheless, he has decided to carry out the expedition on his own even if everyone fails him." Julius now placed his hopes for a successful outcome on recruiting 6,000 to 8,000 infantry, not from the States of the Church, but from the territories of Florence and Ferrara. He sent letters to both governments seeking permission for his condottiere Ramazzotto to recruit this force from their contado populations. Machiavelli commented at this point, perhaps sardonically, that "these matters have the instability [variazione] that Your Lordships see, and he who must write about them day by day has to follow them and therefore deserves to be excused"—almost as if Machiavelli felt a bit embarrassed about sending a daily revised version of Julius's intentions (*LCSG* 5.476.4–10). A day later, he commented that, despite what the French envoy said about Louis's change of heart, Julius "is more eager [piú caldo] than ever" to move on to Bologna and does not seem to have lost hope in the French." "To everyone the undertaking seems audacious [animosa] without France, and all anxiously await the outcome." Machiavelli reported that many still feared Julius might jump for the Venetian offer "as a last desperate measure [per ultima desperazione]." Speculation continued to swirl around Louis's decision not to assist Julius and about Venice's proposal to provide the help that Louis was now refusing the pope. "Time, which is the father of truth, will tell" (*LCSG* 5.477.7–13).

The situation in Perugia was precarious. "Although the cavalry [genti] of the Church are billeted around the city gates and those of Giampaolo are a little more distant," Machiavelli told the Ten, "nonetheless the pope and [cardinals] are at the mercy of [a discrezione di] Giampaolo, not Giampaolo at theirs." Machiavelli may have thought this because, as he says at the end of this dispatch, the infantry that was to have preceded Julius into the city to guard the gates and the piazza had not yet arrived and were still two days away. This may be why, a decade later, Machiavelli wrote in the *Discourses* (1.27.3) that Julius entered the city "disarmato." In the dispatch of September 13 his perception that Julius was more "at the mercy" of Giampaolo than vice versa induces him to contemplate the possibility, even as he dismisses its likelihood, that Giampaolo might attack or arrest the pope: "And if [Giampaolo] does no harm [se non farà male] to him who has come to deprive him of his stato, this is probably because of his good nature and benevolence [sarà per sua buona natura e umanità]. What the outcome will be I do not know; it should become clear in the six or eight days the pope will remain here." The suggestion that Baglioni might have harmed Julius, but refrained from doing so out of his "good nature and benevolence," anticipates, even as it contrasts with, Machiavelli's assertion in the *Discourses* that Giampaolo's failure to act must be attributed to "viltà [cowardice and incompetence]" and *not* to any "bontà" or "conscienza" that might have held him back. To be sure, the two texts make different arguments based on different perceptions of Baglioni. Yet the astonishing hostility toward Julius evident in the *Discourses*—the contemplation of a justified use of lethal force against a belligerent pope come to take away Giampaolo's "stato," and the missed opportunity to carry out a "deed whose courage everyone would have admired" and by which Baglioni "would have left everlasting memory of himself as the first to show the prelates how little those who live and reign as they do are to be esteemed" (*DL* 1.27.5–7)—is already present in the dispatch of September 13 in the notion that, *if* Giampaolo does him no harm, *only* Giampaolo's "good nature and benevolence" will have held him back from justifiable, reasonable resistance against one who intended to deprive him of his "stato." Machiavelli claims Giampaolo said there were two ways of saving his "stato," either with "forza" or with humility and trust in friends who advise him. Preferring the second method, he entrusted his fate to the duke of Urbino (*LCSG* 5.476.11–13), a decision that, for the moment, seemed to turn out well for him. "From what I hear," Machiavelli says in the next day's dispatch, "it seems that the subvention Julius intended to give Giampaolo is beginning to be discussed as a condotta," with some disagreement only about the size of the cavalry Baglioni would be permitted. Machiavelli thought this would be satisfactorily resolved "because matters between Giampaolo and the pope, from what one sees, are continuously improving" (*LCSG* 5.477.15). On September 15, reporting the arrival of infantry from the duchy of Urbino, he speculated that these, "perhaps," were the troops that would remain in Perugia after the pope's departure, according to the agreement (*LCSG* 5.478.6).

Uncertainty still surrounded Julius's plans for Bologna. His desire to proceed was said to be "fervent ['l Papa ci è su caldo]." The Bentivoglio envoy told Machiavelli that Julius was beginning to listen to the Venetians and could "easily" agree to collaborate with them (*LCSG* 5.478.9–10). Machiavelli had conversed at length with Ercole Bentivoglio about the pope's prospects for taking Bologna. A long-time captain of Florence's forces, Ercole had been dismissed in March 1506, after a setback in the Pisan war. Although related to the ruling Bentivoglio, he was excluded from the succession because he had spent his youth in Florence and pursued a career as an independent condottiere, much of it in the service of Florence. He and Machiavelli had developed close ties during their collaboration in the Pisan campaigns, and, as noted in Chapter 1, Machiavelli sent him a copy of the printed edition of the first *Decennale* early in 1506, to which Ercole responded with a warmly laudatory letter. By September, he had entered the service of Pope Julius, but his friendship with Machiavelli allowed him to speak candidly. Admittedly "confused by these doings of the pope," he believed there was only one way Julius could succeed in expelling Giovanni Bentivoglio from Bologna, namely, to force him to spend heavily, for example, by going to Imola and deploying 600 or 700 men-at-arms and 5,000 or 6,000 infantry to conduct raids in the Bolognese countryside during the next winter and destroy crops in the spring. Ercole thought Bentivoglio would not endure such assaults because he was unwilling to spend what little cash he had without being certain of his survival, only to find himself both bereft of funds and in exile (*LCSG* 5.478.13–14).

On September 16 and still in Perugia Julius formally announced in consistory that the long hoped-for French military assistance was ready (*LCSG* 5.479.8). The Ten relayed, in code, to Machiavelli that "Rouen seems to think it would be well to please the pope and give him troops for the Bologna expedition" (*LCSG* 5.481.6–7). Francesco Gonzaga arrived in Perugia and had a long talk with Julius. Six ambassadors from Bologna were expected at any moment. On the 17th Machiavelli was summoned to court but waited all day and never saw the pope. He guessed that Julius was going to ask Florence to ready forces in support of the expedition but must have decided to wait (*LCSG* 5.482.4–6, 12–14). On the 19th word came that the anti-papal exiles of Forlì, supported by Venetian forces, had tried to storm the city's walls with cries of "Marco, Marco." Julius was furious and immediately declared he would send "all his troops," under the command of another nephew, to confront the crisis. But the next day, Machiavelli wrote that he had "changed his mind": he would not send his nephew and might not even send troops (*LCSG* 5.483.4–12). There was no end to the pope's reversals and reconsiderations.

From Perugia Julius went to Gubbio and then to Urbino. On September 25 Machiavelli wrote from Gubbio that the pope was still waiting for the French reply that would determine "whether there is to be peace or war." "Everything depends on the French cavalry, although the pope says that, even without the French, he wants to carry out the *impresa* in any case" (*LCSG* 5.486.7–8). Back in Florence, the Ten were now uncertain about French intentions, telling Machiavelli they had the impression that Louis and his advisers had made no firm decision about assisting Julius and were still giving reassuring, if vague, signals to Giovanni Bentivoglio. "What displeases us above all," the Ten wrote, "is learning that the king of France is urging the pope to make at least some concessions to the Venetians. We alert you to this so that, in whatever way possible, something can be done to stop it" (*LCSG* 5.487.9–12). From Urbino, Machiavelli speculated on the possibilities facing Julius, now describing him as "more eager than ever [ci è su piú caldo che mai]" to take Bologna. By leaving Rome Julius believed he had "shown the whole world his firm determination [el buono animo suo]" to "bring the cities [of the papal dominions] to obedience to the Church and cleanse them of their tyrants" (*LCSG* 5.488.5).

In the same dispatch Machiavelli comments that "those who know [Julius's] temperament [umore] believe that, if he must rush headlong [precipitare] into something, this [the Bologna campaign] is the least dangerous *precipizio* [cliff, precipice] over which he could jump." Given how much he wants this and how far he has come, "one concludes that either the expedition will succeed according to his original plan or he will rush headlong [si precipiti] wherever he thinks it might turn out best for him, or he will deceive himself in some agreement, honorable in appearance if not in actuality. An agreement that seems honorable seems difficult to find. Because of the French, it is not believed he can succeed according to his original wishes; and [without the French] it is greatly feared that he will rush headlong [del precipizio si dubita assai]," presumably into a trap set by the Venetians (*LCSG* 5.488.5–7). Elsewhere Machiavelli uses "precipitare" to connote negative consequences of, or punishments for, ill-advised actions: in *Prince* 23.6, a prince who fails to control the advice he receives "either is ruined by flatterers [precipita per li adulatori]" or suffers diminished esteem because the many opinions he hears cause him to change his mind too often; in *Discourses* 1.24.12–13, Manlius Capitolinus, after saving the Capitol from the Gauls, is found guilty of sedition and punished by being "thrown headlong [gittato precipite] from that same Capitol." In this dispatch Machiavelli similarly uses the term to suggest a potentially ruinous misjudgment. The opinion that, if the pope is determined to rush headlong into some action, the expedition to seize Bologna is the "least dangerous cliff" from which he could jump implies that all his options are risky. The passage seems to be saying that Julius cannot keep himself from headlong rushes into things that could prove ruinous. But, because, having proceeded so far into the expedition, he cannot retreat, the outcome has to be either a successful completion of the original plan (with French assistance); or, if the French fail him, a risky jump—the deal offered by Venice—that might turn out well for him; or, last possibility, a compromise agreement with Giovanni Bentivoglio that Julius might consider "honorable" but which, given how much of his prestige he has invested in expelling Bentivoglio, would dishonor and even shame him. An honorable agreement with Bentivoglio is impossible, and few now believe the French will give Julius the assistance to drive him from Bologna. Many fear, therefore, that he will rush headlong over some other cliff: "del precipizio si dubita assai," where "dubitare" means, as it usually did at the time, fear, not doubt.[27]

[27] Significant differences in punctuation among the editions further complicate the interpretation of the last part of the passage. *LCSG* 5.488 has: "Questo accordo che paia onesto, pare difficile a trovare che li riesca secondo el primo suo desiderio: rispetto a' Franzesi, non si crede; del precipizio si dubita assai." But Vivanti (*Opere*, vol. 2, p. 1029) and Martelli (Machiavelli, *Tutte le opere* [Florence: Sansoni, 1971], p. 594) follow the transcription by L. Passerini and G. Milanesi, *Legazioni e commissarie di Niccolò Machiavelli*, vol. 3 (Florence-Rome: Tipografia Cenniniana, 1876), p. 200, which places a period after

On September 26 the envoy Julius sent to Bologna returned with the reply that "the city is willing to show in every way that it is well disposed toward Holy Church, provided the pope has no intention of altering the *capituli*," the existing treaties between the city and the papacy in which Bologna was guaranteed a large measure of autonomy. If Julius sought to upset these conventions, however, the city "would defend itself," and Bentivoglio was strengthening its defenses. In the same dispatch Machiavelli reported the arrival from France of letters about which Julius "showed himself very happy [molto allegro]" because, as he announced, they brought assurance of the French military assistance he needed. He held in his hand a document he described as containing a list of the military units and captains that were on their way. Machiavelli could not give any details because "Julius did not say more about it" (*LCSG* 5.489.4–7). He must have wondered if Julius was again bluffing, for the next day he wrote that, while the pope "had great hopes" for French support, "according to what one hears, no decision has yet arrived." Nonetheless, he added, "the pope's stubborn determination [ostinazione] to go forward and bring this undertaking to a conclusion increases every day" (*LCSG* 5.491.4–7).

That Julius was still caught between two stronger powers, France and Venice, was the main topic of Machiavelli's dispatch of the 28th in which he reported on a long, closed meeting that included Julius, Duke Guidobaldo da Montefeltro, the Venetian ambassador, and Cardinal Francesco Alidosi. Observers assumed the discussion focused on the guarantees the Venetians sought that the pope would not attack them, presumably in the Romagna cities they still occupied. Machiavelli knew from the Ten that Louis was urging Julius to give Venice some assurance in this regard, and he reports in this dispatch that the pope was open to a spoken promise but not to the formal written commitment the Venetians wanted. Machiavelli thought Julius might be walking into a trap. "The further the pope enters into this undertaking, the more he is committed to it, and the Venetians and the king are waiting for him to get into a difficult situation to make him accede to their wishes [lo aspettono a qualche stretta per farlo calare alle voglie loro]. If the king holds firm with the Venetians, they could succeed." A person "familiar with these negotiations" (Machiavelli does not name him) offered a different view: namely, that "the king thinks he can make the pope knuckle under [calare] with these tactics, but the pope will make *him* knuckle under, such are the spurs [sproni] he will drive into the king's flank if the decision [of the French] about providing troops is not made in the pope's favor." Machiavelli admits he has "no idea what these spurs could be [che sproni si abbino ad essere questi, io non li so]. Your Lordships can make their own judgment" (*LCSG* 5.492.4–7). It has been

"trovare," making what follows a separate sentence: "Questo accordo che paia onesto, pare difficile ad trovare. Che li riesca secondo el primo suo desiderio, rispetto a' franzesi, non si crede; del precipizio si dubita assai." As my interpretation indicates, I believe the second reading makes clearer sense.

suggested that Machiavelli here confidently accepts the unnamed insider's assessment of the pope's ability to "drive spurs into the king's flanks" and was beginning to glimpse, even without knowing what those "spurs" might be, the "ineluctable" and "triumphal" conclusion of the expedition—that he understood at last, after much puzzlement over the yawning gap between the "material possibilities" of Julius's policies and the final outcome that could not be rationally deduced from those possibilities, why Julius was able to bind Louis to his cause and ensure his victory.[28] But if Machiavelli accepted the observer's assertion of Julius's leverage over the king and was beginning to foresee the successful outcome of the expedition, one would expect him at least to speculate what those "spurs" were and not simply tell the Ten to make their own conjecture. In any case, Machiavelli would soon discover that Julius's "triumph" actually came at the cost of serious concessions to the king that weakened the Church in Italy.

On September 28 Julius sent an emissary—curiously, his butler or majordomo ("cubiculario")—to Milan to settle matters with France that were evidently not yet resolved (*LCSG* 5.493.9). On October 3 the Ten wrote to Machiavelli that Louis had made a "firm and clear" decision to provide the soldiers Julius wanted: "It seems there is no longer any doubt of it: they number 500 lances" (*LCSG* 5.496.4). Julius, who was now in Santarcangelo di Romagna, received the news through his own channels, and Machiavelli commented that it "injected so much spirit into the pontiff [messo tanto animo in corpo a questo Pontefice] that it seems to him he has already conquered Bologna and is beginning to think of something still grander." Confident of victory, Julius summoned the Bolognese ambassadors and let them deliver a "long oration" in which, after offering "the obedience of the people of Bologna and their submission to the Church," they brought forth the "capituli" negotiated with several popes and recently confirmed by Julius himself. "They explained" to the pope, Machiavelli says, the city's "*politico vivere*, its abundant religion, and observance of law" (*LCSG* 5.498.5–8). Did the ambassadors actually use the phrase "politico vivere"? Or did Machiavelli paraphrase their characterization of Bologna's right to self-government in terms so central to his own political language? Either way, the ambassadors' bold challenge to the pope's intention to discard the longstanding agreements between Bologna and the papacy clearly made an impression on Machiavelli. So did Julius's reply, to judge at least from the point-by-point summary of it he gave the Ten. The pope countered that, if the Bolognese "people are devoted to the Church," as the ambassadors claim, "they are [merely] doing their duty [faceva el debito suo], obligated as they are to the Church [perché li era obligo]. And because the Church is such a good lord [buon signore] and the people of Bologna good subjects [buon servo], he was coming to them in person to liberate them from the tyrants." As for the "capituli,"

[28] Cutinelli-Rèndina, *Chiesa e religione*, pp. 55–6.

Julius peremptorily rejected any notion of mutual or contractual relationship between lord and subjects: "he cares neither about what other popes did nor about what he himself has done, because he and [former popes] were unable to do otherwise; necessity, not free choice [volontà], had made them ratify those treaties. But the time having come when he can correct them, it would seem to him that if he did not do so he could not justify himself before God." Obliquely mocking Bologna's "politico vivere," Julius said he had come to Bologna to ensure that the city would live well [vivessi bene]," eliding the "politico" dimension of its life. Again alluding to the "politico vivere," he announced that "if he found the method of governance [quello modo di vivere] practiced by the Bolognese to his liking, he would confirm it; if not, he would change it. And if other ways of doing this did not suffice, he had assembled forces to enable him to do it with arms, forces so great as to make Italy tremble [fare tremare Italia], not only Bologna." The bewildered ambassadors, according to Machiavelli, departed saying but few words (*LCSG* 5.498.9–10).

In fact, Julius was still assembling the forces of which he boasted. In this same dispatch Machiavelli wrote that papal cavalry quartered at Santarcangelo would be mustered the next day and "orders were being given to recruit infantry." Julius already counted among his forces the 100 men-at-arms of Marcantonio Colonna that Florence had not yet agreed to provide. But now he wanted them ready to move whenever he needed them (*LCSG* 5.498.11–12). On October 4 Ramazzotto told Julius "he was ready with the infantry," but Machiavelli commented that he did not see any effort at further recruitment. Moreover, several condottieri who had accepted employment in the papal army were losing hope, and "people fear that Julius thinks his 2,000 Italians will suffice for an assault on Bologna even as he is still counting on the 3,000 Swiss" the French wanted to bring with them (*LCSG* 5.500.9–10). When the troops were mustered the next day, Machiavelli counted 600 men-at-arms, 1,000 infantry of the duke of Urbino, 600 recruited by Nanni Morattini of Forlì, and 300 soldiers of the pope's Swiss guard. Ramazzotto's infantry had not yet appeared, but his messenger said he had 4,000 ready whenever the pope wanted them (*LCSG* 5.501.5–7). Julius hired only 750 of Ramazzotto's reported 4,000, and 300 of Morattini's, and gave orders for another 5,000 to 6,000 to be at the ready—from where or whom Machiavelli does not say (*LCSG* 5.502.6). Julius expected the French to bring 600 lances, infantry variously estimated between 3,000 and 5,000, and twenty-four pieces of artillery (*LCSG* 5.501.9; 502.6). Julius was pleased that the Ten allowed him to borrow an (unspecified) number of Florentine infantry. From Machiavelli's comment, these were evidently recruits from the militia he had begun to organize, and he boasted to the Ten that, "if Your Lordships could see the infantry of the duke of Urbino and Morattini, they would neither be ashamed of, nor esteem lightly, those of their own Ordinanza" (*LCSG* 5.501.7). Even at this late date, Julius's forces were hoped for, expected, and arriving piecemeal or perhaps not at all.

Yet the pope had another weapon that he, alone among princes, could wield, the so-called spiritual sanctions that withhold the sacraments from the laity. On October 5 Julius and the cardinals with him, in consistory, imposed "censure" against Bologna (*LCSG* 5.501.8) and two days later an interdict (*LCSG* 5.504.6). Machiavelli already had the impression that Giovanni Bentivoglio's resistance was beginning to weaken [cominci a piegarsi] and that he was "coming down from the ostentatious bravado he had been displaying recently [che si abbassi da quella sua tanta gagliardia che si prometteva a questi dí]" (*LCSG* 5.501.8). The Bolognese attempted to reopen negotiations and even requested that two cardinals be sent to reform the government, but Julius would have none of it (*LCSG* 5.502.7). On October 9 the pope made a formal entrance into Forlì. "If before he was *caldo* about the expedition, now he is *caldissimo*." His troops went ahead to Imola, but he was still waiting for the French forces, believed to be near Modena. (*LCSG* 5.504.6–8). The Bolognese ambassadors presented to Julius the draft of a proposal according to which he could bring only his Swiss guard of 250–300 soldiers into the city and must commit beforehand to a stay of specific length. The indignant pope and cardinals reacted by immediately issuing a bull—"much stronger," says Machiavelli, than the interdict—that declared Giovanni Bentivoglio and his followers "rebels against Holy Church" with plenary indulgences promised to anyone who seized their goods, property, and persons, or even killed them. Julius summoned Bentivoglio's secretary, who had accompanied the pope during the entire expedition, and accused him of having encouraged Bentivoglio and the people of Bologna to remain obstinately disobedient to the Church. Declaring the secretary's behavior deplorable and deserving of severe punishment, but not wishing to violate the rights of a "persona pubblica [a government representative]," he refused him the chance to reply to the pope's accusation and limited his punishment to banishment from the States of the Church. Julius then confronted the Bolognese ambassadors before a crowd of 1,000, as Machiavelli estimated, and denounced the "tyranny" of Giovanni Bentivoglio and those shameless enough to defend it. Julius, he wrote, "spoke scathing words full of venom" (*LCSG* 5.506.3–7).

Julius now felt confident that he had sufficient forces and allies to seize Bologna. In addition to King Louis his allies included the Gonzaga marquis of Mantua, the Este duke of Ferrara, the Montefeltro duke of Urbino, and the humbled Giampaolo Baglioni of Perugia, each with a cavalry contingent. But Florence still had not joined the alliance, and Julius wanted the republic to bend to his will. Still in Forlì, on October 12 he summoned Machiavelli, fully aware that he had witnessed his humiliating treatment of the Bolognese representatives two days earlier. Recalling the request he made "quite some time ago" that Florence make available to him Marcantonio Colonna and his troops, Julius surmised that the governors of Florence, "seeing how far advanced he was" in the campaign to unseat Bentivoglio, must be astonished that he had not repeated the request. He wanted them to know he had waited in order to "accede fully to their wishes" and decided to renew his request only now, when they could "know and see" that the expedition and promised help from the French were assured. The French, he said, were sending the number of troops he had requested, "or more," and in return he had given "money and every other thing they wanted" (*LCSG* 5.508.4). Julius did not specify the number of troops, nor did he say how he paid for them or what "other things" the French had asked for. Later in the dispatch, however, Machiavelli reported that, the day before, the "consistory issued a brief [breve] by which the pope concedes to the king of France" the right of "disposing of the benefices of the duchy of Milan"—a privilege, Machiavelli notes, previously enjoyed by Francesco Sforza.[29] "And this is the last demand [l'ultima domanda] the king made of the pope in these matters" (*LCSG* 5.508.10). The assertion that this was the king's last demand, whether accurate or not, could only have been made by someone in Julius's inner circle. Machiavelli thus learned that the real price Julius paid for French military assistance in taking Bologna was considerably greater than some cash and "other things," as Julius disingenuously told Machiavelli in their private meeting that same day. Surrendering control of benefices in the wealthy Milanese duchy diminished the papacy's power, prestige, and, not least, revenues.[30] Responding on October 13 to a request from the Ten about the location of the French troops, Machiavelli replied that "they say" two-thirds of them were in Parma and the rest with Chaumont (the French governor of Milan), who was delaying his departure until the pope issued the "breve" for the concession of the Milanese ecclesiastical benefices to France (*LCSG* 5.510.5)—a detail that reveals how important those benefices were to the French. The next day, Machiavelli reported that Julius learned that Chaumont was willing to send 500 lances to Parma but had orders not to proceed without more instructions (*LCSG* 5.511.14). The French were pressuring Julius. One wonders whether Machiavelli pondered the contradiction between Julius's boast about defending the rights and liberty of the Church and the weakening of papal power entailed by the surrender to the French crown of control over Church offices in the duchy. In the light of this concession the statement in *Prince* 11 that Julius's successes merited all the more praise because his purpose was "to increase the power of the Church" can be read as deepening the vein of irony of the chapter's opening sentences.

On October 12 Julius again enumerated for Machiavelli his available forces: in addition to the French contingents, he had his own 400 men-at-arms, Baglioni's 150, the 100 *stradiotti* from Naples, 100 light horse from the marquis of Mantua who promised another hundred, and "more than" 100 men-at-arms of the duke of Ferrara. There would be no compromise with Bentivoglio: "So that everyone may

[29] Guicciardini confirms that Julius gave the king the "facoltà di disporre de' benefici del ducato di Milano, come già ebbe Francesco Sforza"; *Storia d'Italia*, ed. Scarano, book 7, ch. 3, p. 662.

[30] The importance for the papacy of controlling benefices is indicated by the inclusion in the interdict of an order for an inventory ("censimento") of all of Bologna's vacant benefices; see Angela De Benedictis, *Una guerra d'Italia, una resistenza di popolo, Bologna 1506* (Bologna: Il Mulino, 2004), p. 71.

know that I want no agreement with messer Giovanni, I have declared a kind of crusade against him [ho pubblicatogli come una cruciata addosso]." Julius also wanted Florence in his camp and told Machiavelli to convey to the Ten his strong desire that Marcantonio Colonna and his 100 men-at-arms come to Imola. "Tell them that, as they can see, I could do without [Colonna's] troops. I want them," Julius ominously intoned, "not for any benefit or honor I would get from having them, but in order to have a just reason [giusta cagione] to do [Florence's governors] favors and give them assistance [beneficarli e favorirli] in things of the greatest importance to them, whenever the opportunity should arise, which will always be the case if the Church is held in the high regard to which I hope to lead it." Julius asked how much time it would take for Colonna's troops to reach Imola. Machiavelli tried to buy time replying that his letter to the Ten would take two days to reach Florence, another two days for Colonna to get the order in Cascina, near Pisa, and "at least" seven days for his troops to march to Imola. Julius said that "seemed like too many days" and urged Machiavelli to send his letter to Florence immediately and let him know when a reply arrived (*LCSG* 5.508.4–6). On the 16th Machiavelli told Julius that the Ten had ordered Marcantonio and his troops to Imola: "As soon as he heard it, completely elated [tutto allegro]," he summoned his datary and the Bolognese ambassador and said to them: 'I want you to hear what kind of friends messer Giovanni has and which of us, he or the Church, is held in higher esteem by his neighbors." He then called everyone to hear him read the Ten's letter and "spoke with great honor and affection of Your Lordships" (*LCSG* 5.513.4–5).

The road from Forlì to Imola goes through Faenza, which was still under Venetian control, and Julius refused to be a "guest" of its Venetian occupiers. So he decided to bypass Faenza and take a four-day detour up into the Tosco-Romagnol mountains, spending two of the four nights at Marradi and Palazzuolo in Florentine territory. Machiavelli warned Julius that these were "luoghi poveri" without many amenities for important visitors. He regretted not knowing of the pope's decision six days earlier when he could have alerted Florentine officials to the papal visit. So he quickly rode ahead to these towns to make what arrangements he could on short notice. From Castrocaro, Julius's first stop, in the valley of the Montone, Machiavelli wrote to the Ten that he was on his way to Modigliana that same evening "ut parem viam Domino [to prepare the way for the Lord]" (*LCSG* 5.513.3–8), echoing the verse in Matthew 3:3[31] that recounts the coming of John the Baptist in the words of Isaiah: "this is he who was spoken of by the prophet Isaiah, saying 'The voice of one crying in the wilderness: Prepare the way of the Lord [Parate viam domini], Make His paths straight.'" If Machiavelli

[31] Noted by the editors in *LCSG*, vol. 5, p. 515, n. 15.

intended some humor, was it aimed at Julius as an improbable vicar of Christ, or at himself as a latter-day John the Baptist who might have wanted, as John did, to denounce the priestly castes as a "brood of vipers"? Or was it a joke (perhaps a disgruntled one) contrasting the "straight paths" to be made for the Lord with the winding, narrow roads through the mountains that Julius's decision to bypass Faenza forced on Machiavelli? The Ten sent gifts of wine, cheese, and fruit to Julius, and the people of each town also gave large quantities of bread, wine, and meat. Machiavelli reported that Julius was "satisfattissimo" with his journey through Florentine territory (*LCSG* 5.518.3).

When Julius arrived in Imola on October 20, a French envoy informed him that the approaching forces—810 lances, 5,000 infantry, 2,000 Swiss, and an unspecified number of Gascons—"should be" at Modena at that moment. Giovanni Bentivoglio, seeing the forces arrayed against him, sent word through Chaumont that he wished to come to terms with Julius. Machiavelli reported the view of (unnamed) observers that, "if Bentivoglio despairs of being able to defend himself with military force, he will throw himself and his children into the pope's arms with guarantees from Chaumont or someone similar and hope to be able personally to come to an agreement like the one Julius reached with Giampaolo Baglioni, by which he might be able to remain in Bologna and not lose the possibility, if the opportunity should present itself, of returning to power." Julius told his cardinals that this proposal was "more honorable" than what the ambassadors had offered in Forlì, but he insisted that Bentivoglio had only two choices: either he could leave with the valuables he could carry, in which case his property in the city would not be confiscated; or he would have to surrender voluntarily and unconditionally (*LCSG* 5.518.4–6). For the moment, Bentivoglio did not yield: he reportedly ransacked a number of convents that chose to obey the interdict, which Machiavelli calls the "bolla della maladizione" (*LCSG* 5.519.5).[32] Three days later, Bentivoglio made the interdict public and gave all religious the option of remaining in the city or leaving. He fortified Bologna's defensive ramparts, gave orders for the recruitment of 3,000 infantry, and engaged the services of several condottieri who had been fighting with Pisa against Florence (*LCSG* 5.522.7–8).

On October 22 Machiavelli reported that French troops were expected the next day in Castelfranco (Emilia), still some fifteen miles from Bologna. One of the French commanders was coming to confer with Julius and the captains of the Italian contingents about how to proceed (*LCSG* 5.519.3). Three days later Machiavelli wrote that the vanguard of the French army had just then left

[32] The "Bolla" is published in L. Frati, *Le due spedizioni militari di Giulio II tratte dal Diario di Paride Grassi bolognese*, in *Documenti e studi pubblicati per cura della R. Deputazione di Storia patria per le Province di Romagna* I (1886), pp. 177–86a. It is analyzed and extensively excerpted in Italian translation by De Benedictis, *Una guerra d'Italia*, pp. 101–11.

Modena—farther away than Castelfranco—and the rest of the army was still in Parma. "It is believed that within the coming week" they would arrive in the area around Bologna (*LCSG* 5.522.3–4). The French commander expected on the 23rd had still not arrived by the 26th when French forces were still just entering Castelfranco. Machiavelli was well aware that the French were in no hurry. Before they reached Bologna, however, Chaumont, in the name of the king, sent an ultimatum to the communal government in Bologna, the Reggimento, to surrender within two days and obey Julius's commands or relinquish the protection Louis had extended to the city and the Bentivoglio family. The Reggimento instructed their ambassadors at the papal court to yield and plead for the lives of Giovanni Bentivoglio and his children (*LCSG* 5.523.6–10). Ten days later, the Bentivoglio left Bologna in the custody of the French, and Julius made ready to enter the city (*LCSG* 5.524.4). Machiavelli did not witness Julius's triumph because the Ten recalled him and sent an ambassador, Francesco Pepi (*LCSG* 5.520.3). In Machiavelli's last dispatch, on October 26, he reported that Pepi had arrived and would soon meet with Julius. "Either tomorrow or the next day, God willing, I'll be on my way home" (*LCSG* 5.523.3–9).

In the last days of the legation Machiavelli made two intriguing comments about Julius. On October 19, during the pope's journey through the mountains, he wrote: "Everyone believes that, if the Bologna expedition is successful, Julius will not waste time before trying something bigger [maggiore cosa]. People think this time either Italy will find safety [si assicurerà] against those who have plotted to swallow it up, or it never will" (*LCSG* 5.517.7). Machiavelli does not say who was plotting to devour Italy, but there is enough attention, in earlier dispatches and other legations, to the aggressive designs of the Venetians to warrant the conjecture that he was referring to Venice.[33] Did Machiavelli and others speculate that Julius would rescue Italy from Venetian expansionism? Just two and a half years later, French and imperial armies, blessed by Julius, inflicted a major defeat and searing humiliation on Venice. Or does "maggiore cosa" refer to the greater plan to liberate Italy from the "barbari"—the French—that dominated Julius's actions in 1510–12? The second comment appears in the dispatch of October 22, referring to the French envoy who was coming to coordinate military plans. Machiavelli reported that Julius "let it be known that, when the envoy arrives, he wants a Florentine ambassador to be present, because they would be discussing the well-being of Italy [avendosi a ragionare del bene d'Italia]" (*LCSG* 5.519.3). Did Machiavelli see unintended irony in the pope's apparent concern for Italy's well-being, foreseeing instead that his decisions, actions, and temperament were leading Italy into the abyss?

[33] *LCSG*, vol. 5, p. 518, n. 4.

"TO DESTROY CHRISTENDOM AND COMPLETE THE DEVASTATION OF ITALY"

Four years later, in June 1510, Machiavelli was sent yet again to the French court where he spent more than two months, mainly in Blois, attempting, in the end successfully but not easily, to dissuade Louis and his ministers from demanding that Florence send troops to Lombardy to assist in defending French positions. Julius had lured away Florence's Colonna condottieri—Muzio departed in 1509 and Marcantonio was severing ties in 1510—and this made the Florentines reluctant to part with any more of their condottieri, especially as they now perceived Julius as a grave danger. He was threatening their merchants and bankers in Rome, had fomented a revolt in French-controlled Genoa, and tried to seize Ferrara, which was formally within the papal states but contractually independent. Had he succeeded, Florence, already militarily weakened, would have been almost entirely surrounded by territories controlled by the increasingly hostile pope. Julius now turned his ire against France, announcing his intention to drive its forces from Italy. He wanted Florence to join him in this war, thereby putting the republic in the impossible position of having to incur the wrath of either Julius or their ally and protector, King Louis, whose demand that the Florentines send troops to support him in Lombardy seemed oblivious to Florence's dilemma vis-à-vis Julius. Machiavelli's mission in France was to make Louis understand the menace Julius represented for Florence and to persuade him not to persist in his request for military assistance.

So important was this mission that, on June 20, 1510, the lifetime gonfaloniere himself, Piero Soderini, sent Machiavelli an "instruzione" in his own name (*LCSG* 6.232). A week later, his brother, Cardinal Francesco Soderini, wrote a personal letter expressing his pleasure at Machiavelli's selection for the mission and great confidence in his prudence and skill. "The decision to send you pleased us very much, with regard to both official business and our private matters [Per rispetto del publico e privato nostro]." "In addition to the duties you will carry out for the patria, we encourage you to be as diligent as possible in keeping [King Louis] and His Holiness the pope in friendly accord [buona unione], which will benefit not only them, but also us and all Italy. We think it essential that they not be alienated from each other, even if disagreements sometimes occur."[34] The cardinal's reference to duties "in addition to" those for the patria is at least partly explained in the "instruction" of his brother Piero, who told Machiavelli to assure the king that Francesco shared his own devotion and loyalty to the French crown and to explain that, "if Francesco has not yet fulfilled his obligation to visit the king, the reason is that the pope has not given him permission to do so." As a cardinal,

[34] *Lettere*, pp. 327–8.

Francesco of course had no choice but to obey Julius in this matter, not only because the pope "is his sovereign lord [suo primo signore]" but also because Julius "is a man so impulsive and hot-tempered [sí rotto e caldo] in his actions, and of such influence and power [di tanta autorità], that princes must treat him cautiously [gli hanno ad avere rispetto]" (*LCSG* 6.232.5–6). Piero uses the same term—"rotto": impulsive, reckless, impetuous—with which Francesco had characterized Julius years earlier, as Machiavelli reported in November 1503. On the basis of this explanation of why Francesco had not visited the king, it has been speculated that Piero may initially have wanted to send his brother on the mission. But this seems unlikely, because, given the known French sympathies of the Soderini and the extent to which Cardinal Francesco had benefitted from Louis's patronage in the matter of benefices, sending the cardinal to negotiate a rapprochement between pope and king would have infuriated Julius. Because Machiavelli was asked to convey to the king the undiminished loyalty of the Soderini brothers, the cardinal's modern biographer conjectures that it "seems likely that Machiavelli was sent as a personal messenger of the Soderini rather than as an official representative of the Florentine republic."[35] This was not the case, however. Despite bringing personal messages from the Soderini—personal messages of political import—there can be no doubt that Machiavelli went to France as the official representative of the republic and the Ten. Piero Soderini's "Instruzione" refers, in its opening sentence, to "everything the Ten will direct you to do" (*LCSG* 6.232.3), and it was the Ten who, of course with Soderini's approval, appointed Machiavelli as "Mandatario e Nuncio della loro Republica" (*LCSG* 6.234.3). The Ten sent him news and further instructions during the legation, and Machiavelli addressed his dispatches to them.

Piero Soderini asked Machiavelli to "tell His Majesty the king on my behalf that I have no desire in this world beyond these three things: the honor of God, the well-being [bene] of my patria, and the well-being and honor of His Majesty, the king of France. And because I believe that the well-being of my patria is not possible without the honor and well-being of the French crown, I cannot treasure the one without the other." Machiavelli was to convey to Louis Piero's concern over the looming conflict between France and Julius and assure him that he wanted nothing more than for the king "to maintain and increase his prestige and power [reputazione e possanza] in Italy." To this end, Soderini wrote, Louis needed to "keep the Venetians beaten down [battuti, afflitti] and maintain good relations with the emperor." Piero also asked Machiavelli to tell Louis "how dismayed" he was that Julius was able to employ the Swiss and that Louis should do everything possible to prevent this. "The support of the Swiss," Soderini explained, "if added to the pope's financial resources and his temperament [natura], would make him

[35] K. J. P. Lowe, *Church and Politics in Renaissance Italy: The Life and Career of Cardinal Francesco Soderini (1453–1524)* (Cambridge: Cambridge University Press, 1993), p. 84.

excessively bold [ardito]" and enable him "to do some bad things [fare qualche male effetto]." Louis should do everything possible to avoid a rupture with Julius, "because, if a friendly pope isn't worth much, an unfriendly one is very harmful." Maintaining good relations with Julius "should not be difficult," Soderini averred, rather too optimistically, "because the pope does not have much firm support on which he can rely" (*LCSG* 6.232.3–13).

While Machiavelli was traveling north, the Ten informed him that Marcantonio Colonna had signed a contract with Julius and accepted papal funds to augment his forces (*LCSG* 6.236.7). Julius wanted him to proceed directly from the territory of Lucca to Bologna and asked the Florentines to let him take the quicker route through Florentine territory. Fearing the pope's anger, the Ten consented and told Machiavelli (in a letter mostly in code) to explain to Louis the reasons for their decision. But they also confessed puzzlement over Julius's bravado. He was preparing an assault on Ferrara and "speaks of it so freely that on the one hand one has to believe he is not acting thoughtlessly [leggermente], but on the other hand we do not see that he has the resources [fondamenti] to do so securely, especially given the opposition of the French." Julius was reported to have said that the king "would not stop him, and, even if he did, he was so well supported [fondato] that he would have no fear. Nonetheless, this *fondamento* he says he has is nowhere in sight." "He must either have great confidence in himself or is planning a well-organized surprise attack." The Ten asked Machiavelli to learn what he could about French plans to defend Ferrara (*LCSG* 6.237.4–12).

In Lyon, on July 7, Machiavelli heard a report that King Ferdinand of Spain had a large fleet in Sicily with 10,000 or more soldiers ready to intervene in Italy, either for his own purposes or on behalf of his "friends." Unsure of the report's accuracy, Machiavelli commented that "nothing would make me believe it to be true if I saw the pope any less audacious than he is against the French." Machiavelli comments sardonically that "because this audacity [gagliardia] of his must be based on something other than his holiness [Santità sua], some preparations must exist or be coming" (*LCSG* 6.239.6–8). From Lyon Machiavelli traveled north and west, arriving at the royal court at Blois in the Loire valley on July 17. The Ten continued to inform him of rumors that Julius's "every thought, plan, and effort" now aimed at stoking a rebellion against French rule in Genoa (6.240.8–9). They interpreted his repeated threats to damage Florentine commercial interests as an attempt to force Florence to align with him and break with France. Yet, "in view of Julius's fever-pitch intensity [visto quanto sua Santità ci è dentro caldo]" in making demands, they feared his objectives went beyond that. The Ten instructed Machiavelli to ask Louis what he planned to do if Florence refused the pope's demands and found itself threatened by him (*LCSG* 6.241.5–19).

In his first dispatch from Blois, written on July 18, Machiavelli reported on a meeting with the king's personal secretary, Florimond Robertet, who welcomed him warmly but warned that Louis was angry over the Ten's decision to allow

Marcantonio to cross through Florentine territory and wanted to know why they did. Machiavelli showed Robertet the letter in which the Ten explained their reasons and was confident that Robertet accepted them. But he was surprised to learn from him that Marcantonio had gone, not to Bologna, but to Genoa, about which Machiavelli said he knew nothing (*LCSG* 6.244.4–11). Later that day, Robertet warned him that the Florentines had many enemies at court willing to slander them when they found a reason to do so and that the Ten should therefore make it clear that Marcantonio's employment by Julius did not have their consent (*LCSG* 6.244.23–6). Machiavelli met with the king and presented the purpose of his mission "with the most affectionate and appropriate words I knew." He pleaded that a matter as relatively insignificant as the passage of Colonna's troops through Florence's territory did not warrant maligning the Ten whose actions "did not deserve such suspicions." Louis said he was certain of the "trust [fede] and loyalty [affezione]" of the Florentines, but the time had come to be even more certain: "Secretary, I have no hostility [nimicizia] toward the pope or anyone. But because new friendships and new hostilities arise every day, I want your Signori to declare without delay what and how much they are willing to do to support me if the pope or anyone else should attack my territories in Italy [li stati miei che io tengo in Italia]." He wanted the Ten to reply immediately, "because I want to know who my friends are and who my enemies are. And tell them that, in return [for a pledge of loyalty], I offer all the forces of this kingdom and will come in person to safeguard [salvare] their stato." Machiavelli assured the king that the Ten "would never fail to honor their agreements with His Majesty and were prepared to do everything reasonable and possible." Louis said he was sure of this but "wished to have specific certainty of it [ne voleva ancora particulare certezza]" (*LCSG* 6.244.12–21).

In this same dispatch Machiavelli responded to the Ten's request that he learn "the basis of the pope's extravagant self-assurance [rigogli] against the French." From what little he was able to gather in the short time he had been at court, it was clear to him that no one knew anything for certain. He relayed the view of "a friend, who nonetheless speaks conjecturally," that Julius's most secure foundations were his financial resources, the Swiss, and the "influence [autorità]" he thinks he has to enlist the cooperation of Spain and the emperor. According to the friend, Julius "must have solid promises" from Ferdinand, because "we saw in the [1506] expedition against Bologna that he left Rome without a firm agreement with the French or anyone else and subsequently brought them over to his side with his audacity [audacia] and influence [autorità]"—an idea reiterated and elaborated in chapter 25 of *The Prince*. (Exactly where the views of the "friend" conclude in this "conjecture" and where Machiavelli's own perception of matters takes over is not altogether clear.) Machiavelli says it was generally believed that the rupture between Julius and Louis was beyond repair, especially given the pope's undisguised determination to seize Genoa. About Julius's Swiss allies,

Machiavelli says "I know for certain" that Julius had just sent them 36,000 ducats for the immediate mobilization of 6,000 infantry, but that the Swiss took the cash and then refused to budge unless they received another 18,000 ducats to pay the soldiers for the first three months. "Some people think" Julius wanted these troops to pry Genoa from the French, but it was unclear whether the duke of Savoy would let them traverse his dominions to reach Genoa. Machiavelli concluded the dispatch by saying that "no one can judge where all this might lead; one can only abide by the results [riportarsene a li effetti], which will become clear day by day" (*LCSG* 6.244.35–45).

On July 21 Machiavelli reported on his conversation with the bishop of Paris (Etienne de Poncher), whom he praised as a man of "calm intelligence with a reputation for wisdom [d'ingegno riposato e tenuto savio]" and considered to be "among those who now govern" France. The bishop emphasized "how great a mistake the pope is making, with no reason to harm anyone, by placing himself and all Italy in danger. If this war happens," he said, "none greater or more unrelenting [ostinata] will ever have been seen, for, as many favors as [Louis] has conferred on the pope and as much as he has desired his friendship, so much the more will he be a merciless enemy; he will persecute him in his stato and his person [seguiterallo ne lo stato e ne la persona: stato signifying papal authority or Church dominions?]." Poncher expressed confidence in Florence's loyalty to France: "you could not be other than good Frenchmen" (allies of the French), "nor does the king think otherwise, for you will see such a quantity of arms readied in Italy for the defense of his possessions and his friends that you will have no cause to fear. The king was not afraid to thwart the pope [Alexander] to save the stato of Arezzo for you and force his boy [figliolo: Cesare] to present himself before the king in Asti with the leather strap [signifying humility and submission] around his neck [con la coreggia al collo]." Now, Poncher advised, the Florentines should do something for the king in return, and do it soon "so that the favor will be the more appreciated, which could redound to your benefit" (*LCSG* 6.246.5–11).

Making the rounds of the king's ministers, Machiavelli next met with the royal chancellor (Jean de Ganay), whom he described (in code) as "hot-tempered and all fury [uomo piú caldo e tutto collera]." Ganay subjected Machiavelli to "a lengthy reprimand [gran rimesta]" over Marcantonio Colonna's passage through Florentine territory and the departure from the royal court of Florence's ambassador (who was, however, about to be replaced). He also accused the Florentines of failing to tell the French everything the pope said to them against France and of not wanting to make it clear to Julius that they would not ally with him. To Ganay's characterization of these alleged failures as "acts of a wicked nature [mala natura] that would make anyone suspicious," Machiavelli replied that no one in Florence believed that conflict between Julius and Louis was inevitable and that it was therefore unnecessary to speak in such accusatory terms (*LCSG* 6.246.12–20). On this same busy day he met with the Spanish ambassador, two imperial ambassadors, and the papal nuncio, Angelo Leonini, described by Machiavelli as a "distinguished and wise signore with much experience in political matters [pratico nelle cose di stato]." (Francesco Soderini had similarly described Leonini to Machiavelli as very wise, worthy, and "amicissimo.")[36] Leonini was "deeply upset and astonished" at how relations between pope and king had so quickly come to undisguised hostility. Machiavelli saw him as more perplexed than anyone concerning the pope's "fondamenti ed ordini," about which he said he knew nothing. "When he thinks about what kind of war this would be and how offensive and defensive operations would be conducted, he shudders with horror [se ne raccapricciava tutto]; he deplores the errors made in France and Italy, whose unfortunate people [poveri populi] and minor principalities [minori principati] would be the first to suffer." According to Leonini, no hope for peace remained (*LCSG* 6.246.23–9).

So Machiavelli had to report that, as regards Julius's "fondamenti," no one knew anything for certain, and, "knowing nothing, they fear everything and everyone." News arrived that Genoese exiles were gathering near the city, and Robertet told Machiavelli, "with a cross look [con non molta buona cera]," that Marcantonio too had arrived there. The Ten, Machiavelli wrote, "can well imagine what is being said here about the pope; the least of the disasters with which they threaten him are withdrawal of obedience, convening a Church council against him, and subverting his temporal and spiritual authority" (*LCSG* 6.246.30–5). The next day Robertet again berated Machiavelli, filling his ears with complaints. The king, he said, "could not be more displeased" that the Florentines had not kept the French informed, especially because "the Ten know better than anyone else in Italy everything [that happens there]." Such "boorishness [salvetichezza]," Robertet said, must come from the Florentines' sense of guilt over not behaving as good allies should. After hearing this, Machiavelli advised his government that, if they did not want to lose their French allies, they had to show them they wanted to be their "amico." He judged that "the wound the pope attempted to inflict on the French [in Genoa] is so grievous, and considered as such by the king, that I believe one can draw this firm conclusion: either the king will avenge himself to his great satisfaction and honor, or he will lose what he possesses in Italy. And he will soon cross the mountains with redoubled force compared to previous years" (*LCSG* 6.248.7–12).

French suspicions of Florentine intentions were allayed by the arrival on July 24 (*LCSG* 6.249.3–4) of two missives from the Ten, written on the 12th (*LCSG* 6.241; *LCSG* 6.242), conveying their decision not to let papal troops cross Florentine territory toward Genoa and to deny Marcantonio Colonna's request to recruit troops within Florence's borders. The next day came the news that the

[36] *Lettere*, p. 328.

attempted revolt in Genoa had failed, over which "this entire court was in celebration [ne è stata oggi in festa]." Machiavelli showed Robertet the letters as soon as they arrived and the next morning read parts of them to the king. Both asserted they had no further doubts about the loyalty of the Florentines. Louis promised that his forces in Italy would respond to any Florentine request for help and made a public announcement that "the Florentines had refused the papal troops passage to Genoa and were his great and good friends" (*LCSG* 6.250.3–11, 22).

At the end of the dispatch of July 26 Machiavelli offered an assessment of Julius's prospects. "This action of the pope," he wrote, referring to the failed attempt to foment rebellion in Genoa, "displeases everyone here, for it seems he is trying to destroy Christendom and complete the devastation of Italy [ruinare la cristianità e fornire di consumare l'Italia]. But because he was not successful in the Genoese affair, there is hope that matters could settle down, if he neither persists in his obstinacy nor sets in motion such wickedness [male], all the more if there are good mediators. Although the outrage the pope sought to inflict on the crown was great, it was not successful. It would also be dangerous [for the king] to seek to avenge himself, because, since there can be no more honorable action against a prince than [one motivated by a desire to defend] the Church, if His Majesty openly attacks the pope he will have to fear drawing the whole world down on himself. So it is assumed the king will easily let himself be advised" not to do so. It depends, Machiavelli continues, on the willingness of the pope, "who should be more chastened [umile] because he has seen the initiative at Genoa fail" and realizes it was more difficult than he had assumed. "If he has become more fearful, ways will not be lacking to reassure him, if, as I say, there are good mediators" (*LCSG* 6.250.31–5).

The idea of mediation was evidently being discussed. Machiavelli reveals that "a worthy and influential notable [personaggio buono e d'autorità]" asked him to request that the Ten use their influence to urge Julius to come to terms with Louis (*LCSG* 6.250.36). A week later, he reported strong support at the court for this proposal. With Genoa secured and Louis feeling more confident, certain "wise and worthy" persons at the court hoped the moment was right for an understanding with Julius, "provided they can find a trustworthy intermediary who could intervene for the good of all Christendom and especially of Italy." It is not clear how far the next two sentences continue to represent the thought of these unnamed "wise and worthy" persons or whether they express Machiavelli's views. It would be easy, he writes, to show the king how dangerous it would be to go to war with the pope, what harm he might suffer, and what expenses he would certainly incur with no assurance of a favorable outcome. Similarly, it would be easy to persuade the pope of the ills such a war could entail, not only for him personally and for the temporal power [stato temporale] of the Church, but for all Christendom. Robertet discussed the matter often with a "man of great *autorità*" (Machiavelli reveals in a postscript that this was the papal ambassador Angelo

Leonini), "who feels sorrow deep in his soul over these matters." Convinced of the need to prevent such a calamity, Robertet asked Giovanni Girolami, a Florentine "who conducts some business at the court" (he was Francesco Soderini's representative there, hence well known to the king's council),[37] to take this proposal to the Ten. Robertet told Girolami he believed the pope would receive a positive response [riscontro] from the king "if [Julius] were willing to soften his stance [quando e' volessi quietare]," which "he should do, if God has not made him obstinate for the destruction of the world." Leonini sought Louis's approval for the plan, urging him to set aside the "iniuria" the pope had inflicted and to agree to a cessation of hostilities. Louis was initially reluctant, not wanting to be the one to back down, but in the end gave his permission for the mediation. Machiavelli offered to write to the Ten to assure them that the undertaking had the king's approval (*LCSG* 6.257.3–18). Girolami hesitated to undertake the mission (perhaps because he feared that, if Julius learned of it, he would be angry with Cardinal Soderini). Both Girolami's reluctance and Machiavelli's decision not to mention that the proposal came from Leonini may reflect their fear that the mediation would fail before it started if Julius got wind of who was behind it. Machiavelli nonetheless urged Girolami to accept and told the Ten, "I did not keep distant from these negotiations [Io non ho fuggito queste pratiche], because I think no more frightful misfortune could befall your city than open hostilities between these two princes, for reasons that even the blind and the deaf see and understand. I believe that any and all ways that can be pursued to bring about an agreement are good." After enumerating the benefits for Florence, Machiavelli again emphasized and justified his own role in arranging the mediation: "All these reasons induced me to take part willingly in these negotiations. If Your Lordships approve, it will please me greatly; if not, please excuse me, because, according to everything I see here, I could not have judged the matter any differently" (*LCSG* 6.257.24–8). In fact, Machiavelli was far from "keeping distant" from the negotiations. If he was not actually the originator of the idea of asking the Ten to make a direct appeal to Julius, he certainly promoted it, motivated by deep (and prophetic) fears of the disaster that would ensue from all-out war between Julius and Louis.

In the event, the effort to induce the pope to embrace reason and peace did not succeed. Hopes for a more "umile" Julius quickly evaporated. The Ten wrote to Machiavelli on July 26 that "it is now clear" that the pope's attempt to foment revolt in Genoa "was completely based on his hopes concerning the [Genoese] exiles and was conducted with so few preparations that it is astonishing to believe" (*LCSG* 6.251.9). They reported that Julius had vented his anger against Florence's ambassador and the Florentine community in Rome. "It should not be surprising

[37] Soderini assured Machiavelli at the beginning of the mission that "Giovanni Girolami will be with you every day" and "will explain what is needed"; *Lettere*, p. 328.

if we go slowly with this, given that we are dealing with a pope like this one, who, having dared to assault Genoa, will have less hesitation in all things concerning us." Having failed in Genoa, "he persists in the same frame of mind, or pretends to," and says he wants to try again (*LCSG* 6.256.7–11). On the same day, August 3, on which Machiavelli wrote to the Ten outlining the plan for approaching the pope with a peace proposal, the Ten were conveying reports from Rome about how "incredibly enraged Julius is with us." The pope was threatening to imprison Florentine merchants and bankers in the Castello or even unleash the Roman mob against them (*LCSG* 6.258.9–10). He repeated these threats the next day, warning Florence not to take any action against him. He was recruiting more cavalry in Bologna, "but not in a very organized way, nor with much urgency" (*LCSG* 6.260.6–10). Two days later, the Florentine ambassador in Rome reported to Machiavelli that Julius was trying to persuade Venice to reassemble the fleet for another attack on Genoa, was "very angry" over military setbacks around Imola, and was having difficulty arranging payments to the Swiss, who would not move without them. "Given all these problems, and if the Swiss cannot pass through [the territory of the duke of Savoy], the speculation here [in Rome] is that, if His Holiness had the possibility of an agreement with the French…he would accept it, although he has said that any agreement must be by his choice [a sua posta]." The ambassador added that "His Holiness often greatly exaggerates these affairs of his [sua Santità usa molto magnificare queste sue cose] in order not to appear shamed [per non mostrare di rimanere in vergogna]." Exactly what the ambassador was referring to is not clear, but it is striking that Cesare Borgia too was said to "magnificare" his strength and resources during his slide into oblivion in 1503 (see Chapter 3, pp. 137, 154). According to the ambassador, "the pope has deceived himself in assuming that the king of Spain is on his side," when, in fact, Ferdinand was openly expressing astonishment over the lack of "fondamento" in the pope's latest ventures. In essence, the ambassador was conveying to Machiavelli an image of Julius—which he evidently assumed would be shared with the French court—as one given to exaggeration, anger, self-deception, and whose aims lacked both coherence and military and diplomatic support (*LCSG* 6.261.2–17).

In early August Machiavelli and Robertet visited King Louis at his hunting ground some ten miles from the court. On the way they "spoke of all the affairs of Italy and of everything about the current situation in a general way," except, Machiavelli notes, that "no one has said anything to me about plans for attacking the pope, for [the French] do not, and never will, fully trust Your Lordships unless they see you armed and openly supporting them. It is their nature to be suspicious, and they are suspicious of you because they consider you particularly wise [savi] and less inclined to take risks. This is why they made the request I sent you in my letter of the 18th [of July]," namely, that Florence make some of its troops available to the king. "Your Lordships should believe, as much as you believe in the gospels, that, if there is to be war between the pope and His Majesty, you will not be able to avoid declaring for one side while disregarding all concerns for the other side." Because Florence will be compelled to make this choice and therefore run some risk, Robertet raised the possibility of territorial acquisitions for Florence (mentioning Lucca and Urbino) in the coming conflict. Machiavelli says he steered clear of the idea ("volsi largo"), uncertain of what the Ten might think. But he knew that his and his government's reticence increased French suspicions that Florence was less than the fully committed ally the French desired. Although he worried that showing no interest in territorial gains in alliance with France, and at the Church's expense (as would have been the case with Urbino), would be seen as a sign that Florence still wavered between pope and king, a few sentences further on Machiavelli suggests that "a good part of Tuscany" could be Florence's reward for "tempting fortune with France." Adherence to its treaty with France, Machiavelli advises, will not suffice, because it addresses only defense and the French "will want to engage you in offensive actions to make you more obligated to them. If war comes, it is believed you will have to declare for the French side in any case or else become their enemy." "Opportunity does not last long [l'occasione ha poca vita], so you must decide quickly" (*LCSG* 6.263.8–29).

On August 13 the chancellor, Ganay, subjected Machiavelli to a harangue that began with a catalogue of the favors France had done for Florence from the time of Charlemagne to Louis XII. Machiavelli's characterization of this part of the speech as "un grande esordio [exordium]" suggests his irritation. According to Ganay, the king was of the opinion that Julius, "instigated by a diabolical spirit that had possessed him," wanted to try again to seize Genoa. Louis, he said, knew of the "several thousand infantrymen [fanti ordinati]" Florence had at its borders—part of Machiavelli's militia—and "wanted them or some similar force ready so as to make the French [royal] house forever indebted to Florence." Machiavelli responded "to them all" (he was evidently speaking to the king's council), explaining that Florence was surrounded by the States of the Church and that a mere suspicion had nearly provoked Julius to confiscate the assets of Florentine merchants in Rome, which would surely happen if Florence made any overt gesture of support for France. The Ten, he said, "knowing [the pope's] anger," had no doubt Julius would put aside every other war and attack Florence. For all these reasons, in addition to the expense of mobilizing the infantry, Florence simply could not make available to France forces on which it depended for its own defense. The council replied in unison that these troops would be needed for only a few days to repulse an attack, and that the Ten should remember that the king had the well-being and interests of the Florentines as much in his thoughts as did the Ten themselves. Apparently in an effort (but an odd one) to reassure Machiavelli of the king's good intentions, they added that Louis was making "such preparations" for war as "would bring to Italy *caelum novum et terram novam*" (*Revelation* 21: in effect, unleashing the apocalypse) "to destroy his enemies and exalt his friends." Although not inclined to be frightened by allusions to apocalyptic scenarios,

Machiavelli must have wondered what such dramatic words meant. Perhaps to allay any worries, the councilors quickly attempted to "show with long and loving expressions how dear to their hearts is the stato of Tuscany and in what esteem they hold it." But the demand for military assistance still stood. Machiavelli was now more than ever convinced that the French "want to involve" the Florentines "in this war," which prompted him again to remind the Ten that they should seek some advantage for Florence in a situation in which there was potentially so much to lose (*LCSG* 6.268.8–14).

In letters to Machiavelli chancery colleagues and friends in Florence described Julius as carried away by his own hyperbolic speech and irrationally determined to attack Genoa. One said, "it is incredible how obsessed [fisso] he is *in questa fantasia* of capturing Genoa, which is in any case laughable." "He still has nothing solid with the emperor, yet thinks he will be his ally, based in my opinion on very weak foundations [fondandosi secondo me molto debilmente]." About the Swiss "nothing is known and, although he can feign [simulare]" an agreement with them, "nevertheless it scarcely seems plausible, given his customary exaggeration and hyperbole [magnificare] in whatever is to his advantage" (*LCSG* 6.269.7–14). Another colleague wrote that "we see this pontiff more inflamed for war every day. He has assembled a large fleet at Civitavecchia and has hired 3,000 or 4,000 infantry; he persuades himself, to judge from how he speaks, that he will succeed in this undertaking" to seize Genoa.[38] Francesco Vettori (whom Machiavelli knew well from their joint mission to the emperor in 1507–8) wrote privately to Machiavelli that he was surprised Marcantonio Colonna had decided to join what turned out to be a failed attempt on Genoa. He had considered Colonna "cautious in his endeavors" and "a man of excellent judgment" and could not understand what had induced him to put his soldiers, his honor, and indeed his life at risk in this action against the French, from which he narrowly escaped onto a Venetian vessel. Vettori was sure the French would not have spared Colonna's life had they captured him. About Julius, he commented similarly, "One cannot say that, since he has been pope, his behavior [governo] has been that of a madman [matto]. In what he has done, he seems to have proceeded quite cautiously. Nonetheless, he starts a war with the king of France, and it is not yet clear that he has any allies other than the half-destroyed and desperate Venetians. And he begins by offending the king in such a way as to make peace impossible any time soon." After summarizing what he considered Julius's inexplicable actions—the Genoa fiasco, his insistence on trying again, and his attack against Ferrara and its pro-French duke—Vettori commented: "In sum, I do not understand this pope or how it is possible that he alone and the Venetians want to start a war against France." Employing the metaphor of card games, he thought Julius was trying to bluff the

[38] *Lettere*, p. 337.

king but wondered whether Louis held the winning hand and planned to march on Bologna, which Vettori said he would welcome: "To tell the truth, I would like the king to take Bologna, gain the victory, and expel the pope from Rome."[39] Vettori would not have so openly expressed his contempt for Julius without knowing that Machiavelli shared it.

On August 18 Machiavelli met again with the king and shared recent reports from Florence and Rome (about Julius's exaggerations and fantasies) over which the king expressed "the greatest pleasure." Machiavelli urged him to "use" the pope's failure to take Genoa as an opportunity to "conclude a good peace" rather than smite him in a war whose consequences no one could foresee. Louis replied, as Machiavelli puts it, "with a forcefulness [efficacia] I would not be able to describe, vowing that, as he had not started the war against the pope, it would not be because of him if peace is not achieved." The king then launched into a long lamentation of grievances over Julius's actions, complaining that, after they defeated Venice (in 1509), he was "unable to placate [dimesticare]" Julius. So, Machiavelli concluded, "although [Louis's] spirit was turned toward peace, he was not neglecting preparations for war." He had just sent 300 lances and 3,000 infantry to Italy, because "he wanted not only to defend himself and his friends but also attack his enemies." Apparently on his own initiative, Machiavelli went directly from this audience with Louis to a meeting of the royal council where, "in the presence of all," he conveyed the same news he had just shared with the king. "I can hardly tell you with what pleasure" they all listened and said that "the mission Your Lordships are carrying out is that of a true and good friend" (*LCSG* 6.272.7–14). Machiavelli thought Louis reluctant to go to war, but if "la forza" leads him to it he "intends to wage the most *onorevole* [grandest, most awe-inspiring and majestic] war ever seen in Italy." In the meantime the king was proceeding with the "Gallican Council" in Orléans, intending to humiliate, and, if possible, dethrone Julius. Prelates were arriving and preparing a formal withdrawal of obedience from the pope. If Louis gained the support of England and the emperor for removing Julius and installing a new pope, he planned to "descend into Italy in the spring [of 1511] with such a large army that it would be a pleasure trip to Rome, not war." Machiavelli added his own hope that the Almighty "might wrest from the pope's body the diabolical spirit the French say has taken hold of him so that he does not cause [Florence] to be trampled and himself buried." Such an attack "would be quite welcome" if the Florentine dominions were located elsewhere (i.e. not surrounded by the States of the Church), "so that these priests could get a big mouthful of the bitterness of this world" (*LCSG* 6.272.23–8). Francesco Vettori had expressed the same wish to see Julius and the Church humiliated.

[39] *Lettere*, pp. 330–2.

The Ten were pessimistic about Julius taking the road of peace and conciliation, to which "he has always been steadfastly opposed." Nonetheless, they sent a second envoy to join their resident ambassador in Rome. Against the French request that Florence ready troops to go into Lombardy, the Ten argued that they could not present themselves as trustworthy mediators between king and pope while undertaking military actions in open opposition to the latter (*LCSG* 6.273.6–12). The news that Modena and Ferrara had fallen to papal troops (in the case of Ferrara revealed to be incorrect a few days later) made the Ten even more reluctant to send forces to Lombardy. They would resist the French demand, not only because Florence's dominions were surrounded by the States of the Church and the pope's client states but also because "all our hired soldiers [captains and condottieri] are the pope's subjects," originating as they did from the papal states. If Florence ordered them to join the French, Julius could, with ecclesiastical censures and threats of confiscation of their properties, coerce them to leave Florentine service. The Ten wanted Machiavelli to explain to Louis that "the pope's purpose is to exalt himself by destroying others [esaltare sé con la ruina d'altri]," and that, "if ever there was need to keep our troops close at hand, it is now, given the actions of this pope from whom we can fear anything at any time." Even after learning that Ferrara had not been captured, the Ten firmly believed that "we cannot feel secure, given that the pope is still planning for war" (*LCSG* 6.275.9–20, 28; *LCSG* 6.276.8; *LCSG* 6.279.5). As they said in a letter to the new Florentine ambassador to the French court, Roberto Acciaiuoli, which was meant to be seen by Machiavelli as well, "the pope's nature is, as you know, unpredictable and reckless [súbita e precipite]. If he has dared to attack such a king as the king of France without cause, and launch an assault against Ferrara when it was defended by the king, he would have even less hesitation [manco respetto] to attack us." "The hostility of a pope like this cannot and must not be left to chance [pigliare a caso]." "We believe it is more in our interest for now to use the shield and not the sword," in other words, better to defend the Florentine dominions from possible attacks by Julius than to go on the offensive by sending troops to assist the French (*LCSG* 6.282.18–19, 29–33). In a follow-up letter to Acciaiuoli the Ten said: "Now we see the pope's entire plan [disegno]; we believe we could be attacked within a few days; such are the rumors—he himself says it, and one sees it being organized [se ne vede l'ordine]" (*LCSG* 6.285.11). The next day, Machiavelli's chancery colleague Antonio della Valle wrote that Julius planned to go not only to Ferrara but also to Parma "and farther still until he expels the king from Italy. This is his *fantasia*, and he thinks he has it all well in hand; he has been saying that he is determined either to die or to be victorious." According to Della Valle, a "major foundation [grande fondamento]" of his plan is to bend Florence to his will either by friendship or by force; he says openly that he plans to overthrow [mutare] this government, which is too French [troppo franzese] and will try anything and everything to bring this about. And he is far enough along [in this aim] that I wish to say nothing more except that there is someone who needs to take good care of himself" (*LCSG* 6.286.4–5, 18–19).[40] Machiavelli no doubt recalled that Cesare Borgia had made similar threats to "mutare" Florence's government.

In another long talk with Robertet Machiavelli tried to persuade the minister that, if Florence sent a significant portion of its forces to Lombardy to support France, thus leaving Tuscany vulnerable to papal attacks, Louis would have the additional burden of defending Tuscany. The best way for Florence to help the French, Machiavelli argued, was to be able to defend itself without French help. He urged Robertet to present these views to the royal council, although he still feared that the French intended to involve Florence in the war. The Gallican Council had moved from Orléans to Tours, and the king, apparently without waiting for its pronouncements, prohibited all appeals from France to Rome concerning ecclesiastical benefices or other issues and declared obedience to the pope null and void within the kingdom. Machiavelli now saw Louis thirsting for revenge against Julius: the French, he wrote, consider "every other wound and every other attack more justified [onesto] and tolerable than what the pope did. Day and night the king thinks of nothing but the wrong he believes was done to him by His Holiness, and he thinks of nothing but revenge" (*LCSG* 6.283.4–17, 33–7).

At the end of August, the French were still pressuring Florence to send troops to Lombardy. Robertet complained to Machiavelli that Florence's willingness to mediate between Julius and Louis was not an acceptable "scusa" for its refusal to comply with the request for military assistance, because the king did not want anyone even to "dream" that the initiative for approaching the pope had come from him. Unable to speak with Louis, who was temporarily indisposed because of illness, Machiavelli went to Chancellor Ganay's house where the royal council was meeting and explained at length (presumably in French) all the reasons why the Florentines considered sending any of their forces out of Tuscany dangerous both to themselves and to the French. To insist on such a demand would be in effect to leave Florence "unarmed in the midst of its enemies." An attack on Florence would force Louis not only to send back to Tuscany the forces he had requisitioned but also to send additional troops of his own. The Ten, Machiavelli said, were confident their French allies recognized that keeping Florentine troops in Tuscany "would be a more effective bit in the pope's mouth [maggiore freno in bocca] than sending them elsewhere." The council members "all listened attentively," Machiavelli reported, "and, when I finished speaking, they declared that I had spoken wisely [prudentemente]." "Within the day," they told him, "they would meet with the king and give me a reply that would satisfy me, because they knew it was necessary to protect [salvare] Your Lordships [i.e. assure Florence's security] and not place you in danger" (*LCSG* 6.287.10–26). The next day, wishing to

[40] The editors plausibly speculate that "someone" alludes to Piero Soderini; *LCSG*, vol. 6, p. 527, n. 8.

leave as little as possible to chance, Machiavelli again visited the king (now apparently recovered) as he was strolling through his gardens and reiterated the battery of arguments he had presented to the council. Louis too said he would think things over and provide a response. Machiavelli then sought out the members of the council individually ("a la spartita"), urging them to solicit a reply from the king as soon as possible. They told him to come to the council meeting that afternoon. After waiting "for a long time" while the councilors discussed the issue, Machiavelli was finally invited in to hear the recommendation they intended to present to Louis. Ganay said the "ragioni" Machiavelli had presented "seemed to be good ones, especially considering the pope's nature [qualità] and the location of your dominion [stato]. They therefore accepted the good intentions [buono animo] of [the Ten], just as if you had sent troops [to Lombardy], and concluded it was best that they remain in Tuscany." Their recommendation required the king's confirmation, which, as Machiavelli added in a postscript, arrived the next day, August 31 (*LCSG* 6.287.27–36). With notable tenacity, Machiavelli secured the agreement his government needed. He even worried that he had been too tenacious. On September 5 he assured the Ten that "I have omitted nothing in these efforts, for I have been so persistent that it was perhaps excessive [mi sono fatto tanto vivo che forse è suto troppo]" (*LCSG* 6.293.13). It took several days for the news to reach Florence from the Loire valley, and in the meantime the Ten continued writing to Machiavelli urging him to make the French understand the risks of their demand. But the mission was complete. On September 10, in his last dispatch, he wrote that there was no need to pursue the issue further, "because everything was resolved on August 31" (*LCSG* 6.297.4). The Ten informed Acciaiuoli of Machiavelli's "opera"—his effort and achievement—in "persuading the king and his ministers not to ask for our troops in Lombardy" (*LCSG* 6.299.6).

Machiavelli had a final meeting with Louis on September 2 to emphasize again the danger Florence faced from Julius's military actions in a broad arc around the Florentine dominions. The king promised not to abandon the republic and boasted of having 15,000 infantry at the ready. Machiavelli suggested that Louis could send 200 lances to Tuscany to strengthen Florentine defenses and "give the pope and his allies in Tuscany something to think about," adding that if Julius "had to start thinking about defending himself, he would be less lackadaisical [meno ozioso] about defense and less aggressive [meno galiardo] on offense." The king liked the idea but said he had to wait six or eight days to see what the Swiss were doing. Robertet showed Machiavelli the letter in which Louis informed Chaumont in Milan that, because Julius "wants to overthrow the government [mutare lo stato] of Florence," the king would no longer ask the Florentines to send troops to Lombardy. When Machiavelli remarked to Robertet that the time had come for the French to get tough with Julius ("che si facessino vivi con questo Papa"), Robertet replied that "they knew they had to give the pope a real pummeling [una mazzata da dovero]; as he said this, he snickered [sogghignò], as if to say 'and let it be soon' [quasi dicessi: ‹E' fia presto›]" (*LCSG* 6.288.8–17). A few days later, Robertet said "it would be foolishness [mocheria] to think the pope would launch a war against the king" (*LCSG* 6.293.9). Yet Machiavelli was skeptical that Louis and his ministers paid the requisite attention to preparations and tactics. He worried about the king's well-known reluctance to spend money and the absence of skilled administrators, both in France and Lombardy. The loss of Georges d'Amboise (Rouen), who had died in May, was particularly troubling to Machiavelli. "God grant that time not reveal, to the detriment of the king and others, how important the death of the legate is," because "the king was not accustomed to managing matters closely when Rouen was alive and now he neglects them." Nor do his ministers assume responsibility: "so the patient dies as the doctor ignores him and the caregivers [the ministers] neglect him." As Machiavelli was conversing with Robertet, a painter brought a portrait of Rouen. Robertet sighed and said to the image: "If you were alive, we would be in Rome with our army," words that confirmed Machiavelli's fear of how much Rouen's death would damage France (*LCSG* 6.288.26–9).

Julius rejected the mediation the French asked the Florentines to undertake in search of a settlement. The Ten told Acciaiuoli and Machiavelli that, in meetings with Florence's ambassadors, Julius "angrily exploded with many threats [venuto in collera, proruppe in assai minacci] against us, as if we had attacked him or wanted to. No words could be found to calm him.... No one has any idea how he can be engaged in discussion [ragionamento] as long as he holds on to these hopes to which he is so strongly attached.... With such opinions and self-assuredness [confidenzia], he is proceeding to Bologna...like one carried forward by sheer will [volontà] and hope of victory." In a last, and long, harangue with the Florentine ambassadors Julius said his aim was "to extricate Italy from bondage [cavare di servitù] and from the clutches of the French. He loudly lamented the obstacles we [Florentines] had put in his way, again threatening us" with ecclesiastical censures, punitive actions against the Florentine community in Rome, military assaults, "and every bad thing one could fear from an armed enemy.... From having thought we could be the authors of peace, it seems we have exacerbated his animosity [avere esacerbato l'animo suo] and provoked him to do us harm." And later in the letter: "It is astonishing how much he promises [si promette] himself a positive outcome of these promises [promesse] of his, which he bases on the arrival of the Swiss, a coup in Genoa, the acquisition of Ferrara, and the negative feelings of the [Italian] people toward the French" (*LCSG* 6.289.7–17). In another letter the Ten told Acciaiuoli that Julius was as convinced as ever of victory and was continuing to threaten and intimidate the Florentines: "He could not behave more menacingly [sinistramente] toward us with his words and threats; already throughout the Marche he has publicly ordered the confiscation of the assets of our *nazione*. We don't yet know the whole truth of this, but we greatly fear it is so, in view of his tactics and purpose, namely, to get us to take his side" in the war (*LCSG* 6.294.7–9). In mid-September, telling Acciaiuoli that Julius would soon arrive in Ravenna, the Ten commented: "Few are those who dare to judge what the pope will do: some believe that, following his initial plan, he will come in any event to Bologna. They base this on his nature etc., and on the *fumo di gloria* to visit the territories he himself regained" (*LCSG* 6.301.6–8). It is an ironic oxymoron, "fumo [smoke]" suggesting something unsubstantial and evanescent, "gloria" pointing to the pope's arrogant presumption of victory. The combination captures the view of Julius impelled by an inflated sense of glory resting on flimsy and fleeting foundations.

"ENTICED BY THIS GOOD FORTUNE OF HIS"

Pope Julius's seemingly irrational actions during the 1506 expedition prompted Machiavelli to theoretical speculation in the *Ghiribizzi al Soderino* (a letter to Piero Soderini's nephew Giovanbattista), written sometime between Julius's entry into Perugia on September 13 and his departure eight days later. Machiavelli was baffled by the risk Julius took going into Perugia with only a small guard, which led him to wonder why "different procedures produce the same outcome [con varii governi conseguire una medesima cosa]," or, as he restates it, "operating in divergent ways gains the same result [diversamente operando avere uno medesimo fine]." After reviewing examples of rulers and generals who achieved similar results with diametrically opposed methods, he states: "many who carefully measure and weigh" every aspect of their actions "do [not] attain their objectives."[41] Julius did not "measure and weigh" his actions beforehand and yet was successful. Machiavelli was puzzled by his disregard for the prudent calculation of means and ends that conventional wisdom and accepted practice assumed essential for success. "Why it happens that different procedures are sometimes beneficial and sometimes harmful in equal measure I do not know, but would very much like to know." He ventures a hypothesis: "just as nature has given to each person a distinctive look," so it has also given each person distinctive intellectual and imaginative faculties ("diverso ingegno e diversa fantasia"), which determine in each person a particular "modo di procedere," an innate and immutable way of acting and behaving in the world. The immutability of each person's "way of proceeding" encounters, in the world, the variability of "the times" and of the "ordine/i delle cose [structure/order/pattern of events]." Machiavelli does not say, here, how the times vary or what he means by the "ordine" of events. He proceeds directly to the conundrum, namely, that each individual's "way of proceeding" yields success only when it is compatible with the times and order of things and will fail when it

[41] Opinions differ about whether "non/not" should be inserted in this sentence. In any case, Machiavelli clearly thinks Julius did *not* "carefully measure and weigh" his actions.

is out of harmony with them. Two persons acting in their different ways can attain the same result if, in each case, the "way" matches what the times require. The "times" and "order of things"—factors external to, and beyond the control of, individual actors—determine success and failure. Machiavelli suggests, conjecturally, that one wise enough to recognize and understand [conoscessi] changing times and circumstances would always enjoy "good fortune" and keep clear of ill fortune, "and it would come to be true that the wise man controls the heavens and the fates." But he immediately qualifies this as purely theoretical and, in fact, impossible: "such wise men do not exist," because people are unable to control their own nature ("comandare alla natura loro"), from which "it follows that fortune changes [la fortuna varia] and controls men and keeps them under its yoke [sotto el giogo suo]."[42] Fortune, here representing the changing times and order of things, determines success and failure. Machiavelli's poem "Fortuna," probably written in 1506 and dedicated to the same Giovanbattista Soderini, likewise underscores the innate predisposition to act in a certain way and, hence, the power of Fortune, now personified as a woman. If one enjoys success, she will reverse her wheel—a metaphor for changing "times and circumstances"—and transform success into failure. "Because you cannot "change your persona [temperament]," Fortune "abandons you in the middle of your journey." Here too, Machiavelli speculates that, if one could understand the changing times and leap from wheel to wheel, one would always be successful and happy—a hypothesis no sooner proposed than quashed: "Because this ability is denied us by the occult power [virtú] that rules us, our situation changes with her course."[43]

But the problem Julius represented was more complicated. His "modo di procedere" may have been immutable, but Machiavelli cannot have meant this to apply to his tactics, which displayed a bewildering kaleidoscope of twists and reversals in which he constantly changed his mind and forgot or overturned each day what he had decided or tried the day before. As Machiavelli commented in early September 1506, "those who know the pope say that nothing fixed in one place can be found there the next day" (*LCSG* 5.464.5). The sense in which Julius's way of doing things was unchanging is, paradoxically, that it was *always* changing, often without apparent reason; he acted on impulse, never adequately studying the advantages and disadvantages of a particular course of action, needlessly placing himself in danger (as in Perugia), and repeatedly going forward on the basis of hasty, ill-considered assumptions or expectations. What puzzled Machiavelli was that Julius ignored the norms of prudence but was nonetheless successful.

[42] *Lettere*, pp. 239–45. But see the reorganization of the text by Carlo Ginzburg in *Nondimanco. Machiavelli, Pascal* (Milan: Adelphi, 2018), pp. 43–65, and Michael McCanles's valuable reading of the *Ghiribizzi* in *The Discourse of* Il Principe, pp. 1–9.

[43] Machiavelli, *Capitoli*, ed. Inglese, vv. 106–20, pp. 118–19.

That, apparently, is what "the times" required, at least in 1506, but what if the "times" changed?

In *Prince* 25 Machiavelli confronts the problem of fortune's seemingly ineluctable power with the example of Pope Julius. It is a commonly held opinion, he begins, that "the things of this world are so controlled [governate] by fortune and God that men are unable with their prudence to harness them [correggerle], indeed they have no answer [remedio: antidote] whatsoever." This "opinion" is given "more credence in our times because of the great instability [variazione] of events." Acknowledging that he too has "sometimes and in some measure inclined toward this opinion," Machiavelli must be alluding to the *Ghiribizzi* and the poem "Fortuna." Now he announces his intention to salvage "our free will [libero arbitrio]" by limiting the omnipotence that common opinion attributes to fortune. He proposes possible solutions, first suggesting that fortune is the "arbiter" of only half of human actions and leaves the rest, "or almost," to us, then likening fortune to a river where embankments can be built to limit the damage of inevitable floods. Italy, he adds, is a country without embankments and dikes and hence without shelter (*P* 25.1–8). Turning to fortune's power over individuals and specifically to the question of why a prince can be successful one day and destroyed the next without having changed his "natura," Machiavelli asserts, alluding to the analysis of Cesare Borgia in chapter 7, that "the prince who relies on fortune will come to ruin when fortune changes." He echoes the *Ghiribizzi*: success comes if one's "modo del procedere" is compatible with the times; conversely, failure ensues when the times are discordant with one's way of doing things. People achieve the same objectives in different ways—with caution or impetuousness, with violence or cunning, with patience or without it; and among those who employ the same methods, some succeed and others do not. It all depends on whether one's way of doing things is in conformity with the "times." And, once again, he affirms that "no man is wise enough [sí prudente] to know how to adapt" to changing times. One who habitually operates with "caution [rispetto]" will come to ruin when the times call for "impeto [impetuousness]," and vice versa (*P* 25.10–17).

This brings Machiavelli to Pope Julius, who "proceeded in his every action impetuously" and invariably met with success because the times and circumstances were in harmony with this way of proceeding. Reviewing the Bologna campaign of 1506, he notes that both Venice and King Ferdinand of Spain opposed it, and with the king of France Julius had had "discussions [ragionamenti]," but no firm agreement. "Nonetheless, [Julius] personally undertook that campaign with brazenness and daring [ferocità e impeto]." The Venetians and Ferdinand hesitated to do anything to stop him, and Julius got the support of King Louis, who "wanted an alliance with the pope in order to humble the Venetians and decided he could not deny the pope the use of his forces without openly offending him." Machiavelli concludes this brief review by saying that Julius's "impetuous move" gained him what "no other pope could have achieved even with the greatest human prudence." For if he had waited in Rome to be able to commence the campaign with agreements and assurances of assistance in place, "as any other pope would have done," he would never have succeeded, because the king of France would have found countless reasons to postpone providing assistance, and Venice and Spain would have created innumerable worries for him. Machiavelli provides just this one example of Julius's successes; he will "leave aside" his other deeds, because they "were all similar and successful," adding that the "brevity" of his reign prevented him from experiencing the opposite result that would have been his fate "if times had come that called for caution [respetti]." In that case, Julius would have come to ruin because "he would never have been able to deviate from those ways to which nature predisposed him" (*P* 25.18–24). In the light of Machiavelli's oft-repeated assertion that individuals never change their "modo di procedere," the chapter's (in)famous conclusion—"that it is better to be impetuous than cautious, because fortune is a woman who must be beaten and shoved about to keep her down" (*P* 25.25–7)—cannot imply a choice between impetuosity and caution. Machiavelli can only mean that those who are impetuous have a better chance of avoiding the disastrous consequences of Fortune's turn of the wheel. Chapter 25 never rejects the underlying conviction that people are, as we might say today, hard-wired from the outset.

From the title of *Discourses* 3.9—"How necessary it is to change with the times, if one wishes always to have good fortune"—one might be forgiven for thinking that Machiavelli changed his mind about the possibility of "changing with the times." In fact, however, the chapter reiterates and strengthens his belief that "people always act as [your] nature compels you to [secondo ti sforza la natura]." He contrasts Fabius Maximus (Cunctator, the Delayer), whose slow and cautious tactics, employed "per natura e non per elezione," were exactly what was needed when Hannibal was at peak strength in Italy, with Scipio Africanus, who boldly took Roman armies to Africa to defeat the Carthaginians and was likewise the right man for the moment. Republics, Machiavelli says, have longer life and longer-lasting good fortune than principalities because the "diversità" of their citizens enables them to find ones with the qualities and temperament required at any given time (*DL* 3.9.1–12). He then discusses two modern examples, Piero Soderini and Pope Julius. Soderini, he says, conducted himself in all things with "compassion [umanità]" and "equanimity [pazienza]," and this allowed him and his patria to prosper for as long as the times were compatible with his ways. But when the times called for different methods his inability to change resulted in his and his patria's downfall. Pope Julius did everything with "daring [impeto]" and in haste and "frenzy [furia]," and, because the times were compatible with his ways, he was successful in all his endeavors. But he too would have come to ruin if times requiring different methods had supervened (*DL* 3.9.13–16). The odd thing, of course, is that Soderini's decade as lifetime gonfaloniere of the Florentine republic from 1502 to 1512 almost exactly coincided with Julius's pontificate from 1503 to

1513; the "times," it seems, could be different in different places at the same moment. In *Discourses* 3.44.6–8, asserting (in the title) that "many times one achieves with *impeto* and *audacia* what would never be achieved with *modi ordinari*"—methods that followed accepted and lawful norms—he cites Julius's refusal to wait patiently for the replies he needed from France and Venice to carry out the 1506 campaign. Instead, he took the initiative, left Rome with whatever troops he could scrape together, and headed for Bologna, telling the Venetians to stay neutral and expecting troops from France. Fearing Julius's anger ("indegnazione") if they refused or delayed, the French and Venetians complied with his wishes.

In these chapters Machiavelli makes no mention of Julius's failure to seize Genoa from the French in 1510 or the 1511 revolt in Bologna that restored the Bentivoglio under the protection of King Louis. Had Machiavelli provided a fuller account of Julius's pontificate, he might have concluded that he did indeed encounter "times and circumstances" incompatible with his "way of proceeding," not only in the setbacks at Genoa, Ferrara, and Bologna but also in the defeat of the Spanish-papal armies at Ravenna (in 1512), from which he had to be rescued by the Swiss. Instead, in *Prince* 25, by omitting these reversals and near disasters, and by asserting that Julius was successful in all his undertakings because of his impetuosity, Machiavelli leaves the impression that he thought of him as one who mastered fortune. The image of Julius in chapter 25 has appealed to those who see in it the impetuous, aggressive, always successful prince Machiavelli allegedly yearned for. As we have seen, however, Machiavelli's perception of Julius in the legations of 1503, 1506, and 1510 puts his "impetuosity" in a quite different light. As Francesco Soderini also did, he saw Julius as reckless, unstable, and irrational, given to fits of rage, lusting for revenge, and obsessed with ambitions and desires that would have destroyed him had the Swiss not come to his rescue in 1512. Machiavelli no doubt remembered the letters he and Roberto Acciaiuoli received from the chancery near the end of the 1510 legation that describe Julius as "showing himself every day bolder [piú animoso], foreseeing great results [grandi effetti] for himself, *enticed by this [good] fortune of his* [invitato da questa sua fortuna]" (*LCSG* 6.284.11), and "hoping for victory, *enticed and led by this [good] fortune of his* [invitato e condotto da questa sua fortuna]" (*LCSG* 6.285.6; emphases added). In these formulations impetuosity does not control fortune; on the contrary, fortune "entices" and "leads" one to impetuosity.

In the *Discourses* Julius is portrayed as given to furious passions and wild fantasies. In three of the chapters in which he appears Machiavelli emphasizes his "furore" (fury, rage, frenzy) (*DL* 1.27.4), "temerità" (recklessness, irrational audacity) (*DL* 1.27.5), "impeto/furia" (violence, passion, aggression) (*DL* 3.9.15), and "audacia" (insolence, brazenness) (*DL* 3.44.1). In *Discourses* 2.24 he cites Julius's error in constructing, after the expulsion of the Bentivoglio in 1506, a fortress in Bologna that proved to be of no benefit to him. But this is more than just another example of what Machiavelli considered the dubious utility of fortresses. He uses it to underscore in particular their uselessness for rulers who abuse and mistreat the people. He notes that the papal governor installed by Julius (in 1508) so severely tormented the people of Bologna that they rose in rebellion against Julius's rule and welcomed back the Bentivoglio. Julius thus "lost his fortress, which did him no good; on the contrary, it harmed him." The governor, although he is not named in this passage, was, as Machiavelli knew, Julius's notoriously cruel advisor and collaborator, Cardinal Francesco Alidosi, known to Machiavelli from both the Bologna expedition of 1506 and the Rome legation of 1503 when he described him as "el primo uomo" in Julius's entourage (*LCSG* 3.263.4). Omitting Alidosi's name and referring to the "governatore" merely as the executor of Julius's policies makes Julius the real perpetrator of the savagery that sparked rebellion in Bologna: Julius, Machiavelli says, "had the people brutalized [faceva assassinare] by a governor of his." (Although "assassinare" here means to torment or mistreat, Alidosi did actually have a large number of Bolognese citizens executed.) Julius's agency is further emphasized in the observation that, "if he"—and Julius is the only available subject—"had conducted himself differently," the fortress "would have been useful to him" (*DL* 2.24.24–5). A cruel governor carrying out the brutal policies of the "prince" recalls Cesare Borgia's similar use of Ramiro de Lorqua. The comparison can be extended. Needing to rid himself of Ramiro when the cruelties became excessive, Borgia had him murdered in the piazza of Cesena. In Julius's case (although Machiavelli does not include this) he sent his nephew Francesco Maria della Rovere, the duke of Urbino, to fight the French outside Bologna while Alidosi defended the city from within. When Bologna rebelled and welcomed the French, Julius was irate with both Francesco Maria and Alidosi, who both feared punishment from Julius but also hated each other. Francesco Maria seized the opportunity and killed Alidosi in the streets of Ravenna,[44] thereby inflicting the same retribution that Borgia visited upon messer Ramiro. Machiavelli's compressed summary of how the mistreatment of the Bolognese people led to the loss of the fortress and the city—and to the ruthless governor's assassination—underscores the consequences of Julius's own inept and cruel administration.

Nor does Julius escape reproach for the same failure to create his own arms—and hence for constant dependence on mercenary and foreign arms—that undermined Cesare Borgia. Chapter 13 of *The Prince*, which criticizes Julius for his employment of Spanish auxiliaries (in 1511) after his failure to capture Ferrara with Italian mercenaries, follows the denunciation at the end of chapter 12 of mercenaries who, by corrupting Italian arms, created the conditions in which Italy was led to "slavery and humiliation." Employing Spanish auxiliaries was a "bad choice [mala elezione]," and "throwing himself into the hands of a foreigner

[44] Guicciardini, *Storia d'Italia*, book 9, ch. 18, ed. Scarano, vol. 2, p. 931.

[Ferdinand of Spain] could not have been more ill-advised," for, as he notes, these auxiliaries and the rest of his Holy League were defeated by the French at Ravenna in 1512. Julius was saved only by his "buona fortuna," when his Swiss allies invaded Lombardy, drove the French out of Italy, and spared him the reprisals that King Louis would certainly have inflicted (*P* 13.1–4). Engaging Spanish auxiliaries resulted in adding both Spain and the Swiss to the mix of foreign powers who "humiliated" Italy.

Returning for a moment to *Discourses* 1.12.20, where Machiavelli says the Church was not so weak that it could not call on foreigners to defend it against anyone "too powerful in Italy" who threatened its temporal possessions, we may recall that his examples of such interventions "in our own times" are the defeat inflicted on Venice by France in 1509 and the expulsion of the French by the Swiss in 1512—the very events adduced in *Prince* 11.5 as victories by which Julius brought the Church to "grandezza." A very different perspective on these events emerges as Machiavelli lays bare the complicity of Pope Julius in the humiliation of Italy. After restating that the Church's inability to bring all Italy under its control while not allowing anyone else to do so was why the country could not unite under a single head and consequently suffered disunity and weakness that left it prey to "powerful barbarians" and anyone who attacked it, Machiavelli angrily repeats that "we Italians owe this debt to the Church and to no one else" (*DL* 1.12.18–21). He knew of course that no one more than Julius had brought this about. On August 26, 1513, he expressed his full rancor against Julius in a private letter to Francesco Vettori—something he could not do in *The Prince*. Fearful of the Swiss threat, he told Vettori that he wished some "remedy" could be found to protect Italy from these fierce warriors from the mountains. "And if France is not a sufficient [remedy], I cannot see any other, and I shall begin to weep with you over our ruin and servitude, which, if it does not come today or tomorrow, will occur in our time. Italy will have this debt with Pope Julius and with those who fail to provide a remedy—if any is now possible."[45]

[45] *Lettere*, p. 419. On this letter, see my *Between Friends: Discourses of Power and Desire in the Machiavelli-Vettori Letters of 1513–1515* (Princeton: Princeton University Press, 1993), pp. 167–75.

5
Momentous and Natural Enmities

Why was Italy so "broken"? Machiavelli does not give just one answer. We could say he gives a hundred (he might have written *mille*, or *infiniti*—countless) reasons. Nor does he make a clear separation between the portrayal and denunciation of the broken world and the attempts to explain it. Diagnosis and etiology are constantly intertwined. Although it would be more accurate to say diagnoses and etiologies in the plural, Machiavelli does offer an overarching multi-faceted analysis, pursued with increasing complexity throughout his writings, that connects the various dimensions of his inquiry. It is not hidden in esoteric language. Indeed, he outlines its foundations in unambiguous terms at the beginning of the *Discourses on the First Ten Books of Livy*. However, because he introduces it in the context of Roman history that dominates the opening chapters of the *Discourses*, its full relevance for his interpretation of Italy's crisis is often overlooked. Its essence, as he expresses it in the introductory chapter of book 3 of the *Florentine Histories*, lies in the "gravi" (grievous, momentous, dangerous) and "naturali" (deeply ingrained, natural, structural) "nimicizie" (enmities) between the elite classes of wealth and power and the rival class(es) of professional, merchant, and generally less wealthy groups that vied for power with the elites. Machiavelli usually calls the elite classes "nobili" or "grandi," and their antagonists the "popolo" (or "plebe [plebs]" in the Roman context). He found fault with both classes but was more consistently and sternly critical of the elites whose power, wealth, and ambition he saw as a persistent threat to law and constituted authority—the state, as we would say—whose survival and viability, he believed, depended on efforts by other classes to constrain the elites. If princes, mercenaries, and popes were the agents of the crisis, its root causes lay deeper in Italy's social structures, family politics, and history. Machiavelli's originality as a political theorist consists above all in his perception of the social foundations of politics and government.

Machiavelli was acutely aware that those most responsible for "breaking" the Italian world came from, or were raised to power by, the elite classes: Italy's princes and leaders of republics; mercenaries; and the Church's hierarchy, both popes and cardinals. He saw the chief aim of all three groups—the broad, interconnected (and to a considerable extent intermarried) network of princely, ecclesiastical, and military families—as that of advancing the ambitions and defending the interests of their families and their class. To be sure, they often clashed—princes, republics, popes, and mercenaries in all possible conflictual combinations—but in the end they safeguarded the network. Machiavelli's attention to the elite's methods of

Machiavelli's Broken World. John M. Najemy, Oxford University Press. © John M. Najemy 2022.
DOI: 10.1093/oso/9780199580927.003.0005

preserving its power, which he saw as a principal source of Italy's dysfunction and weakness, led him to theorize the phenomenon historically and conceptually. This chapter focuses on his evolving theory of the nature of elite power—its aims, assumptions, and characteristic methods of self-preservation.

"PRINCES CANNOT HONORABLY SATISFY THE POWERFUL WITHOUT HARMING OTHERS"

Machiavelli's new direction is adumbrated in *The Prince*, theoretically elaborated in the *Discourses on Livy*, and exemplified and illustrated in the *Florentine Histories*. At its core, it rests on the premise that government and politics are shaped by the interests of, and conflicts among, society's constituent parts and that an understanding of the success or failure of polities, whether princely or republican, needs to be grounded in the analysis of social structures, class interests, and institutions. *The Prince* is best known as an inquiry into the attributes, conduct, virtues, vices, and failures of princes—issues that never ceased to stimulate Machiavelli's interest and ire. This is in large part a function of its status as a work, ostensibly of counsel, addressed and dedicated to princes. Despite its many departures from conventional ethical norms, the focus on princely virtues (in whatever sense of the term) and vices was not essentially new. Despite the radical twists he gave to the old "mirror of princes" literature, overturning traditional precepts concerning the virtues princes needed and the ones they should (sometimes) disregard, the conceptual framework itself of virtues and vices derived from earlier political discourses, especially that of the humanists and their classical forebears, for whom the success or failure of princes depended on moral education and morally informed choices.

The Prince does not systematically inquire into the social foundations of power and princely rule. But several chapters assume that an understanding of princely power requires awareness of society and subjects. It is already present, obliquely, in the dedicatory letter's assertion that "to know well the nature of princes it is necessary to be of the people [essere populare]" (*P* Dedica.5). Chapter 2 says it is easier to maintain hereditary principalities, in which subjects are "accustomed to the bloodline of their prince," than new ones. A prince born into a long-established ruling family—he cites the Este of Ferrara—is a "principe naturale" to whom his subjects are "naturalmente" well-disposed (*P* 2.4–5). Chapter 3 analyzes what he calls the "mixed principality" in which a prince of one state acquires new territories ("stati") whose language, customs, and political institutions differ from those of his original principality. These differences, he asserts, citing the example of Louis XII's conquest of Milan, confront a prince with particular difficulties he must take into account if he is to maintain his new acquisitions (*P* 3.8–11). In chapter 4 Machiavelli contrasts the Turkish monarchy, whose subjects are all equally subservient to the "signore" (the sultan), with the French kingdom, governed by the king but also by barons who have "territories [stati] and subjects" of their own and owe their status in the kingdom not to the favor of the king but to the antiquity of their lineages. These barons are "acknowledged and loved by their subjects," and the king cannot deprive them of their privileges without grave risks to himself. Hence, conquering the "dominion [stato] of the Turks" would be difficult because of the uniform obedience of all his subjects, but, once conquered, maintaining it would be easy because of the absence of an intermediate category of local or regional rulers like the French barons. Conversely, conquering the kingdom of France would be easier because barons often act on their own and sometimes even collaborate with invaders; but maintaining such a conquest would be difficult on account of the independence of these same barons who might organize revolts against the conqueror (*P* 4.5–15). The difference between the two monarchies consists in their contrasting internal structures, which produce different relationships between prince and subjects. The fifth chapter explains that a prince who acquires a city accustomed to living as a republic under its own laws will encounter considerable difficulties because "in republics there is greater vitality, greater hatred, and greater thirst for vengeance, and the memory of their former liberty will not let them rest." The options available to such a prince are to destroy the city, to go and live there, or to govern it "by means of [con il mezzo]"—in cooperation with—"its own citizens" (*P* 5.1–3). Here too pre-existing structures and customs condition the kind of government a new prince can construct and the degree of power he can enjoy.

The next four chapters (6–9) all consider the various contexts in which a "private citizen" (or simply a "privato" if he was not previously a citizen or subject of the state he acquires) becomes prince. Chapter 6 introduces four legendary founders and lawgivers (Moses, Cyrus, Romulus, and Theseus), all of whom, Machiavelli claims, rose from private to princely station (although it is not clear why he thought Cyrus, the son of a king and heir to a dynasty, was "privato" in either sense). "Privati" can become princes through either virtú or fortuna, both of which "can mitigate, in part, many difficulties, but those who have depended less on fortune have lasted longer." These four founders, Machiavelli asserts, took only the opportunity ("occasione") from fortune; the rest they accomplished with "their own arms and virtú," which enabled them to do the most difficult and dangerous thing a prince can accomplish: to take the lead in introducing "new institutions [nuovi ordini]." The nature of the societies over which these founders ruled plays little or no role in Machiavelli's analysis, apart from the servile status of the Hebrews whom Moses led out of bondage. The people play a larger role, however, in the brief mention of Savonarola, who, Machiavelli says, introduced new ordini but then fell victim to strong opposition because he lacked the necessary arms to defend them. Savonarola "failed [ruinò] amidst his new institutions [ordini nuovi] once the multitude ceased to believe him: and he had no way to hold firm those who had believed him or to make disbelievers believe in him" (*P* 6.5, 10, 17, 23). The chapter's one modern example is of a would-be lawgiver who, lacking the durable support of the people, failed.

Chapter 7 on Cesare Borgia has already been discussed above in Chapter 3. Here we may notice that Borgia's story continues the discussion of those who rise from a private station to become princes. Unlike the founders of chapter 6, he tried, unsuccessfully, to do so with "the arms of others and with fortune." Cesare did not come from the territories he seized, did not go to live there, and did not create an armed force he could call his own from the population of his conquered territories. There is but a single moment in Machiavelli's account in which Cesare evinces an awareness of the conditions and needs of the people: convinced that he had won the "friendship" of the people of the Romagna for having liberated them from incompetent signori who pillaged more than governed them, Borgia thought it necessary to give the region "good government" in order to "bring peace and make [the people] obedient to princely authority." He entrusted the task to Ramiro de Lorqua and claimed that he succeeded in pacifying and uniting the region. But, fearing that Ramiro's cruelties and "excessive power" would "become hateful," Borgia had him killed "to placate the minds of the people and win them over entirely" (*P* 7.22–8). The sudden collapse of Borgia's little empire after the death of Alexander makes it clear that neither Ramiro's alleged success nor his spectacular elimination succeeded in winning the loyalty of the people. Borgia is the cautionary example of an ambitious prince who fails to establish a relationship of reciprocal interests and mutual advantage with subjects.

Breaking away from the binary virtú/fortuna, chapter 8 identifies crime as a third way in which one rises from a private station to become a prince. His two examples are Agathocles, whom Machiavelli calls the king of Syracuse, in the fourth century BCE, and Oliverotto (Eufreducci) da Fermo, one of the condottieri who conspired against Borgia and then fell into his trap at Senigallia in December 1502. Agathocles accomplishes his rise to princely status in a conspiracy with the Carthaginians, who were enemies of Syracuse, and with their collaboration he had all the city's senators and wealthy citizens massacred. Although he sees no reason not to consider Agathocles a great military captain, Machiavelli quickly adds that his unbridled cruelty, inhumanity, and countless crimes make it impossible to include him among "the most excellent men" (*P* 8.9–11). Machiavelli no doubt wanted his reader to contrast the negative example of Agathocles with the virtuous Hiero (discussed at the end of chapter 6), a later prince of Syracuse, who also rose "from a private station to become prince" but did so with virtú. The Syracusans made him prince of the city after he liberated them (from marauding mercenaries, as Machiavelli could have added). He approvingly summarizes Hiero's creation of new military forces: "when he had alliances and soldiers that were his own, he was able on this foundation to erect any structure"—to build anything he wished. "He was of such virtú, even as a private citizen, that he who writes about him"—the reference is to Justin—"says he lacked nothing to rule except the title" (*P* 6.26–9). Machiavelli says nothing similar about Agathocles. In the unambiguous treatment of Oliverotto da Fermo, the second example of chapter 8, there is no attempt, as with Agathocles, to attribute to him one kind of virtú and deny him another. Oliverotto achieved power in the city of Fermo by massacring its leading citizens, including the uncle who raised him. He besieged the city's magistrates who, out of fear, were "forced to obey him and form a government in which he became the prince." Oliverotto secured his principality through fear and terror, and Machiavelli uses him as an example of cruelties "badly used"—repeated and drawn out—which make it necessary for a prince "always to have his hand on his sword, unable to trust subjects [né mai può fondarsi sopra e' sua sudditi]" who "cannot feel safe on account of the frequent and recurring abuses" he inflicts on them (*P* 8.22–8).

The theme of the social foundations of power and politics emerges prominently in chapter 9, on the "principato civile." Here, for the first time in *The Prince*, Machiavelli explores in some depth the various ways "privati" become princes. The term "principato civile," if not oxymoronic, is at least paradoxical. In Machiavelli's lexicon "civile" usually refers to republican government. Having rigorously separated "principati" from "republiche" in the first sentence of the first chapter, he now proposes a seeming hybrid—princely status within a republic, or, given the "civile" prince's original status as a citizen, a principate that develops from within a republic. Although Florence is named only once and quickly (concerning an episode from the fourteenth century), most of the chapter appears to allude to the city's more recent history. But views differ over precisely which period—assuming he meant to refer to just one—he had in mind. Was it the period of Medici domination from 1434 to 1494, in which Cosimo, Piero, Lorenzo, and the younger Piero increasingly acted (and were treated by foreign governments) as if they were princes, but within what was still formally, and in many respects functionally, a republic? Or was Machiavelli pointing to the period from 1502 to 1512, in which Piero Soderini presided over a robustly popular republican government as lifetime gonfaloniere—a prince-like, yet constitutional office to which he was elected? There are intriguing arguments in support of both hypotheses,[1] but the conceptual core of the chapter addresses an issue that could be applied to either period, or, possibly, even to the post-1512 restored Medici regime, which was still, formally, a republic.

[1] The interpretation of chapter 9 has given rise to many, often contrasting, interpretations. Some of the principal studies are: Gennaro Sasso, "Principato civile e tirannide," in Sasso, *Machiavelli e gli antichi*, vol. 2, pp. 351–483; Giorgio Cadoni, "Il principe e il popolo," in Cadoni, *Crisi della mediazione politica* (Rome: Jouvence, 1994), pp. 93–165; Paul Larivaille, "Il capitolo IX del *Principe* e la crisi del ‹principato civile›," in *Cultura e scrittura di Machiavelli* (Rome: Salerno Editrice, 1998), pp. 221–39; and Romain Descendre, "Of 'Extravagant' Writing: *The Prince*, Chapter 9," in *The Radical Machiavelli: Politics, Philosophy and Language*, ed. F. Del Lucchese, F. Frosini, and V. Morfino (Leiden-Boston: Brill, 2015), pp. 56–72.

Machiavelli theorizes the situation in which "uno privato cittadino" becomes "principe della sua patria" with the support and consent ("favore") of his fellow citizens. Again departing from the first chapter's either/or construction of states acquired with virtú or fortuna, he says that to acquire a "principato civile" one needs neither "all virtú" nor "all fortuna" but something he ambiguously calls "astuzia fortunata"—cunning, or cleverness, assisted by good fortune or luck. However this citizen prince acquires his principate, it is not by having his own arms; nor, apparently, does not having his own arms mean he is necessarily dependent on mercenaries. What he needs, and obtains with his "astuzia fortunata," is the support of either the "grandi"—the wealthy and powerful elite families—or the "popolo." Here Machiavelli introduces the two classes whose contrasting and incompatible desires will provide the analytical framework of the *Discourses*. Anticipating the analysis he will pursue in that work, he identifies the essential difference between the classes: the popolo "desires not to be dominated or oppressed by the grandi, and the grandi want to oppress and dominate" the popolo. From the conflict between these opposing desires, Machiavelli says, comes one of three possible results: "principato" or "libertà" (republican government) or "licenza" (a state of lawlessness). In the *Discourses*, he will contend that tyranny too can result from a particular kind of dysfunctional interaction between these classes, but here he focuses on the first of these potential outcomes, namely the "principato" that he defines as "civile," and explains why this kind of prince should prefer the support of the popolo over that of the grandi. A "principato civile" can be created by the grandi who, if they fear "they cannot resist the popolo, turn their favor to one of their own" and make him prince so that, "under his protection, they can vent their desire [sfogare il loro appetito]" to oppress the popolo. It can also be created by the popolo when they realize they cannot resist the grandi and similarly give their favor to one man (not, or not necessarily, one of their own), make him prince, and expect him to defend them with his power/authority ("autorità"). The civil principate is, therefore, the creation not so much, or at least not entirely, of the "cunning" and "fortunate" citizen raised to power, but of one of the social classes that seeks and uses power to dominate its rival class or avoid domination by it (*P* 9.1–3). It is unclear at this point whether Machiavelli thinks the "civil prince" can choose between these two sources of support.

The differences between the classes, however, subvert the apparent symmetry of their desires and fears. Machiavelli asserts that the citizen prince who achieves this rank with the support of the grandi will experience greater difficulty in maintaining it than one who achieves it with the support of the popolo. This is so because the grandi, who know he is "one of them" and rose from their ranks, consider themselves his equals, making it difficult for him to "command" and "manage" them. No such problem occurs if the prince achieves power with the favor of the popolo, which is generally willing to obey him, in return, of course, for the "defense" he provides against oppression by the grandi. Moreover, the prince cannot satisfy the desires of the grandi "honorably" and "without injury" to others, because their fundamental desire is to oppress and dominate the rest of the population. He can, however, satisfy the desires of the popolo, because its aim "is more honorable [piú onesto] than that of the grandi." Against a hostile popolo a prince can never be secure because of their greater numbers; because the grandi are fewer in number, it is possible for him to gain security ("assicurare") against them (*P* 9.4–7). But Machiavelli will express doubts about this last assertion.

Actually, Machiavelli seems to be of two minds about which class poses the greater danger to the citizen prince. He will resolve this ambivalence in the *Discourses*, but here he presents two sides of the question. Having declared that the grandi are less of a threat because there are fewer of them, he qualifies this: in addition to the possibility that they, like the popolo, might "abandon" him, the grandi could also revolt against him ["gli venghino contro"], which suggests that, despite being fewer in number, they could be the more active and potentially more violent threat. Machiavelli gives no examples here, but he may have been thinking of the machinations of the Florentine ottimati (as the city's grandi were often called by this time) and the coup, aided by foreign arms, that drove Piero Soderini into exile in 1512. Or was he thinking of attempts by earlier generations of ottimati to curtail the power of the Medici (as in 1465–6, after Cosimo died) or destroy the regime (as in the unsuccessful bloody Pazzi conspiracy of 1478 or the expulsion of Piero di Lorenzo in 1494)? Perhaps it was a bit of retrospective wishful thinking that prompted him to add that, while the prince "has to live with the same popolo," he can "make and unmake" the grandi "any day" and give or deny them prestige "as he pleases" (*P* 9.8–9).

The chapter's central contentions are that one who becomes prince with the favor of the popolo must maintain their friendship, whereas he who becomes prince "against the popolo" and with the favor of the grandi "must before all else seek to win over the popolo." This, he adds, "will be easy if he undertakes to defend" the popolo (against the grandi). In whatever way the citizen prince attains his position, the support of the popolo is essential to his success. Avoiding discussion of how it is possible to win the popolo's favor, because the ways "vary according to circumstances," Machiavelli concludes that "for a prince it is necessary to have the popolo as his ally [amico], for otherwise, when adversities come, he has no remedy"—no other solution, no way of surviving the adversities (*P* 9.14–18). Machiavelli may have intended this as advice to the repatriated Medici, who had just secured what could be thought of as a "principato civile" attained with the favor of the ottimati who ousted Soderini. If so, Machiavelli was urging them to change course and gain the favor of the popolo for their own greater security.

Machiavelli refutes the "trite proverb" according to which "he who builds on the popolo builds on mud." But the refutation is not entirely coherent. First, he says the proverb is accurate when a "private citizen" relies on the popolo to rescue him from enemies or the magistrates. "In such a situation, he could indeed often find himself deceived" and discover that he had "built on mud." He gives two examples: the Gracchi brothers in Rome, and Giorgio Scali in Florence. As we shall presently see, Machiavelli says the Gracchi incautiously revived Rome's old agrarian law for a more equitable distribution of land to benefit the plebs and the peasantry. The law incensed the nobles and led to civil war, ultimately causing the ruin of the republic. There are two problems with using the Gracchi as an example here: first, they were elected magistrates, not "private citizens," when they ran afoul of their enemies; second, they were opposed and assassinated not by plebeian supporters who turned against them but by the enraged senatorial aristocracy that would have lost land and wealth as a result of their reforms. Giorgio Scali, although he came from an elite Florentine family, was one of the leaders of the popular government from September 1378 to January 1382, when violent upper-class opposition overwhelmed that government and he was executed. As we shall see, Machiavelli devotes considerable attention to him in the *Florentine Histories*, recounting his loss of favor with the "multitude," which had previously "worshipped him," and his denunciation of the people's inconstancy and ingratitude. The people may have failed to protect Scali, but in the *Histories* Machiavelli emphasizes that the counterrevolution that toppled the popular government emerged from the wealthy elite class. It is on this point that the two examples share an important feature: in both cases, upper-class reformers encountered violent opposition from their own class for having promoted policies that favored the lower classes. The episodes point to conflicts between the classes—an issue Machiavelli apparently did not wish to elaborate in a work addressed to the very upper-class Medici. So he veers away from these examples and concludes, rhetorically, that a prince who builds on the people, who knows how to "command, has courage, does not lose heart in adversities," and who keeps the multitude emboldened with his courage and his governing ordini will have created good foundations and will never find himself deceived by the multitude (*P* 9.20–2).

The chapter's last paragraph is its most difficult and perplexing section. "These principati" (but at least one manuscript has "principi"), Machiavelli begins, "usually encounter mortal danger [periclitare] when they are about to rise from civil to absolute status [da lo ordine civile allo assoluto]." But which "principati"? All "principati civili"? Those that "build on" the popolo or the "multitude"? Or all new "principati"? Machiavelli attempts to explain this tantalizing but ambiguous first sentence saying that "These princes either govern by themselves, or through the magistracies; if through the latter, their government [stato] is weaker and more imperiled, because they are completely dependent on the citizens who sit on these magistracies, who in times of adversity could easily deprive the prince of his power [stato], by either abandoning or opposing him." Facing such dangers, "the prince is not able to seize absolute power [autorità assoluta] in time," because citizens and subjects, accustomed in such circumstances to taking commands from the magistrates, will not obey his orders. "In unstable times he will always have few whom he can trust, for such a prince cannot rely on what he sees in peaceful times when the citizens need the regime [stato]"—"stato" here signifying the informal construct of power that sits uneasily alongside, and sometimes overwhelms, the institutional framework of government. In "tempi quieti" everyone professes loyalty to him, but in "tempi avversi, when the regime [stato] needs the citizens, the prince will find very few" on whom he can rely. "And this undertaking [esperienza: that of assuming absolute authority] is all the more dangerous in that it can be tried only once." Machiavelli concludes that a "wise prince must therefore conceive of a way in which his citizens will need the regime [stato] and him at all times and in all circumstances, and then they will always be loyal to him." Binding the citizens to the regime binds them to the prince as well (*P* 9.23–7).

Some interpretations of this paragraph see it as encouragement to the post-1512 Medici to establish "absolute power"—"assoluto" deriving from the expression of the jurists, *legibus solutus*, unencumbered, unfettered by laws—and to do so before "times of adversity" intervene to make such a bold move more difficult and dangerous. Other interpretations give greater weight to Machiavelli's emphasis on the grave danger civil princes encounter in attempting to "rise" from "civil" to "absolute" rule, from princely government bound by law to one unconstrained by law. Compounding the danger is the fact—and Machiavelli presents it as a fact—that one can try to do this only once, presumably because a failed attempt would bring the prince into disrepute. The paragraph admits of these two (and possibly more) readings. However, the second seems more likely in view of what Machiavelli says in the *Discourses*, namely, that "a prince unfettered by laws [sciolto dalle leggi] will be more ungrateful, erratic, and lacking in prudence than the people" (*DL* 1.58.18) and "a prince who can do what he pleases is mad [pazzo]" (*DL* 1.58.33). Moreover, "absolute" power is twice associated in the *Discourses* with tyranny (*DL* 1.9.13; *DL* 1.25.6). It seems improbable that Machiavelli was urging the Medici to institute a tyranny, but, if it was his intention to encourage them to seize "absolute power" as a euphemism for tyrannical rule, what would have dissuaded him from directly saying so? This question leads to another: why does Machiavelli raise this issue in *The Prince* and specifically in chapter 9? The "principato civile," with its genesis in the "astuzia fortunata" of a private citizen who becomes "principe della sua patria" with the favor of his fellow citizens, certainly reminded readers—and he hoped Pope Leo would be the most consequential of his readers—of the "stato" established by Leo's great-grandfather, Cosimo de' Medici. Leo did in fact hope, in the early days of the restored Medici regime, to resume the kind of governance created by Cosimo—informal (or limited formal) control by the Medici through patronage, ad hoc councils, and manipulation of elections—in cooperation with the leading ottimati families. That the unnamed "private citizen" of chapter 9 becomes "principe della sua patria" obviously echoes the posthumous decree that declared Cosimo *pater patriae*. This suggests that Machiavelli may have been advising the Medici, if they were intent on establishing a "principato," to resurrect Cosimo's limited, camouflaged, quasi-princely fifteenth-century regime. Machiavelli no doubt assumed that Leo knew of his father Lorenzo's pretense that he had less power than he actually did, as when he wrote, "I am not the lord [signore] of Florence, only a citizen with some influence [con qualche auctorità]."[2] Yet, among the restored Medici and some of their supporters, impatience with republican institutions that hampered the tight control they sought kindled a desire to sweep out the republic and install a formal principate. In 1518, Leo and the younger Lorenzo clashed over the latter's wish to do just that, and Leo prohibited his nephew from carrying out what seemed to him an excessively drastic departure from tradition.[3] But the question was constantly in the air after the Medici returned to power in 1512.

If chapter 9 silently refers, not only to the regime Cosimo installed beginning in 1434 but also, and more urgently, to the post-1512 debate over whether the Medici should reconstitute Cosimo's hybrid system of governance or cancel the inconvenient republic altogether, the last paragraph comes into clearer focus. With the caution required by his precarious status, Machiavelli refrains from overtly linking the "principato civile" to the Medici, past or present. But the distinction he makes at the beginning of the chapter between civil princes who come to power with the favor of either the grandi or the popolo would certainly have reminded contemporary readers that in 1512 the Medici seized power with the favor and collusion of many of the grandi. Cosimo, by contrast, although he certainly did not lead a popular movement or government (as an old Medici legend would have it), consolidated the victory over his rivals in 1434 by exiling hundreds of members of the opposing, equally elite, party headed by the Albizzi family. Despite those draconian penalties, he and his son Piero and grandson Lorenzo faced repeated challenges from other elite families of their own class who, considering themselves their social equals, resented the outsized power and control the Medici wielded. After Cosimo died in 1464, his former lieutenants sought to restore traditional republican government, as they understood it, to the hands of leading ottimati and without the emergency councils and electoral manipulations of the Medici. In 1478, the anger and bitterness of a large swath of ottimati resulted in the Pazzi conspiracy and a bloodbath of retribution. And no one needed to remind Leo that the fall of the regime and the long exile into which the future pope and his brothers were sent in 1494 was the work of disaffected ottimati who resented the overbearing and—as some said—tyrannical younger Piero. Machiavelli was warning Leo and his family that a regime built on the support of the ottimati would face the constant threat of their ambitions and grievances. The possibility of "rising

[2] Letter to Pierfilippo Pandolfini, November 26, 1481, in Lorenzo de' Medici, *Lettere*, vol. 6, ed. Michael Mallett (Florence: Giunti-Barbèra, 1990), p. 100.

[3] See Rosemary Devonshire Jones, *Francesco Vettori: Florentine Citizen and Medici Servant* (London: Athlone Press, 1972), pp. 137–9.

from civil to absolute rule" may allude to the advice Leo was getting from the proponents of a clean break with the republic. But Machiavelli cautions that yielding to this temptation is when civil princes run grave risks, in part, but not only, because "a prince in danger will not be able to seize absolute power in time."

The last paragraph does not explicitly identify from whom the danger to the civil prince comes. But Machiavelli has already done so in a passage in the middle of the chapter just after saying that the civil prince can "make and unmake" grandi and give or deny them prestige as he pleases. He then makes distinctions that qualify that assertion, in a collective profile of the grandi that he offers as a guide to how the civil prince must differentiate between those on whom he should bestow prestige and those from whom he should withhold it. Some grandi, he says, "act in ways that obligate them to your fortunes," and these the prince should honor and love, "provided they are not avaricious [rapaci]." (Machiavelli does not comment here on avaricious grandi who do commit themselves to the prince; he will do so in the *Discourses.*) Grandi who do not bind themselves to the prince fall into two groups. If their failure to do so stems from "cowardice [pusillanimità] and inborn lack of courage," the prince should make use of them, particularly if they are good advisers. But against grandi who refrain from committing to him "per arte" (motivated by treachery, guile, and cunning) and "per cagione ambiziosa" (spurred by immoderate and calculated ambition)—"signs that they think more of themselves than of the prince"—he must protect himself and fear them as if they were "openly declared enemies [scoperti nimici], because in times of adversity they will always seek to destroy him [ruinarlo]" (*P* 9.10–13). This is the heart of chapter 9 and the key to the interpretation of the last paragraph: a stern admonition to beware of the avarice, treachery, and deceit of those grandi who, out of perfidy and ambition, deny the prince their allegiance and are "always" waiting for the opportunity to overthrow him.

Writing this in 1513, it seems inconceivable that Machiavelli was not also alluding to the expulsion of Piero Soderini just the year before. That the removal of Soderini was the result of a conspiracy of intransigent ottimati is clear from contemporary accounts. Bartolomeo Cerretani's *Dialogue on the Revolution in Florence*, written in the early 1520s, dramatically recounts the collusion in August–September 1512 between the ottimati conspirators, led by Giovanni di Bernardo Rucellai, and the commander of the Spanish army, Ramon de Cardóna, in pressuring Cardinal Giovanni de' Medici, who was waiting outside the city, to accept their plan for a "mutatione"—the overthrow of the popular republic. As Cerretani says, these ottimati believed that bringing the Medici back as rulers and not merely citizens was the best way to preserve and enhance their own power in the city, and they "waited for the opportunity [occasione]" to bring down Soderini and the republic and "fare nuovo stato."[4] Francesco Vettori, who, as "commissario

[4] Bartolomeo Cerretani, *Dialogo della mutatione di Firenze*, ed. Giuliana Berti (Florence: Olschki, 1993), quoted passages at pp. 26 and 32.

generale," was responsible for internal defense as the Spanish army, with the permission of the pro-Medici ottimati, plundered the countryside and threatened the city, describes, in his history of Italy between 1511 and 1527, the moment when hostile ottimati forced Soderini into exile. On August 31, 1512, four young "nobili"—Bartolomeo Valori, Paolo Vettori (Francesco's brother), Gino Capponi, and Antonfrancesco degli Albizzi—stormed into the palace and told Soderini he had to leave both to spare the city a terrible sack (by the Spaniards) of the sort that had just been inflicted on Prato and to escape harm to himself.[5]

Among Machiavelli's writings, the short memorandum to the Medici party known as "Ai Palleschi" (as the Mediceans were called) supports the reading offered above of chapter 9 of *The Prince*. Written in early November 1512, after the Medici and their ottimati allies had completed the "mutatione" and just before Machiavelli was dismissed from his posts on November 7, it is an apparently unsolicited admonition to the Medici that their new regime ("stato") would put itself in danger by investigating Piero Soderini for alleged misdeeds during his tenure as standard-bearer, as his "enemies" wanted. Their motive, says Machiavelli, was to "destroy his reputation among the people," "not to benefit this [new Medici] stato, but to increase their own prestige." Finding Soderini guilty would bring his "enemies" greater favor with the popolo, but would "not at all be in the interest of this stato, which needs to find some way of making them hated, not admired [benvoluti], by the people, so that they will have more need of being allied [uniti] with the [Medici] stato." Soderini's accusers wanted to diminish the people's hatred for themselves for their own benefit not that of the Medici. Incriminating him would "wreck the reputation of one who is already gone [exiled] and can do no harm and would increase the reputation of those who are here [a chi è in casa] and can at any time damage" the Medici stato. Here Machiavelli not only reveals the depth of his own rancor against the grandi but also puts his finger on the essential triangulation of political forces in Florence. In identifying Soderini's enemies as "those who play the whore [puttaneggiono] between the popolo and the Medici" he makes it clear, if it were not already, that these radical ottimati wanted to incriminate Soderini to free themselves of the opprobrium in which the people held them for having opposed and exiled him. But the regime's interest, Machiavelli insists, is to disrupt any alliance between the people and the grandi and make the latter dependent on the regime,[6] which is exactly what he says at the end of chapter 9, namely, that the civil prince "must devise some way in which his citizens will always and in all circumstances have need of the stato/regime and of him; and then they will be constantly loyal to him." The grandi will need the stato and its prince only if they fear the people.

Grandi and popolo play smaller roles in the rest of *The Prince*. After chapter 9, they do not reappear together until chapter 19's discussion of how princes must

[5] Francesco Vettori, *Sommario della Istoria d'Italia*, in *Scritti storici e politici*, ed. Enrico Niccolini (Bari: Laterza, 1972), pp. 140–4.

[6] *SPM*, pp. 582–4.

avoid contempt and hatred, particularly from the popolo. To prevent conspiracies, Machiavelli writes, "well-ordered states and wise princes have diligently sought not to make the grandi despair and to satisfy and keep happy the popolo." With an irresistible play on words, he says that, because of the "benivolenzia populare" enjoyed by the Bentivoglio of Bologna, that city's popolo rose up and killed the conspirators who (in 1445) assassinated Annibale Bentivoglio. A prince "should respect [stimare] the grandi but never let the people hate him." Hatred and contempt brought about the downfall of many Roman emperors, and the lesson for modern princes is to avoid the hatred of the people (*P* 19.15–19, 24, 61–2). Chapter 20 asserts that a new prince should not offend the people by disarming them or building fortresses, which only show that the prince fears his own people more than foreigners. "The best fortress is not to be hated by the people" (*P* 20.7, 29). Grandi and popolo make a final joint appearance in chapter 24's denunciation of the Italian princes who lost their states in the storms that began in 1494. Citing the king of Naples, the duke of Milan, and "others" (presumably Piero de' Medici, father of the dedicatee of *The Prince*), Machiavelli says that, in addition to sharing deficiencies in military preparations, "some of them either had a hostile popolo, or, if they had the friendship of the popolo, did not know how to find security [assicurare] against the grandi." So crucial is the prince's relations with these classes that Machiavelli declares: "without these weaknesses, states that have enough strength to keep an army in the field are never lost" (*P* 24.5–6). Next to military preparedness, the essential elements of a prince's ability to maintain his state are the friendship of the popolo and the skillful containment of the ambitions of the grandi. The chapters of *The Prince* that most directly address the question of why and how princes lose their states—9, 19, and 24—are the ones in which the dialectic grandi/popolo is most prominent.

"POSSESSING MUCH, THEY CAN, WITH GREATER POWER AND FORCE, OVERTHROW GOVERNMENTS"

Machiavelli deepens the implications of this conflict in the *Discourses on Livy*. After the opening chapter on the origins of cities, in chapter 2 of book 1 he considers the different kinds ("spezie") of republics as preparation for understanding the particular nature and character of the Roman republic. He first distinguishes between republics (or cities—here using the terms interchangeably) that receive their laws all at once from a single lawgiver (his example is Lycurgus of Sparta) and those that get their laws "by chance, piecemeal, and in the course of events [a caso e in piú volte e secondo li accidenti]," as happened in Rome. Although a republic whose laws are established ("ordinate") in such a way by a single wise lawgiver that it has no need to revise or reform them "can be called happy," Machiavelli quickly reveals that he is more interested in cities whose laws evolve through the trial and error of events over time, which, he says, involves "some degree of unhappiness." Such cities will undertake reform only when persuaded by some necessity that entails risk and danger—and, as Machiavelli soon explains, inevitable disagreements and conflicts (*DL* 1.2.3–5).

Pervading the opening paragraphs of *Discourses* 1.2 is the lexical family of ordini, whose specific meanings are indispensable to a correct comprehension of Machiavelli's texts. Laws and ordini are closely related, Machiavelli says, but not identical: ordini are the more permanent, structural institutions and norms, akin to "constitution" in our political language; laws are ad hoc enactments or regulations that address particular issues. In *Discourses* 1.18 Machiavelli identifies the chief ordini of the Roman republic as follows: "the authority [autorità] of the people, the senate, the tribunes, and the consuls, the way of nominating and electing magistrates, and the way of making laws. These ordini varied little or not at all with events." (One wonders why religion is not in this list.) By contrast, the "laws [leggi] that constrained [frenavano]" citizens did change: Machiavelli cites as examples the law against adultery, the sumptuary laws, the law against certain ways of seeking offices and securing election, which he calls the law "dell'ambizione," and "many others" (*DL* 1.18.8–11). The verb "ordinare" means to institute, order, establish, constitute, or organize. A city or state with good ordini is well constituted or well ordered ("bene ordinato"). A lawgiver who establishes the ordini is an "ordinatore." Lycurgus, Machiavelli writes (now back in *Discourses* 1.2.4), gave Sparta its laws so well "ordinate" that it lived securely under them for eight hundred years with no need for correction or conflict and without corruption (the weakening or undermining of the ordini). The reflexive form of the verb, "ordinarsi," when applied to a polity means to give itself ordini, and "riordinarsi" denotes reforming or re-establishing its ordini. Cities without a lawgiver like Lycurgus, says Machiavelli, must frequently "riordinarsi." Ordine (singular) is the condition of having well-functioning laws and ordini. A city lacking good ordini or whose ordini have been corrupted is "in disordine" or "disordinata" (*DL* 1.2.2–9). In just this second chapter of book 1 of the *Discourses* there are thirty-three instances of these related forms from the root "ordinare," but, as we shall see, the family is larger still. An action or procedure in conformity with the ordini is "ordinario"; one that violates the ordini is "estraordinario" with the prefix *estra* or *stra* in the vernacular (from Latin *extra*) signaling outside, or beyond, the ordini. One of the common mistakes in English translations of Machiavelli is to render "ordinario" as ordinary and "estraordinario" (or "straordinario") as "extraordinary." The conceptual specificity of Machiavelli's political language is lost with such *faux amis*. In this study, Machiavelli's use of these key terms will be regularly highlighted.

"Wishing therefore to discuss what the ordini of the city of Rome were, and what events brought it to its perfection," Machiavelli continues in chapter 2, he first reviews the traditional typologies of government. He does so, however, not in his own voice, but following "some who have written about republics," who say that "republiche" (here the genus meaning states of all types) can be subdivided into three "stati" (here in the sense of governments or constitutional systems), which they call "principato," "ottimati" (from Latin *optimates*, literally "the best," signifying government by nobles or elites), or "popolare" (government by the non-noble popolo). "Other [writers], and, according to many, wiser ones," speak of six types of government, three of them very bad ("pessimi"), and three others "good in themselves," but so easily corruptible that they too become "pernicious." The three "pessimi" ones are corruptions of the three good ones. Echoing a common motif of the similitude of virtues and related vices, Machiavelli says the three bad kinds are each so similar to the good government closest to them (and of which they are corrupt forms) that they easily jump ("saltano") from one to the other. Hence, the "principato" easily becomes "tirannico"; government by "ottimati" easily becomes government of the few ("stato di pochi") or oligarchy; and "popolare" becomes "licenzioso" (in which people live unrestrained and without respect for the laws). Machiavelli echoes Polybius in emphasizing the precarious instability of the types: "If a lawgiver [ordinatore] institutes [ordina] one of the three [good] kinds of government in a city," what he establishes will last for only a short time "because nothing can prevent it from sliding into its contrary on account of the similarity of the virtue and the vice," which is to say the similarity of the virtuous form to its corrupted evil twin (*DL* 1.2.10–13). This typology derives from Polybius, whom Machiavelli particularly has present here, and is also found in Aristotle, Plato, and others. Although not original with Machiavelli, it serves the important purpose of underscoring the fluidity and mutability of all forms of government. He will make extensive use of this notion in presenting the founding of governments as an ongoing process that responds to changing circumstances and clashing interests.

Still in chapter 2, Machiavelli summarizes (without acknowledging the source) Polybius' theory of the "cycle of constitutions," written in the past tense as if he were outlining the actual historical origins of political society. First, the people came together to form a community and initially selected the strongest and bravest among them for defense. As emerging ideas of right and wrong led to laws, punishments for transgressors, and the "knowledge of justice," they turned instead to the wisest and most just among them and made him "principe." Subsequent princes came to power by hereditary succession, "not by election," and, as they adopted sumptuous and lascivious ways of life, they provoked the hatred of their subjects. The now fearful prince responded with violence, from which a tyranny was born. Conspiracies and plots to bring down the tyranny came from those citizens who exceeded the others in four things: "generosità," here meaning nobility of spirit, altruism, and benevolence; "grandezza d'animo," greatness of spirit; "ricchezza," wealth; and "nobilità," which denotes family prestige, not noble titles, especially in this mythical ur-moment of the genesis of political society. In one important respect Machiavelli modifies Polybius, adding "ricchezza" to the list of the conspirators' qualities.[7] Detesting the notion of a single ruler, these "potenti" constituted a collective "governo" and "conducted themselves [si governavano] according to the laws they instituted," subordinating their own interests to the common good, and managed [governavano] private and public matters with the greatest diligence." This was the government of the "ottimati." The emphasis on how they "governed" contrasts with the absence of the term in the preceding account of the princely regime. But, as happened with the "principato," subsequent generations of ottimati abandoned the virtues of the founders, turning away, specifically, from "civile equalità"—which, as we shall see, is the bedrock notion of republican government for Machiavelli—and embraced "avarizia," "ambizione," and the dishonoring ("usurpazione") of women. Thus the government of the "best" became government of the few, with no concern for any "civilità"—the norms and laws of good government. The multitude, which had willingly accepted the leadership of the "liberators" who overthrew tyranny, now turned against the oppressive ottimati and instituted a popular government ("stato popolare"). But this too lasted only a short time as it degenerated into "licenza," in which there was no fear of either private citizens or public officials: "everyone lived as he wanted, and every day a thousand wrongs were committed." To escape this state of license, either compelled by necessity or led by "some good man," the principate was reinstated (by whom Machiavelli does not say). "This," he says, concluding the summary of Polybius, "is the *cerchio* [circle, or cycle] in which all states [republiche] revolve in governing themselves" (*DL* 1.2.14–24).

It is often assumed that the Polybian "cycle of constitutions" provides the conceptual foundation of the *Discourses*. Actually, Machiavelli undermines it in these same pages. At the outset, he says "these changes of government occur by chance [a caso]" (*DL* 1.2.14). (The meaning of "a caso" will become clearer from its next appearance.) And, immediately after asserting that "this is the cycle" through which all states are governed, he qualifies it with the observation that "they rarely return to the same governments because no state [republica] can have long enough life to pass many times through these changes." States lacking "prudence [consiglio] and military force" can be overwhelmed by a "better constituted [meglio ordinato]" state. In these and other ways, Machiavelli distances himself from the natural necessity of Polybius' cycle by injecting the contingency of history. In view of the inherent defects of the simple kinds of government, he says, prudent lawgivers have preferred governments that incorporate all three uncorrupted forms—principato, ottimati, and popular government—"so that each watches [guarda: checks up on] the other" (*DL* 1.2.24–7). Why then does Machiavelli devote so much attention to the Polybian theory even as he rejects it as an explanation of historical change? His purpose may have been—and the effect certainly

[7] Noted by Giorgio Inglese in *DL*, p. 196, n. 18.

is—that it allowed him to introduce, early in the *Discourses*, the idea that collective social actors make and unmake governments—that political constitutions are created, modified, and destroyed in the turmoil of the divergent interests of social classes and their conflicts. With Polybius, he introduces the nobles and the popolo as consequential, even decisive, actors, together with princes and lawgivers, in the making of states and governments. In his summary, the earliest inhabitants "gathered together" and selected one of their number as the leader, thus creating the original "principato"; qualified, powerful citizens destroyed the tyranny that the principate became; and the multitude led the revolt against the government of the few into which the ottimati had degenerated. These are the protagonists of Machiavelli's approach to history, and they provide the transition to his interpretation of Roman history.

"But let us come to Rome," Machiavelli declares near the end of chapter 2 and immediately draws from his critique of Polybius' theory two foundational ideas. The first is the absence of a preordained or inevitable outcome. Unlike Sparta, he says, whose founder, Lycurgus, provided all the laws that city needed to prosper in liberty for a long time, in Rome historical events ("accidenti") drove its development, such that "il caso" did what a single "ordinatore" did not do (*DL* 1.2.30). Machiavelli's "accidenti" are not random or freakish occurrences lacking cause or connection to what precedes and follows; they are not, in short, accidents. They are the contingent events of history, what happened but did not need to happen or could have happened differently, the results of choices and aims that could have been formulated or implemented differently. Hence, in this context, "il caso" is not pure chance, luck, or randomness. It is the sum of the "accidenti," the overall result of contingent events. This meaning of "il caso" is confirmed by its use in *Discourses* 1.6, where Machiavelli says the custom in Venice of designating as "gentili uomini" all those admitted to government was the result of "il caso," not of the wisdom of legislators, and then gives a historical explanation of how the original inhabitants formed their government and decided on this designation (*DL* 1.6.7–8). The second foundational idea of Machiavelli's analysis of Rome is that these contingent "accidenti" of history were the result of "disunione"—conflict, disunity, dissension—between the plebs and the senate, the specific Roman instantiations of the collective actors to which he refers, in summarizing Polybius, as, respectively, the "multitude" and the "potenti" citizens of nobility and wealth. The motor of Roman history was the confrontation of these classes. Lacking a single founder, Rome's ordini were initially defective; yet the kings who ruled before the birth of the republic gave it good laws and institutions (including, as Machiavelli will say in *Discourses* 1.9, the senate) and put it on the "right road" toward a "vivere libero," which is to say, a republic. The creation of the republic removed the title of "king" but vested the powers formerly held by the kings in two consuls. At that point, with its consuls and senate, Rome had "only" two of the three forms ("qualità") of government—"principato" and "ottimati"—and needed to add the third, the "governo popolare." But the nobility did not willingly yield power, and a revolt by the "popolo" was needed to bring about the "creation of the tribunes of the plebs," which brought the third element into a share of government. With all three elements now included, the "stato" of the republic gained greater stability and, being "mixed [mista]," made for a "perfect" (or complete) republic. Machiavelli ends chapter 2 by reaffirming that Rome came to this "perfection" through the "disunion" of the plebs and the senate (*DL* 1.2.31–6). Hereafter, however, he will show less interest in the "perfection" of the "mixed constitution" composed of monarchical, aristocratic, and popular elements and focus instead on how conflicts between the plebs and the nobles shaped Rome's history.

The office of the tribunes, Machiavelli writes in chapter 3, was the first result of these conflicts. For as long as the Tarquin kings ruled, the nobles kept their arrogance and hatred of the people "hidden" and acted "humanely" toward them. Machiavelli calls it a deception ("inganno") perpetrated by the nobles because they feared the power of the kings and any alliance between king and plebs. He thus underscores the bad faith and ill will of the nobles before the creation of the tribunate, indeed even before the emergence of hostilities with the plebs. Once the kings were removed, the nobles, no longer fearing royal power and punishment, began to "spit out against the plebs the poison they had kept in their breasts and injured them in all the ways they could." It thus became necessary to create a "nuovo ordine"—a new permanent magistracy—that would have the same restraining effect on the nobles that the kings had had. "After much turbulence, many riots, and the risk of conflict [pericoli di scandoli] between the plebs and the nobles, it was agreed, for the security of the plebs, to create the tribunes," who were given sufficient powers and prestige ("riputazione") to mediate between the plebs and the senate and "resist the insolence [insolenzia] of the nobles" (*DL* 1.3.4–9). Machiavelli will often emphasize the "insolenzia"—haughtiness, arrogance, impudence—of elites in both Rome and Florence. For the moment, we notice the awkward combination of the tribunes' role as mediators and their duty to "resist the insolence of the nobles" and guarantee the "security of the plebs."

Chapter 4 presents Machiavelli's most revolutionary, counterintuitive, and original political argument, namely, that the "disunione"—conflicts—between the plebs and the senate "made the Roman republic free and powerful," an assertion that Francesco Guicciardini found incomprehensible, protesting that "to praise disunion is like praising the illness of a sick person for the efficacy of the remedy prescribed for him."[8] From classical antiquity to Augustine to the Renaissance humanists (to limit the picture to the time before Machiavelli), the essential and unquestioned goal of political theory was to identify and establish the conditions

[8] Francesco Guicciardini, *Considerazioni sui ‹Discorsi› del Machiavelli*, in *Opere di Francesco Guicciardini*, ed. Lugnani Scarano, vol. 1, p. 616.

for concord, harmony, and peace.[9] Machiavelli broke with this tradition radically and unequivocally. Referring to the turbulence and riots that led to the institution of the tribunate, he begins chapter 4 with what seems at first a tangential comment—almost an afterthought—on those disturbances: "I do not wish to omit discussing the tumults that occurred in Rome from the death of the Tarquins to the creation of the tribunes." But then he jumps—feet first, we might say—into the biggest questions of Roman history. He wants to say "some things against the opinion held by many, who maintain that Rome was a chaotic [tumultuaria] republic, full of so much turbulence [confusione] that, if good fortune and military virtú had not compensated for its defects, it would have been inferior to every other republic" (*DL* 1.4.2). How, he asks, did the Roman republic become so powerful and create so vast an empire? Was it owing to good fortune, or military prowess? Did either or both of these overcome the "defects" of a republic that lacked social cohesion and concord? And how did Rome for so many centuries maintain the liberty of a republic of laws? How did it achieve this in the face of so much internal turbulence—so much indeed that many of Machiavelli's contemporaries considered Rome inferior to peaceful and "serenissima" Venice? While not denying that fortune and military strength aided the growth of Roman power, Machiavelli insists that, where good arms exist, there must be "buono ordine"—a good political constitution—and rarely does this combination not entail good fortune as well (*DL* 1.4.3). "Buono ordine" precedes military strength, and good fortune is a consequence, not a cause, of both.

Machiavelli addresses Rome's critics in a sentence that encapsulates the central insight of the *Discourses*: "I say that those who condemn the tumults between the nobles and the plebs seem to me to denounce the very things that were the primary cause that kept Rome free, and that they pay more attention to the disturbances and shouting to which the tumults gave rise than to the good effects they produced." Machiavelli faults the critics of Rome in particular for not considering that "in every republic there are two different *umori*"—collective temperaments, inclinations, attitudes—"that of the popolo and that of the grandi." Because he occasionally likens the state to the human body, the "humors" in this sentence might seem to refer to—and do remotely derive from—the ancient medical theory of the body's four humors (blood, phlegm, yellow bile, and black bile) whose interactions allegedly determine the prevalence of one of, or a balance among, the four personality types—respectively, sanguine, phlegmatic, choleric, and melancholic. But Machiavelli did not have a naturalistic concept of the state. For him, "humors" signify the sum of the dispositions, opinions, and behaviors of social groups. He uses the term where we might say "classes," a concept for which there

[9] See Gabriele Pedullà, "‹Concordia parvae res crescunt›? Breve storia di un ideale politico europeo," in Pedullà, *Machiavelli in tumulto. Conquista, cittadinanza e conflitto nei ‹Discorsi sopra la prima deca di Tito Livio›* (Rome: Bulzoni, 2011), pp. 11–80.

was as yet no specific term in Italian. The four humors have no relevance to what he writes at the end of chapter 2 concerning the three elements that constituted the "perfect republic" in Rome, and even this tripartite composition of the state now gives way to the binary popolo/grandi, or plebs/senate in the Roman context. Most of Machiavelli's critics would not have objected to the notion that every republic, indeed every state, has an elite class of grandi (nobles, ottimati) and a non-elite but politically active class, called the popolo in his Italy and the plebs in ancient Rome. But many could not understand or accept what follows in the same sentence, namely, that "all the laws enacted to the benefit of liberty emerge from the disunion" between the plebs and the senatorial nobility. He makes the remarkable and unexpected assertion that these conflicts, decried by so many as defects and weaknesses of the Roman polity, were, in his understanding, the incubators of liberty, law, and, over time, the military power that forged the empire. He notes that the tumults were not particularly violent or frequent—eight or ten decrees of exile, he says, and a handful of executions—in the "more than three centuries" (actually four) between the expulsion of the Tarquins and the agrarian reforms attempted by the Gracchi late in the second century BCE. Rome cannot rightly be considered a "disorderly [inordinata]" republic, he declares, in view of the many instances of virtú it produced, which were the fruit of good "educazione" (upbringing, acculturation), itself the result of good laws that resulted from those "tumulti" that many thoughtlessly condemn. Machiavelli insists that the "tumulti" produced not exiles or violence against the common good but "laws and ordini" that enhanced "public liberty [publica libertà]" (*DL* 1.4.2–7). "Publico" in Machiavelli often refers to the government or state, and "publica libertà" can be understood both as the liberty of the state and liberty protected by the state. He will soon tell us against whom this liberty needs to be protected.

Machiavelli acknowledges that some might say the tactics and methods employed in these "tumulti" were "illegal [straordinarii]" and "almost savage [efferati]"—the people and senate shouting against each other, chaotic running through the streets, shops closed, and the withdrawal of the plebs ("partirsi tutta la plebe") from the city. Such things are indeed frightening, he responds, but "every city must have ways for the popolo to express its ambition, especially those cities that want to avail themselves of the popolo in important matters." The "withdrawal of the entire plebs from Rome" refers to the secession of 494 BCE that resulted in the creation of the tribunes, and to this Machiavelli adds that, when the plebs sought the passage of a law, they either did some of the things already mentioned or refused to register for military service (literally, "to give their names"). This alludes to the most important of the ways Rome "availed itself of the popolo," namely in the armies, and explains the leverage the plebs enjoyed. Central to Machiavelli's view of the republic's liberty and expansive power was that its armies consisted mostly of its own plebeian citizens, a topic on which he will say more in later chapters. For the moment, he concludes chapter 4 with the observation that "the desires of free peoples are rarely harmful to liberty," because these desires "originate from being oppressed or from the fear of being oppressed" by the nobles. The Roman plebs' fear of oppression by the senatorial nobility was at the root of the tumults and the reason why they agitated for the institution of the tribunes. "And if the tumults brought about the creation of the tribunes," Machiavelli concludes this foundational chapter, "they are worthy of the highest praise, because, in addition to their part in popular governance, they were instituted for the guardianship [guardia] of Roman liberty" (*DL* 1.4.8–12). The assignment of the tribunes to this (still undefined) role again raises questions about their function. Were they representatives and protectors of plebeian interests, or mediators whose task was to resolve differences and limit violence between the plebs and the nobles, or defenders *supra partes* of the correct functioning of the state's institutions? Machiavelli may have viewed the tribunes in all three roles as circumstances warranted.

Having asserted that the tribunes served as "guardians of Roman liberty," in chapter 5 Machiavelli asks whether it is more secure to place the guardianship of liberty—in any state—in the hands of the popolo or in those of the grandi. From the question alone, before it is answered, it is clear that Machiavelli assumes the "guardianship of liberty" must belong to one of the two classes. And because he has already said that in Rome this guardianship was assigned to the tribunes of the plebs, it can safely be anticipated that his answer will be, in general, that it is more secure to assign this task to the plebs than to the nobles. Among the "most necessary" things the founders of republics have instituted is the guardianship of liberty, he begins, and the longevity of republics depends on how wisely they decide to whom it should be entrusted. Because in every republic there are "uomini grandi" and "popolari," he says some doubt has surrounded the question. Sparta and Venice assigned this responsibility to the nobles; ancient Rome "placed it in the hands of the plebs." Machiavelli acknowledges that there are valid arguments on both sides. If the issue is judged according to the outcome ("il fine loro"), namely, the long life of the Spartan and Venetian republics, we would choose the nobles. But if one assesses the question by examining what he calls the "ragioni"—the rationale or principles underlying the choice—one sees that the guiding principle of the Roman approach is that "one must entrust the guardianship of a thing to those who have the least desire to seize it [usurparla]"—to arrogate it to themselves. "And without doubt," he affirms, restating what he had written in *Prince* 9, "one sees in the nobles great desire to dominate" and in non-nobles "only the desire not to be dominated." Hence, non-noble citizens have a "greater desire to live free [vivere liberi], being less able than the nobles to hope to seize [usurpare] liberty for themselves. It is reasonable," therefore, that the "popolari," if they are "entrusted with guarding liberty, will have greater care of it and, not being able to seize it themselves, will not allow others to do so" (*DL* 1.5.2–8). The liberty whose protection is entrusted to the popolo is, of course, "publica libertà," the liberty enshrined in, and protected by, the republic's laws and ordini. The people need this liberty for protection against domination by the nobles, whereas the latter seek to seize it for themselves. Throughout the *Discourses* and in the *Florentine Histories* Machiavelli will explain at length how nobles tried, often successfully, to do this.

Assessing the rationale of those who prefer to entrust the guardianship of liberty to the "powerful [potenti]," Machiavelli says they allege two positive consequences: first, that it "satisfies the ambition of the nobles, who, having a greater role in the republic with this cudgel of power [bastone] in their hands, would have reason to be more content"; and, second, that it "removes from the agitated spirits of the plebs a kind of influence/power [autorità] that can cause endless conflicts and discord and is apt to bring the nobility to a degree of desperation that with time can have harmful consequences." Those who promote the Spartan/Venetian model, Machiavelli notes, adduce Rome itself as an example where, "because the tribunes of the plebs possessed this authority it was not enough for them to have one plebeian consul; they wanted both consuls" from the plebs, and afterwards all the other offices of government. "Even this was not enough for them, for, impelled by the same fury, they began in time to worship those men they thought could bludgeon the nobility, whence came the ascendancy of Marius and the ruin of Rome" in the civil wars. Still in chapter 5, but anticipating the more extended comparison of the Roman and Spartan/Venetian systems in his next chapter, Machiavelli hurriedly concludes that the choice between them depends on whether a republic wants to create a territorial empire. If it seeks empire, it should do everything as Rome did; if it is content to "maintain itself" without expansion, it should do as Venice and Sparta did (*DL* 1.5.9–14). In chapter 6, Machiavelli delves deeper into this distinction, explaining that Rome's imperial ambition required "employing the plebs in war" and "opening the way for foreigners" to become citizens, both of which "gave the plebs strength, greater numbers, and countless opportunities to cause disturbances [tumultuare]"—but also enabled the Romans to assemble immense armies and conquer vast territories. The Venetian way, by contrast, blocked the admission of foreigners to citizenship and did not allow the "popolani"—citizens denied access to the ruling class of the "gentili uomini"—to have any role in matters "in which they might acquire power [autorità]," thus depriving them of the strength and means to "cause disturbances" but also foreclosing the possibility of expansion. As we have seen, Machiavelli was aware that Venice had, in fact, created a maritime empire and later expanded its dominions on the Italian mainland in large part with mercenary armies—of which Machiavelli was severely critical because they proved incapable of defending these acquisitions—but also with "money and cunning [astuzia] (*DL* 1.6.7–11, 17–28).

Before leaving chapter 5, however, Machiavelli opens a critical new line of inquiry. The question of which class is best entrusted with the guardianship of liberty remains in doubt, he says, if one does not know "which class [umore] of men is more harmful [nocivo] in a republic, those who desire to preserve honor [l'onore] already acquired or those who wish to acquire what they do not have." Machiavelli then restates these two positions as "those who wish to acquire" and "those who fear losing what they have acquired" (*DL* 1.5.12–15). The preservation or acquisition of "onore" alludes to political power ("onori" in the plural often meant political offices), but the fear of losing what has been acquired hints at issues of wealth and economic power. Machiavelli will connect and highlight them at the end of the chapter. First, however, to shed light on which men are more "nocivi" in a republic, he turns to an episode in Livy (9.26) from the late fourth century BCE. In Machiavelli's summary, the plebeian Gaius Maenius (Machiavelli incorrectly calls him Marco Menennio) was appointed dictator (in effect, a special prosecutor) with Marcus Folius, Master of the Horse, as his deputy to investigate certain "conspiracies" against Rome in Capua. Machiavelli says the popolo (Livy says the senate) added to their mandate the investigation of electoral improprieties in Rome: "to find out who, through ambition and illegal means [per ambizione e modi straordinari], was scheming to reach the consulate and other political offices [onori]." Livy's characterization of these crimes no doubt caught Machiavelli's eye: the alleged perpetrators had "colluded and conspired to obtain high offices for themselves against the public welfare [or republic: adversus rem publicam]." As already noted, Machiavelli refers in *Discourses* 1.18.11 to the Roman laws against electoral bribery and corruption—called "de ambitu," literally "going around," to solicit support for election through bribery—as laws on "ambizione." In Machiavelli's account, the nobles, fearing that the dictator's wide-ranging prosecutorial powers would take aim at their entire class, planted rumors that not they but the non-nobles (Livy calls them "new men") were the ones who sought to obtain offices "per ambizione" and with "modi straordinari." Indeed, they accused the dictator himself of these illegalities. So grievous was the accusation against him that he resigned his position and submitted himself to the judgment of the people (of the consuls, according to Livy). He was acquitted and fully vindicated. Because nobles and non-nobles had accused each other of excessive ambition and illegal electoral practices, Machiavelli says "it was much debated [si disputò assai] who is more ambitious, he who wants to preserve [what he has] or he who wants to acquire [what he does not possess]." There is no such "debate" in Livy, but Machiavelli wants to address the question. Although he believes that either of these desires can be the "cause of very great disturbances [tumulti grandissimi], nonetheless, most often they are caused by those who possess [da chi possiede], because the fear of losing [what they have] generates in them the same desires that exist in those who want to acquire." Those "who possess" are the nobles, and the fear of losing what they have makes them want to acquire more, "because men do not think they possess securely if they do not acquire still more than they have." The wealthy, in short, are not content to preserve or maintain what they have; the fear of losing what they possess intensifies their avarice. This, in turn, negatively affects those who have less, because "the dishonorable and ambitious behavior [scorretti e ambiziosi portamenti]" of those who possess much "arouses the desire to possess in the breasts of those who do not possess, either to avenge themselves by despoiling [the wealthy of their possessions] or to gain access for themselves to those riches [ricchezze] and offices [onori] they see being badly used by [the nobles]" (*DL* 1.5.15–20). Riches and honors are now linked, resulting in a more conflictual view of relations between the classes than what until now has been presented.

Machiavelli then offers another—and critically consequential—reason for why "those who possess" more often cause "tumulti" and are more "nocivi" in a republic: "possessing much, they can with greater power and force overthrow governments [possedendo molto, possono con maggiore potenza e maggiore moto fare alterazione]" (*DL* 1.5.19). "Alterazione" means revolution; "fare alterazione" is to overthrow or undermine governments, not merely cause disturbances or troubles or bring about change. Machiavelli here claims that the wealth of nobles and grandi allows them to build forms of private power that can subvert law and enervate constituted authority and institutions. It is their ability to weaken the state (or government) itself that Machiavelli offers as the explanation of why the grandi are the more dangerous of the classes and, therefore, why the non-elite classes must be the guardians of liberty. Machiavelli's contention is, in essence, that the popolo, lacking the wealth that sustains private power, must rely on the state and its laws, magistracies, and courts for protection against the determination of the grandi/nobles to dominate the people and debilitate law and institutions. The grandi, by contrast, with their "maggiore potenza," made possible by great wealth, do not need the state—or, at most, need it for the more limited purposes of securing their privileges and safeguarding their wealth. The threat they pose to the state lies in the "modi privati" and "modi straordinari" that they wield in violation of legal, or constitutional, procedures and constraints. Machiavelli's focus on the greater wealth, and hence power, of the grandi magnifies his initial emphasis on their desire to dominate the people and accumulate wealth, and it leads him to focus on the instruments, means, and resources with which nobles pursued these ambitions. The difference between the classes becomes less a question of greater or lesser desire to dominate or acquire and more a function of their divergent views on government and law. Thus, the question of which class can better "guard liberty"—when liberty is understood as "public liberty," hence a free, functioning constitutional order—answers itself: wealthy nobles, far from guarding the liberty of the state, aim to supplant or even destroy it.

Among the reasons Machiavelli offers at the end of chapter 6 for why the "tribunician authority" was necessary for the guardianship of liberty in Rome is the great benefit of the tribunes' "power of accusation" (*DL* 1.6.38). Chapter 7 opens by declaring that "No more useful and necessary authority can be given in a city to those entrusted with the guardianship of liberty than that of being able to bring charges [accusare] before the popolo or some magistracy or council against citizens who sin in any way against free government [lo stato libero]." What Machiavelli calls "accusations [accuse]" are, in modern terms, indictments by a magistracy, which he sharply distinguishes from unofficial accusations—which are, at worst, mendacious slander—for which there is no possibility of adjudication or defense. Legal indictments prevent, or at least discourage, unofficial accusations by requiring accusers to bring their charges before a constituted magistracy that has the authority to decide if the charges are true or false. The "very useful" effects of this ordine are, first, that fear of being indicted will deter citizens from engaging in actions against the "stato"—"sinning against free government"—knowing they will be swiftly punished; and, second, it provides a way of venting the "omori"—here meaning antagonisms or animosities—that arise against this or that citizen. The importance of legal mechanisms for adjudicating accusations is that in their absence—if they cannot be resolved "ordinariamente," according to the ordini—unregulated accusations find resolution in "modi straordinari," in extralegal, hence private, channels, "which cause a republic to go completely to ruin." Nothing, he asserts, contributes more to a republic's stability than to "organize [ordinare]" it so that the antagonisms that agitate it have a way of being resolved that is "ordinata dalle leggi"—established by the laws. To illustrate the utility of formal indictments, Machiavelli recounts from Livy (2.34–5) the story of the patrician Coriolanus, from just after the first secession of the plebs and the creation of the tribunes, when Rome's nobles were angry because they believed the office of the tribunes gave the plebs too much power. An "enemy of the popular party," Machiavelli calls him (Livy says particularly of the "tribunician power"), Coriolanus advised that it was time to "punish the plebs and deprive it of the authority/power [autorità] it had taken to the detriment of the nobility." Rome was suffering from a shortage of foodstuffs, and Coriolanus planned to starve the plebs into surrendering their newly won political authority by withholding grain from the people. When the people got wind of Coriolanus' scheme, "they became so angry they would have killed him in a riot [tumultuariamente morto] as he left the senate, if the tribunes"—the very magistracy he sought to destroy—"had not summoned him to appear and defend himself" (*DL* 1.7.2–7). Machiavelli omits the rest of Livy's account—Coriolanus' refusal to appear, his sentence of exile, and his collaboration with Rome's enemies in war—but the importance of the episode for Machiavelli is that the tribunes, a state magistracy, intervened to prevent mob justice and entrust Coriolanus' fate to a trial.

The story of Coriolanus elicits a theoretical commentary—one of the most revealing passages of the *Discourses*—about ordini and the danger of private actions that subvert them. Machiavelli begins by reiterating the either/or of ordini and their absence: when these "modi ordinari" (legal procedures) do not exist, recourse is had to "straordinari"—here a noun meaning illegal actions—which, "without doubt, produce much worse consequences." Machiavelli does not claim that perfect justice always prevails in cases adjudicated within the ordini. But if, he says, a citizen is punished "ordinariamente," even if wrongly convicted, little or no "disordine" results for the republic, "because the conviction [esecuzione] occurs without private forces [forze private] and without foreign forces [forze forestieri], which are what destroy the vivere libero" of republics. Punishment via "modi ordinari" occurs instead with "forze e ordini publici," which have "specific limits and constraints [termini loro particulari]," namely, rules and procedures defined by law. The crucial contrast here is "private" vs. "public" (and we shall see in a moment why Machiavelli adds "foreign" to "private"). "Disordine"—the negation and violation of the ordini—occurs when punishments or acts of retaliation, whether just or unjust, are inflicted by private initiative, influence, or coercion. Machiavelli does not associate "disordine" with unjust convictions arrived at "ordinariamente." When punishment is dispensed "ordinariamente," it is done with public authority and does not exceed the constraints of legal procedures "in ways that ruin a republic." Private accusations and private punishments undermine the ordini and destroy the republic; legal indictments adjudicated according to the ordini and the laws protect the republic.

Returning to the episode of Coriolanus, Machiavelli asks the reader to "consider how much harm would have come to the Roman republic if he had been killed *tumultuariamente*"—by the enraged people in a riot without legal procedures. This would have been "a punishment inflicted by private citizens against private citizens [offesa de' privati a' privati]." In rapid succession, Machiavelli outlines the steps by which "straordinari" actions damage and ultimately ruin a republic. Injury ("offesa") by "privati" against "privati" generates fear ("paura"); fear searches for protection ("difesa"); for such protection, people seek "partigiani" (supporters, allies); from "partigiani" come factions ("parti"); and from factions results the destruction of cities. In the case of Coriolanus, Machiavelli concludes, those (the tribunes) who had the legal authority ("autorità") to handle the matter did so, and all the evils that could have resulted "if it had been managed with private power [autorità privata]" were avoided (*DL* 1.7.8–11). Machiavelli uses "autorità" here in two different senses (as reflected in the translations): "autorità" as influence, power, or prestige unconnected to any legal right, hence the ability to punish others with private power or wealth; and "autorità" as the legal right and responsibility to enforce laws and decree punishments, as in the case of Coriolanus and the tribunes. The danger of private power supplanting public ordini is the conceptual heart of chapter 7, and it pervades much of the rest of the *Discourses*, book 1 of the *Art of War*, and the *Florentine Histories*.

To illustrate just how dangerous such private power could be, Machiavelli cites two violent episodes from Florence's recent history: the murder in 1498 of Francesco Valori, the political leader of the Savonarolan party; and the expulsion of Piero Soderini and the dismantling of the republic of the Great Council by

Florentine ottimati aided by the Spanish army sent by Pope Julius to restore the Medici to power in 1512. Although Machiavelli does not name the Medici in connection with either event, they are central to both. The episode involving Valori (discussed in Chapter 4 in the context of Savonarola's failure to uphold the right of appeal) serves as a negative twin to the story of Coriolanus.[10] A prominent Medicean before 1494, Valori was among the ottimati who led the revolt that expelled Piero de' Medici and his brothers from the city. As Savonarola's influence grew and helped shape both the new republican constitution of the Great Council and the mix of religion and politics that dominated the three and a half years of his ascendancy, Florence's elite families divided into factions for and against him. Valori emerged as a partisan in the Savonarolan camp, and, with his election as standard-bearer of justice for January–February 1497, became the friar's chief political ally in the councils of government. In April of that year, the exiled Piero de' Medici arrived with a contingent of soldiers at the city gates and attempted, unsuccessfully, to overthrow the republic and return by force of arms. Soon thereafter, revelations of a conspiracy within the city in support of Piero led to the arrest of several prominent citizens. A hastily convened ad hoc advisory council declared them guilty and sentenced them to death. When they sought to appeal their sentence to the Great Council, as they had the right to do according to the law promoted by Savonarola himself for the protection of supporters of the defunct Medici regime, a bitter controversy erupted. Although the Signoria favored (by a narrow margin) allowing the appeal, a majority in the ad hoc council feared that a successful appeal and acquittal would cause a popular uprising. Valori took the lead in arguing against the appeal (despite his alliance with Savonarola) and made an impassioned and threatening speech that caused the Signoria to reverse its earlier decision and disallow the appeal. The five conspirators, all friends of the Medici, were executed that very evening. Piero Parenti says Valori was now Florence's most powerful citizen—although he was no longer in office—and "the city was governed according to his bidding." Nonetheless, Parenti adds, Valori faced the "hatred" of the families of the executed conspirators.[11] Less than a year later, in April 1498, as Savonarola's prestige in the city waned and his enemies subjected him to accusations and ultimately to torture and execution, Valori too became a target of the anti-Savonarolans. On Palm Sunday 1498 a mob attacked the Dominican church of San Marco where Savonarola and his associates lived. Failing to find Valori there, they went to his home, sacked and burned it, and murdered him and his wife (an unusual occurrence that reveals the depth of their hatred, as wives were not usually harmed in episodes of political violence).

[10] The following background is gleaned from the chronicle of Piero Parenti and from Alison Brown, *Piero di Lorenzo de' Medici*, pp. 243–70. Many other sources, primary and secondary, analyze the episode.

[11] Parenti, *Storia fiorentina*, ed. Matucci, vol. 2, pp. 119–26.

One of the attackers spit on Francesco's corpse, saying "Valori, you will no longer govern us."[12]

For Machiavelli and his contemporaries, these events were seared into memory (in more vivid and bloody detail than this brief summary allows), and his comments on Francesco Valori in *Discourses* 1.7 cannot be fully understood without an awareness of the impact of those events. "We have seen in our own times what havoc [novità] was inflicted on the republic of Florence when the multitude was unable to vent its animus legally [ordinariamente] against one of its citizens." Valori, Machiavelli says, was "thought by many to be ambitious and a man who aimed, with his boldness [audacia] and arrogance [animosità], to rise above the *vivere civile*," by ignoring the laws and civic norms. Machiavelli himself may or may not have shared this opinion of Valori.[13] Here he attributes it to Valori's enemies, who, however, lacked legal avenues for accusing him, even as he appeared (at least to them) to operate outside the bounds of the *vivere civile* and the ordini, causing them to believe he sought tyrannical power. The lack of constitutionally established procedures for indicting him and adjudicating guilt or innocence meant that Valori's opponents could punish him only by extra-legal means of their own and that, likewise, his only defense against them was his faction, the quintessential form of private power. "Because in the republic there was no way to stop him except with a faction [setta] opposed to his own, it happened that, since his only fear was of extralegal measures [modi straordinari], he began gathering supporters who would defend him." Machiavelli alludes to Valori's murder without directly mentioning it, saying that those who opposed him, "having no legal way [via ordinaria] to subdue him," had recourse to "illegal ways [vie straordinarie] even to the point of violence [in tanto che si venne alle armi]." The lesson he draws is this: "if it had been possible to oppose him through legal means [per l'ordinario], extinguishing his power [autorità] would have hurt him alone. But because it had to be done through illegal means [per lo straordinario], the result was that it harmed not only him but many other distinguished citizens" in his faction and among the Savonarolans (*DL* 1.7.12–13). The lack of established ordini for handling accusations and resolving grievances caused political retribution to erupt through factions, destroying the lives and reputations of many others in addition to the one suspected of harboring tyrannical ambitions.

Machiavelli's second example in chapter 7 is the expulsion of Piero Soderini in 1512 by his ottimati enemies and the Spanish army they invited to threaten the city and apply the needed pressure. Again, no contemporary reader needed reminding that Soderini, since 1502 the lifetime standard-bearer of justice of the

[12] Parenti, *Storia fiorentina*, ed. Matucci, vol. 2, p. 165.

[13] Mark Jurdjevic analyzes the differences between this assessment of Valori and the laudatory portrait in Machiavelli's *Nature di uomini fiorentini* (in *OS* vol. 1, p. 76); see his *Guardians of Republicanism: The Valori Family in the Florentine Renaissance* (Oxford: Oxford University Press, 2008), pp. 63–95.

republic of the Great Council, had defended the popular republic against members of his own elite class who wanted an oligarchic government more friendly to their interests. Soderini had also held firm to the French alliance that was the cornerstone of the republic's foreign policy and enforced (albeit less successfully as time went on) the law prohibiting Florentines from having contact with the exiled Medici. Against the wishes of many ottimati, he allowed Machiavelli to organize and recruit the militia from the surrounding subject territories. Soderini's removal from office led quickly to the return of the Medici, the dissolution of the Great Council, and Machiavelli's dismissal from his posts. Machiavelli's long association with Piero Soderini and his brother, Cardinal Francesco, was probably the chief reason why suspicion fell on him in early 1513, resulting in his arrest and torture, and why the Medici refused to have anything to do with him for many years. What, with considerable and understandable understatement, he calls the "event [accidente]" concerning Piero Soderini in 1512 was the traumatic turning point of both his life and that of the Florentine republic. Machiavelli's summary of the "event" is vague and veiled. He does not name the ottimati who brought Soderini down, among other reasons because of the prominent role in the "mutatione" of both Paolo Vettori, Francesco's brother, and Giovanni Rucellai, son of Soderini's arch-nemesis Bernardo Rucellai and Nannina de' Medici, the elder Lorenzo's daughter and Pope Leo's sister. Machiavelli's *Discourses* took shape some years later in discussions held in the gardens of the Rucellai family hosted by Cosimo Rucellai, Giovanni's nephew and Bernardo's grandson. Machiavelli's friendship with Cosimo (the *Discourses* are in fact dedicated to him and Zanobi Buondelmonti) would have made it awkward to highlight the critical role Cosimo's uncle played in bringing down Soderini and the popular republic and reinstating the Medici.

Machiavelli contends that the expulsion of Piero Soderini occurred "because in the republic there was no procedure for indictments [accuse] against the ambition of powerful citizens." Anticipating the potential objection that the Otto di guardia (a police magistracy whose jurisdiction had expanded until it became, under the Medici, the chief criminal court) provided such a procedure, he says that "accusing a powerful citizen before eight judges is not sufficient in a republic," because "the few always act in the manner of the few," and consequently "many judges are needed." The underlying assumption here is that the powerful can easily influence a small number of judges, who will rarely convict a powerful citizen. In the case of Soderini, says Machiavelli, "if the proper procedures had existed" and "if his conduct in office had been blameworthy [vivendo lui male]," his opponents "would have indicted him and in this way vented their anger without bringing in the Spanish army." "If," on the other hand, "he was blameless, they would not have dared to initiate an action against him for fear of being accused themselves" if their accusations proved baseless. In other words, for a court to adjudicate an indictment and punish the accused, it must be presented with reliable evidence, the absence of which could entail an indictment against the accuser for calumny. Either way, the aspersions against Soderini, which caused so much controversy and strife, would have disappeared. Formal indictments requiring accusers to provide corroborating evidence or face charges for slander themselves would, Machiavelli contends, obviate the need for "private or foreign forces" in resolving accusations. The absence of a system of public indictments opens the way for recourse to either or both of these, and Machiavelli's inclusion of "foreign forces" pointedly alleges that the ottimati, lacking legal procedures for accusing and removing Soderini, resorted to bringing into Tuscany the Spanish army that sacked Prato, killing thousands, and terrorized Florence. "Whenever foreign forces are called by one faction [parte] of men in a city, one can assume that this results from its defective ordini and from the absence of a procedure [ordine] for venting their malicious antagonisms without illegal methods [modi straordinari]." This can be done, Machiavelli reiterates, "by arranging for indictments [to be litigated] before a large number of judges" (*DL* 1.7.14–17). How a republic handles—or fails to handle—partisan vilification determines how much power private factions will have and the degree to which they might rely on foreign intervention to defeat their enemies.

Machiavelli pursues the same issue in chapter 8 from the perspective of the "pernicious" effects of slanders, calumnies, and defamatory accusations—malicious rumors, in effect—unchecked by formal indictment and adjudication. Here he makes the difference explicit: "Calumnies have no need of witnesses or other evidence to confirm them, so that anyone can be slandered by anyone. But not everyone can be accused [legally indicted], because [legal] accusations require truthful confirmation [riscontri veri] and specific details that demonstrate the truth of the accusation." Lawful charges are brought "before magistrates, popular assemblies, or government councils; slanders are bandied about in city squares and public arcades [logge]." Calumnies are more common in cities that are "meno ordinate" (lacking the ordini needed for indictments). The "ordinatore" of a republic must therefore make it possible to indict any citizen "without fear or hesitation." Slanderers must be severely punished, especially when institutional avenues are available for the adjudication of accusations against those they defame in the "logge." "Where this matter is not properly organized [bene ordinata], serious illegalities [disordini grandi] will ensue, because slanders anger citizens but do not punish them, and those angered seek revenge, hating rather than fearing the things said against them" (*DL* 1.8.8–13). Slanders, in short, engender division and conflict.

Machiavelli again illustrates the difference between lawful indictments and unlawful accusations with examples from Roman and Florentine history. Whereas "in Rome this matter was *bene ordinata*, it has always been *male ordinata* in our city of Florence," where this "*disordine* has done great damage" (*DL* 1.8.14–15). His Roman example (which opens the chapter) is the episode, drawn from Livy

(6.14–20), of Manlius Capitolinus' attempt to win a following among the plebs by "sowing various malicious rumors [oppinioni sinistre]." Manlius alleged that "private citizens" had usurped public funds, which, "if recovered, could be converted to public benefit [publica utilità], either by lowering the taxes of the plebs or relieving their private debts." The accusations excited the plebs, who held meetings and initiated disturbances. The senate, disliking what they saw as Manlius' dangerous manipulation of the plebs, appointed a dictator to adjudicate the case and restrain Manlius' vehemence. The dictator and Manlius appeared together "in publico"—possibly indicating a large public gathering (Livy says they met in the Comitium) or an arraignment in court (he also says Manlius came to "the tribunal")—the former surrounded by many nobles and Manlius by his plebeian supporters. Asserting that the senate was as eager as the plebs to know the truth, the dictator asked Manlius to name the "privati cittadini" he believed were concealing the "treasure." Manlius offered no specifics, saying it was unnecessary to tell the senators what they all knew. Because he was unable, or unwilling, to name names (and, presumably, provide evidence) the dictator found him guilty of slander (*calumnia* was a crime in Rome) and jailed him. The episode reveals, Machiavelli comments, how "detestable" calumnies are: no remedy ("ordine") should be spared to eliminate them, and there is not a better way than increasing the possibilities for public indictments (*DL* 1.8.2–9). Machiavelli curiously omits Livy's conclusion of the story: Manlius was released and continued his rabble-rousing and accusations. The senators decided that only violence could stop his threats, but the tribunes intervened and indicted him. His still undiminished favor among the people required the convocation of the "concilium populi," which, however, declared him guilty and sentenced him to death. Indictment by the tribunes and conviction by the people's assembly saved Rome from open warfare between the senate and the plebs.

In Florence, by contrast, Machiavelli says, still in chapter 8, slander and calumny were pervasive and had destructive consequences: "Anyone who reads the histories of this city can see that many calumnies targeted citizens involved in its important affairs," especially accusations of peculation and corruption. The absence in Florence of legal procedures to adjudicate such charges gave rise to "hatred, which led to conflict [divisione], from conflict came factions [sette], and from factions ruin. If there had been an institutional procedure [ordine] for indicting citizens and punishing calumniators, the endless conflicts [scandoli] would not have occurred" (*DL* 1.8.16–19), because, whether citizens were convicted or acquitted, they would not have been able to harm the city and many fewer would have been indicted than had been slandered in the absence of a legal procedure. Machiavelli adds another and particularly injurious effect of unchecked calumny. "These calumnies have been among the things some citizens have used to achieve "grandezza"—political power—and they are "especially useful when aimed at powerful citizens who oppose their ambition." The conflict envisaged here is between a citizen who strives for "grandezza" by slandering other "potenti" citizens who try to stop him. "Taking the side of the people," the one seeking "grandezza" gains their support by persuading them of the slanders he directs against his rivals.

Machiavelli then turns to a Florentine example, from the early fifteenth century, in which ambitious citizens used slander to weaken political opponents. His barebones summary of the episode here in the *Discourses* (he will give a much more detailed account in the fourth book of the *Florentine Histories*) states that, when Florence went to war against neighboring Lucca (in 1430), Giovanni Guicciardini (brother of Francesco Guicciardini's great-grandfather) was appointed civilian commissioner to direct military operations. Because of "either his poor conduct of the war or ill fortune," Giovanni failed to capture Lucca. Some accused him of taking a bribe from the Lucchesi, a slander, Machiavelli says, "promoted by his enemies that reduced him to complete desperation." He wanted to entrust his defense to the capitano del popolo (one of the commune's judicial officials) but "was never able to vindicate himself because there were no *modi*"—no institutions—"in the republic through which he could do so." As a result, bitter controversies erupted between Giovanni's "friends," who "were the majority of the powerful citizens [uomini grandi]"—leading members of the elite families—"and those who sought a political coup [fare novità] in Florence," i.e. to overthrow and replace the ruling group. The disputes sparked by the slandering of Giovanni Guicciardini grew to such proportions, writes Machiavelli, that it caused the "ruin of that republic." Machiavelli stops there and concludes the chapter by commenting that Manlius Capitolinus was a calumniator, not a (legal) accuser, and that the Romans knew how "calumniators had to be punished." What he omits to say here is that Giovanni Guicciardini's slanderers were the Medici. It was the Medici party, led by Cosimo, that wanted to "fare novità." Their challenge to the ruling group led to Cosimo's rise to power and the exile of the opposition leaders, initiating sixty years of Medici domination and causing, Machiavelli contends, "the ruin of the republic" (*DL* 1.8.20–9). The unverified accusation against Giovanni Guicciardini expands the seemingly narrow issue of how republics should deal with slanders—and why formal indictments are needed to curb them—into the larger problem of how ambitious citizens take advantage of the absence of legal procedures for handling calumnies to gain power through fear and factions. Did Machiavelli intend an analogy between this episode in the conflicts that brought the Medici to power in the fifteenth century and the slanders hurled at Piero Soderini by pro-Medici ottimati who returned the family to power almost a century later? Was he implying that the campaign of calumny against Soderini followed the same playbook that had raised the Medici to power in the 1430s? If so, he may have intended the story of Giovanni Guicciardini to serve as a warning to the ottimati of his own time—and to Francesco Guicciardini in particular—that they could find themselves victims of a tyranny they helped to create.

"MEN OF AMBITIOUS AND RESTLESS SPIRIT"

In chapter 55 of book 1 of the *Discourses* Machiavelli constructs a general theory of the role of the elite and noble classes in Italian history, integrating his perception of the aims and methods they employed to protect their power with an assessment of the effects of these methods on both the equality he considers the prerequisite of republican liberty and the process of its corruption. Praising the abundance of goodness ("bontà") and religious devotion of the Roman plebs, Machiavelli declares: "In truth, where this goodness is lacking, one cannot hope for anything good," as is the case in countries that have become "corrupt, as Italy is, above all others," but to some degree also France and Spain as well. If one does not see as many "disordini" in these countries as occur daily in Italy, this is because "they have kings who keep them united, with not only their virtú but also the ordini of those kingdoms, which are not yet broken [guasti]." The one area of Europe in which "goodness" and "religion" are still strong is "la Magna"—Germany—where "many republics live free and observe their laws [so strictly] that no one, neither internally nor from without, dares to subjugate them" (*DL* 1.55.6–9). The small German republics Machiavelli has in mind here include the Swiss cities whose military prowess had stirred his admiration and his anxiety, both evident in the 1513 correspondence with Francesco Vettori.[14] As evidence of their exceptional respect for the laws, Machiavelli notes that, when their magistrates impose a 1 or 2 percent levy on each citizen's taxable wealth, they leave it to the citizens themselves to follow their "conscience" in deciding how much to pay. He claims that these free, law-abiding cities maintain their uncorrupted "goodness"—"so rare that it remains in this one country alone"—in two ways. One is that they rigorously restrict contacts, commerce, trade, and all social relations with their less virtuous neighbors, protecting themselves from the customs of France, Spain, and Italy, "which together account for the corruption of the world." The second way in which "they have preserved an uncorrupted republican life [vivere politico]" is by not "permitting any of their citizens to be, or to live in the manner of, a *gentiluomo*; on the contrary, they maintain among themselves *una pari equalità* [a uniform equality]." They are, moreover, "very hostile to the signori and *gentiluomini* in that country, and if any of them happen to fall into their hands they kill them as instigators of corruption and the cause of all conflict" (*DL* 1.55.10–17).

Aware that the term "gentiluomini" might be unfamiliar to many of his readers (it was used, with a different meaning, in Venice, but not in Florence), Machiavelli explains that "gentiluomini" are those who live "opulently [abbondantemente]" from the income of landed possessions, but are uninvolved in direct cultivation of

[14] See my *Between Friends*, pp. 136–75.

the land or any other activity necessary for one's livelihood; hence they are "oziosi [at leisure]." As the repudiation of such persons by the virtuous Swiss cities already presages, these "gentiluomini" are "pernicious in every republic and every country." (That they are dangerous *in*—not only to—republics suggests that they exist in some republics.) Machiavelli then defines a second group even more dangerous to republics. "More pernicious still are those who, in addition to the aforementioned sources of wealth [fortune], rule over walled towns and have subjects who obey them [comandano a castella, e hanno sudditi che ubbidiscono a loro]" (*DL* 1.55.18–19). "Castella" are fortified towns (not castles) whose inhabitants are under the jurisdiction of—and in this sense "obey"—these "more pernicious" lords. Machiavelli will later call them "signori di castella," sometimes leaving ambiguous whether they are a species of, or distinct from, the leisurely "gentiluomini." He considers them "more pernicious" because they exercise private, yet territorial, power that weakens principalities and republics alike.

"Gentiluomini" and "signori di castella" are, for Machiavelli, crucial to understanding Italy's political geography. Four regions of Italy, he says, are "full of these two kinds of men": the kingdom of Naples; the "terra di Roma" (approximately the old Patrimony of Saint Peter and modern Lazio); the Romagna; and Lombardy (which, as noted, was then the entire area north of the Po). Their dominant presence in these regions has prevented the formation of republics: "no republic or *vivere politico* [constitutional government] has ever emerged" in these areas "because these kinds of men are completely hostile to any *civilità*." "Vivere politico" and "civilità," the first echoing the Aristotelian language of politics, the second from Roman political discourse, both denote independent communities characterized by observance of laws and governance by the citizens themselves. We may think of "civilità" as the cluster of cultural traditions, behaviors, and institutions that make a "vivere politico" possible. Machiavelli uses these terms, and also "vivere libero," more or less interchangeably, and in the sentence just quoted both are functionally synonymous with "republica." In regions dominated by "gentiluomini" and "signori di castella," "introducing a republic would not be possible." The only kind of state feasible in such areas is a "regno"—a monarchy. And "the reason," Machiavelli explains, is that "where the matter [materia, here meaning society, the people] is so corrupt that laws are not sufficient to halt the corruption, it is necessary to institute, together with the laws, a greater force, namely, a monarchical hand [una mano regia] which, with absolute and exceptional power, can restrain the extreme ambition and corruption of the powerful" (*DL* 1.55.20–3). "Corruption" is the condition in which laws and ordini are undermined, disregarded, or non-existent, and here Machiavelli directly links it to the "ambition of the powerful." Entities dominated by the two kinds of nobles are "corrupt" in this very specific sense. In such circumstances weakened laws cannot remedy their own ineffectualness, and the only solution is an absolute monarch who has the brute force to control the nobles. Machiavelli puts it even more starkly when he asserts, a paragraph later, that "anyone who wants to institute a republic where there are many gentiluomini cannot do so unless he first neutralizes [spegne] all of them" (*DL* 1.55.27).

The converse of the incompatibility of republics and powerful landed nobilities lies in the "example of Tuscany," where, Machiavelli says, three republics, Florence, Siena, and Lucca, have long existed. Tuscany's other cities, he admits, are no longer free but have reacted to their subjugation (to Florence) in ways that reveal a desire to regain their liberty. The survival of republics and the yearning for republican liberty by formerly free republics in Tuscany are owing to the fact that "in that region there are no signori di castella and no, or very few, gentiluomini." In the *Florentine Histories* (2.32.19–20) Machiavelli observes that, after the failure in 1340 of an armed uprising by the magnate Bardi and Frescobaldi families, who were allowed to "return unimpeded to their castella" in the countryside, Florence's government passed a law prohibiting any citizen from "possessing castella within twenty miles of the city." This, presumably, is the basis of his assertion that there were no longer any signori di castella in Tuscany. On the contrary, "there is so much equality that a wise man with knowledge of ancient republics [antiche civiltà] could easily introduce a *vivere civile*" (*DL* 1.55.24–5). This is a provocative and perplexing statement. If three major cities in Tuscany were still republics, and if republican spirit and institutions survived in former republics now subject to Florence, why would it be necessary to introduce a *vivere civile*? Machiavelli might be implying that even Florence, Siena, and Lucca were republics in name only because they were controlled by powerful families or strongmen. He may be hinting that Florence under the Medici and Siena under the Petrucci lacked the attributes of true republics and, being closer to principates ruled by a single family, were as much in need of a restoration of a true *vivere civile* as were Pisa, Arezzo, and other cities in Tuscany under Florentine rule. Or is Machiavelli intimating that the spirit of "equality," which he says still survives throughout the region, would allow a "wise man with knowledge of ancient republics" to introduce a *vivere civile* throughout the whole of Tuscany? Did he entertain the possibility—or at least the desirability—of forging a unitary state in Tuscany, or in the territories under Florentine rule? Such a state would have eliminated the unequal relationship between the dominant city and the so-called subject cities and instituted legal equality and citizenship throughout the territories—as the Romans did on a much grander scale. Intriguing as this possibility is, it remains speculative.[15]

After the digression on Tuscany's republics, Machiavelli returns, still in *Discourses* 1.55, to the incompatibility of republics and gentiluomini, turning the issue around and asking if and how it would be possible to establish a "regno" or a "principato" where great "equalità" exists. Equality, for Machiavelli, means a

[15] Alissa M. Ardito explores this possibility in *Machiavelli and the Modern State:* The Prince, *the* Discourses on Livy, *and the Extended Territorial Republic* (Cambridge: Cambridge University Press, 2015).

uniformly applied legal system for the entire population: equality under the law, with all citizens subject to the same laws in the same measure. Equality excludes the private jurisdictions exercised by "signori di castella," by persons claiming to be subject to other legal regimes, or by powerful individuals asserting de facto privilege, or private law. This equality is not economic (although economic factors, as we shall see, do figure significantly where legal inequality prevails). Machiavelli hypothesizes that "one who wishes to create a "regno" or a "principato" where there is great equality will never be able to do it unless he draws out [trae] from that equality many men of ambitious and restless spirit [d'animo ambizioso e inquieto] and makes them gentiluomini in fact, not just in name, by granting them castella and lands and giving them gifts of wealth and subjects." It would be necessary, in short, to destroy equality by creating ex novo a class of gentiluomini. But only a powerful monarch ruling over vast territories could create nobles and endow them with lands and subjects and jurisdiction over the same. Machiavelli sees this hypothetical monarchical overlord and the nobles he creates as mutually supportive. "Placed in their midst," surrounded by his newly fashioned signori di castella, he "preserves his power, as they in turn secure their ambition through him." Everyone else, in this scenario, will be "compelled to endure the yoke that only coercion [forza], and nothing else, can make them endure." Landed nobility and monarchy are, in short, natural allies, each supporting and depending on the other, while the rest of the population is forced to submit. This scenario alludes, obviously if obliquely, to the controversial question in the years in which Machiavelli was writing the *Discourses*, namely, whether the Medici would (or should even try to) transform the republic into a principate. Although he does not address it directly, he underscores its enormous difficulty. "Creating a republic in a country suited to be a *regno* and creating a *regno* in a country suited to be a republic" are both undertakings for men of rare "intellect [cervello] and power [autorità]. Many have wanted to do it, but few have known how to accomplish it" (*DL* 1.55.27–9). At the end of the chapter he counsels against such wrenching mutations and advises that "one who wishes to create a republic should do so where there is great equality, and, conversely, one who wishes to establish a principate should do so where there is great inequality. Otherwise the result will be distorted [sanza proporzione] and of short life" (*DL* 1.55.35). But the question of transforming Florence into a principate was very much in the air after 1512 until it was accomplished two decades later, after the destruction of the last republic, by Emperor Charles V, Pope Clement VII (Giulio de' Medici), and their ottimati allies. When Machiavelli writes that to create a principate where there is great equality would require "drawing out from that equality many men of ambitious and restless spirit" and turning them into "gentiluomini in fact, not just in name," who else, in a presumptive Florentine scenario, can these "ambitious and restless" men be if not the ottimati, many of whom schemed to restore the Medici to power in 1512?

Machiavelli reiterates the fundamental conclusion of chapter 55—that the private jurisdictions, prerogatives, and privileges of signori di castella and gentiluomini are antithetical to republics, which must be built on the equality of citizens in law—in the *Discursus florentinarum rerum*, written between late 1520 and early 1521. The *Discursus* was his contribution to the discussions solicited by Cardinal Giulio de' Medici (Leo's cousin) concerning Florence's constitutional future. Addressing Leo and Giulio, Machiavelli seeks to persuade them, with the same arguments elaborated in *Discourses* 1.55, that only a republic is suitable for Florence: "Your Holiness should understand that, in all cities where there is great equality among citizens, one cannot create a principate except with the greatest difficulty. And in those cities where there is great inequality among citizens one cannot create a republic except with the greatest difficulty." He cites Milan as an example of the latter case. "To seek to create a republic in Milan, where there is great inequality among citizens, it would be necessary to eliminate its entire nobility and bring the nobles to equality with the other [citizens]." The reason, he adds, why it would be necessary to deprive the nobility of its separate legal status is that among themselves they are so "estraordinarii" that "the laws are not sufficient to restrain them; it requires a strong voice [una voce viva] and a monarchical power [una potestà regia] to subdue them." As "estraordinarii" suggests, Machiavelli's point is that Milan's nobles so completely flout the ordini—the institutions and norms of a *vivere civile*, above all equality—that laws are powerless to restrain them. Only a "potestà regia," implicitly above the laws, can control the private power of nobles. (This "potestà regia" may be, for Machiavelli, similar to that of the Roman dictator, whose temporary authority to suppress anyone attempting to gain influence "through private means" he refers to in *Discourses* 3.28.14 as "il braccio regio.") Turning to the Florentine converse of the Milanese situation, he says: "if one wishes to institute a *principato* in Florence, where a very great equality exists, it would be necessary first to introduce inequality" and to create many "nobili di castella e ville," who, "together with the prince, would keep the city and the whole region suffocated with arms" and with "l'aderenzie loro"—with the clients and partisans of their private factions. Imposing a principate where equality prevails requires creating a nobility in possession of its own territorial bases, its own arms, and factions of fighters and clients. Machiavelli drives the point further. "A prince alone, deprived of a nobility, cannot sustain the weight of a principate. There needs to be an intermediary [mezzo] between him and the people to help him sustain it. This is evident in all princely states, especially the kingdom of France where the gentiluomini rule [signoreggiono] the people, the barons [principi] rule the gentiluomini, and the king rules the barons." Machiavelli wants to impress upon Leo and Giulio just how complicated and difficult it would be to convert Florence from its centuries-long attachment to equality and the republic. "Creating a principate where a republic would work well [starebbe bene] and creating a republic where a principate would work well are difficult things, and, being difficult, inhumane and unworthy of anyone who wishes to be considered compassionate and good," as Machiavelli assumes Leo and Giulio wished to be. "I will therefore leave aside any further discussion of the principate [as a solution for Florence] and will speak of a republic, because Florence is an entity most suitable to assume the form [of a republic]" (*Discursus* 48–53)[16]

In *Discourses* 1.55 Machiavelli alludes only briefly to the presence in republics of "ambitious and restless men" and the danger of their potential collaboration with a would-be prince in subverting republican equality. But in chapter 37 of book 1 he recounts the most spectacular example in Roman history of the threat represented by "ambitious" men in republics: the reaction to the attempted revival of Rome's agrarian law by the Gracchi late in the second century BCE. Particularly noteworthy in Machiavelli's treatment of this complex episode is that, while emphasizing the permanence and danger of noble ambitions, the chapter opens and closes with criticism of the Roman plebs, attributing to it a large share of the responsibility for Rome's descent into the civil wars that began over the contentious agrarian law and ended, Machiavelli says, with the ruin of the republic. Not satisfied with gaining security against the nobles with the creation of the tribunes, something it did "out of necessity," the plebs began contesting the nobility "out of ambition," demanding to share with them both political offices ("onori") and wealth ("sustanze"). "From this came the disease [morbo: pathology] that gave rise to the disputes over the agrarian law and ultimately caused the republic's destruction." The metaphor echoes Livy's characterization (2.41.5) of the original agrarian law as a "pestilential [pestilens] gift" that ultimately did more harm than good to the plebs. Whatever its defects in timing and application, however, Machiavelli did not think the law's objectives were unjust; he agreed with its aim of distributing conquered property more widely to the plebeians on the principle that "well-ordered republics must keep the state [il publico: the state's treasury] rich and their citizens poor" (a maxim reiterated in *DL* 2.19.8), by which he meant not allowing great accumulations of private wealth. Despite conflating the provisions of the first agrarian law (of 486 BCE) and the second (of 367 BCE), Machiavelli conveys the virulence of the controversy with the comment, borrowed from Livy (2.41.3), that "it was never possible to speak of this law in Rome without the city being turned upside down over it." It damaged the economic fortunes of the nobles, he writes, by limiting the amount of land a citizen could possess, thus making it necessary to share newly conquered lands with the plebs, forcing many nobles to cede some of the lands they already held, and denying to many further acquisitions. Over the centuries, Machiavelli says, the "uomini potenti" used every means to deflect, delay, and weaken the enforcement of the law. In time, however, Rome's expansion throughout Italy and far beyond made

[16] *SPM*, pp. 631–2.

the more distant conquered land less desirable and seemed to put an end to the controversies (*DL* 1.37.6–15).

The law "lay as if asleep" until the Gracchi revived it, and, once reawakened, it "wholly destroyed Roman liberty" because the "power of its adversaries was redoubled. And so much hatred was ignited between the plebs and the senate that they came to fighting and bloodshed beyond all civic norms and customs [fuori d'ogni modo e costume civile]." With the "publici magistrati" powerless to stop the recourse to violence, and "because neither of the factions [fazioni]"—neither the nobles nor the plebs—"any longer placed hope in them" (in the "publici magistrati") "they turned to private remedies [rimedi privati], as each of the parties [parti] sought a leader [capo] who could defend it." ("Fazioni" and "parti" are here synonymous, both referring to the classes of nobles and plebeians.) Machiavelli makes a point of noting that the plebs took the first step in this direction by selecting Marius as its "capo" and getting him elected consul seven times. "Having no remedy against this disaster [peste]," the nobility chose Sulla as its leader. Civil war ensued, and, "after much bloodshed and reversals of fortune, the nobility emerged victorious." Decades later, Machiavelli adds, the conflicts revived with Caesar in Marius' role and Pompey in Sulla's. Caesar's victory made him "the first tyrant in Rome, and the city was never again free." That, Machiavelli concludes, was "the beginning and end of the agrarian law" (*DL* 1.37.16–21).

In a remarkable passage in which he critically reads his own text, Machiavelli acknowledges that some, seeing this denunciation of the conflicts sparked by the resumption of the agrarian laws, might conclude that he has contradicted what he wrote "elsewhere" (in *Discourses* 1.4) about the beneficial effects of conflict for Roman liberty. "Although we demonstrated elsewhere how the hostilities [inimicizie] in Rome between the senate and the plebs kept Rome free—because from those hostilities emerged laws that favored liberty—and for this reason the outcome of the agrarian law might seem incompatible [disforme] with that conclusion, I say that this does not make me retreat from that opinion." Anticipating the reader's potential puzzlement over the apparent inconsistency, Machiavelli explains why the disastrous result of the contention over the agrarian law does not invalidate his view that "inimicizie" between the nobles and the plebs were beneficial to Roman liberty. His answer highlights the ceaseless ambition of the nobles: the "ambizione" of the grandi, he says, "is so great that, if not beaten back [sbattuta] with various means and methods, it quickly brings a city to ruin" (*DL* 1.37.22). He acknowledges that, in this confrontation, both classes resorted to "private methods" and armed conflict and even that the plebs did so before the nobles. But Machiavelli still insists that the agrarian laws were necessary, because, viewed in longer historical perspective, the relentless ambition of the nobles is the overriding cause of all such conflicts. Nobles and grandi had always sought and still seek constantly to augment and protect their wealth, and, as he says in *Discourses* 1.5, they assume that the only secure way to protect their wealth is to increase it. Such avariciousness and obstinate preservation of what they possess are intrinsic to their nature and not, as for the plebs, a defensive, albeit sometimes exaggerated, reaction to noble ambition. For their part, the plebs' role over the centuries was to place one obstacle after another—tribunes, magistracies, distributive laws, occasional dictators—that might limit or constrain the nobles' inexorable ambition and greed. The constant, permanent aim of the noble class, by contrast, is to undermine and weaken magistracies like the tribunes and to circumvent laws, such as the agrarian legislation, designed to rein in its arrogance and restrict its power and wealth. Elite resistance to these attempts never ends. Inevitably—sooner if the plebs/popolo is weak, later if its laws and ordini are strong and effective, but inescapably in either case—the nobility undermines and, if it can, destroys the people's laws and institutions in order to preserve and augment its power and wealth. It may have been—and ultimately was—a losing battle for the people, as Machiavelli's argument implies. But if the plebs had not joined the fight, Rome would not have enjoyed liberty for several centuries and would never have acquired its empire. "If, therefore," Machiavelli continues, "the agrarian law took three hundred years to make Rome a slave"—its liberty finally destroyed in the civil wars—"it would perhaps have been reduced to servitude much sooner if the plebs, with this law and its other aims [appetiti], had not constantly applied a brake to [non avesse sempre frenato] the ambition of the nobles." This shows, Machiavelli comments, "how much more men value wealth [la roba] over political offices [gli onori]. Rome's nobles were always willing to share political offices with the plebs" without inciting strife with illegal measures ("sanza scandoli straordinari"). "But when it came to *la roba*"—wealth, property, possessions—"their obstinacy in defending it was so great that the plebs resorted to the illegalities [straordinari] discussed above to achieve their aims." Machiavelli concludes that the "intention" of the Gracchi—the "initiators [motori]" of this "disordine"—"deserves more praise than their wisdom [prudenza]," conveying approval of their objectives but disapproval of both the incautious and mistimed decision to revive agrarian legislation and the "straordinari" means they adopted to defend the law (*DL* 1.37.22–6).

This is, to be sure, a decidedly pessimistic vision of the prospects for social justice on any solid and lasting footing. Machiavelli sees noble ambition and the determination to acquire and defend wealth at all costs as relentless constants, occasionally challenged and sometimes forestalled, even for long periods, by the non-noble classes, but never definitively quelled. He believes the Roman plebs was justified, indeed had no choice but to attempt to restrain the excesses of noble ambition; otherwise, liberty and the republic would never have taken root. He reiterates this conclusion in *Discourses* 3.11.2–4, asserting that the "power of the tribunes of the plebs" was "great and necessary, as we have many times said, because otherwise it would not have been possible to apply a brake to the ambition of the nobility, which would have corrupted the republic much sooner than it did." Although the people and their tribunes could sometimes become overbearing and occasionally needed to be reined in, such excesses did not diminish the need for a constant "brake on the ambition of the nobility."[17]

"CITIZENS OF RENOWN"

Machiavelli's analysis of noble ambition in republican Rome and in his Italy and Florence focuses on the pursuit of private power through factions. He distinguishes factions, which he usually calls *sette* (less often *parti*, which can have other meanings in other contexts), but only occasionally *fazioni* (which can also mean military battles), from social groups or classes, which he calls *umori* and sometimes *parti*. He portrays both the noble and popular classes as the ubiquitous, permanent, but not unchanging, motors of history, social formations that emerge naturally in every society from the patterns of unequal distribution of wealth. Factions, by contrast, he sees as smaller, temporary groupings, tactically assembled, malleable, and created by powerful grandi who possess the necessary resources and influence to attract adherents from both their own class and the popular classes. Machiavelli understands factions, both in Rome and in the Italian cities, as built on patronage ties: on the ability of powerful patrons to attract followers and clients who give loyalty in return for a variety of favors including financial assistance and protection in disputes and in the courts. Reflecting Florentine usage, Machiavelli often calls these clients *amici* (friends) and also *partigiani*, members of the patron's *parte*. A patron expected his *partigiani* to serve him in a variety of ways: by supporting him in clashes with rival factions, in the councils of government, in the pursuit of offices, and in demonstrations of street power that included gatherings, in moments of crisis, at the patron's home. A large and cohesive faction gave the patron prestige and leverage over rivals and, if especially powerful, even over government and public authority. Factions were the forms of private power through which, Machiavelli contends, the wealthy and powerful deflected the laws, pressured magistrates to do their bidding, and resisted the attempts of the plebs or popolo to limit their wealth or power. Manlius Capitolinus' attempt to attract a following among the plebs by spreading rumors of peculation by certain citizens is, for Machiavelli, a classic example of faction-building (and manipulation of the people) in the pursuit of private ambition.

Friendships ("amicizie"), according to Machiavelli, were the building blocks of factions. In *Discourses* 1.46, paraphrasing Livy (3.65), he says that in Rome "whenever the plebeians were peaceful...young nobles took to offending them." Nobles may have thought their youth were excessively abusive ("feroce") toward the

[17] John P. McCormick analyzes Machiavelli's recommendations for containing the ambition of the elite classes in *Machiavellian Democracy*.

plebs, yet they nonetheless preferred that, if anyone was to engage in excesses ("trapassare il modo"), it should be their young men, not the plebs. "The logic of such events [l'ordine di questi accidenti] is"—Machiavelli now translates Livy—"that, in trying to escape fear, men instill fear in others; the injury they seek to evade they inflict on others, as if it were necessary either to offend or be offended." Machiavelli adds his own conclusion: "One sees from this in what way, among others, republics fall apart, and in what way men climb from one ambition to another." He links this ladder of ambition to the problematic aspect of "amicizie" with the passage from Sallust's *Catilina* (51.27) in which Caesar says that "all bad precedents have their origin in good beginnings" (Sallust actually says "in good things"). Machiavelli then illustrates Sallust's dictum asserting that friendship, seemingly a good thing, can have negative consequences. "Citizens who live ambitiously in a republic"—"ambiziosamente" again signaling the thirst for personal power—"seek, above all, not to be offended [or injured: offesi] by either private citizens or the magistrates." To this end, "they seek friendships, which they acquire in ways honorable in appearance [in apparenza oneste], with either financial assistance or protection against the powerful." But behind these apparently honorable ways lies something insidious: "Because it seems virtuous [pare virtuoso], it easily deceives everyone, and nothing is done to stop it." If an ambitious citizen persists in this without any opposition, Machiavelli continues, "private citizens fear him and the magistrates deal with him very cautiously [gli hanno rispetto]." Once he achieves this status, it is "very dangerous" to try to oppose him, and the only choices are either to eliminate him ("spegnerlo") or, if he is allowed to continue, to accept the undisguised loss of liberty—"servitù manifesta"—that his power and influence now entail. If both citizens and magistrates fear offending "him and his friends," it will not be long before they think they can "offend anyone as they please." Personal bonds of loyalty and obligation that generate such fear, weakening the magistrates and the laws, are among the ways in which the seeming virtue of friendship subverts liberty.

Discourses 1.46 concludes with a warning that republics should have among their ordini ways of preventing citizens from "engaging in wickedness [fare male] under the cover of doing good [sotto ombra di bene]" and ensuring that they acquire the kind of "renown that benefits liberty and does not harm it, as we shall discuss in its place." The reference is to *Discourses* 3.28, which reprises the theme of "doing evil under the cover of good" with the more specifically political warning, as the chapter title puts it, "that many times, beneath a merciful act [una opera pia] is hidden the beginning of tyranny [si nasconde uno principio di tirannide]." The seemingly "merciful act" that Machiavelli selects as an example is the scheme of Spurius Maelius, a "very wealthy" Roman but not a noble, who bought large amounts of grain during a famine to distribute to the plebs. In so doing, "he gained such a loyal following among the people [tanto concorso di popolo in suo favore]" that the senate, mindful of the potentially dangerous consequences of his liberality, appointed a dictator who investigated the matter and had him executed. Livy tells the story in greater detail (4.12–15), including the accusation—which Machiavelli strangely omits even as his chapter title alludes to it in mentioning tyranny—that Spurius Maelius aimed to become "king" with the popular support his liberality won him among the plebs. The danger he represented was precisely that "tanto concorso di popolo," the formation of a faction bound to him by his merciful acts. Machiavelli comments that this and similar acts, which "seem merciful and cannot justifiably [ragionevolmente] be condemned, become malicious and very dangerous to republics unless quickly suppressed" (*DL* 3.28.2–4).

"Looking more closely at the matter," Machiavelli acknowledges that republics cannot survive or be well governed without "citizens of renown [cittadini riputati]." Yet, citizens' "riputazione"—fame, distinction, eminence, power—"is the cause of tyranny in republics." Machiavelli does not mince words here: he does not say that citizens' "riputazione" *can* cause tyranny or *sometimes* causes tyranny; their "riputazione" *is* the cause of tyranny. To forestall this eventuality, a city needs laws that encourage citizens to pursue the kind of prestige and renown that benefits and does not damage its liberty (as he says in *Discourses* 1.46). It is therefore necessary to "examine the ways by which [citizens] gain renown," which are either "public [publici]" or "private [privati]." Public ways include "offering good advice" and, "better still, doing deeds that redound to the common benefit." Renown so acquired and untainted by ulterior motives is not dangerous. But renown acquired "per vie private" is "very dangerous and entirely harmful." Private ways include doing favors for individuals by lending them money, arranging marriages for their daughters, defending them from the magistrates, and other similar "privati favori." With such "favors," powerful men with money and influence create factions whose members are beholden to them. What is worse, the politics of private favors and factions undermines the institutions of government. Such "vie private" make those receiving favors into "partigiani"—clients in the patron's faction—and encourage them [danno animo] to think they can "corrupt public authority and violate the laws [corrompere il publico e sforzare le leggi]." Rome, Machiavelli notes approvingly, instituted rewards for citizens who gained renown in public ways and punishments for those, like Spurius Maelius, who did so with private methods. Among these punishments, he includes "indictments [accuse]" and the appointment of a "dictator" with emergency powers to force wayward citizens back into line ("dentro al segno") (*DL* 3.28.5–15). In chapter 34 of book 1 Machiavelli affirms the beneficial effects of the office of the Roman dictator precisely in the context of the danger of powerful men who command the loyalty of factions. "For a man to be harmful [to the republic] and seize unlawful power [autorità istraordinaria], he needs to possess many assets that he can never have in a republic that is not corrupt; he must be very rich and must have many clients and followers [aderenti e partigiani], which he cannot have if the laws are observed" (*DL* 1.34.8). This places the very existence of factions outside the laws and ordini. Factions flourish and expand where the laws have weakened or ceased to function. Corruption, in Machiavelli's political language, is the subversion of the sphere of public law by private power.

In the immediately preceding chapter Machiavelli illustrates the danger of an "ambitious" noble who rises to power with a strong faction behind him. Approaching the issue tangentially from the question of whether it is better to confront a danger to a republic head-on or "temporize," Machiavelli says such dilemmas more often arise from internal than external causes, as when a "citizen is allowed to take more power [piú forze] than is *ragionevole*, or when a law that is the nerve and life of a free constitution begins to be corrupted." The first part of this sentence says more than might appear upon first reading. Tempted as we are to read "ragionevole" as "reasonable," "ragione" also means justice, right, and law; hence, the phrase implies "more power than is just or justifiable, more power than one should have by right." The implication that such power transgresses the laws becomes explicit in the second part of the sentence: "when a law that is the nerve and life of a free constitution [vivere libero] begins to be corrupted [si comincia a corrompere]." Such dangers are difficult to recognize at first, Machiavelli asserts, because people generally look with favor on the beginnings of things, especially if "achieved by young men who seem to have in them some virtú." But this is quickly revealed to be less benign. "For if in a republic a young noble rises up who displays *virtú istraordinaria*, the eyes of all citizens begin to turn toward him and, without careful forethought [sanza alcuno rispetto: heedlessly], they compete to honor him, such that, if he has even a minimum of ambition, with the combination of advantages given him by nature and by this circumstance [accidente: the favor he enjoys], he quickly reaches a position in which the citizens, when they become aware of their error, have few possibilities of opposing him" (*DL* 1.33.4–8). The appealing (and apparent) virtú of a political newcomer has become a dangerous combination of ambition and "virtú istraordinaria," endangering the ordini and threatening the republic. Because of their imprudent rush to curry favor with him, however, even the citizens who now realize the seriousness of their error are powerless to stop him.

Only at this point does Machiavelli reveal that, among the "many examples" of this phenomenon, the only one he intends to discuss is Cosimo de' Medici, "from whom," he is quick to say, "the Medici family had the beginnings of its "grandezza [power]." It is of course the most delicate example of all. Cosimo, he says, acquired so much "riputazione" with the "favore" he gained "from his prudence and the ignorance of the other citizens that he began to instill fear into the stato," here meaning the regime, or *reggimento*, as the Florentines referred to the inner circle of powerful citizens who controlled the government through private influence and informal channels. Cosimo became so powerful that those who opposed his rise to power "considered it dangerous to attack him and even more dangerous to let him go on" acquiring more power. Niccolò da Uzzano, the passage continues, "considered in those times most expert in political matters [nelle cose civili]," having himself failed in the beginning to recognize the danger of Cosimo's growing "riputazione," knew that to try to stop him after he had acquired such influence would spell the ruin of "their stato [dello stato loro]"—the plural possessive "loro" making it clear that Machiavelli means the regime. Uzzano therefore blocked attempts to free the city of Cosimo, but after Uzzano died Cosimo's enemies ignored this advice and exiled him. Cosimo's faction then manifested its power and determined the outcome: "Hence it happened that his faction [parte], indignant over this injustice, soon recalled him and made him *principe della repubblica*"—"principe," of course, in the sense of first citizen, but unmistakably alluding to the family's future aspirations. Machiavelli audaciously compares Cosimo's success to Caesar's: "This same thing happened in Rome with Caesar" whose virtú initially had the support of Pompey and other prominent citizens. But not long afterwards their "support turned into fear," and they resorted to "solutions that accelerated the ruin of their republic" (*DL* 1.33.9–14). What Machiavelli does not say directly about Cosimo is implied in the comments about Caesar.

Dangerous citizens of renown are in evidence also in Machiavelli's explanation of the military dimension of the Roman republic's collapse. As conquests extended far beyond Rome, the increasing distances altered relations between the generals and the army's plebeian soldiers. In *Discourses* 2.33 he praises as "very wise" the senate's policy of allowing army commanders ever greater freedom to make battlefield decisions, as it became more difficult for the senate to have adequate knowledge of the conditions and circumstances of far-flung campaigns. Giving commanders "unhampered authority [commissioni libere]" to conduct campaigns as they judged best was, Machiavelli says, prudent and effective. If the senate had insisted on sharing the tactical management of a campaign, it would have made its commander "less attentive and slower, because it would not have seemed to him that the glory of victory was his alone" if he had to share it with the senate. The senate therefore allowed the commanders to be on their own so that "the glory would be all theirs." Machiavelli does not comment here on the obvious danger of generals claiming the glory of victory for themselves, but in *Discourses* 3.24 he explains that this policy led to another that was central to Rome's decline. The expansion of the territorial empire, he says, caused the senate not only to give the generals a free hand in their campaigns but also to grant prolongations of their commands ("prolungazione delli imperii"), "which in time destroyed the republic." However necessary the extension of commands may have been because of the increasing distances and the impracticality of replacing commanders in the midst of faraway sieges or campaigns, Machiavelli says two serious problems resulted. The first was that renewing commands meant that fewer men gained the experience of commanding armies, eventually reducing the prestige ("riputazione") of command to only a few. The second was more serious: "a citizen who remained as commander of an army for a long time obtained it"—the army—"for himself [se lo guadagnava] and made it his *partigiano*, because, with time, the army forgot the senate"—the public authority that had sent it into war—"and recognized [the commander] as its *capo*." Machiavelli claims, in effect, that repeated extensions of command inevitably bound armies to their generals with ties of obligation, favor, and loyalty not unlike those of political factions, and that the weakening of ties to the senate and the republic's laws corrupted the armies with the private power of military patrons who each made his army his client/*partigiano* and whose "renown" undermined public authority. This, Machiavelli concludes, "was how Sulla and Marius were able to find soldiers to follow them against the *bene publico*. This was how Caesar was able to seize [occupare] his patria"—to take tyrannical power (*DL* 3.24.10–13). Rome's late republican warlords were manifestations of the disastrous privatization of military forces and the transformation of the republic's armies into their own armed factions.

The public/private dichotomy also informs Machiavelli's assessment of the relative benefits of severity and leniency in military commanders. In *Discourses* 3.22 he compares two "excellent commanders" from the fourth century BCE, Manlius Torquatus and Valerius Corvinus. Equal in virtú, triumphs, and glory, he writes, they differed enormously in how they treated their soldiers. Manlius engaged "in every kind of severity" (*DL* 3.22.3)—even executing his own son, a shocking act that Machiavelli mentions two other times in the *Discourses*: in 2.16.5, where he says it kept the spirits of his soldiers obedient and resolute; and in 3.34.18, where he finally explains that, according to Livy (8.7), Manlius inflicted the terrible punishment because his son had disobeyed orders not to engage in duels with the enemy. In 3.22.19 Machiavelli presents him as "one of those who, with the severity [asprezza] of their commands, maintained military discipline in Rome." Valerius was the complete opposite: he treated his soldiers with kindness, affability, and familiarity (*DL* 3.22.3). Yet both were highly successful generals, and both received praise from historians (including Livy). This, says Machiavelli, makes the question of "which is the more praiseworthy way" of dealing with soldiers "debatable [disputabile]" and "difficult to decide." After considering arguments on both sides (*DL* 3.22.25–31), Machiavelli concludes that Manlius' method is "more praiseworthy and less dangerous" for a citizen commander who "lives under the laws of a republic," because "his way is entirely to the benefit of the *publico*"—the state, or republic—"and in no way concerns private ambition [non risguarda in alcuna parte all'ambizione privata]." If one is "strict with everyone and loves only the common good, it is not possible to acquire *partigiani*," because one who conducts himself as Manlius did "does not acquire *particulari amici*"—personal allies—"which, as was said above, we call *partigiani*." Severity of the sort practiced by Manlius "could not be more useful or desirable in a republic, for it does not lack benefit to the state [utilità publica] and because there can be no fear of private power [potenza privata]." By contrast, familiarity and kindness, as employed by Valerius, create "much fear about the personal good will [particulare benivolenza]" the captain "acquires with the soldiers, which, during a long tenure of command, has negative consequences for liberty" (*DL* 3.22.32–5). Hence, severity is preferable in a citizen commander of a republic's army. But to princes who command their own armies Machiavelli recommends that they emulate Valerius and practice kindness with their soldiers. Princes, he says, must seek "obedience and love" in their soldiers and subjects (an apparent departure from the advice about love and fear in *Prince* 17). A prince can secure obedience by respecting the ordini and being considered valorous ("virtuoso"); but he wins love with "affability, kindness, compassion, and Valerius' other qualities." "Being personally well liked [bene voluto particularmente] and having the army as his *partigiano*"—bound to him by ties of loyalty and personal obligation—"are compatible with the other aspects of his status" as a prince. But for a citizen to command an army as his "partigiano" does not comport with his duty "to live under the laws and obey the magistrates." Therefore, Machiavelli concludes, "Valerius' approach is useful in a prince and pernicious in a citizen, not only for his country, because "it paves the way for tyranny," but also for himself, because, "when the city begins to be fearful of how" he treats his soldiers, "it will be compelled to protect itself to his detriment" (*DL* 3.22.36–42).

The principles that a republic (1) must prevent ties of personal obligation and loyalty between commanders and soldiers; (2) must not allow commanders to pursue private political agendas; and (3) must ensure that soldiers acknowledge the republic as their ultimate head were central to Machiavelli's vision of the Florentine militia.[18] Florence, he says in the 1506 memorandum outlining the militia's structure, the *Cagione dell'Ordinanza*,[19] "must provide for arms only through public legislation [deliberazione pubblica]" (3). The banners of all the militia units must display the image of the "lion"—the Marzocco, the symbol of Florence—"so that all your soldiers will be bound by affection to one and the same thing, will acknowledge only the public emblem [segno pubblico], and thereby become its *partigiani*" (15). To prevent improper use of the militia by a magistrate or "persona privata," the militia units were under the authority not of a single "superiore" but of several government committees, recognizing in each "un pubblico e non un privato." Unit leaders must not "assume more authority than is appropriate for them," and to this end constables must be regularly rotated to different posts and not assigned to localities in which they were born or owned property (35–8). The "Provisione della Ordinanza," the law, drafted by Machiavelli, that instituted the militia, detailed these regulations and threatened with capital

[18] Andrea Guidi expertly analyzes Machiavelli's writings on the militia in *Un Segretario militante. Politica, diplomazia e armi nel Cancelliere Machiavelli* (Bologna: Il Mulino, 2009).

[19] *SPM*, pp. 470–6 (passages cited by numbered sentences).

punishment any squad captain who "raises his flag"—in effect, mobilizing his unit—"for any private conflict [alcuna fazione privata], or on behalf of any private person [per conto di alcuno privato]" or anyone who assembles militiamen because of personal "animosities [inimicizie]" or "any private conflict."[20]

[20] *SPM*, pp. 477–92, cited passages at 489–90.

6
Family and Faction

Machiavelli knew more about Florentine factions than ancient Roman ones, and the *Florentine Histories* contain both more examples of factions in historical context and greater detail concerning their formation, function, and danger to the state. Whereas in Rome the nobility was identifiable as the senatorial class, Florence had no titled nobility, no social category endowed with formalized privileges or separate legal status, and no institution that defined an aristocracy like the Roman senate or the Venetian Maggior Consiglio. This is what Machiavelli means when he writes, in several places, that "equality" prevailed in Florence and made the city unsuitable for princely government. Yet he was of course well aware that Florence had an elite class that sought, no less than Rome's nobility, to establish its dominance in state and society and protect itself against challenges to its power. In certain texts and contexts he avoided calling Florence's elite class a nobility. For example, in the 1520–1 *Discursus florentinarum rerum*, he divides the Florentines into three categories: the "primi, mezzani e ultimi,"[1] characterizing the "primi [first]," not by legal criteria or titles, but as those "of haughty temperament [d'animo elevato] who believe they deserve to take precedence over others [pare loro meritare di precedere agli altri], and who must be satisfied in organizing a republic" (57–9). In a text in which he seeks to persuade Pope Leo and Cardinal Giulio de' Medici to approve a republican constitution, which he explicitly contrasts with the princely regime in Milan supported by its nobility (49), he had good reason not to call Florence's "primi" nobles. Needless to say, Machiavelli did not accept the subjective claims of superiority and rightful precedence of Florence's "primi"; indeed, his critique of their politics and self-image is a major theme of the *Histories*. Moreover, as the following chapters will show, his historical perspective reveals a constantly changing elite class that was not always politically pre-eminent. And in the *Discursus*, far from establishing institutional primacy for the "primi," he insists on the necessity of satisfying the aspirations of the "universale" by reopening the Great Council (73–80) and instituting a popular restraint, with veto power, over the executive committees dominated by the "primi" (82–6).[2] Yet, if he was to

[1] *Discursus*, in *SPM*, pp. 621–41 (passages cited by numbered sentences).

[2] On the veto power he would give the Sixteen gonfalonieri, see my *History of Florence* (Oxford: Blackwell, 2006), p. 439; McCormick, *Machiavellian Democracy*, pp. 103–7; and my "Machiavelli's Florentine Tribunes," in *Renaissance Studies in Honor of Joseph Connors*, 2 vols., ed. M. Israëls and L. A. Waldman (Florence: The Harvard University Center for Italian Renaissance Studies, 2013), vol. 2, pp. 65–72.

Machiavelli's Broken World. John M. Najemy, Oxford University Press. © John M. Najemy 2022.
DOI: 10.1093/oso/9780199580927.003.0006

have any chance of persuading Leo and Giulio to accept his recommendations, he needed to assure them that their "friends" and allies—the "primi"—would "take precedence" in a reformed republic.

"SEEKING TO DEPRIVE EACH OTHER OF POWER, THEY ALL LOST IT"

In the *Florentine Histories* the terminology Machiavelli uses for the elite class varies with time and political circumstances. Through the first half of the fourteenth century, he uses "nobili" to refer to only a portion of this class, namely the elite families designated as magnates whom he calls either "nobili" (collectively "nobilità") or "grandi." Magnate status neither denoted nor conferred privilege. It deprived the families so designated of the right to hold major communal offices and subjected them to injurious penalties for specified crimes against non-magnates. Assigning families to magnate status was a political decision of the popular governments of the 1280s and 1290s, based on the families' reputation for violence and contempt for communal law. Many, but not all, were older families that traced their lineage and prominence back to the twelfth century and constituted the original nuclei of the Guelf and Ghibelline parties. Their leadership in the hostilities that engulfed the city in civil and foreign wars in the thirteenth century was in most cases the determining factor in their relegation to magnate status. Two-thirds of the magnates were prominent Guelfs or Ghibellines, roughly the same number from each party. But a full third of the magnates belonged to the merchant and banking elite. On the other hand, many powerful and wealthy elite families escaped designation as magnates. Magnates, in short, did not constitute a social class. The popular governments of the 1280s and 1290s strategically divided the elite class, designating seventy-two elite lineages as magnates while leaving dozens among the non-magnates, possibly to incentivize the latter to accept the popular government's reforms and institutions and conform to its norms. It is essential to bear in mind that, when Machiavelli refers to "nobles" in the period before the mid-fourteenth century, he means only the magnate portion of the elite class.

Although the term *magnates* was common in the Latin statutes and legislation of the thirteenth and fourteenth centuries, Machiavelli never uses its vernacular equivalent, *magnati*, probably because the chroniclers rarely used it. For the century or more in which the magnates were a prominent, legally defined category within the broader elite, he does not refer to the many equally wealthy and powerful non-magnate elite families as either *nobili* or *grandi*. He calls them instead the *potenti*, the *primi cittadini*, or, more often, *popolani nobili*, *popolani potenti*, or *popolani grandi*. Despite the use of *popolani* in these expressions, the non-magnates among the elite must not be confused or conflated with the social popolo. Legally, all non-magnates of whatever class were *popolani*. Hence, the legal category of *popolani*—all non-magnates—included both elite families and the wider community of smaller, less wealthy families who generally had little knowledge of their ancestry going back more than a couple of generations and in many cases even lacked surnames. This social popolo consisted of non-elite merchants, shopkeepers, notaries, and artisans who filled the ranks of the city's guilds. Although many of Machiavelli's *popolani nobili* were families of relatively new wealth and political prominence, they did not constitute a social class distinct from the magnates, among whom there were also families that had acquired wealth and influence as recently as the second half of the thirteenth century. Later in the *Florentine Histories*, writing about the period after many magnate families regained *popolano* status and the political importance of the magnate category declined, Machiavelli occasionally refers to the entire elite class as *nobili* (and once as grandi), but more often as the *potenti*, *primi cittadini*, or *primi uomini*. Despite this varied nomenclature, these terms all referred to the social elite of great families, both magnate and non-magnate.

Up to the 1340s, and in some respects until the end of the fourteenth century, Machiavelli treats the magnates as a distinct political group, portraying them as arrogant, overbearing, and disdainful of civic norms and communal law, as did the popular governments and the chroniclers who were his chief sources. Their often violent attempts to throw off the yoke of punitive legislation and exclusion from major offices ended with their defeat in street battles in 1343—the "rovina de' nobili," as Machiavelli puts it (*IF* 2.42.3). Yet he does not depict their "rovina" as the end of elite misconduct and discord. Introducing the political conflicts of the 1350s, he writes that, with the power of the magnates suppressed, "it seemed that no further cause of division remained in Florence. But the ill fortune of our city and its defective ordini generated hostility between the [non-magnate] families of the Albizzi and the Ricci, which divided Florence much as the antagonisms of the Buondelmonti and Uberti and later of the Donati and Cerchi had divided the city" (*IF* 3.2.2). Three chapters later, Machiavelli has a speaker tell the Signoria that some may have thought no further cause of conflict remained after the "old nobility's overbearing haughtiness and insufferable ambition" had been quelled. On the contrary, he says, the "superbia e ambizione" of the grandi were not extinguished ("non si spense"); "they were instead wrested from them [fu loro tolta] by our popolani"—by the powerful non-magnate elite families who adopted the worst characteristics of the magnates and, "following the custom of ambitious men," sought power in the republic through "discord and have again divided the city" (*IF* 3.5.17–18). Although the magnates had lost power, Machiavelli has the speaker insist that "our popolani" took on the same aggressive and destructive impulses that characterized the magnates. As we shall see, hostilities between family-based factions remain central to Machiavelli's narrative long after the "ruin" of the magnates in the mid-fourteenth century.

Machiavelli depicts Florentine elite factions as emanations of private family power. In *Histories* 2.3 he follows Florentine legend in tracing the Guelf-Ghibelline conflicts of the thirteenth century to a dispute in 1216 (1215 in Florentine dating) between two groups of families over a pledge of marriage broken by Buondelmonte Buondelmonti, who heedlessly yielded to the persuasions of a woman of the Donati family to forsake his betrothed from the Amidei family and marry her daughter instead. He hastily made this ill-considered decision, Machiavelli writes, "giving no thought to the promise he had given [fede data] or to the offense he was committing in breaking his word, nor indeed to the evils that could result" (*IF* 2.3.1–6). Buondelmonte becomes a synecdoche of his class, embodying its impulsive and destructive inability to adhere to civil customs and norms. His breach of faith filled the Amidei and their chief allies, the Uberti, with indignation and thirst for revenge: only his death, they concluded, would be a fitting "vendetta" for the offense. But killing Buondelmonte, far from resolving the conflict, "divided the entire city." Two great coalitions of elite families formed: one led by the Buondelmonti and Donati, the other by their archenemies, the Uberti and Amidei. Machiavelli highlights their strength in numbers and their many fortified compounds and impregnable towers in the city center, which allowed them, he says, to fight for years without victory for either side. "These hostilities never ended with peace, only with truces; and in this way, depending on how events unfolded, they were sometimes quelled, at other times inflamed" (*IF*.2.3.7–13). The methods of conflict resolution, in other words, had only temporary and minimal success and often made things worse. Machiavelli, like other writers before him, lets the episode serve as an iconic original moment of the destructive behavior of Florence's elite.

By positioning the Buondelmonti episode at the beginning of his narrative of Florentine history, Machiavelli emphasizes that factions within the city's elite families preceded and melted into the formation of the pro-imperial Ghibelline and anti-imperial Guelf parties. The Uberti and their allies sided with the Emperor Frederick II in the Ghibelline party; the Buondelmonti and Donati and their allies became anti-imperial Guelfs. Borrowing from the chronicle of Giovanni Villani,[3] Machiavelli lists thirty-seven Guelf families and twenty-nine Ghibelline families, adding that many "populari" families joined these coalitions of "famiglie nobili," so that "almost the entire city was corrupted [corrotta] by these divisions" (*IF* 2.4.1–5). The Guelf and Ghibelline families he names were all later declared magnates. Whether the "populari" families in this passage are non-magnate elite or the social popolo is not clear; either way, Machiavelli is calling

[3] The indispensable guide to Machiavelli's sources in book 2 is Cabrini's *Per una valutazione delle "Istorie fiorentine" del Machiavelli*. Gian Mario Anselmi provides a general overview of Machiavelli's sources in *Ricerche sul Machiavelli storico* (Pisa: Pacini Editore, 1979).

attention to the influence exerted by the magnates in drawing non-magnate allies into their camps. This, he will show, was a constant feature and important measure of the strength of Florentine factions: the more allies a faction could pull into its orbit, the stronger it would be in confrontations with rivals. The assertion that "almost the entire city" was "corrupted" by these factional divisions alerts us to Machiavelli's understanding of "corruption" as the spread of private power.

Factions originating in family ties and attracting allies from beyond the family circle are constants in the *Florentine Histories*. Throughout, Machiavelli underscores the decisive role in factional solidarity, not only of blood relatives but also of relatives by marriage ("parenti") and friends ("amici"). Recounting the Buondelmonti murder, he notes that the Amidei and Uberti were "linked by ties of marriage [per parentado congiunti]." To decide a course of action they met with many other "parenti" (*IF* 2.3.7–8). Whenever "nobles" injured non-nobles, Machiavelli says, they sought to evade punishments with the help of their "parenti" and "amici" (*IF* 2.12.2). During the May Day festivities of 1300, bands of young members from magnate families rode on horseback through the city "with their friends" to watch the dances in the city streets (*IF* 2.17.6). When a member of the Cerchi family decided for his safety to leave the city and take shelter in his country properties, he did so "with many of his friends" (*IF* 2.20.3). Corso Donati, leader of the Black Guelf faction and widely suspected of aiming to become tyrant of Florence, finding himself besieged by communal troops trying to arrest him, barricaded himself in the family compound with his "partigiani" and then attacked the besiegers "with many others of his most powerful and trusted friends" (*IF* 2.23.7–9). In 1340 the magnate families of the Bardi and Frescobaldi attempted a rebellion and placed their hopes for success in the "nobles of the countryside and other *amici*" of theirs. To counter the threat, some citizens urged the Signoria to sound the bell and call the popolo to arms, but the gonfalonier of justice and one of the priors opposed the idea "because they were *parenti* of the Bardi." When the rebellion collapsed, the Bardi fled the city "with their friends" (*IF* 2.32.11–19). The Ricci, "with their friends," lost no opportunity to hinder the plans of the Albizzi (*IF* 3.4.8). Seeing the first outbreak of violence by workers and artisans in 1378, two members of the Strozzi family went into hiding in the city, believing that, "because they had many *parenti* and *amici*," they would be safe once the tumults subsided (*IF* 3.10.12).

Machiavelli highlights the speed with which confrontations between elite factions originating in private disputes escalated into hostilities and violence that overwhelmed the city. In the story of Buondelmonte's broken pledge of marriage, divisions instantly formed and quickly expanded. The same pattern is evident in Machiavelli's account of the split around 1300 of the Guelf party into Black and White factions. He introduces the two magnate families that led these factions, the Donati and the Cerchi, as both "very potent in wealth, nobility, and men"—"men" indicating their large followings of "friends" and clients (*IF* 2.16.1). He ascribes the escalation of their clashes to an incident when the Donati youth and their "friends" on horseback stopped to watch women dancing and a group from the rival Cerchi, "similarly accompanied by many nobles" and eager to see the dances, also arrived. Not recognizing who was in front of them, the Cerchi pushed their horses forward and collided with the Donati, who took offense and drew out their weapons, provoking the Cerchi to do likewise. A brawl ensued with many injures on both sides. "This tumult [disordine]," Machiavelli comments, "was the beginning of much evil [male], because it divided the whole city, both the popolo and the grandi." Here too, as he does with the Buondelmonti episode and again following Villani, Machiavelli lists the major families in each faction: seventeen magnate families among the Whites, joined by many "famiglie popolane"; and nine magnate families among the Blacks. He also notes that certain families were themselves divided between the factions, thus underscoring the constant tendency of the elite, even within families, to divide and turn against itself. Nor, he points out, was this split limited to the city: the contado (presumably its powerful families) also divided between Blacks and Whites (*IF* 2.17.5–10). After the Black Guelfs enlisted the help of Pope Boniface VIII and the French prince Charles of Valois to exile the Cerchi and their allies and take control of the city (in 1301–2), they too divided into warring factions. Several of the most prominent Black leaders broke with Corso Donati and joined the attack that resulted in his death (*IF* 2.23).

Machiavelli establishes a direct and repeated link between the elite's disruptive and violent factionalism and the response of the popolo, which created institutions and laws to restrain the elite and protect its own security. Machiavelli's fundamental article of indictment against the elite is its contempt for the laws and magistrates and its subversion of communal institutions. The absence of any mention of the city's magistrates or laws in his account of the Buondelmonti murder conveys the elite's disdain for constituted authority. A few pages later (*IF* 2.5), he admiringly describes the constitution of the first government of the popolo (known later as the "primo popolo") and its huge militia of citizens and contado residents, created (in 1250) by "uomini di mezzo"—citizens neutral between the warring Guelfs and Ghibellines—who instituted a "framework of free government [forma di vivere libero]" (*IF* 2.4.7–9) to rein in excesses of the elite Guelfs and Ghibellines. Machiavelli comments that "with these military and civic ordini the Florentines laid the foundation of their liberty" (*IF* 2.6.1), thus highlighting the link between liberty and ordini. Guelfs and Ghibellines, he points out, coexisted for some years under the primo popolo, which tried to remain neutral between the parties. But when it was learned that Ghibellines were secretly negotiating with Manfred, the Hohenstaufen heir of Frederick II, the government of the primo popolo summoned the leaders of the chief Ghibelline family, the Uberti. "Not only did they not obey [the summons]," Machiavelli writes, "but they also took up arms and barricaded themselves in their homes." The popular government forced the Ghibellines into exile. But two years later (1260) a Sienese, Hohenstaufen, and Ghibelline army inflicted the massive defeat on the Florentines at Montaperti (*IF* 2.6.8–10), sending the Guelfs into exile and "abolishing the magistracies and every institution [ordine] that manifested any semblance of the city's liberty," thus provoking the "extreme revulsion [grande odio] of the entire people" (*IF* 2.7.2–3).

Restored to power, the Ghibellines ruled for six years but were in turn defeated by Charles of Anjou, invited by the papacy into Italy to rid itself of the danger of encirclement by the Hohenstaufen (*IF* 2.8). As the Ghibellines went into exile, the elite Guelf families returned and assumed power (1267). Just as the Ghibellines "did not obey" the government of the primo popolo, Machiavelli portrays the victorious Guelfs as contemptuous of the law and the magistrates and eager to resume factional conflicts. Florence under the Guelfs "was in a sorry state [assai mala condizione], because the Guelf nobility had become arrogant [insolente] and had no fear of the magistrates. Every day they committed many murders and other acts of violence; those who committed these crimes were not punished because they were protected [favoriti] by one or another of the nobles." Again Machiavelli says that "noble insolence," this time of the Guelfs, spurred a popular response, as the "capi del popolo" seized the initiative to "restrain [frenare] this insolence" and "bridle the powerful [tenere i potenti in freno]." In 1282 (Machiavelli notes the year) they created the priorate of the guilds as the commune's new chief executive magistracy. "As became clear in time," he comments, "this magistracy was the cause of the ruin of the nobility, as the popolo excluded the nobles [i.e. magnates] from the priorate." The magnates' own internal conflicts, he adds, prevented them from effectively opposing the popolo's reforms: "the nobles allowed this to happen, because they were not united; as they sought to deprive each other of power, they all lost it" (*IF* 2.11.1–9).

By this time—the end of the thirteenth century—the chief conflict was no longer, Machiavelli asserts, between Guelfs and Ghibellines. The Guelfs had won that long war. The conflicts that now heated up were "those that naturally occur in all cities between the powerful [potenti] and the popolo." He restates what he had written in *Prince* 9 and *Discourses* 1.5 about the fundamental difference between the two classes: "because the popolo wants to live according to the laws, and the powerful want to rule over the laws [comandare a quelle], it is not possible for them to co-exist [cappiano insieme]." The "potenti" intensified their antagonism toward the popolo: "every day some member of the popolo" was "ingiuriato"—offended, attacked, injured, or humiliated—"and the laws and magistrates were not sufficient to avenge the wrongs" committed by nobles, "because every noble shielded himself [si difendeva] from the power of the priors and the capitano [the judicial official created by the primo popolo] with the help of his "parenti" and "amici" in order to circumvent the laws and evade prosecution and punishment. Accusers needing corroborating witnesses to prove the "ingiurie" committed against them "could find no one willing to testify against the nobles," so great was the fear of retaliation. "Thus, in a short time, the city fell back into the same disorders [disordini], and the popolo suffered the same attacks at the hands of the grandi" (*IF* 2.12.1–2, 8). So, for the third time in the narrative, escalating transgressions by the elite provoked a response from the popolo. A new popular government, supported by the city's increasingly influential guilds, came to power under the leadership of Giano della Bella, who, although "from a very noble family, was a lover of the city's liberty." Giano "instilled into the leaders of the guilds the courage" to promulgate the Ordinances of Justice (of 1293), which, among other provisions Machiavelli mentions, excluded the magnates from the governing priorate and made all members of a magnate family liable to punishment for crimes committed by any one of them. Predictably, the magnates vehemently resisted the restriction on their political influence and what had until then been de facto immunity from prosecution. Not only, says Machiavelli, did Giano della Bella feel the hatred of the "potenti," who considered him the "destroyer of their power [potenza]"; he also was the target of resentment from the "popolani ricchi"—the non-magnate elite families—who "thought his power [autorità] was excessive" and who seized the first opportunity ("occasione") to discredit and remove him. When, two years later (1295), Corso Donati was surprisingly acquitted after participating in a brawl "in which many nobles took part" and a "popolano was killed," an angry crowd seized weapons and went to Giano demanding that he enforce the anti-magnate laws of the Ordinances "of which he had been the author [inventore]." Giano, says Machiavelli, "wanted [Donati] punished," but he did not tell the crowd to lay down their arms and encouraged them to take their grievance to the Signoria. Instead they seized and sacked the palace of the judicial official who had acquitted Donati. This displeased "all the citizens," and Giano's enemies, hoping to bring him down, accused him of inciting the popolo to violence. The crowd offered to protect him, but he preferred to spare the city further violence on his account and decided to "leave, voluntarily, the city he had liberated from servitude to the powerful [potenti]" (*IF* 2.13.1–12).

The magnates, Machiavelli says, now had "high hopes of recovering their preeminence [dignità]. Realizing that their troubles resulted from their own divisions," they put aside their differences and, presenting a united front, sent representatives to the Signoria to ask for revisions of the Ordinances of Justice that would make convictions more difficult. Fear that the Signoria might respond favorably angered the popolo, and the city was suddenly "in arms." Armed magnates gathered at several points in the city, and "popolani in great numbers assembled under their banners at the residence of the Signoria." Recounting this sudden flare-up of potential mayhem, Machiavelli introduces an episode, largely of his own invention, in which a group of peacemakers consisting of "popolari," "nobili," and "certain well-respected religious" intervene and persuade both sides to lay down their arms (*IF* 2.14.1–6). His sources give the barest notice of this intervention. Villani (*Cronica* 9.12) briefly mentions the mediation of "frati di buona gente,"[4] and Leonardo Bruni (*History* 4.43) says only that "good men interceded and urged [the opposing sides] to make peace."[5] Attributing his own views to the peacemakers, Machiavelli has them remind the magnates that their "arrogance [superbia] and nefarious conduct [cattivo governo]" are what caused them to lose their office-holding rights and become subject to the punishments prescribed in the Ordinances. They tell the magnates that "taking up arms now to regain with force what they let be taken from them as a result of their own internal divisions and wicked behavior was nothing more than a desire to destroy the patria and make their situation worse." The popolo, Machiavelli has the mediators say, "is greatly superior to [the magnates] in numbers, wealth, and animosity [odio, toward their opponents]" and, moreover, "the 'nobility,' which they claim gives them precedence over others [mediante la quale e' pareva loro avanzare gli altri], has no teeth"—literally, does not fight ("non combatteva"). "If matters came to arms, [their alleged nobility] would be revealed to be an empty name [uno nome vano], unable to defend them against so many." Machiavelli here ascribes to the magnates the same assertion of superiority and "precedence" he had imputed to the "primi" of the early sixteenth century in the *Discursus florentinarum rerum* and exposes their self-declared "nobility" as delusional on every level, including that of martial valor. The peacemakers had a warning for the popolo too, namely, that "it is not prudent always to want a total victory and not wise to make men desperate, because those who have no good reason to hope do not fear [committing] evil." The popolo should bear in mind that "the nobles had honored the city in wars and that it is therefore neither good nor just to persecute them with such hatred." In this fictionalized scene the voices of moderation prevail: the popolo agrees to make it a bit more difficult to bring accusations against magnates (*IF* 2.14.6–9), both parties lay down their arms, and the popolo remains in control of the government (*IF* 2.15.1–2). Left unexplained is the seeming contradiction between the judgment that the magnates lacked the strength to defeat the popolo and the assertion that they had "honored the city" fighting in its wars.

"ALL WHO WANTED ANY *ESTRAORDINARIA* THING TURNED TO HIM"

Machiavelli represents the rupture of the Guelf elite into the factions of White Guelfs, led by the Cerchi family, and Black Guelfs, led by the Donati, as among

[4] For the edition of Villani cited here, see Chapter 4, note 8.

[5] Leonardo Bruni, *History of the Florentine People*, 3 vols., ed. and tr. J. Hankins (Cambridge, Mass.: Harvard University Press, 2001–7), vol. 1, p. 384; passages cited by book number and numbered subdivisions. Machiavelli may have read Bruni's *History* in the 1476 Florentine translation by Donato Acciaiuoli, more easily available to modern readers in *Istoria fiorentina di Leonardo Aretino*, 3 vols. (Florence: Felice Le Monnier, 1855–60); cited passage in vol. 1, p. 459.

the most traumatic events in Florence's early history. Occasional manifestations of enmity in the late 1290s escalated into dangerous clashes, including the brawl at the May Day festivities of 1300 between brigades of young men from both families and their friends that left many injured and, by "dividing the whole city, was the origin of much iniquity [di molto male principio]" (*IF* 2.17.5–9). With "the whole city in arms," Machiavelli says, the "Signori [the priorate] and the laws were overwhelmed by the rage of the powerful [dalla furia de' potenti vinte]" (*IF* 2.18.3). Initially weaker than their White rivals, the leaders of the Blacks, including Corso Donati, met and decided to ask the pope (Boniface VIII) to send "someone of royal blood" to aid their cause. Machiavelli's comment that the meeting of the Blacks "came to the attention" of the Signoria suggests that it had been held in secret. Echoing Villani (9.42), who describes the meeting as a conspiracy ("consiglio e congiura"), but following more closely Leonardo Bruni's account (4.56) that the accusation came from the Whites, Machiavelli says the latter denounced it as a "conspiracy against liberty [una congiura contro al vivere libero]" (*IF* 2.18.5). He may have agreed, perhaps also seeing the appeal to an obviously foreign "prince of royal blood" as similar to the ottimati's invitation to the Spanish army to remove Soderini and restore the Medici in 1512 and as another example of how "defective ordini" permit factions to summon foreign forces, as he writes in *Discourses* 1.7. The sudden flare-up from a minor confrontation to a state of incipient civil war, with all the important families lined up on one side or the other, mirrors the rapidity with which Buondelmonte's broken betrothal led to the violent division of the entire elite.

The foreign prince invited by Boniface was Charles of Valois, "brother of the king [Philip IV] of France." In Machiavelli's telling Charles "armed all his amici and *partigiani*"—his Black Guelf allies—"which made the popolo so fearful that he might deprive them of their liberty" that "everyone took up arms and waited in their homes to be ready in the event that Charles made a move." Machiavelli says the Cerchi and the Whites had brought on themselves the "hatred" of the multitude because they "conducted themselves arrogantly [superbamente]" when their faction was in power. Hence, Corso Donati and the Blacks deemed the moment propitious to bring Charles to Florence (*IF* 2.19.2–6). Machiavelli may be referring here to Vieri de' Cerchi's contemptuous rejection of Pope Boniface's advice to end the feud with the Donati and make peace: Vieri told the pope that "peace presupposes war, and since there was no war between him and the Donati, he did not know why it was necessary to make peace" (*IF* 2.17.3). Machiavelli could also be alluding to the White party's indifferent response a few months later to the attempted mediation by the papal legate, Cardinal Matthew of Acquasparta, who encountered "difficulties" dealing with the Whites who, believing themselves the stronger of the factions, thought they had less to fear (*IF* 2.17.12). Whatever the reason, Machiavelli's assertion that the multitude hated the Cerchi puts both factions in a bad light. The antipathy toward the Whites, he says, encouraged Corso

Donati, then in exile, to return to the city, confident that the French prince would support him and that the popolo would not oppose the Blacks. Corso and the Black exiles entered the city (on November 5, 1301) "without being hindered by anyone." Friends of Vieri de' Cerchi urged him to meet Corso, but he refused, "saying he wanted the popolo of Florence, against whom [Corso] was coming, to punish him." This was Vieri's third misguided assumption and missed opportunity. "The opposite occurred," says Machiavelli: Corso "was welcomed, not punished, by the popolo and Vieri was forced to flee in order to save himself." As the Blacks, accompanied by Charles's troops, entered the city, the Cerchi and other leaders of their faction, with no hope of support from the popolo, retreated to their countryside strongholds and went into exile (*IF* 2.19.7–9).

Yet Machiavelli's judgment of Corso Donati and the Blacks is more critical. He devotes more attention to Corso than to Vieri, in part of course because the latter never returned from exile whereas Corso remained a commanding, but also dangerous and destructive, presence in Florence until his death in 1308. Entering the city in November 1301 under the protective umbrella of Charles's forces, he gathered many followers ("assai amici e popolo"), broke into the communal jail and released the prisoners, forcibly removed the priors from office just days after their election, and appointed a new Signoria entirely from the Black party. Corso's henchmen and followers then engaged in five days of violence and plunder against the properties of the Whites (*IF* 2.19.8). Soon thereafter, another crisis "put the whole city once again in an uproar" when Corso Donati's son, Simone, assaulted and killed Nicola de' Cerchi (a brother of Corso Donati's wife, a fact not mentioned by Machiavelli but highlighted by Villani [9.49]). Simone also died of wounds suffered in the attack. No punishments were forthcoming, however, because, as Machiavelli says, the Black party was "protected" by the new priors they had chosen, an example, so Machiavelli implies, of how elite factions corrupt justice and subvert the laws. To hide the "infamia [opprobrium]" that Simone's murderous attack brought on them, the Blacks alleged—perhaps with forged documents, Machiavelli suggests, as does Villani—a conspiracy by the Cerchi to retake power. This accusation led (in March 1302) to the conviction, banishment, confiscation of properties, and destruction of homes of all the Cerchi and their followers in the White party, including, Machiavelli notes, "the poet Dante" (*IF* 2.20.3–8).

Machiavelli makes Corso Donati the emblematic figure of the magnates' recklessness, vainglory, and self-destructiveness. Following the 1301 coup, the city was peaceful, he says—with one exception: "Messer Corso alone was agitated [inquieto], because it did not seem to him that he held the rank [grado] he believed he deserved in the city." What Corso "believed he deserved" Machiavelli does not say in his own voice, preferring to let Corso's enemies express their perception of his ambition. The source of Corso's unhappiness, even after his faction had expelled its rivals, was that Florence still had a "governo popolare" and that "the republic was administered by many inferior to him." "Goaded by these miseries [passioni], he resolved to give his dishonorable intention an appearance of honor with an honorable pretext [adonestare con una onesta cagione la disonestà dello animo suo]" (*IF* 2.21.1–2). Machiavelli often underscores attempts to cover the dishonorable with a mask of false honor (among other places, as we shall soon see, in the speech in *Histories* 3.5 that denounces the baneful history of Florentine factions). He says Donati "slandered [calunniava] many citizens," accusing them of administering public finances for private benefit ("privati commodi"). Asserting that they should be identified and punished, he posed as a defender of honest administration of public resources. Machiavelli points to the sinister aspect of his plan: his "opinion" found favor, not only among those who shared his dishonorable purpose of removing "inferior" citizens from government but also with those who, from "ignoranzia," assumed that Corso was motivated by "love of country." Machiavelli depicts Corso as a demagogue, beguiling and misleading the people with false accusations and slanders for the purpose of augmenting his own power. We have seen that in *Discourses* 1.8 Machiavelli exposes the corrosive effect of "calunnie" in the absence of procedures for adjudicating them on the basis of evidence and witnesses. In spewing slander without evidence or fear of being refuted in a legal inquiry, Corso's demagoguery parallels that of Manlius Capitolinus, who similarly accused certain "private citizens" of embezzling public funds and, in so doing, gathered a following among Rome's plebeians. In the Florentine case, however, the citizens Corso slandered enjoyed "favor with the popolo" and "defended themselves." The dispute escalated from "modi civili"—from what was permitted by law and the ordini—and "recourse was had to arms [si venne alle armi]." Once again, the city was suddenly and perilously divided—Corso, with many grandi (including Florence's bishop who came from the magnate Tosinghi) and "some popolani" on one side; on the other, the Signoria and the "majority of the popolo"—and "there was fighting in several parts of the city." The Signoria had to ask Lucca for help in quelling the strife. Order was re-established, and the popolo preserved its liberty and control of government ("rimase il popolo nello stato e libertà sua"). But, Machiavelli adds, there was "no punishment for those who had incited the armed conflict" (*IF* 2.21.3–6).

Just one chapter further on, Machiavelli again says the "city would have been peaceful if it had not been unsettled [perturbata] yet again by the restless spirit [animo inquieto] of messer Corso." Machiavelli then provides this portrait of Corso (2.22.11–15)—the first extended profile of a Florentine citizen in the *Histories*:

> To give himself notoriety [reputazione], he always held views contrary to those of the most powerful citizens. Whichever way he saw the popolo leaning, he directed his influence [autorità] there in order to make them more well-disposed [benivolo] toward him, with the result that he was the leader [capo] of all the

> conflicts and uprisings [novità], and all those who wanted any *estraordinaria* thing turned to him. For this reason, many renowned citizens hated him, and their hatred visibly grew to the point where the party of the Blacks openly split, for messer Corso made use of private forces and power [forze e autorità private], while his adversaries relied on the government [stato]. So influential was his demeanor, however, that everyone feared him. Nonetheless, to deprive him of popular support—which is easy to extinguish in this way—they spread the word that he wanted to seize tyrannical power [che si voleva occupare la tirannide]. It was easy to persuade people of this, because his style of life exceeded all civic norms. This opinion of him greatly increased when he married a daughter of Uguccione della Faggiuola, the very powerful leader of the Ghibelline and White party in Tuscany.

The portrait has two dimensions. On the one hand, Corso embodies the political style of his elite class in inciting division and tumult, currying the people's favor to serve his own ambition, assisting others in the pursuit of illegalities ("alcuna cosa estraordinaria"), thus acquiring partigiani, and above all, relying on the "private forces" of his faction. On the other hand, the portrait depicts Corso as aspiring to rise above his social peers and even above the narrow circle of the leadership of the Black Guelf party. Although, according to Machiavelli, his adversaries, in order to deprive him of the popolo's favor, exploited the accusation that he sought to make himself tyrant of Florence, Machiavelli's profile suggests it was not far from the truth. Such an ambition is implied in his interpretation of why, in 1304, Corso took no part in the street battles between the factions (during which an immense fire consumed a great part of the city center). Unlike Villani (9.71), who claims Corso stayed away from the tumults because he was ill with gout, Machiavelli ascribes his absence to the more sinister motive of planning "more easily to become the master [arbitro] of both parties [Blacks and Whites], when, tired of fighting, they come to an agreement" (2.21.16–17).

Corso's marriage into a noble non-Florentine family—something Florentines of the time almost never did—and to a daughter of the chief of the Tuscan Ghibellines no less, fed the perception of his tyrannical aspirations. Following Villani (9.96) and Bruni (4.106), Machiavelli says the marriage alliance persuaded his adversaries to take up arms against him. His antagonists now included the long-time leaders of the Black Guelfs who had been his comrades-in-arms (all magnates of course), and the "majority of the popolo." The Signoria submitted a formal "accusa"—an indictment—to one of the judicial magistracies, charging him with seeking to make himself "tyrant" of Florence "with the help of Uguccione." In the "space of two hours" the indictment produced a summons, which Corso ignored, and then conviction for contumacy as a "rebel," which cost him all protections of the law. The Signoria and the neighborhood militia companies of the popolo immediately set out to bring him to justice, but Machiavelli says Corso feared neither public awareness that his former allies had abandoned him, nor the judgment of the court, nor the authority of the Signoria, nor the multitude of enemies arrayed against him. He barricaded the streets of his neighborhood (San Pier Maggiore) and took refuge in the compound of family residences stoutly defended by his "partigiani." In the daylong battle, with many killed and wounded on both sides, the forces of the popolo, "although numerous," were unable to break through until they entered nearby houses and attacked from inside. Corso and his "most trusted friends" broke out of the compound, fled toward the city gate of Porta alla Croce, and headed east until the pursuing troops captured them in Rovezzano, two miles out. Machiavelli claims that Corso, so as not to let his enemies see him defeated and, as he feared, "torn to pieces," fell from his horse as the soldiers led him back to the city, and one of them cut his throat. The monks of San Salvi collected his remains and unceremoniously ("senza alcuno onore") buried him (*IF* 2.23.1–12).

Although Machiavelli often omits dates, in this case he notes that Donati's demise occurred in 1308 (*IF* 2.24.1) and, as Giovanni Villani had done (9.96), also provides an epitaph (*IF* 2.23.13–14):

> This was how messer Corso met his end. His patria and the party of the Black Guelfs owed him many things, both good and bad. If he had had a more serene spirit [animo piú quieto], his memory would be a happier one. Nonetheless, he deserves to be counted among the exceptional citizens [rari cittadini] that our city has had. In truth, his volatility [inquietudine] prevented his patria and his party from acknowledging their debts to him, and in the end it brought death to him and many ills [mali] to his patria and his party.

In asserting that Corso's party owed him some "good things," Machiavelli no doubt alludes to the uncontested dominance he gave the Black Guelfs in the coup of 1301. But he makes no mention of benefits to, or debts owed him by, the patria. Apart from Corso's restless and agitated spirit, never content with the victories and power he achieved, relentlessly clashing with opponents, and dividing even his own faction in pursuit of further personal ambition, the essence of Machiavelli's negative judgment of Corso Donati lies in his continual subversion of the laws and institutions of the communal government as he facilitated illegalities and "availed himself of his private forces and power." The comment that, despite all, Corso "deserves to be counted among the *rari* citizens our city has had" links him in Machiavelli's narrative to that other, and much more successful, manipulator of private methods in the service of "estraordinaria" ambition a century later, Cosimo de' Medici. As we shall see, Machiavelli associates Cosimo too with aspirations to tyranny in ways that echo his portrait of messer Corso.

The rest of book 2 of the *Histories* is dominated by several attempts by the magnates to overturn the governing group and rescind the laws that barred them from the Signoria and subjected them to the penalties prescribed in the Ordinances of Justice. Each episode was more violent than the preceding one, but they all failed. The first was a plot (in 1323) by a group of "nobles" to secure the repatriation of Guelf exiles. The Signoria promised to allow "Guelf rebels" to return if they joined the defense of Prato against Castruccio Castracani of Lucca. Machiavelli says 4,000 exiles accepted the offer. But after the Florentine army of 20,000 infantry and 1,500 cavalry dissuaded Castruccio from an open battle and he returned to Lucca (*IF* 2.26.5–7), the Signoria withdrew the offer of repatriation for the exiles, whereupon magnates in the city, "in order to see if they could obtain by agreement what they had not been able to obtain by force," asked the Signoria to reconsider. The Signoria refused, Machiavelli writes, because the "universalità" was firmly opposed to any concession to magnates or exiles. "The indignant magnates," reversing tactics, then attempted to accomplish "by force" what they failed to get through entreaties: they conspired with the exiles to have them approach the city while armed magnates within prepared to support them. But the plot was revealed, and when the exiles arrived they found "the city in arms, mobilized"—"ordinata" (the popular militias readied)—"to repulse those without." The magnates in the city "were so frightened that no one dared take up arms." Many citizens wanted to punish the conspirators, but, "although everyone knew who the guilty [delinquenti] were, no one dared name, let alone accuse, them." To sidestep these fears, Machiavelli says, the Signoria instructed the members of the legislative councils each to write, in secret, the names of the "delinquenti" and deliver them to the capitano del popolo, who indicted and fined three magnates, Amerigo Donati, a Frescobaldi, and a Gherardini. Machiavelli comments that the judge was perhaps more lenient "than their crimes deserved" (*IF* 2.27).

The second episode is from 1340, when "new causes of subversion [nuove cagioni di alterazioni]" appeared. This involved abuses of power by non-magnate "potenti cittadini" from elite families who sought to "increase or protect their power" in two ways: by limiting eligibility for political offices to themselves and their "amici," and by appointing judicial officials who would render judgments favorable to them and detrimental to their enemies. So important did they consider having judicial officials who would do their bidding that, in addition to the "rettori ordinarii [constitutionally appointed magistrates]," they added another "estraordinariamente"—in violation of the communal statutes—to whom they gave full power ("ogni autorità") over citizens. This official, in undisguised support of the ruling "potenti," maliciously prosecuted many persons, including the wealthy magnates Piero de' Bardi and Bardo Frescobaldi. Closely following Villani here, Machiavelli makes it clear that the controversy originated with the non-magnate "cittadini potenti" who ignored communal law in creating an extra-constitutional official to punish their adversaries. The offended magnates, "being nobles and by nature arrogant [naturalmente superbi], hence unable to tolerate the wrongs unjustly inflicted on them at the bidding of a few powerful citizens," organized a conspiracy that included many "magnate families [famiglie nobili] together with some families of the popolo"—non-magnate elite—"who disliked the tyranny of those in power." The conspirators assembled large numbers of armed men in their homes, ready to raise a revolt and kill the hated official and the ruling group on All Souls' Day when "everyone would be in church praying for their departed," after which they intended to appoint a Signoria of their choosing and "reform the government [lo stato riformare]" with a "nuovo ordine" (*IF* 2.32.1–7). Machiavelli echoes Villani (12.118), who says they wanted to "abolish the office of the priors," institute a "nuovo stato," and, "according to some, undo [disfare] the popolo"—dismantle the popular institutions created in the 1280s and 1290s.

Before the conspirators could carry out their coup, one of them—from the Bardi family—revealed the plot to a brother-in-law from the Alberti, a powerful non-magnate family of wealthy bankers. With the conspiracy exposed, there were demands for the Signoria to call the people to arms. But, as Machiavelli notes, the standard-bearer of justice at that moment, Taldo Valori, and one of the priors, Francesco Salviati, "were related by marriage [parenti] to the Bardi" plotters and advised against calling the militias, warning more generally against "arming the people for every slight thing, because power given to an undisciplined multitude never did any good." They thought it better first to learn the "truth of the matter" and then have the guilty punished "civilmente" (in established judicial proceedings) than to act precipitously on the basis of unconfirmed reports and run the risk of destroying the city. Machiavelli thus highlights the family support—even among affinal kin—that the magnate conspirators had in the Signoria itself. In the event it was not enough: popular anger forced the Signoria to summon the people in arms to the piazza. The Bardi and Frescobaldi, "determined to win with glory or die without shame," also took up arms, defending themselves in their Oltrarno quarter, barricading the bridges, and hoping for help from the "nobles of the contado" (the many magnate families in the surrounding countryside) "and other friends of theirs." But they were soon surrounded by "popolani," and an agreement was negotiated whereby most of the Bardi and Frescobaldi "and their friends," except those who had taken up arms, were allowed to leave the city and go to their "castella"—their contado strongholds. In the aftermath of the failed revolt, Machiavelli notes, the commune of Florence purchased from the Bardi the "castello" of Mangona and that of Vernio, north of Florence, and passed the law (noted in Chapter 5) prohibiting any citizen from owning "castella" within twenty miles of the city (*IF* 2.32.8–20).

Defeating the Bardi and Frescobaldi, Machiavelli comments, "was not enough for those who were governing" the commune, "for, as always happens, the more power men have, the worse they use it and the more arrogant [insolenti] they become." To the official whose abuses had provoked the magnates to rebel, the ruling group added another with jurisdiction over the contado and with such broad powers that no one under any suspicion could live safely either in or outside the city: "the magnates were so infuriated that they were ready to sell the city and themselves in order to gain revenge. They waited for the opportunity, which presented itself well and which they used even better" (*IF* 2.32.22–3). Machiavelli here alludes to the invitation to the French-Neapolitan nobleman Gualtieri di Brienne to take control of Florence's government in the deepening military and financial crisis of the early 1340s. This is the third attempt by the magnates in the *Florentine Histories* to overturn the existing political order. "Unhappy for the reasons explained above," the grandi believed the time had come for them "to be able to satisfy their burning desire [spegnere lo incendio loro] [even at the cost of] the ruination [rovina] of the city, thinking there was no other way to subdue [domare] the popolo that had tormented them than to accept the rule of a prince" who would reward their virtú and restrain the "insolenzia" of their tormentors: "they had great hopes for the benefits they would gain if [Brienne] acquired his principate through them." What the grandi so ardently desired was liberation from the political disenfranchisement imposed by the Ordinances of Justice, in return for which, as Machiavelli says, they were prepared to jettison the popular republican constitution that had excluded them from the Signoria since 1293 and replace it with a princely regime, which, Machiavelli implies, would have been tantamount to the "rovina" of the city. Confident that Brienne would reward their support, the magnates encouraged him "to seize total power [pigliare la signoria del tutto]" (*IF* 2.33.13–15). Brienne's rule is, for Machiavelli, an example of how tyranny originates: one class or party raises up a strongman to subdue its rival only to see him dominate both.

Machiavelli makes it clear, nonetheless, that the invitation to Brienne to make himself lord of Florence did not come from the magnates alone. He names several non-magnate elite families ("famiglie popolane") who added their support: Peruzzi, Acciaiuoli, Antellesi (Dell'Antella), and Buonaccorsi—all merchant-banking families "burdened by debts" and nearing bankruptcy. These were wealthy families of the same class and social stature as the magnates but who had escaped designation as such. Machiavelli does not explain the financial crisis they were facing, saying only that, unable to "pay their debts" from their own assets, they tried to meet their obligations with "other people's money" and, "with the enslavement [servitú] of the patria" under Brienne, "to free themselves from enslavement [servitú] to their creditors" (*IF* 2.33.16) thereby securing their financial survival. Despite their differing motivations in this risky plan, Machiavelli underscores the complicity of both sectors of the elite class in delivering Florence into the hands of an ambitious foreigner. For the endangered merchant bankers, the motivation was to preserve their commercial and banking empires. Some magnates were similarly motivated (the Bardi and Frescobaldi were also merchant bankers whose companies were in difficulty), but all magnates shared the incentive to roll back the punitive legislation and disenfranchisement inflicted on them by the Ordinances of Justice. Machiavelli makes it clear that the elite class as a whole—magnate and non-magnate, merchant bankers or not—came together to safeguard class-wide interests.

Machiavelli inserts in the narrative, just before Brienne becomes signore of Florence, an invented speech in direct discourse—the first such speech in the *Histories*—delivered by one of the incumbent priors to Brienne. The unnamed prior warns him that "those who are now your friends and who urge you to take this decision will try to do away with you as soon as they have defeated their enemies under your command" (*IF* 2.34.12). The Signoria, he says, is deeply disturbed by Brienne's debasement of the city's institutions, especially his plan to summon the people to the piazza of the church of Santa Croce (where he resided) to approve his demand for "la signoria libera" (*IF* 2.34.4–5)—unhampered lordship. Such plebiscites, which the Medici would often use, had no legitimate place in Florentine legislative procedures. The orator accuses Brienne of "seeking unconstitutionally [estraordinariamente] that which we have not granted you constitutionally [per l'ordinario]" (*IF* 2.34.8)—by law and statute. He warns that the Florentines' love of liberty has been preserved through generations and is enshrined in public buildings and the banners of "liberi ordini" (*IF* 2.34.15–16). Brienne's response was to have his henchmen sack the government palace, expel the priors, and tear up the banner of the popolo (*IF* 2.35.8). He prohibited the Signoria from meeting in the palace, confiscated the banners of the standard-bearers of the companies of the people (the neighborhood militias), repatriated the Bardi and Frescobaldi, and abolished the Ordinances of Justice (*IF* 2.36.1). To this point, he was satisfying the wishes of the magnates.

Brienne quickly revealed, however, that he had his own agenda and would not exclusively serve magnates' interests. Among the policies that alienated the wealthy citizens who had raised him to power Machiavelli includes the cancellation of "assignments [assegnamenti]"— revenue from indirect taxes pledged (as Machiavelli read in Villani, 13.8) to repay communal creditors who made large loans during the costly war against Lucca (in the late 1330s). Machiavelli mentions this in just one sentence (*IF* 2.36.2), without explaining that the loss of these promised repayments could not have come at a worse moment for the endangered companies. The elite families also deplored the cruelty of Brienne's administration of justice, especially the execution of members of the Medici, Rucellai, and Altoviti families (*IF* 2.33.17) and many monetary penalties. But Machiavelli does not let the elite's disillusionment with Brienne obscure their initial willingness to accept a princely regime to safeguard their interests. He makes it clear that the families that championed Brienne had no qualms about the illegitimacy of his rule or his degradation of communal magistracies. But what enraged them most of all was his alliance with the "plebe." Machiavelli says Brienne was suspicious of the grandi because "he could not believe that the haughty [generosi] spirits typical of the nobility would be content obeying him." Machiavelli generally advised princes to govern in alliance with the people rather than the nobles, who, as he says in *Prince* 9, consider themselves the prince's equals and are consequently more difficult to control. He has Brienne reflect this advice in deciding to transfer his favors to the "plebe," "believing that, with their support and with foreign arms, he could sustain his tyranny" (*IF* 2.36.3–6).

Just a year after Brienne became "signore" of Florence in 1342, the same elite families that had supported his assumption of power conspired to expel him. Machiavelli names the leading families, both magnate and non-magnate, in each of three conspiracies. In the first, led by Bishop Acciaiuoli from the powerful non-magnate banking and trading family, Machiavelli lists the magnate Bardi, Rossi, Frescobaldi, and Scali and the non-magnate Altoviti, Magalotti, Strozzi, and Mancini. The second group was led by the magnates Manno and Corso Donati (a descendant of the famous Corso) and included the magnate Pazzi, Cavicciuli, and Cerchi, and the non-magnate Albizzi. The magnate Antonio Adimari was the leader of the third group whose principal families were the non-magnate Medici, Bordoni (Bordini in Machiavelli's spelling), Rucellai, and Aldobrandini. Machiavelli's lists, however incomplete, show that the magnate and non-magnate sectors of the elite were (temporarily) burying their differences in the effort to be rid of the hated tyrant. Not all magnates were on board, however. He notes that a Brunelleschi and a Buondelmonti urged Brienne to send his cavalry through the streets to frighten the populace and kill suspected plotters. Machiavelli repeats Villani's story (13.16) that Brienne rejected this advice but concocted instead an even more terrible plan to invite three hundred citizens to a meeting at which he allegedly intended to kill or imprison them all. Knowing it was a trap, the invited citizens stayed away. The conspirators acted quickly and drove Brienne from Florence on July 26, 1343 (*IF* 2.36.16–30). "All heads of families, both *nobili* [magnate] and *popolane* [non-magnate elite]" met to organize the assault, except for some of the (magnate) Buondelmonti and Cavalcanti and "those four families of the popolo" whose precarious financial situation had persuaded them to support Brienne's rise to power. They initially broke with the other elite families, joining the "butchers and others of the lower class [infima plebe] who came armed to the piazza in [Brienne's] defense." When they saw the strength of the assembled conspirators, however, "they changed their minds." The elite class that Machiavelli portrayed as nearly unanimously in favor of Brienne's seizure of power he now depicts as all but united in bringing him down. He notes that some magnates took advantage of the chaos to destroy the public records of judicial convictions: one or more members of the Donati broke into the "publica camera" (the earliest repository of official documents) and burned the archive of the podestà (*IF* 2.37.1–9). They were, evidently, quite thorough in their vandalism, for today nothing survives before 1343 in the archives of the podestà and the other judicial officials.

Despite the temporary rapprochement of "grandi" and "popolane" families, reflected in the even division of the governing committee of fourteen created immediately after Brienne's expulsion (*IF* 2.37.13), Machiavelli shows that elite unity did not last long. The reform committee of fourteen gave the magnates a third of the seats in an expanded priorate and half the posts in all other offices. With this (very temporary) reorganization of government, Machiavelli suggests, perhaps facetiously, that "the city would have regained some peace if the grandi had been content to live with the moderation required in civic life [con quella modestia che nella vita civile si richiede]. But they did the opposite. As private citizens, they wanted no equals [privati, non volevono compagni] and in the magistracies they wanted to be signori"—bosses. Daily occurrences of magnate "insolenzia e superbia" angered the popolo, "who lamented that, for one tyrant eliminated, a thousand had been born. So much did the impudence [insolenzie] on one side and resentments [sdegni] on the other increase that the popolani leaders remonstrated with the bishop [Acciaiuoli] over the dishonorable behavior [disonestà] of the grandi and their unsatisfactory cooperation with the popolo [la non buona compagnia che al popolo facevano]" (*IF* 2.39.1–7). The popolani leaders soon insisted that the magnates be removed from the priorate, which, Machiavelli says, "gravely angered their spirits." He has Ridolfo de' Bardi, head of the powerful magnate family and merchant company, say that the magnates "would defend their [rights to] public offices [onori] in the face of the same risk with which they had regained them." But when they saw the "whole popolo in arms," they thought better of fighting and stayed safely in their homes. The magnate priors left the palace, and offices of government were again in the hands of only non-magnates (*IF* 2.39.11–15).

Just days later, however, the magnates made one last, and futile, effort to reverse their fortunes. Machiavelli devotes considerable attention to these clashes and the significance of the magnate defeat. Seeing their opportunity in hostilities (in late September 1343) between the popolo and the "plebe minuta" over grain shortages and prices, the grandi hoped, Machiavelli says, "they could justly [ragionevolmente: by right] regain by force that which had been unjustly taken from them by force" (*IF* 2.40.4). They armed themselves and requested help from "friends" as far away as Lombardy. The Signoria likewise assembled an armed force and appealed to neighboring cities for assistance. The two components of the elite prepared for pitched battles in the streets, and both invited help from outside Florence. But in this last gasp of the magnates their antagonists expanded to include a broad coalition of non-magnate elite families together with the neighborhood militia companies of the social popolo, all under the "gonfalone [banner]" of justice that was the symbol of the constitution of 1293 (*IF* 2.40.10). The forces of the "popolani" who met the magnates in the streets now included guildsmen, artisans, and laborers—the elements of Florentine society that were about to enter the political stage and which dominate the third book of the *Histories*.

Following his chronicle sources, Villani and Marchionne di Coppo Stefani, Machiavelli describes the initial positioning of leading magnate families at strategic points in the city center, which they soon abandoned, however, having no chance against the armed neighborhood companies. "Three-quarters of the city," he says, "were in the hands of the popolo; only one quarter remained under the control of the grandi, but it was the most difficult": the Oltrarno, to which the magnates blocked access by barricading the bridges over the river. Having tried and failed to break through on two bridges, the companies of the popolo concentrated their attack on the Carraia bridge as the weakest of the four because it lacked towers and because several non-magnate elite families from this area, particularly the Capponi, joined in the attack. Machiavelli further notes that, once the popular militias overran the magnate families of that neighborhood, all the non-magnate elite families of the Oltrarno joined the militias, implying that, until then, some had been hedging their bets, uncertain which way to lean. The Bardi were the largest and most powerful of the magnate clans, and, even in these dire straits, "neither the defeat of the other [magnates], nor the united popolo arrayed against them, nor the dwindling hope of help [from outside Florence] could frighten them, determined as they were to die fighting or see their houses burned and sacked rather than voluntarily submit to the will of their enemies." But this was, as Machiavelli reveals, only bravado. They held out for a while, but when six of the militias went up the hill of San Giorgio behind the Bardi defenses and descended toward their palazzi, "the assault caused them to lose courage and sealed the victory of the popolo." The Bardi left the bridges to defend their homes, as the assailants breached the barricades on the Ponte Vecchio and put the Bardi to flight. Many found refuge in nearby homes of elite families (only one a magnate family). At the end of the battle, "the lowest ranks [la parte piú ignobile] of the popolo"—Machiavelli does not say what mix of lower guildsmen, artisans, or workers this group consisted of—"thirsty for plunder, pillaged and sacked the Bardi houses and destroyed and burned their towers with such rage [rabbia] that even the cruelest enemy of Florence would have been ashamed of so much destruction" (*IF* 2.41).

What did Machiavelli think of the hopeless and quixotic obstinacy of the Bardi who resolved to "die fighting"? Actually, he mentions no deaths in the assault, and Villani too (13.21) says "no notable person, and few others, died." Twice in the space of a few days, Machiavelli has the magnates thunderously declare their readiness to defend to the death their rights and honor, only to describe them losing their nerve and either staying secluded in their homes (*IF* 2.39.14) or running to safety provided by sympathetic neighbors (*IF* 2.41.15). What, then, are we to make of the oft-quoted sentences in book 2's final chapter? "This destruction [rovina] of the nobles was so great and so weakened their party [parte] that never again did they dare take up arms against the popolo; on the contrary, they became ever more amicable and humble [umani e abietti]," to which Machiavelli adds that this is why Florence was bereft not only of arms but of all "generosità." As already noted, "generosità" in Machiavelli's texts usually means consciousness of highborn status and implies the haughtiness, boldness, or fierceness thought to be characteristic of nobles. But the martial performance of the magnates in the conflicts of 1340 and 1343 was, as Machiavelli shows, anything but fierce. Whatever admirable contributions magnates had made to Florence's wars were far back in the past. Florentines of all classes were ceasing to fight in the city's wars, and dependence on mercenaries steadily increased. So there may be some sarcasm in the assertion that the "rovina" of the magnates made Florence militarily weak. Machiavelli's preferred solution for the republic's military needs was certainly not its old warrior elite, which he saw as more interested in dominating the rest of society than defending the patria. The remedy he favored for the republic's defense had its origins in those neighborhood militias that trapped the Bardi and forced them to flee in 1343.

"FAMIGLIE FATALI"

The opening chapter of book 3 of the *Histories* amplifies and complicates the judgment Machiavelli offers of the defeat of the magnates at the end of book 2. Some interpretations see in this famous introductory chapter evidence of a turn in Machiavelli's thinking away from the radically popular stance of the *Discourses on Livy* to a more conservative politics grounded in greater appreciation of the elite class. Certain sentences, lifted out of context, can give that impression, but an integrated analysis, read against the background of book 2, suggests a different interpretation.

Evoking the arguments of chapters 4 and 5 of the first book of the *Discourses*, Machiavelli opens the chapter by affirming that the momentous ("gravi") and inevitable ("naturali") conflicts between "popolari" and "nobili" occur because "nobles want to rule [comandare], and *popolari* do not want to obey." But the assertion that these hostilities are "the cause of all the ills [mali] that occur in cities" appears to deviate from the opinion in *Discourses* 1.4 that conflicts between the classes were the foundation of Rome's liberty and expansive power. Machiavelli modifies the picture as the chapter unfolds. The "popolari" of this chapter are not the non-magnate elite he calls "popolani" in book 2. There is never a question in book 2 of the governing non-magnate elite "obeying" the magnates. As he looks ahead to the social conflicts of book 3, Machiavelli here uses "popolari" to refer to the broad social popolo—the non-elite guildsmen, local merchants, notaries, and artisans. In the last chapter of book 2, in a brief mention of the reorganization of government offices following the 1343 defeat of the magnates, Machiavelli refers to three categories of popolo—"potente, mediocre e basso." The "potenti," he mistakenly says, were given two seats in the priorate (which from 1343 consisted of eight members), the "mediocri" three, and the "bassi" three. Machiavelli took this inaccurate information from Villani (13.22), who reports the same apportionment of seats among "grassi," "mediani," and "artefici minuti [lower guildsmen]." In fact, the new popular government's electoral reform law of October 1343 says only that three of the eight priors in each term had to come from the fourteen minor guilds, the rest from the seven major guilds.[6] What is significant, despite the error, is Machiavelli's distinction between the "potenti" of the popolo—elite non-magnates—and the non-elite popolo that he divides into "mediocre" and "basso." The first sentence of *Histories* 3.1 is not about the conflicts between magnate and non-magnate elites, which, however "gravi," were certainly not "naturali" in Machiavelli's understanding. Here "popolari" refers to the non-elite popolo—the combination of "mediocri" and "bassi."

The introductory chapter proceeds to a number of contrasts between ancient Rome and Florence, mostly to Florence's disadvantage. But it begins with something they shared. Hostilities between "nobili" and "popolari" kept Rome "disunited [disunita]" and Florence "divided [diviso]." The "effects," Machiavelli says, were different in each city, but the reason for this is that, on the Roman side of the comparison, he considers in this chapter only the hostilities of the ancient republic's "beginning" ("le nimicizie che furono nel principio in Roma"), thereby excluding the degeneration of Rome's hostilities into civil war in the aftermath of the reforms of the Gracchi and the emergence of the warlords with their private armies. With this important limitation, Machiavelli can say that in Rome hostilities were resolved by debating and laws, but in Florence by fighting and the exile and death of many citizens. In Rome, he continues, hostilities always increased military virtú; in Florence, they completely extinguished it. These two contrasts are both, apparently, to Rome's favor. But the next one is not: Roman "nimicizie," he says, "led that city from equality [ugualità] of citizens to a very great inequality [disaguaglianza]; those in Florence brought [the city] from inequality to an astonishing [mirabile] equality." Equality—the absence of a nobility claiming separate status and privilege—is, for Machiavelli, essential to republics; conversely, the presence of a nobility is a grave danger to them. We have already seen that in the *Discursus florentinarum rerum* he affirms that Florence's equality renders it suitable for republican government only. To state that Rome's otherwise beneficial hostilities led to a "very great inequality" clearly alludes to the later, disastrous, period of Rome's republican history: the formation of large-scale factions and private armies led by strongmen who contended for power in violation of the ordini. Without for the moment commenting on how this third divergence of "effects" favors Florence, Machiavelli claims that its cause was the "different objectives [diversi fini]" of each city's popolo: whereas Rome's popolo sought to enjoy offices together with the nobles, Florence's popolo fought to have the government to itself without the "nobles." Because the desire of the Roman popolo was "more

[6] See my *Corporatism and Consensus in Florentine Electoral Politics, 1280–1400* (Chapel Hill: University of North Carolina Press, 1982), p. 142.

reasonable [or just: "ragionevole]," he says, Rome's nobles yielded to the demands of the plebs without resorting to arms. After some disputes, they agreed to a law that satisfied the popolo while allowing the nobles to keep their offices.

By contrast, Machiavelli says, the aim of Florence's popolo was "harmful and unjust [ingiurioso e ingiusto], so much so that the nobility [the magnates] prepared to defend itself with greater force." Florentine hostilities consequently resulted in bloodshed and banishment of citizens, and all the laws were made to the advantage of the victors, not for the common benefit. The "victories" of Rome's popolo increased military valor (made Rome "piú virtuosa"), because the "popolani, being able to participate in the administration of magistracies, armies, and military commands with the nobles, fully acquired the same virtú [the nobles] had; hence, as [Rome's] virtú grew, its power did likewise." But in Florence, "with the victory of the popolo, the nobles lost political offices, and if they wished to reacquire them it was necessary for them not only to be, but to appear, similar to the popolani in their behavior [governi], spirit [animo], and way of life [modo del vivere]." From this, Machiavelli continues, came the changes in family heraldry and names that the nobles made "in order to seem like the popolo [per parere di popolo]." This may refer to the transfer by the popular government (in October 1343) of many magnates to the ranks of the popolo (briefly noted in *IF* 2.42.2) in order, as Machiavelli interprets the measure, "to weaken" the magnates. It may also refer to the decisions by various branches of magnate clans in the following decades to separate from their parent lineages, assume new surnames, and gain admittance to the popolo.[7] Repeating what he wrote at the end of book 2, Machiavelli says the result of the changes imposed on the magnates was that their "virtú in arms and prideful spirit [generosità di animo] were extinguished," qualities that "could not be rekindled in the popolo where they did not exist, so that Florence became ever more humble and *abietto*" (*IF* 3.1.5–7). The temptation to translate "abietto" as abject, in the sense of despicable or contemptible, may be too difficult to resist, but in 2.42 Machiavelli pairs "abietto" with "umano," saying the magnates became steadily more "umani e abietti" as their defeat cast them down from their "haughty spirit"—their hauteur and prideful arrogance in being well-born and superior. Here "abietto" is compatible with "umano" and closer to one sense of Latin "abiectus" meaning of low or common station. Magnates who wanted to regain office-holding rights had to accept a common status equal to that of other citizens: they had "to be and seem like the popolo" in all aspects of their lives, to display the moderation required of citizens in civic life, as Machiavelli says in 2.39. In this sense to say that Florence became ever more

[7] On the readmission of magnates to the legal popolo, see Christiane Klapisch-Zuber, *Ritorno alla politica. I magnati fiorentini 1340–1440* (Rome: Viella, 2009); for the 1343 legislation mentioned by Machiavelli, pp. 182–4. Original French edition: Paris: Éditions de l'EHESS, 2006.

"umile e abietto" is to refer not to abjectness as cowardice or wretchedness but to its ever more inclusive legal equality.

It is precisely to Florence's increasing equality that Machiavelli's argument moves. In the next sentence he writes that, "whereas Rome, with its virtú converted to arrogance [superbia], brought itself to a situation in which it could not sustain itself without a prince, Florence has arrived at a stage in which it could easily be reconstituted [riordinata] by a wise lawgiver [savio datore di leggie] into any form of government [qualunque forma di governo]" (*IF* 3.1.8). The terms "datore di leggie" and "riordinata" make it clear that he is referring to a republic of laws and ordini. Moreover, his use here of the present perfect—Florence "has arrived [è pervenuta]"—rather than the simple past (*pervenne*) implies a connection to the present in which he is writing. If Machiavelli hoped that Giulio de' Medici, who, after the conspiracy of 1522, had shut down discussions of Florence's constitutional future (in which Machiavelli advocated a republican solution in the *Discursus*), might be the "savio datore di leggie" or might appoint one, it was no longer prudent to suggest openly in the *Histories*, commissioned by and dedicated to Giulio (as Pope Clement VII), that Florence could or should be reorganized as a republic. This may be why Machiavelli writes "any form of government," and not republic, in this passage. In any event, the importance of this concluding contrast is that it puts into a different light the contrasts that favor Rome and reveals the implications of the one difference that does not favor Rome, namely, that Rome went from equality to inequality and rendered itself unable to sustain a republican order, whereas Florence went from inequality to an "astonishing equality," thus creating the conditions for a genuine republic. The utter defeat of the magnates, who, Machiavelli says, had been accustomed to seeing themselves as above the rest of the citizenry, compelled them to accept the "modestia" of the "vita civile," thus establishing the legal equality of citizens essential for a republic. This, in Machiavelli's estimation, is the signal achievement of the early Florentine popolo.

"These things," Machiavelli continues, referring to the historical process by which Florence reached the "astonishing equality" that makes it possible for a wise lawgiver to reorganize the government, "can clearly be seen" from "the preceding book," which has "shown the origins [principio] of the city's liberty" (*IF* 3.1.9). Far from decrying Florence as a failed polity, as *Histories* 3.1 is often read, Machiavelli affirms Florence's attainment of equality as a precondition for republican liberty. He does not say the city had fully achieved this liberty; he has shown its "principio" and the potential it possessed after the republic's first century. Obstacles remained that subverted this potential, as the rest of the *Histories* will demonstrate, but Florence was not "broken" from the outset: the demise of its liberty was a historical process attributable to specific historical actions and actors. This reading of 3.1 confirms and amplifies the judgment in the *Histories*' proem, where, having emphasized how many and complex Florence's "divisioni" were, Machiavelli affirms: "And in truth, according to my judgment, I believe nothing reveals so much the power [potenza] of our city as that which came from these divisions, which would have had the force to destroy any great and powerful city. Nonetheless, ours always seemed to become greater [maggiore]" (*IF* proemio.8–10). By the middle of the fourteenth century, the chief result of these "divisioni," as book 2 reveals, was the relegation of the nobles to equality with other citizens. If this is so, how should we interpret Machiavelli's characterization of the aims of Florence's popolo as "unjust" and "injurious," especially its unwillingness to compromise with the grandi? The answer may be that the popolo's objectives, however punishing and "injurious" to the magnates, were indispensable for achieving equality and the potential for a free, well-ordered republic. Founding or protecting republics, Machiavelli often reminds us, requires severity against those who attempt to destroy or subvert them. Brutus' acquiescence in the execution of his sons, who conspired against the still infant Roman republic, serves as Machiavelli's iconic model of the stern discipline needed to protect liberty. Florence's magnates did not suffer loss of life or exile, except as inflicted among themselves or by Brienne. The "injury" they suffered was being forced to "seem like the popolo."

Machiavelli does not, however, lose sight of the continued presence of an elite, if no longer of magnates, still pursuing private, family, and factional interests, as the most serious obstacle to the republic's survival. In book 3, chapter 2, he again underscores the elite's intra-class hostilities, which, though less violent, kept Florence in a state of tension. When the freelance mercenary company of Fra Moriale arrived in Tuscany in 1353 (he says; it was actually 1354), frightening all the cities of the region, Florence readied arms for defense "publicamente"—by government order. But "many citizens" did so on their own, among them the elite but non-magnate families of the Albizzi and Ricci, who "took up arms for their own security [per salute propria]." Machiavelli's source here is Stefani's chronicle, which says the Albizzi brought "soldiers [fanti]" from the Casentino right into their family palazzo in the city.[8] The Albizzi and Ricci, he adds, were "full of hatred" for each other, each seeking to subdue the other "to gain leadership [principato] in the republic." They did not come to violence and "confined their feuds to the councils and magistracies." But "the whole city was armed," and a dispute in the city center gave rise, "quite by chance [a sorte]," to a rumor that the Albizzi were about to assault the Ricci and the latter were coming for the Albizzi. "The whole city was in an uproar," Machiavelli writes, and only "with difficulty were the magistrates able to restrain both families and prevent a battle that had been randomly [a caso] rumored and for which no one was to blame." Although it came to nothing, the episode had the effect of "reigniting the animosities" of the two families, each now

[8] Marchionne di Coppo Stefani, *Cronaca fiorentina*, ed. Niccolò Rodolico (Città di Castello: Lapi Editore, 1903) Rerum Italicarum Scriptores, tome 30; (reprint ed. Reggello [Florence]: FirenzeLibri, 2008), rubric 662, p. 245.

"seeking, with greater determination, to acquire partigiani"—the followers, clients, and allies who filled the ranks of factions. That they avoided "privata violenzia" in this instance and channeled their quarrels through the institutions of government ("per la via ordinaria") Machiavelli ascribes to the magistrates being more respected ("reveriti") than previously because of the "equality into which the citizens had come as a result of the ruin of the magnates [grandi]" (*IF* 3.2.5–9). Although he frames the episode, in one sense, as a portent of the non-magnate elite's ongoing predisposition, no less ingrained than that of the magnates, to intra-class hostilities that could throw the whole city into chaos, he also suggests that cutting the magnates down to size not only increased the security of the popolo but also strengthened the institutions and influence of government.

A less violent elite politics, according to Machiavelli, generated new kinds of private power in the hands of great families. The Ricci sowed discord by introducing (in 1354) a law banning Ghibellines from communal office (*IF* 3.3). In fact, no actual Ghibellines remained in Florence, only the descendants of Ghibellines exiled generations earlier who quietly became Guelfs. Machiavelli says the Ricci proposed the measure out of "ambition" and because they assumed the law would hurt their Albizzi rivals, whose ancestors had long before immigrated from the Ghibelline city of Arezzo. The plan backfired when Piero degli Albizzi embraced the law, turned it against his opponents, and increased his power with this new instrument of intimidation as one of the leaders of the Parte Guelfa, which arrogated to itself the right to name suspected Ghibellines and "warn" them against accepting political offices. As the Albizzi promoted the Parte's campaign of proscriptions, the Ricci, realizing their error, tried to stop it. Machiavelli charges both families with destructive "ambizione." As tensions rose between them, they took opposite positions on foreign as well as domestic issues. By the early 1370s, the hostility between them created "great anxiety [sospetto grandissimo] and fear of every kind of ruination" (*IF* 3.4.8).

At this point in the narrative, with factional divisions again threatening the peace of the city, Machiavelli inserts (*IF* 3.5) a salient analysis of the evils of factionalism in a speech to the Signoria made by the leader of a group of citizens who, "motivated by love of the patria," had met in secret to discuss the "disordini" created by the Albizzi and Ricci. Like all the speeches in direct discourse in the *Histories*, it is Machiavelli's literary creation, especially in its lengthy elaboration, rhetorical flourishes, and broad historical perspectives. However, unlike many of them, this one builds on an actual speech attested in the historical record of an advisory meeting convened by the Signoria in April 1372 at a moment of high tension between the factions. The year 1372 is almost exactly the chronological mid-point of the 242 years of Machiavelli's narrative from the primo popolo of 1250 to Lorenzo de' Medici's death in 1492. From this Archimedean vantage point Machiavelli, through his speaker, looks back to the troubled past of Florentine elite factionalism and ahead to the future.

The Latin summary of the speech delivered to the advisory meeting survives in the archival series of the *Consulte e pratiche*.[9] Filippo Bastari, a citizen unaffiliated with either faction and from a family of middling importance somewhere on the murky border between the elite and the higher echelons of the social popolo, tells the Signoria that he and other concerned citizens had met to discuss the "great division that is harming the community." Unity among citizens, he insists, is essential to liberty. Decrying the influence of powerful private citizens, Bastari declares that those who seek something from the commune should go, not to "individual private citizens [singulares cives]," but to the Signoria. This would "eradicate ambition" and prevent anyone "from vaunting himself as being above the commune [ne aliquis supra comune se mostret]." The Signoria "should look with favor on those citizens"—Bastari refers to himself and his concerned colleagues—who "strive for the commune to be above all citizens." The Signoria and their advisory colleges should be "the heads of the city, not any private citizens [non aliqui privati cives]." The chronicler Stefani heard (or heard of) Bastari's speech and summarized it, with particular attention to Bastari's emphasis on protecting liberty. In Stefani's version Bastari and his group say they want to "proclaim the liberty [narrare la libertà] under which this city has lived and must live." Those "who have made themselves heads of factions [capi di setta]" are "malevolent" persons who "accuse, harass, and ruin anyone not of their faction." Stefani explains that, because an Albizzi partisan had criticized Bastari and his group for discussing public matters outside the palace and in secret, Bastari had to defend his group's decision to meet. In Stefani's version, he pleads with the Signoria—"We held our meeting in order to be free. O Lord Priors, give us liberty"—and justifies his actions as motivated by the desire to preserve liberty.[10]

Bastari's speech was made to order for Machiavelli's critique of Florentine factionalism. In his adaptation and elaboration Machiavelli does not name the speaker, although his anonymous orator begins by explaining, just as Bastari does in Stefani's account, why he and his colleagues were justified in meeting "privately" to discuss "public" affairs. They were fearful, he says, "about meeting by private arrangement, even if for a public purpose [cagione publica], thinking we might be either considered presumptuous or blamed as being motivated by ambition." But because they saw many other citizens meeting regularly both in the public spaces of the city's arcades ("logge") and in their homes, "not for any public benefit [publica utilità] but for their own ambition [per loro propria ambizione]," they concluded that, if those who gathered "for the ruin of the republic" did so without fear, those who meet "for the public good and benefit" should not fear to do so either. "The love we bear our patria," the speaker says, "is what persuaded us

[9] Archivio di Stato di Firenze, *Consulte e pratiche* 12, f. 11r; published in Gene Brucker, *Florentine Politics and Society, 1343–1378* (Princeton: Princeton University Press, 1962), pp. 252–53n.

[10] Stefani, *Cronaca*, rubric 731, p. 281.

to meet and now motivates us to come before you," the Signoria, "to speak of the evil [male], already great and continuously growing in our republic," which they declare themselves ready to assist in extinguishing. The Signoria should be able to succeed if it is willing to leave aside "privati rispetti"—hesitations induced by fears of offending powerful private citizens—and use its authority through "publiche forze"—the laws and the power to punish those who violate them. The exordium of the speech turns repeatedly on the public/private dichotomy.

Machiavelli's orator then provides a diagnosis and etiology of the "male" that he defines as "the common corruption of all the cities of Italy, which has corrupted and continues to corrupt your city" and whose essence, as he will make clear, is factionalism and private power. He provides historical perspective: after escaping imperial tutelage, Italy's cities lacked a "powerful restraint [freno] able to correct" their own missteps and consequently organized their governments "not as free cities but divided by factions [sette]," from which came all the other "mali" and "disordini." Corruption and factions are repeatedly juxtaposed: the noun "corruption," the adjective "corrotto/a," and the verb "corrompere" cumulatively appear seven times in the speech, and factions—"setta/e" and "parte/i"—ten times. He identifies the manifestations of corruption. No "unity" or "friendship" exists among citizens, except those involved in "some wickedness [sceleratezza]" directed "either against the patria or against private citizens"; because piety ("religione") and "fear of God" have been extinguished in everyone, vows and oaths are honored only as long as they are useful in deceiving others; hence, malicious ("nocivi") men gain praise for being clever, while good men are ridiculed as fools. "In truth, everything that can be corrupted and everything that can corrupt others come together in the cities of Italy: the young are indolent, the old lascivious, and both sexes and all ages are full of dissolute customs, which good laws, being vitiated by wicked behavior [dalle cattive usanze guaste], cannot correct."

The speaker ties the degeneration of mores and morality to the plague of factions, asserting that with laws rendered ineffective and ethical norms ignored, citizens become prey to "avarizia" and "the hunger, not for true glory, but for repute stained with disgrace [vituperosi onori], which generates hatreds, hostilities, disputes and factions that, in turn, cause death, banishment, the affliction of good men and the exaltation of wicked men." Good men, he says, "trusting in their innocence, do not search, as the wicked do, for someone to protect and honor them with illegal methods [estraordinariamente]; hence, "unprotected and disrespected," they come to ruin. Here Machiavelli alludes to patrons—factional leaders whose followers seek protection from magistrates, laws, taxes, or other powerful bosses in return for allegiance and service to the patron. "From this," the speaker explains, "come the power of factions [parti] and devotion to them, for wicked men align with factions out of avarice and ambition, good men out of necessity. Most pernicious of all is to see how factional bosses [i motori e principi di esse] camouflage [adonestano] their purpose and objective with pious language [piatoso vocabolo]" (as Machiavelli said of Corso Donati). Still referring to the heads of factions, the speaker avers that, "although they are all enemies of liberty, they suffocate it under the guise of defending either a regime of ottimati or a popular government." Implied here is that Ricci defenses of liberty and the Albizzi campaign for loyal Guelf government were both mystifications of their true aims. The reward for the victory they desire is not the glory of having liberated the city, "but the satisfaction of outdoing [superare] all others and seizing power [principato] in the city"—an echo of Machiavelli's characterization of the "primi" in the *Discursus florentinarum rerum* as those "of haughty temperament who think they deserve to take precedence over others." Once a city falls under the sway of such ambitious men, the orator continues, "there is nothing so unjust, cruel or avaricious they dare not do." Consequently, "the ordini and laws are made for private, not public, benefit; wars, peace, and alliances are made not for the common glory but for the satisfaction of a few."

Addressing Florence's experience of this corruption common to all the Italian cities, the orator claims that "our city is more stained by these *disordini* than any other," for its laws, statutes, and civic ordini have always been, and are still, enacted according to the "ambition of the victorious faction," not the requirements of a "vivere libero." Moreover, factions destroy each other and subvert themselves: the expulsion of a defeated faction or the termination of a conflict gives rise to another: "in cities that want to maintain themselves with factions more than with laws, it is inevitable that, when a faction finds itself without opposition, it divides, because it cannot protect itself against the same private methods [modi privati] it had earlier contrived for its own security." Machiavelli's speaker here identifies a critical weakness of factional politics, namely, that the instruments of private power employed by a faction to defeat its enemies will inevitably be used against it. Florence's whole history, the orator asserts, demonstrates this. Everyone assumed that the defeat of the Ghibellines meant the Guelfs would long rule the city in peace, but within a short time the Guelfs divided into White and Black factions. Even after the Whites were banished, "the city was never without factions," which frequently appealed to foreign forces to defeat their rivals: "giving to others what we could not or did not want to possess by agreement amongst ourselves, we surrendered our liberty now to King Robert, now to his brother, then his son, and most recently to the duke of Athens [Brienne]." Dependence on foreign power, however, never brought stability or ended factional hostilities. "We have never established the unity to live in freedom, and we are not willing to submit" to others. Despite Brienne's cruel tyranny, "which ought to have made us wiser, as soon as he was expelled we again took up arms and fought each other with greater hatred and rage than ever before, with the result that our former [antica] nobility was vanquished and submitted to the will of the popolo." It was again assumed that "no cause of division or faction remained in Florence, restraints having been applied to the arrogance [superbia] and intolerable ambition of [the magnates] who, it seemed, had been the cause" of the divisions. But "experience" proved this to be fallacious, because, as the speaker says in a passage cited earlier, "the arrogance [superbia] and ambition of the grandi were not extinguished; they were instead wrested from them [fu loro tolta] by our popolani"—not the social popolo, but the non-magnate elite families, who, "following the ways of ambitious men, seek pre-eminent power in the republic, and, having no other way to do so except through discord, have once again divided the city." Machiavelli now has his speaker identify the perpetrators of these ills: "It is decreed from above," that "in all republics there must be fateful/fatal families [famiglie fatali] born for their destruction [rovina, i.e. of the republics]. Of such families our republic has had a greater abundance than any other; not one, but many have tormented and afflicted it, as the Buondelmonti and Uberti first did, then the Donati and the Cerchi, and now—what a shameful and absurd thing!—the Ricci and Albizzi torment and divide it." Pondering this roster of "famiglie fatali" that culminates with the Albizzi—the antagonists that the Medici defeated in their rise to power sixty years later—could any reader fail to see an allusion to the ambitions of the Medici family, especially after the catastrophic siege of Florence and the final destruction of the republic, caused in large part by the avarice and duplicity of the Medici pope Clement VII?

The speaker reassures the Signoria that he "has not recalled the city's corrupt customs and its past and ongoing divisions" to frighten them, but to remind them of "their causes" and encourage them not to despair of being able to rein them in. One reason for hope is that the power of "those old families," he claims, came in large part from the support they had from "the princes" (the reference is to emperors, kings, and popes), which rendered the city's ordini and "modi civili" inadequate to restrain the families. Now, however, "the empire has no strength, no one fears the pope" (the papacy was then in Avignon), "and the whole of Italy and this city have reached a condition of such equality [è condotta in tanta ugualità] that the city can rule itself [che per lei medesima si può reggere]." In this somewhat ambiguous sentence "equality" seems to combine two distinct but related ideas. The "equality" of "Italy as a whole" presumably refers to the independence of each of its states and their ability to govern themselves without interference from external powers. Because Italy's elite classes often depended on foreign support to maintain dominance within their cities, the diminished strength of emperors, popes, and the Angevin monarchy make Italy's governments better able to restrain the excesses of their elites. The "equality" of "this city" alludes to the subordination of the magnates to the norms and institutions of the popolo—the equality of all citizens in law. In these circumstances restraining family factions and bridling the elite's constant striving for private power should be—or should have been—easier.

The speaker concludes with another expression of optimism that echoes book 3's introductory chapter. "Despite past instances pointing to the contrary," he declares, "this republic of ours" can both preserve unity and institute the needed reforms, "provided Your Lordships [the Signoria] are prepared and willing to do it." The speaker and his colleagues, reiterating that they are "motivated by love of the patria and not by any private partiality [non da alcuna privata passione]," exhort the Signoria to "extinguish the illness that sickens us, the rage that consumes us, the poison that kills us." They should ascribe the "disordini" of the past not to the "nature of men," but "to the times"—to the contingencies of history. Times change, he says, and for this reason "you can hope for better fortune through better ordini"—improved laws and institutions—and "overcome the malice" of fortune "with wisdom [prudenzia]." His final thought returns to the necessity of grasping the fundamental problem: success will depend on "restraining the ambition of men who nurture factions" and abolishing institutions that do the same, and building instead on ordini compatible with a true "vivere libero e civile." He urges the Signoria "to do it now, with the benevolence of the laws, rather than, by delaying, make it necessary for others to do it with support of arms"—an allusion to the upheavals of 1378.

"ALL WHO COME TO GREAT WEALTH AND POWER DO SO THROUGH FRAUD OR FORCE"

Following this speech—the centerpiece of Machiavelli's analysis of Florentine corruption—he reviews the popular challenges to elite dominance in the decade 1372–82: attempts to restrain the Albizzi and Ricci factions and curtail the Guelf Party's "anti-Ghibelline" campaign; the war against the papacy; the 1378 reforms promoted by a revived guild community, which sparked the insurrection of woolworkers and artisans; and the guild government of 1378–82 that brought hostilities between elite and popolo to a fever pitch and temporarily displaced the elite from its customary hold on power. The broader trajectory of Machiavelli's narrative after 1382 through the rest of book 3 and into book 4 recounts the recovery of the elite, the resurgence of factional politics, and the expansion of "extraordinary" private power, culminating in the ascendance of the Medici.

The Signoria of March–April 1372, inspired, Machiavelli says, by the orator's speech, created a committee of fifty-six citizens to "provide for the security [salute] of the republic" and diminish the influence of factions. Although the committee produced many important reforms, as both the official record of its proceedings and the chronicler Stefani reveal,[11] Machiavelli asserts its overall failure before even mentioning its accomplishments. Because the reformers were "more intent on curtailing existing factions than removing the causes of future ones, they achieved neither," and, consequently, they "made one faction"—the

[11] Summarized by Brucker, *Florentine Politics*, pp. 254–6; Stefani, *Cronaca*, rubric 732, p. 282.

Albizzi—"more powerful" than its rival. He describes two of their principal enactments: procedures by which a citizen injured in his person or property could petition to have the assailant declared a magnate, with attendant penalties and loss of political rights; and the suspension for three years of office-holding rights in the Signoria of three leading Albizzi, including Piero di Filippo, and three Ricci. The reformers' error, Machiavelli explains, was not extending the suspension to the office of the captains of the Guelf Party: "If the palace of the Signoria was closed to Piero [degli Albizzi], the palace of the Guelf [Party], where he had great power [autorità], remained open to him, and if, before this, he and his followers were zealous [caldi] about issuing warnings [ammunire: political proscriptions]," after this "ingiuria" they were "caldissimi" (*IF* 3.6). The problem to which Machiavelli alludes, and the likely "cause" of the future factional enmities that he believes the reformers neglected, was the anomalous place of the Parte Guelfa in Florence. From one angle it was a communal magistracy, often included in ad hoc reform committees and balìe; from another, it was a private association, governed by its own regulations and statutes and enjoying considerable freedom to act independently of the communal government. This became an acute issue when the Parte assumed the right to identify "Ghibellines" and "warn" them not to accept political offices.[12] Machiavelli says the "audacity" of the Parte captains "increased so much that they heedlessly [senza alcuno rispetto] proscribed not only those who merited it but anyone they wanted, spurred by whatsoever rapacious or ambitious motive." Indeed, he calls the Parte a "faction [setta]" and characterizes the arbitrariness of its actions as "insolente." The captains and "setta" of the Guelfs became powerful because everyone, afraid of being "ammunito"—tagged as Ghibellines—"fawned on them [gli onorava]" (*IF* 3.3.6–9). Machiavelli notes that a 1366 law, promoted by the Ricci, required that proscriptions of "Ghibellines" be confirmed by a larger committee, which "moderated in good measure the power of the [Parte] captains" and reduced the number of proscriptions. But by the early 1370s, the Parte regained strength, its arrogance and independence increased, proscriptions resumed, and the leadership, especially the Albizzi, "capo di questa setta," grew more powerful (*IF* 3.4).

Machiavelli maintains that the failure to curb the Parte Guelfa undermined the reforms of 1372. As the bastion of the pro-Guelf and pro-Church elite, it strenuously opposed the war against the papacy, which, Machiavelli says, was supported by the "universale" and a few elite families hostile to the Albizzi—the Ricci, Alberti, and Medici. Machiavelli praises the popular magistracy that administered the war, as he admiringly says, "con tanta virtú e tanta sodisfazione dello universale" (*IF* 3.7.6–8). But the Parte's fierce opposition so magnified its "audacity" and "arrogance," and hence its defamatory attacks against the war's supporters, that its

[12] Brucker provides a detailed account in *Florentine Politics*, pp. 202–21.

captains "were more feared than the Signoria itself; people felt less reverence in the presence of the Signoria than in that of the Parte leaders, greater esteem for the Parte palace" than for the palace of the Signoria. "No ambassador came to Florence without instructions to visit their captains." Paying greater respect to private power than to government officials was, Machiavelli believed, a subversion of the proper order of things. He even says that, because "the audacity of the Guelfs was intolerable and no one knew how to subdue them, people thought it would be necessary to resort to arms to determine which of the two seats [of power, the Guelf Party or the Signoria] would prevail." On the side of the Guelfs were "all the old nobles [the magnates]," and a majority of the "piú potenti popolani"—the most powerful non-magnate elite families. On the other side were all the "popolani di minore sorte"—the social popolo. Machiavelli re-emphasizes the distinction between the non-elite popolo and the "potenti popolani" to make it clear that most of the elite—magnate and non-magnate—were closing ranks against the social popolo. The leaders of the "setta guelfa," he writes, seeing the strength of their adversaries, believing that "the whole city was hostile to them," and worried that the election of an unfriendly Signoria might put them in grave danger, "saw no other solution" except to banish their opponents and "seize the palace of the Signoria by force," thus "limiting the government entirely to their faction [reducendo tutto lo stato nella setta loro] in imitation of the old Guelfs who lived securely in the city only after banishing their adversaries" (*IF* 3.8.6). The aim was, in effect, a coup d'état, which, if successful, would have absorbed Florence's government into a private association of elite families: a particularly egregious inflation of the elite's persistent aim of weakening any government it did not control. There was no coup, but the Guelfs conducted a relentless campaign of accusations of Ghibellinism, thereby provoking a furious controversy that came to a head early in 1378.

The Parte leaders, Machiavelli recounts, aware that the procedures for drawing names from the electoral purses would result in one of their chief antagonists, Salvestro de' Medici, becoming standard-bearer of justice for May–June 1378, attempted, unsuccessfully, to manipulate the process and prevent his election. Having already identified the Medici among the opponents of the Parte's excesses, Machiavelli introduces Salvestro as one who, although born into an "elite non-magnate family [nobilissima famiglia popolana], could not abide the oppression of the popolo by a few powerful men." Determined to put a stop to this "insolenzia," he and a number of "nobili popolani," elite enemies of the Parte and the Albizzi, drafted a proposal, which they intended to present to the legislative councils, to re-promulgate the Ordinances of Justice "against the grandi" and curtail the powers of the Guelf party. Machiavelli follows the chronicler Alamanno Acciaioli's report that, when the proposal failed to win the approval of the Signoria's advisory colleges of the Twelve and the Sixteen, Salvestro made a dramatic appearance before the large legislative council of the popolo, asserting that he had been elected standard-bearer to "safeguard the government [vigilare lo stato], chastise the insolence of the powerful, and modify the laws that were leading the republic to ruin." He threatened to resign his office if his "just undertaking" was rebuffed by the "malice of men" (*IF* 3.9). His ally Benedetto Alberti (from the wealthy banking family that, like the Medici, opposed the Albizzi and the Parte) "called the people to arms" in the piazza. This, Machiavelli says, "was what sparked greater turmoil [tumulto] and put the city in arms." The now frightened advisory colleges quickly reversed course and approved Salvestro's proposals. The Parte captains, who had gathered allies in their palace "to discuss how they should defend themselves against the ordine of the Signoria," "fled to their homes" in fear of the uprising (*IF* 3.10.2–3).

Over several chapters, Machiavelli recounts the rapidly evolving events from the June balìa that rescinded all proscriptions for "Ghibellinism," the attacks against the palazzi of Parte leaders, the reforms sponsored by the guilds in early July, the revolutionary demands of artisans and wage laborers for guilds of their own (and, hence, a share of political offices), the expulsion of the incumbent Signoria, a second day of violence, and, in August, the emergence and violent suppression of the politically radicalized unskilled laborers (the Ciompi, although Machiavelli never uses the name). Inferring Machiavelli's opinion of these complex events is not easy. On the one hand, he characterizes the demands of the artisans and minor guildsmen in July as "disonorevoli e gravi" (*IF* 3.15.5) and deplores the "audacity and great presumption" of the August revolutionaries who wanted veto power over the Signoria (*IF* 3.17.3–6). Indeed, he famously praises the "woolcomber" (*IF* 3.16.1), Michele di Lando, chosen as standard-bearer of justice during the July insurgency, for the zeal and ruthlessness with which he put down the August rebellion: "unable to tolerate such arrogance," Machiavelli says, Michele violently suppressed "con estraordinario modo una estraordinaria insolenzia" (*IF* 3.17.7): "estraordinaria insolenzia" applied to the wage laborers' demand for unconstitutional veto power, "estraordinario" applied to the violence with which Michele di Lando stopped them. These are, however, the only appearances of *e/straordinario* in all the chapters Machiavelli devotes to the 1378 convulsions. He does not characterize the uprisings of June or July as the work of factions (neither *sette* nor *fazioni*) or as violations of the ordini (with one indirect exception, in 3.11.5, in which unnamed persons "who placed their hopes in *disordini*" persuade the guildsmen to banish and destroy their enemies). Machiavelli was well aware of the days of violence inflicted against family palaces and those of the podestà and the Wool guild, all apparently planned actions that included arson and theft in certain cases, only arson in others, but not attacks against persons.[13] By contrast, several of the perpetrators were summarily executed. Once, in

[13] "Lettera d'anonimo sul Tumulto dei Ciompi," in *Il tumulto dei Ciompi. Cronache e memorie*, ed. G. Scaramella (Bologna: Zanichelli, 1917–34), p. 142. Referring to the violence of 20 July, the writer comments: "Tutti questi arsono senza alcuna ruberia, et senza fare a nessuno male nella persona."

chapter 14, he calls the insurrectionists "congiurati [conspirators]" and their plan to seize power a "congiura." He refers to those who carried out the June riots as "predatori" (*IF* 3.10.15) and to the violent episodes in June and July as "wickedness [mali]" (*IF* 3.14.10). But he reserves "estraordinario" and "insolenzia" (combined) for the unconstitutional demands of the unskilled workers in August—when no violence occurred, except in their suppression—evidently considering their demand for veto power over the government's decisions a transgression of the ordini that justified Michele di Lando's "estraordinario modo." Until that point, whatever the faults and crimes of the revolutionaries, Machiavelli does not claim that their politics crossed the line from ordinario to straordinario, presumably because they presented their demands for a share in government and other reforms in lawful petitions approved by the communal councils. In short Machiavelli does not see the uprisings of 1378 as a recurrence of Florence's pathology of factionalism. They were certainly divisive, but not manifestations of the private power of factions, which he believed emanated exclusively from the wealthy elite.[14] He saw the tumults of June and July as legitimate expressions of the aims and grievances of social groups (or classes), much like those of the early Roman plebs.

Moreover, although he denounced some of the revolutionaries' actions, Machiavelli evinces a remarkable understanding of the economic and institutional bases of their grievances that is directly relevant to his critique of the wealthy elite. In chapter 12, explaining that wage-laborers "felt hatred for the wealthy citizens and guild leaders" because they were "not compensated for their work as they believed they rightly deserved," he reaches back to the origins of the organization and control of labor in the Florentine woolen cloth industry. In the thirteenth century, Machiavelli explains, "when the city divided into guilds...each guild got its own governance and leaders, who rendered judgments in civil cases involving its members" (*IF* 3.12.3–4). (That the guilds actually took shape earlier and that Florence did not exactly "divide into guilds" does not vitiate Machiavelli's argument.) As the guilds increased in number and power, he continues, a distinction arose between more and less influential guilds, and a de facto alliance developed between the popolani (wealthy non-magnates) of the major guilds and the old families of the Parte Guelfa against the minor guilds. For an understanding of working-class grievances, the crucial fact that Machiavelli foregrounds is that the guilds excluded from membership the many trades in which the "popolo minuto" and the "plebe" labored, especially those who worked for subsistence wages in the various stages of the production of woolen cloth. "Without guilds of their own,"

[14] Nor, with the same single exception of the August insurgents, does Machiavelli associate the political movements of 1378–82 with "licenzia," the corruption of popular government in the Polybian cycle of constitutions he summarizes in *DL* 1.2. The term appears only once in book 3, adverbially in chapter 22, where he says that Michele di Lando suppressed the "unleashed multitude" that was destroying the city "licenziosamente."

these workers were subject to the disciplinary regimes of the major guilds for which they performed essential labor. Lacking any voice or representation in the guilds that supervised them and regulated their work, wage laborers who "were not satisfactorily compensated for their labors or in any way mistreated [oppressati] by their employers had no recourse other than to the magistracy of the guild to which they were subject, from which they did not believe they received the justice they considered their due." Well aware of the crucial role played in the 1378 uprisings by workers in the woolen cloth industry, Machiavelli mentions in particular the role of the Wool Guild. "Of all the guilds, the one with the greatest number of these subjects [sottoposti] was and is the Wool Guild, which, being very powerful and surpassing the others in influence, supported [i.e. employed] and still supports, through its manufacturing firms, the majority of the *popolo minuto* and the plebs" (*IF* 3.12.6–8). The Wool Guild, therefore, became a particular target of workers' grievances, as Machiavelli states in the next chapter: "the men of the plebs, those subject to the Wool Guild as well as to other guilds, were filled with anger [sdegno] for the above-stated reasons" (*IF* 3.13.1). Machiavelli's analysis of the workers' grievances focuses on the legal, institutional, and economic power of the wealthy entrepreneurs who used their influence in government and the guilds to their own advantage and to the detriment of the workers. He thus represents the workers' grievances as rational and the uprisings of June and July as logical expressions of those grievances. However much he disliked some of their demands and actions, Machiavelli's analysis separates working-class anger from stereotypes of workers and the poor as inherently vicious and prone to violence.

His explanation of the workers' plight in chapter 12 precedes and underlies the speech in chapter 13 by an unnamed "courageous and experienced" worker who encourages his fellow "plebei" not to let fear prevent them from evading punishment and "living in greater liberty and contentment [sodisfazione]."[15] To escape punishment for the violence already committed in June, he advises them to "redouble" the acts of arson and theft and involve more of their fellow workers in such misdeeds, "because when many do wrong no one is punished" (*IF* 3.13.5–6). Machiavelli's anonymous speaker then launches into a critique of the elite's wealth and pretensions to "nobility." "Do not be frightened by that antiquity of bloodlines with which they reproach us. All men have the same origin, all come from an equally long line of ancestors, and nature has made them all the same." He exhorts the plebs to embrace this "natural" equality of all people and deconstructs the external appearances and contingencies of wealth and poverty on which the elite's

[15] On the speech, see Gabriele Pedullà, "Il divieto di Platone. Niccolò Machiavelli e il discorso dell'anonimo plebeo (*Ist. Fior.* III, 13)," in *Storiografia repubblicana fiorentina (1494–1570)*, ed. J.-J. Marchand and J.-C. Zancarini (Florence: Cesati, 2003), pp. 209–66; and Yves Winter, *Machiavelli and the Orders of Violence* (Cambridge: Cambridge University Press, 2018), pp. 167–91.

claim to "nobility" rests. "Strip us all of our clothes and in our nakedness you will see we are all alike. If we were dressed in their clothes, and they in ours, we would without doubt seem noble and they would not, because it is only poverty and wealth that make us unequal." Neither remorse nor scruples of conscience should hold them back because, "where there is fear of hunger and imprisonment, fear of hell has no place," and because wealth, far from conferring or denoting nobility, is always and inevitably ill-gotten: "all those who come to great wealth [ricchezze] and power [potenzia] do so through either fraud or force. To hide the sordid reality [bruttezza] of [the wealth] they acquire, they bestow an honorable appearance on what they have usurped with deceit or violence by giving it the false name of earnings [sotto falso titolo di guadagno adonestano]" (*IF* 3.13.9–13).[16] The wealthy "hide" the dishonorable origins of their riches with dissembling language that ennobles the theft, "guadagno" performing the same masking function as the nobles' fine clothes. The speaker underscores the coercion and deceit behind social and economic inequality—natural equality distorted and denied by false appearances, dishonesty, and fraud. Although Machiavelli had previously left the issue of wealth largely unexamined in affirming equality as the essential foundation of republics, the speaker's emphasis on economic inequality suggests that legal equality alone is insufficient for a well-ordered republic. And, if some degree of economic justice is also necessary, would it be the plebs' task to bring about, if not equality, at least a more equitable distribution of wealth, just as legal equality was achieved by the popolo in its struggle with the magnates?

But does Machiavelli share his anonymous worker's critique of wealth? The answer depends on the level of wealth. Among the benefits of political liberty, he says in *Discourses* 2.2.44–7, is that it allows men to acquire wealth "without fear of it being taken from them." In a "vivere libero" "riches multiply to a greater degree," from both agriculture and the trades ("arti"). This evidently assumes modest levels of wealth, acquired by households from labor in fields and shops. The implied context of household and family is confirmed by the assertion that being able to use one's wealth [beni] to raise one's children instills greater willingness to marry and procreate. Machiavelli's view of great wealth is different. We recall the assertion in *Discourses* 1.5.18–19 that "those who already possess much" are especially dangerous to republics because their resources allow them to overthrow governments. In *Discourses* 1.37.22–5, discussing the Roman nobles' fierce opposition to the Gracchi's land reforms, he writes that fear of losing wealth impels the wealthy to defend it with extreme violence. He praises the Romans for keeping the

[16] Cabrini observes that the speeches in *Histories* 3.5 and 3.13 share—through "adonestare"—a similar unmasking function, which Machiavelli also "proudly claims for himself in the dedication" of the *Histories*, declaring that he has never wanted to camouflage "una disonesta opera con una onesta cagione" or hide "una laudevole opera, come fatta a uno contrario fine" (*IF* Dedica.8); Anna Maria Cabrini *Interpretazione e stile in Machiavelli. Il terzo libro delle ‹Istorie›* (Rome: Bulzoni, 1990), pp. 44–5, n. 52.

public treasury rich and the citizens poor (*DL* 2.19.8), adding that poverty induced the Romans to strive for offices with virtú; indeed, he "could demonstrate at length—if others had not done so many times—how poverty produces so many better results than do riches, how the former has brought honor to cities, countries, and religions, while the latter has brought them to ruin" (*DL* 3.25.17). As we shall see, his account of the rise of the Medici confirms his skeptical, sometimes hostile, attitude toward great private wealth. The passages just cited suggest that, while he certainly did not exculpate the insurrectionists of 1378 for their crimes, Machiavelli had considerable sympathy for the anonymous worker's unmasking of great wealth, especially as a marker of "nobility."

Two chapters earlier, in *Histories* 3.11, Machiavelli attributes a very different speech—also his invention—to Luigi Guicciardini, the standard-bearer of justice in the Signoria that assumed office on July 1, 1378. The textual proximity and specular opposition of these paired orations make it clear that Machiavelli intended them to be read against one another.[17] They are usually thought to highlight the contrast between the worker's rhetoric of class hostility and violence and the fictional Guicciardini's pleas for moderation and compromise. However, even assuming that the worker in 3.13 voices only the perspectives and grievances of his class, one must ask whether Guicciardini's speech is any less an expression of his own class's rhetoric and strategies. Guicciardini addresses the guild representatives who, in June, had demanded punishments of the Parte Guelfa leaders. Now, in early July, the guildsmen were presenting more demands. (It was later in July that the artisans and wage-laborers announced their program.) Addressing the guild leaders, Guicciardini declares: "we have tolerated with patience the uprisings," which "began through no fault of ours [senza nostra colpa]." "We" might refer to the Signoria, or, because in June he and his fellow priors were not yet in office, to the wider elite. That the uprisings had occurred "senza nostra colpa" overlooks the Parte's role in precipitating the crisis with its barrage of politically motivated proscriptions. "Having indulged you on so many and such difficult demands, we hoped the agitations would at some point cease." Deploring the requests for more punishments and banishments for the Parte, Guicciardini ominously warns that, "as your shamelessness [disonestà] grows, so does our displeasure." The Signoria, he intones, "had hoped to be dealing with men who had in them some benevolence [umanità] and love for their patria, and we thought we could overcome [vincere] your ambition with our benevolence. But experience now tells us that, the more humbly we conduct ourselves and the more we acquiesce [in your demands], the more arrogant you become [tanto piú insuperbite] demanding still more dishonorable things." Guicciardini rebukes the guildsmen

[17] See Gennaro Sasso, *Niccolò Machiavelli*, 2 vols. (Bologna: il Mulino, 1980–93), vol. 2, pp. 287–358, esp. 304–32; and Marina Marietti, *Machiavelli. L'eccezione fiorentina* (Florence: Cadmo, 2005), pp. 200–18 (on Machiavelli's use of "antilogia").

without considering the origins of, or rationale behind, their grievances. He contrasts "our" "umanità," "pazienza," and "liberalità" with "your" "disonestà" and "ambizione"—a claim of moral superiority based on elite social status. He admonishes that "if we speak in this way, it is not to offend you but to make you reconsider [farvi ravvedere: reassess yourselves]. We will let others tell you what you want to hear; we will tell you what is useful for you." Guicciardini recalls the demands the government had already accepted. "You wanted to deprive the Parte captains of their power; it was done. You wanted the lists of citizens eligible for the captaincy of the Parte destroyed and reforms instituted; we agreed to do it. You wanted office-holding rights restored to citizens proscribed [by the Parte]; we allowed it. Following your wishes, we have pardoned those who burned homes [of Parte leaders] and despoiled churches. To satisfy you, we sent many honored and powerful citizens into exile. At your request," the re-promulgated Ordinances of Justice "have again restrained the magnates." Guicciardini preceded this list of accepted demands by asking, "Tell us, by your faith, what more can you honorably ask of us?" He reiterates, with evident impatience: "What end will these demands of yours have?" And, echoing Cicero's invective against Catiline: "How long will you abuse our liberality?" He makes the elite magnanimous victims: "Do you not see that we bear defeat with greater patience than you accept victory?" These sentences echo the speech in Livy (3.67–8) by the consul Titus Quinctius Capitolinus, who similarly appeals to the plebs and their tribunes to set aside their grievances and hostility to the consuls and senate and urges them to cooperate in confronting Rome's approaching enemies. Like Guicciardini, Quinctius lists the plebs' demands, each followed by "it was done"; "we agreed to it"; "we allowed it." But to read Quinctius's speech as an "appeal to embrace concord and moderation, to set aside party differences in the name of the greater good of the patria,"[18] overlooks the anger and disdain with which he scolds and berates the plebs. Machiavelli's Guicciardini and Livy's Quinctius both express their class's unexamined, privileged sense of aggrieved entitlement and moral superiority.

Luigi Guicciardini reproaches the guild leaders for the harm they inflicted on the city. "To what will all your divisiveness [disunioni] lead this city of yours?" He claims that internal discord caused Florence's submission to Walter of Brienne, oddly calling him "your private hired soldier [privato condottieri vostro]" and forgetting that it was angry magnates and imperiled merchant bankers who brought Brienne to Florence. Milan (in the early 1350s) and the papacy (in 1375–8), he says, were unable to defeat a "united" Florence, omitting to mention that it was the Parte Guelfa's furious opposition to the war against the Church that plunged the city into crisis with an escalation of anti-Ghibelline proscriptions, thus setting in motion the uprisings of 1378. He insists instead that it is the

[18] As the editors of the Edizione Nazionale do in *OS*, vol. 1, p. 322, n. 10.

guildsmen who have weakened the city by dividing it. "Why then do you want your discord to make a slave [serva] in peacetime of a city that remained free even after wars with so many powerful enemies? What will you gain from your discord other than servitude?"

Guicciardini then shifts his litany of accusations to the acts of arson and theft (on 22 June), asking if the perpetrators expect to gain anything but poverty from the "possessions you have robbed us of." The stolen wealth, together with "our business enterprises [industrie nostre], are what feed [nutriscono] the entire city." Without this wealth, he admonishes, "we will no longer be able to feed it. Those who seized it as ill-gotten gain will not know how to preserve it, and the result will be famine and poverty." Assuming that only the already wealthy know how to turn their wealth into economic benefit for the whole city, he argues in effect that prosperity depends on letting the wealthy use their wealth as only they know how. His paternalism, its benevolence taken for granted, prevents him from seeing what Machiavelli will explain in chapter 12, namely, that political power and control of law and institutions—what the plebeian orator calls "forza"—thwart economic justice. Guicciardini ends his speech by telling the guildsmen to cease and desist. "These Signori and I command you and, if honor permits, beg you to make a firm resolve and be satisfied with the things we have decided. And if you want something different, be willing to ask for it civilly, not with uprisings and arms. If your requests are honorable, they will always be granted, and you will not give evil men opportunity to bring ruin upon your patria by exploiting and bringing blame and opprobrium on you."

At the conclusion of Guicciardini's speech, Machiavelli comments that "these words, because they were true [perché erano vere], deeply touched the spirits of the citizens, who graciously thanked the standard-bearer" for having fulfilled, for them the duties of a "buon signore," and for the city those of a "buono cittadino," declaring their willingness "to obey what they had been instructed to do" (*IF* 3.11.18). If these "citizens" were the guildsmen Guicciardini had addressed, we must wonder about their alleged compliance, given that Machiavelli knew very well that they did not in fact "obey" his directives. After the second wave of attacks on elite palaces (on July 20), guildsmen and workers together presented the revolutionary petitions that created a guild for laborers and artisans (soon expanded to three guilds, with a third share of the seats in the Signoria), expelled the incumbent Signoria, including Luigi Guicciardini, held a new electoral scrutiny that radically restructured the office-holding class, and enacted far-reaching fiscal reforms. So why does Machiavelli say that docile guildsmen were moved by Guicciardini's words "because they were true"? A passage in Alamanno Acciaioli's chronicle suggests a possible answer. According to Acciaioli, sometime in the first half of July, the guilds demanded that more citizens be declared magnates, exiled, or otherwise deprived of office-holding rights. To prevent this, he says, the Signoria "commanded the guild leaders not to engage in further agitations" and implored them to make any additional requests "peacefully and quietly. Requests deemed just and appropriate would be gladly approved." Acciaioli, who was a prior and hence Guicciardini's colleague in the Signoria, does not attribute these admonitions specifically to the standard-bearer, but they are in essence what Machiavelli has Guicciardini say to the guild leaders, who, Acciaioli adds, "were satisfied with the priors' command."[19] Saying that Guicciardini's words "were true" and "deeply touched the spirits of the citizens," Machiavelli may have been paraphrasing Acciaioli's comment that the guild leaders "furono contenti del comandamento de' priori."

But the historical Luigi Guicciardini's view of the insurgents was far from the composed and admonitory posture of the fictional speech in *Histories* 3.11. A fragment of the historical Guicciardini's account of the events shows him quite hostile to those who, as he says, promoted the legislation against the Parte Guelfa, re-issued the Ordinances of Justice against the "grandi" and "gientili uomini," orchestrated the burning of "many homes and palaces of Guelf citizens and members of the Parte," and "plunged the city of Florence into arson and theft." At the beginning of his term of office, he writes, "certain wicked men, Ghibellines and persons proscribed by the Parte" wanted "our priorate" to banish Parte members. "They also wanted us to promulgate ordinances against the Parte and destroy it totally [disfalla a fatto]." Guicciardini says he tried to prevent this: "And I, Luigi, declaring my opposition, was determined not to allow it." Accusing those who demanded the exile of Parte leaders of organizing the workers' uprising, he asserts that, after the Signoria got wind of the insurgents' plans and arrested three of their leaders, a large crowd, enraged by reports that these prisoners were being tortured,[20] occupied the piazza and demanded their release. Guicciardini himself was a target of the fury of the crowd, which crossed the Arno and torched his and his relatives' palaces. Under the threat of more violence, the legislative councils approved the insurgents' petitions, and the next day the crowd forced the Signoria to resign: "they expelled us all from the palace" and "appointed new priors and a new standard-bearer of justice to the harm and shame of the Guelfs of Florence."[21] Machiavelli may not have known Guicciardini's account, but Acciaioli, whose chronicle he knew well, says that while he, Acciaioli, "had no intention of leaving" the palace, the "cowardly [vile e codardo] standard-bearer"—Guicciardini—"was weeping for his children and wife," and, as the staff and guards slipped away, "the craven and wretched [vile e triste] standard-bearer secretly took leave of his companions without saying a word."[22] Machiavelli, in fact, echoes Acciaioli's devastating judgment of Guicciardini: "These disagreements magnified the fear of the Signori and the anger [sdegno] of the popolo, so much so that the

[19] *Cronaca di Alamanno Acciaioli*, in *Cronache e memorie*, p. 18.
[20] Acciaioli says one was tortured with "several hoists" of the strappado; *Cronache e memorie*, p. 22.
[21] *Cronache e memorie*, p. 49. [22] *Cronache e memorie*, p. 32.

standard-bearer, preferring to finish his term of office in shame [vergogna] rather than by confronting danger, appealed to Tommaso Strozzi, who took him from the palace and led him home" (*IF* 3.15.14). In the light of this rebuke of Luigi Guicciardini, how likely is it that Machiavelli embraced the words spoken by his fictional Guicciardini as "true"?

In the popular government in power from September 1378 until early 1382, Machiavelli says, the guildsmen "di minore qualità" enjoyed more power than the "nobili popolani." The Signoria was, indeed, overwhelmingly staffed in this period by non-elite guildsmen, with very few priors from elite families. This, he explains, was the price the "nobili popolani" had to pay for the acquiescence of the other two workers' guilds in the suppression of the wage-laborers' guild. Machiavelli focuses on this government's near-permanent state of siege at the hands of the grandi and their allies among the exiles. The governing group lived in constant fear of "malcontents" in the city who "plotted, or were believed to be plotting, insurrections [cose nuove] every day"; outside the city, plotters openly collaborated with foreign powers to foment division and undermine the government (*IF* 3.18.4–9). The most destabilizing event of these years was the arrest and execution in December, 1379, of Piero degli Albizzi and several other prominent citizens (Machiavelli names six, but there were many more) for conspiring with exiles and foreigners to stage an armed revolt. Following Leonardo Bruni's whitewashing account (9.16–17), Machiavelli says "no proof of guilt was found and the capitano del popolo declined to convict them."[23] But "enemies of the accused so incited the wrath of the popolo against them" that they were sentenced to death. Machiavelli knew how traumatic these executions were for Florence's elite families and how much, as we shall see, they poisoned the memory of this popular government for many decades. He reflects on the irony of Piero's fate—"neither the prominence [grandezza] of his family nor his former renown as the most honored and feared of all citizens helped him"—and inserts an anecdote in which Piero, at a banquet to which he invited many citizens, finds, hidden in a cup, a nail that was "interpreted" as a reminder that, having arrived at the top of fortune's wheel, he should use it to stop the wheel from descending to the bottom.[24] The wheel's inexorable turn, Machiavelli implies, sealed not only Piero's fate but also that of the popular government: after his execution, "the city was engulfed in bewilderment [confusione]; both the vanquished and the victors lived in fear. Yet the most poisonous [maligni] consequences resulted from the fears of those who controlled the government, as every little thing made them heap more injury on the Parte Guelfa" with condemnations, proscriptions, banishments, and "new laws and ordini to strengthen the stato." The "stato" here is the popular government, but

[23] According to Robert A. Fredona, *Political Conspiracy in Florence, 1340–1382*, Ph.D. dissertation, Cornell University, 2010, pp. 181–213, there was abundant evidence of a vast "criminal" conspiracy.

[24] Cabrini analyzes the anecdote and its sources, *Interpretazione e stile*, pp. 130–5.

the next sentence points to its fatally sectarian character: "all these things harmed those who were suspect to their faction [fazione]" (*IF* 3.19.3–8).

This is the only time Machiavelli attaches "faction" to any of the popular movements, uprisings, or governments of 1378–82. That he does so here implies a judgment that this last popular government was being subverted by private ambitions and animosities among its leaders. He identifies its four "principi," all from elite families: Benedetto Alberti, Salvestro de' Medici, Giorgio Scali, and Tommaso Strozzi, (*IF* 3.18.6). The first two had led the assault on the Parte Guelfa, supported the reforms of the summer of 1378, and remained influential allies of the government installed in September 1378. To the latter two Machiavelli imputes "insolenzia," asserting that with their "autorità [influence]" they exceeded the power of the magistrates because everyone feared being persecuted by them. Hence, their "governo [leadership]" seemed "tyrannical and violent" to everyone. Scali and Strozzi, Machiavelli implies, acted more in the manner of party bosses, managing things behind the scenes and superseding the authority of the elected magistrates. Feeling ran especially high over Scali's "insolenzia" when (in January 1382) "one of his followers [uno suo familiare]" was indicted and jailed for falsely accusing a citizen of conspiring against the "stato." After trying, unsuccessfully, to use his influence [autorità]" to liberate him, Scali, together with Tommaso Strozzi "and a multitude of armed men stormed and sacked the captain's palace and freed the prisoner. "This action," says Machiavelli, "filled the city with so much hatred against [Scali] that his enemies believed they could destroy him and free the city not only from his clutches but also from those of the plebe" (*IF* 3.20.1–4). But to do so they needed the agreement of Benedetto Alberti.

Machiavelli describes Benedetto as "very rich, compassionate [umano] and austere [severo], one who cherished the liberty of his patria and so strongly disliked tyrannical ways that it was easy to get him to agree to Scali's downfall." What had made Alberti an opponent of the "popolani nobili" and the "faction" of the Guelfs, Machiavelli says, was their "insolenzia" and "tyrannical ways." But seeing the "capi della plebe" acting in similar ways caused him to take his distance from them as well." Although he points with apparent approval to Benedetto's love of liberty and the patria and his hatred of "modi tirannici," Machiavelli also underscores his shifting loyalties. Perhaps to dramatize this hint of a guilty conscience for betraying a former ally, Machiavelli places Benedetto among the onlookers at Scali's execution. Seeing him, Scali calls out: "And you, messer Benedetto, are you allowing this injustice [ingiuria] to be done to me, which, were I in your place, I would never allow to be done to you? But I tell you that this day is the end of my misfortune [del male mio] and the beginning of yours" (*IF* 3.20.7–12). The execution of Scali and several of his closest allies threw the city into turmoil: Machiavelli says "many citizens took up arms in support of the Signoria and the capitano, while many others did so out of ambition or personal fears [per loro ambizione o per proprii sospetti]" (*IF* 3.21.1). Machiavelli portrays the last days of the government of 1378–82 as beset by personal enmities, "tyrannical ways," and the division of the city into armed bands—all fueled by the ambition and insolence that Machiavelli saw as the pathology of factionalism.

One wonders if this dismal end of the fourteenth-century resistance to elite misrule in Florence caused Machiavelli to contemplate its parallel in the experience of the Roman plebs. Just as Rome's plebs, attempting to effect a more equitable distribution of wealth, resorted, when confronted with the furious opposition of the nobles, to arms, violence, and "rimedii privati" that destroyed Roman liberty, the Florentine popolo, having sought, initially with constitutional methods, to curb the excesses of the Parte Guelfa and create a more equitable distribution of power, similarly resorted, when frightened by the incessant, subversive conspiracies of an elite dislodged from its customary dominance, to draconian measures that pushed the enraged elite to precipitate the government's violent overthrow. Noble "ambizione," Machiavelli repeatedly reminds us, is so relentless that, unless constantly beaten back by popular challenges, however flawed or ill-timed, "it quickly brings a city to destruction" (*DL* 1.37.16–18).

7
Faction and Regime

Machiavelli and Francesco Guicciardini had very different judgments of Florence's ruling group in the half-century between the collapse of the popular government in 1382 and the victory of Cosimo de' Medici in 1434. Twice, in the *Storie fiorentine* and the *Dialogo del reggimento di Firenze*, Guicciardini extolled this regime as the best government Florence ever had. He begins the *Storie* with a brief mention of the Ciompi revolt, noting that his ancestor Luigi was standard-bearer of justice in 1378, and with some hostile comments on the government of 1378–82, controlled, he says, by "uomini plebei" and the "moltitudine," and guilty of having perpetrated "many terrible [brutte] things," especially the execution of Piero degli Albizzi, Donato Barbadori, and "many other innocent" citizens. Stability "finally" came, he says, with the "stato" of 1393 when, with Maso degli Albizzi (Piero's nephew) as standard-bearer of justice, the chief offices were restricted to "well-born and wise men [uomini da bene e savi]," resulting in several decades of "great unity and security." This was not surprising, Guicciardini opines, because "men were exhausted by the turbulence of the past and gladly found repose" in the stable governance ("vivere ordinato") that began, he says, in 1393. Praising this government for the strength and unity it displayed in the wars against Giangaleazzo Visconti of Milan and King Ladislaus of Naples and in the conquest of Pisa, he calls it a time of "many successes." Internally, Florence kept itself "free, united, and governed by well-born, good, and valorous men [uomini da bene e buoni e valenti]"; abroad, the Florentines "defended themselves against very powerful enemies and extended their territorial dominion [imperio]. It is justly said," he concludes, "that this was the wisest, most glorious and happiest government our city has ever had."[1]

In the early 1520s Guicciardini reiterated this judgment in the *Dialogo del reggimento*, a lengthy imagined conversation over two days among four prominent Florentines, set at the end of 1494 or beginning of 1495, after the expulsion of the Medici and the creation of the Great Council, the defining institution of the broadly based popular government. The interlocutors are Bernardo del Nero, the influential Medici adviser who was executed in 1497 for concealing information about Piero de' Medici's conspiracy to overthrow the government by force; Piero Capponi, a proponent of oligarchic government from a family of longstanding

[1] Guicciardini, *Storie fiorentine*, ed. Montevecchi, ch. 1, pp. 77–80.

Machiavelli's Broken World. John M. Najemy, Oxford University Press. © John M. Najemy 2022.
DOI: 10.1093/oso/9780199580927.003.0007

prominence; Paolantonio Soderini, brother of Piero and a Savonarolan who was influential in re-orienting the post-Medici republic away from the oligarchic plan promoted by many ottimati, including Piero Capponi, and toward the broad-based popular constitution centered on the Great Council; and the author's father, Piero Guicciardini, also a Savonarolan. The first day is devoted to evaluating the defunct Medici regime, in preparation for a discussion on the second day of what shape the republic should assume now that a government of the few, as Bernardo says, was "out of consideration" (because of the institution of the Great Council). Capponi, however, does not see why a government of the "cittadini principali e di più qualità [leading citizens of greater rank]" should not still be possible. To support his opinion, he recalls the "stato" of the early fifteenth century when, as he says, Maso degli Albizzi, Niccolò da Uzzano, and his own great-grandfather Gino presided over a government of "leading citizens of the highest worth" that "was not, however," Capponi insists, "so restricted [stretto] that it was not free." Capponi repeats Guicciardini's laudatory characterization in the *Storie* of that ruling group, namely, that it was without upheavals or revolutions ("sanza mutazione") and admirably defended itself against powerful foreign enemies. So much did it enlarge the city's dominion in Tuscany and its own reputation that "in the opinion of everyone who has spoken or written of these matters, Florence never had a stato more ably governed or more honored." The memory of that exemplary government, Capponi says, is what made his group of ottimati hopeful of reviving it after the Medici were exiled (and before the proponents of the Great Council gained the upper hand). Capponi believes there was no danger of tyranny, because "no one was so deluded as to think he could aspire to supremacy [che pretendessi alla superiorità]." He is convinced, moreover, that the fear of falling back into one of "the two extremes"—a broad popular government ("una larghezza populare") or the "return of Piero [de' Medici]"—would have kept the small group of "leading citizens" tightly united.

Bernardo del Nero counters Capponi's idealization of the pre-Medici ruling group and casts doubt on whether something like it could have been revived in 1494. Given the animosities and ambitions [emulazioni e ambizioni] that generate "disunione," Bernardo says, it is likely that among the ottimati someone would have aspired to a position of pre-eminence. Two factors, according to Bernardo, lay behind what he too agrees was the unity of the pre-Medici regime, both of which, he says, are lacking in the post-1494 world. The first is that (as Guicciardini had already written in the *Storie fiorentine*), after so many and such wrenching revolutions of the late fourteenth century, the "men of greatest worth" were "exhausted and desperate" and hence motivated to remain united in order to ensure their collective rule. The memory of the Ciompi and the succeeding popular government of 1378–82, in which the "uomini da bene" had been "battered" as in no other time and "nearly all the best men" suffered oppression and persecution, was a powerful incentive for unity. Bernardo's second reason echoes, as we shall see, Machiavelli's explanation in the *Discursus florentinarum rerum* that the lengthy and difficult wars against Milan and Naples forced that regime's leaders to put aside rivalries and cooperate in saving the city from foreign threats. Whereas in the *Storie* Guicciardini had viewed these wars as evidence of Florentine power and the regime's successful management of affairs, in the *Dialogo* Bernardo sees them as the reason why it did not break apart into factional conflicts. Bernardo goes still further in echoing Machiavelli's critique in the *Discursus* of the pre-Medici oligarchy, telling his listeners that, if they "read the chronicles well," they will see "it was not a free government, because everything was in the hands of a few citizens, and the popolo did not have, one might say, any part in it at all. Nor was it peaceful, Bernardo affirms: there were in fact frequent upheavals and disruptions; as soon as they finished securing and stabilizing their leadership [governo], new divisions erupted among them and the factions that produced the events of '33 and '34 emerged" (the exile of Cosimo de' Medici and his return the next year).[2] When Guicciardini wrote the *Dialogo*, he knew Machiavelli's brief but trenchant critique of the pre-1434 "stato" in the *Discursus* of 1520–1, and the more nuanced evaluation of the pre-Medici oligarchy spoken by Bernardo reveals the influence of that critique on Guicciardini himself.[3] But Guicciardini never relinquished his nostalgia for that leadership group, which was, after all, the only instance in the century and a half from 1382 to the 1520s of a Florentine government entirely in the hands of those "men of worth"—like himself—to whom he always attributed the qualities he believed necessary to save the republic from both (Medici) tyranny and broad-based popular government.

In the *Discursus* Machiavelli judges the pre-Medici regime negatively. He begins by asserting that Florence has never had either a republic or a princely government ("principato") with its requisite features. Referring to the Medici regime, he says "one cannot consider a principato stable where things are done according to the wishes of one man and decided with the agreement [consenso] of many." Then referring to the pre-Medici regime, he adds, "Nor can one believe a republic will last long if it does not satisfy the social classes [umori] whose [interests] must be satisfied if republics are not to collapse. The truth of this can be seen from the stati the city has had since 1393"—the same year Guicciardini identifies as the beginning of stable and successful governance by the "uomini di più qualità." The fundamental flaw, in Machiavelli's view, of Maso degli Albizzi's reforms in that year was that "they wanted to give [Florence] the constitution [forma] of a republic governed by ottimati." The implication that a republic cannot, or should not, be "governed by ottimati" of itself contradicts Guicciardini's

[2] Francesco Guicciardini, *Dialogo del reggimento di Firenze*, ed. Gian Mario Anselmi and Carlo Varotti (Turin: Bollati Boringhieri, 1994), pp. 44–8.

[3] Gennaro Sasso illuminates their long dialogue in "Guicciardini e Machiavelli," in *Francesco Guicciardini 1483–1983* (Florence: Olschki, 1984), pp. 3–130.

notion of an ideal republic. But Machiavelli has more to say about the weaknesses of Florence's early fifteenth-century regime: "It had so many defects that it did not last more than forty years and would have lasted less than that if the wars with the Visconti, which kept it united, had not occurred." He faults the electoral system for approving citizens for high office in scrutinies many years before their names were extracted from the purses, with the result that some of those approved will have become unsuitable for office in the intervening years. Another defect was the lack of any way of instilling fear in the "uomini grandi"—Guicciardini's "uomini da bene e savi"—to dissuade them from "creating factions [sette], which are the ruin of a stato." Related to this was another "disordine" of "no little importance," namely, that "private citizens [gli uomini privati] were giving counsel on public affairs [ne' consigli delle cose pubbliche]." Powerful citizens not in any official capacity and motivated, such is the implication, by personal or factional interests, had too much influence over government. "This enhanced the reputation of private citizens and diminished that of public officials, thereby reducing the prestige [autorità] and reputation of the magistrates, which is contrary to any *ordine civile*," i.e. to any well-ordered polity or republic.

Machiavelli also thought the Signoria had too little prestige ("poca riputazione") and, seemingly paradoxically, too much "autorità," which might seem to contradict the idea that the influence of "uomini privati" undermined the Signoria's "autorità." But he has something quite specific in mind. In two areas, he believed, the Signoria had excessive "autorità"—the authority to dispose of the life and property of citizens without appeal and the power to call the people to a "parlamento." To clarify this second point: parlamenti were ad hoc assemblies of citizens, usually in the piazza of the palace of the priors, called by the Signoria to obtain uncounted voice assent for measures that might not have gained approval from the constituted legislative councils. Parlamenti had no place in Florentine statutory law or legislative procedure. No rules regulated them, which made it possible, even easy, for powerful bosses and factions, if they controlled the Signoria, to manipulate them. The Medici, as Machiavelli well knew, made strategic use of parlamenti during their sixty years in power, and the popular government that succeeded the Medici in 1494 prohibited them. In *Histories* 3.25, as we shall see, Machiavelli observes that in 1393 Maso degli Albizzi, who, as standard-bearer of justice, dominated the Signoria of September-October of that year, asked a parlamento to authorize a balìa—a temporary committee with the power to promulgate decrees that did not need approval by the legislative councils. In addition to completing the political destruction of the rival Alberti, this balìa issued a series of electoral reforms that consolidated the Albizzi faction's control of government and largely determined the composition of the office-holding class for the next forty years. These are the reforms Guicciardini praises so warmly. In the *Discursus* Machiavelli explains, just after discussing the events of 1393, that the power to call parlamenti meant that the Signoria was no longer the "defender" of the "stato" (here akin to our sense of the "state") but had instead become the instrument for bringing about its ruin whenever a "citizen of renown [cittadino reputato]" was able either to dominate the Signoria or pull strings behind the scenes: "la potessi o comandare o aggirare" (the feminine pronoun—"la"—referring to the Signoria). The Signoria's excessive and extra-constitutional power to summon parlamenti thus enhanced the private, behind-the-scenes power of influential citizens. Although, in explaining this "defect," Machiavelli alludes to Maso degli Albizzi and the parlamento of 1393, everyone knew it was the Medici who made frequent and controversial use of this device. The emphasis on the dangerous influence of a "cittadino reputato" in manipulating the Signoria echoes the memorable assertion in *Discourses* 3.28 that, while a republic needs its "cittadini riputati," their "riputazione" is the cause of tyranny in republics. Yet the Signoria itself, he claims in the *Discursus*, lacked "reputazione" because it often included men of low station ("uomini abietti") and young men, and because their terms of office lasted only two months. The ability of powerful "big men" to manipulate the Signoria was a further cause of its declining prestige. To all these "disordini" was added another that, as Machiavelli says, was as significant as all the rest ("che importava il tutto"), which is that the "populo" did not have "la parte sua" in government. "All these things, considered together, made for innumerable [infiniti] disordini."[4] Machiavelli does not elaborate here on the people not having their part in government, but the brief comment anticipates his call, later in the *Discursus*, for a restoration of the Great Council.

"THE KINDS OF DUPLICITY WITH WHICH THINGS HAPPEN IN THIS CITY"

In the *Histories* Machiavelli expands his critique of the pre-Medici regime. He begins with the counter-revolution of 1382, which terminated the popular reforms, suppressed the remaining two of the three workers' guilds created in 1378, reduced the allotment of seats in the Signoria of the traditional minor guilds, and restored the "nobili popolani" and "guelfi" to power (*IF* 3.21.6–7). He quickly asserts that "this regime [stato] was no less abusive [ingiurioso] toward the citizens nor any less oppressive [grave] at the outset than the government of the plebe [of 1378–82] had been." Countering the myth of the elite's unity, he notes the banishment of several "nobili popolani" who had been "defenders of the plebe" (*IF* 3.22.1) and the factional divisions that soon erupted. Benedetto Alberti became suspect to the regime's leaders because he disapproved of the "banishments and death sentences" decreed by the counterrevolution of 1382 and "condemned them publicly and privately." Hence, the "principi" of the new "stato"

[4] *Discursus*, in *SPM*, pp. 624–6.

feared him, "considering him one of the plebe's chief allies." They "also believed he had consented to the execution of Giorgio Scali, not because he disliked his methods, but in order to take sole power in the government [per rimanere solo nel governo]. His words and actions so increased their fears that the entire ruling faction [tutta la parte che era principe] kept their eyes glued on him to seize the opportunity to destroy him" (*IF* 3.22.3–4). Machiavelli highlights the fears, rivalries, and thirst for personal power that, according to Guicciardini, were lacking in this leadership group.

The tension between private and public underlies Machiavelli's account of the fall of Benedetto and the Alberti. After the acquisition of Arezzo (1384), Florence organized "grandiose celebrations" in which "public and private magnificence" was on display. "Many families competed with the commune [a gara con il publico] in their festivities, but the family that outdid all others in ostentatious magnificence was the Alberti, whose extravagant displays and jousting pageants were not those of a private family [non d'una gente privata] but worthy of any prince." This, Machiavelli says, "increased the rancorous envy toward the Alberti, which, added to the suspicion that the regime [lo stato] harbored toward messer Benedetto, was the cause of his downfall." His enemies seized on a convenient pretext (in 1387)—his son-in-law, Filippo Magalotti, drawn for the office of standard-bearer of justice, was found not to have reached the requisite age—to accuse Benedetto of aiming for too much power and posing a danger to the "stato." Drawn in place of Magalotti was Bardo Mancini, "a man completely hostile to the plebs and an enemy of Benedetto" (*IF* 3.23.1–6). Mancini created a balìa—with full powers to confront the alleged emergency—which promptly exiled Benedetto and "warned" the rest of the Alberti. Machiavelli dramatizes Benedetto's departure from Florence by having him address his "consorti" and allude, proleptically, to the fate awaiting them all. No one should be surprised, Benedetto tells his elders ("padri e maggiori"), that "fortune has destroyed me and threatened you," "because this has always happened to those who seek to be good among the wicked and who defend what the majority wish to destroy." In addition to the echo of the dictum in *Prince* 15 about good men coming to bad ends among so many who are not good, this is the beginning of a thorough excoriation of the pre-Medici regime. As love of the patria caused him, Benedetto says, to ally with Salvestro de' Medici and then turn against Giorgio Scali, it also "made me hate the practices of those who now govern [the city]," and who, because they cannot be punished, brook no criticism. Benedetto claims to be "content, by means of my exile, to free them from their fear not just of me but of anyone they know is aware of their tyrannical and criminal [scelerati] ways." Machiavelli has Benedetto say that by punishing him they threaten others. He is sorry, not for himself, because the honors that a "free" patria gave him cannot be rescinded by a patria that has become "serva"—a slave (to tyrants). "It sorrows me that my patria is left as prey to a few [in preda di pochi], subject to their arrogance [superbia] and avarice." Benedetto then forecasts the catastrophe that is about to descend on his entire family: "I sorrow for you, because I fear that the evils that for me finish today are just beginning for you and will pursue you and inflict greater harm on you than what they have done to me." He encourages them "to steel themselves against every affliction and conduct themselves in such a way that, if adversity comes—for much will indeed come—everyone will know it has befallen you in your innocence and without any fault of yours" (*IF* 3.23.7–12).

Beginning with the banishment of Benedetto, Machiavelli makes the persecution of the Alberti a defining manifestation of the factional animosities that, contrary to Guicciardini's judgment, lacerated the post-1382 regime, not unlike earlier divisions of Guelfs and Ghibellines and Black and White Guelfs. Benedetto's fate frames Machiavelli's assessment of the regime. In book 4, when Rinaldo degli Albizzi tries to persuade Giovanni de' Medici to sign on to his plan to subdue the popolo by halving the number of minor guilds and bringing magnates back into government, Giovanni advises caution with the example of Benedetto. "If you recall past events," Giovanni tells Rinaldo, "and the kinds of duplicity [inganni] with which things happen in this city, you would be less enthusiastic about your plan, because those who counsel it, once they take power from the people with your support, will take it away from you with the people's help.... And it will happen to you as it did to messer Benedetto Alberti, who, following the advice of those who did not wish him well and assenting to the downfall of messer Giorgio Scali and messer Tommaso Strozzi, was soon thereafter banished by the same persons who had advised him" to concur in their destruction (*IF* 4.10.4). Machiavelli presents Benedetto and the Alberti as victims of the regime's corrosive and deceitful enmities. But the Alberti were not the only victims of the balìa of 1387. Machiavelli names six members of prominent families who were exiled, together with a "great number" of minor guildsmen. Seven entire families were "warned" and lost the right to political office. To "deprive the lower guildsmen [artefici plebei] of more power," the balìa reduced the minor guilds' share in the Signoria and, to strengthen the ruling group's hold on the Signoria, instituted a small pool of carefully selected citizens of proven loyalty to the governing faction ("de' piú confidenti allo stato") from which two of the priors in each term would be drawn (*IF* 3.24).

Machiavelli thus depicts an insecure regime that feared rivals within its own ranks as much as the still smoldering ambitions of artisans and guildsmen. Both fears play prominent roles in his account of the events of 1393, which, as we have seen, more than a century later were still central to Machiavelli's and Guicciardini's interpretations of Florentine history. With factional animosities very much alive ("tuttavolta vegghiavano gli umori delle parti"), Maso degli Albizzi became standard-bearer of justice (for the term September-October 1393) and made it his highest priority to avenge the execution of his uncle Piero. Although Benedetto Alberti had died in exile, Maso determined to punish the rest of the family and found the "occasione," as Machiavelli says, in an informant's report that two Alberti had been plotting with exiles. The Signoria had them arrested and, with the city suddenly in turmoil, summoned a parlamento which created the balìa that promptly banished "many citizens," carried out electoral reforms (actually far more consequential than Machiavelli's brief reference suggests), exiled "almost all the Alberti," and "warned" and sentenced to death "many guildsmen." Machiavelli says the guilds and the popolo minuto, "believing they had been robbed of honor and life, rose up in arms over the many wrongs [ingiurie] inflicted on them" (*IF* 3.25.6–9). Commentators have suggested that Machiavelli inverts cause and effect here, arguing that the death sentences were a consequence of the guildsmen's actions, not the reason they took up arms,[5] and that, in so doing, he furnishes a justification for their recourse to arms against the balìa.[6] This is possible, given the harsh punishments that awaited them at the conclusion of the unrest. But Machiavelli's source for these events relates that two artisans were in fact killed before the parlamento created the balìa. Machiavelli may have exaggerated in claiming that "many guildsmen" were killed, but two deaths could certainly have triggered an angry reaction. In any case, he says a part of the crowd came to the piazza (of the Signoria), while another group ran to the home of Vieri (Machiavelli gives his name as Veri) di Cambio de' Medici, "who, after the death of Salvestro, had become the leader of the family" and "begged him to seize control of the regime [prendere lo stato] and liberate them from the tyranny of those citizens"—not named, but presumably the ruling faction—"who were destroyers of good men and the common good" (*IF* 3.25.10–12).

Machiavelli's chief source, the anonymous contemporary *Cronica volgare di anonimo fiorentino* (formerly attributed to Piero Minerbetti), tells a somewhat different story. When "the city erupted in turmoil"—exactly why is not clear—"all the citizens prepared to fight, and many ran into the piazza shouting 'Long live the popolo and peace, and the Parte Guelfa, the good citizens [li buoni cittadini].'" Some armed guildsmen went to the palace of the capitano del popolo, seized one of the banners of the popolo's militia, and returned to the piazza shouting "Long live the popolo and the guilds." Hearing the guildsmen chant this unwelcome slogan, many of the "buoni cittadini" assaulted them and forced them to shout "Long live the popolo and the Parte Guelfa." A dyer and his "compagno" "refused to do so" and were immediately attacked and killed. The Signoria gave a banner of the Parte Guelfa to Rinaldo Gianfigliazzi and a banner of the popolo to Donato Acciaiuoli, and "everyone"—presumably all the guildsmen—followed the banner of the popolo. The chronicler comments that "on this day it was clearly seen that the guilds wanted to separate themselves from the good citizens [dividersi da'

[5] See Vittorio Fiorini's commentary in Niccolò Machiavelli, *Istorie fiorentine* (Florence: Sansoni, 1894; reprint edn. 1962), p. 352.
[6] Cabrini, *Interpretazione e stile*, p. 164.

buoni cittadini]," the latter already identified as supporters of the Parte Guelfa. The guildsmen then "said to messer Vieri and messer Michele de' Medici that one of them should take and carry the banner of the popolo held by Acciaiuoli. They all wanted to join them in forcibly seizing it." But no one wanted to do what the guildsmen demanded, "neither messer Vieri nor anyone else of the Medici family; they wanted instead to hold fast to the good citizens under whose rule they wanted the city to remain." The chronicler adds that "many believed that, if the Medici family had wanted to ally with the guildsmen, there was a great danger that the city might have come under the rule of their grasping hands [le loro branche: literally their claws]. For it is believed that many other citizens would have followed them."[7]

In Machiavelli's version there is no mention of a group that challenged the guildsmen with chants of "Long live the Parte Guelfa." Instead he gives the impression that the guildsmen split into two groups for tactical reasons and that the Signoria designated Gianfigliazzi and Acciaiuoli as their "capi" because they were more acceptable to the "plebe" than anyone else and in order to calm them ("adormentargli," literally put them to sleep). Machiavelli also significantly embellishes the chronicler's report that the guildsmen asked Vieri de' Medici to seize power. He has them ask him to do so in order to "liberate them from the tyranny of those citizens who were destroyers of the good [men: de' buoni] and the common good," switching "buoni" from the partisans of the Parte Guelfa to the guildsmen and artisans. Particularly striking is Machiavelli's elaboration with a new twist of the chronicler's comment that the city would have fallen under the "claws" of the Medici if Vieri had done what the guildsmen asked of him. He writes: "All those who have left any record of those times agree that, if messer Vieri had been more ambitious than good," he could easily have made himself "principe" of the city—"principe," as always in such contexts, meaning leading citizen, but alluding, here as in *Discourses* 1.33, to the princely ambitions of the later Medici. Vieri, he says, could have succeeded in taking power, because "the egregious injuries suffered, rightly or wrongly, by the guilds and their allies had so inflamed the desire for revenge that all they lacked to satisfy their wishes was a leader to show them the way" (*IF* 3.25.11–13).

Moreover, whereas the anonymous chronicler says only that Vieri and Michele de' Medici did not accept the guildsmen's "offer" and that, consequently, matters went no further, Machiavelli tells a more complicated and perplexing story. He says Vieri urged calm upon the guildsmen saying he "wished to be their defender provided they let themselves be advised by him." He then went to the Signoria to proclaim that, while he was not sorry to have lived his life in such a way that the people of Florence had great affection for him ("lo amasse"), he did regret that

[7] *Cronica volgare di anonimo fiorentino*, ed. E. Bellondi, in *Rerum Italicarum Scriptores*, vol. 27, pt. 2 (Città di Castello, 1915–18), pp. 179–80.

some—the guildsmen who appealed to him—"had formed an opinion of him that his past life did not warrant." Insisting that he had never shown himself to be "scandaloso"—a sower of discord—or "ambizioso," Vieri said "he did not know how it had come about that some believed he was a restless agitator who incited discord [mantenitore degli scandoli come inquieto] or nurtured ambitions to seize the government [occupatore dello stato come ambizioso]. He begged the Signoria not to impute the ignorance of the multitude to any error [peccato] on his part" and urged them to be satisfied with "half a victory" in restoring the city's security rather than aim for a "complete" victory that might result in its devastation. The Signoria, Machiavelli says, praised Vieri and asked him to return to the guildsmen and persuade them to lay down their arms. Vieri agreed and assured the guildsmen that he had "found in the Signoria great good will toward them." They could be assured of their security, he said, if they put down their arms, showed themselves "more humane than arrogant and made requests rather than threats," and if they followed his advice. Trusting in his promises, they returned to their homes (*IF* 3.25.14–22). But Machiavelli acknowledges that matters did not turn out as Vieri promised. Once the guildsmen put away their arms, the Signoria and the balìa sent an armed security force of 2,000 citizens who were "loyal to the regime [confidenti allo stato]" to take control of the piazza. "Having made these preparations," Machiavelli says, "they exiled and killed many guildsmen who had been especially aggressive [feroci] in the tumults." Some think Machiavelli exaggerates the actual deaths as opposed to death sentences in absentia for contumacy.[8] However, according to an eyewitness chronicle, "seven men were killed in Florence on that day, two of them in the piazza of the Signoria."[9] Machiavelli claims the measures taken by the balìa were "intolerable" to the victims and "odious" even to the "buoni cittadini," who believed that "a stato that needs to defend itself with such violence cannot be considered good and secure" (*IF* 3.26.1–3).

The entire episode—the guilds' appeal to Vieri de' Medici; his speech to the Signoria; his request, backed by the Signoria's promise of safety, that the guildsmen lay down their arms; and the violent betrayal of that promise—is extremely puzzling. In the first place Machiavelli's source for the second half of these events has yet to be discovered. Some think he invented the story.[10] This is possible, but Machiavelli did not just make things up out of whole cloth, and it might be hasty to assert that he did so in this case. If the second part of the episode is, shall we say, creative embellishment on his part, it is surely significant that this occurs in connection with a member of the Medici family and at the crucial juncture in the

[8] Editors' note in *OS*, vol. 1, p. 364, n. 3.

[9] *Alle bocche della piazza. Diario di anonimo fiorentino (1382–1401)*, ed. A. Molho and F. Sznura (Florence: Olschki, 1986), p. 160.

[10] Fiorini, in the edition cited above, p. 353: "Io credo che di qui alla fine del § il M. abbia seguita la propria fantasia." Cabrini considers and excludes all the possible extant sources; *Interpretazione e stile*, p. 167, n. 63.

consolidation of the leadership that controlled the republic for the next forty years before Cosimo put his party in power. One hypothesis, proposed by Mark Jurdjevic, connects the episode involving Vieri in 1393 with Machiavelli's accounts of the roles of two other family members: Salvestro, who supported the guilds' demands for reform in 1378; and, as we shall presently see, Giovanni di Bicci, Cosimo's father. Jurdjevic observes that all three are said by Machiavelli to have cultivated the support of the people, who regarded them as defenders of their interests against the Albizzi-led Parte Guelfa in Salvestro's case and against the Albizzi ruling group in the cases of Vieri and Giovanni di Bicci. According to this interpretation, Machiavelli saw Vieri's "refusal to seize the government," as the guildsmen wanted him to do, in "a positive light." Although invited by an excited multitude to take personal power, Vieri remains a dutiful citizen. He reports to the Signoria the crowd's misguided request and loudly announces that he would never dream of stirring up discord for the sake of ambitions he did not in any case harbor; he agrees to persuade the guildsmen to put down their arms and trust in his, and the Signoria's, good faith. Vieri did not "refuse leadership of the aggrieved guild community," but he did disapprove of "armed confrontation" and preferred to "resolve the city's conflict through debate rather than violence." Jurdjevic speculates that, in Vieri as also in Salvestro and Giovanni di Bicci, Machiavelli intended to furnish the Medici of his own day with examples of family members from the past who respected moderation and civil methods in politics.[11]

This is an intriguing hypothesis, but can it be reconciled with Machiavelli's account of the grim outcome of Vieri's promises to the guilds? Once the guildsmen put down their arms, Machiavelli says, the "Signori" recruited and sent to the piazza a militia that engaged in mayhem. The anonymous chronicler reports that it was the balìa that ordered the Signoria and the Otto di guardia to recruit these 2,000 citizen militiamen and, in addition, to hire 300 infantrymen and 200 Genoese crossbowmen, "all of whom were to stay continuously in the piazza of the Signoria and reside nearby." According to the author of the *Cronica volgare*, "the captain of the balìa seized two of the citizens who shouted 'Long live the popolo and the guilds'...and had them decapitated." The chronicler gives their names, and they are not the same two who, before the balìa began its work, were assaulted and killed for shouting the same thing. He also reports that the captain interrogated and convicted in absentia twenty three more guildsmen and artisans and had another executed merely for appearing as the sentences were being read.[12] That it was the balìa that organized the violent repression assumes significance in light of the fact that Vieri was among its members,[13] and, as such, not

[11] Jurdjevic, *Great and Wretched City*, pp. 165–77; cited passages on Vieri, pp. 167–8.
[12] *Cronica volgare di anonimo fiorentino*, ed. Bellondi, pp. 181–2.
[13] *Alle bocche della piazza*, ed. Molho and Sznura, p. 155.

only knew of the military force hired to police the piazza and the three cases of capital punishment but must also have participated in the deliberations that led to this outcome.

The pivotal assertion in Machiavelli's account claims that "many disliked so much violence," including the Medici "to whom it seemed that they had deceived the people [e ai Medici ai quali pareva avere ingannato il popolo]" (*IF* 3.26.4).[14] The passage alludes to Vieri himself having deceived the people, and, although it is not clear whether Machiavelli thinks Vieri knowingly participated in the deception, the fact that he was at least its instrument must raise questions about Machiavelli's view of him. Was he the naive dupe of the Signoria and the balìa, and hence of Maso degli Albizzi? Did they deceive him? Or was Vieri a witting perpetrator of the deception? If the latter, does the episode function as a murky prefiguration of deceptions employed by the fifteenth-century Medici who more than once disingenuously claimed to be defenders of the people in order to suppress their own rivals. The *inganno* of which Vieri was either victim or perpetrator is recalled, as already noted, in book 4 when Giovanni di Bicci refuses to take part in Rinaldo degli Albizzi's plan to weaken the influence of the people and reminds him of the kinds of "inganni" that propelled events in Florence. And there is another echo of Vieri's story in Machiavelli's portrait of Giovanni di Bicci. After the guildsmen ask Vieri to seize the "stato," Vieri's kinsman, Antonio de' Medici, despite having "nurtured personal animosity [particolare inimicizia] against Vieri for some time, encourages him to seize command [pigliare il dominio] of the republic." Machiavelli has Vieri reply: "Your threats did not frighten me when you were my adversary, nor will your advice damage me now that you are my friend." Where Machiavelli found this, or whether he invented it, is not known. He may or may not have known that Antonio de' Medici was Vieri's nephew, became his business partner in 1386, and inherited the Florence branch of the company when Vieri retired in 1392.[15] To my knowledge (and, as far as I know, that of others who have investigated the matter),[16] no source mentions Antonio's advice to Vieri. But Machiavelli's invention—if that is what it is—of a close relative encouraging the head of the Medici family to seize power too closely matches Alamanno de' Medici's similar advice to Giovanni di Bicci, in chapter 11 of book 4, to adopt a more aggressive political agenda for it to be a coincidence.[17] If Pope Clement VII, who as Cardinal Giulio de' Medici approved Machiavelli's commission to write the *Histories*, actually read the book, he may have noted with satisfaction his

[14] Following Allan Gilbert's translation, Jurdjevic, *Great and Wretched City*, p. 170, reads this as saying that the Medici "felt that the Signors [the Signoria] had deceived the people." The Signoria did indeed deceive the people, but Machiavelli says the Medici felt that *they*, the Medici, had deceived the people.

[15] Raymond de Roover, "Gli antecedenti del Banco Mediceo e l'azienda bancaria di messer Vieri di Cambio de' Medici," *Archivio storico italiano* 123 (1965): 3–13.

[16] Cabrini, *Interpretazione e stile*, p. 166.

[17] Noted by Jurdjevic, *Great and Wretched City*, p. 167.

distant ancestor's principled decision, as a good citizen, not to seize the "stato" and not to accept the guildsmen's request to make himself "principe" of the city. But was he pleased that, in Machiavelli's interpretation, Vieri cooperated in the deceit and enabled the violence with which the crisis was resolved?

The banishments of 1393 did not diminish rivalries within the elite. The remaining chapters of book 3 recount episodes of opposition to, or conspiracies against, the governing inner circle—or accusations of the same concocted by it to discredit political opponents. Among those who "disliked the violence" of 1393 was Donato Acciaiuoli, who, "unable to live contentedly amidst so much wickedness [tanti mali]" and unwilling to exploit "public adversity [il comune danno] for personal gain [privato commodo], as most people do," tried (in 1395–6) to build support for repatriating the exiles and restoring political rights to the "ammuniti." There was no other way, he told many people, "to calm the popolo and mollify the passions of the factions." Failing to achieve his aims through legislation, Machiavelli writes, Acciaiuoli let frustration get the better of him and incautiously blurted out that, if the government refused to do this through institutional channels, "it would be achieved with arms." Someone reported the comment to the "principi del governo," who quickly indicted and banished Acciaiuoli together with Alamanno de' Medici and all his descendants, the aforementioned Antonio de' Medici, and "many minor guildsmen" (*IF* 3.26.4–12). The inclusion of the Medici among these exiles suggests that the Signoria saw a conspiracy here, but Machiavelli does not say this and leaves open the suspicion that the regime's leaders may have invented a conspiracy to rid itself of political opponents.

There were still, however, many "malcontents" in the city who, together with numerous exiles, hatched in 1397 what Machiavelli unambiguously describes as a conspiracy to re-enter the city, kill Maso degli Albizzi, and incite a rebellion among the popolo. The exiles included members of the Cavicciuli (a branch of the Adimari), Ricci, Spini, and Girolami families, and, once again, Antonio de' Medici, "all young, audacious, and willing to tempt fortune [tentare ogni fortuna] in order to return to the patria." Convinced that they could rouse the "discontented" popolo to revolt, aided within by the Ricci, Adimari, Medici, Mannelli, "and many other families," they secretly slipped into the city and hid in the homes of the Cavicciuli, waiting for Maso to leave his home. Nothing went according to plan. They killed two persons of the "opposing faction," but Maso escaped harm and the Signoria had the conspirators captured and executed—another bungled affair of elite families. Machiavelli devotes much attention to the conspirators' failure to rouse the multitude, which on this occasion showed no interest in rebellion. Despite the conspirators' cries of "popolo, arms, and liberty" and "death to the tyrants" as they went running through the streets, crowds gathered only to stare at them and at each other, Machiavelli says, unmoved by the would-be "liberators." Implying that the families who conspired against the regime miscalculated in expecting to exploit for their own purposes what they assumed was the discontent of the popolo, Machiavelli comments that "the promoters of the tumult, seeing that neither words nor actions sufficed to embolden the citizens, realized too late how dangerous it is to want to liberate a people determined to remain enslaved [servo]" (*IF* 3.27.1–9).

One last conspiracy "of greater importance" closes the third book of the *Histories*. Together with Duke Giangaleazzo Visconti of Milan, with whom Florence had been at war for ten years, Florentine exiles schemed to assassinate the "leaders of the stato" and "reform the republic as they wanted." Within the city, the ringleader was Samminiato de' Ricci, who, searching for allies, revealed the plot to one of the Cavicciuli, who in turn reported it to the Signoria. A balìa ordered the execution of Samminiato and imposed rebel status—thus removing the legal protections afforded to citizens—on six other members of the Ricci, six Alberti, two Medici, three Scali, two Strozzi, an Altoviti, an Adimari, and "molti ignobili." It also "warned," and deprived of office-holding rights for ten years, the entire families of the Alberti, Ricci, and Medici. Of the Alberti, only messer Antonio was exempt from the "ammonizione"—until the balìa discovered that he too had been corresponding with the conspirators, whereupon, "to prevent the Alberti from continually endangering the regime [stato]," it exiled all members of the family over the age of 15 (*IF* 3.28). The city was peaceful, Machiavelli says, from the expulsion of the Alberti in 1400 until 1433, the "only" exception, he quickly adds, being a conspiracy by the Alberti to force their way back in 1412, which resulted in another balìa that worsened their punishments. But he shortens the period of internal peace again, noting that, after eight years of calm following the end of the war with King Ladislaus of Naples in 1414, new wars with Milan erupted, "which reignited factional hostilities that only ended with the collapse of the stato that had governed" from 1381/2 to 1434 (*IF* 3.29).

"AGENTS OF SERVITUDE"

The first two chapters of book 4 constitute the conceptual hub of Machiavelli's critique of the pre-Medici regime. They need to be considered as two parts of a whole, and perhaps not even two distinct parts, given that, as the manuscripts reveal, Machiavelli did not divide the text into chapters. The essence of the critique is that the leadership so weakened the ordini—the laws and institutions of the republic—that, by the beginning of the fifteenth century, Florence could no longer be classified as "bene ordinata" because it was not governed through "good laws and good ordini" and was therefore incapable of liberty. This is the hinge of the *Florentine Histories*, the historical moment—actually a long generation—in which the republic lost the institutions and norms that had, until then, produced ever greater equality (in Machiavelli's sense of the term) by restricting the ambition of the elite class, both the magnates and the "popolani nobili" who had inherited their aims and methods.

To appreciate the full significance of book 4's proemial chapter, it is useful to begin at the end of the second chapter, where Machiavelli identifies "two errors" of the "nobili popolani" that caused their downfall. First, they became "insolenti" because of their "uninterrupted hegemony [continuo dominio]." "Insolente," we recall, is one of Machiavelli's two most frequent characterizations of elite classes, the other being "ambizioso." "Insolente," "insolenzia," and related forms appear a combined twenty times in books 2 and 3 and the first two chapters of book 4 of the *Florentine Histories*, denoting excessive, offensive, and overbearing behavior and brazen arrogance. If the elite's "insolenzia" was not new, it was now immutable, because of the leadership's "continuo dominio"—its monopoly of power. The governing faction not only rebuffed popular challenges; it also eliminated rivals from within its own class, both achieved with the balìe and/or parlamenti of 1382, 1387, 1393, and 1400. In Machiavelli's interpretation the suppression of the popolo and the elimination of rival elite factions converged, because the elite families that opposed the Albizzi—chiefly the Alberti, Ricci, and Medici—had supported the popular government of 1378–82. This faction, "which enjoyed more favor with the multitude [piú favorita dallo universale], was predominant for only three years and was defeated in 1381[2]. But it could not be completely extinguished because the majority of the city" shared its "umore"—its inclinations and opinions. Although not eradicated, the faction of the Alberti, Ricci, and Medici was "reduced to almost nothing" by "the frequent parlamenti and ongoing persecutions of their leaders between '81[/2] and '400." The severe blows ("battiture") of banishment, confiscation of property, and, for those who escaped exile, prohibition against holding office made their faction pitiful ("umile") and almost destroyed it. But the resurgence of the Medici is the chief topic of book 4, and Machiavelli says the "memories of the wrongs" done to them left in their breasts a hidden desire for revenge. This connects to the second "error" of the regime's leaders, namely, that, "because of resentments [invidia] among themselves and their long control of the stato [regime], they did not pay sufficient heed, as they should have, to those who could damage them" (*IF* 4.2.4–8), namely, the Medici.

Machiavelli's summary in chapter 2 of the ruling group's "errors" helps us understand the context and polemical force of the first chapter, which addresses the weaknesses of "cities"—plural, but the focus is Florence—that are not "bene ordinate" but "are governed as republics." Such cities vary their "governi e stati" between "servitú" and "licenzia," and not, "as many believe," between "libertà" and "servitú." Liberty, in other words, is impossible without good ordini, and republics without good ordini, as Florence had become by 1400, so Machiavelli believes, can oscillate only between "licenzia" and "servitú." In such conditions the "ministri" (agents who serve or promote) of "licenzia," who are the "popolari," honor only the "name of liberty"—not liberty itself—because, in the absence of healthy ordini, no one is willing to be "subject to the laws or to men" (*IF* 4.1.1–2). "Licenzia," as Machiavelli says in the *Discourses*, denotes the corruption specifically of popular government: without the rules and restraints of good laws and good ordini, the "stato popolare" slides into a state of "licenza" in which no one fears either "private" citizens or "public" officials, "everyone lives as he pleases," and "consequently a thousand wrongs [ingiurie: injustices, offenses] are committed" (*DL* 1.2.23).

The agents of "servitú" are the "nobili," which here refers to the entire wealthy elite. In this passage "servitú" is domination by the "nobles," not submission to a prince or a foreign power, two meanings it has elsewhere in Machiavelli's writings. As with the agents of "licenzia," the agents of "servitú" only nominally and superficially honor liberty and refuse to be "subject to the laws or to men." Later in the chapter Machiavelli redefines the alternatives facing republican cities that are not "bene ordinate" as tyranny ("tirannico") and license ("licenzioso)," implying that "servitú" ministered by nobles is, or can be, a form of tyranny (a theme to be explored in due course). Neither in "licenzia" nor under "servitú"/tyranny, Machiavelli says, can a city find stability, because "good men" do not like "servitú," and "wise men"—the "savi," generally denoting the elite class, but often with irony—do not like "licenzia." Hence, both of these corrupt conditions generate disaffection and dissension. A "stato [regime]" of "servitú" "can easily do much harm," whereas one of "licenzia" "can do good only with difficulty." Under "servitú," "insolent men have too much power," as "do foolish men [gli sciocchi]" under "licenzia." In the chapter's last sentence Machiavelli asserts that these defective forms of governance can be "maintained" only "by the virtú and fortuna of one man." It requires skill and ingenuity, in other words, to keep afloat an inherently unstable city that lacks good ordini, but he does not say whether the "fortuna" he also thinks necessary is good luck or, more troublingly, dependence on others. In any case, such a man, even with all his virtú and fortuna, cannot be a long-term solution, because "death can remove him and mishaps can render him ineffective."

This hypothetical "maintainer" is not be confused with the "wise, good, and powerful citizen" Machiavelli hypothesizes earlier in the chapter as capable of legislating the missing ordini. If such a legislator emerges in a city that lacks good ordini—and Machiavelli immediately acknowledges that this rarely ("rade volte") occurs—and creates laws that calm the "umori" (the passions and divisions) of the "nobili" and the "popolani," that city "can be called free and its government considered stable, because, being founded on good laws and good ordini, it has no need of the virtú of one man to maintain it." Machiavelli thus distinguishes the rare event of creating good ordini in a corrupt city, which eliminates the republic's dependence on the virtú of one man, from the more common need to "maintain" a defective republic with virtú and/or fortune, which can only be a short-term fix. Machiavelli does not say what happens when the caretaker of a defective republic dies or is swept aside by the accidents of history.

At the beginning of chapter 2, Machiavelli links the pre-Medici regime to his theory of the dependence of defective republics on the virtú of one man. "The stato [regime] that began in 1381/2 with the death of Giorgio Scali," he writes, was "sustained" first by the "virtú" of Maso degli Albizzi and then (after his death in 1417) by that of Niccolò da Uzzano (also a member of the balìa of 1393 and subsequently a highly respected and influential figure until his death in 1431). Machiavelli names five additional "cittadini di autorità [influential citizens]": Bartolomeo Valori (who played a key role in the electoral reforms of 1393); Nerone di Nigi (Dietisalvi, who survived the Albizzi group's downfall in 1434 and became a loyal Medici ally); Rinaldo degli Albizzi (Maso's son, on whom more below); Neri di Gino (Capponi, who maintained a degree of independence between the Medici and their opponents in a distinguished diplomatic and military career, including a prominent role in Florence's victory at Anghiari in 1440), and Lapo Niccolini. There is nothing surprising about Machiavelli's choice of these seven citizens; all were from elite families and among the leaders of the regime in the half century between 1382 and 1434. Maso degli Albizzi, Niccolò da Uzzano, and Bartolomeo Valori each served as standard-bearer of justice three times. Lapo Niccolini did so five times in addition to two terms as a prior. Several of them were elected many times to the Signoria's advisory colleges of the Twelve and the Sixteen. But many other members of elite families had similar office-holding careers, and, aside from Rinaldo degli Albizzi who, despite holding office less frequently, was perhaps the most influential figure in Florentine politics after his father's death, one may wonder why Machiavelli chose the remaining four "influential citizens" in preference to many others. Are they only examples? Or do they have something in common? Intriguingly, although Machiavelli does not mention this, four of the seven, including Lapo Niccolini, served on one or the other of the balìe that managed the war against Pisa in 1405–6, as did Gino Capponi, the father of Neri. In any case, there are clearly two categories here: a first tier of two men whose virtú "sustained the stato," and five others characterized as "influential citizens." Especially noteworthy is the relegation of Rinaldo degli Albizzi to the second group, despite his central role in Florentine and Italian politics in the 1420s and 1430s. That Rinaldo, in Machiavelli's estimation, was not among those whose virtú "sustained the stato" foreshadows the critical assessment of him in books 4 and 5.

Book 4's opening chapters telescope the origins and development of the conflict that would bring down the pre-Medici regime. In chapter 3, Machiavelli introduces what he could have offered as a third and indeed the worst of the ruling group's errors, namely, that "they daily rekindled the hatred of the multitude [nello universale]" with their "sinistri modi." "Sinistro" can mean offensive, injurious, damaging, or wicked. Guicciardini attaches to the term the sense of domineering, arrogant, illegitimate, or even tyrannical (for example, in so characterizing the actions and attitudes of Piero de' Medici that alienated Medici allies and led to the expulsion of 1494).[18] Machiavelli depicts the behavior of the leaders with some combination of these meanings, identifying their "sinistri modi" as the cause of the hatred he says they engendered in the population at large. At the same time, either by failing to exercise adequate vigilance over lurking dangers because they had no fear of them, or (paradoxically) by creating dangers through mutual resentments amongst themselves, the regime's leaders opened the door "for the Medici family to regain influence [autorità]." Giovanni di Bicci de' Medici, whom he describes as "very rich and by nature benevolent and compassionate [benigno e umano]" began the family's revival when he was elected to the Signoria (for the term of July-August 1402). Curiously, Machiavelli adds that this occurred "by concession," or agreement, of those who controlled the government. Machiavelli knew that in those years the names of citizens approved in a scrutiny were placed in pouches and drawn by lot, in some cases many years after the scrutiny. In the half-century before 1434 only once, in the exceptional circumstances of 1393, was sortition (the drawing by lot) set aside and the priors handpicked for the next term by the balìa. Giovanni di Bicci was a member of that balìa, which suggests that at that time, despite the punishments visited on other branches of the family, he was in the good graces of the Albizzi faction. Moreover, the two-month term in which he served as prior in 1402 was a time of crisis, with the city fearing imminent attack from the forces of Giangaleazzo Visconti of Milan. The year before, the commune had relied on Giovanni, already a very wealthy banker, to supply the huge sum of 200,000 florins promised to the emperor, Rupert of Bavaria, for military aid against Giangaleazzo. None of this suggests that the ruling group made, or had to make, any kind of "concession" for Giovanni to be elected to the Signoria. Machiavelli may have assumed that, because other Medici suffered exile (and in one case execution) for conspiring against the leadership, Giovanni's election required some special approval. If he made such an assumption, it is an early indication that he viewed the rise of the Medici as the result of errors and willful blindness on the part of the preceding regime.

Even at this early moment, Niccolò da Uzzano enters the narrative as the prophet of the regime's self-destruction. The multitude, Machiavelli says, was overjoyed at the election of Giovanni di Bicci as prior, because "it seemed" to them they had gained a "defender" against the hated oligarchs. If it "seemed" so to them, to "wiser heads" the multitude's joy was cause for concern, because they saw "old passions [gli antichi umori]"—between elite and popolo—"beginning to revive." Machiavelli continues: "And Niccolò da Uzzano did not fail to warn the other citizens of this, showing how dangerous it was to support [nutrire] one who enjoyed so much favor with the multitude, and how it was easy to confront problems [disordini] at the outset, but difficult to remedy them once they have been

[18] Francesco Guicciardini, "Del modo di assicurare lo stato alla Casa de' Medici," in Palmarocchi, ed., *Dialogo e discorsi*, pp. 267–81 (at p. 276).

allowed to grow." Uzzano thus associates Giovanni's reputation as a "defender" of the "multitude" with "disordini" and adds the warning, ominous for the ruling group, that he saw in Giovanni many characteristics that "exceeded those of messer Salvestro," whose fierce opposition to the Parte Guelfa and the Albizzi had ignited the revolutions of 1378. Yet, because Uzzano's peers ("uguali") resented his prestige, no one, says Machiavelli, listened to him (*IF* 4.3.1–6).

"IT PAINED THEM NOT TO BE ABLE TO START A WAR WITHOUT FINANCIAL SACRIFICE TO THEMSELVES"

Controversies over foreign policy and taxes divided the city in the 1420s. The "piú reputati," Machiavelli says, favored securing arms and taking the initiative to meet the reviving threat from Milan, whereas "many others," either out of "invidia" of the ruling group (the context implies hostility more than envy) or from fear of war, believed it too risky to provoke the Milanese. The influence ("autorità") of the former prevailed: mercenaries were hired and new taxes levied. The taxes hit the "minori" more than the "maggiori" citizens and filled the city with bitterness, as everyone denounced the "ambizione" and "avarizia" of the "potenti," "accusing them of starting an unnecessary war to satisfy their own desires and oppress and dominate the popolo" (*IF* 4.4.4–6). According to Machiavelli, Giovanni de' Medici discouraged a headlong rush to war (*IF* 4.5.5), but those in favor had greater sway and (in 1424) the Ten sent troops into the Romagna who suffered a major defeat (*IF* 4.6) at Zagonara (east of Imola and north of Faenza). "The entire city of Florence," Machiavelli says, "sorely grieved over the news of this defeat, including the grandi who had promoted the war." But the popolo was outspokenly furious. "In all the city's piazze the popolo castigated [the grandi] with abusive words, bemoaning the taxes they had to endure for a war started without cause." Elaborating on the accusations he found in his (nearly exclusive) source for book 4, the *Istorie fiorentine* of the early fifteenth-century historian Giovanni Cavalcanti,[19] Machiavelli fashions a collective indictment spoken by unnamed citizens of the popolo: "Their plans and the objectives they were pursuing have now been exposed: not to defend liberty, which is their enemy, but to enhance their own power, which God has justly diminished. Nor is this the only undertaking in which they have burdened the city with taxes. There have been many; the war against King Ladislaus [of Naples] was similar to this one" (*IF* 4.7.1–4).

Machiavelli dramatizes the ruling group's response to the growing agitation of the angry popolo. "To calm, with good words, the passions stirred by the multitude," the Signoria convened a meeting of many citizens (in mid-1426) at which

[19] Giovanni Cavalcanti, *Istorie fiorentine*, ed. Filippo Luigi Polidori (Florence, 1838–9), vol. 1, book 2, ch. 21, pp. 65–7; in the edition by Guido Di Pino (Milan: Aldo Martello Editore, 1944), pp. 39–40.

Rinaldo degli Albizzi (in his first active appearance in Machiavelli's narrative) "spoke at great length." Through the fourth book and into the fifth, Machiavelli portrays Rinaldo as a complex figure who, as we shall see, plays a crucial part in the collapse of the pre-Medici "stato." Machiavelli introduces him by imputing personal political motives to his pursuit of a war so hated by the people: "he aspired, with his own abilities [le virtú sua] and the memory of his father, to the highest rank in the city." Rinaldo tells the gathering that "it is not wise to judge things by their outcomes [effetti], because many times things planned well [bene consigliate] do not have a good result [fine] and things poorly planned have a good result," implying that the defeat at Zagonara neither proved that the leadership had started a war for dishonorable reasons nor invalidated the wisdom of their decision. If the Florentines had not confronted the Milanese in the Romagna, Machiavelli has Rinaldo say, they would have had to do so in Tuscany. Rinaldo deflects the protests over taxes, cautioning that no one should be frightened by the costs or by future taxes: "it was right to adjust the taxes, and future military expenses will be less than in the past." He encourages his listeners to "imitate their fathers"—their ancestors—"who, because they did not lose courage in any adversity, always defended themselves against any and all princes" (*IF* 4.7.7–12). Rinaldo's speech, says Machiavelli, sufficiently calmed the citizens to allow new mercenaries to be hired (*IF* 4.8.1).

Yet the furor over taxes did not subside. Closely following Cavalcanti's account,[20] Machiavelli says a committee of twenty citizens, "emboldened" by seeing the "potenti cittadini" humiliated after Zagonara, unhesitatingly and drastically increased assessments on the wealthy. At first, the "cittadini grandi," in order to appear more honorable, lamented the burden on all citizens, not just on themselves, and proposed a general reduction for everyone. But the legislative councils refused to approve any reduction and prescribed draconian, even capital, punishments for those refusing to pay the assessments. Machiavelli magnifies Cavalcanti's reports of strife and clashes, asserting that some were killed and others wounded and that "it seemed the parties [parti] would come to the spilling of blood." The "uomini grandi," who were "accustomed to deference [ad essere riguardati]," could not tolerate the disrespect and threats of violence directed at them. The "others"—Machiavelli has not yet said who they are—insisted that everyone be taxed "equally." Facing this crisis, many of the "primi cittadini" decided on a radical plan to "retake the government [ripigliare lo stato]," because "their own insufficient diligence had encouraged men to resume active political involvement [riprendere le azioni publiche] and emboldened the leaders of the multitude." Cavalcanti says the leading citizens wanted to evade higher taxes and restore good government to the republic, but Machiavelli heightens the stakes by attributing to the "potenti cittadini" the intention of "retaking the government" in a struggle against citizens

[20] Cavalcanti, *Istorie* 3.1, ed. Polidori, vol. 1, pp. 71–4; ed. Di Pino, pp. 45–6.

who were reasserting themselves in political life. With permission from the standard-bearer of justice, Lorenzo Ridolfi, and one of the priors, Francesco Gianfigliazzi, some seventy citizens from elite families met in the church of Santo Stefano al Ponte to hear Rinaldo's advice and recommendations. Machiavelli pointedly notes that Giovanni de' Medici was not among the seventy (*IF* 4.8.2–8).

Doubts have been expressed about the accuracy of Cavalcanti's version of these events because of the vehemence of Rinaldo's denunciation of the guildsmen and the radical, even inflammatory, nature of his proposals. But controversy over war and taxes was indeed intense in these years.[21] What is relevant here is that Machiavelli regarded the speech reported by Cavalcanti as compatible with his own view of Florence's "grandi." Both Cavalcanti and Machiavelli represent the Santo Stefano meeting as an unofficial and private, even if large, gathering to confront a perceived emergency, not as a formal advisory meeting (*pratica*). Irregular, private, and secret meetings were common in these years, but they were also illegal, and laws were passed to prohibit and punish them. Requesting permission from the Signoria to convene such a meeting was no doubt an attempt to deflect accusations of illegality. Cavalcanti says the group's leaders knew that the two members of the Signoria whom they approached shared their views and would give their approval.[22] Machiavelli does not repeat this detail but does say that, after preliminary discussions, the worried "primi cittadini" decided, with the "licenzia" of Ridolfi and Gianfigliazzi, to "assemble the entire group at once [ad un tratto]" (*IF* 4.8.7). Even with permission granted, the participants had good reason not to let the event become widely known, given the fury with which Rinaldo denounced the popolo. In Cavalcanti's version he delivers a blistering attack on the city's guildsmen as the authors of all the city's—and the elite's—woes.[23] Machiavelli has Rinaldo begin by saying that the "negligence" of the leadership had allowed the city once again to come under the power of the "plebe," from which it had been rescued "by their fathers in 1381 [1382 modern style]." Recalling the "iniquity" of the government that ruled from 1378 to 1382, Machiavelli's Rinaldo voices the wildly exaggerated accusation that every one of the seventy men present had a father or other ancestor killed by that "stato." The city was falling back into the same dangers and "disordini," he says, with the "multitude" imposing taxes as it saw fit, and, unless some "maggiore forza" or

[21] See Anthony Molho, *Florentine Public Finances in the Early Renaissance, 1400–33* (Cambridge, Mass.: Harvard University Press, 1971), pp. 74–87 and passim; Gene Brucker, *The Civic World of Early Renaissance Florence* (Princeton: Princeton University Press, 1977), pp. 472–81; Dale Kent, *The Rise of the Medici: Faction in Florence, 1426–1434* (Oxford: Oxford University Press, 1978), pp. 213–20; Elio Conti, *L'imposta diretta a Firenze nel Quattrocento (1427–1494)* (Rome: Istituto Storico Italiano per il Medio Evo, 1984), pp. 119–37; and Arthur Field, *The Intellectual Struggle for Florence* (Oxford: Oxford University Press, 2017), pp. 38–52.

[22] Cavalcanti, *Istorie* 3.1, ed. Polidori, p. 73; ed. Di Pino, p. 46.

[23] Cavalcanti, *Istorie* 3.2, ed. Polidori, pp. 78–86; ed. Di Pino, pp. 48–52.

"migliore ordine" restrained it, it would soon be filling the magistracies as it pleased. If that happened, Rinaldo warns, the multitude would replace those present and "destroy the stato that ruled the city with such glory for forty-two years." Florence would either be governed "chaotically [a caso] by the whim of the multitude," with one part of the city (the multitude) living "licenziosamente" and the other part (the elite) "pericolosamente," or under the rule of one man who would make himself "principe" of the city (alluding possibly to the Medici). Machiavelli's Rinaldo continues: "Everyone who loves the patria and his own honor should bestir himself and remember the virtú of Bardo Mancini, who, by destroying the Alberti, rescued the city from the dangers it then faced" (a reference to the balìa of 1387). At the heart of the problem, according to Rinaldo, were the broad-based scrutinies that the ruling group's own "negligence" allowed. He alludes to the increased numbers of citizens approved in the scrutinies for major offices in claiming that the government palace abounds with "new men of low birth [uomini nuovi e vili]" (*IF* 4.9.1–3). In reality, although Machiavelli may not have known this with any precision, despite the approval in the scrutinies of large numbers of citizens (over 1,000 in 1411 and 2,000 in 1433), the numbers of "new men" reaching the Signoria—the first of their families to do so—were quite small. Machiavelli has Rinaldo reflect the elite's traumatized memory of 1378–82 and its fear, real or manipulated, of the popolo.

As does Cavalcanti, Machiavelli has Rinaldo propose a plan he believes is the only way to save the elite from suffering renewed rule by "new men" and the "plebe" (which, in this context, denotes the non-elite and minor guildsmen). He advocates restoring office-holding rights to the magnates ("rendere lo stato ai grandi") and reducing the number of minor guilds from fourteen to seven, which he says would diminish the influence of the "plebe" (and the guild community as a whole) in the legislative councils. "Prudenza," he says, consists in knowing how "to make use of people [sapersi valere degli uomini] according to the times." Just as their "fathers"—their ancestors going back several generations—"made use of the plebe to suppress the insolence of the magnates, now that the magnates have become humble and the plebe insolent, it is well to restrain the plebe's insolence with the help of the magnates" (*IF* 4.9.4). Rinaldo recommends, in effect, nothing less than abrogating the Ordinances of Justice and overturning the guild constitution of 1293 (as the magnates themselves had occasionally tried to do until 1343). Many formerly magnate families had since been integrated into the ranks of the "popolani" (i.e. non-magnate) citizens with full office-holding rights: the Gianfigliazzi, one of whom, as prior, approved the Santo Stefano meeting, are a prime example. To restore such rights to all remaining magnates would have accelerated a process that was already underway (and which the Medici completed after 1434).[24] But cutting the number of minor guilds in half would have

[24] See Klapisch-Zuber, *Ritorno alla politica*, especially pp. 311–45.

seriously weakened the political presence and influence of the entire guild community. Especially for the fourteen minor guilds, the full complement of twenty-one guilds established in 1293 was a non-negotiable sine qua non of the popular constitution. Reducing their number had been tried once before; in 1348, when the Black Death was killing a huge percentage of the population, an emergency balìa controlled by elite families decreased the minor guilds from fourteen to seven—but the measure was rescinded just two years later.

Rinaldo makes the most scandalous of his proposals when, in Machiavelli's narrative, he turns to the problem of how to effect these changes. It could be done either by deception ("inganno") or force ("forza"), he asserts, but force would be easy because, as he notes, several attendees at the Santo Stefano gathering were at that time serving on the magistracy of the Ten, which administered military affairs and the hiring of troops. They could, Machiavelli has Rinaldo say, "secretly bring soldiers into the city" (*IF* 4.9.4). In Cavalcanti Rinaldo raises the idea even more prominently, suggesting that two or three thousand infantry could be brought into the city to occupy the piazza, under the pretense of mustering them for review. "All laws," says Cavalcanti's Rinaldo, "however efficacious and just they may be, are dependent on force [stanno suggette alla forza], for in the final analysis the sword is the authoritative judge [il competente giudice]."[25] Machiavelli's Rinaldo proposes the idea more matter-of-factly but still envisions nothing less than a coup d'état and military occupation of the city center to impose radical political changes. Machiavelli lets the outrageousness of the idea speak for itself, perhaps because, as we shall see, Rinaldo attempted a similar resort to force in 1434, and because in subsequent decades the Medici too often employed their own or mercenary troops to suppress opposition and ensure the success of their agenda. Machiavelli's opinion of such methods is unambiguous: utilizing "forze private" and "forze forestieri," he says in *Discourses* 1.7, to change or overthrow a government is the mark of a city with defective ordini, and, as he says in *Histories* 4.1, the pre-Medici "stato" was not "bene ordinato." The willingness of the old magnates to use their power to overthrow governments, Machiavelli insists, was still alive in the "nobili popolani" of the fifteenth century.

Machiavelli says everyone at the Santo Stefano meeting praised Rinaldo's recommendations, including Niccolò da Uzzano who proclaims everything Rinaldo said to be "true" and his solutions "good and certain"—but only if they could be implemented without openly dividing the city, which he was sure would happen unless they persuaded Giovanni de' Medici to sign on. If the plotters secure his cooperation, Uzzano continues, the multitude would lack the "leadership and forces" required to mount serious opposition; otherwise, the plan will not succeed "without arms," and even with arms they would risk failure. Everyone agreed they had to convince Giovanni de' Medici to join their cause, and the task

[25] Cavalcanti, *Istorie* 3.2, ed. Polidori, vol. 1, pp. 86–7; ed. Di Pino, p. 52.

was assigned to Rinaldo himself (*IF* 4.9.5–8). In Cavalcanti's account Giovanni declines to support the plan, warning that it would be dangerous to deprive the popolo of the "favors [beneficii]" granted them by Rinaldo's father Maso.[26] Machiavelli too has Giovanni recall these benefits: a reduction in the price of required purchases of salt; cancellation of taxes for those assessed at less than half a florin; and protection from creditors on days when the large communal councils met. But Machiavelli significantly expands the grounds on which Giovanni de' Medici rejects Rinaldo's plan from material benefits to an ethical principle of good citizenship and a lesson in good tactics for one who seeks the favor of the people. Machiavelli's Giovanni says "he believes it the duty of a wise and good citizen not to alter the customary ordini of his city, for nothing offends men as much as changing them." Giovanni criticizes both of Rinaldo's proposals as wrong-headed: those who have never had the right to hold office (at least not for a long time, namely the magnates) will value less gaining that right and have less cause to lament not having it; by contrast, those accustomed to having it (the guildsmen) will never cease agitating to regain it. The offense done to the latter would be much greater than the favor done for the former. Hence, Rinaldo and his group would find themselves with many enemies, above all the people, determined to avenge the wrong done to them. This is where (as already noted) Machiavelli has Giovanni warn Rinaldo not to fall into the same trap that doomed Benedetto Alberti, who let himself be persuaded to consent to the destruction of Giorgio Scali and Tommaso Strozzi, only to find himself banished by the very persons who had urged him to do so. Giovanni foresees that those imploring Rinaldo to destroy the power of the popolo would then turn against him and destroy his power with the help of the popolo that will have become his enemy (*IF* 4.10.1–5)—spoken, ironically, by the founder of the family dynasty that would in turn exile Rinaldo and his faction.

Machiavelli was more attentive to the economic and fiscal dimensions of politics than is often assumed.[27] He introduces them at crucial junctures, usually in connection with resistance by elites to attempts to limit their wealth. The best-known example is the analysis in *Discourses* 1.37 of the violent opposition of the Roman nobility to the land reforms of the Gracchi. Another is his account of the resistance of the Florentine grandi in 1426–7 to more burdensome tax assessments, first in their willingness to use military force in the episode just recounted and, in the next year, in their reaction to the Catasto, the new method of assessing forced loans. For both Cavalcanti and Machiavelli, the novelty of the Catasto was the implementation of standardized criteria for assessing taxable wealth in place

[26] Cavalcanti, *Istorie* 3.5, ed. Polidori, vol. 1, pp. 94–5; ed. Di Pino, pp. 55–6.

[27] Now amply demonstrated by Jérémie Barthas, *L'argent n'est pas le nerf de la guerre. Essai sur une prétendue erreur de Machiavel* (Rome: École Française de Rome, 2011); and his "Machiavelli, the Republic, and the Financial Crisis," in *Machiavelli on Liberty and Conflict*, ed. D. Johnston, N. Urbinati, and C. Vergara (Chicago and London: University of Chicago Press, 2017), pp. 257–79.

of subjective estimates, or, as Machiavelli puts it, "that tax burdens must be allocated by the law, not by men." This resulted in much higher assessments for the "cittadini potenti": Cavalcanti claims that under the old system Niccolò da Uzzano never had assessments greater than 16 florins and now found himself with a tax burden of 250 florins.[28] Machiavelli interprets the Catasto and the controversies it generated in terms of class interests: the new system, he says, "set limits to the tyranny of the powerful [pose in parte regola alla tirannide de' potenti]," who could no longer intimidate the "minori" and use threats to keep them silent in the legislative councils. The people at large (the "universale") welcomed the Catasto, whereas the "potenti" suffered it "with the greatest displeasure." What "frightened" the grandi even more than the Catasto itself was the popolo's desire to make it retroactive—to collect back taxes from the rich on the basis of the revised assessments. "To defend themselves against" this, the wealthy "never ceased condemning it" (*IF* 4.14.1–8). Machiavelli repeats from Cavalcanti's account[29] the role played by Giovanni de' Medici in persuading those who advocated retroactive adjustments of taxes to abandon the idea because it would seriously divide the city (*IF* 4.14.12–13).

Machiavelli builds on Cavalcanti's account[30] in reporting the reasons why the wealthy believed the Catasto, and especially the plan (never realized) for retroactive reassessments, was the height of injustice. They complained that many persons concealed cash, which was therefore not taxed, to which (according to both Cavalcanti and Machiavelli) the Catasto's supporters replied that uninvested liquid wealth should not be taxed because it yields no profit. If and when it is invested and generates profit, its existence would become known and it would be taxed. Another objection of the wealthy was that "those who leave their businesses to govern the republic should be taxed less, because it is not right for the city to have the benefit of both their wealth and their talents [industria]" in governing the city, while it takes only taxes from "the others." According to Machiavelli (who rephrases and elaborates Cavalcanti on this point), defenders of the Catasto replied that, if the politically active citizens "do not like exerting themselves for the republic, they should stop and not trouble themselves over it, because the republic would find devoted [amorevoli] citizens who would have no difficulty assisting it with both taxes and wise counsel." The wealthy should be satisfied with "the numerous benefits and honors that accrue to those who serve in government, without wanting to be exempt from taxes." Machiavelli adds a third reason (which Cavalcanti does not clearly state) why the banking and commercial class hated the Catasto, namely, that it taxed investments and capital ("beni mobili") that "one can possess today and lose tomorrow." The Catasto's defenders, he says, replied that tax assessments can be adjusted as the value of

[28] Cavalcanti, *Istorie* 4.8, 4.12, ed. Polidori, vol. 1, pp. 197, 214; ed. Di Pino, pp. 108, 116.
[29] Cavalcanti, *Istorie* 4.12, ed. Polidori, vol. 1, p. 218; ed. Di Pino, pp. 117–18.
[30] Cavalcanti, *Istorie* 4.12, ed. Polidori, vol. 1, pp. 214–16; ed. Di Pino, pp. 116–17.

investments fluctuates. But the elite's real and never acknowledged objection, Machiavelli writes, echoing Cavalcanti, was that "it pained them not to be able to start a war" without financial sacrifice to themselves ("sanza loro danno"), knowing that now they too would have to contribute to the costs. If the new fiscal system had been adopted sooner, Machiavelli comments, Florence would not have fought the wars against Ladislaus of Naples and Duke Filippo of Milan, which he, like Cavalcanti, claims "had been fought, not out of necessity, but to enrich [riempire: fill the pockets of] the citizens" (4.14.8–11)—Machiavelli's mordant rejoinder to Guicciardini's encomiastic celebration of the regime's "glorious" successes in war and expansion of the "imperio."

Machiavelli asserts (*IF* 4.15.5) that the Florentines spent three and a half million ducats in the five-year war against Milan that ended in 1428 and got nothing except "poverty and internal discord" for their expense and effort. When "the war abroad ended, the war within recommenced," and once again the Catasto was a focal point of controversy. Unable to tolerate it but seeing no way to eliminate it, the "cittadini grandi" looked for ways to make the Catasto disliked by others. Summarizing Cavalcanti,[31] Machiavelli writes that the grandi "reminded the officials" that the Catasto law required them to register the assets and properties of inhabitants of the district—the subject cities beyond Florence's contado—"in order to ascertain if there were properties of Florentine citizens among them." In fact, the Catasto did extend to all residents of the district. But many of its cities maintained, by agreement with Florence, their own laws and statutes, including fiscal regulations, and some strongly protested against the requirement that their inhabitants submit declarations of their wealth. The subject city of Volterra, Machiavelli notes, sent a delegation (in 1429) to contest this violation of their rights. According to Cavalcanti (a point Machiavelli overlooks), the Catasto officials denied violating Volterra's rights, saying they only wanted to ensure that Florentines were not defrauding the Catasto by fictitiously registering assets under the names of Volterran citizens. Machiavelli says Florence arrested and imprisoned eighteen members of the delegation, "angering the Volterrans" (*IF* 4.15.4–11) and sparking a short-lived revolt that ended when pro-Florentine Volterrans murdered the leader of the uprising and surrendered the city to two Florentine military commissioners, one of whom, Rinaldo degli Albizzi, was waiting outside the city with troops (*IF* 4.17)—a prefiguration of the more violent conflict between Florence and Volterra in the time of Lorenzo de' Medici.

"SLANDERING THEM WITH EVERY DECEPTION AND SKILL"

Machiavelli makes of Rinaldo both the instigator and epitome of the recklessness that brought down the pre-Medici oligarchy. At first, he blames the disastrous war

[31] Cavalcanti, *Istorie* 5.1, ed. Polidori, vol. 1, pp. 257–9; ed. Di Pino, pp. 139–40.

against Lucca, begun in 1429, on "the ambition of men" (*IF* 4.18.1). A few sentences later, however, he says "it was commonly believed" that Rinaldo persuaded the mercenary captain Niccolò Fortebraccio to initiate assaults against Lucca under the pretext of "some fictitious grievance [sotto qualche fitta querela]," promising him he would promote a war and ensure Niccolò's appointment as Florence's commander. When news of Fortebraccio's first successful attacks reached Florence, the "majority" favored a campaign to acquire Lucca. Among the grandi, the advocates of war, Machiavelli writes, included both the "Medici faction" and Rinaldo, who was motivated "either by his opinion that it would be a useful undertaking for the republic or by personal ambition, believing he would be hailed as the author of the victory [capo di quella vittoria]." Opposing the war, Machiavelli claims, were Niccolò da Uzzano and his faction. Actually, things were not so simple, as both the Medici and Albizzi factions counted supporters and opponents. But it is true that Rinaldo favored the war from early on and got himself appointed commissioner, while, within the Medici group (headed by Cosimo after his father Giovanni's death in 1429), initial reluctance gave way to increasing administrative and financial involvement. Machiavelli's inclusion of both Rinaldo and the Medici in the rush to war is only part of his explanation of the fateful decision. He attributes much of the impetus to the popolo. "It seems an incredible thing," he comments, "that such different views about launching a war could exist in the same city." This refers not only to contrasting positions among the elite factions but also to the divergence between the popolo's views of the recently concluded war against Milan and the war against Lucca: "the citizens and popolo who had condemned the war against Duke Filippo, undertaken for the defense of [Florence's] liberty, now, after such great expense and so much suffering, vociferously demanded war against Lucca to suppress the liberty of others." Conversely, those who had favored the earlier war now denounced this one. This shows, Machiavelli comments, how much "opinions vary with time, how much more eager the multitude is to seize what belongs to others than to protect its own, and how men are more motivated by hope for gain than by fear of loss." Niccolò Fortebraccio's initial successes "filled the popolo of Florence with hope" for territorial gain, as did reports from Florentine officials that captured towns were asking to be taken into the Florentine dominion and the prediction that "soon the whole contado of Lucca would be acquired" (*IF* 4.18.1–10).

Aware of the clamor for war, the Signoria, Machiavelli writes, convened a large council of 498 citizens to debate the issue (*IF* 4.18.14). Machiavelli has Rinaldo, speaking for the pro-war coalition, emphasize the strategic utility of acquiring Lucca and the ease, so he believed, of conquering it (*IF* 4.19.1–4). But Machiavelli devotes more space to the speech against the war that he attributes to Niccolò da Uzzano. "Florence has never engaged in a more unjust endeavor," Uzzano begins, "or a more dangerous one, or one from which greater harm could result." Lucca, he notes, has many times welcomed exiled Florentine Guelfs and, when not ruled by a tyrant, has never attacked Florence. Machiavelli says Uzzano objected to despoiling a friendly city of its wealth but knew this argument carried little weight because "in life today little attention is paid to what is just and unjust." So he has Uzzano predict that Florence would spend huge sums and run great risks in such a war, and, instead of conquering Lucca, would liberate it from its tyrant (Paolo Guinigi) and turn a weak, subjugated, but friendly city into a hostile and free one that, in time, would become an "obstacle to the power [grandezza] of the [Florentine] republic" (*IF* 4.19.5–14). In a secret vote, Machiavelli claims, only 98 of the 498 assembled citizens dissented from the decision to go to war. The Ten appointed Astorre Gianni and Rinaldo as civilian commissioners, giving each a contingent of troops. Their campaigns, Machiavelli says, "had unhappy outcomes, not because they did not capture many towns, but because both were blamed for their conduct of the war." Gianni allowed his troops to sack and destroy the town of Seravezza, northwest of Lucca (*IF* 4.20), some of whose inhabitants escaped to Florence where one of them made an impassioned speech of aggrieved accusation. Machiavelli himself calls the attack an "atrocità" for which the Ten recalled and punished Gianni (*IF* 4.21), although he later notes that the escalating antagonisms between the factions, with slanders flying back and forth, "caused the sins of Astorre Gianni to be exaggerated" (*IF* 4.26.7).

Rinaldo, on the other hand, faced very different charges. He was "vilified [diffamato]," Machiavelli writes (*IF* 4.22.1), for conducting the war "for his own benefit [utilità], not that of the Florentine people." He was accused of relinquishing any desire to seize Lucca itself and of being content to "pillage the countryside" to fill his own estates with livestock and his home with booty. Because the loot taken by his armed partisans ("satelliti"—his private military force) was not enough for him, he purchased more from the soldiers, so that "from a commissioner he became a trafficker [tale che di commissario era diventato mercatante]." Machiavelli takes the phrase directly from Cavalcanti, who, however, rejected as "abominable hearsay" rumors that Rinaldo had become a "mercatante" of spoils taken from the field of battle and "bought plundered loot from the soldiers and sent it to Monte Falcone"[32] (the Albizzi villa in the lower Arno valley, not far from Lucca). Machiavelli calls the accusations "slanders [calunnie]," seemingly exonerating Rinaldo but without commenting on the substance of the charges. Yet he strongly disapproves of Rinaldo's reaction. "These slanders unsettled his righteous and proud spirit [mossono lo intero e altiero animo suo] more than was fitting for a dignified man. So much did they unnerve him, that, in his anger at both the magistracy [of the Ten] and the citizens, he returned to Florence without waiting for, or requesting, permission." Machiavelli describes him going to the Ten to lament the difficulty of serving a divided city and a people that does not observe its laws. He complains that one who successfully completes a mission receives no

[32] Cavalcanti, *Istorie* 6.13; ed. Polidori, vol. 1, p. 321; ed. Di Pino, p. 173.

praise, whereas one who makes a mistake is condemned by everyone, and one who loses (presumably a battle) is slandered. Machiavelli has Rinaldo say that, although "a friendly faction [parte] persecutes you out of envy, and a hostile faction does so from hatred, nonetheless he has never shirked a mission that would benefit his city because of fear of false accusations." After these denunciations of the failings of his fellow citizens and declarations of his own unalloyed loyalty and willingness to sacrifice for the city, Machiavelli has Rinaldo confess that the dishonorable slanders he has suffered have changed him, destroyed his patience, and caused him to change his nature ("fattogli mutare natura"). He ends the diatribe by asking the Ten to do more to defend citizens against slanders, for they themselves might become targets of the same, and then they would understand how injurious false slanders are to men of integrity ("uomini interi"). Machiavelli says the Ten "tried to mollify" Rinaldo and replaced him with two new commissioners, Neri di Gino Capponi and Alamanno Salviati (*IF* 4.22.1–6). Machiavelli knew, but does not say, that both were Medici allies.

Machiavelli further darkens the picture of dysfunction when he introduces the next commissioner in the Lucca war, Giovanni Guicciardini. After a major defeat (in December 1430), recriminations intensified and the "universale" blamed those who administered the war, Rinaldo again being a particular target. "But more tormented than anyone was messer Giovanni Guicciardini," accused—Machiavelli does not yet say by whom—of deliberately failing to bring the war to a successful conclusion when he had the opportunity to do so, because, it was alleged, he "had been corrupted [corrotto] with money, a sum of which he sent home"—in effect, that he used his position as commissioner for personal profit and accepted bribes to subvert military operations. "So loud did these denunciations and accusations become that the capitano del popolo, impelled by these public rumors and prodded by those of the opposing faction [quelli della parte contraria]," summoned Guicciardini to appear before his court (*IF* 4.25.11–13). In the next chapter Machiavelli reveals that the Medici party was behind this slander, naming Averardo de' Medici (Cosimo's cousin) as the author of a veritable campaign of calumny (*IF* 4.26.6–7). In the *Discourses* (1.8), we recall, Machiavelli identifies Guicciardini's victimization by unchecked slander as the event that triggered the confrontation between the factions and led to the Albizzi group's downfall.[33] Although he expresses no opinion concerning the veracity of the charges against either Rinaldo degli Albizzi or Giovanni Guicciardini, he emphasizes that the crux of the accusations in both cases was malfeasance motivated by personal gain—private gain over public interest and duty.

[33] Cavalcanti reports the accusations against Giovanni Guicciardini only as what the "plebea turba" said, with no mention of the "opposing faction"; *Istorie* 6.16, ed. Polidori, vol. 1, p. 326; ed. Di Pino, p. 175.

"The war for Lucca was fought by this so divided city," Machiavelli says, "in which factional passions were inflamed [si accesono gli umori delle parti]" (*IF* 4.26.5). From the general dysfunction of factional discord, Machiavelli narrows the explanation for the slanders against the commissioners to a tactic of defamation pursued by the Medici faction to discredit those who were administering the war. Although "Cosimo's party was the one that favored" the war, the management of military operations was largely in the hands of many "from the opposing party"—the Albizzi faction—because they "were more prominent in government [piú reputati nello stato]." Because the Medici were unable to break the opposition's political control of the war, Machiavelli claims, they set about "slandering them with every deception and skill [con ogni arte e industria]" they could muster. Whenever setbacks occurred—and he says there were many—blame went "not to fortune or the strength of the enemy, but to the commissioner's unwise judgment [poca prudenzia]." "This," Machiavelli claims, "is what led to the exaggeration of Astorre Gianni's sins. This is what caused Rinaldo degli Albizzi to be so resentful and to abandon his post without permission. This again is what caused the capitano del popolo to summon [in effect, to indict] Giovanni Guicciardini." Without giving further specifics, Machiavelli says "all the other accusations against magistrates and commissioners arose from this." Not all accusations were false: "those that were true were magnified, those not true were fabricated, and the people, who ordinarily hated [slanders], believed both the true and the false ones" (*IF* 4.26.5–7). The essence of the infirmity was that factional hostilities so distorted people's judgment that they began to believe all manner of things they had previously rejected.

Machiavelli's indictment of the pre-1434 ruling group culminates in the long speech (*IF* 4.27) he has Niccolò da Uzzano make in response to an appeal from another of the leaders, Niccolò Barbadori, to join a plan to rid the city of Cosimo de' Medici. This famous chapter also contains Machiavelli's initial critique of Cosimo's aspirations to tyrannical power. In presenting both in one speech, he makes clear the inextricable link between the dysfunctions of the pre-1434 regime and the danger to liberty and the republic represented by Cosimo, his family, and party.

Only in a limited sense is Giovanni Cavalcanti the source of Machiavelli's version of Uzzano's speech. For several reasons, some of which Machiavelli maintains in his version, Cavalcanti's Uzzano advises against what he considers the dangerous plan to neutralize or remove Cosimo. In Cavalcanti, the core of the speech is a stinging diatribe against Rinaldo degli Albizzi, in which Uzzano describes him as even "more ruthless, arrogant, and erratic [più inumano e superbo, ed è voltante]" than his father, and as one who values his friends no more than his enemies and treats everyone as disposable ("ogni uomo ha per cencio"). He accuses Rinaldo of having "thrown himself into the arms of the Medici" to secure appointment to the war magistracy of the Ten, and of wanting "our downfall" more than Cosimo's in order to enhance his own power and "grandigia [ostentatious arrogance]," which he cannot achieve without "our ruin." "He wants his desires to be received by the people as laws" and "certainly intends to deceive us." If he succeeds in the plan to banish Cosimo, Cavalcanti's Uzzano continues, "the result will be his own ruin, discord among the citizens, and the destruction of the republic."[34]

In the preliminary draft of chapter 27, Machiavelli intensifies the invective against Rinaldo spoken by Cavalcanti's Uzzano: "Did Lucifer himself ever display as much arrogance [superbia] as he does? He wants his words to be incontrovertible judgments [sentenze] and his desires to be laws. Was there ever in any man so much capriciousness [inconstanza] as in him? Many times we feared he would side with our adversaries, and this war for Lucca is proof of it, for he supported it against us and to the advantage of the opposing [Medici] party."[35] Machiavelli deleted this passage from the final text, evidently preferring that Uzzano's speech be less a personal attack on Rinaldo and more a critical evaluation of the regime. Because it departs in significant ways from what Cavalcanti has Uzzano say, and given the absence of other sources, we must assume that the speech Machiavelli attributes to Uzzano reflects his own judgment. Machiavelli says Uzzano and the other leaders of the faction ("parte" replacing "stato" in the draft) fully recognized and often discussed "queste cosí fatte cose e modi estraordinari [the things done in these ways and these illegal methods]." Because the preceding chapter concludes with a description of the slanders the Medici party used to attack commissioners and magistrates of the opposing faction, these "things" and "illegal methods" obviously allude to the campaign of calumny. Underscoring the corrupting illegality of politically motivated slander, Machiavelli says Uzzano was the "first" among those who disliked "le vie straordinarie" (*IF* 4.27.1).

"FLYING TOWARD TYRANNY"

Uzzano and his colleagues were confronted with a dilemma, Machiavelli writes: to do nothing would be dangerous; to confront the problem openly would be difficult. Uzzano admonishes Barbadori to exercise caution, warning that "those who want to banish Cosimo from Florence must, before all else, measure their strength [forze] against his," by which he presumably means the support each faction enjoys. Machiavelli then has Uzzano deconstruct the common perception of the opposing parties: "You [plural: the leaders of his faction] have christened this party of ours the *parte de' nobili* and the opposing party that of the *plebe*. Even if the truth [verità] corresponded to these labels"—and Uzzano clearly believes it does not—"victory [over our opponents] would in any event be

[34] Cavalcanti, *Istorie* 7.8, ed. Polidori, vol. 1, pp. 384–6; ed. Di Pino, pp. 205–6.
[35] *OS*, vol. 2, p. 847.

doubtful, and we would have to be more fearful than hopeful" in view of what happened "to the city's old nobility [antiche nobilità: the magnates], who were destroyed [spente]" by the people. Uzzano says his party should be still more fearful because of its fractiousness by contrast with the unity of their adversaries. Even "our families and households are divided" between the factions: one of the sons of Maso degli Albizzi, Luca, being "envious of Rinaldo," joined the Mediceans; Luigi Guicciardini's son Piero is hostile to Giovanni (the tormented commissioner) and "favors our adversaries"; both Tommaso and Niccolò Soderini, moved by "hatred for their uncle Francesco, work against us." And Neri di Gino (Capponi) and Nerone di Nigi (Dietisalvi) have never declared their allegiance clearly enough "for us to know whether they are more our friends or theirs" (of the Medici). Machiavelli thus underscores the intractability of the ruling faction and the extent to which its members transferred loyalties because of personal animosities or grudges (*IF* 4.27.1–10).

Machiavelli then has Uzzano return to the doubt he expressed about whether theirs is the party of the "nobles." "If we take a good look at who they are and who we are, I do not know why our faction [parte] deserves to be called noble any more than theirs." If, he says, the ruling group's stronger claim of nobility rests on the large following the Medici have among the people ("seguitati da tutta la plebe"), this "puts us in a worse condition and them in a better one, and if the conflict is to be resolved either by arms or by votes, we will not be able to hold them off." "If we still enjoy our pre-eminence [dignità]" ("reputazione" in the draft),[36] "this results from the longstanding prestige [reputazione antica] of this regime [stato], which it has maintained for fifty years." Machiavelli was being quite precise here. The "stato" to which Uzzano alludes dated from the overthrow of the popular government in 1382, and the (perhaps invented) conversation between Barbadori and Uzzano, set during the Lucca war, had to have occurred before the latter's death in 1431 or 1432. Yet this "dignità," Uzzano warns, is a facade: "if it were put to the test and our weakness were exposed, we would lose it." Uzzano tears down one further claim by the regime's leadership to "nobilità" and "dignità." If "you were to say that the just cause [giusta cagione] that motivates us would bring credit to us and deprive [the Medici] of it, I would reply that this justice [giustizia] needs to be understood and believed by others as we do. But it is entirely the opposite." The "just cause that impels us is based on the fear that he [Cosimo] may make himself principe of this city." Before Machiavelli lets Uzzano explain the reasons behind this fear, he has him caution that, however just the cause, it will not salvage the "dignità" of the ruling group because, "if we have this fear, others do not; even worse, they accuse us of what we accuse him" (*IF* 4.27.11–14). Behind this counter-accusation of the "others" is Machiavelli's

[36] *OS*, vol. 2, p. 845.

own indictment of the regime, already foreshadowed in the proemial chapter of book 4, namely, that they had destroyed the city's liberty and reduced the republic to the unhappy alternatives of "servitú" and "licenzia."

Enumerating "the actions of Cosimo that make us fear him," Uzzano outlines what later emerges as the essence of Machiavelli's critique of the Medici. Cosimo, he says, helps "everyone" with his money, not only private citizens but also the "publico" (the communal treasury), and not only Florentines but also the city's hired condottieri. He supports "this and that citizen who needs something from the magistrates" and "promotes this and that friend of his into high office with the goodwill he enjoys among the people." "So," Uzzano ironizes, "it would be necessary to adduce as the reasons for banishing him that he is compassionate, thoughtful, generous and loved by everyone [piatoso, oficioso, liberale e amato da ciascuno]." He asks, rhetorically: "Tell me: what law is it that prohibits, blames, or condemns in men compassion, generosity, and love?" Uzzano's point is that, when seen through the eyes of those who benefit from Cosimo's largesse and influence, his alleged misdeeds and transgressions become—or seem to be—virtues. Uzzano does not leave matters there. He immediately delivers the grim judgment that "these are all methods that propel men flying toward princely power ("che tirino gli uomini volando al principato"). In the draft version, Machiavelli's judgment is more damning: there he wrote that these methods propel men "flying toward tyranny [volando a la tirannide]."[37] But in revising the passage, he evidently thought better of accusing the great-grandfather of his book's dedicatee, Pope Clement VII, of tyrannical ambitions. Machiavelli does not let Uzzano dwell on the extent to which Cosimo's apparent virtues were leading the republic down a dangerous path. He points, instead, to the lamentable fact that people do not see Cosimo's "methods" for what they really are and that no one (apparently beyond the inner circle of the ruling group) recognizes these methods as the building blocks of tyranny. Nor, Uzzano adds, are "we able to help them understand this, for our own ways [i modi nostri] have destroyed our credibility [fede: trust]." Moreover, "the city, which by its nature is given to factionalism [che naturalmente è partigiana] and, having always lived with factions [vivuta in parte], is corrupt, is unable to listen to such charges" (*IF* 4.27.15–18). Machiavelli's Uzzano turns the blame for the people's inability to see the danger back onto the leadership itself. The implied judgments of Cosimo in this passage are certainly damning, but the focus is on the complicity of the opposing faction in rendering the city blind to Cosimo's strategy and deaf to the warnings about his aspirations, if not to tyranny, at least to princely power.

The people's failure to understand the direction in which things were moving, which Uzzano blames on the factionalism engendered by the ruling group, is among

[37] *OS*, vol. 2, p. 846.

the chief reasons why he advises that it would be a mistake to banish Cosimo. Another is the strength of Cosimo's party. With so many "friends" (clients and partigiani) who, if he were to be exiled, would "burn with desire" for his return, how could the leadership prevent this? Exiling more of Cosimo's "chief allies" would only make more enemies; and, once repatriated by his faction, Cosimo would not be the same man: "you would banish a good man and he would return a wicked [cattivo] one; his nature would be corrupted [corrotta] by those who bring him back, for, once in their debt, he would not be able to defy them." Here too, the imperatives of factional obligations—in both directions between patron and clients—would cement loyalties and exacerbate antagonisms. In the draft version, Machiavelli made the point more starkly: Cosimo "would be compelled to transgress all civic norms [trapassare ogni civiltà], because he would have to satisfy many wicked [malvagi] men who vow to follow him not for his sake but for their own rage [rabbia]."[38] Furthermore, any attempt to have him killed would fail if pursued through the magistrates—i.e. by legal means—because "his wealth and your corruptible dispositions [gli animi vostri corruttibili] will always save him" from such a fate (*IF* 4.27.19–21)—the allusion is to bribery.

Uzzano's final accusation against the Albizzi faction is directed against Rinaldo himself. Exiling or otherwise eliminating Cosimo "would bring no benefit to our republic, because, if you liberate it from Cosimo, you make it a slave to messer Rinaldo." Uzzano claims to be "among those who wish no citizen to exceed the others in power and influence [autorità]. But if one of them must prevail, I do not know what reason would make me love messer Rinaldo more than Cosimo." (At this point in the draft, Machiavelli inserted part of the invective against Rinaldo spoken by Cavalcanti's Uzzano, including the denunciation of his arrogance as worse than Lucifer's.) "May God preserve this city," Machiavelli has Uzzano say in the revised text, "from any of its citizens becoming its principe. Even if we deserve this because of our sins, may God save us from having to obey him [lui]" (in the draft, "from having him as prince"). The referent of "lui" is ambiguous: Rinaldo or Cosimo? Perhaps it does not matter, given that Uzzano had just professed not to see a reason to prefer one to the other. Still, he concludes with a focus on Cosimo. He warns his party's leaders not to pursue a course of action that would be dangerous in every way, and not to think that they, few as they are, could oppose the will of the many. Uzzano delivers a final charge of corruption against both Cosimo and the pre-Medici regime: "all these citizens, partly through ignorance and partly through malice, are prepared to sell this republic; and so much is fortune their friend that they have found their buyer [comperatore]." With this savage metaphor—missing in the draft—Machiavelli links Cosimo's great wealth and the venality of the ruling faction, saying in effect that Cosimo used his money to buy

[38] *OS*, vol. 2, pp. 846–7.

the republic—to make it his own—and had no trouble finding sellers willing to consummate the transaction. Uzzano's last bit of advice to Barbadori expresses the forlorn hope that some Florentines might steer clear of both the sellers and the buyer: "Live modestly and, as far as liberty is concerned, be fearful of our party as much as of theirs" (*IF* 4.27.22–5).

"ONLY THE PATRIA THAT LOVES ALL ITS CITIZENS EQUALLY DESERVES TO BE LOVED BY ALL ITS CITIZENS"

Although Uzzano's advice, Machiavelli writes, cooled Barbadori's enthusiasm for the drastic plan to remove Cosimo, after Uzzano died and the war ended (in 1433) Rinaldo's continued scheming threw the city into crisis. "Believing he was now the undisputed leader of the faction [solo principe della parte]," Machiavelli says, Rinaldo assumed he could act on his own, ignoring the unwritten norms of collective leadership and even urging an armed uprising to deal with the threat of Cosimo. He "repeatedly implored and badgered" all the most influential citizens "to take up arms to liberate the patria from the man who was inevitably leading it into servitude through the wickedness [malignità] of a few and the ignorance of many." Machiavelli repeats Cavalcanti's story[39] that Rinaldo, "knowing" Bernardo Guadagni's name would soon be drawn for the office of standard-bearer of justice, paid Guadagni's back taxes to make him eligible and then plotted with him to have Cosimo killed. Machiavelli assumes a more neutral posture, blaming both Rinaldo's "modi" and those of the "parte avversa" (the Medici) for the climate of fear and apprehension that was building. Rinaldo tells Guadagni that the "faction of the nobles" was counting on him to do what they believed necessary to resolve the crisis. He impresses on Guadagni that the only solution is to eliminate ("spegnere") Cosimo, "for he alone, through the favors that his excessive wealth [immoderate sue ricchezze] makes possible, left them defenseless. He has climbed so high that, unless something is done, he will become principe" of the city. It is Guadagni's duty as a "good citizen," says Rinaldo, to remedy the situation by "calling the people to the piazza" (for a parlamento) "and retaking the government [ripigliare lo stato] in order to restore to the patria its liberty." He reminds him that "Salvestro de' Medici unjustly undermined the power of the Guelfs, to whom, because of the blood shed by their ancestors, the government [governo] belonged" (*IF* 4.28.1–9). Machiavelli thus depicts Rinaldo, a private citizen, instructing the republic's standard-bearer to initiate a coup d'état, not unlike what the "primi cittadini," with Rinaldo in the lead, had believed necessary in their anger over taxes in 1426 (*IF* 4.8). He urges Guadagni not to be afraid, because

[39] Cavalcanti, *Istorie* 9.3–5, ed. Polidori, vol. 1, pp. 497–507; ed. Di Pino, pp. 265–9.

"friends would quickly be ready to assist him with arms." And, in fact, as Machiavelli notes, after Cosimo's arrest "messer Rinaldo came from his house with many armed men and occupied the piazza in front of the palace with his entire faction [tutta la parte]" (*IF* 4.28.10–13). Again, but not for the last time, Machiavelli underscores Rinaldo's willingness to trample the republic's constitutional procedures and resort to force to achieve his objectives.

During his detention in the palace tower, Cosimo feared a death sentence from the magistrates, Machiavelli says, "but feared even more that his enemies"—above all, Rinaldo—"might have him killed extra-judicially [estraordinariamente]" (*IF* 4.29.2)—assassinated. The decision to exile Cosimo "went against the wishes of messer Rinaldo, who wanted to eliminate him [lo voleva spegnere]" (*IF* 4.29.12). Machiavelli has Rinaldo tell his supporters that, with Cosimo still alive and the city full of his "friends," he sees "their own ruin already assured by their having let themselves be won over by the entreaties, tears, and the hard cash [danari] of their enemies"—a reference to the bribe Cosimo paid to Guadagni to spare his life—and predicts, about those "danari," that "they'll reimburse the principal [il capitale] and pay interest [usura] with torture, death, and exile." The only recourse, he advises, is to "fortify ourselves in the city" to be able to "expel our enemies by force of arms," since "it was not possible to drive them out with legal procedures [con i modi civili]" (*IF* 4.30.2–5)—here again Rinaldo's willingness to use force. In August 1434, when the extraction by lot of name-tickets yielded a Signoria (for September-October) consisting of Medici friends and "partigiani," Rinaldo again recommends to his frightened faction that they take up arms. They should, he advises, call the people to the piazza, institute a balìa, prevent the priors-elect from taking office, replace them with ones favorable to their own group, destroy the lists of citizens approved in past electoral scrutinies, and hold a new scrutiny to approve their "friends" for office. According to Machiavelli, while many in Rinaldo's party agreed, many others, among them Palla Strozzi, considered it "too violent" and likely to bring opprobrium down on them. They therefore decided to let the priors-elect take office, but with the understanding that, if it became clear that the new Signoria "wanted to overturn" things ("volessero alterare"—shorthand for recalling Cosimo and banishing his enemies), Rinaldo's party "would have time to take up arms" and do what was necessary "per la salute comune [collective security]." One could read "salute comune" as referring to the common good of the city (with its echo of the Roman maxim "salus populi suprema lex"), but in the context of a plan for armed resistance against the elected Signoria it must refer to the safety and protection only of Rinaldo's faction. The Albizzi leadership intended to keep a watchful eye on this suspect Signoria; "if they got wind" of any action against their faction ("contro alla parte"), they intended to defend the regime with force of arms (*IF* 4.30.13–18).

The new Signoria, Machiavelli says, initiated contact with the leaders of the Medici faction and summoned Rinaldo and other leaders of his party. This triggered the revolt: Rinaldo "emerged from his home with a large contingent of armed men," joined by Ridolfo Peruzzi, Niccolò Barbadori, "many other citizens, and numerous unemployed mercenaries [assai soldati...sanza soldo] who were in Florence." They met, as prearranged, in the piazza of Sant'Apollinare (today piazza San Firenze), behind the palace of the Signoria. The unexplained detail about "soldati" who happened to be in the city hints at the possibility of a more sinister arrangement between Rinaldo and unnamed condottieri he may have invited into the city to assist in controlling the Signoria and preventing Cosimo's return—if so, the kind of thing Machiavelli condemns in *Discourses* 1.7. In the event, however, several of Rinaldo's prominent allies lost their nerve: Palla Strozzi did not appear with his armed retainers; nor did Giovanni Guicciardini, who, as commissioner, had suffered the vicious slanders of the Medici a few years earlier. Although prodded and scolded by Rinaldo, they made their excuses. After several attempts to rouse him to action, Palla Strozzi finally appeared, but unarmed and accompanied by only two attendants. In Machiavelli's version of this famous encounter, Rinaldo reproves Palla for his dereliction ("negligenzia") and lack of loyalty and courage, telling him he is mistaken if he thinks the Medici will spare him death or exile for his refusal to act against them. Machiavelli has Rinaldo console himself with the satisfaction, even if the revolt ended in disaster, of not having failed to warn of the danger with prudent counsel and not having shirked the duty to meet it with force. By contrast, Rinaldo tells Palla Strozzi and the others that they will live with redoubled sorrows knowing they had betrayed their patria three times (an allusion to Peter's three denials of Jesus?), first in saving Cosimo's life (by accepting bribes), then by not heeding Rinaldo's advice, and finally by not coming to the patria's rescue arms in hand. Palla is said to have mumbled something that no one understood, turned around, and gone home (*IF* 4.31.1–10). Most of Machiavelli's readers knew that Cosimo rewarded Palla's indirect, but crucial, contribution to the Medici victory with a decree of exile that the regime regularly renewed until he died thirty years later.

With the defection of key allies, Rinaldo lost control of the situation. Machiavelli writes that, although the Signoria told Rinaldo (disingenuously) that they had not discussed Cosimo's repatriation, Rinaldo was not reassured and still wanted to remove the Signoria by force. But his allies were losing courage. Ridolfo Peruzzi said all he wanted was for Cosimo to remain in exile, not a confrontation in which blood might be spilt, and would therefore obey the Signoria's summons. Machiavelli summarizes the reasons why the attempted coup failed: Rinaldo's fatal hesitation, Palla's loss of courage, Peruzzi's defection, and the waning enthusiasm of Rinaldo's followers (*IF* 4.31.12–18). With the insurgents "disarmed," the pro-Medici Signoria brought in troops to secure the city and created a balìa, which immediately repatriated Cosimo and exiled Rinaldo, Peruzzi, Barbadori, Strozzi, and "many other citizens." So numerous were the exiles, Machiavelli comments, that "few cities in Italy did not have some, and many cities outside Italy were full of them." Consequently, he comments, "not only was Florence deprived of many worthy men [uomini da bene] but also of much wealth [ricchezze] and talent [industria]" (*IF* 4.33.1–2). Curiously, Machiavelli will have the exiled Rinaldo say these exact words trying to persuade the duke of Milan that, because Florence had lost so much "ricchezze" and "industria" with the exiles, the duke would have no trouble attacking and defeating the weakened city (*IF* 5.8.11).

Machiavelli took from Cavalcanti[40] the story of how Rinaldo let himself be persuaded by Pope Eugenius IV (who was then residing in Florence because the barons had once again thrown Rome into chaos) to lay down his arms and trust in the Signoria's promises that no harm or punishment would come to him if he ended the standoff. There are, however, significant differences between Cavalcanti's account and Machiavelli's briefer version of Rinaldo's reply to the pope (*IF* 4.32). Omitting Cavalcanti's accusation that Eugenius deviously lured Rinaldo into a trap, Machiavelli has Rinaldo say only that he "trusted" him "too much." Cavalcanti has the embittered Rinaldo lament his failure to request the intervention of the condottiere Niccolò Piccinino—whose soldiers were waiting just beyond Florence's borders[41]—and thereby avoid his grim fate. In Machiavelli's narrative, Rinaldo leaves aside such regrets and, in defeat, becomes, or pretends to be, a stoic defender of the very rule of law he had so often been ready to subvert in his angry zeal to crush his enemies. He tells Eugenius that, having had ample experience of "fortune's games" and placed "little trust in the good times, adversities wound me less." Even if fortune never wishes to smile on him again, he adds, "I will always set little value on living in a city where the laws have less power than men [dove possino meno le leggi che gli uomini]." The irony, of course, is that Rinaldo's entire career, as Machiavelli describes it, suggests little respect for this principle—an irony that underscores the hypocrisy of this sudden conversion and newfound allegiance to "the laws" that Rinaldo embraces in the anguish of defeat and the inevitability of exile. Machiavelli has Rinaldo continue: "only that patria in which it is possible to enjoy securely one's wealth and friends is desirable, not one in which these things can easily be snatched away and in which friends, fearing for themselves, abandon you in your time of greatest need" (alluding to his former allies who failed to join the attempted revolt). Machiavelli's Rinaldo is of course oblivious to the irony of lamenting the absence of loyalty and true friendship in an armed uprising against the government in order to destroy a rival. He embraces exile as the more honorable state, even if it means turning his back on the travails of the patria: "wise and good men have always thought it less painful to hear of the ills of their patria" from afar "than to witness them" up close and

[40] Cavalcanti, *Istorie* 10.10, 12, 18–19, ed. Polidori, vol. 1, pp. 580–3, 585–7, 606–10; ed. Di Pino, pp. 307–9, 310, 320–2.

[41] Cavalcanti, *Istorie* 10.19, ed. Polidori, vol. 1, pp. 608–9; ed. Di Pino, pp. 321–2.

"consider it more glorious to be an honorable rebel [onorevole ribello] than a citizen slave [stiavo cittadino]" (*IF* 4.33.3–6).

Yet Machiavelli's Rinaldo is not an "honorable rebel." Together with "the other leaders of the Florentine exiles," Machiavelli has him appeal to Duke Filippo Maria Visconti of Milan to start a new war against Florence for the purpose of securing his repatriation. Rinaldo delivers a long speech to the duke seeking to justify asking a former enemy to make war against his patria. No one should be surprised, Rinaldo says, that "we come full of hope to beg for your help." He claims to have "evident and justifiable reasons [manifeste e ragionevoli scuse]" both for past actions against Milan and for the appeal he now makes to the duke. The wars Florence fought against Milan and the Visconti he justifies on grounds of patriotic self-defense: "no good man will ever reprove one who seeks to defend his patria," "nor was it ever our aim to harm you [iniuriarti], but only to protect our patria from harm." Whenever the Florentines were victorious on the battlefield and saw the duke inclined to peace, "we desired it more than you." Cleverly but tortuously, he argues that Florence's willingness to make peace with the Visconti after the wars of the past should persuade him that "we have never done anything that would make us fear that we could not secure any favor from you" (*IF* 5.8.2–4). In Cavalcanti's shorter account, Rinaldo does not go beyond this opening part of Machiavelli's version, asking the duke to help him and the other exiles return to Florence, seeking the duke's good will by contrasting the more conciliatory stance of his own generation with the bellicose policies of their elders, claiming that, when Filippo Maria's father (Giangaleazzo) died (in 1402) while at war with Florence, "we" did not pursue the war "with you," and reminding the duke that he, Rinaldo, was among those who negotiated peace (in 1433).[42]

Machiavelli's Rinaldo says more. He is at pains to justify "our imploring you to wield against our patria the very arms against which we so tenaciously defended it." Florence, he insists, cannot rightly deplore the exiles' appeal to Filippo Maria, because "only the patria that loves all its citizens equally deserves to be loved by all its citizens, not one that reveres a few more than all others" (*IF* 5.8.5). In view of Rinaldo's repeated attempts to diminish the political rights of the guildsmen and to urge his faction to seize power by force, one wonders what Machiavelli intended in having Rinaldo speak out this high-minded appeal to the equality of all citizens. Is it little more than sanctimonious cant? Or does it suggest a deeper critique? We do not know if Machiavelli read Leonardo Bruni's *Panegyric to the City of Florence*, but he could not have been unfamiliar with the claim, expressed there and elsewhere in Bruni's writings, that the Florentine republic was founded on the principle of equality. In the *Panegyric*, Bruni writes: "Nowhere on earth is law more equal for all [ius magis equum sit omnibus]. Nowhere else does so

[42] Cavalcanti, *Istorie* 12.11, ed. Polidori, vol. 2, p. 52; ed. Di Pino, p. 360.

much liberty flourish, and nowhere is there such uniform—equalized—treatment of greater and lesser citizens [maiorum cum minoribus exequata condicio]."[43] In the "Oration for the Funeral of Nanni Strozzi," Bruni asserts that the design of Florence's government "aims especially at the liberty and equality of all citizens [ad libertatem paritatemque civium maxime omnium]." Because it is "equal for all [equalis est omnibus]," the Florentines call it "popular" government. "Liberty is equal for all [equa omnibus libertas], subject only to the laws." Bruni extends the principle of equality to citizens' access to office: "The hope of reaching office and gaining distinction is equal for all [omnibus par]." "This is true liberty," "equality of law among citizens, and equality of access to government [paritatem esse iuris inter se civibus, paritatem reipublicae adeunde]."[44] In letting Rinaldo parrot, and twist to his own purposes, notions of liberty and equality patently undermined by his—and his class's—actions and ambitions, Machiavelli reveals the ideological hollowness of the pre-Medici elite.

Machiavelli also has Rinaldo use language from *Discourses* 3.1 in referring to states as "mixed bodies" that occasionally require healing. Still justifying his entreaty to the duke of Milan to attack Florence, he says: "Let no one condemn arms taken up against the patria, because cities, although they are mixed bodies [corpi misti], are similar to human bodies [corpi semplici]. Just as in the latter many times illnesses occur that cannot be healed without fire and steel [sanza il fuoco o il ferro], so also in mixed bodies it often happens that so many problems arise that a compassionate and good citizen, even if violence [il ferro] is necessary, would commit a greater sin leaving them untreated than administering treatment." Rinaldo identifies the illness, asking, rhetorically, what greater "malattia" could befall the body of a republic than "servitú" (*IF* 5.8.6–7), here referring to the loss of political liberty that he believes Cosimo was inflicting on the city. Machiavelli expects his readers to remember the first two chapters of book 4 of the *Histories*, where he says that it was in the half century between 1382 and 1434 that even the possibility of liberty was destroyed, after which Florence no longer oscillated between liberty and "servitú," "as many believe," but rather between the "servitú" imposed by the nobles and the "licenzia" of the "popolari"—even as they all praise "the name" of liberty. Machiavelli's Rinaldo champions "liberty," asserting that, whereas Duke Filippo Maria had once fought to deprive the Florentines of their liberty, he could now restore it to them (*IF* 5.8.14)—by repatriating Rinaldo and the other exiles. Machiavelli's Rinaldo is one of the "nobles" who "praise the name of liberty" as they undermine its foundations. Again seeking to justify his request that Visconti attack Florence, Machiavelli's Rinaldo speaks a

[43] Leonardo Bruni, *Laudatio Florentine Urbis*, ed. Stefano U. Baldassarri (Florence: SISMEL-Edizioni del Galluzzo, 2000), p. 33.

[44] Text in Susanne Daub, *Leonardo Brunis Rede auf Nanni Strozzi* (Stuttgart and Leipzig: B.G. Teubner, 1996), pp. 281–300, quoted passage at 285; relevant passages also in Hans Baron, *The Crisis of the Early Italian Renaissance* (Princeton: Princeton University Press, 1966), pp. 556–7.

line from Livy that is also famously quoted in *The Prince*: "Only wars that are necessary are just, and arms are sacred [pietose: compatible with devotion to the patria] if there is no hope without them." Rinaldo claims not to know what necessity could be greater than "ours"—except that "ours" refers to his faction—or what "pietà" could exceed that which rescues the patria from "servitú": "it is therefore most certain that our cause is sacred [piatosa] and just" and that "we" and "you"—the exiles and the Visconti duke—must so consider it. He says defeating the Florentines will be easy because of their internal animosities and lack of unity, which make it difficult for them to invest their wealth in war, for men are willing to contribute their patrimonies when wars are fought for honor, glory, and their own benefit, especially if they hope, when peace returns, to regain the wealth that wartime taxes take from them. But they are not willing to do so, Rinaldo continues, when they are oppressed both in war, enduring damage inflicted by the enemy, and in peacetime, suffering the "insolenzia" of those who rule them. Much more harmful to a people than the rapaciousness of foreign enemies is the avarice of its own citizens: the former, they hope, will end; the latter never ends (*IF* 5.8.8–13).

The prognostications of Machiavelli's Rinaldo were, of course, erroneous. Subjugating Florence, far from being an "impresa facile" for the duke of Milan, was not possible. Machiavelli shows Rinaldo and his fellow exiles still urging Filippo Maria to invade Tuscany several years later, telling him that the Florentine people, "exhausted by taxes and the insolence of the powerful," would surely rise up against the Medici regime (*IF* 5.26.4). But after Florentine forces under the command of Neri Capponi defeated the troops of Filippo Maria's captain, Niccolò Piccinino, at Anghiari in 1440 (*IF* 5.33), the exiles' cause was hopeless. Machiavelli says Rinaldo went to live in Ancona, and from there made a pilgrimage to the Holy Sepulcher. Shortly after returning, he died (in 1442) on the day of his daughter's wedding: "in this," Machiavelli comments, "fortune favored him, because he died on the least unhappy day of his exile." There follows an enigmatic epitaph: "He was a man honored in every turn of fortune; but still more honored he would have been if nature had caused him to be born in a united city, for many of the qualities that harmed him [lo offesono] in a divided city would have rewarded him in a united city" (*IF* 5.34.7–8). Given that Rinaldo did so much to divide Florence, we may wonder what Machiavelli meant.

8
Regime and Repression

HOW TO WRITE ABOUT THE MEDICI

Machiavelli's interpretation of the ascendancy and domination of the Medici should be seen as part—a very large part, to be sure—of his more general critique of wealthy elites. For all the peculiarities of the regime's history, including the several crises that nearly brought it down and the one that did in 1494, in Machiavelli's judgment the Medici shared the ambitions, avarice, pursuit of private power, and willingness to resort to violence to protect that power that were characteristic of Italian elites. But the Medici took the techniques and refinement of private power to a new level, gradually undermining the uneasy compromise the pre-1434 elite had maintained with republican norms and instituting practices of unofficial personal rule without precedent in Florentine history. Machiavelli was well aware of this transformative dimension of the Medici domination, but he was also cognizant of the difficulty, and delicacy, of describing and assessing it. Writing about the Medici in a work commissioned by Cardinal Giulio de' Medici, and dedicated to him when he was Pope Clement VII, posed special problems for Machiavelli, whose service to the republic that succeeded the Medici in 1494 and close association with the republic's standard-bearer, Piero Soderini, made him unpalatable to the restored Medici. Consequently, they shunned him for several years after 1512. When a rumor reached Rome in early 1515 that Giuliano di Lorenzo was planning to employ Machiavelli, Cardinal Giulio, presumably conveying instructions from Pope Leo, warned Giuliano not to have anything to do with Machiavelli.[1] But in 1518 and 1519 friends of Machiavelli negotiated a rapprochement that resulted in Medici-sponsored performances of *Mandragola*, a few "commissioni" on behalf of the regime, and, in 1520, the commission to write the *Florentine Histories*. The inevitable importance of the Medici in Machiavelli's interpretation of Florence's history is matched by the risks of constructing a critical perspective on their place in that history. In short, when writing about the Medici, Machiavelli had to be careful.

In the proem of the *Florentine Histories* Machiavelli establishes the centrality of the Medici to his narrative by asserting that his original intention was to begin in

[1] Letter of the papal secretary Pietro Ardinghelli to Giuliano de' Medici, in Oreste Tommasini, *La vita e gli scritti di Niccolò Machiavelli*, 2 vols. (Turin-Rome: Ermanno Loescher, 1883–1911; reprint edn. Naples: Istituto Italiano per gli Studi Storici and Il Mulino, 1994–2003), vol. 2, pp. 1064–5.

Machiavelli's Broken World. John M. Najemy, Oxford University Press. © John M. Najemy 2022.
DOI: 10.1093/oso/9780199580927.003.0008

1434, "the time when the Medici family, through the merits of Cosimo and his father Giovanni, assumed more *autorità* [influence and power] than any other [family] in Florence" (*IF* proemio.1) There are reasons to doubt that this had actually been Machiavelli's original plan: first, the attention he devotes to the "defects" of the pre-1434 regime in creating the conditions for Cosimo's rise to power; and second, the fact that, because much of books 5 and 6 (and some of books 7 and 8) deal extensively with events outside Florence, Machiavelli actually wrote more about pre-1434 Florence than about the sixty years of Medici dominance. Inventing a fictitious original plan to begin in 1434 was, first of all, a way of signaling the rise of Cosimo as the crucial turning point of Florentine history; second, it allowed him to establish the famous contrast with the two influential humanist historians of Florence, Leonardo Bruni and Poggio Bracciolini. Machiavelli says he believed he could begin in 1434 because they had covered in detail ("particularmente") everything before that date. Again, this should not be taken literally. Bruni's history begins with the city's Roman foundations and the vicissitudes of imperial Rome, moves quickly through the medieval period, and begins a continuous narration of Florence's history from the thirteenth century to the end of the wars against Giangaleazzo Visconti in 1402. Bruni does not deal with the pre-Medici regime of the first third of the fifteenth century to which Machiavelli attributes signal importance in book 4 of his *Histories*. Poggio's history begins in 1350, thus omitting the entire century from the first popular government of 1250 to the 1340s, to which Machiavelli devotes his second book. Bruni and Poggio clearly did not cover "in detail everything" before 1434. Machiavelli's criticism of these predecessors is that, while they were "most diligent" in recounting the wars fought by the Florentines, when it came to "domestic discord [civili discordie] and internal hostilities [intrinseche nimicizie] and their effects," they were "either entirely silent" or "described them so briefly" as to provide no utility or pleasure to their readers. Machiavelli speculates that they did so either because they considered such matters unimportant or because they feared offending the descendants of those about whom they might have had to "speak ill [calunniare]." Dismissing both reasons as "unworthy of great men," he asserts, first, that "history can teach or give pleasure if it describes things in detail," and, second, that nothing is more useful to "citizens who govern republics" than histories that "demonstrate the causes of hatreds and divisions in cities" (*IF* proemio.1–4), thereby enabling them to learn how to preserve unity from [predecessors] who gained wisdom from the dangers they experienced. It has often been noted that, while the criticism that they neglected internal conflicts is largely true of Poggio, it is inaccurate for Bruni, who, despite his decision not to continue beyond 1402 and thus not to investigate how hostilities within the pre-1434 elite paved the way for the rise of the Medici, does in fact say a great deal about domestic political conflicts in the thirteenth and fourteenth centuries, albeit coming to judgments quite different from those of Machiavelli.[2] With friends and patrons in both the Medici and Albizzi camps, Bruni had good reason not to enter the contentious territory of factional discord that split Florence's elite in the early fifteenth century. Curiously, Machiavelli's criticism of Bruni alludes to a dilemma he himself decided not to face, namely, the problem of how to write contemporary history without offending the powerful. Just as Bruni declined to extend his history into the time of his career as chancellor and into the factional divisions between the Albizzi and Medici parties, Machiavelli similarly did not continue his history beyond Lorenzo's death in 1492, thus avoiding the controversies surrounding both the collapse of the Medici regime and the agitated politics of the republic of the Great Council that he witnessed during his years in the chancery. Despite their undeniably different perspectives on the interpretation of Florence's history before 1400, Machiavelli might have felt some kinship with Bruni as he pondered the dangers of navigating the rapids of the history of his own time.

The dilemma is immediately evident in the dedication, where Machiavelli says that "in describing the goodness [bontà] of Giovanni [di Bicci], the wisdom [sapienzia] of Cosimo, the kindness [umanità] of Piero, and the magnificence and prudence [magnificenzia e prudenzia] of Lorenzo," he fears he may have transgressed Clement's command to avoid flattery ("adulazione"). He asks forgiveness from Clement and all readers who disapprove of such flattering descriptions as "not very trustworthy [poco fedeli]," thereby hinting that such characterizations of the pope's ancestors are not the full truth. He could not have done otherwise, he pleads, because he had either to describe these family leaders with the same praises he found in the "memorie [sources]" on which he relied, or, by keeping silent about them, to appear grudging ("invido"). But this was not, of course, the choice Machiavelli actually faced. He then raises the question, disingenuously declaring it to be specious, that surrounds everything he wrote about the Medici: "And if, under their distinguished deeds was concealed, as some say, an ambition opposed to the common good, I who do not recognize it am not obliged to discuss it." So not all the sources were filled with praise: "some say" different things. Machiavelli here simultaneously identifies the kernel of the dilemma—the "ambizione" of the Medici—and, despite the rhetorical deflection, suggests that he has in fact recognized it: "for in all my narratives I have never wanted to camouflage a dishonorable deed with an honorable pretext, nor conceal a praiseworthy deed as done for an opposite purpose." In other words, he has always called things as he sees them and will continue to do so. In fact, as we shall see, there is no doubt that

[2] Michelle Clarke astutely assesses Machiavelli's critique of Bruni in *Machiavelli's Florentine Republic* (Cambridge: Cambridge University Press, 2018). Gary Ianziti's *Writing History in Renaissance Italy: Leonardo Bruni and the Uses of the Past* (Cambridge, Mass.: Harvard University Press, 2012) is a comprehensive, magisterial study of Bruni's historical writings.

Machiavelli did recognize in the Medici an ambition that was corrosive of both law and liberty. Yet he could not, for obvious reasons, openly accuse them of nurturing such ambition. Anticipating how he would present the truth of their role in Florence's history while avoiding the Scylla of fawning panegyric and the Charybdis of risky condemnation, at the end of the dedicatory epistle he reverses his earlier fear of having transgressed Clement's directive not to engage in flattery, now saying: "How far I am from flattery can be seen in all the parts of my history, and especially in speeches and private discussions, both in direct and indirect discourse, which preserve, without any reticence, in both substance and presentation, the pertinent disposition [il decoro dello umore] of the speaker" (*IF* Dedica.6–9). Machiavelli thus highlights the speeches, opinions, and conversations of the actors in the *Histories* as crucial to grasping his interpretation.

Donato Giannotti, Machiavelli's younger contemporary, recounted, in a letter of 1533, a conversation in which Machiavelli had told him something quite similar. About the "sincerità" (truthfulness, straightforwardness) of the "historia," Giannotti quotes him as saying: "I cannot write this history from the time when Cosimo seized the government [prese lo Stato] to the death of Lorenzo as I would if I were free from all hesitations [rispetti]"—free of anxiety about possible consequences. "The actions will be accurate and I will omit nothing, except that I will leave aside a discussion of the general causes [cause universali] of things; in other words, I will speak of the events and facts [casi] that occurred when Cosimo seized the government; [but] I will leave aside a discussion of how, and with what means [mezzi] and shrewdness [astutie], one attains such heights. Anyone wishing to understand this should carefully note what I will have his adversaries say, because what I am not willing to say as coming from myself I will have his adversaries say." Giannotti claims Machiavelli said this to him many times.[3] In a 1524 letter to Guicciardini Machiavelli hinted at the same dilemma, asserting that he would "pay ten soldi" to "have you at my side and show you where I am [in the narrative]. Now that I am at the point of having to deal with certain matters"—almost certainly the Medici, given the date of the letter—"I would need to know from you whether I cause excessive offense [offendo troppo] in praising [esaltare] or in denigrating [abbassare] things." Because "offendo" is not followed by a direct object, it is not clear whether Machiavelli was worried about offending his readers or the Medici, particularly Pope Clement. He tells Guicciardini he will "proceed with his own counsel"—in effect, decide for himself: "I will make every effort to [write] in such a way that, as I speak the truth [dicendo il vero], no one will be able to complain [nessuno si possa dolere]."[4]

Promising to respect the "dignity and truth of history," Machiavelli concludes the dedication by declaring that "no one who correctly considers my writings can

[3] Donato Giannotti, *Lettere italiane*, ed. Furio Diaz (Milan: Marzorati Editore, 1974), p. 35.

[4] *Lettere*, p. 539.

reproach me for being a flatterer [adulatore]." "I have therefore made every effort, Most Holy and Blessed Father, in these descriptions of mine, while not staining the truth [non maculando la verità], to satisfy everyone; and perhaps I will have satisfied no one." If that is the case, he says, he will not be surprised, "because I believe it is impossible, without offending many, to narrate the events of their times" (*IF* Dedica.10–14). In 1525, when Machiavelli finished the eighth book of the *Histories* at the death of Lorenzo de' Medici in 1492, many who lived through the latter decades of the fifteenth century were still living, including Clement. One wonders if he read the book closely enough to find reason to be offended.

As noted earlier, Machiavelli mentions the role of the Medici family in several turbulent moments of the fourteenth century—in the street battles of 1304 in which the great fire destroyed the inner city; in the conspiracies against Walter of Brienne; and in the final defeat of the magnates—giving the impression of a quite unruly lot.[5] We have seen that he devotes considerable attention to three prominent Medici before Cosimo—Salvestro, Vieri, and Giovanni di Bicci. Salvestro is favorably portrayed as a defender of the laws and staunch opponent of the excesses of the Parte Guelfa who was determined to "castigate the insolence of the powerful." Vieri is presented more ambiguously: while refusing the guildsmen's invitation to seize the "stato," he also declined to "liberate them from the tyranny of the citizens who were destroyers of good men and the common good" and feared he had "deceived the people" by persuading them to lay down their arms. Machiavelli's account of Vieri's role foreshadows his representation of the fifteenth-century Medici in its mix of protestations of civic virtue, claims to defend the people, but also actions that undermined civic norms and popular interests.

There is ambiguity as well in the portrayal of Cosimo's father, Giovanni di Bicci. Machiavelli depicts him as a virtuous citizen who rejects Rinaldo degli Albizzi's plan for a seizure of power by force of arms. He has Giovanni say "he believes it the duty of a wise and good citizen not to undermine the customary ordini of his city" (*IF* 4.10.2), that he "was not for supporting factions, but for extinguishing them," and that "he desired nothing more than the unity of the city." But Machiavelli also introduces the aggressive voice of his "followers"—his faction: "molti che seguivano le parti sue"—who were "unhappy" with these sentiments and would have liked him to be "more dynamic [piú vivo]." In particular, Alamanno de' Medici (Giovanni's nephew), possessed of a "feroce" (bold, feisty, brazen) temperament, "never stopped inciting him to persecute his enemies and favor his friends, denouncing his detachment [freddezza] and his restrained [lento] ways, which, he said, were why his enemies, with no hesitation, were concocting schemes against him that would one day result in the ruin of his family

[5] An impression supported by Gene Brucker's study of archival and chronicle sources in "The Medici in the Fourteenth Century," *Speculum* 32 (1957): 1–26.

and friends." Machiavelli leaves uncommented the contrast with Cosimo, who "also urged [his father] in the same way."[6] Despite these exhortations and prognostications, Giovanni "did not waver from his intention," even as his "parte"—his faction—was already in evidence ("scoperta") in the manifestly divided city (*IF* 4.11.2–4). Giovanni may have denounced factions and claimed to want only unity, but Machiavelli makes it clear that his loud and powerful faction wanted more.

Machiavelli's Giovanni makes a deathbed speech to his sons, Cosimo and Lorenzo, that borrows important elements from Giovanni Cavalcanti's version in which Giovanni tells his sons that his legacy consists in both great wealth ("infinite ricchezze") and "the favor of every good citizen and the multitude of the people, which has always chosen our family" as its "tramontana stella"—its north star or lodestar, and hence its unfailing beacon and guide. He instructs them to be benevolent to the poor and the humble and assist them in adversity, and not to "try to turn the government palace into their own shop [il palagio non esercitate in farne bottega]." They should instead wait until they are called before going there and should not give counsel against the will of the people. "I leave you free of all blemishes [netti di tutte le macule], because none was ever committed by me, and thus I leave you heirs of glory, not of infamy." Leaving this world, Giovanni is happy, but "happier still would I be if I did not see you involved in a faction [se in setta non vi vedessi entrare]."[7]

Machiavelli echoes many of the same themes in chapter 16 of book 4. In his version, too, Giovanni dies happy, knowing that he leaves his sons "wealthy, in good health, and in circumstances that allow you, if you follow in my footsteps, to live honored in Florence and in everyone's good graces." He claims not only never to have wronged, or injured ("offeso"), anyone, but indeed to have given assistance to everyone as far as he was able. Machiavelli's Giovanni gives the same political advice spoken by Cavalcanti's Giovanni but adds the arresting notion of "taking" only the right amount of the "stato": "As for the stato, if you wish to live securely, take of it [toglietene] only as much as is given to you by the laws and by men." Following this principle "will never bring you resentment [invidia] or risk [pericolo], for what makes men hated is what they take for themselves, not what is given to them. You will always have more of it [ne arete molto piú—i.e. of the stato] than those who, wanting the share of others, lose their own and, before losing it, live in constant anxiety" (*IF* 4.16.2–4). Giovanni's "stato" hovers between power (the unofficial but very real influence of party leaders) and the regime (the faction's control of government). The idea that bits and pieces of it can be given

[6] The subject of this sentence—"Inanimava ancora al medesimo Cosimo suo figliuolo"—is unclear. Did Cosimo pressure his father in the same way Alamanno did? Or did Alamanno exhort Cosimo in the same way he urged Giovanni? The usual reading is the former.

[7] Cavalcanti, *Istorie fiorentine* 5.3, ed. Polidori, vol. 1, pp. 261–3; ed. Di Pino, pp. 141–2.

and taken (and sometimes taken without being given) underscores Machiavelli's notion of the private, transactional nature of factional politics. On the other hand, the restraint Giovanni counsels—to take only what is given by the laws and by men—gestures, at least as far as the laws are concerned, to legal and statutory norms, and hence to respect for institutions. That "men" can also give shares of the "stato" to others, however, reverts to the politics of private influence and bartering. Giovanni's advice, seemingly born of good sense and civic equity, is, upon closer inspection, caught between regime and government, between private and public concepts of politics. In the light of Machiavelli's subsequent analysis of the Medici regime's studied conflation of public and private, Giovanni's speech seems a first, albeit apparently innocent, expression of this intentional ambiguity, a foreshadowing of a regime built on taking more and more of the "stato" into its hands. Giovanni continues his advice to Cosimo and Lorenzo by telling them that, "with these skills [con queste arti], among so many enemies and so much contentiousness, I have not only maintained but increased my renown in this city" (*IF* 4.16.5–7). If they do otherwise, he warns them, they will come to no happier end than those who have ruined themselves and their families. But is "arti" in the phrase "con queste arti" meant as skills, or as cunning, trickery, and guile?

Enlarging upon Cavalcanti's laudatory portrait, Machiavelli adds that Giovanni was "merciful, generous with alms, not only to those who begged for assistance but many times also to those who did not ask. He loved everyone, praised good men, and had compassion for wicked men. He never sought political offices but held them all, and never went to the [government] palace unless he was called. He loved peace, hated war, assisted those in [financial] difficulty, and promoted general well-being [le prosperità aiutava]." These are all ritual terms of praise. But the next sentence curiously points, by way of negation, to what would later be a troubling aspect of Medici power: "He was averse to theft of public funds [alieno da le rapine publiche] and a supporter of the common good." The oddity of praising Giovanni for non-commission of the crime of embezzlement points ahead to the fiscal irregularities of later Medici. "He died very rich financially, but richer still in reputation and good will. This inheritance, both in the goods of fortune as in those of the spirit, Cosimo not only maintained, but increased" (*IF* 4.16.9–16).

"TINGED IN BLOOD"

As noted in Chapter 5, before Machiavelli undertook to write the *Histories* he had already commented on Cosimo's rise to power in chapter 33 of book 1 of the *Discourses* in a discussion of how a republic should deal with an "inconveniente" it has ignored and whose danger has become greater and more difficult to correct. "Inconveniente" in Machiavelli's Italian is much stronger than "inconvenience" in English. Inconveniences can be tolerated, ignored, or easily corrected, but they pose no great danger. The "inconveniente" analyzed in *Discourses* 1.33 is a danger that, if not remedied early, threatens the health and even the survival of the republic; if allowed to grow, it is wiser to temporize and hope that it dissipates on its own than to attempt to root it out with rash measures, because, "almost always, those who try to quash it make it even stronger and accelerate the damage [male] that is feared from it." His first example is the failure of Rome's early neighbors to realize the growing danger in their midst: by the time the "inconveniente" of Roman power had grown so large that it made neighboring peoples fearful, it would have been better to temporize than try to eliminate it. In republics, Machiavelli says, such problems typically arise from within. He cites two frequent kinds: "allowing a citizen to gain more strength [forze] than is lawful [or justified]," and "the corruption of a law that is the nerve [nervo] and life of a free polity [vivere libero]." If a "young noble" who possesses "virtú istraordinaria" emerges and captures the admiring attention of fellow citizens, they will "heedlessly compete to honor him." And if he has a modicum of "ambition," his natural gifts—virtú and youth—and the citizens' favor quickly raise him to a position from which it is difficult to remove him. Implicitly comparing the threat Rome posed to its neighbors to the growing power of this ambitious citizen of "virtú istraordinaria" underscores the gravity of this "inconveniente." Cosimo is Machiavelli's example. Pope Clement may have been pleased to see Cosimo described as a man of extraordinary virtú honored by so many citizens (as he no doubt would have understood the phrase), but he was probably unaware that the first hint of Cosimo's threat to the republic lies precisely in the characterization of his virtú as outside the ordini, beyond the constitutional norms of the republic. Machiavelli acknowledges Cosimo's political skill—his virtú—but by calling it "istraordinaria" he already points to Cosimo's ascent to power through his faction, wealth, private influence, and "riputazione"—his renown, which, as Machiavelli says in *Discourses* 3.28, is the cause of tyranny in republics. Still in *Discourses* 1.33, he says Cosimo "acquired such "riputazione" from his wisdom ("prudenza") and the citizens' ignorance that he began to cause fear "in the stato," namely, among the leaders of the Albizzi regime, who therefore banished him, only to see his "parte"—his faction—secure his recall and make him "principe della republica." Just how much of a threat to the republic this "inconveniente" actually proved to be Machiavelli makes clear adding that "the same thing happened in Rome with Caesar," whose favor among the other senators quickly turned to "fear that caused them to adopt a solution"—assassination—that "accelerated the ruin of their republic" (*DL* 1.33.1–14).

In *Discourses* 1.52, still pondering how Cosimo could have been stopped, Machiavelli asserts that in corrupt republics (in which private and factional politics have already rendered the ordini ineffective) there is "no better, less divisive, or easier way" of opposing the "ambizione" of some citizen than to adopt the same methods he uses to reach his goal, or, as Machiavelli puts it, "preoccupandogli quelle vie [preempting those paths]" on which one sees him moving—to get ahead of him with the same techniques. In Cosimo's case this was his "strategy [stile] of favoring the people," the policy of cooptation through favors and generosity. If "the citizens who were competing with him had done the same," they would have deprived Cosimo, without uprisings or violence, of the "weapons of which he made most use." This, Machiavelli says, would have been a "much better choice for his opponents than banishing him from Florence" (*DL* 1.52.1–5). The chapter title states that this method is the "most secure and least divisive way of repressing the arrogance [insolenzia] of one rising to power in a republic." Machiavelli thus attaches to Cosimo his two fundamental characterizations of the destructive politics of the elite classes: "ambizione" and "insolenzia." Finally in the *Discourses*, as an example of the theory that all republics and religions, if they are to survive, must periodically return to their "beginnings," the opening chapter of book 3 recalls—as an ironic example—that "those who governed the regime [stato] in Florence from 1434 to 1494 used to say that it was necessary to retake [ripigliare] the stato every five years." "And what they called 'retaking the stato' was to implant in men the same terror and fear they instilled in them" when they took it the first time. Because, with time, Machiavelli says, people forget their fear and dare to try to change things and "speak ill" (of those in power), it was necessary to return the stato to its beginnings and instill another heavy dose of fear and terror. In this parody of the return to beginnings, and without mentioning Cosimo's name, Machiavelli exposes the Medici regime as constantly in need of keeping citizens in a state of fear in order to survive (*DL* 3.1.24–6). This is one of Machiavelli's most scathing judgments of the Medici regime.

In the 1520–1 *Discursus florentinarum rerum*, written for Medici eyes (or so Machiavelli hoped), Cosimo's "stato" is said to have "inclined more toward a principate than a republic." It lasted longer than its predecessor, he says, for two reasons: first, because it was created "with the favor of the people"; and second, because it was managed ("governato") by the wisdom ("prudenza") of "two men of the likes of Cosimo and his grandson Lorenzo." The first reason—that the Medici were the party favored by the people (and their adversaries the party of the nobles)—belongs to the lore of Medici propaganda. As noted in Chapter 7, Machiavelli debunks it in the *Histories* (*IF* 4.27.11) when he has Niccolò da Uzzano say: "I do not know why our faction deserves to be called noble any more than theirs." Machiavelli's second reason for the longevity of Cosimo's stato (which he considers to have extended through the time of Lorenzo) is standard flattery inserted to win the benevolence of Pope Leo and Cardinal Giulio. But Machiavelli undercuts the images of popular favor and skillful leadership in the next sentence, asserting that the regime's major weakness was that "what Cosimo wanted had to be deliberated by so many." This refers to the statutory legislative councils (of the people and the commune), which, as Machiavelli tactfully omits to mention here, sometimes refused to approve the plenipotentiary balìe needed to authorize the election officials selected by the Medici to ensure that the executive offices were staffed by loyal Mediceans. The "weakness" was such that "many times they came dangerously close to losing it"—the stato. "From this came the many parlamenti"—the manipulated ad hoc plebiscitary assemblies in which the crowd mumbled its approval of the regime's intentions—"and the many exiles" of political opponents "that occurred during that regime" (*Discursus* 9–10). Camouflaged by praise of Cosimo and Lorenzo and the people's alleged approval, Machiavelli puts his finger on the regime's need—precisely because it was not a true principate—to resort frequently to the extra-constitutional remedy (often imposed by force with soldiers ringing the piazza) of bypassing the legislative councils. Because of this fundamental weakness, he concludes that it would not be feasible, in the conditions of the 1520s, to recreate Cosimo's regime. "No stable stato can be established unless it is a true principate or true republic" (*Discursus* 43).

The outlines of Machiavelli's perception of Cosimo and his stato were thus already sketched out as he began to write the *Histories*. In 4.26 he offers a first, short portrait of Cosimo. After Giovanni's death, Machiavelli says, Cosimo conducted himself with greater "boldness [animo]" in political affairs, and with "greater zeal [studio] and more liberality with friends than his father had done." "Animo" denotes spirit and courage but also hints at animosity, or aggressiveness, suggested as well by the observation that the difference between Cosimo and Giovanni was such that the enemies of the Medici "who had been pleased by Giovanni's death were distressed [si contristavano] seeing what Cosimo was like." As for Cosimo's "liberality with friends," Machiavelli immediately underscores its crucial role in his acquisition of power. He was "very wise, solemn and gracious with others, always generous [tutto liberale], always kindly [tutto umano]." Referring to the period before his exile and return, Machiavelli says "he never attempted anything against the Parte [Guelfa] or against the stato [of the Albizzi]; he devoted himself to assisting [beneficare] any and all and making many citizens his partigiani with his liberality." His "liberality," therefore, was strategic: the chief method he used to build a large party of loyal followers. In enlarging his influence and exercising power through a faction composed of partigiani, Cosimo continued the privatized politics of the Albizzi regime. But in doing so with the liberality made possible by his vast wealth, he represented something new and far more dangerous. This is why Machiavelli says the opponents of the Medici were deeply distressed "seeing what Cosimo was like [vedendo quale era Cosimo]" and why his prominence "increased the anxiety [carico: worry, trepidation] among those in power." In a particularly revealing sentence Machiavelli says Cosimo "believed [giudicava] that, in this way, he would be able to live as secure and powerful as anyone else; or, should the ambition of his adversaries bring matters to the straordinario"—"venendosi per la ambizione degli avversarii allo straordinario"—"he would be victorious with his arms and the support he enjoyed [essere e con le armi e con i favori superiore] from those who benefitted from his liberality" (*IF* 4.26.1–3). Machiavelli here provides the essence of the assessment he will subsequently elaborate. Cosimo's political rise depended on his wealth and his faction of partigiani, and in any conflict between the factions—by definition "straordinario" and extra-constitutional—he was confident he would prevail with the arms and supporters funded by his wealth. Of course, these resources themselves belonged to the sphere of the "straordinario," including the ominous suggestion of the use of private arms.

As we have already seen, Machiavelli claims, also in *Histories* 4.26, that the Medici faction instigated the campaign of slander against those who managed the Lucca war. Avoiding mention of Cosimo by name, he attributes the campaign to Averardo, Cosimo's cousin, "and the others" (*IF* 4.26.6). The next chapter openly characterizes these attacks by the Medici in terms of the unlawful "extra-ordinary," asserting that these "modi estraordinari di procedere" were "rightly [ottimamente]" recognized as such by Niccolò da Uzzano and the other leaders of their party, who discussed ways of countering Cosimo's "modi" but found nothing suited to their purpose, for it "seemed to them dangerous to let the thing grow stronger [lasciare crescere la cosa] and difficult to challenge it" (*IF* 4.27.1). In the draft Machiavelli did not equivocate, bluntly writing that it was dangerous "to let *Cosimo* grow stronger [lasciare crescere Cosimo]." This is the chapter in which Uzzano lays out "the actions of Cosimo that make him suspect to us"—actions that, to those who do not see their true purpose, seem to reflect the virtues of compassion, solicitude, and liberality.

The central elements of Uzzano's indictment of Cosimo are confirmed by Rinaldo degli Albizzi's lament that the "favors" Cosimo extended to citizens with his "enormous wealth" kept the opposition party weak (*IF* 4.28.8), and by similar judgments in Machiavelli's own voice of Cosimo's liberality and pursuit of power through his wealth. The first example is the ease with which Cosimo, while imprisoned, secured the funds with which to bribe the standard-bearer of justice, Bernardo Guadagni, into allowing him to be exiled instead of executed as Rinaldo wanted (*IF* 4.29). Another episode that underscores the leverage of Cosimo's faction and wealth even during his exile (and the fear it engendered in the Albizzi party) is the discovery of a letter written to Cosimo by his ally Angelo Acciaiuoli (later one of the regime's chief lieutenants) in which Acciaiuoli encouraged him to "get some war started"—from exile!—because "he believed that, since the city would need money" for the war, "it would find no one [else] to provide it, and the citizens would be freshly reminded of [Cosimo] and want to have him returned." Even when the letter fell into the hands of the magistrates and Acciaiuoli was arrested, tortured, and banished, this "did not restrain in any way the faction [umore] that supported Cosimo" (*IF* 4.30.10–12). Cavalcanti recounts the episode in more detail,[8] but in his version Acciaiuoli says to Cosimo only that sooner or

[8] Cavalcanti, *Istorie*, 9.28, ed. Polidori, vol. 1, pp. 554–7; ed. Di Pino, pp. 293–4.

later the rulers of Florence would become involved in another war and need the great sums that only Cosimo could provide. Machiavelli has Acciaiuoli advise the exiled Cosimo actually to start a war, implying a degree of influence that only he, with his great wealth as a private citizen, could finance. To any reader aware of the huge loans Cosimo made to the public treasury—and Machiavelli has Uzzano (correctly) say that he was already doing this before 1433—the magnitude of the republic's dependence on Medici wealth to fight its wars, both before and during Cosimo's thirty years at the helm, comes into stark relief. Book 4 ends with Cosimo's return from exile in 1434 to what Machiavelli calls "a great demonstration of affection [benivolenzia] amid a great throng of people [con tanto concorso di popolo]"—the latter being the same phrase Machiavelli uses in *Discourses* 3.28 to describe the popularity of Spurius Maelius whose "liberality" the Roman senate found so dangerous. Everyone, Machiavelli says, warmly greeted Cosimo as "benefattore del popolo" and "padre della patria" (*IF* 4.33.9–10).

The beginning of Cosimo's regime is not quite so joyous in Machiavelli's narrative. In chapter 4 of book 5 he exposes the nature of the regime in terms that echo what he writes in *Discourses* 3.1: that those who administered the regime said "retaking" the stato every five years meant renewing the "terror and fear" they had created at the regime's origin. Employing the classic technique of deflecting blame from the king to his ministers, Machiavelli says those who had effected Cosimo's return and many others who had been "wronged" (by the Albizzi party in 1433–4) "resolved without any qualms [sanza alcuno respetto]" to guarantee the security of their regime ("assicurarsi dello stato loro"). He attributes a series of punitive actions, not to Cosimo, but to the Signoria of November-December 1434 (which, Machiavelli omits to mention, had been handpicked by the Medici election secretaries and the Signoria of September-October that recalled Cosimo, hence not drawn by lot according to traditional practice). "Not content with what their predecessors had done in support of the [Medici] faction," the new Signoria lengthened the sentences of banishment for many exiles and added "many others" to the ranks of those forced to leave the city. Underscoring the extent to which political persecutions were determined by personal and family antagonisms, Machiavelli says these added punishments were motivated by "wealth, marriage connections, and private enmities [le ricchezze, i parenti, le nimicizie private]." He then makes, albeit via partial and then retracted denial, an astonishing comparison: "And if these proscriptions had been accompanied by [the shedding of] blood, they would have been similar to those of Octavian and Sulla." As he had likened Cosimo to Caesar in *Discourses* 1.33, here he compares the nascent regime's large number of banishments to those of the Roman warlords Octavian (Caesar's heir and later the first emperor) and Sulla, infamous for his cruelty as general of the armies of the nobles against Marius and the forces of the people in the civil wars sparked by the agrarian laws of the Gracchi. Withdrawing the conditional ("if these proscriptions had been accompanied by blood"), Machiavelli corrects himself by pointing out that they were "in fact to some degree tinged in blood [nel sangue s'intignesse]." He cites specific cases. The Signoria executed the son, Antonio, of the standard-bearer of justice, Bernardo Guadagni, who had first plotted with Rinaldo degli Albizzi to kill Cosimo but then accepted a bribe to replace capital punishment with exile. And this was followed by the execution of four other citizens. Machiavelli names two of them, Zanobi Belfradelli and Cosimo Barbadori, explaining that they had violated the terms of their banishment by going to Venice, and that the Venetians, "valuing their friendship with Cosimo more than their own honor," arrested and sent them back to Florence where "they were shamefully [vilmente] put to death." This, comments Machiavelli sarcastically, "conferred great prestige [reputazione] on the parte"—the Medici faction, although he does not identify it as such—"and instilled the greatest terror in its enemies." Having removed from the city "all those who were enemies of, or suspect to, the regime [stato]," they—again, no mention of either Cosimo or the Medici—sought to strengthen their "parte" by repatriating some of those exiled by the former regime, including the Alberti, and granting popolano status to most of the remaining magnates (*IF* 5.4.1–5).

Machiavelli summarizes the legislative enactments and electoral mechanisms employed to fortify the regime's control. New scrutinies filled the purses with the names of Medici "friends" and removed those of their "enemies"; handpicked priorates (no longer drawn by lot from the purses) assured that the most important magistracies of government would be filled with the "leaders of their faction [principi della setta loro]"; and the police magistracy of the Otto di guardia was given the authority to inflict capital punishment ("autorità sopra il sangue"). No exile could return without the approval of thirty-four of the thirty-seven members of the priorate and its two advisory colleges, the Twelve and the Sixteen. Writing letters to, or receiving letters from, exiles was prohibited, and "every word, every gesture, every practice that displeased those in power [quelli che governavono] in any way was severely punished." Finally, if anyone suspect to the regime was unaffected by these measures, new tax laws were enacted to punish and intimidate them. "And so, in a short time," Machiavelli concludes, "having exiled and impoverished the entire enemy faction, they secured their regime [dello stato loro si assicurorono]." Machiavelli paints an astonishing picture of punitive and repressive control—without attributing any of it directly to Cosimo. It is the "parte"—the faction headed by Cosimo—that takes control of the magistracies, the law, the police, and the electoral and fiscal institutions in order to punish its enemies and reward its friends (*IF* 5.4.6–8).

It might seem curious that, following the detailed account of Cosimo's exile and return and the consolidation of the regime, the next two books of the *Histories* relegate him to the background. In book 5 he appears in only three of thirty-five chapters, and in book 6 he figures in just four of thirty-eight chapters. Only the last decade of his thirty years in power are discussed in any detail, and even these consequential years from 1455 to 1464 are compressed into the first four chapters of book 7, just before the summary of Cosimo's life and the obligatory portrait. In books 5 and 6 Machiavelli turns his attention away from Florentine domestic politics to the wider theater of Italian inter-state relations in which he makes Francesco Sforza the dominant figure. He recounts Sforza's career as a mercenary captain who fought for Florence, Venice, and Milan, quarreled again and again with Duke Filippo Maria Visconti, married his daughter nonetheless, fought against Venice, suppressed the Ambrosian Republic, and became duke of Milan (see above, Chapter 2). Cosimo is by no means absent from all this: Machiavelli makes clear how critical his financial and diplomatic support was to Sforza's success. And he attributes to Cosimo the realignment of the alliances among the Italian states as a consequence of making Sforza the Medici regime's chief ally and protector.

Machiavelli generally hides Cosimo's role (much as Cosimo himself did) in these diplomatic and military affairs, crediting decisions and actions to the "Florentines." But he brings him front and center in two foreign policy episodes concerning Sforza. The first is Cosimo's unusual in-person appeal to Venice not to break ties with Sforza. After leaving (temporarily) the service of Visconti (1435), Sforza signed on as captain of the Florentine-Venetian-papal league fighting against Milan. Still eager to marry Filippo Maria's daughter, however, and therefore reluctant to offend the duke, Sforza resisted taking his troops north across the Po. The frustrated Venetians wanted to terminate their contract with him, but Cosimo, Machiavelli writes, "believing that with his prestige [reputazione] he could persuade them" not to do so, went to Venice himself and spoke at length to the senate (1438), surveying the conditions of "lo stato di Italia"—an odd and intriguing use of "stato"—and arguing that, if Venice ended its alliance with Sforza and he reunited with Filippo Maria, Venice would "return to the sea" (i.e. lose its mainland possessions) and Florence would risk its "independence [libertà]." The reply Machiavelli attributes to the Venetians is not reported in any known source and quite likely expresses Machiavelli's own view of Sforza (and all mercenaries). He has the Venetians tell Cosimo they were not accustomed to paying mercenary captains who work for others: "So let the Florentines pay [Sforza] if they wish, since he works for them. For the security of their own dominions, the Venetians believe it more urgent to diminish his arrogance [superbia] than to continue to pay him. Men's ambition knows no bounds, and if he were paid without providing service, he would soon demand something still more dishonorable and dangerous. They therefore think it necessary to curb his insolence once and for all and not let it grow to the point of becoming incorrigible" (*IF* 5.14.2–6). Cosimo returned home empty-handed.

A year later Sforza overcame his reluctance, taking his forces north and liberating Verona and Brescia from the sieges of Filippo Maria's captain, Niccolò Piccinino. Visconti blamed "the financial assistance and support of the

Florentines" for his failure to capture those cities (*IF* 5.26.1) and responded by sending Piccinino into Tuscany. Machiavelli's account of the Florentine victory over Piccinino at Anghiari in 1440, while mentioning Cosimo only once, comments on the restrictive nature of the regime. The Florentines, he writes, "were not frightened" by the arrival of Piccinino's army, but they took measures to "keep firm control over [tenere fermo] the government." Although they had earlier had a "terrore grandissimo" of the exiles led by Rinaldo degli Albizzi, the Florentines now "had little to fear," Machiavelli suggests, "because of the affection [benivolenzia] Cosimo enjoyed among the people and because major offices were restricted to a small group of powerful men [intra pochi potenti], who with severity maintained tight control in the event that malcontents sought political changes" against the regime. Machiavelli no doubt realized that these two explanations were at odds with each other. Why was severity against "malcontents" needed if Cosimo enjoyed "benivolenzia" among the people? This seems an ironic juxtaposition of Medici propaganda about the contentment of the people with the more complex reality of a fragile regime that faced a good deal of internal opposition. Neri Capponi, whom Machiavelli often places at the center of Florentine diplomatic and military efforts in books 5 and 6 (unlike Cosimo), "kept [the Florentines] alive with hope" by bringing troops back from Lombardy. Machiavelli says Capponi found the city in "disordini" and fear—an assessment that likewise contradicts the assertion that the Florentines "had little to fear" because of the tight control of the government by a few powerful men. Capponi, one of the two civilian commissioners, succeeded in stopping Piccinino's depredations and defeated him at Anghiari. In these events it is Capponi who leads, decides, and achieves the victory. Machiavelli pointedly notes that the other commissioner was a Medici—not Cosimo but his distant cousin Bernardo (*IF* 5.31.1–3, 10)—and praises both commissioners for their "diligenzia" in quickly preparing the disorganized Florentine camp to meet the enemy (*IF* 5.33.2–3). They were welcomed back to Florence "with wonderful expressions of joy" by the "principi del governo" and the people and given all "the highest honors" usually awarded to "trionfanti" (alluding to ancient Roman triumphs) (*IF* 5.35.12–13). In all this Cosimo is conspicuously absent.

Cosimo's influence, on the other hand, is abundantly clear in Machiavelli's dramatization of the controversies in Florence (in *Histories* 6.23, briefly summarized in Chapter 2) over his support for Sforza in the struggle for Milan. This is the second episode in which he portrays Cosimo intervening prominently, and this time successfully, to promote his foreign policy goals. Machiavelli invents (or embellishes) a debate, situated in late 1449 or early 1450, weeks or at most a few months before Sforza's triumph, that articulates the domestic tensions over Cosimo's personal alliance with Sforza. At this point, Machiavelli writes, the Florentines "had not declared for either of the parties and had given no help to Sforza, either when he was defending the Milanese or later." But this was true only for the government of Florence. Machiavelli immediately distinguishes Cosimo's private initiatives from the government's "public" stance: "When Count Francesco was isolated and had no one to whom he could turn"—Machiavelli refers here to the period after Filippo Maria's death, which caught Sforza unprepared and without allies—"he urgently sent requests to the Florentines for help, both to the government [publicamente allo stato] and privately to friends [privatamente agli amici], and especially to Cosimo de' Medici, with whom he had long had a durable alliance [amicizia] and by whom he had always been faithfully assisted [fedelmente consigliato] and generously subsidized [largamente suvvenuto] in his every undertaking." "Nor," Machiavelli says, "did Cosimo fail him in this moment of dire necessity: indeed, as a private citizen [come privato] he abundantly subsidized him and encouraged him to pursue the campaign" to take Milan. Machiavelli says Cosimo pressured the Florentines to assist Sforza; he wanted the "city"—the Florentine government—to provide Sforza with funds from the public treasury: "Desiderava ancora che la città publicamente lo aiutasse." This, Machiavelli says, is where Cosimo "encountered some difficulty." Machiavelli has the "highly influential [potentissimo]" Neri Capponi, the hero of Anghiari, oppose both Cosimo's policy of funding Sforza and his insistence that the government assist him as well. He has Capponi say it would not be to Florence's benefit for Sforza to take Milan, believing instead that the "well-being [salute] of Italy" would be better served if Sforza ratified the peace agreement (the treaty of Brescia, September 1449) between Venice and the Milanese, according to which (as Machiavelli explains in the preceding chapter) Venice promised to defend the Ambrosian Republic and Sforza agreed to relinquish his claims to Milan (*IF* 6.22.1–7). Capponi warns that, if Sforza takes Milan (as Cosimo wished), the combination of his military strength and such a large territorial entity ("tanto stato") would be so "formidable" that, if Sforza is already "intolerable [insopportabile]" as a count, he would be "insopportabilissimo" as a duke. "It would be better for the republic of Florence and for Italy," Capponi advises, "for Sforza to keep his reputation in military affairs" and "for Lombardy to be divided between two republics"—the Ambrosian and the Venetian; and the best way to accomplish this, he concludes, is "not to finance" Sforza and to maintain Florence's traditional alliance with Venice (*IF* 6.23.1–8).[9]

With Neri Capponi's challenge to Cosimo on a foreign policy issue so critical to Medici fortunes, Machiavelli calls attention to the fissures within the regime. Capponi's arguments, he writes, "were not accepted by Cosimo's friends." By making the "friends" the first to speak in defense of Cosimo's policies, Machiavelli

[9] Machiavelli may have known of Capponi's pro-Venetian sympathies from Giovanni Cavalcanti's *Trattato politico-morale*: "il nostro eccellentissimo Neri...consigliò la Repubblica che per nulla da' Veneti si partisse"; in Cavalcanti, *Istorie*, ed. Polidori, vol. 2, p. 517. But the arguments spoken by Capponi and Cosimo seem to be largely Machiavelli's invention.

highlights his leadership of a powerful faction and the support of loyal allies ready to speak for him, unlike Capponi, who apparently speaks for himself. These "friends" not only defend Cosimo's views; they also impugn Capponi's motives, accusing him of expressing views opposed to those of Cosimo, "not because he thinks they are in the best interests of the [Florentine] republic, but because he does not want Sforza, Cosimo's ally, to become duke [of Milan], believing that, if this happened, Cosimo would become too powerful." Machiavelli thus reveals that at stake in the dispute over foreign policy was the Medici regime's need for foreign support to strengthen itself and fend off internal opposition. Although the debate is framed as a question of whether Florence should provide the assistance and cash Sforza requested, it was equally about whether Cosimo should be allowed to enlist Sforza as an external protector to help the Medici become still more powerful in Florence. After the "friends" speak, Machiavelli has Cosimo directly dispute Capponi's views, "explaining why assisting Sforza is extremely useful to both [Florence] and Italy." The essential objective was to prevent Venice from swallowing up the Milanese duchy. Machiavelli's Cosimo claims that "it is an unwise opinion to believe that the Milanese can keep themselves free, because the conditions [qualità] of the citizenry, their way of life, and their entrenched factional divisions [le sette antiquate] are inimical to any form of civile governo." There is a notable irony in having Cosimo, the undisputed head of the most powerful *setta* Florence had ever known articulate Machiavelli's own analysis that the prevalence in Milan of powerful factions—the "sette antiquate"—preclude liberty. It is inevitable, Machiavelli has Cosimo say, either that Sforza will become duke of Milan or that the Venetians will become Milan's "signori." Cosimo rejects Capponi's warning that the Milanese might submit to Venice because of their "deep anger" against Sforza: they will not do so, Cosimo says, because Sforza, unlike the Venetians, has his "parte"—his faction—in Milan (*IF* 6.23.9–11). Machiavelli thus has Cosimo, the master of regime politics who knew better than anyone the necessity of a loyal faction for maintaining power, imply that, in this respect, Sforza's regime would not be so different from his own.

Although the "conflicting opinions kept Florence in suspense," in the end Cosimo of course prevails. Machiavelli says ambassadors were sent to Sforza to negotiate an agreement, but only if they judged him strong enough to win and take Milan (*IF* 6.23.12). While traveling north, they learned of Sforza's triumphant entrance into the city (Machiavelli gives the precise date: February 26, 1450), invited by the Milanese themselves who, having strenuously opposed him, were dying of starvation and saw no chance of rescue (*IF* 6.24.1, 9, 16–21). The ambassadors' mission was now merely to offer Florence's congratulations to the new duke. Machiavelli says Sforza enthusiastically welcomed the ambassadors and the prospect of a close alliance with the Florentines, because he knew that, against "the strength of the Venetians, he could not have in Italy more loyal or stronger allies." The Venetians, recognizing that the Florentines' former fear of, and zeal in opposing, the Visconti had been transferred to themselves, now "sought the ruin" of their former ally. This, Machiavelli says, was the origin of the diplomatic realignment of the major Italian states—Florence and Milan allied against Venice and Naples (*IF* 6.25.2–4). Although this historic alliance shift was largely engineered by Cosimo, his name appears only later in the chapter when Machiavelli has him deliver "a long and wise oration" to disgruntled Venetian ambassadors, in which he emphasizes the many benefits Venice received from the thirty-year alliance with Florence, specifically "how much *imperio* [territory] Venice had acquired with Florentine money, soldiers, and counsel" (*IF* 6.25.8). Ostensibly offering the Venetians solace for the reversal of alliances, Machiavelli's Cosimo also hints at the Florentines' resentment over the one-sided results of the alliance they were abandoning.

For the last fifteen years of Cosimo's life (he died in 1464) and into the time of his son Piero and grandson Lorenzo, the Sforza dynasty was indeed the chief ally and indispensable protector of the Medici regime in several domestic crises. In *Histories* 7.19, recounting the aftermath of the failed attempt in 1465–6 by Cosimo's former lieutenants to prevent Piero from succeeding to his father's role as head of the regime, Machiavelli has the exiled leaders of the movement recall with bitterness how Cosimo ignored the wishes of other citizens in making the fateful decision to throw Medici and Florentine money and influence behind Sforza. Addressing the Venetian senate, the exiles sought to "incite the free men [of Venice] against the [Medici] tyrants, the compassionate against the wicked." They appealed to the deep grievance they said the Venetians should nourish, pleading with them to remember that the Medici deprived them of the "imperio" of Lombardy when Cosimo, against the will [fuora della volontà] of the other citizens and against the [Venetian] senate, supported and subsidized Francesco [Sforza]." Here Machiavelli has the anti-Medicean exiles express what he hesitated to say explicitly in summarizing the debate in book 6, namely, that Cosimo pursued his own interests and objectives and disregarded the opinions of "other citizens." A closer look at 7.19 (see Chapter 9) will show that the exiles associated such heavy-handed hijacking of the decision-making process with tyranny.

"INTOLERABLE AND VIOLENT"

The rivalry between Cosimo and Neri Capponi is a recurring theme of this part of the *Histories*. It was never, of course, an even contest. Machiavelli constantly emphasizes Cosimo's great wealth and formidable faction, whereas Neri stands apart from factions and speaks for the interests of the republic. Comparing them, Machiavelli outlines in *Histories* 7.1 the distinction between public and private paths to "riputazione [renown]" and in 7.2 says Neri was one of those who gained renown "per vie publiche," so that he had many "amici" but few "partigiani," whereas Cosimo had both "public and private paths to power open to him" and consequently had both many friends and many "partigiani." The historical Neri Capponi sometimes cooperated with the Medici but generally maintained a cautious independence.[10] He was, as Machiavelli portrays him, a major figure in Florentine diplomacy and the civilian management of military operations, serving often as military commissioner, most notably at Anghiari. But when he publicly objected to Cosimo's reversal of Florence's longstanding alliance with Venice, he was quickly removed from the inner group of Cosimo's trusted diplomats and commissioners.[11] Although Capponi could never be entirely aloof from factional politics, the contrast Machiavelli draws between him and Cosimo is largely accurate. In the *Histories* Capponi appears often, and almost exclusively, in military and diplomatic contexts, whereas Cosimo, by contrast, never holds a military office and serves on just one diplomatic mission.

Machiavelli underscores more than differences of opinion between Cosimo and Capponi. As early as Capponi's victory at Anghiari in 1440 (and perhaps because of it), he says Cosimo saw him as a threat and became apprehensive about his growing influence and prestige: "Among the distinguished [reputati] citizens in government was Neri di Gino Capponi," whose "reputazione" Cosimo "feared more than that of any other man, because to the great trust [credito] he had in the city was added the trust he had among the soldiers [soldati], for, having many times been the head of the Florentine armies [as civilian commissioner], he had won them over with his virtú and merits." The "soldati" referred to here are probably mercenaries, especially given that the episode Machiavelli is about to recount involves one of them. "The memory of the victories attributed to [Neri] and his father Gino," who, Machiavelli notes, "had vanquished Pisa [in 1406]," made Neri "loved by many and feared by those who wanted no coequals [compagnia, i.e. no competition] in governing" Florence. (No reader had to wonder to whom Machiavelli was referring here.) Among the commanders in the Florentine army, says Machiavelli, Baldaccio d'Anghiari was "most excellent" in war, unsurpassed in Italy for "virtú" of body and spirit, and an infantry commander whose reputation earned him his troops' complete loyalty. Baldaccio was a "close friend [amicissimo]" of Neri Capponi who loved him for his "virtú" (plural: his many skills and strengths). This, Machiavelli says, without naming Cosimo or the Medici, "caused great fear [sospetto] in other citizens" who, "believing it dangerous to dismiss [Baldaccio] and even more dangerous to keep him, decided to eliminate him [spegnerlo]" (*IF* 6.6.2–6). Machiavelli lets the reader absorb the shocking brevity and inexplicability of the steps here: we are not told why Capponi's friendship with a trusted and skillful condottiere caused "other citizens" to be so fearful

[10] Dale Kent, *The Rise of the Medici*, pp. 201–3.

[11] Riccardo Fubini, "Diplomazia e governo in Firenze all'avvento dei regimi oligarchici," in Fubini, *Quattrocento fiorentino, politica, diplomazia, cultura* (Pisa: Pacini Editore, 1996), p. 81.

as to want to have Baldaccio killed—other than their not wanting any rivals for power. Baldaccio's murder was arranged by a Medici partisan, Bartolomeo Orlandini, then serving as standard-bearer of justice, who bore a deep grudge against Baldaccio. Machiavelli explains (partly in *IF* 5.30 and partly in 6.6) that, in 1440, when Niccolò Piccinino was looking for a way to enter Tuscany, Orlandini was sent with a contingent of infantry to guard the strategic town of Marradi. As soon as Piccinino's forces approached, however, Orlandini fled, "vilmente" according to Machiavelli, and left the town undefended. Baldaccio, disgusted by Orlandini's "viltà [cowardice]" publicly denounced him. Humiliated and angry, Orlandini "greatly desired revenge" (*IF* 6.6.2–9).

With the encouragement and connivance of "other citizens"—the same euphemism—Orlandini, now standard-bearer in 1441, invited Baldaccio into the government palace, where a group of "armed young men," brought in by Orlandini, killed him and threw his body to the streets where it was mutilated. "For the whole day they made of it a spectacle [spettaculo] for all the people" (*IF* 6.7.1–9).[12] "Spettaculo" is the same word Machiavelli uses in *Prince* 7 to convey the horror and effect on the people of Ramiro de Lorqua's mutilated body in the piazza in Cesena; the echo here of that "spettaculo" hints at an equivalence between these two murders arranged, or allowed, by Cesare Borgia and Cosimo. The murder of Baldaccio also provides a parallel to the 1465 murder of Iacopo Piccinino (discussed above in Chapter 2). Like Cosimo, who feared the prestige of Neri Capponi and Baldaccio, Francesco Sforza, fearing the popularity Piccinino enjoyed among the Milanese, connived with Ferrante of Naples to have him killed. In the light of Baldaccio's murder—in the government palace, no less—Machiavelli's comment on Piccinino's murder applies as much to Cosimo as it does to Sforza and Ferrante: "Our Italian princes feared [temevano] and extinguished [spegnevano] in others the virtú they themselves lacked, so that, with no virtú remaining in anyone, they exposed [Italy] to the ruin that shortly thereafter afflicted and destroyed it" (*IF* 7.8.7)—"temere" and "spegnere" appearing in both episodes.

Machiavelli comments that Baldaccio's murder "diminished in part Neri's influence/power [potenzia] and deprived him of prestige and allies." But "the men of the regime [cittadini dello stato]" wanted more "because ten years had passed since the inception of their stato" and they were seeing many persons display "more boldness in speech and actions than was appropriate." Therefore, in order not to lose the stato, they deemed it necessary to retake it" (as Machiavelli says, in

[12] Cavalcanti recounts and denounces the "abominevole morte di Baldaccio" in the *Seconda storia*; see *Istorie*, ed. Polidori, vol. 2, pp. 160–3. Although the episode has received scant attention from modern historians, Guicciardini deemed it important enough to include in the *Storie fiorentine*, ed. Montevecchi, pp. 84–5, as did Vespasiano da Bisticci in the *Comentario della vita di messer Giannozzo Manetti*, in *Le vite*, ed. Aulo Greco, 2 vols. (Florence: Istituto Nazionale di Studi sul Rinascimento, 1976), vol. 2, pp. 535–6.

Discourses 3.1, they periodically did) by enhancing the influence [autorità] of their "friends" and destroying that of their enemies. They therefore created a new balìa in 1444, which tightened the manipulation of elections by "giving the power to elect the Signoria to a few," put trusted allies in key positions, extended the banishments of the exiles, and denied office-holding rights to the election officials ("accoppiatori") of the former regime (of the Albizzi)—which Machiavelli calls the "stato nimico." "And in these ways they regained power and influence for themselves and deprived their enemies and those suspect to them of their audacity [orgoglio]" (*IF* 6.7.9–12). Machiavelli describes this veritable coup d'état, sparked by a horrific murder, without even mentioning Cosimo or the Medici.

At the beginning of book 7, announcing his intention to return to Florence's internal history after devoting the preceding book (two books actually) to events "in Lombardia e nel Regno," Machiavelli muses that some readers will perhaps have found excessive his attention to events outside Florence. But the city's history, he insists, cannot be fully and properly understood apart from the context of peninsular events, especially the wars in which Florence became involved. His emphasis on the interrelatedness of domestic politics and foreign policy—evinced by his focus on Cosimo's support for Francesco Sforza and the formal alliance with Milan into which he led Florence—structures much of the narrative in books 7 and 8. Machiavelli's criticism of Leonardo Bruni in the *proemio* for (allegedly) ignoring Florence's domestic history must therefore not be misunderstood as a preference for a municipal history within the walls, as it were. Machiavelli knew from his chancery experience how inextricably linked were internal developments and external challenges, especially under the Medici whose power depended in great part on external support.

Before resuming the narrative, and still in the first chapter of book 7, Machiavelli revisits, and links, two principal components of his political thought: discord and the question of when and why it is harmful or beneficial; and the public and private roads to renown and power. Although both are familiar to readers of the *Discourses* and the *Histories* up to this point, here Machiavelli combines and applies them to his interpretation of the Medici regime. He restates the fundamental premise first presented in *Discourses* 1.4, namely, that conflict is inevitable in republics—"Those who hope a republic can be united are greatly deceived by this hope"—and then distinguishes between two kinds of divisions in republics: "some conflicts [divisioni] harm republics and others benefit them; harmful are those accompanied by factions [sette] and partigiani; conflicts that occur without factions benefit republics. Founders of republics cannot prevent enmities [inimicizie], but they must ensure that there are no factions." This takes Machiavelli to the two different ways of gaining renown. "One must know, therefore, that citizens acquire renown in two ways in cities: either through public channels [vie publiche] or with private methods [modi privati]." The connection is, of course, that factions are built with "private" ways of acquiring renown.

Explaining the difference again, as he had in *Discourses* 3.28, Machiavelli says a citizen can gain renown "publicamente"—on behalf of and through the institutions of the "publico"—by winning a battle, capturing a city in war, wisely carrying out a diplomatic mission, and giving sage and useful counsel to the republic. Renown gained in these ways is beneficial to the republic because it is "based on a common good [fondata sopra un bene commune], not a private good [bene privato]." It is not, in other words, done for private or personal advantage. Private methods of winning renown include doing favors for individual citizens; defending citizens from the magistrates (not from the excesses of the magistrates, as some read this, but from rigorous enforcement of the laws); assisting people financially; promoting citizens into office without regard for merit or qualifications ("immeritamente"); and—here he adds something new—ingratiating oneself with the "plebe" with public games and gifts. These actions produce "sette" and "partigiani"—factions and the clients beholden to them. Although "it is not possible to prevent intense animosities" even among citizens who pursue renown through public channels, they cannot harm the republic if they lack "partigiani" loyal to them. On the contrary, such citizens are actually beneficial, because in order to succeed in their endeavors they necessarily strive to bring glory to the republic and keep a watchful eye on everyone else to ensure that no one "transgresses civic standards [i termini civili]"—the rules and norms established by laws and ordini. With everyone acting in accordance with these standards, each will be on the lookout for anyone seeking to evade them.

Yet Machiavelli immediately declares that Florence's "inimicizie" "always occurred with factions and were therefore always harmful." Victorious factions remained united only as long as an opposing faction still existed; once the rival faction disappeared, the dominant faction itself divided, because neither fear nor internal discipline [ordine infra sé] held it together any longer." Applying this generalization to the origins of the Medici regime, Machiavelli says Cosimo's "parte," after coming to power, remained "united and lenient [umano] for a time because the defeated party was still large and full of powerful men." During these early years, "amongst themselves" the members of the Medici party "made no mistakes"—they avoided rifts or feuds—"and did nothing to make the popolo hate them." Consequently, whenever the regime "needed the people in order to retake power [ripigliare la sua autorità]"—the allusion is to the required approval by the legislative councils of periodic reauthorizations of balíe through which the Medici manipulated electoral procedures and, hence, the government—"it always found the people willing to give its [the regime's] leaders the authority and power they wanted." Machiavelli notes that they secured reauthorizations by the councils "ordinariamente [constitutionally]" six times in twenty-one years between 1434 and 1455 (*IF* 7.1.5–14). For as long as the regime remained united, the combination of its power ("potenzia") and the benevolence ("grazia") it enjoyed with the people ensured its success in getting from the people what it wanted

(*IF* 7.2.2)—and needed: the acquiescence of the legislative councils to legitimate the regime's extra-constitutional controls. Apart from foreign and military affairs and Baldaccio d'Anghiari's murder, Machiavelli has little else to say about these first twenty years of Cosimo's regime.

The attention to domestic politics revives in 1455, when the Medici party temporarily lost control of the institutions essential to its power and stability. In that year, "with Neri Capponi having died" (actually not yet: he died in 1457) and the "parte nimica" eliminated, "the regime [stato] encountered difficulty in reconfirming its power [nel riassumere la autorità sua]" (*IF* 7.2.3). Curiously, Machiavelli does not connect the regime's problems to the end of the long years of war, first with the Peace of Lodi between Milan and Venice in 1454 (to which Cosimo reluctantly adhered) and then with the promulgation of the Lega Italica in early 1455, which persuaded many Florentines that the time had come to end the extra-constitutional stranglehold on elections and government that had been justified and deemed necessary for twenty years by the wars and the threats posed by the exiles. Marco Parenti makes this clear in his memoirs. As "proposto" (chairman for the week) of the priorate of March-April 1454, he ensured the passage of Florence's ratification of the Peace of Lodi one day before a new war tax would have been levied. In May the statutory councils terminated the most recent balìa, instituted in 1452 and extended for five additional years at the end of 1453. The greatest blow to the regime came in June 1455, when handpicked ("a mano") elections of the priorate were terminated and sortition reinstituted. Suddenly, Cosimo lost the mechanisms on which he had relied to impose his and the regime's will on the committees of government. With the resumption of the traditional extraction of name tickets by lot for staffing the Signoria, Parenti commented that "the citizens believed they were regaining some degree of liberty."[13] Machiavelli writes almost the same words about the people's reaction to the regime's loss of electoral controls: "to the generality of citizens it seemed that they had regained their liberty" (*IF* 7.2.7).

It was Cosimo's own powerful friends, Machiavelli says, who caused the regime's loss of control, because they no longer feared the now defunct opposition party and "were keen to diminish [Cosimo's] power." The desire on the part of Cosimo's chief allies to rein him in, he adds, "initiated the divisions that followed in '66" (when, as Machiavelli will show and we shall see, many of the same Medici allies sought to prevent Piero from succeeding to Cosimo's leadership role). In emphasizing that the regime's own chief lieutenants were among the major voices in 1454–5 that favored terminating the balìa and returning to traditional electoral procedures Machiavelli again underscores the structural weakness of government by faction. Cosimo had to choose between two possible courses of action. He

[13] Marco Parenti, *Ricordi storici 1464–1467*, ed. Manuela Doni Garfagnini (Rome: Edizioni di storia e letteratura, 2001), pp. 111–12.

decided not to attempt to "retake the stato by force with the partigiani" who remained loyal to him and opted instead to stand back and let the "friends" who favored this weakening of controls come to the realization that they were depriving, not him, but themselves of "lo stato e la reputazione." This was so, Machiavelli writes, because the people believed, not only that they had regained their liberty, but also that the "magistrates would hand down sentences according to their own judgment, not according to the wishes of the powerful." The people, Machiavelli implies, assumed that impartial justice meant they no longer had to curry favor with the powerful and that they had regained liberty not only from Cosimo but also from the grandi. Consequently, the regime's lieutenants, accustomed to seeing their homes full of "salutatori"—clients paying their respects and bringing gifts—"now saw them empty" of visitors and offerings; "they saw that they had become equal to those they used to consider inferior" in rank and influence. "No longer were they respected and honored; indeed, they were often mocked and derided, as people talked about them and the republic in the streets and the piazze without any compunction [senza alcuno riguardo]." Consequently, Cosimo's former lieutenants "quickly recognized that they, not Cosimo, had lost the stato." Machiavelli reveals that they lost more than respect and honor: "what most frightened the grandi and gave Cosimo the best opportunity to make them rethink" what they had done was the "revival of the Catasto of 1427." The original Catasto law, according to which, as Machiavelli says in book 4 and now repeats, "laws, not men" determined tax burdens (i.e. objective legislated standards, not the subjective judgment of individuals with conflicts of interest), had been set aside by the Medici regime as Cosimo let public finance return to the old system of forced loans assessed by neighborhood committees. In early 1458, in the third year of government freed from Medici controls, the Signoria and legislative councils approved a resumption of the Catasto, which, if implemented, would have imposed more onerous fiscal burdens on the wealthy. This, Machiavelli says, was intolerable to the grandi and caused those who had abandoned Cosimo in 1455 to "rethink" what they had done and recognize their error (*IF* 7.2.3–11). Just as the Gracchi's land reforms provoked the Roman nobility to drastic opposition, the revival of the Catasto caused the Florentine grandi to set aside their differences and "go to Cosimo and beg his willingness to rescue both themselves and himself from the clutches of the plebe and restore to the regime [stato] the prestige [riputazione] that made him powerful and them honored" (*IF* 7.3.1). Machiavelli shines an unflattering light on the elite's overriding concern to preserve its wealth, and, if this required submission to Cosimo, their willingness to pay the price.

Cosimo agreed, Machiavelli writes, but he wanted a law passed "ordinariamente" (by the statutory councils), with the "consent [volontà] of the people, and not by force [per forza]; he wanted no talk at all about force." In view of the violent outcome, as we shall see, attributing these high-minded sentiments to

Cosimo is devastating irony on Machiavelli's part. When the councils rejected the proposal to create a new balìa, the "cittadini grandi" went back to Cosimo and, "with every expression of deference [umilità]," begged him to agree to a parlamento. Again he refused, because he wanted to compel them to "fully recognize their error" (*IF* 7.3.2–3). Cosimo did not of course want matters to go beyond his ability to control them, and Machiavelli says he found the right moment to act when Luca Pitti, a member of the regime's innermost circle, a frequent elector of the Signoria, and Cosimo's chief lieutenant over twenty years, became standard-bearer of justice (for the term July-August 1458). Machiavelli, always aware of the underlying bad faith within factions, says Cosimo wanted Pitti to take the needed measures so that, if blame [biasimo] were incurred, it would be imputed to Pitti, not to himself. When the legislative councils again rejected proposals for the creation of a balìa, Pitti threatened them with "injurious words full of arrogance [superbia]." Resorting to coercion, he filled the government palace with armed men, summoned the people to the piazza, and "with force and arms" made them "assent to what they had not voluntarily agreed to." He "resurrected [riassunto; recaptured] the regime [lo stato], created a balìa," and resumed "a mano" elections to ensure the selection of a Signoria agreeable to the stato. In addition, Machiavelli says, "in order to give this government, which they had instituted by force, an inception in terror [con terrore], they banished, among others, messer Girolamo Machiavelli and deprived many others of their right to office" (*IF* 7.3.5–8). The "forza" that Machiavelli says Cosimo had prohibited was not only implemented but converted to "terrore"—just as Machiavelli says, in *Discourses* 3.1.25, the Medici characterized the means by which the regime regularly reasserted its power.

Machiavelli does not explain that Girolamo Machiavelli was his second cousin once removed, a distinguished jurist and public figure well known to his father Bernardo (a jurist himself), and an outspoken critic of the regime.[14] He was arrested by the regime's police in a roundup of opposition figures, some of whom were tortured and others banished. After his banishment, because he failed to maintain the required distance from Florence, he was declared a rebel. Machiavelli says he traveled around Italy trying to prod other governments "contro alla patria." Betrayed by one of them, he was arrested, brought back to Florence, (tortured, although Machiavelli does not mention this, for obvious reasons perhaps too painful), and died, or was killed ("fu morto"), in prison (*IF* 7.3.8–9). Apart from the letters and the dedications and proems of Machiavelli's works, this is the only appearance of the family name in his writings. Adduced as an example of the

[14] On Girolamo Machiavelli, see the entry by Raffaella Zaccaria in *Dizionario biografico degli Italiani*, vol. 67, pp. 72–5; and Catherine Atkinson, *Debts, Dowries, Donkeys: The Diary of Niccolò Machiavelli's Father, Messer Bernardo, in Quattrocento Florence* (Frankfurt am Main: Peter Lang, 2002), pp. 38–40.

violence with which the regime reasserted its control in 1458, Girolamo's victimization also reminds the reader—and was perhaps so intended—of Machiavelli's ordeal in 1513: examples, both, of the brutality with which the Medici, like Sforza, Ferrante, Borgia, and most princes, dealt with those they did not trust and silenced anyone tempted by dissent.

Machiavelli's assessment of this tougher Medici regime could not be more severe. The "governo" that emerged from these events, he says, "was, for the eight years it lasted, intolerable and violent" (*IF* 7.4.1). He says eight years presumably because he considered that it lasted beyond Cosimo's death (in 1464) to 1466, when another challenge to the regime resulted in still more oppressive controls. But the important point is his characterization of this regime as "insopportabile e violento." Again he diverts opprobrium from the Medici themselves to Cosimo's lieutenants, particularly Luca Pitti. Cosimo, Machiavelli says, was by now "old and exhausted" and, because he could not attend to public affairs as he once did, "a few citizens plundered [predavano] the city." He notes that Luca Pitti was richly rewarded for his successful management of the 1458 crisis—the gifts bestowed on him were rumored to be worth twenty thousand ducats, and his prestige rose to such heights that he, Machiavelli surmises, not Cosimo, was governing the city. He built for himself two "splendid and regal [regii]" residences, one of which—Palazzo Pitti—was "in every way greater than anything built by a private citizen up to that time." Cosimo had already constructed his new family palace, about which the same observation had often been made. These comments underscore the latent rivalries among the faction's leaders that would erupt again in 1465–6. In assembling the resources for his building projects, Machiavelli adds, Pitti "omitted no illegal means [alcuno estraordinario modo]," taking gifts from citizens and accepting contributions from rural communes ("comuni e popoli interi"). Recent studies of Florentine patronage have shown how factional bosses extended their private networks into the contado and dominion cities, which often gave them gifts to secure favors and tax reductions, win appointments for lucrative ecclesiastical positions, and gain political or administrative offices. Machiavelli thus reveals that Pitti was now doing what the Medici had long done. Such gifts amounted to bribery, and this may be what Machiavelli means in saying that "a few citizens were plundering the city." Pitti was not alone in this: "Other citizens" among the elite, "if they did not build [as lavishly] as he did, were no less violent and rapacious than he was, such that, if external wars were not destroying Florence, it was being destroyed by its own citizens" (*IF* 7.4.1–10). Machiavelli presses further his accusation of the inner circle's rapacity: when Cosimo died, those who, because of rivalries within the regime, "did not love him" but saw that while he was alive the "reverence" in which his chief lieutenants held him somewhat tempered their "rapacity," feared they would be ruined without the constraints of Cosimo's presence. They put little hope in his son Piero, Machiavelli asserts, seeing him as a "good man" who would, nonetheless, because of his infirmity (a severe case of gout) and inexperience in politics, be obliged to act very cautiously in dealing with his father's former lieutenants. "Without a bit in the mouth," they would be "unrestrained [strabochevoli] in their rapacity" (*IF* 7.5.1–4).

"EXTRAVAGANCES CONSTANTLY ON DISPLAY CAUSE MORE RESENTMENT THAN THOSE CAMOUFLAGED IN HONOR"

Machiavelli's portrait of Cosimo occupies the rest of chapter 5 and all of chapter 6 of book 7. In a work dedicated to a pope who was Cosimo's great-grandson it can be considered a rhetorical requirement, but it is not without subversive elements. Cosimo was, Machiavelli begins, the "most renowned and famous citizen—of those who were not military leaders [di uomo disarmato]—that not only Florence, but any other city whose history we know, has ever had. He surpassed everyone in his time not only in influence/authority [autorità] and wealth [ricchezze], but also in liberality and wisdom [prudenzia]." "Wealth" and "liberality" announce what is to come. "Among the other qualities that made him the leading citizen [principe] of his patria" was being "liberale" and "magnifico" over and above all other men—the munificence that allowed him to make so many citizens and even some foreigners his clients and partigiani. The extent of his liberality, Machiavelli says, "became even more apparent after his death," when an inventory of his assets revealed that there was no citizen of any standing in Florence to whom Cosimo had not lent large sums of money. Even without being asked, he made loans when he became aware that some "uomo nobile" was in need. "Magnifico" alludes to the civic virtue—so-called by Aristotle and St. Thomas—of *magnificentia*, which, in the fifteenth century, became associated with lavish expenditures on great civic and ecclesiastical building projects. Cosimo's magnificence, Machiavelli writes, "was evident in the abundance of buildings" whose construction and decoration he financed: the many churches, monasteries, and convents in both the city and the contado, some of which Machiavelli lists; and his own "private homes," including the family palace in the city and four residences in the countryside, "all more suited to kings than private citizens [non da privati cittadini, ma regii]"; and, finally, a hospital for poor and sick pilgrims in Jerusalem. On all of them, Machiavelli repeats, he spent "a very great sum of money" (*IF* 7.5.6–11).

Machiavelli introduces the ethical (and political) dilemma posed by a level of spending whose "magnificence" entailed the risk that Cosimo might seem to have been raising himself above other, theoretically equal, citizens. Traditional norms discouraged and even prohibited excessive displays of wealth, and Machiavelli suggests how Cosimo protected his image: "Although these residences and his other works and deeds were those of a king, and he alone was the leading citizen [principe] in Florence, he was, nonetheless, so restrained by his prudence that he never transgressed civic moderation [civile modestia]. In his demeanor with others [conversazioni], with his servants, in horse riding"—presumably meaning that his horses were modestly caparisoned—"in every aspect of how he lived and in the marriage alliances" he arranged, "he was always like any *modesto cittadino*, because he knew that extravagances [cose estraordinarie] constantly on display cause more resentment [invidia] than those camouflaged with honor [con onestà si ricuoprono]." Characterizing these "magnificent" expenditures as "estraordinarie" and affirming Cosimo's awareness of their need for "honorable" camouflage, Machiavelli alludes to their perceived transgression of civic moderation and suggests that, to avoid other citizens' resentment, Cosimo disguised with honorable pretexts—philanthropy and religious devotion—the extravagant funding of churches and convents that might otherwise have been judged negatively for a private citizen. Machiavelli leaves unanswered, even unasked, the question of what "honorable" pretext, in the case of his many sumptuous private residences, would have allowed Cosimo to escape the opprobrium of excess that generates resentment. To illustrate his "civile modestia," he turns instead to the marriage alliances, noting that Cosimo did not marry his children and grandchildren into the families of "principi" (here meaning noble and titled rulers) and was content to contract marriages with other Florentine families (*IF* 7.5.12–13). Machiavelli will later contrast Cosimo's policy in this regard with that of his son and grandson.

Turning to Cosimo's expertise in governance and politics, Machiavelli claims that no one in his time equaled his understanding of both princely states ("stati de' principi") and republics ("civili governi"), and that this is what allowed him to "hold together a regime [tenne uno stato]" for thirty-one years amid the vicissitudes of fortune and in such an unstable city and volatile citizenry. He was "prudentissimo" (here bridging prudence and wisdom), saw problems from afar, and prepared for them. This allowed him to overcome the "ambizione" of both fellow citizens and many [foreign] princes with his good fortune and practical judgment ("con tanta felicità e prudenzia"). Praising Cosimo's success in dealing with other states, Machiavelli claims (with notable exaggeration) that, when the Venetians were allied with Cosimo (stated as if he were a sovereign ruler), they were always victorious; when not allied with him, they were always defeated by the Visconti or Sforza dukes; when they allied with Alfonso of Naples against Florence, Cosimo used his financial leverage all over Italy ("il credito suo") to "empty" both Naples and Venice of cash and force them to accept his terms of peace. All the crises he faced, both in the city and beyond, "ended gloriously for him and badly for his enemies. Consequently, domestic conflicts [civili discordie] in Florence always increased his prestige [stato: stature], and external wars augmented his power [potenzia] and renown." The "civili discordie" of this passage are factional rivalries, and Cosimo's successful management of them did indeed strengthen his command of domestic politics. More troubling is the suggestion that foreign wars likewise enhanced his power and prestige, for some Florentines believed he manipulated the city's foreign policy for his own benefit. Machiavelli mentions that Cosimo "added" two towns and two valleys to the Florentine dominions, but he does not link his political "wisdom" in any specific way to the well-being of the republic. In Machiavelli's pages his political sagacity seems narrowly focused on the typical aims of factional bosses: "Thus his virtú and fortune crushed his enemies and exalted his friends" (*IF* 7.5.14–18).

In chapter 6 Machiavelli continues—and in part rewrites—the portrait. He begins with a quick mention of ordeals ("travagli") that Cosimo suffered and overcame: his narrow avoidance of a death sentence in 1433 and the year-long exile; and, earlier, his flight in disguise from the Council of Constance after the deposition of Baldassare Cossa, Pope John XXIII of the Pisan obedience, whose pontificate had been so profitable for the Medici bank. Having survived these perilous moments, Machiavelli says, Cosimo lived in great happiness and success. Again he highlights his wealth: "Partaking in his good fortune were not only those close to him in political matters [nelle imprese publiche], but also those who managed his business affairs [tesori] throughout Europe, as a result of which many Florentine families gained great wealth"—he names the families of the Medici bank's managers: Tornabuoni, Benci, Portinari, and Sassetti: "all who trusted in his prudence and good fortune got rich." Machiavelli again mentions Cosimo's lavish spending on churches and philanthropy. He praises his "natural wisdom [naturale prudenzia]," despite the lack of formal education ("Fu senza dottrina"). He gives many examples of his quick and often cutting wit, including one that raises disquieting issues. "When some citizens told him after his return from exile that the city was being damaged [si guastava] by the banishment of so many distinguished men," Cosimo is said to have "replied that a damaged [guasta] city is better than a ruined [perduta] one, that two yards of red cloth suffice to make a distinguished man [uomo da bene], and that regimes [stati] are not held with rosaries in hand [co' paternostri in mano]." Machiavelli thus has Cosimo mockingly dismiss the large number of banishments he decreed in 1434–5 (which Machiavelli himself likens to those of Sulla and Octavian). This flippant response to the hardship inflicted on many citizens and families, and on the city itself, "gave his enemies reason to slander him as a man who loved himself more than his patria, and this world more than the next" (*IF* 7.6.1–12). Machiavelli pushes beyond this sensitive topic to Cosimo's patronage of "men of letters," especially philosophers, mentioning John Argyropoulos and Marsilio Ficino, "whom Cosimo dearly loved." He concludes this part of the portrait affirming that Cosimo's "wisdom [prudenzia], his riches, his way of life and good fortune made him feared and loved by the citizens of Florence, and wondrously esteemed by the rulers [principi], not only of Italy, but of all Europe" (*IF* 7.6.13–16). Noteworthy here is the claim that the citizens both feared and loved him.

Machiavelli then redraws the picture. "In the last years of his life, Cosimo experienced the most grievous sorrows," including the death of one son, Giovanni, and the debilitating infirmity of the other, Piero. Also "causing anguish to his spirit" was Cosimo's feeling that he had not made an "honorable" addition to Florence's territorial "imperio" (*IF* 7.6.18–20). Machiavelli had just written (in chapter 5) that Cosimo "added" to the republic's territorial dominions the towns of Sansepolcro and Montedoglio (the latter once near Sansepolcro but now under the waters of the artificial Lago di Montedoglio) and two valleys, the Casentino and the Val di Bagno. But now he says Cosimo was distressed because he believed he had not made an "honorable acquisition" for the "imperio." This is puzzling, first, because both Sansepolcro and the Casentino were actually very significant additions to the dominion. But was Cosimo responsible for them? The Casentino came under Florentine control bit-by-bit much earlier; by 1402 only the town of Poppi was still in the hands of the [Counts] Guidi of Battifolle, and in 1440, after the victory at Anghiari, it too submitted to Florence.[15] Cosimo served on the Dieci di balìa, the magistracy that supervised military operations, for three six-month terms in 1439, 1440, and 1441, and he may have participated in the settlement that brought Poppi into the Florentine dominion. But whatever role he played in the military success that made this possible seems to have gone unrecorded. Nor is it known if Cosimo ever claimed to have "added" the Casentino to the dominion or if he ever expressed regret at not making an "honorable acquisition." Did Machiavelli invent Cosimo's "distress" in order to call attention, obliquely, to his lack of direct involvement in territorial acquisitions and to underscore the contrast with Neri Capponi, the hero of Anghiari? Complicating this is the assertion that Cosimo was especially sorrowful because "he believed he had been deceived by Francesco Sforza," who "had promised that, when he became lord of Milan, he would undertake a campaign to give Lucca to the Florentines." On becoming duke, however, he broke that promise and preferred to enjoy his new duchy in peace. Was it Lucca that Cosimo (in Machiavelli's perception) regretted not having added to Florence's dominion? Machiavelli says Sforza's broken promise caused Cosimo much grief because of the "effort and expense" he devoted to "making powerful an ungrateful and disloyal man." We wonder what has become of the glorious outcomes Machiavelli claims Cosimo achieved for himself and his friends. The culminating sorrow of his last years, Machiavelli tells us, was the illness that prevented him from attending to "matters public and private" with his customary diligence. Consequently, he saw the city "destroyed [distrutta] by its citizens" (presumably his own lieutenants) and his "wealth dissipated by his sons and [bank] managers" (*IF* 7.6.23).

Despite these troubles, Machiavelli says Cosimo died "pieno di gloria" and was posthumously awarded the title "Padre della patria" (actually Pater patriae) by "public decree," so inscribed on his tomb slab in San Lorenzo. Mention of this

[15] Giovanna Benadusi, *A Provincial Elite in Early Modern Tuscany: Family and Power in the Creation of the State* (Baltimore: Johns Hopkins University Press, 1996), pp. 15 and 22.

singular honor prompts Machiavelli to offer an explanation of why, in writing about Cosimo, he has "imitated those who write the lives of princes, not those who write the histories of peoples [universali istorie]," in a book in which he proposed to write of "the things done at home and abroad by the Florentine people" (*IF* proemio.1). "This should surprise no one," Machiavelli explains, "because, since [Cosimo] was an exceptional [raro] man in our city, I have found it necessary to praise him *con modo estraordinario*." This could mean that he considered Cosimo "raro" in the sense of especially admirable and that this required a more exalted approach to writing his life. On the other hand, "estraordinario" has negative connotations for Machiavelli, signaling a transgression of what is lawful. In a republic grounded, in principle, in the equality of all citizens before the law, no man should be so "raro" as to be above the ordini and "civile modestia." But "estraordinario" in this sentence actually modifies Machiavelli's own "modo" of writing about Cosimo: is the portrait itself "estraordinario" and hence transgressive?

"IN ALL ITALY THERE ARE NOT SO MANY INSTANCES OF VIOLENCE AND GREED AS IN THIS CITY"

In the two years after Cosimo died in 1464 the handful of prominent citizens who for thirty years had been his chief lieutenants tried to prevent his son, Piero, from succeeding to the same position of unquestioned leadership within the party and control over government that Cosimo had enjoyed. They sought to restore traditional electoral procedures (as in 1455–8) and collegial leadership based on equality among themselves and Piero. To judge from the contemporary sources, none of this was done in secret and there was no plot to banish the Medici. The alleged conspiracy to kill Piero, which Machiavelli reports in chapter 15 of book 7 of the *Histories*, was invented, we now know, by Piero's loyalists to discredit the reformers.[16] Machiavelli may not have known this, and, as the narrative of the *Histories* approached the conspiracy that assassinated the duke of Milan in 1476 and the Pazzi conspiracy in 1478, it may have seemed obvious to him that the attempt to diminish Piero's power also involved conspiracy and assassination. He refers several times to the protagonists as "congiurati," sworn conspirators. His chief reason for considering the reform movement a conspiracy may have been that, while not concealed, it emerged from breakaway elements within the Medici party, not from government magistracies. Machiavelli paints a negative picture of the "congiurati" that emphasizes their private grievances against the Medici. He

[16] Nicolai Rubinstein, "La confessione di Francesco Neroni e la congiura antimedicea del 1466," *Archivio storico italiano* 126 (1968): 373–87. Francesco's interrogators added to his confession the fabricated plot to kill Piero.

regarded the means by which they pursued their objectives, the movement's failure, and the confrontation that brought the city to the brink of violence as products of factional dysfunction.

Machiavelli's account of the reformers' motives begins with Dietisalvi Neroni. Cosimo so trusted this pillar of his regime that he instructed Piero to follow Dietisalvi's advice concerning the Medici bank, family finances, and "the regime [lo stato]." "Wishing to obey his father in death as he had in life," Piero had Dietisalvi examine all the bank's accounts and Medici enterprises to identify problems or signs of mismanagement. "Promising to do so with diligence and in good faith," Dietisalvi found problems everywhere (Machiavelli calls them "disordini"). But what spurred Dietisalvi, Machiavelli affirms, was more his "own ambition than any love for Piero or favors received from Cosimo. So he thought it would be easy to deprive Piero of his prestige [reputazione] and the status [stato] bequeathed to him by his father." Although Machiavelli does not say so explicitly, Dietisalvi's bad faith also implies poor judgment on Cosimo's part in entrusting the family's financial fortunes to him. Dietisalvi's advice "seemed honorable and legitimate [onesto e ragionevole]," but "underneath," Machiavelli says, "was hidden Piero's ruin." Having uncovered the precariousness and risks of Medici enterprises, Dietisalvi told Piero that "the most honorable way to put his affairs in order was to try to collect the sums owed to his father by many persons, both foreigners and citizens." Machiavelli underscores the implications of this advice by reminding the reader that "Cosimo had been exceedingly generous [liberalissimo] in sharing his wealth with everyone in order to acquire partigiani in Florence and amici outside" the city. Hence, there were many debtors and their outstanding debts were substantial. Trusting that Dietisalvi's advice was "good and honorable," Piero demanded repayment of the loans and was suddenly confronted with the anger of many who "carelessly [sanza rispetto] spoke ill of him and slandered him as ungrateful and avaricious" (*IF* 7.10.2–11). Hatred of Piero spread among merchants who blamed him for their resulting business failures (*IF* 7.11.9).

Of the other protagonists of the movement—Luca Pitti, Agnolo Acciaiuoli, and Niccolò Soderini—Machiavelli says they saw the disaster into which Piero had fallen and "decided to deprive him of his prestige [reputazione] and power [stato]." He ascribes disinterested motives only to Soderini, who "wanted the city to live in greater freedom [piú liberamente] and be governed according to the judgment of the magistrates," and not, by implication, according to the wishes of party chiefs manipulating the magistrates (*IF* 7.11.3). The records of the consultative assemblies (the Consulte e Pratiche) show that Soderini did indeed express such views and promoted reforms based on them when he became standard-bearer of justice in November 1465.[17] He was an uncle of Piero Soderini, and it

[17] Guido Pampaloni, "Fermenti di riforme democratiche nelle Consulte della Repubblica fiorentina," *Archivio storico italiano* 119 (1961): pp. 241–81. Soderini's speech is on 242–4.

may have been a satisfying coincidence that Machiavelli could, with no distortion of the facts, attribute to Niccolò motives grounded in the common good akin to those of his nephew, thus separating Niccolò from the selfish and private motives of the other "congiurati." Machiavelli devotes a chapter to Niccolò's term as standard-bearer, calling attention to the large crowd ("quanto concorso") of admirers from both the elite ("onorati cittadini") and the people that accompanied him to the palace with enthusiastic expectations that he would protect the "safety [salute] and liberty" of the city. Soderini proposed a new scrutiny for the executive offices with the aim of "filling the purses with citizens who loved the *vivere libero*." But his good intentions, says Machiavelli, were undermined by the other "capi" of the "congiurati," who, out of envy, did not want to see the regime reformed under his "authority [autorità]." In Machiavelli's view rivalries and jealousies among the movement's leaders scuttled the best chance they had to realize their goals (*IF* 7.14).

Personal ambition and animosities, Machiavelli says, motivated the other leaders of the movement. Luca Pitti "had become so powerful [grande] that he was indignant at the prospect of having to be subservient to Piero" and wanted to "succeed" to Cosimo's role of undisputed leadership of the party. Dietisalvi considered Pitti "not suitable to be the head of government" and assumed that, once Piero was out of the way, the top spot would be his. Agnolo Acciaiuoli nurtured "personal animosities [particulari odii] against the Medici" because of a decision Cosimo made concerning the broken marriage of Agnolo's son, Raffaello, whose wife, Alessandra de' Bardi, had suffered "mistreatment" by both her husband and father-in-law and was rescued by her Bardi kin. At stake was her "huge dowry." The dispute was entrusted to Cosimo, who, despite having no legal training or authority in such matters, decided that the Acciaiuoli would return the dowry and Alessandra could decide for herself whether she would return to her husband's household. Agnolo considered this a betrayal of his long friendship with Cosimo, and, "having been unable," as Machiavelli says, "to gain revenge [vendicarsi] against Cosimo, decided to do so against his son." Machiavelli implicitly accuses all the "congiurati," except Niccolò Soderini, of bad faith, noting that, although motivated "by a great variety of grievances [tanta diversità di umori], they nonetheless announced one and the same justification [publicavano una medesima cagione] of their actions, namely, that they wanted the city to be governed by the magistrates and not by the decisions of a few" (*IF* 7.11.1–8). Machiavelli sees this as an attempt to camouflage ambition and private rancor. Accusing them of what he now calls "sedizione" as well as hypocrisy and deceit, he says they were confident of victory "because the majority of citizens followed them, deceived as they were by the word 'liberty' that the leaders adopted as their banner [insegna: slogan, emblem] in order to confer a semblance of honor on their undertaking [per adonestare la loro impresa]" (*IF* 7.11.11). In Machiavelli's view this was a fight inside a faction that was breaking apart, with no honor on either side, and a demonstration that, in a factional regime, dissent could only be conspiracy.

Deepening their resentments, Machiavelli claims, was Piero's decision to marry his son Lorenzo to Clarice Orsini from the Roman noble family. Similar to the reaction provoked by Corso Donati's marriage to the daughter of Uguccione della Faggiuola (*IF* 2.22.15), Piero's opponents saw his rejection of a Florentine marriage for Lorenzo as evidence that he considered the city too small for his and his family's ambitions ("che la città piú come cittadino non lo capeva": literally, that the city could no longer contain him as a citizen) and that he was therefore preparing to establish a "principato," because, so they reasoned, "he who does not want his fellow citizens as in-laws [parenti] wants them as servants [servi]" and "not as friends" (*IF* 7.11.10). Feeling the sting of this insult above all were the stalwarts of the Medici faction. Machiavelli points here to another dysfunction of private politics built on factional ties of patronage and marriage alliances. The Medici always insisted they were not superior in rank or standing to the city's leading citizens. This was of course a fiction, but a crucial one that held the faction together. He cites no specific evidence to show that the prospect of Lorenzo's marriage to Clarice contributed to the growing resentment against Piero; in fact, the chronology of events (which Machiavelli may not have known with precision) does not support his claim; the earliest indication of Medici interest in the Orsini *parentado* is the description of Clarice by Piero's wife (and Lorenzo's mother), Lucrezia Tornabuoni, written to Piero from Rome in March 1467,[18] a year after the conclusion of the political crisis. But Machiavelli was following his source, Giovanni di Carlo, who, according to the summary of his (unpublished) chronicle, the *Libri de temporibus suis*, claims that, in addition to negotiating the marriage, Piero was seeking help from Milan against his domestic antagonists.[19] The implication is that both pursuits were motivated by his need for allies beyond Florence.

Machiavelli says Francesco Sforza's death in early 1466 exacerbated and accelerated the "divisioni" in Florence (*IF* 7.9.8 and 7.10.1). His successor, Galeazzo Maria, sent ambassadors to Florence to confirm existing agreements that allegedly included annual subventions to Milan. Actually Florence had not promised annual payments, but there had been episodic subsidies to Francesco from both Cosimo and the Florentine government. In Machiavelli's telling, the reformers seized the occasion to announce, "publicly in the councils," their disapproval of any subsidy, arguing that the agreement had been made with Francesco, not Galeazzo, and that Florence could not expect the same benefits from Galeazzo, "who lacked his father's virtú." Machiavelli also has them assert that "if any

[18] Lucrezia Tornabuoni, *Lettere*, ed. Patrizia Salvadori (Florence: Olschki, 1993), pp. 62–3.

[19] Gaia Pieraccioni, "Note su Machiavelli storico. I—Machiavelli e Giovanni di Carlo," *Archivio storico italiano* 146 (1988): 635–64 (at 657).

citizen"—alluding to Piero—"wants to hire [Galeazzo] for his military strength [potenzia], it would be contrary to the *vivere civile* and liberty of the city": in other words, a private agreement between Piero and Galeazzo would be illegal, and any government subsidy would divert public funds to Piero's private defense. Machiavelli has Piero counter these arguments by asserting that it was unwise to abandon so necessary an alliance ("amicizia") out of miserliness ("avarizia") and that nothing was so beneficial to the republic and all Italy as Florence's alliance with the duke of Milan: without it, the Venetians would attack the duchy and depose Galeazzo, bringing the "destruction of the [Florentine] republic" (*IF* 7.12.7–9). In the event, as Machiavelli notes (*IF* 7.13.1), no subsidy was approved. The "congiurati" were gaining the upper hand: Machiavelli mentions the list of citizens who signed the oath in support of the movement (May 1466) but omits to say that they did so in the very public setting of the palace of the Signoria, that they numbered over four hundred and included, in addition to the leaders, members of many elite families and scores of families of the popolo and guildsmen. Nor does he acknowledge that the signers swore to defend liberty and the "government of the many," the selection of the Signoria by lot, and the freedom of all citizens "to give counsel and express their judgments on public matters."[20] By ignoring the number and social diversity of the signatories, the open, public character of the event, and the movement's declared aims, Machiavelli leaves the reader unaware of its broad popular support and reduces the oath, in effect, to propaganda by the "conspirators." But he does say that Piero was stunned by the quantity and stature ("qualità") of the signatories and instructed his lieutenants to compile a list of his own supporters (*IF* 7.13.13–14).

Machiavelli says hostilities were emerging into the open ("dimostrarsi aperte") but also, rather contradictorily, that both groups were meeting at night (he even gives locations). To sustain the impression of conspiratorial secrecy, he describes one of the reformers' nighttime meetings as a "private conference [particulare consiglio]" on how to achieve their objectives. All were in favor of "diminishing the power of the Medici," he writes, but they had different ideas about how to proceed. One group—Machiavelli calls it the more moderate ("la piú temperata e modesta")—wanted to refuse a reauthorization of the balìa, which, they assumed, would restore authority to the legislative councils and magistrates, quickly undermine Piero's influence, and ruin his credit and commercial enterprises, as long as he was prevented from "using government funds" to shore up his weakened finances. In this way "liberty" would be recovered "without banishments or the shedding of blood." Any use of force, they thought, would entail "many risks," and by not resorting to any "cosa straordinaria" against Piero they would deprive him of a pretext "to gather arms or search for allies"; but if he did, he would incur so

[20] Guido Pampaloni, "Il giuramento pubblico in Palazzo Vecchio a Firenze e un patto giurato degli antimedicei (Maggio 1466)," *Bullettino senese di storia patria* 71 (1964): 212–38.

much blame and suspicion as to hasten his ruin and give others justification to overthrow him. Machiavelli outlines the views of a second group that was dissatisfied with the time it would take for these outcomes to materialize. Time favors Piero, they insisted, not them. If they adhered to lawful measures ("cose ordinarie"), they would face many risks and Piero none, because the magistrates, even if hostile to him, "will let him enjoy the city"—allow him to maintain contacts with allies and supporters—and "his friends will make him *principe*, just as happened in '58 [with Cosimo]," which would destroy the movement. This second group wanted to avoid a repetition of that outcome in which a restoration of constitutional electoral procedures that failed to undermine the private sources of Medici influence would leave the door open for their "friends" to re-establish and even strengthen the family's control. They therefore advised neutralizing Piero ("spegnerlo") while passions were "inflamed against him," asserting that the way to do this was to arm the city and engage the marquis of Ferrara (Borso d'Este) to provide further protection. They aimed to be ready as soon as a Signoria favorable to them emerged from the electoral purses (*IF* 7.13.1–11).

According to Machiavelli, the failure of Niccolò Soderini's priorate to effect the political reforms many citizens expected strengthened Piero's party, which also benefitted from a number of "neutrals," who, detecting a shift in the political winds, joined Piero's side. The reformers now realized they had to act, and "what they had not been able, or not wanted, to do through the magistrates"—through the institutions of government—"they resolved to accomplish by force." Machiavelli says they decided to kill Piero and, to this end, bring the marquis of Ferrara into the city; with their own troops in the piazza, they would demand that the new Signoria institute a "stato" (magistrates in this context) according to their wishes (*IF* 7.15.1–3). Already aware of his opponents' plans from an informer who attended their meetings (*IF* 7.13.12–13; 7.15.5), "Piero decided to be the first to take up arms and seized on the opportunity [presented by] his adversaries' negotiations [pratiche] with the marquis of Ferrara." He "pretended [finse]," Machiavelli says, "to have received a letter from Giovanni Bentivoglio of Bologna informing him" that Borso d'Este's troops were in the mountains north of Pistoia and moving toward Florence. "With this warning, Piero took up arms and came to the city with a great multitude of armed men" (*IF* 7.15.5–8).[21] But the Milanese ambassador in Florence reported that Piero did in fact receive such a letter and, moreover, that Borso's troops were coming to Florence "at the request of Piero's adversaries."[22] Knowing that his opponents had conspired with Borso was what Piero needed to justify bringing the "grande moltitudine" of armed men

[21] Machiavelli's source for Piero's having pretended to receive a letter from Bentivoglio is Giovanni di Carlo; see Manuela Doni Garfagnini's review of the evidence in the "Introduzione" to her edition of Marco Parenti's *Ricordi storici*, pp. 3–50 (37–40 on Giovanni di Carlo).

[22] Nicolai Rubinstein, *The Government of Florence Under the Medici (1434 to 1494)*, 2nd edn. (Oxford: Clarendon Press, 1997), p. 184, n. 5.

into the city (recruited from the Medici-controlled territories of the Mugello and the Romagna fiorentina through patronage networks).[23] Both parties now armed themselves, although, Machiavelli notes, Piero's did so "with better organization [migliore ordine], like ones who came prepared," whereas his adversaries "were not yet organized according to their plans" (*IF* 7.15.9).

Machiavelli says Dietisalvi Neroni visited Piero often during these turbulent days to discuss unity and advise him, but also "the better to conceal" his intentions (*IF* 7.15.4). Now, with Medici forces occupying the piazza of the Signoria, Dietisalvi asked the Signoria to persuade Piero to lay down his arms and also urged Luca Pitti to stay committed to the plan. Niccolò Soderini—"more energetic than anyone [piú vivo che alcuno]" and accompanied by "all the plebe of his quarter" (of Santo Spirito, in the Oltrarno)—went to Pitti's home and begged him to mount his horse and go to the piazza; if they acted quickly, Soderini said, victory could still be theirs, but if he stayed in hiding at home he would either be shamefully overpowered by armed enemies or ignominiously deceived by unarmed ones and, when it was no longer possible to act, would regret not having done so. If he wanted to destroy Piero, he could easily accomplish it; if he wanted to reconcile with him it would be better to dictate terms rather than have terms dictated to himself. "These words," Machiavelli says, "did not move messer Luca," who gave the impression of having been "turned [svolto] by Piero with promises of new marriage alliances and new agreements."[24] Pitti urged Soderini to lay down his arms and return home (*IF* 7.15.10–13). Machiavelli's account of the challenge of the "congiurati" essentially ends there, especially as some of their supporters, seeing the Medici faction well-armed and its adversaries "unarmed," were switching sides (*IF* 7.16.2–3).

Machiavelli sees the events of 1465–6 as a factional struggle. "The leading citizens, heads of the factions [primi cittadini, capi delle fazioni]," he says, met in the government palace to discuss "reconciliation." But because Piero's illness prevented him from attending, "they all, except Niccolò Soderini, decided to go meet him at his home"—the Medici palace: a symbolic demonstration of where power had now shifted. Machiavelli's account makes the meeting seem less a reconciliation than a defiant declamation by Piero of his victory. One citizen expresses regret over the turmoil and asserts—in a weak combination of accusation and submission—that "greater blame lay with him who first took up arms. Not knowing what Piero, who had been the first to do so, now wanted, they had come to hear his wishes, which, if compatible with the welfare of the city, they were

[23] Marco Parenti estimated Piero's private army at 6,000; *Ricordi storici*, p. 132. The Milanese ambassador said they numbered 8,000; Rubinstein, *Government of Florence*, p. 186, n. 3.

[24] Marco Parenti, *Ricordi storici*, p. 130, reports that Pitti was tricked into believing that Piero had agreed to a marriage between his son Lorenzo and Pitti's "fanciulla," whereas Piero meant, not Lorenzo, but his brother-in-law Giovanni Tornabuoni (Lucrezia's brother). Machiavelli says only that Piero agreed to a marriage between Tornabuoni and Pitti's "nipote."

prepared to follow." The evidence available to us makes it difficult to determine who actually was the first to consider the use of force and ask for outside help, and the ambiguity pervades Machiavelli's account as well. But he does not let Piero overlook the reproach that he had been the first to resort to arms. Machiavelli frames Piero's defense of himself not as a denial that he had been the first, but with the argument that "he who causes civic strife is not the one who first takes up arms, but the first to give cause that arms be taken up." If his now defeated opponents "had given more thought to how they had acted toward him, they would be less surprised at what he did to save himself, for they would see that the nighttime meetings, the subscriptions, and the schemes to take his life and deprive him of the city [tôrgli la città] made him resort to arms." Ignoring the fact that thousands of his troops occupied the piazza della Signoria, Piero claims that "his arms never left his residences," which he says "demonstrated that they were intended purely for defense, not to attack anyone else." Machiavelli has him insist further that he desired nothing beyond "his own security and tranquility [quiete]," with no mention of the safety and peace of the city. Proof of this, Machiavelli has him say, is that, when the authority of the balìa ended (in September 1465), he never considered any "estraordinario modo" to restore it and was quite satisfied, if his opponents were as well, "to let the magistrates govern the city." Machiavelli has Piero say, in effect, that his not resorting to unlawful and unconstitutional measures to reauthorize the balìa shows that his aims were limited to ensuring his own security. For Machiavelli, of course, introducing military forces to resolve a political impasse was the most damaging of extra-ordinary solutions. He has Piero say to his defeated foes, apparently with an imagined straight face, that Cosimo and his children were always able to live with honor in the city with or without a balìa and that, in 1458, their opponents, not the Medici, had reinstituted it (*IF* 7.16.3–8). In letting Piero utter such manifest distortions of recent events Machiavelli illustrates the emerging mystification of Medici power: the denial that they, merely private citizens, wanted anything more than their own safety and security.

Still in the same speech, Machiavelli has Piero go on the attack. He has become aware, he says, that his now humbled former antagonists believe they and he cannot exist in the same city—something he would never have believed or even imagined of these former allies of his father. Turning to Dietisalvi, who had precipitated Piero's financial crisis with deliberately damaging advice, and his brothers, he reproaches them "with stinging words full of indignation" for the favors they received from Cosimo, for the trust the Medici had placed in them, and for their great ingratitude. Machiavelli says Piero's words made some of those present want to assault the Dietisalvi brothers—and that they would have done so if Piero had not stopped them. Piero ends the harangue and returns to conciliatory reassurances, declaring that he would accept everything they and the

Signoria decided, and that, as for himself, he only wanted to live in peace and security (*IF* 7.16.9–12).

Having let Piero express indifference concerning a resumption of the balìa, Machiavelli immediately underscores his hypocrisy. As soon as a pro-Medici Signoria was installed for September-October 1466, "all matters having been prepared in advance," the standard-bearer of justice "summoned the populace to the piazza and created a new balìa, entirely from Piero's faction." The balìa quickly appointed magistrates "according to the wishes of the new stato," allowing Piero's party to take complete control of government offices. According to Machiavelli, this "frightened the leaders of the opposing faction" and caused them to flee the city: Agnolo Acciaiuoli went to Naples, and Dietisalvi Neroni and Niccolò Soderini to Venice. They were declared rebels and lost all legal protections. "Many other citizens" were banished to a variety of locations. "Nor was this enough," Machiavelli remarks: a procession was decreed to give thanks to the Almighty "for the preservation of the stato [regime] and reunification of the city," and during these "solemnities certain citizens were seized and tortured" (including Francesco Dietisalvi Neroni), with "some executed and others exiled" (*IF* 7.17.2–7). The extant sources do not mention executions, and Machiavelli's assertion that "some were killed," if erroneous, reflects his aim of portraying Piero's repression as especially punitive.[25]

Machiavelli comments separately on the fate of Luca Pitti, who, from having been a leader of the opposition, is portrayed as succumbing to fear, or pressure, and switching sides in return for promised favors only partly fulfilled. When the crisis was over, "he remained in Florence, trusting in the marriage alliance and Piero's promises." The trust was, of course, misplaced: "there was no more noteworthy illustration [esemplo] of the unpredictability of events [variazione di cose]," Machiavelli writes, "than messer Luca Pitti, who suddenly learned the difference between victory and defeat, dishonor and honor." Nominally, Pitti emerged on the winning side as an ally of Piero, but he was shunned and humiliated for having betrayed the movement he initiated and he lost the power he once had as a trusted lieutenant in the Medici party. Machiavelli paints a haunting picture of Pitti in the aftermath of Piero's victory. "In his home, to which so many citizens had previously flocked, great solitude prevailed. On the street, his friends and relatives feared not only to walk with him, but even to greet him, because some had lost the right to hold office, others had lost property, and all were equally threatened," presumably with still greater punishment if they were seen to befriend Pitti. "The splendid residences he had begun were abandoned by the builders; the favors once offered him had turned to insults; honors to vilification.

[25] Guicciardini says Piero was "clementissimo" in decreeing punishments; *Storie fiorentine*, ed. Montevecchi, ch. 2, p. 100. Rubinstein expresses the same judgment; *Government of Florence*, pp. 189–90.

Many who had given him valuable gifts expecting favors now demanded their return, as if they had been loans. Those who had regularly lauded him to the skies now denounced him as ungrateful and violent." Machiavelli ponders Pitti's failure: "And so he regretted, too late, not having trusted [the advice of] Niccolò Soderini and not having preferred to die with honor, arms in hand, than to live dishonored among victorious enemies" (*IF* 7.17.4, 8–10). Machiavelli's requiem for Pitti carries the message that, where factions reign, one's choices are either subservience to the faction in power or a dangerous roll of the dice that could cost one everything.

Agnolo Acciaiuoli appealed to his old friendship with Cosimo as grounds for reconciliation with Piero. Machiavelli evidently saw the letters they exchanged in September 1466,[26] just weeks after Acciaiuoli's banishment. "I laugh over what I see," Acciaiuoli wrote, maintaining that, as he had helped Cosimo return from exile, Piero should do likewise for him. Machiavelli rewrites the letter, changing the opening to "I laugh over fortune's games and how, according to her whims, she makes friends into enemies and enemies into friends." He has Acciaiuoli remind Piero of the risks he took in remaining loyal to Cosimo in 1433–4 and his unfailing devotion to him and the Medici family. Defending the stance he took in 1465–6, he says he was motivated by Piero's illness and the tender age of his sons to give the "regime [stato]" a "form" that would protect the patria from ruin after Piero's death. He did what he did, "not against you, but for the benefit of my patria. Even if it was an error, it deserves to be erased by my good intentions and past actions." He cannot believe he "will not find clemency in you or that my many merits must be obliterated by one misstep." In Piero's actual reply he acknowledges Acciaiuoli's loyalty to Cosimo, says he has forgiven the offenses committed against himself, and wants "to remain in your debt as far as it concerns me personally [privatamente]." But the "republic cannot and must not forgive so lightly," and therefore he too "cannot, will not, and must not forgive the *ingiuria publica*"—the wrong done to public authority. Machiavelli has Piero mock the opening line of the letter he attributes to Acciaiuoli. Piero actually wrote: "Your laughter has prevented me from crying, even as I was sorry about your misfortune." Machiavelli gives it the following twist: "Your laughter gives me reason not to cry; because if you were laughing in Florence, I'd be crying in Naples"—i.e. Piero would be the one in exile. Machiavelli's Piero acknowledges that Acciaiuoli was a loyal ally of Cosimo but reminds him that he was amply rewarded and that, as his debt to the Medici was greater than theirs to him, he must now pay the penalty for his offenses. Machiavelli's Piero sets aside the public-private distinction by which Piero simultaneously claimed to be able to forgive Acciaiuoli "privately" while the republic "cannot forgive so lightly," and has Piero employ the entirely private calculus of reciprocal obligations, favors, rewards, and penalties

[26] Published in *Laurentii Medicis Magnifici vita auctore Angelo Fabronio*, vol. 2: *Adnotationes et monumenta* (Pisa, 1784), pp. 36–7.

that structured factional bonds. Hence, his Piero rebuffs Acciaiuoli's plea that he did it all for love of country: "love of the patria does not excuse you, for no one will ever believe that this city was less loved or less exalted by the Medici than by the Acciaiuoli." Even love of the patria, for Machiavelli's Piero, is reduced to private competition. Because he lost the competition, Acciaiuoli is told he must "live dishonored there [in exile], since you did not know how to live here with honor" (*IF* 7.18.2–12).

The other banished adversaries, Dietisalvi Neroni and Niccolò Soderini, appealed to Venice, lamenting to the doge, in Machiavelli's telling, that "they suffered exile for no other error than having wanted their patria to live within its laws, and its magistrates, not a few citizens [Medici insiders], to be honored." Piero and his followers, they assert, "were accustomed to living like tyrants [vivere tirannicamente]; they deceitfully [con inganno] took up arms, deceitfully made [the opposition] lay down theirs"—as Vieri de' Medici did in 1393—"and deceitfully banished them from their patria." "Nor," Machiavelli has them say, "were they satisfied with this, for they used God as a go-between [mezzano] to persecute many others who remained in the city with assurances" for their safety (*IF* 7.19.1–9). Referring to the procession of September 1466, held to "give thanks to God for having saved and reunited the city" but used by the Medici to trap more of their opponents (*IF* 7.17.7), Machiavelli (in a passage cited earlier in this chapter) has the exiles tell the doge that Piero's faction made "God an accomplice [partecipe] in their betrayal, as they jailed and killed many citizens"—"a wicked and nefarious deed." They exhort the Venetian senate, "because it has always been free, to have compassion for those who have lost their liberty." Merging his voice with theirs, Machiavelli says the exiles "were thus rousing free men against tyrants and compassionate men against the wicked" (*IF* 7.19.9–11).

Machiavelli allows the exiles a rhetoric of liberty at war with tyranny, but the very fact of their appeal to Venice also implies, perhaps with greater relevance to Machiavelli's assessment, that in a republic dominated by factions there is no possibility of honorable opposition. In Medici Florence political defeat meant exile. And for the exiles the only recourse—other than Stoic resignation—was to incite foreign powers to attack their homeland. In asking the Venetians to make war on Florence the exiles of '66 were following in the footsteps of those of '34 who appealed to the Visconti of Milan and those of '58 who asked many "principi" for help. The Venetians, whether moved by the exiles' pleas, as Machiavelli asserts, or seizing an opportunity to weaken Florence, sent their captain, Bartolomeo Colleoni, to the Romagna borderlands, where, together with the ever-ready Este forces, he attacked a few towns. Minor clashes with Florentine forces, now led by Federico da Montefeltro, came to nothing. Once it became clear that the revolt against the Medici "promised by the rebels" would not occur, the parties reached a truce. The exiles, "deprived of all hope," dispersed to a variety of places: Dietisalvi to Ferrara, and Niccolò Soderini to Ravenna, where, "with a small pension from the Venetians, he grew old and died." Machiavelli offers a last thought about Soderini: "He was considered a just and courageous [animoso] man, but irresolute and slow in making decisions; this made him lose, as standard-bearer of justice, the chance for victory that later, as a private citizen, he sought but failed to regain" (*IF* 7.20.1–5, 12–17).

Machiavelli judges the regime that emerged from the confrontation of 1465–6 as harshly as he does Cosimo's regime after the coup of 1458. The victors "did not consider they had won unless they persecuted, not only their enemies, but also those suspect to their faction, with every kind of *ingiuria*," depriving many citizens of office-holding rights and exiling many more: "this increased their power and everyone else's dread [spavento]. And they wielded this power without any restraint [sanza alcun rispetto] and governed in such a way that it seemed God and fortune had given them the city as prey." Machiavelli spares Piero direct responsibility, claiming he "knew little about all this and, owing to his infirmity, was unable to stop what little he knew" (*IF* 7.21.1–4). "The city was greatly tormented [afflitta] by its own citizens, and Piero was unable to curtail their ambition because of his infirmity. Nonetheless, in order to unburden his conscience [sgravare la sua conscienza] and see if he could cause them to be ashamed, he summoned them to his home" and denounced their many misdeeds. Never would he have believed, Machiavelli has him say, that the "ways and practices" of his friends could cause him to love his enemies or that victory could make him wish for defeat. He had assumed that the men of his party might have recognized some "limit or moderation in their greed" (plural: nelle cupidità loro) and that, having avenged themselves against their enemies, they might have considered it sufficient to live "with security and honor in their patria." But he was greatly deceived, he says, because he underestimated the "inborn ambition [naturale ambizione] of all men, and especially yours." "It is not enough for you," Machiavelli's Piero says, "to be the leading citizens [principi] of so great a city and for you few to enjoy" the offices "that formerly were held by many citizens. It is not enough for you to have divided amongst yourselves the wealth of your enemies. It is not enough for you to torment everyone else with punitive tax assessments, while you, free of them, enjoy all the public emoluments as you persecute everyone else with all manner of *ingiuria*." More accusations follow: "You despoil your neighbors of their property; you sell justice; you evade the judgments of the courts; you oppress peaceful men and exalt the insolent. Nor do I believe that in all Italy there are as many examples of violence and greed [avarizia] as there are in this city." After a series of rhetorical questions in which, switching to the first-person plural, Piero asks "why we" want to destroy and disparage a city that has given "us" life, victory, and honor, he turns to threats: unless "you" cease acting in ways that "make me sorry to have emerged victorious, I will make you sorry to have abused the victory." Machiavelli comments that they did not put an end to their wicked ways ("sinistre operazioni") and adds that, if Piero had not died soon thereafter (in 1469), he would doubtless have repatriated all the exiles in an effort to curb the rapacious acts [rapine] of his allies within (*IF* 7.23.2–11).

Piero's harangue against the rapacity and avarice of his own faction is Machiavelli's most extreme indictment of the Medici regime.[27] It is doubtless an old rhetorical device, but an effective one, to have the "prince" enumerate and denounce the sins of those who govern in his name. But Piero's condemnation of the crimes of his regime must also implicate himself, either for concealing his complicity or for losing control of his faction. Either way, Machiavelli points again to the failures of factional leadership, the ease with which a chain of command, bound only by personal loyalties and unregulated by law, can degenerate and succumb to private avarice and ambition. Machiavelli's final sentences on Piero are filled with double-edges. "Death obstructed his most honorable intentions" of putting an end to the rapacity and bringing the exiles home. Piero's patria was unable fully to know his "virtú e bontà" because his father lived almost as long as he did, and the few years he had after Cosimo's death were "consumed" by "civic disputes [contenzioni civili]" and his infirmity. He was buried in San Lorenzo next to his father, and "his funeral rites were celebrated with the pomp that such a citizen deserved." His two sons, Lorenzo and Giuliano, "gave everyone hope they would be men most useful to the republic, but their youth nonetheless frightened everyone" (*IF* 7.23.12–15).

[27] This is also the assessment of Felix Gilbert, "Machiavelli's *Istorie fiorentine*: An Essay in Interpretation," in *Studies on Machiavelli*, ed. M. Gilmore (Florence: Sansoni, 1972), p. 86; and of Marina Marietti, *Machiavelli. L'eccezione fiorentina*, p. 154.

9
Repression and Conspiracy

"UNICA AUTORITÀ"

Putting Lorenzo into historical perspective was a greater challenge for Machiavelli, in part because of personal and family connections. Machiavelli's father had contacts in Lorenzo's circle, particularly with the chancellor Bartolomeo Scala. Machiavelli himself evidently knew Lorenzo's youngest son, Giuliano, well enough at least to appeal for his help with three sonnets written either from prison or shortly after his release in 1513.[1] Another poem addressing "giovanetto giulío" may suggest a pre-1494 personal friendship with Giuliano.[2] The burgeoning myth of Lorenzo further complicated attempts at an objective, critical view of him. Especially after the return of the Medici in 1512 and the elevation of his son Giovanni to the papacy in 1513, Lorenzo's fame inspired paeans to his philosophical and practical wisdom; his (alleged) clemency toward enemies; his crucial role in maintaining the peace and balance of power of Italy; the reverence in which he was allegedly held both in Florence and among Italy's princes; and his cultural patronage and so-called "magnificence." As already noted, Machiavelli expressed concern to Guicciardini in 1524 about what he was writing regarding the Medici in the *Histories*, hoping that, "even as I tell the truth, no one will have cause to complain."[3] Telling the truth about an already legendary figure whose progeny ruled both Florence and the Church was no easy matter.

Hints of a demythologized Lorenzo begin with Machiavelli's account of the negative reaction, even within Medici circles, to his marriage into the Roman baronial family of the Orsini, which fed the perception that the Medici were becoming too grand for their fellow citizens. That the Medici were elevating themselves above their compatriots in ways deemed offensive is a major theme of the eighth and last book of the *Histories*. Machiavelli addresses it in the book's introductory chapter where he theorizes the transition from the acquisition of ever greater power by a faction to the complete absorption of the institutions of government by and into the regime—the ultimate privatization of the republic. Piero's defeat of the opposition from within his own party in 1466 was, for Machiavelli, the crucial point of no return. "After the Medici regime [stato]

[1] "Rime," ed. A. Corsaro and N. Marcelli, in *SPP*, pp. 277–83.

[2] Ibid., pp. 242–4. Robert Black summarizes the different views on the poem's interpretation and dating in his *Machiavelli*, pp. 24–9.

[3] *Lettere*, p. 539.

Machiavelli's Broken World. John M. Najemy, Oxford University Press. © John M. Najemy 2022.
DOI: 10.1093/oso/9780199580927.003.0009

vanquished all the adversaries who had openly [apertamente] locked horns with it, if the family wanted to take sole power [unica autorità] in the city and distinguish itself from [si spiccasse: transcend, surpass] the other families [but still] within the republican constitution [col vivere civile], it also needed to subdue families that covertly [occultamente] schemed against it." That the Medici sought "unica autorità" within the "vivere civile" suggests that, in Machiavelli's view, their aim at the time was not to establish a principate, but rather to elevate themselves to unquestioned supremacy without modifying the basic structure of the republic, in other words, to circumvent the barrier—implicit in the "vivere civile"—against such supremacy. Overcoming overt opposition was no longer enough; the regime now needed to thwart the still hidden opposition that could emerge into conspiracy—in effect, to prevent potential opponents from even contemplating dissent. "As long as the Medici vied with other families on the basis of equality of influence and prestige [di pari di autorità e di riputazione]," Machiavelli says, "citizens who resented their power could openly oppose them without fear of being persecuted as soon as they expressed opposition." This was so because the Medici had not yet acquired complete control over the institutions of government: as Machiavelli puts it, the "magistrates were free," able, in other words, to exercise their authority according to the laws and not at the whim of the private power of factions. "But after the [Medici] victory of '66, the entire stato [regime and government] was so concentrated in the hands of the Medici, who acquired so much power [autorità], that those who were unhappy with it had either to endure it patiently or, if they wished to eradicate it, attempt to do so secretly and by means of conspiracies" (*IF* 8.1.3–5).

Machiavelli's critical argument here is that after 1466, because no possibility remained for open dissent through institutions, potential dissidents were forced to choose between abject acquiescence and covert plots. In effect, the very supremacy sought by the Medici created the conditions in which the only way of challenging their stato was through conspiracies, themselves private, outside the ordini, and in violation of the laws. Conflict conducted through private factions and in contravention of the ordini, Machiavelli believed, can only lead to the supremacy of one faction and the suppression of constitutional channels for dissent, converting all opposition into competing manifestations of privatized politics. Whereas Machiavelli initially characterized the reformers of 1465–6 as "congiurati," here he implicitly acknowledges that they began their challenge to the Medici "apertamente" (by restoring traditional methods of electing the Signoria and re-establishing the lawful powers of elected magistrates). Once this movement was squelched, however, the Medici sought to nip in the bud any incipient dissent. Political opposition perforce became conspiratorial.

The consequences go still further. Still in the opening chapter of book 8, Machiavelli reiterates one of the major conclusions of his examination of conspiracies in *Discourses* 3.6, namely, that because conspiracies "rarely succeed, they most often result in disaster for the conspirators and greater power [grandezza] for those they target." Almost always, he continues, a "principe" attacked by a conspiracy "rises to greater power and many times, if he is a good [buono] prince, turns into a bad [cattivo] one." With the Pazzi conspiracy looming in the first half of book 8, "principe" here refers to both monarchical rulers and the quasi-prince, Lorenzo, of Florence's still republican polity. That Lorenzo is, for Machiavelli, among the "princes" who, having survived conspiracies, become "bad" is clear from *Discourses* 3.6.135, where, after saying that the conspiracy succeeded only in killing Lorenzo's brother Giuliano, he comments that "those who survive" such conspiracies "become more intolerable and more cruel [acerbi], as Florence, Athens, and Heraclea know" ("Heraclea" referring to the assassination of "Clearco, tiranno di Eraclea" [*DL* 1.16.19–22]). Finishing the first chapter of book 8, Machiavelli outlines the steps by which this occurs. The experience of surviving a conspiracy, he says, makes princes live in fear; fear makes them seek security; and the search for security causes them to "ingiuriare [hurt, provoke, offend]" rivals and even those merely suspected of potential dissent, which generates the "hatreds" that often cause a prince's ruin. The effort to control a city through the private bonds of patronage and clientage that structure factions undermines laws and ordini, requires the victory of one faction, drives all opposition into illegal conspiracy, and ultimately causes the regime built on the victorious faction's private power to self-destruct. In these few lines, and without mentioning his name, Machiavelli identifies Lorenzo's political Achilles' heel: the mistrust of any dissent, which caused him to see conspiracy in all opposition, the impulsive recklessness with which he inflicted punishments and humiliations on perceived opponents, thus provoking real conspiracies, and the construction of an edifice of control built on fear and insecurity that, although it did not destroy Lorenzo himself, caused his regime to crash and burn little more than two years after he died.

Book 8's introductory chapter thus makes it clear that, in his account of Lorenzo's regime, Machiavelli will not embrace the myth of his successful management of politics in Florence or the preservation of peace in Italy. On the contrary, he highlights the vulnerabilities of a regime with spindly legs built on the privatized politics of a faction that saw enemies everywhere, became ever more punitive and oppressive, and consequently made real enemies who nearly destroyed what Cosimo had built. Machiavelli begins by emphasizing the precariousness—despite the victory of 1466—of the transition from Piero to Lorenzo, who enters the narrative in the protective shadow of the longtime loyal Medici ally Tommaso Soderini. Unlike his brother Niccolò, Tommaso remained a faithful Medicean through the troubles of 1465–6, and his "wisdom and influence [prudenzia e autorità]," Machiavelli writes, earned him great prestige "not only in Florence but indeed among all the princes of Italy." After Piero died, the "entire city" looked to Tommaso Soderini for guidance, as "many citizens," considering him the "head [capo] of the city," visited him at home, and "many princes wrote to him." But he wisely knew he had to make clear to the citizens that they should pay their respects, not to him, but to the Medici, and Machiavelli says he did not even reply to the letters from foreign princes. "To make manifest in deeds what he advised in counsel," Soderini took the initiative to assemble all the leaders of Florence's "noble" families, together with Piero's young sons, Lorenzo and Giuliano, in the "convento di Santo Antonio,"[4] where he "pronounced a long and solemn oration" on the conditions of the city and Italy and the aims of its princes. If the assembled family heads, Soderini said, "wanted a united and peaceful city, secured against internal divisions and foreign wars, it was necessary to defer to [osservare] these young men and preserve the prestige of their family." Lorenzo himself then spoke "with such solemnity and modesty as to give everyone hope that he would be what he later became." The family elders all swore an oath to "accept the brothers as their sons and to be as fathers to them" and to honor them as "principi dello stato [leaders of the regime]" (*IF* 7.24). This was an unofficial and private meeting, but it was not secret. Machiavelli may or may not have known that the original plan was to gather 150 influential citizens but that, according to the Milanese ambassador in Florence, more than seven hundred attended.[5] In effect, Soderini and the heads of all families of any prominence jumped in immediately (the very day Piero died, December 2, 1469, and a day before his funeral) to safeguard the supremacy of the Medici. Without overt comment, Machiavelli points to the problem of succession in factions that act as if they were governments and, in particular, to the weakness of Lorenzo's succession, as many, both in and beyond Florence, assumed that Tommaso Soderini, the regime's elder statesman, and not Lorenzo, would assume the reins of power. Machiavelli did not have to remind his readers that regimes built on factions did not and could not have firm rules of succession unless and until one family instituted a de jure principate with hereditary succession, something the Medici were not (yet) prepared to attempt and that the city's elite class (both allies and adversaries) were not (yet) prepared to accept.

In Lorenzo's first decade at the helm Machiavelli focuses on a series of violent episodes that emerged from the remnants of the confrontation between the Medici and the would-be reformers of 1465–6: from Lorenzo's tendency to see conspiracy everywhere, and from the inevitable resentments generated by all-or-nothing factional politics in which there could be no sharing of power or spoils. He first recounts, at surprising length (three chapters), an attempted revolt (in 1470) in the nearby city of Prato (within the Florentine dominion). The instigator was Bernardo Nardi, whose family, Machiavelli says, was among those that allied

[4] This is, most probably, the church of Saint Anthony of Vienne, founded in 1358 and located at the northern end of Via Faenza; see Placido Landini, *Istoria dell'oratorio e della venerabile arciconfraternita di Santa Maria della Misericordia della città di Firenze* (Florence: Peratoner, 1843), p. 52, n. 3. Vasari also mentions it in his life of Duccio.

[5] Rubinstein, *Government of Florence*, p. 199.

"with the party of Luca Pitti" in 1465–6. Nardi had been exiled and subsequently declared a rebel for his part in the brief war in which Venice sent Bartolomeo Colleoni to attack Florentine territory. "Unable to endure exile and seeing no other way to effect his return to Florence," Nardi "decided to try something that could spark a new war." Machiavelli says he had "conoscenza grande"—a large circle of acquaintances—in Prato and even more in the contado of nearby Pistoia. He also "knew" that the Pratesi harbored deep resentment against the "stato"—the Medici regime—for the manner in which they were "arrogantly and avariciously ruled." Nardi gathered a number of supporters in Prato—Machiavelli twice refers to them as "congiurati" (*IF* 7.26.4; *IF* 7.27.1)—and enlisted one of the most prominent of the Florentine exiles, Dietisalvi Neroni, who promised he could secure military support from Bologna and Ferrara. To encourage his following in Prato, Nardi claimed he had a secret group of plotters ("intelligenzia") in Florence who would emerge as soon as they knew Prato was united behind him. Machiavelli shows Nardi reconstituting in exile a faction from anti-Medici elements and plotting foreign military intervention (*IF* 7.25).

Nardi overestimated anti-Medici sentiment in Prato, and the revolt collapsed before it could receive any assistance. Machiavelli uses the episode to show how factional ambitions and resentments could hijack an entire city for personal and family aims. Nardi's group seized the fortress and the communal palace and took the Florentine podestà in Prato prisoner, threatening to kill him. He made high-minded appeals to the Pratesi, reminding them of their "former liberty and present condition." But he misjudged the mood of a city he thought he could exploit or manipulate: the communal magistrates would have none of it and declared their loyalty to Florence. Machiavelli says Nardi was captured and executed (*IF* 7.26–7) but, curiously, despite his considerable attention to the episode, does not mention the many other executions, which are confirmed in the sources. Nor does he mention Lorenzo. Although still very young and closely advised by the regime's elders, Lorenzo was of course fully aware of the role played in the Prato revolt by the exiles of 1465–6 and would subsequently be determined never to let either exiles or rivals within Florence challenge his control. Machiavelli dubs the event a "harbinger [presagio] of future woes" (*IF* 7.25.1).

The first test of this determination came two years later (1472) in the much bloodier conflict with another subject city, Volterra, over control of a recently discovered alum mine. Machiavelli presents this tragedy (*IF* 7.29) as an example of the process, outlined in book 8's introductory chapter, by which a "principe," having survived a conspiracy, lives in fear and seeks greater security through excessive punishment of all opposition, real or perceived. As Machiavelli recounts the conflict, the Volterrans, who discovered the mine, realizing how profitable it could be and needing investment partners with enough influence ("autorità") to protect the enterprise, brought "some Florentine citizens" into the company. Giving no names, Machiavelli evidently assumes his readers know that Florentines able to "protect" the company with their "autorità" could only be Medici allies and/or Lorenzo himself. Controversy emerged in Volterra over where the mine's profits were going. Machiavelli describes the protests as a defense of public rights against private interests: the city councils "asserted that it was not appropriate [non essere conveniente] that an enterprise originating on public lands [ne' terreni pubblici] be turned toward private gain [privata utilità]." They sent ambassadors to Florence to argue their case. Resolution of the dispute was entrusted to "certain citizens"—only later does Machiavelli say they were Florentines—who ruled in favor of the original investors, "either because," Machiavelli suggests, "they had been bribed [corrotti]" or "because they thought it was right" to preserve the original arrangement. The arbiters concluded "that the desire of the Volterran people to deprive their fellow citizens of the [fruits] of their efforts and their business was not just" and that "the mine belonged to the private citizens [a' privati]" who had formed the company "and not to the people" of Volterra. But they also concluded that "it was proper that [the investors] should pay a certain amount of money each year by way of acknowledging [the Volterran people] as the legal proprietor [in segno di ricognoscerlo per superiore]." Machiavelli interprets this ill-fated compromise to mean that, however just the rights of the investing partners were, the people of Volterra did not relinquish their rights as ultimate titleholder. It is possible that Machiavelli knew, from the non-Florentine sources he relied on (in at least one case openly anti-Medicean), that this insistence on the people's rights was indeed how the Volterran government justified revoking the company's ownership and seizing the mines.[6] His interpretation of the conflict rests on the same conceptual framework of the conflict between public authority and private interests that pervades the *Florentine Histories* (and not on the notion, promoted by the Medici and frequently repeated by modern historians, that Volterra rebelled against Florentine rule). The Volterrans reacted to the arbiters' findings with "increased agitation and hatred," demanding what they believed had been taken from them. The "particulari"—the private investors—wanted to keep what they had acquired, "as confirmed by the judgment [sentenzia] of the Florentines." Violence broke out—Machiavelli does not call it a rebellion—and one of the original Volterran investors was killed along with "many others" whose homes were also sacked and burned.

Volterra again sent ambassadors to Florence with a proposal that Machiavelli represents as follows (*IF* 7.30): if the Signoria of Florence were willing to maintain the longstanding agreements, the "capituli antichi" (which gave Volterra substantial autonomy in its internal affairs but required payment of taxes to Florence and acceptance of a Florentine official who controlled security and military matters), the city of Volterra would continue its time-honored submission to Florence

[6] Allegretto Allegretti, *Diari sanesi*, columns 774, 779–80, in *Rerum Italicarum Scriptores* 23 (1733); *Cronache volterrane*, in *Archivio storico italiano*, Appendice 3 (1846): 328–32.

("sua antica servitú"). Machiavelli says there was "considerable disagreement" in Florence over how to respond. He ascribes the more conciliatory stance to Tommaso Soderini, who advised that the Volterrans should be welcomed back "in whatever way they wished to return." It was "the wrong time," he said, "to ignite a fire so close that it might consume our city as well," especially given the possible reactions by the other Italian powers. Machiavelli has Soderini recall the old proverb according to which "a lean agreement is better than a fat victory." It was Lorenzo, according to Machiavelli, who advocated the more belligerent solution: "Lorenzo believed this an opportunity for him to show how valuable he could be with his advice and wisdom [quanto con il consiglio e con la prudenzia valesse]." This implies that he feared appearing weak and was looking for a chance to prove otherwise, especially because he was urged in this direction "by those who were envious of [or who resented: avevono invidia] the influence [autorità] of messer Tommaso [Soderini]." Machiavelli thus points to Lorenzo's sense of vulnerability and to strains within the leadership of the party: taking a hard line against Volterra was a way for him to assert his independence vis-à-vis the older and more experienced Soderini—an example of how insecurity and rivalry within factions could shape events as fateful as the decision to punish Volterra. Lorenzo opted for an "impresa"—a military undertaking—"to castigate the arrogance of the Volterrans, asserting that, if they were not disciplined as an unforgettable example, others would not hesitate to act similarly, for the slightest reason, without deference or fear." In Machiavelli's interpretation Lorenzo's precariousness and fear of the slightest challenge to his primacy pushed him to an extreme solution. His decision, as Machiavelli represents it, had nothing to do with the justice or injustice of the Volterrans' case. They were told they could not ask for mutual observance of the "capituli," because they themselves had violated them: they had either to submit to the judgment of the Florentine Signoria or face war. Machiavelli describes the overwhelming superiority of the troops Florence was able to assemble under the command of Federico da Montefeltro against the few and unreliable forces available to the Volterrans. Aware of the impossibility of their position, "those poor citizens" of Volterra offered to surrender to the Florentine commissioners, who, instead, opened the gates and let the besieging troops into the city to carry out the infamous sack and massacre that Machiavelli describes as "the destruction and plunder of the city, pillaged and raided for an entire day, with neither women nor holy places spared." As for Lorenzo's responsibility, he says only that "The Florentines received the news of the victory with the greatest joy," and "because it had been entirely Lorenzo's *impresa*"—in the sense that he wanted and approved the attack—"it greatly increased his prestige [reputazione]."

Machiavelli closes his account of the Volterra calamity with a possibly apocryphal anecdote: "one of Lorenzo's closest allies reproached messer Tommaso Soderini for the advice" he had given: "What do you say," the unnamed Medicean asks Soderini, "now that Volterra has been taken?" Soderini replies: "I think [Volterra] has been lost, because, if you had taken it with a compromise [d'accordo], you would have got both profit and security; now that you have to keep it by force, it will cause you weakness and anxiety in bad times, and vexation and expense in peacetime" (*IF* 7.30.14). In the draft it is not "one of Lorenzo's closest allies" who asks the question, but Lorenzo himself.[7] Removing the direct confrontation between Lorenzo and Soderini in the final version has the effect not only of obscuring Lorenzo's attempt to scold Soderini but also of hiding Lorenzo's anxiety—his need for confirmation of his success in handling the crisis. In both versions, however, Machiavelli lets Soderini have the last—and highly critical—word on a course of action dictated, as his account implies, by Lorenzo's need to prove himself up to the task of managing the Medici stato and protecting his own power.

"MADE DEAF BY THE FORTUNE AND LIBERALITY OF THE MEDICI"

"The beginning of this eighth book," Machiavelli writes in the introductory chapter, "is placed between two conspiracies"—"one, already recounted [in *IF* 7.33–4] that occurred in Milan" (the 1476 assassination of Duke Galeazzo Maria Sforza), "the other yet to be recounted," namely, the Pazzi conspiracy of 1478. More than half of book 8 is devoted to the Pazzi plot against the Medici and the war that erupted in its aftermath between Florence and two of the conspiracy's principal architects—Pope Sixtus IV and King Ferdinand of Naples. Machiavelli's long chapter on conspiracies in the *Discourses* (*DL* 3.6) and this opening chapter of the last book of the *Histories* both convey the dismal view he had of conspiracies, because they mostly fail and because princes who survive them become initially more powerful but also more suspicious and more inclined to violent and unjust rule. He approaches the Pazzi conspiracy from both angles: as a spectacular example of the failure of conspiracies, and as a manifestation of the culminating stage of the deterioration of regime politics—the corrosion and eventual implosion of political systems built on private favors and factional power.

Machiavelli constructs the origins of the Pazzi conspiracy from affronts, injuries, and insults traded between the Medici, Lorenzo in particular, and the leaders of rival elite families, and inflamed by the grievances and ambitions of Sixtus and Ferdinand. He identifies a first sign of trouble in the ease with which, in 1474, Ferdinand lured Federico da Montefeltro away from his contract with Florence (*IF* 7.31.10–15). He points to Pope Sixtus's "many efforts" to disrupt the "stato" in Florence, including the appointment to the archbishopric of Pisa of Francesco

[7] *OS*, vol. 2, p. 901.

Salviati, who, as the pope well knew, was "hostile" to the Medici. The Florentine Signoria (handpicked by Lorenzo's inner circle) denied Salviati possession of the see, infuriating the pope and exacerbating the acrimony. Machiavelli says Sixtus also extended "great favors" in Rome to the Pazzi family and "deprecated [disfavoriva] the Medici in every action" (most importantly, by removing them from the office of Depositary of the Apostolic Camera, thus depriving the Medici bank of lucrative papal accounts, and replacing them with the Pazzi). Machiavelli introduces the Pazzi as the "most splendid of all Florentine families," for both their "ricchezze" and "nobilità" and says the same of the family's head, Iacopo, "knighted by the Florentine people for his "ricchezze" and "nobilità" (*IF* 8.2.1–5). Whether or not the "nobilità" of the Pazzi alludes to their having been magnates, it was only in the early fifteenth century that they gained office-holding rights. In 1422 Iacopo's father, Andrea, successfully petitioned for "popolano" status, and in 1434 two more family members (along with many other families) were released from magnate status by the balía that recalled Cosimo de' Medici. Several Pazzi subsequently held major offices as Medici allies. Iacopo himself reached the office of standard-bearer of justice in 1469 and was made a knight by "the popolo," as Machiavelli says, meaning that the honor was awarded by the legislative councils.[8] Knighthood, however, did not confer "nobility." Machiavelli explains that Iacopo was made a "cavaliere" because he was wealthy and already possessed "nobilità," not that his "nobilità" derived from the knighthood. The same paired terms appear a third time in this chapter when Machiavelli recounts that Cosimo, aware of the "ricchezza e nobilità" of the Pazzi, married his granddaughter Bianca (in 1460) to one of Iacopo's nephews. Cosimo "was hoping," Machiavelli says, "that the marriage alliance would unite the families and remove the enmities and hatreds that often result from *sospetto* [resentment and fear]" (*IF* 8.2.7). Until now, Machiavelli has said nothing about resentments or hatreds between the families, but it seems clear that all three events—the marriage alliance, Iacopo's election as standard-bearer, and his knighthood—were aspects of a strategy to neutralize the rivalry fueled by the expanding wealth and influence of the Pazzi.

The result, however, was not what the Medici hoped for, and it was Lorenzo's fears that ignited the conflagration. "Those who were advising Lorenzo showed him how very dangerous it was, and hazardous to his political influence [autorità], for wealth and power [stato] to be combined in [the same] citizens." This was the nub of the matter. The Medici had long enjoyed great wealth, unprecedented political power in Florence, and extensive influence in Rome and throughout Italy. But a regime built on factional bonds of patronage and clientage could not allow any other family—this is Machiavelli's point—to challenge the unique

[8] On the Pazzi's attainment of "popolano" status and office-holding rights, see Lauro Martines, *April Blood: Florence and the Plot against the Medici* (Oxford: Oxford University Press, 2003), pp. 65, 94–5; and Klapisch-Zuber, *Ritorno alla politica*, pp. 193, 415–16.

double primacy of the Medici in "ricchezze" and "stato." As a result of the warning Lorenzo received, "messer Iacopo and his nephews were not granted the high level of offices [quelli gradi di onore] they believed they deserved, compared to other citizens," and this, Machiavelli affirms, "was the cause of the initial anger of the Pazzi and the initial consternation among the Medici; the growth of the one fueled the growth of the other." This explanation of the origins of the conspiracy thus identifies Lorenzo and his advisers as the instigators of the suspicion and fear between the two families. Machiavelli cites the punishing treatment of the Pazzi by Florentine courts and police, something that could only have happened under orders or pressure from Lorenzo. In court actions against other citizens the Pazzi were "not well regarded by the magistrates." The police magistracy of the Otto di guardia subpoenaed Francesco de' Pazzi (son of Iacopo's brother Antonio) from Rome (where he was director of the Rome branch of the Pazzi company) for what Machiavelli calls a "frivolous reason [leggieri cagione]." The Pazzi lamented these affronts "with defamatory and indignant words," which "increased the slurs" directed at them and the "resentment [sospetto] felt by others" (*IF* 8.2.8–10).

The example Machiavelli highlights of Medici abuse of power to damage the Pazzi involved a disputed inheritance. Giovanni de' Pazzi, Francesco's brother, was married to a daughter of the "very wealthy" Giovanni Borromei, who died without male heirs and bequeathed his fortune to his daughter (which would have made the funds available to her Pazzi husband for investment). But Borromei's nephew Carlo seized some of the assets, triggering a legal dispute that was resolved by a law—an ad hoc, retroactive legislative enactment—that "deprived Giovanni de' Pazzi's wife of her father's inheritance and assigned it to Carlo." Despite the passive voice ("fu fatta una legge"), Machiavelli immediately asserts that the Pazzi knew this "ingiuria" was entirely owing to the Medici ("al tutto dai Medici ricognobbono"). Lorenzo's name is missing in these sentences, but his direct involvement becomes clear in the next one, which relates the rebuke he received from his brother Giuliano, who "many times expressed regret [si dolfe]" over the episode, "saying he feared that, by wanting things too much [per volere delle cose troppo], everything might be lost" (*IF* 8.2.11–13).[9] Machiavelli makes this ominous warning a prophecy of the violent conspiracy that exploded shortly thereafter and a portent both of Giuliano's own martyrdom and of how close the Medici indeed came to losing everything. But Lorenzo, Machiavelli says, would not listen. "Hot with youth and power [caldo di gioventú e di potenzia]," he writes, "Lorenzo wanted to control everything and wanted all to acknowledge that everything came from him [che ciascuno da lui ogni cosa ricognoscesse]" (*IF* 8.3.1), this last phrase echoing the assertion that the Pazzi "ricognobbono" the

[9] Machiavelli did not invent this. He found Giuliano's warning in Giovanni di Carlo's *Libri de temporibus suis*; see Marcello Simonetta, *The Montefeltro Conspiracy: A Renaissance Mystery Decoded* (New York: Doubleday, 2008), pp. 108, 228.

loss of the Borromei inheritance as the work of the Medici. Machiavelli similarly uses the word at the beginning of the *Vita di Castruccio Castracani*, where he affirms that all men who have done great things have risen from lowly origins because fortune wants to demonstrate that she, not "prudenza," makes men great and that "everything must be acknowledged as coming from her [da lei si abbi a ricognoscere il tutto]"[10]—an assertion of the ultimate patronal power, namely, recognition that the patron dispenses all things, both favors and punishments.

Machiavelli says the Pazzi, described yet again as possessing "so much nobility and such great wealth," could not abide the affronts and began plotting revenge. After enumerating the major participants in the conspiracy (in addition to several members of the Pazzi, he mentions Girolamo Riario, Francesco Salviati, Pope Sixtus, King Ferdinand, and the pope's condottiere Giovanbattista da Montesecco) and explaining the motives of each, the shifting plans of action, and the decision to kill Lorenzo and Giuliano (*IF* 8.3–5), Machiavelli says the Medici brothers "were aware of the Pazzi's bitter feelings against them" and of their desire to deprive them of the "autorità dello stato"—the power they enjoyed as heads of the regime. "But they did not fear for their lives, believing as they did that, even if [the Pazzi] attempted something, they would do it *civilmente*," within the framework of the laws, "and not with great violence. Unconcerned for their own safety, therefore, they simulated friendship with them" (*IF* 8.6.4).

The attack in the cathedral failed to kill Lorenzo who, wounded, found refuge in the sacristy (*IF* 8.6.5–9). With the plot having gone awry and the city in chaos, Francesco de' Pazzi begged his uncle Iacopo to make an appeal to the people and "call them to liberty and arms." Iacopo, Machiavelli writes, "despite being old and inexperienced in such upheavals, in order to make a last test of their [the conspirators'] fortune [ultima esperienzia della fortuna loro], mounted his horse and, with perhaps a hundred armed men readied earlier for such a mission, went to the piazza of the [government] palace, calling the people and liberty to his aid." The failure of this pathetic appeal provided the moment for Machiavelli's brief but trenchant judgment of the effect on the Florentines of almost a half-century of Medici dominance: "because the one [the people] had been made deaf by the fortune and liberality of the Medici, and the other [liberty] was unknown in Florence, no one answered him" (*IF* 8.8.1–4). Once again Machiavelli underscores both the strategic use of wealth—"liberalità"—in establishing Medici power and its corrosive effect on the inclination of citizens to defend their liberty. Machiavelli pictures messer Iacopo in the piazza, "fearful [dubio]," as the priors high up in the palace "greeted" him with threats and a barrage of rocks. In this moment of hopelessness he is approached by Giovanni Serristori, whom Machiavelli identifies only as Iacopo's brother-in-law, although

[10] *OS*, vol. 1, p. 8.

he may have expected readers to know that the Serristori were loyal Mediceans, raised from obscure beginnings to prominence and wealth. Serristori rebukes Iacopo for the mayhem the Pazzi had unleashed and urges him to return home; he mocks Iacopo for hypocrisy, telling him "that other citizens held the popolo and liberty as close to their hearts as he did" (*IF* 8.8.5–6). Guicciardini, in the *Storie fiorentine*,[11] and Poliziano, in the *Coniurationis commentarium*,[12] both recount Iacopo de' Pazzi's futile ride to the piazza and the shower of rocks from the palace. But neither mentions the detail of Giovanni Serristori's rebuke, which Machiavelli either found (perhaps in Giovanni di Carlo) or invented. The function of Serristori's intervention lies in the contrast between what he says about liberty and Machiavelli's assertions, in his own voice a few lines earlier, that the people had been made "deaf" by the "liberality" of the Medici and that liberty was unknown in Florence. Serristori, by contrast, scolds Iacopo for a false appeal to a liberty to which, as he insists, many others were as devoted as he, and without resorting to violence. His is the voice of a Medici partisan who had benefitted, politically and financially, from loyalty to his patrons and who promotes the regime's ideology that Florentine liberty was alive and well. Lorenzo's political survival depended on Medicean "liberality." Once it was evident that the plot had failed and the Pazzi were being hunted down, Machiavelli says, "there was no citizen, armed or otherwise, who did not go" to the Medici palace in the Via Larga, "offering himself and his worldly goods" to Lorenzo: "so great was the fortune and favor that the family had acquired through its wisdom and liberality" (*IF* 8.9.7).

"CONSIDER WHERE EVIL FORTUNE HAS BROUGHT OUR FAMILY, WHICH, AMONG FRIENDS, RELATIVES, AND EVEN IN CHURCH, IS NOT SAFE"

Machiavelli's most salient interpretive commentary on Lorenzo's regime is the long speech he has him deliver in chapter 10 of book 8 to his most loyal followers after the violence of the Pazzi conspiracy subsides, a speech that acknowledges both the strengths and weaknesses of the bonds that held the regime together. Lorenzo makes no such speech in Guicciardini's *Storie fiorentine*, which Machiavelli knew well,[13] in Poliziano's *Commentarium*, or in Piero Parenti's

[11] Guicciardini, *Storie fiorentine*, ed. Montevecchi, ch. 4, p. 123.

[12] Angelo Poliziano, *Della congiura dei Pazzi (Coniurationis commentarium)*, ed. Alessandro Perosa (Padua: Antenore, 1958), p. 40: Poliziano writes that Iacopo "undertook to tempt fate [fortunam tentare aggressus]" and "called the people to arms [populum ad arma convocat]"—but apparently not to liberty.

[13] Gaia Pieraccioni shows that Machiavelli borrowed details and certain locutions from the *Storie*; see her "Note su Machiavelli storico. II—Machiavelli lettore delle *Storie fiorentine* di Guicciardini," *Archivio storico italiano* 147 (1989): 63–98.

chronicle.[14] Machiavelli may have expanded the hints of such a speech in Niccolò Valori's *Vita di Lorenzo de' Medici*,[15] which briefly summarizes Lorenzo's exhortations to civic concord, situated at approximately the same point in the succession of events that Machiavelli chose for the longer speech he attributes to Lorenzo, namely, after the conspirators' failure to kill him and just as Sixtus and Ferdinand decide to achieve their objectives with war and the papal weapons of excommunication and interdict. Valori says Lorenzo zealously promoted civic concord and always bound the citizens together with "ties of benevolence." Claiming to use Lorenzo's own words, he says Lorenzo "regularly told the citizens that 'just as a healthy body is not disturbed by heat or cold, so cities, whose members are the citizens, can withstand any external assault if the citizens are united.' He said the same of Italy: if united [in concordia], it has nothing to fear; divided [in discordiis] it would perish in a short time."[16]

Because Sixtus insisted the war was being waged against Lorenzo, not the Florentine people, Machiavelli's Lorenzo, needing to justify his relationship with the people,[17] "assembled in the [government] palace, together with the Signori, all the high-ranking [qualificati] citizens, in excess of three hundred." He begins by saying he does not know whether to grieve or rejoice over what has happened: "When I consider with how much treachery and hatred I was attacked and my brother murdered, I cannot but be saddened and sorrow with all my heart and soul. But when I consider how swiftly and with how much zeal and love and with what unanimity [unito consenso] the entire city defended me and avenged my brother, I must not only be joyous but also exult and glory in my whole being [in tutto me stesso esalti e glorii]."[18] Machiavelli then has Lorenzo cast doubt on the unanimity he has just extolled, declaring that this experience has made him realize he has more enemies in the city than he had thought, even as it has also shown him he has more ardent and devoted "amici" than he had believed. On balance,

[14] Piero di Marco Parenti, *Storia fiorentina I 1476–78, 1492–96*, ed. Andrea Matucci (Florence: Olschki, 1994), pp. 12–20.

[15] On the *Vita*, see Mario Martelli, "Le due redazioni della *Laurentii Medicei Vita* di Niccolò Valori," *La Bibliofilia* 66 (1964): 235–63; Catherine M. Kovesi, "Niccolò Valori and the Medici Restoration of 1512," *Rinascimento* 27 (1987): 301–25; Roslyn Pesman Cooper, "Political Survival in Early Sixteenth-Century Florence: The Case of Niccolò Valori," in *Florence and Italy: Renaissance Studies in Honour of Nicolai Rubinstein* (London: Westfield College, University of London, 1988), pp. 73–90; and Riccardo Fubini, "Lorenzo de' Medici tra eulogia e storia: la *Laurentii Medices vita* di Niccolò Valori," in *Il Principe e la storia*, ed. Tina Matarrese and Cristina Montagnani (Novara: Interlinea Edizioni, 2005), pp. 439–63. Alison K. Frazier has recently proposed that the author of the *Vita* may actually be the humanist and notary Angelo Angeni: "Who Wrote the First *Life* of Lorenzo de' Medici?" in *Renaissance Studies in Honor of Joseph Connors*, vol. 2, pp. 59–64.

[16] *Vita di Lorenzo de' Medici scritta in lingua latina da Niccolò Valori*, ed. Enrico Niccolini (Vicenza: Accademia Olimpica, 1991), pp. 60–1. This edition contains both the Latin and vernacular versions of the *Vita*, whose relationship and dating have been much discussed; see the bibliography in n. 15 above.

[17] On Lorenzo's speech, particularly what Machiavelli has him say concerning the regime's need for identification with the people, see Sasso, *Niccolò Machiavelli*, vol. 2, *La storiografia*, pp. 477–85.

[18] A possible, but, if so, incongruous, echo of Dante when he meets the great philosophers and poets in Limbo, *Inferno* 4.120: "che del vedere in me stesso m'essalto."

however, he feels compelled to grieve so much the more over the attacks as they were "unprecedented and undeserved by us." Underscoring the rarity of such treachery, he asks his listeners to consider "where evil fortune has brought our family, which, among our friends, our in-laws [parenti: his sister Bianca being married to a Pazzi], and in church"—the attack occurred in Florence cathedral—"is not safe." Having just given thanks for the devotion of his family's "amici," Lorenzo now laments their betrayal. People who face mortal danger usually look to their "amici" and "parenti" for succor, he says, but "we found ours armed for our destruction." Lorenzo now portrays the conspiracy as a manifestation of the faithlessness and treachery of "amici" and "parenti"—"we are murdered by those to whom others look for protection. Where parricides and assassins find safety, the Medici found their murderers." Only the Almighty has rescued them: "God, who has never in the past abandoned our family, has again saved us and taken up the defense of our just cause." Machiavelli turns the speech into a rebuke and bitter accusation against the "amici" and "parenti" with whose support the Medici had built their "just cause" (*IF* 8.10.5–13).

Lorenzo turns to the injustice of the conspiracy. "What wrong [ingiuria] did we do to anyone to deserve such hunger for vengeance?" Machiavelli has Lorenzo distinguish between private and public "ingiurie," insisting that "we never privately wronged [mai privatamente non li offendemmo] those who have revealed themselves as our enemies." In other words, if they wronged anyone, they did so legally, through government institutions. "If we *had* wronged them [privately]," he chillingly adds, "they would not have had the possibility of wronging us." The Medici would not, in other words, have left their enemies able to retaliate. "They blame us for public wrongs/injustices [publiche ingiurie]"—for unjust punishments inflicted on them by the government or the courts, behind which they claimed to see the hand of the Medici (an allusion to the quickly concocted and retroactively applied law on inheritance)—"but I know of no such wrong done to them." In making such charges, Lorenzo asserts, "they do injustice more to you than to us, more to this palace and to the majesty [maestà] of this government than to our family," for in so doing they imply that "you"—the Signoria and the three hundred "cittadini qualificati" in attendance—"unjustly inflict injuries on your citizens for our sake, which is very far from all truth" (*IF* 8.10.14–16).

Machiavelli's Lorenzo confuses private and public. He denies that the Pazzi were wronged either by the Medici acting as private citizens or by the government they controlled. But in the next breath he acknowledges the unofficial and yet openly recognized power enjoyed by the Medici: "Anyone seeking the truth will discover that our family has always been exalted with such unanimity by you for no other reason than that it has exerted itself to win over everyone with kindness, liberality, and favors." Lorenzo asks, rhetorically, how, if the Medici have honored citizens outside the family, they could have wronged their own "parenti"—the Pazzi. He considers two possible motives for their conspiracy: either a desire for domination or envy of the power/influence ("autorità") of the Medici. If their motive was a "desiderio di dominare" (the fundamental attribute Machiavelli ascribes to "nobles" and grandi in the *Discourses*), "it reveals itself, indeed condemns itself, as grotesque, ambitious, and damnable." But if they acted out of "hatred and envy of our power/influence [autorità], they wrong you, not us, since you yourselves gave [this autorità] to us." Machiavelli has Lorenzo engage in a verbal sleight of hand here in order to create the semblance of a plausible distinction between the Pazzi "desire to dominate" and the "autorità" enjoyed by the Medici. Neither Lorenzo nor his family or faction had any legally or constitutionally confirmed "authority." "Autorità" here, as often in Machiavelli, is influence, prestige, unofficial power, and there is precious little to distinguish Medici "autorità" from the "domination" the Pazzi allegedly seek—power outside the ordini of the laws and statutes. But Lorenzo has to maintain and justify the distinction. So Machiavelli has him argue that there are two kinds of "autoritadi" distinguished by the means of their acquisition. "The *autoritadi* that men usurp"—take illegally—"deserve to be hated" (obviously referring to the Pazzi and acknowledging that they too sought a form of "autorità"), "but not those that men earn [si guadagnano] through liberality, kindness, and generosity [munificenza]" (*IF* 8.10.15–18). The kind of "autorità" the Pazzi desire, Lorenzo says, is stained by usurpation and, as he might have added, by violence. By contrast, he asserts, the legitimacy of Medici "autorità" rests on private acts of beneficence enabled by wealth and liberality. Machiavelli does not let Lorenzo claim the *ordinaria autorità* defined and warranted by law, statute, and election.

Lorenzo claims his family never attained any level of "grandezza" to which it was not "spurred [spinta, literally pushed] by this palace"—by the government—"and by your unanimous agreement [dallo unito consenso vostro]." This "consenso" is not active consent: neither the Florentines at large, nor the legislative councils or executive committees ever approved Medici "grandezza" or "autorità." It is tacit, passive consent assumed to be general or even unanimous (hence "unito consenso"), precisely because there was never any formal mechanism to express consent or dissent. Lorenzo supports this view of the legitimacy of his family's power with reference to his grandfather and father. Cosimo did not return from exile, he asserts, "with arms or violence, but rather with your *consenso* and *unione*." (Lorenzo chooses, obviously, to overlook the exiles—and executions—that caused Machiavelli to liken the proscriptions of 1434–5 to those of Sulla and Octavian.) And his father, Piero, "old and infirm, did not defend the regime [stato] on his own; it was rather you who defended it with your *autorità* and benevolence." Lorenzo claims that he, "still a youngster [fanciullo]" when his father died, would not have maintained his family's position "were it not for your counsel and assistance." In the culminating conflation of public and private he declares that his family "would not have been, and still would not be, able to rule [reggere] this republic if you had not ruled, and did not still rule, together with [my family]."

Machiavelli here lets Lorenzo lapse into asserting that the Medici were co-rulers with the inner circle of the regime: "reggere," like Latin "rego," means to wield supreme, sovereign power. On the one hand, Lorenzo insists he is a private citizen; on the other, he asserts for his family a right to rule allegedly bestowed by the unanimous consent of the political class. Hence, there can be no justification for hatred or envy of, or opposition to, the Medici. If anything, Machiavelli has Lorenzo say, the Pazzi, former magnates, should "hate their ancestors whose arrogance [superbia] and avarice cost them the esteem that our [Medici ancestors] were able to acquire with endeavors contrary to theirs." Lorenzo then asks: even if we "concede" (hypothetically of course) "that the wrongs inflicted by us against [the Pazzi] were great and that they justly desired our ruin, why did they attack the government palace? Why ally with the king and the pope against the liberty of this republic? Why break Italy's long peace? For this they have no justification at all. They should have attacked those who wronged them and not confused private animosities with harm to the republic [non confundere le inimicizie private con le ingiurie publiche]" (*IF* 8.10.19–24). Because they attacked both the Medici and the government palace, and induced foreign powers to launch a war against Florence, Lorenzo, whose entire speech has conflated public and private, now, in a neat reversal, accuses the Pazzi of confusing public and private—of attacking the public sphere in order to settle private grievances. Lorenzo's words bespeak his own confusion of private and public, which is, at bottom, the essence of Machiavelli's critique of Medici politics.

Machiavelli has Lorenzo finish the long speech by declaring that, if it were true that, as the pope and king insist, they wage war against him alone, he would gladly sacrifice himself to save the city. But he is sure it is not true, for "the powerful always conceal the wrongs they commit with some less dishonorable pretext [con qualche meno disonesto colore]." "But if you believe otherwise,"—namely, that the war is actually being waged for the sole purpose of removing Lorenzo—"I will put myself in your hands," for "you are my fathers, you are my defenders, and I shall gladly do whatever you instruct me; nor will I refuse, if you so wish, to finish this war, begun in the blood of my brother, with my own." (In having Lorenzo pledge to revere the Signoria and the three hundred citizens as "voi miei padri, voi miei defensori," was Machiavelli ironically echoing what Callimaco says Lucrezia said to him in *Mandragola* V.4 after their night together, when she declares, with transparent insincerity not noticed by Callimaco, "tu mio padre, tu mio defensore"?) The citizens, Machiavelli says, "could not hold back their tears" while Lorenzo spoke. One of them replies that "the city acknowledges the many benefits" received from Lorenzo and his family and that he can be assured that they will maintain his "reputazione" and the "stato" with the same alacrity with which they avenged his brother's death and saved Lorenzo's life. He will no sooner lose the "stato," they tell him, "than they will lose their patria" (*IF* 8.10.25–9), an affirmation of equal loyalty to the regime and to the common homeland of all Florentines.

Lorenzo's speech is followed in the narrative by Florentine preparations for the war unleashed by Pope Sixtus and King Ferdinand, whose forces invaded and occupied much of the dominion. As we have seen, Machiavelli had written of Sixtus that he was "the first pope who showed how many things previously considered to be transgressions [errori] could be hidden under pontifical authority," including "ambitious" nepotism (*IF* 7.22.5–8). He cuttingly speculates that Sixtus's death (in 1484) may have been caused by his sorrow over the coming of peace (*IF* 8.28.3). The decision to wage war against Lorenzo "did not lack justifications," Machiavelli writes, articulating Sixtus's own stated rationale that "it is a pope's duty to extinguish tyrannies, persecute the wicked, and exalt the good" (*IF* 8.11.5). He suggests that Sixtus's claim to be at war only with Lorenzo influenced the refusal of the Venetians to come to Florence's aid: "As the war was being waged against private citizens [fatta a privati]," the Venetians denied they were obligated to assist the Florentines in "private quarrels [private cause]," because "inimicizie particulari [personal or private hostilities]" should not be settled "publicamente"—by governments (*IF* 8.12.3).

Machiavelli's account of the war presents a quite different picture of the regime from that implied in Lorenzo's speech. His emphasis on the anxiety, dissension, and outright opposition to Lorenzo after military setbacks undermines the notion of the regime's "unito consenso." By the end of 1479, "the citizens were openly and without hesitation accusing one another and denouncing the mistakes committed in the war. They laid bare the fruitless expenditures and unjustly imposed taxes. And they boldly talked of such things, not only in meetings of private citizens [ne' circuli, intra i privati], but also in the councils of government [ne' consigli publici]." The regime was imperiled because dissent was finding expression in government institutions supposedly under the tight control of the Medici party. One citizen, Machiavelli says, "summoned sufficient audacity [prese tanto ardire] to turn to Lorenzo and say: 'this city is exhausted and wants no more war' and he [Lorenzo] must therefore think of peace." Machiavelli has Lorenzo respond to this demand by addressing a closed meeting (not a formal council) of "those *amici* he judged most loyal and wise"—the regime's inner circle. This private gathering decided that the best option was to break the alliance between Sixtus and Ferdinand by "winning over the king" and that, to achieve this, Lorenzo should go in person to Naples. Having decided on this course, says Machiavelli, Lorenzo entrusted both the city and the "stato" to Tommaso Soderini, then serving as standard-bearer of justice. Only when he reached Pisa, Machiavelli makes a point of noting, did Lorenzo write to the Signoria to explain "the reason for his departure." Further underscoring how entrenched the subordination of public to private had become, Machiavelli says that, when the Signoria received Lorenzo's letter, they appointed him "ambassador on behalf of the Florentine people," both "to honor him and allow him to negotiate peace with the king with greater prestige, giving him the *autorità* [in this case the *legal* authority] to form an alliance with the king as he thought best for his republic" (*IF* 8.17.3–9). This official authority, granted after Lorenzo had arrogated de facto power to himself as a private citizen, was a face-saving gesture for a government excluded from both his decision to go to Naples and whatever agreement he might bring back.

A big part of the legend that formed around Lorenzo derives from his allegedly great success in securing the peace that saved "his republic." Machiavelli, by contrast, emphasizes the opposition to Lorenzo in Florence during his visit to Naples, the precariousness of the negotiations, and the less than satisfactory peace he achieved. To be sure, he reports Ferdinand's admiration of Lorenzo, as does Valori's *Vita.*[19] The king, says Machiavelli, was so impressed by the "greatness of [Lorenzo's] spirit, the quickness of his intellect, and his wise judgment" that he "began to think he would send him home as an ally [amico] rather than detain him as an enemy." But he kept him in Naples from December 1479 to March 1480, in order, Machiavelli adds, to get a deeper understanding not only of Lorenzo but also of "the city." Yet Ferdinand's hospitality was not motivated solely by admiration for Lorenzo, as Machiavelli immediately explains: "for Lorenzo had no lack of enemies in Florence who would have liked the king to detain him and deal with him as he had with Iacopo Piccinino," the condottiere Ferdinand murdered in 1465 in collusion with Francesco Sforza. These domestic enemies, "simulating grief" over the danger Lorenzo faced, "spoke about it all over the city, and in public deliberations they opposed anything that would have helped Lorenzo. In these ways they promoted a rumor that, if the king kept Lorenzo in Naples for a long time, there would be a coup [si muterebbe governo] in Florence."[20] This is why, according to Machiavelli, Ferdinand delayed releasing Lorenzo—"to see if an uprising [tumulto] would break out in Florence." No coup or revolt occurred, and Machiavelli says that Lorenzo, already "grande" when he departed, returned home "grandissimo," "welcomed by the city with the joyfulness that his exceptional attributes and recent achievements deserved and for having risked his own life to bring peace to his patria" (*IF* 8.19.1–7).

In fact, however, not everyone was happy. Venice and Pope Sixtus were angry at being excluded from the separate peace between Florence and Naples, and in Florence "everyone" therefore feared that the peace would be the prelude to a new war. Because of these fears, Machiavelli writes, without naming Lorenzo, the "leaders of the regime [principi dello stato] decided to narrow the ruling group [ristrignere il governo]" and limit "important deliberations to a smaller number" of citizens in a Council of Seventy, to which they gave "the greatest possible authority [autorità] over vital matters" (April 1480). This new "ordine inhibited

[19] Valori, *Vita*, p. 64; noted by the editors of the *Histories*, in *OS*, vol. 2, p. 742, n. 2.

[20] There were such rumblings in Florence, and Machiavelli could have known of them from his father Bernardo's friend, chancellor Bartolomeo Scala, who sent warnings to Lorenzo urging him to return quickly (see Alison Brown, *Bartolomeo Scala 1430–1497: Chancellor of Florence* [Princeton: Princeton University Press, 1979], pp. 95–6); or indeed from Bernardo himself.

[fece fermare l'animo] anyone who wanted political changes" (*IF* 8.19.9–11). Apparently assuming that most readers knew of the revolutionary import of the Seventy and how far it undermined traditional republican institutions, Machiavelli does not describe the new council's structure or functions. The members of the Seventy were chosen, some directly and others indirectly, by Lorenzo and his inner circle, and remained in office for five years. They elected the Signoria, decided which proposals could be submitted to the older legislative councils, appointed the security magistracy of the Otto, and elected from within their own membership new magistracies that oversaw military and fiscal policy. Although such a radical transformation of government of course required the cooperation or acquiescence of the regime's leading citizens, Lorenzo managed the entire reform and thereafter exercised unimpeded supervision over elections and government decisions.[21] The Seventy was the culmination of the regime's seizure of power and the relegation of the republican constitution to irrelevance. Yet Machiavelli obscures Lorenzo's direct role in its creation, as he similarly downplays Cosimo's hand in the reforms of 1458.

The peace with Ferdinand did not restore to Florentine control all the fortresses seized by Neapolitan troops during the war. It was the Ottoman attack at Otranto (August 1480) that turned the king's attention south and forced him to hand over the strongholds (*IF* 8.20). Machiavelli comments: "thus force and necessity, not written agreements and obligations, make princes honor their promises." With the fortuitous reacquisition of the fortresses, Lorenzo "regained the prestige [riputazione] that first the war and then the peace, when there was fear of the king, had taken from him." The assertion that the peace he negotiated was as responsible as the war for Lorenzo's loss of prestige is a sharp rejection of the legend of the heroic mission to Naples. Even more remarkably, Machiavelli adds that "in those days there was no lack of persons who openly slandered him [calunniasse] and asserted that, to save himself, [Lorenzo] had sold out [venduta] his patria, and that, as towns had been lost in the war, liberty would be lost in peace." The accusation by these unidentified critics that Lorenzo was responsible for Florence's "loss of liberty" no doubt alludes to the reforms of 1480 that radically restricted power to trusted Medici insiders. But Machiavelli quickly adds that, once the towns lost in the war were recovered and the city regained its former prestige (no mention of liberty regained, however), "in Florence, a city eager to talk [di parlare avida], which judges matters by their outcomes [dai successi] and not by the wisdom [consiglio] of the actions taken, all the talk changed [si mutò ragionamento], and Lorenzo was praised to the skies, as people said that his prudence [prudenzia] was able to gain in peace what evil fortune had taken from him in war and that his wisdom and judgment did more for him than arms and

[21] Rubinstein, *Government of Florence*, pp. 226–44.

military force did for the enemy" (*IF* 8.22.3–5). If Machiavelli seems here to echo the myth, he also reprimands the Florentines for heaping praise on Lorenzo for a successful outcome that actually owed more to the Ottoman attack at Otranto, and for losing sight of their stolen liberty as they celebrated his alleged wisdom and prudence.

After the Pazzi conspiracy and the mission to Naples, Machiavelli has little more to say about Lorenzo until the famous portrait in the final chapter. He appears in a minor and mostly ceremonial role in Florence's capture of Pietrasanta in 1484. The seizure of the stronghold that dominated the town was accomplished, Machiavelli says, by the newly appointed commissioner and loyal Medicean Antonio Pucci, whose "umanità" and "affabilità" restored courage to a demoralized Florentine army. With victory assured, "Lorenzo thought he should go to the [army's] camp so that matters could be concluded with greater prestige [reputazione]" (*IF* 8.31.5–7). In his notes on events from 1464 to 1501 (the "Spogli") Machiavelli makes the point more caustically: Pucci's "virtú" brought about the successful capture of the fortress and Pietrasanta's submission, whereupon "Lorenzo went to the camp to have the glory."[22] In the same border war Machiavelli says the Florentines would have attacked the town of Sarzana "had it not been for Lorenzo de' Medici's illness, for he suffered not only from the gout inherited from his father but also from terrible stomach pains, so much so that he was forced to go to the baths [of Porretta] for a cure" (*IF* 8.31.12). A third instance of Lorenzo's marginal role in military matters is kinder to him. In a subsequent and successful attempt to capture Sarzana in 1487 his arrival "in campo" caused "the soldiers to take heart" and the people of the town to lose courage and "freely and unconditionally yield to Lorenzo" (*IF* 8.33.12–13). Machiavelli notes two ways in which Lorenzo sought to reestablish good relations with the papacy. He negotiated the marriage of his daughter Maddalena to Innocent VIII's son, Francesco Cybo, "believing this would bring him great *reputazione*" (*IF* 8.33.1–3), and he successfully persuaded Boccolino Guzzoni, the rebel lord of Osimo (in the papal dominions), to restore the town to papal control in return for an invitation to Florence where he "lived most honorably"[23] (until he made the mistake of going to Milan where Ludovico il Moro had him killed) (*IF* 8.34.1–2). Machiavelli tactfully omits to mention that the reward for assisting Innocent in Osimo was a cardinal's hat for Lorenzo's 13-year-old son Giovanni.

In the concluding portrait of Lorenzo Machiavelli briefly mentions what he calls Lorenzo's "governo particulare [personal governance]" of Faenza which allowed him to control the city through a Florentine commissioner. He explains the origin of this arrangement in the preceding chapter (*IF* 8.35). In 1488 Faenza's signore, Galeotto Manfredi, was murdered in a plot hatched by his wife

[22] *OS*, p. 962.
[23] Valori mentions these events: *Vita*, pp. 71, 75, 79.

(Francesca) and her father, Giovanni Bentivoglio, signore of Bologna, who entered the city with forces led by a condottiere in the service of Ludovico Sforza of Milan. The people of Faenza, especially the inhabitants of the Val di Lamone, resisted the invasion, took Bentivoglio prisoner, and appealed to the Florentine commissioner, Antonio Boscoli, to take control of the city. The Florentines, unhappy about Manfredi's murder and the Bolognese signore's armed entry into the city, nonetheless liberated Bentivoglio and his daughter and, Machiavelli says, assumed protection of both the city and Galeotto's infant son Astorre, "according to the wishes of the entire popolo" of Faenza (*IF* 8.35.1–9). As Niccolò Valori states in the *Vita* and modern historiography confirms,[24] Lorenzo did indeed intervene to guarantee Bentivoglio's safety, protect Astorre, and secure Florentine control over Faenza. Strangely, Machiavelli does not mention Lorenzo in his account or the fact that, in order to preserve Florentine influence in the Romagna, he needed to persuade the king of Naples, Ludovico Sforza's ally, not to intervene militarily, an eventuality that could have ignited a peninsula-wide conflagration. Lorenzo's "governo particulare" in Faenza depended on Neapolitan acquiescence.

"SEMPRE IN FESTA"

The last chapter of the *Histories* (8.36) contains the famous portrait of Lorenzo. Although it incorporates many elements that were already coalescing into the heroic myth, its paradoxes and incongruities, especially the reversals of fortune between success and adversity, triumph and sorrow, problematize, perhaps even undermine, what might seem to be unqualified panegyric. Machiavelli comments on Lorenzo's initiatives to embellish the city, promote its cultural splendor, enhance its security, and promote the fortunes of his family. He highlights Lorenzo's literary skills and patronage of leading humanists and philosophers. But there is little to nothing about Lorenzo's leadership of the Medici party, his management of Florentine government, or his role in diplomacy and foreign policy.

"Once the Sarzana war ended," the portrait begins, "the Florentines lived in the greatest happiness until Lorenzo died in 1492," because, with peace having come to Italy through his "senno [wisdom]" and "influence [autorità]," he turned his attention to making "himself and his city *grande*." In addition to the ambiguity of "grande" (powerful? prestigious?) the juxtaposition, almost conflation, of Lorenzo and the city is puzzling. In fact, the examples Machiavelli adduces, in a continuation of the same sentence, are family events: first, the marriage he arranged for his eldest son, Piero, to Alfonsina (of the Neapolitan Orsini); second, the cardinalate he secured for his second son, Giovanni, which, Machiavelli comments, "was

[24] Valori, *Vita*, p. 80. On Lorenzo and Faenza, see Marco Pellegrini, *Congiure di Romagna. Lorenzo de' Medici e il duplice tirannicidio a Forlì e a Faenza nel 1488* (Florence: Olschki, 1999), pp. 89–142.

all the more notable, indeed totally unprecedented, because he was elevated to such a rank before he reached the age of 14"; and third, the marriages of his daughters: he names the husbands—Iacopo Salviati, Francesco Cybo, Piero Ridolfi, and Giovanni (di Pierfrancesco) de' Medici—but omits the daughters' names. For his third son, Giuliano, Lorenzo did not live long enough to arrange any "estraordinaria fortuna." Machiavelli implies that Lorenzo assumed all these arrangements would make himself and "his" city "grande." Piero's marriage into the Orsini was crucial for protecting the family's standing and power. Of Giovanni's red hat, Machiavelli adds, perhaps a bit cheekily, that it was "a ladder to enable his family to rise to the heavens." Could Lorenzo (or Machiavelli) have imagined the circumstances in which a Medici princely dynasty would one day descend from his daughter Lucrezia's marriage to Iacopo Salviati?

The first reversal of fortune comes with the revelation that "in his other private matters," particularly as regards "la mercanzia" (his financial enterprises and chiefly the Medici bank), Lorenzo was "infelicissimo," unlucky and unhappy, because of the "disordine" of those who administered his businesses "not as private citizens, but as [if they were] princes." Yet these were the same trusted long-term managers to whom the Medici had always delegated the management of the bank. Machiavelli says "so much of his liquid assets [mobile] was spent"—he does not say by whom—"that it was necessary for the patria" (the public treasury) "to assist him with great sums of money."[25] Yet we know it was Lorenzo himself who paid little attention to the accounts and, as a private citizen, spent his wealth as if he were a prince, confident of being bailed out by the treasury. Consequently, Machiavelli says, "in order not to tempt fate further," Lorenzo gave up commercial activities and turned instead to more stable investments, buying land and properties in several parts of the dominion, which, "for the income [they provided] and the type and magnificence of their buildings were more befitting a king than a private citizen [non da privato cittadino, ma regie]." Twice in a few lines, Machiavelli underscores Lorenzo's and his ministers' temptation to spend like royalty.

Lorenzo then turned his attention, Machiavelli says, to "making his city more beautiful and greater [maggiore]," promoting the construction of new streets and buildings in the city's uninhabited spaces (projects well documented by modern scholarship). He attributes to Lorenzo a program of strengthening the dominion's defenses: "so that the city might live more peacefully and securely within its dominion [perché in nel suo stato piú quieta e secura vivesse]"[26] and to keep his

[25] How he availed himself of public funds is elucidated by Alison Brown, "Lorenzo, the Monte and the Seventeen Reformers: Public and Private Interest," in Brown, *The Medici in Florence: The Exercise and Language of Power* (Florence: Olschki; and Perth: University of Western Australia, 1992), pp. 151–211.

[26] The most commonly cited English translations misread this sentence: "stato" is the territorial dominion (we have seen that Machiavelli frequently uses it in this sense), not "the state." And the

enemies at a greater distance, he "fortified the walled town of Firenzuola in the mountains toward Bologna," "initiated the construction of the fortress of Poggio Imperiale in the direction of Siena," and, in the direction of Genoa, "closed off that route to potential enemies with the acquisition of the towns of Pietrasanta and Sarzana" (not, of course, exactly *his* "acquisition"). Echoing Valori's *Vita*,[27] he says Lorenzo kept his "friends" in power in nearby cities with payments and subsidies ("stipendii e provisioni"), including the Baglioni in Perugia, the Vitelli in Città di Castello, and the "governo particulare" in Faenza, all of which, Machiavelli says, were "like secure bulwarks [fermi propugnaculi] for his city." The irony, perhaps well intended, is that Pietrasanta and Sarzana did nothing to stop the army of Charles VIII from marching into the Florentine dominion in 1494 and brutally sacking the town of Fivizzano on the way. Nor did the fortress at Firenzuola impede the incursion of Cesare Borgia and his condottieri in 1501, and the fortress at Poggio Imperiale (Poggibonsi) was built *after* Neapolitan troops had occupied much of the southern portion of the dominion in the war that followed the Pazzi conspiracy. Machiavelli thought fortresses generally useless (*P* 20 and *DL* 2.24), and he may be hinting here at the futility of Lorenzo's efforts to secure the dominion.

The portrait justly praises Lorenzo's cultural patronage and literary accomplishments. "He profoundly revered those who excelled in any skill [arte]," especially men of letters ("litterati")—Machiavelli mentions Poliziano, Landino, Demetrio "greco" (Chalcondylas), and Giovanni Pico della Mirandola, "uomo quasi che divino," who, "touched by Lorenzo's munificence," settled in Florence. Lorenzo himself "marvelously delighted in architecture, music, and poetry" and "wrote not only much poetry himself, but also a commentary on his poems." He founded the "studio" (university) in Pisa "so that Florentine youth could be trained in literary studies" and invited the "most excellent men in Italy" to teach there.

"He was supremely loved by fortune and by God, and all his undertakings consequently enjoyed success while those of his enemies ended badly." Oddly enough, Machiavelli cites the Pazzi conspiracy and two other attempts on his life—and the penalties meted out to the would-be assassins—as evidence of how fortune and God smiled on him. Lorenzo survived all these plots, but his brother did not and the war that followed the Pazzi plot put Lorenzo and the city in grave danger from which they escaped only with some unexpected help from the Turks. When Machiavelli comments that Lorenzo's "way of living, his prudence, and good fortune" earned him the admiration and esteem of princes in and beyond Italy, one

subject is "città" from the preceding sentence, not Lorenzo, as the feminine adjectives "quieta" and "secura" make clear. The sentence does *not* say that Lorenzo fortified Firenzuola "so that he might live in his state more quietly and safely."

[27] Valori, *Vita*, p. 71.

wonders in what, exactly, this "way of living" consisted. His luck in surviving assassination plots and wars? The king of Hungary, the (Mameluke) Sultan (of Egypt), and the "gran Turco" (the Ottoman Sultan), Machiavelli writes, all expressed friendship and deep respect for Lorenzo in a variety of ways, including the Ottoman ruler's extradition of his brother's assassin. "All this," says Machiavelli, made Lorenzo widely admired in Italy, "where his reputation for wisdom grew daily, because he was eloquent and witty in discussing things, sagacious in making decisions, and quick and bold in executing them."

From Lorenzo's wisdom, eloquence, and wit, the portrait takes another change of direction, this time to his vices. Affirming first that no vices can be adduced "that could stain his many virtú," Machiavelli immediately qualifies this blanket exoneration: "he was astonishingly engrossed in sexual affairs [nelle cose veneree maravigliosamente involto], delighted in the company of witty and sarcastic men and in childlike games more than was appropriate for such a man. He was often seen joining his children in their games." Then comes the famously enigmatic statement: "Considering the light-hearted, sensuous, and serious" sides of Lorenzo, "one saw two different persons in him, combined in an almost impossible combination [quasi con impossibile coniunzione congiunte]." The implication that sexual excess, the company of sharp-tongued wags, and playing games with his children were Lorenzo's only vices starkly differs from Guicciardini's darker portrait of Lorenzo's relentless sexuality, cruelty, vindictiveness, and especially his paranoia, suspicion, and fear.[28] Machiavelli obviously could not say such things in a book he was about to present to Lorenzo's papal nephew, but we shall see that he too hints at a darker side.

From being supremely loved by fortune and God, in his last years, Machiavelli says, Lorenzo fell into "constant suffering" from illness and "intolerable stomach pains." Yet there was "no one," he adds "in Florence or Italy who ever died with such a reputation for wisdom [prudenzia], or whose death brought such grief to his patria." "All his fellow citizens"—this was not true, as contemporary chronicles reveal—"and all the princes of Italy mourned his death." They had good reason to be sorrowful, Machiavelli explains, because, "with Italy deprived of his *consiglio* [wisdom, judgment, prudence]," no one was able to forestall the calamity that engulfed Italy two years later.

I have left for last the most intriguing passage of the portrait (*IF* 8.36.10). "In these peaceful times," Machiavelli writes, presumably referring to the years after the wars of the 1480s, Lorenzo "kept his patria constantly in festivities [Tenne...sempre la patria sua in festa], with frequent jousting tournaments [giostre] and theatrical performances [rappresentazioni] of ancient deeds and triumphs. His purpose [fine] was to keep the city in abundance [abundante], the

[28] Guicciardini, *Storie fiorentine*, ed. Montevecchi, ch. 9, pp. 178–81.

people united, and the nobility honored." Machiavelli here combines several elements from Niccolò Valori's *Vita*: the many "feste," games, and different sorts of entertainments, including "the most magnificent theatrical performances," and Lorenzo's love of "giostre" and horse racing. About the "abundance" of all things, Valori writes: "External affairs having been settled with maximum dignity to the republic, and with domestic matters so peaceful that nothing more could be desired, virtue was esteemed, the people were in liberty, the nobility honored, and the city had the greatest abundance of all things [e la città di tutte le cose abondantissima; summa rerum omnium copia]."[29] Although Machiavelli once again notably omitted the phrase about liberty, it seems clear that he pondered these scattered elements in the *Vita* and brought them together in a memorable statement of Lorenzo's purpose ("il fine suo") in this politics of festival, entertainment, and abundance.

Machiavelli's emphatic combination of these themes tellingly evokes the famous "panem et circenses" verses of Juvenal's tenth satire, in which the poet says that the people of Rome, "having cast aside their political responsibilities and no longer conferring commands or the insignia of office, remain subdued, eagerly desiring only two things: bread and the circus races." Juvenal ties the Roman people's desire to be well fed and entertained to the abdication of their former and abandoned role in government as the nascent imperial order replaced the republic.[30] In Machiavelli's passage "giostre" and "rappresentazioni" have the function of Juvenal's "circenses," and, as any Florentine would have recognized from the name of the office of the Magistrato dell'Abbondanza which managed the grain supply, keeping "la città abundante" clearly alludes to bread. Keeping the city "abundante," the popolo united (hence calm, quiet and well fed), the elite honored (and satisfied) and everyone entertained with "giostre" and "rappresentazioni" was Florence's version of the conditions in which Juvenal says the Roman people relinquished their political vocation and became passive—the conditions in which Iacopo de' Pazzi's desperate appeal to the Florentine people to answer the call of liberty went unheeded.

That Machiavelli intended an allusion to Juvenal's verses in the portrait of Lorenzo is, moreover, confirmed by a direct quotation from the same tenth satire in *Discourses* 3.6.20–4, where, discussing the injustices ("ingiurie") that induce victims to seek revenge against tyrants, he pinpoints the role of the Medici in triggering the Pazzi conspiracy: "The chief reason [maggiore cagione] the Pazzi conspired against the Medici was the inheritance of Giovanni Borromei that was taken from them by order" of the Medici. It was well known that Lorenzo

[29] Valori, *Vita*, pp. 74, 83, 85 (in the vernacular text) and 129–30, 140–1 (in the Latin text).

[30] Juvenal, *Satire* 10, vv. 78–81: "iam pridem, ex quo suffragia nulli / vendimus, effudit curas; nam qui dabat olim / imperium, fasces, legiones, omnia, nunc se / continet atque duas tantum res anxius optat, / panem et circenses."

arranged the ad hoc law that deprived Borromei's daughter and her Pazzi husband of her father's inheritance. From identifying this "chief reason" behind the conspiracy, Machiavelli segues smoothly to "another reason, a very great one," that causes men to conspire against a prince, namely, the "desire to liberate the patria that he has usurped [occupata]" and deprived of its liberty. "This is the cause that impelled Brutus and Cassius against Caesar," Machiavelli writes, thereby indirectly associating Lorenzo with Caesar and the Pazzi with his slayers. Implicitly characterizing usurpers of liberty as tyrants, Machiavelli continues: "No tyrant can protect himself from this hatred except by relinquishing his tyranny. And, because no [tyrant] ever does so, there are very few who do not end badly, whence came that verse of Juvenal":

> Few kings go down to the son-in-law of Ceres [Pluto] without wounds and mayhem, and few tyrants go there by means of a natural death.[31]

The verse (two actually) is from the same tenth satire, and it appears just thirty lines after the "bread and circuses" verse, following a rebuke of those whose immoderate reach for power and wealth brings on their frightful ruin. Juvenal's prime example is Sejanus, the ambitious prefect of the Praetorian Guard to whom Tiberius, who preferred life in Capri, delegated the powers of the imperial office. But Sejanus wanted more and conspired to gain the imperial title for himself; he was discovered, executed, and derided, Juvenal writes, by "Remus' mob, who always support whoever comes out on top" (v. 73). Sejanus too is present in *Discourses* 3.6. Asserting that conspiracies are hatched by prominent men or members of a prince's family whose motives derive from either favors or injuries received from the prince, Machiavelli cites three examples from Roman history, the third of which is Sejanus' plot against Tiberius (*DL* 3.6.41). Sejanus is a link between Machiavelli's allusion, in the portrait of Lorenzo, to Juvenal's condemnation of tyrants and the diagnosis of conspiracy in *Discourses* 3.6, where "the Medici" are placed in the company of tyrannical usurpers of liberty who end badly. The quest for the "highest place," for supreme power, by any and every artifice, Juvenal says, similarly destroyed "those like Pompey and Crassus and him who reduced the Roman people to servitude" (vv. 110–11), namely Caesar. The verses about the brutal fate of tyrants quoted by Machiavelli in the *Discourses* immediately follow (112–13). "Tyrants" and "tyranny" figure prominently (at least twenty-one times) in *Discourses* 3.6; Lorenzo is mentioned four times and alluded to a fifth time in the passage explaining how the Medici angered the Pazzi to the point of murderous conspiracy.

[31] *Satire* 10, vv. 112–13: "Ad generum Cereris sine caede et vulnere pauci / descendunt reges, et sicca morte tyranni."

Juvenal's *Satires* are sardonic meditations on the self-harm that results from excessive desire for power and wealth. The verses of the tenth satire that focus on the lust for power and how it often destroys those who constantly crave it caught Machiavelli's eye and may have led him to reflect on Lorenzo's purposes—pacifying the people and securing his power—in keeping Florence "sempre in festa." Did Juvenal's cautionary examples of self-defeating aspirants to tyrannical power prompt Machiavelli to regard Lorenzo—who, although he narrowly escaped a brutal death, nonetheless suffered "wounds and mayhem"—as one of those who pursue the "summus locus" by any "arte," who "crave excessive honors and wealth," and who construct edifices of such great height that their fall causes immense devastation (Satire 10.104–7)? This is precisely the admonition Machiavelli has Giuliano give his brother Lorenzo before the attack by the Pazzi, "fearing that, by wanting too much, everything would be lost" (*IF* 8.2.13).

10
Corruption and Tyranny

Steadily developing in the narrative of the *Florentine Histories* is the sequence of stages through which, according to Machiavelli, elite ambition generated factions as the dominant political units, eventually resulting in the victory of a single faction (what I call regime) and reducing, as the introductory chapter of book 8 states, all opposition to conspiracy. Each stage further weakens and undermines the ordini—the laws and institutions—of what Machiavelli calls the "publico" and we call the state, in a degenerative process that he calls corruption. The final stage is the condition in which the regime of a triumphant faction, having rendered the ordini ineffectual, is threatened or assailed by conspiracy (sometimes aided by foreign intervention) and transforms itself into a tyranny. Machiavelli does not overtly call the Medici tyrants. He came close: as noted earlier, the draft version of *Histories* 4.27 characterizes Cosimo's methods as those of men "flying toward tyranny"; the exiles of 1466 denounced Piero de' Medici and his followers of "living tyrannically"; and, as suggested in Chapter 9, Machiavelli indirectly hints that Lorenzo pacified the city with tyrannical methods. But Machiavelli's ideas about tyranny were evolving away from traditional notions of the injustice or illegitimacy of despotic princes. More significant to him was the kind of tyranny that emerged in republics from the corruption of the ordini and the privatization of power, which opened the way for regimes that lived, and sometimes died, by the "straordinario," respectively, of faction and conspiracy. For Machiavelli, there was no inevitable cycle of the forms of government as schematized in Polybian anacyclosis (which he outlines and then undermines in *Discourses* 1.2), no cyclical redemptive return, accomplished by men "made wiser by misfortune and adversity," from "disordine" and "rovina" back to "ordine," "virtú," "gloria," and "buona fortuna" (as sketched in the introductory chapter of book 5 of the *Histories*). Even in this imagined return from the depths, in which hitting bottom somehow automatically produces a remedial upward bounce, he quickly adds that this occurs only if it is not "suffocated" by "una forza estraordinaria." The progression from ambition to broken ordini to faction to regime to conspiracy and, finally, to endemic corruption and tyranny is what Machiavelli found in the study of Italy's past and the experience of its troubled present.

Machiavelli did not, however, consider the descent into corruption irremediable. He believed it could be halted, as the Romans did by expelling the Tarquins

Machiavelli's Broken World. John M. Najemy, Oxford University Press. © John M. Najemy 2022.
DOI: 10.1093/oso/9780199580927.003.0010

and establishing a popular republic that lasted four centuries until noble ambition and avarice (as he says in *Discourses* 1.37) catapulted Rome into civil war, and as the Florentines did by instituting and protecting the Ordinances of Justice to contain noble (magnate) ambition and arrogance, and, two centuries later, by creating the republic of the Great Council, which lasted eighteen years until the ottimati conspired with foreign powers to overthrow it and restore the Medici. Machiavelli believed that the degenerative process that begins with the corruption of law and institutions by the wealthy and powerful could be resisted. That the Romans succeeded in doing so for several centuries is the chief reason why they are the principal focus of his theorizing. Noble dominance can be at least interrupted or diminished by strengthening the ordini and returning to "beginnings," as he says in *Discourses* 3.1—to the first principles of law, equality, and limitations on the intrusion of private power into the public sphere. Such resistance is always difficult and sometimes violent; in certain cases it is necessary to "kill the sons of Brutus."

But it is never possible to destroy noble ambition completely. Machiavelli was equally convinced that elite avarice and desire to dominate inescapably revive and return to capture, weaken, or erase the laws and institutions created to tame them. It had always been and would remain a perpetual struggle. The survival of the ordini, and hence of liberty, depended on the constant efforts of the non-noble classes—the popolo/plebe—to set limits on the power and wealth of the elite class and prevent it from building factions strong enough to overwhelm the ordini. He believed this happened in Rome for many centuries and, mutatis mutandis, in Florence's early history. He briefly notes other attempts in Italy's recent past. In fourteenth-century Rome Cola di Rienzo, "chancellor" of the popular government, drove out the senatorial families, made himself tribune and head of a revived Roman republic, and restored the city to its "antica forma" with "such a reputation for justice and virtú" that all Italy honored him (*IF* 1.31.1). Other attempts to tame elite power discussed or mentioned by Machiavelli include Florence's popular uprisings in the 1370s, Milan's Ambrosian Republic in 1447–50, and Genoa's popular revolt in 1506–7 (briefly alluded to in D^2 vv. 97–9: the "severe strife [grave disparer]" between "gl'ottimati e 'l popul genovese"). But for most of the fifteenth century the wealthy and powerful established firm control and kept popular challenges at bay. Machiavelli saw the Medici regime as a prominent instance of the elite hegemony that was dominant throughout Italy, a regime in which a private faction gradually eroded laws and constitutional government, brooked no rivals, and consequently became vulnerable to conspiracy. The Medici regime was the example Machiavelli knew best of the process of corruption to which elite ambition inevitably tends. As for whether the Medici were tyrants, he lets the reader read, as it were, between the lines.

"DECEIVED BY FALSE GOOD AND FALSE GLORY, THEY TURN TO TYRANNY"

"The cities of Italy are full of tyrants," Dante wrote in *Purgatorio* 6.124–5. Machiavelli might have agreed that not much had changed. He too denounced tyrants. The title of chapter 10 of book 1 of the *Discourses* states: "The founders of a republic or a kingdom are praiseworthy in the same measure as the founders of a tyranny are reprehensible [vituperabili]." Yet, he comments, although no one facing the choice would not praise the former and condemn the latter, "nonetheless, nearly all, deceived by false good and false glory, whether willingly or through ignorance, let themselves fall into the ranks of those who deserve more blame than praise and who, although able to create a republic or a kingdom to their everlasting honor, turn to tyranny [si volgono alla tirannide]" (*DL* 1.10.8–9). The temptation of tyranny is here figured as nearly universal, built into the psychology of princes who, having power, want still more (as Juvenal warns in *Satire* 10). Although Machiavelli does not accept the inevitability of the Polybian cycle of constitutions, he does seem to agree that "principalities easily become tyrannical," because, "as a prince begins to be hated and, because of that hatred, fearful, he soon shifts from fear to injurious actions [offese] and suddenly a tyranny is born" (*DL* 1.2.12, 17).

Yet Machiavelli does not use the terms "tyrant" and "tyranny" consistently.[1] He often appears to assume that many of Italy's signori and princes were tyrants, even without the descent into abusive behavior alluded to in *Discourses* 1.10. He often seems unconcerned with distinguishing princes from tyrants. For example, in *Discourses* 1.27.2, discussing Pope Julius's 1506 campaign to remove both the Bentivoglio of Bologna, who "had held the *principato* of that city for a hundred years," and Giampaolo Baglioni, "tyrant of Perugia," Machiavelli does not trouble to explain why he calls Baglioni a tyrant but says the Bentivoglio held the "principato." To defend the implication that the Bentivoglio were not tyrants, he might have mentioned the *capitoli* of 1447 that regularized Bologna's status vis-à-vis the papacy (and for which, as we saw, Julius had nothing but contempt) and Pope Sixtus IV's conferral on Giovanni Bentivoglio of the title of "principe" of the Bolognese office of the Sixteen in 1473.[2] Further muddling matters, on the other hand, Machiavelli says Julius "had sworn an oath against all the tyrants who were occupying the cities of the Church," including the Bentivoglio. In the chapter on conspiracies in the *Discourses* he calls Pandolfo Petrucci, the signore of Siena, a tyrant (*DL* 3.6.19), as he does Aristotimus, "tiranno" of Epirus (*DL* 3.6.72); the Magus who usurped the kingdom of the Persians (*DL* 3.6.74); Nabis "tiranno" of

[1] On Machiavelli's ideas of tyranny, see Giovanni Giorgini, "The Place of the Tyrant in Machiavelli's Political Thought and the Literary Genre of the *Prince*," *History of Political Thought* 29 (2008): 230–56.

[2] De Benedictis, *Una guerra d'Italia*, pp. 86–98.

Sparta (*DL* 3.6.76); Diocles and Hippias, "tiranni" of Athens (*DL* 3.6.132); and the "tiranni" Clearchus and Satirus of Heraclea (*DL* 3.6.133). In the *Florentine Histories* he explains that when the emperors "abandoned" Italy (in the thirteenth century) some cities became free [republics] while many others were "seized" by "tiranni" (*IF* 1.26.2). He cites the dueling policies of Pope Benedict XII and Emperor Ludwig of Bavaria with regard to "tyrants" who had de facto control of cities within, respectively, the States of the Church and the imperial territory of Lombardy: to all the "tyrants" of Lombardy Benedict gave titles and legitimate possession of their cities "in order to gain as allies those who had usurped" power, and to prevent the emperor from making himself "signore" of Italy; Ludwig retaliated by granting all the "tyrants" of the States of the Church "imperial authority" over their cities (*IF* 1.30.1–2). Such a passage suggests that "tyrants" existed in the eye, or propaganda, of the beholder. These are instances in which Machiavelli, echoing common usage, labels as tyrants rulers who lacked titles and in some cases usurped power and who therefore ruled, as the jurists said, ex defectu tituli. Yet rulers with legitimate titles could also be tyrants for Machiavelli. He calls the rule of the Berengars in the ninth and tenth centuries a "tirannide" despite the fact that the first Berengar had been installed as king of Italy by a pope (*IF* 1.12.2, 12). He sometimes attaches the label of tyrant to rulers, whether titled princes or untitled signori, without commenting on either the nature of their conduct or the legitimacy of their title. He refers to the fourteenth-century Visconti and "the other tyrants of Lombardy" (*IF* 2.29.8; 2.30.8), thus implying that the early Visconti, like the unnamed signori of other cities, were tyrants. Lucca's early fifteenth-century signore, Paolo Guinigi, is repeatedly referred to as that city's "tiranno" in the speeches in the *Florentine Histories* in which Machiavelli has Rinaldo degli Albizzi and Niccolò da Uzzano debate the wisdom of waging war on Lucca (*IF* 4.19). In his own voice, too, Machiavelli calls Guinigi a tyrant (*IF* 4.25.9). In such instances it is difficult to see how he differentiates tyrant from signore or prince.

Abusive and cruel behavior by princes, but also by officials who were not princes, could earn the appellation of tyrant from Machiavelli. The punishments meted out (in 1316) by Lando da Gubbio, Florence's executor of the Ordinances of Justice, who had been hired by one faction, were so brutal that another faction, "determined to be free of such disreputable tyranny," appealed to King Robert of Naples to remove him (*IF* 2.25.9–17). Following deep-rooted Florentine tradition, Machiavelli brands as tyranny the rule of Walter of Brienne, who was granted emergency powers (in 1342) for a limited time but then, Machiavelli says, established a "tirannide" with support from the plebs and foreign arms (*IF* 2.36.6). When Archbishop Angelo Acciaiuoli, from a family that initially supported Brienne's appointment, became aware of his "tirannici modi," he sought to make amends for his error by leading one of the several conspiracies formed to oust him (*IF* 2.36.17). The unnamed citizen who makes the long, impassioned speech against factions recalls Brienne's "acerbo e tirannico" spirit (*IF* 3.5.17). Without expressing disagreement, Machiavelli reports the accusations of tyranny by the citizens of Milan against two of the Sforza. When Francesco Sforza allied with Venice (in 1448) against the Ambrosian Republic he had pledged to protect, the aggrieved Milanese, Machiavelli says, considered him a traitor (*IF* 6.20.2) and begged the Venetians to "follow the custom of republics" and support the cause of Milanese liberty, not that of a "tiranno" (*IF* 6.21.8). Duke Galeazzo Maria Sforza was detested, Machiavelli writes, for his numerous acts of cruelty and fell victim to assassins who swore an oath to liberate their patria from the "tirannide" of "the prince" (*IF* 7.33.5–7). These are examples of tyranny defined by abuse of power or immoral behavior—ex parte exercitii, in juristic theory. But Machiavelli makes no programmatic use of the distinction between tyrants ex defectu tituli and ex parte exercitii.

In *Discourses* 1.9, discussing Rome's origins and founders, Machiavelli says Romulus' institution of the senate and strict adherence to its advice made the later transition from monarchy to republic an easy matter of substituting two consuls for the king. This shows, he says, that Rome's foundational ordini were "more in accord with a free and civic government [vivere civile e libero] than with an absolute and tyrannical one [uno assoluto e tirannico]" (*DL* 1.9.13). In Machiavelli's lexicon "vivere civile" and "vivere libero" are usually synonymous with republic, and here they are contrasted with a tyrannical order, also characterized as "assoluto," which refers to the concept in Roman law of the emperor "exempted from the laws," princeps legibus solutus. He reiterates the equation of tyranny with "absolute power" in *Discourses* 1.25.5–6, asserting that one who wishes to institute either a "vivere nuovo e libero" (a new republic) or a "vivere politico" (a constitutional polity) "either through a republic or a kingdom" must allow the changes to retain something of the old order. But he who intends to create a "potestà assoluta," which "the ancient authors call tyranny [tirannide], must change everything." Here tyranny is seemingly disengaged from both a lack of legitimate title and cruel and abusive rule.

In *Discourses* 2.2 Machiavelli characterizes princely tyranny and theorizes its consequences in two passages contrasting tyranny and liberty. Ancient peoples, he says, had greater desire for liberty and greater hatred of tyranny than modern peoples have. The love of the "vivere libero" among the ancient peoples of Italy—he mentions the Etruscans ("Toscani"), Romans, and Samnites—is easy to understand when one considers that "cities have never expanded, either in territory or wealth, except when they are in a condition of liberty." He declares it "truly astonishing to behold to what level of greatness Athens rose in the hundred years after it liberated itself from the tyranny of Pisistratus." But the "most marvelous" example is the greatness Rome achieved after freeing itself from its kings. "The reason for this is easy to comprehend, because what makes a city great is the common good [bene comune], not private good [bene particulare]." The common good is sought, he adds, "only in republics, where everything that enhances the common good is done, and, however much it may damage this or that private citizen, so many more benefit from it that they are able to support it against the resistance of the few who might be harmed by it." But "the opposite happens," Machiavelli says, "when there is a prince, because most of the time what benefits him hurts the city, and what is good for the city hurts him." Here Machiavelli envisions the prince as engaged in a private enterprise for his own profit, not for the good of the city, "such that, as soon as a tyranny overtakes a republic [vivere libero], the least bad thing that happens to the city is that it no longer makes any progress [non andare piú innanzi] or grows in power or wealth." Tyranny is identified with the prince's alleged inclination to attend solely to his private interests: the prince/tyrant, he says, keeps for himself any expansion of territory or gains in wealth, and, far from growing and expanding, cities ruled by such a prince/tyrant "will decline [tornano indietro]." Even if the tyrant is "virtuoso"—possesses military valor and political skill—and with this virtú "acquires new territories, this benefits him alone and not the republic, because he cannot place citizens over whom he exercises tyrannical power in important positions, no matter how worthy and good they might be, and does not want to have to fear them." Similarly, he cannot add the territories he acquires to the jurisdiction or governance of the city whose tyrant he is, "because making the city powerful does not benefit him. It is in his interest to keep the dominion [*stato*] divided," because he wants "each town and district to acknowledge *him*"—not the city—"as its lord" (*DL* 2.2.5–19).

Later in *Discourses* 2.2, following the famous passage, discussed above in Chapter 4, in which he blames Christianity for the modern world's tepid attachment to liberty, Machiavelli contrasts the effects of the "vivere libero" of antiquity and the "vivere servo" of his time. "All cities and regions that live in freedom," he reiterates, "make great advances in every way." Population increases because people enter into marriages more freely and gladly procreate children knowing they can raise them "without fearing that their wealth [patrimonio] will be seized." They know their children are not only born free and not slaves but also can become, through their talents ("mediante le virtú"), leading citizens ("principi"). This implies a contrasting lack of such opportunities under a prince/tyrant who fears appointing his best citizens to important offices. In free cities wealth multiplies, both from agriculture ("dalla cultura") and from the artisan and merchant trades ("dalle arti," the professions organized in guilds), because "everyone willingly increases [his wealth] and seeks to acquire those goods he knows he can enjoy. Whence it happens that men compete with one another in pursuit of private and public advantages [commodi], both of which wonderfully increase." By contrast with this utopia of liberty, in the dystopia of the "vivere servo" the "opposite of all these things happens." The harsher the servitude, the more do countries lacking liberty decline from former prosperity (*DL* 2.2.44–8).

Machiavelli then veers off in an unexpected direction, declaring that, "of all the harsh forms of servitude, the harshest is that which subjects you to a republic: first, because it lasts longer[3] and there is no hope of escaping it; second, because the aim of a republic is to enervate and weaken all other bodies [politic] in order to expand its own. A prince who subjugates you does not do this." If republics impose the worst kind of servitude and are, almost by their nature, predatory whereas "a prince who subjugates you does not do this," one wonders what has happened to the prince/tyrant who, at the beginning of this same chapter, is portrayed as doing only what profits himself, keeping for himself the territories and wealth he acquires, and refusing to appoint his subjects to important positions because he cannot trust them. Machiavelli reverses this earlier image of the prince, now saying that a prince will *not* rule in such a way as to deprive the city or the people of the enjoyment of both the "private and public benefits" of expanding wealth and territory. Aware, no doubt, of the contradiction he has introduced, he resolves it, in effect, by splitting the prince. A prince will not "do this"—will not deny benefits to his subjects—"provided he is not some barbarous prince, a destroyer of countries and annihilator of all forms of civic life [under the laws], as are the oriental princes [qualche principe barbaro, destruttore de' paesi e dissipatore di tutte le civilità degli uomini, come sono i principi orientali]."[4] If a prince inclines to "humane and lawful norms [ordini umani e ordinarii]," unlike the allegedly "barbarous" oriental princes, "in most cases he will love equally all the cities subject to him and will let them keep all their professions and almost all their traditional ordini." Machiavelli here conjures an image of the good prince as the embodiment of the ordini that sustain "civilità"—the constitutional legitimacy and ethical norms of well-ordered republics—in effect making him a synecdoche of the well-ordered republic. One way of understanding this is that, aware of the inconsistency in his argument, Machiavelli needs to evoke the barbarian destroyer of all "civilità" in order to distance the good prince from the tyranny he earlier implies is inherent in all princes. He makes a further distinction to save his argument. Under a prince imbued with "ordini umani e ordinarii," "even if cities cannot expand as free cities, they do not come to ruin as enslaved cities, it being understood that [this applies] to the servitude of cities subject to a foreigner"—a foreign prince—"because I have already spoken above about cities subject to one of their own citizens" (*DL* 2.2.49–52). Oddly, the more benevolent prince is the foreign one (provided he is not an "oriental" barbarian!); the more oppressive

[3] Grammatically, the subject "la" in the phrase "perché la è piú durabile" could refer either to "servitú" or "republica." "Servitú" seems more plausible because the comment that there is little hope of escaping it refers to servitude. But the two possibilities overlap, since the republic that endures longer can inflict longer-lasting subjugation on other cities.

[4] I examine Machiavelli's notions of European and other cultures in "Machiavelli between East and West," in *From Florence to the Mediterranean and Beyond: Essays in Honour of Anthony Molho*, 2 vols., ed. D. Ramada Curto, E. R. Dursteler, J. Kirshner, and F. Trivellato (Florence: Olschki, 2009), vol. 1, pp. 127–45.

prince is he who rises to power from the population of the city itself. With these two distinctions, Machiavelli safeguards his contention that foreign princes who incorporate cities into their dominions, and who respect and govern them according to the ordini, will allow to their subjects almost all the benefits of liberty, if not liberty itself. It is the homegrown prince who represents the greater danger. But there is much ambiguity in this argument, which leaves hanging the question—which Machiavelli confronts elsewhere—of why the home ground produces princes who inhibit growth and confiscate gains in wealth and territory.

"THOSE WHO PROSPERED UNDER TYRANNY WILL CONSPIRE TO RESTORE IT"

It is not only princes who behave tyrannically in Machiavelli's reading of history. As already noted, he characterizes a few Florentine citizens as would-be tyrants or as tyrannical in their inclinations, aims, or actions. To deprive Corso Donati, the leader of the Black Guelfs, of his popularity among the people, his enemies circulated the accusation that he "wanted to seize tyrannical power [occupare la tirannide]," which, Machiavelli adds, "was easy to get people to believe, because his way of life transgressed all civic norms [ogni civile misura trapassava]" (*IF* 2.22.14). They submitted a formal accusation denouncing Donati's intention to "make himself tyrant" of Florence with the support of his father-in-law, the Ghibelline Uguccione della Faggiuola. Donati was indicted, convicted, and declared a rebel (*IF* 2.23.1–4). About Michele di Lando, who suppressed the most radical of the revolutionary workers in 1378, Machiavelli hypothesizes that, if he had had "wicked and ambitious" intentions, the republic would have lost its liberty and fallen into a "tyranny greater than that of [Walter of Brienne]"—a surprisingly dark shadow over a figure Machiavelli claims to admire as "one of the few who have benefitted their patria" (*IF* 3.17.5–13). Machiavelli appears to confirm the accusation by the exiled opponents of Piero de' Medici that he and his followers were living "tirannicamente" when he adds that the exiles were inciting the Venetians "against tyrants" (*IF* 7.19.8–11). And he attributes tyrannical ambitions to private citizen Cosimo de' Medici in the draft of Niccolò da Uzzano's speech in *Histories* 4.27.

Most intriguing, however, is Machiavelli's imputation of tyranny to groups, and specifically to elite classes. After the collapse of their government in Florence in 1266, the leading Ghibelline families were hated both by the returning Guelfs, who had spent years in exile, and by the popolo, "who vividly remembered the tyranny" of their rule (*IF* 2.9.10). In 1340 a faction of "powerful citizens," illegally ("estraordinariamente") manipulating the appointment of judicial officials, hired a new "Captain of the Guard" who so abused his powers and wronged so many citizens that a conspiracy quickly formed among those who "disapproved of the tyranny [tirannide] of those who were governing" and had appointed him (*IF* 2.32.1–6). After the expulsion of Walter of Brienne in 1343, magnates briefly dominated the communal government, and their "insolence and arrogance" caused the outraged popolo to lament that, "in place of one eradicated tyrant, a thousand more have been born" (*IF* 2.39.6). Many Florentines judged the popular government of 1378–82 to be "tirannico e violento" because the power of private citizens "exceeded that of the magistrates." Benedetto Alberti consented to Giorgio Scali's execution because he disliked his and the other popular leaders' "modi tirannici" just as he had previously opposed the "tyrannical ways" of the Parte Guelfa (*IF* 3.20.2–9). When Benedetto himself was exiled in 1387, he bade farewell to his assembled family members declaring, ironically, that he was glad to free the ruling faction of its "fear not only of him but of any [like him] who understand their tyrannical and wicked ways" (*IF* 3.23.9). In all these instances tyranny is collectively exercised by, or attributed to, parties or classes.

The tyranny of ruling classes and factions becomes a frequent theme in the *Histories* from the end of the fourteenth century. The guildsmen who appealed to Vieri de' Medici in 1393 to protect them from oppression by the Albizzi faction begged him to liberate them from the "tirannide" of "those citizens who were destroyers of good men and the common good" (*IF* 3.25.12). In 1397 the conspirators who plotted to kill Maso degli Albizzi ran into the streets yelling "Popolo, arms, liberty" and "Death to tyrants" (*IF* 3.27.6). In his own voice Machiavelli says the controversial Catasto of 1427, whose method of assessing household wealth compelled the rich to pay more, "set some limits to the tyranny of the powerful [pose in parte regola alla tirannide de' potenti]" (*IF* 4.14.5). Mariotto Baldovinetti, who opposed Rinaldo degli Albizzi's desperate plan for an alliance with the old magnate families to block the rise of Cosimo de' Medici, asserted that it made no sense to have recourse to the "certain tyranny" of the magnates "in order to flee the uncertain dangers of the plebs" (*IF* 4.30.8). Once Machiavelli reaches the period of Medici domination, mentions of tyranny largely disappear, no doubt from considerations of prudence, except in the judgment of the opponents of the Medici. Although, despite coming close, in the *Histories* he stops short of pinning the label of tyrant on Cosimo and Lorenzo, in the *Decennale* of 1504 he characterizes the Medici domination with the metaphor of the "yoke [basto] that oppressed" the Florentines "for sixty years" (D^1 vv. 26–7).

In chapters 16–18 of book 1 of the *Discourses* Machiavelli theorizes collective tyranny and its origin in corruption. Chapter 16 analyzes the difficulty of preserving newly won liberty in cities previously accustomed to living under a prince. If "corruzione" has "completely entered" the body politic, there is no hope at all of maintaining liberty. In cases where corruption has not spread very far—where the good still outweighs "what is ruined [guasto]"—a city that wins its liberty faces the hostility of those who had profited under the former princely regime: "the polity [stato] that becomes free makes enemies, not friends, of members of factions [si fa partigiani inimici e non partigiani amici]." Put differently, a city that acquires or reacquires its liberty inevitably provokes the enmity of the "partigiani [adherents]" of the old regime who find themselves unable to reap the same favors and financial benefits under the new polity, now administered with laws and ordini, that they were accustomed to enjoying under the previous regime, which, with the example of the Tarquins in mind, Machiavelli calls "tyrannical." "All those who profited [si prevalevono] from the tyrannical regime [dello stato tirannico] by feeding off the riches of the prince [pascendosi delle ricchezze del principe] become hostile partigiani" in the state that acquires its freedom. This is so because, "deprived of the ability to profit [valersi], they cannot live content and are all compelled to try to restore the tyranny [ripigliare la tirannide] in order to recover their influence [per ritornare nella autorità loro]" and the material benefits this influence made possible. This is a crucial point for Machiavelli. The prince who cultivates a faction of "partigiani" and rewards them using his own—or, worse, the city's—wealth to keep their loyalty is, implicitly, a tyrant. But the tyranny resides not only in the prince; it pervades the "stato tirannico," the regime supported by a collaborative alliance of prince and "partigiani." With the replacement of the "stato tirannico" by a free polity, these "partigiani," having lost former privileges and benefits and unable any longer to benefit from the departed prince's favor, become antagonistic toward the new order and an obstacle to the preservation of liberty. This occurs, Machiavelli notes, even in cities in which the corrupt alliance of prince and "partigiani" has not spread beyond themselves. Central to this understanding of tyranny is the symbiotic relationship between the prince and those who derive advantages, favors, and benefits from him—designated as "partigiani" because their loyalty is to the "parte"—the private interest, both that of the prince/tyrant and their own—not to the "publico." Seeking to restore the principality and the old order from which they were accustomed to deriving benefit, they become enemies ("inimici") to the free "stato." Hence, Machiavelli says, a free polity makes, and can only make, the partisans of the old order "its enemies and not its friends." Tyranny resides in the ambition and avarice of the "partigiani" who grasp for wealth and power under the prince/tyrant; it is *they* who seek to "retake the tyranny." In the same chapter Machiavelli calls these subversive malcontents the "sons of Brutus," likening them to the nobles who plotted to restore the monarchy of the Tarquins, "as [Livy's] history shows," "for no other reason than that they could not profit illegally [non si potevono valere straordinariamente] under the consuls [of the republic] as they had under the kings. To them, the people's liberty had become their servitude" (*DL* 1.16.5–11).

In chapter 17 Machiavelli delves deeper into the link between corruption and tyranny. Corruption that has infected the entire body politic, Machiavelli says, is an absolute barrier to liberty and republican government. To demonstrate this, he contrasts two great turning points of Roman history: the overthrow of the Tarquin monarchy that gave birth to the republic; and the domination of the

Julio-Claudians from Caesar to Nero ("la stirpe cesarea") that consolidated imperial governance and made the recovery of liberty impossible. The Tarquins were corrupt, Machiavelli says, but the citizens (excepting the "partigiani" who "fed off" the monarchy) were unaffected by their corruption and, once the monarchy was abolished, were able "easily to arrange to live in freedom and under a constitutional order [liberi e ordinati]." However, "considering the level of corruption to which the kings had fallen, if two or three more successions had ensued, and if the corruption that was in them had begun to spread through the members," it would have been "impossible ever again to reform Rome." Just in time, therefore, Rome lost its corrupt monarchical head ("capo") while its trunk ("busto")—the populace—was still healthy ("intero"). By contrast, Machiavelli says, centuries later, when the "stirpe cesarea" became extinct, Rome was unable even to begin to return to liberty. The reason for this "diversity of outcomes" is that, under the Tarquins, the Roman people were "not yet corrupt," whereas by the time of Nero the people was "corrottissimo." Recalling the power of oaths that Numa had inculcated in the Romans, Machiavelli says that, when the Tarquins were expelled, "it was sufficient to have [the people] swear an oath never to allow anyone to rule as king in Rome." But in the later age of complete corruption "the influence [autorità] and severity of Brutus and all the eastern legions" (which he and Cassius commanded) "were not enough to keep [the Roman people] willing to preserve the liberty that he, in emulation of the first Brutus, had restored to them." Machiavelli attributes the Roman people's refusal to defend their liberty to "the corruption that the factions led by Marius [le parti mariane] had implanted in the people." Exactly in what way the "Marian factions," or Marius himself, who led the army of the plebs in the civil wars, corrupted the people Machiavelli does not say here, but he quickly adds that, when Caesar became "capo" of the Marian faction, "he was able to blind the multitude so that it did not recognize the yoke it placed on its own neck." Here Caesar, more than Marius, is figured as the corruptor of the Roman people (*DL* 1.17.2–8). Yet, as we have seen, for Machiavelli the moment of no return in Rome's descent into irremediable corruption was the recourse to "rimedi privati" set in motion by noble opposition to the agrarian law of the Gracchi. While affirming that such laws were necessary to stem the relentless "ambition" of the nobles, Machiavelli acknowledges that it was the party of the plebs, led by Marius, that first took up arms. His unprecedented and never equaled seven consulates, to three of which he allegedly elected himself, were, Machiavelli says, a "scourge [peste]" (*DL* 1.37.18–19). Machiavelli accuses him, together with Sulla, of having initiated the damaging process of factionalizing and privatizing Rome's armies (*DL* 3.24.12).

Still in *Discourses* 1.17, Machiavelli briefly cites Milan and Naples as examples of cities that can never be made "liberi"—can never be republics—because their "membra" are "tutte corrotte." About Naples, he adds nothing more here; concerning Milan, he says only that, after Filippo Maria Visconti died, the Milanese wanted to return to liberty (with the Ambrosian Republic) but "did not know how to maintain it." Hence, it was Rome's "great good fortune that its kings became corrupt and were expelled before the corruption spread to the city's vital organs [nelle viscere]." With a nod back to chapter 4 of book 1, Machiavelli asserts that the absence of corruption ("incorruzione") in the body politic of early republican Rome explains why the "countless tumults," in which the citizens pursued "good purposes, did not harm but actually benefitted the republic" (*DL* 1.17.10–12). At the end of chapter 17, he adds the crucial notion, the fundamental reason why he believes polities like Milan and Naples can never sustain liberty, namely, that "corruption and the weak capacity for a free way of life result from inequality [inequalità]" (*DL* 1.17.16), which, as he explains in *Discourses* 1.55, consists above all in the privileges and forms of private power that nobles (or grandi) create to distinguish themselves from the people (and dominate them).

Machiavelli also introduces into the discussion of corruption in *Discourses* 1.17 an issue that was, we may presume, much on his mind since he wrote the last chapter of *The Prince*, namely, whether and how it is possible to eradicate corruption and restore liberty. Despite having already asserted that corrupt cities liberated from princely regimes cannot preserve liberty, he tests this pessimistic conclusion with a series of hypotheses. First, a corrupt city can never regain liberty, he says, "*unless* [se già]" the goodness and virtú of one man "keep it free." But he immediately points to the obvious limitation of this solution, namely, that "this liberty will last only as long as his life," after which the city will revert to its "former tyranny" (*DL* 1.17.4). Ten or so sentences later, he ventures a second hypothesis: "In a corrupt city" even "constitutionally created laws [leggi bene ordinate]" are of no help, "*unless* [se già] they are enforced by one who, with exceptional force [estrema forza], makes them be observed, so that the matter [materia: the people] becomes good." Machiavelli does not explain or even broach the question of what this "estrema forza" might consist of, or how it could restore the people's "goodness." But here again skepticism instantly undercuts the imagined solution: "I do not know if this has ever happened or if it is possible that it could happen, because, as I have just said, if it does occur that a city in decline because of the corruption of the people [materia] raises itself" out of the corruption, "this happens through the virtú of one man then living, not through the virtú of the people [universale] upholding good ordini." However, "as soon as he dies, the city returns to its former condition." And "the reason is that no man can live long enough to have sufficient time to accustom a city," to liberty and/or new ordini. "And if one man of very long life or the succession of two consecutive able [virtuose] men does not reform the city, as soon as they are gone it will come to ruin"—"*unless* [se già] with much danger and bloodshed, he causes it to be reborn [la facesse rinascere]." This hypothesis too Machiavelli places in doubt: "Corruption and a weak aptitude for liberty derive from inequality," he says, and "if one wishes to bring a city to equality, it is necessary to have recourse to the greatest illegalities [grandissimi straordinari]," which, however, he quickly adds, "few know how, or want, to use" (*DL* 1.17.13–16).

Three times, therefore, the hypothesis that a strong or very able man might be able to restore liberty in a corrupt city elicits both a negating skepticism that affirms its unlikelihood or impossibility and, simultaneously, a statement of the circumstances or conditions in which the impossible/unlikely might after all be possible. First, a corrupt city cannot attain liberty, unless the goodness and virtú of one man bring it to freedom. Second, in a corrupt city even well-established laws are of little use, unless they are executed by one man who, with "exceptional force," succeeds in enforcing them. Third, if an able reformer fails to revive good customs, the city will come to ruin, unless, "with much danger and bloodshed" he brings it to new life. But this would require him to engage in "the greatest illegalities," which few men know how, or wish, to use. The first two hypotheses envision figures of either exceptional goodness and virtú or unshakeable willingness to use great force. Both are declared highly improbable or impossible. With regard to the third hypothesis, Machiavelli does not (yet) say that it too is improbable or impossible. Can a city be rescued from corruption and "disordine" with violence and "grandissimi straordinari"? He addresses this question in the next chapter.

Chapter 18 begins by presupposing ("presupporrò"), for the sake of argument, as it were, a "very corrupt" city in which "there are neither laws nor ordini sufficient to check a universal corruption," i.e. a situation in which corruption has affected all strata of society (*DL* 1.18.2–4). Such corruption was growing, he says, in the electoral and legislative procedures of the Roman republic, both of which, over time, came to be dominated, not by good or qualified men, but by the "powerful." These two functions of government, he affirms, are regulated by the quasi-permanent structural ordini, which rarely change. With the ordini increasingly corrupted, new ones were needed if Rome was to remain free. In theory, Machiavelli writes, reforming the ordini could be done either all at once ("a un tratto") or piecemeal ("a poco a poco"). But both ways, he quickly adds, are "almost impossible." To renovate the ordini "a poco a poco" requires a wise man ("uno prudente") who sees the problem from afar as it originates. But finding such a person is unlikely, and, even if one emerges, he might not be able to persuade others to follow his lead. This leaves the hypothetical possibility of revising the ordini "a un tratto." The first problem here is that, although everyone may see the debased state of the ordini, it is difficult to correct them because "constitutional procedures [termini ordinari] will not suffice," precisely because the ordini have been corrupted and are no longer properly functioning. It would therefore be necessary, Machiavelli says, to have recourse to the "straordinario, which is to say, to violence and arms, and to become, before all else, principe of the city in order to control it as one wishes [poterne disporre a suo modo]" (*DL* 1.18.8–26). This is, in effect, where Machiavelli left the question at the end of chapter 17. Once again he asserts the impossibility of the imagined remedy, but this time for a new reason. "To institute new ordini [riordinare] in a city for constitutional government [al vivere politico] presupposes a good man [uomo buono]," whereas "to become principe of a republic by violent means presupposes a wicked man [uomo cattivo]. For this reason one finds that it very rarely happens that a good man will want to become principe through wicked means [vie cattive], even if his purpose is a good one, or that an evil man [uno reo], having become principe, will want to do good [operare bene], or that it will ever occur to him to use for good the power he has acquired wickedly" (*DL* 1.18.27). Machiavelli here has recourse to what he presumes are general psychological predispositions, grounded in the most basic of ethical categories of good and bad/wicked, to deny the possibility that "good men" will want to achieve power through the "vie cattive" of "violence and arms" in order to institute new ordini and rescue a city from corruption, or, vice versa, that "bad men" with no qualms about seizing power in this way will ever be inclined to use their power to repair the corruption of their cities. In addition to acknowledging the evident contradiction of instituting new ordini by means of the "straordinario," Machiavelli's argument rests on his long-held assumption, first stated in the 1506 *Ghiribizzi*, that every person is endowed by nature with a particular—and unchanging—way of seeing things and acting in the world. "Good" men are temperamentally disinclined to use "wicked means" even for good purposes, and "bad" men are similarly disinclined to use for good ends power achieved with "wicked means," if for no other reason than doing so would undercut their power. In this telling passage Machiavelli seems finally to relinquish the tempting delusion of the strongman who can accomplish good ends through violent and wicked means.

From these considerations Machiavelli derives the "difficulty, or rather the impossibility, of preserving or creating a republic in corrupt cities." But, having just enunciated this firm conclusion, he then appears to reverse himself, almost in deference to the old delusion. "And if, nonetheless, a republic must be created or preserved in such a city, it would be necessary to bring it [ridurla] more toward a monarchical government [stato regio] than a popular government [stato popolare]." Does Machiavelli mean that, to preserve or institute ex novo a republic in a corrupt city would, paradoxically, entail transforming it into a monarchy? The rest of this sentence opens up a way of interpreting this: "so that those men who, because of their arrogance [insolenzia], cannot be disciplined [corretti] by the laws would in some way be reined in [frenati] by an almost monarchical power [una potestà quasi regia]. To try to make them good by other means would be either a most cruel undertaking or completely impossible" (*DL* 1.18.28–30). That the purpose of the "potestà quasi regia" is to suppress "insolenzia"—Machiavelli's favorite characterization, along with "ambizione," of the noble and wealthy classes—underscores his conviction that the corruption that undermines republics comes from these classes, sometimes becoming so rampant that laws are powerless to correct or restrain it. It is sometimes suggested that this "almost monarchical power" is the "principato civile" of *Prince* 9. But there are problems with making this connection. The political context envisioned in *Prince* 9 is very different from that of *Discourses* 1.18. First, the life-and-death struggle of the republic that permeates *Discourses* 1.18 is missing in *Prince* 9. Second, whereas the "principato civile" of *Prince* 9 arises with the support of the people, there is no mention of any role or support of the people in this part of *Discourses* 1.18, which addresses a situation in which the powerful, with their "insolenzia," ride roughshod over the laws and need to be "frenati" by a power greater than the laws. The circumstances envisioned here more nearly approximate the incompatibility of republics and overmighty "gentiluomini" (and "signori di castella") of *Discourses* 1.55, where Machiavelli says, perhaps not coincidentally again after mentioning Naples and "Lombardia" among the regions dominated by "gentiluomini," that establishing a republic in such regions is not possible except by eliminating these nobles who are so "pernicious" to republics: "to reorganize [riordinare] such regions, if one had the power to do it, there would be no other way than to establish a *regno* [monarchy]. The reason is this: where the matter is so corrupt that the laws do not suffice to restrain it, one must institute, together with [the laws], a greater force, namely, a monarchical hand [una mano regia], which can, with absolute and exceptional power, put an end to the extreme ambition and corruption of the powerful" (*DL* 1.55.20–3). This passage revisits the hypothesis introduced in *Discourses* 1.18, and once again the problem is the "ambition and corruption of the powerful" that overwhelm and suffocate republics. Only an "absolute" monarchical power can quash this suffocating dominance. But does Machiavelli envision the emergence of a healthy republic once the "ambition and corruption of the powerful" have been brought to heel? We might think so, given that the discussion in chapter 18 begins with the hypothesis of creating or maintaining a republic in a corrupt city. But what then happens to the "mano regia"? Does it simply disappear once its work is done? Who or what could remove it? Or, if it remains, is the subjugation of overweening noble corruption achieved at the cost of the republic itself? Is this Machiavelli's inescapably tragic dilemma?

"YOUNG NOBLES BECAME FRIENDLY TO TYRANNY FOR A LITTLE PROFIT"

Rome is of course Machiavelli's greatest example of tyranny arising from within a republic. In *Discourses* 1.29, discussing whether the people or princes are more ungrateful, he says cities seeking to maintain their liberty often make the mistake of injuring, or offending, citizens they should reward and fearing those whom they should trust. In an already corrupt republic misdirected ingratitude is the cause of "great evils" that often cause a city "to come more quickly to tyranny." Julius Caesar, he says, "took by force what ingratitude denied him" (*DL* 1.29.18–19).

Given what Machiavelli says about Caesar elsewhere in the *Discourses*—that he is more "blameworthy [biasimevole]" than Catiline (who openly conspired against the republic) and that he sought to possess Rome "in order to ruin it [guastarla]" (*DL* 1.10.13–14, 30)—the suggestion that Caesar's tyranny resulted from the ingratitude of the Roman people might seem puzzling. Machiavelli's reasoning is that, in a corrupt republic, as he says Rome was by Caesar's time, denying him that to which he at least believed he was entitled provoked him to seize tyrannical power. He later calls him the "first tyrant in Rome" (*DL* 1.37.20). Machiavelli may have had in mind what he writes in *Discourses* 1.33, namely, that Pompey and others initially supported Caesar's virtú (his military skill and valor), but that their favor turned to fear and made them adopt "remedies" that "accelerated the ruin of the republic" (*DL* 1.33.13–14). In *Discourses* 1.34 Machiavelli rejects the view that Caesar seized tyrannical power through the office of the dictator and disputes the opinion of "some writers" that, if the office and title of dictator had not existed, "Caesar would not have been able to legitimate his tyranny under any constitutional title [sotto alcuno titolo publico adonestare la sua tirannide]." "It was not the title or rank of dictator" that destroyed Roman liberty, Machiavelli asserts, "but rather the power [autorità] acquired by citizens through lengthy military commands [la diuturnità dello imperio]," as he explains more fully in chapter 24 of book 3. The dictators, by contrast, were appointed, and their powers precisely defined, "secondo gli ordini publici [according to constitutional procedures] e non per autorità propria [not through private, or personal, influence]." Hence, "they always benefited the city" (*DL* 1.34.2–5). Dictators were selected for limited periods of time ("a tempo") to resolve specific problems without necessarily consulting other magistrates, but they were not allowed to do anything "to weaken the stato" (here meaning the state and its constitutional orders): they were prohibited from depriving either the senate or the people of their power, undoing established ordini, or creating new ones (*DL* 1.34.9). Such a magistracy would be useful, even necessary, in modern republics, Machiavelli avers, to enhance their ability to confront emergencies. But he insists that the office of the dictator was not the vehicle that brought tyranny to Rome.[5]

What did put Rome on the road to tyranny, Machiavelli declares, were "the magistrates created and the powers [l'autoritadi] bestowed through unconstitutional procedures [per vie istraordinarie]." For a citizen to be able to harm the republic and seize "autorità istraordinaria," Machiavelli says he must possess many assets that he cannot have in an uncorrupted republic: he must be "very rich" and have many "followers and clients [aderenti e partigiani], which he cannot have where the laws are observed" (*DL* 1.34.6–8). The real danger lies in great

[5] On the Roman dictator, see Marco Geuna, "Extraordinary Accidents in the Life of Republics: Machiavelli and Dictatorial Authority," in *Machiavelli on Liberty and Conflict*, ed. D. Johnston et al., pp. 280–306.

wealth and the private factions wealth can build. In *Discourses* 1.35 Machiavelli introduces his major example from Roman history of how tyranny emerged from elected magistrates: the Decemviri, or, as he calls them, the Dieci (instituted in 451 BCE). Despite being chosen by a legal and open vote ("per suffragii publici e liberi") and given the power to promulgate new laws, the Decemviri were so injurious to liberty that "in time they became the tyrants of Rome and, without any compunction [sanza alcuno rispetto], usurped its liberty." Whereas the appointment of dictators did not entail the removal of established magistracies or a reduction of their powers, when the Romans elected the Decemviri they "annulled" the offices of the consuls and tribunes. The Ten were given "the power to make laws and do anything the Roman people could," the full authority, in other words, of the *populus romanus*. With no one to control or rein them in, they quickly became "insolenti." Because the Decemviri were instituted by "a free and open vote," Machiavelli needs to explain that, when he says the "power granted by a free vote never harmed any republic," he is "presupposing that the people will never grant such authority without establishing its due limits and duration." This did not happen in the case of the Decemviri (*DL* 1.35.2–10). In a coda to chapter 35, commenting on instances in which such limits are omitted or not observed, he says it "does not help that the materia [the people] is uncorrupted, because absolute power [una autorità assoluta]"—which he believes the Decemviri possessed once they became unbridled and "insolenti"—"will in a short time corrupt the matter" and make "amici" and "partigiani" for itself." This intriguing assertion reveals Machiavelli's perception of the circularity of corruption: unchecked power, characterized as "absolute" and by implication tyrannical, even if granted by an open vote of the people, fortifies and protects itself—from the people, from the constitutional magistracies, and from potential rivals—by creating a faction of followers and clients. "Nor does it hurt them [Né gli nuoce]"—referring to the holders of "autorità assoluta"—"if they are poor" or do not have "parenti" (wealth and a wide circle of family loyalists being the building blocks of factions), "because riches and every other kind of support will immediately come to them" (literally, come running: "gli corre dietro"), "as we shall discuss in detail concerning the election of the Decemviri" (*DL* 1.35.12–13). Absolute power, Machiavelli suggests, attracts financial support and legions of clients. This reverses what Machiavelli usually presents as the more normal chain of causation in which wealth attracts followers from which factions, and then tyrannies, are built. Here absolute power draws wealth and followers to itself. This is also why, seeing no opposition to their power, and "encouraged by the ambition of [their leader] Appius [Claudius]," the Decemviri became "insolenti" (*DL* 1.35.9).

The brief introduction to the tyranny of the Decemviri in chapter 35 is the first part of an analysis that resumes in chapter 40, where Machiavelli adds to the explanation the roles played by the social classes of the nobility and the plebs. The Decemvirate was created, he begins, "after many disputes and clashes between the people and the nobility" over the need for new laws to strengthen Rome's liberty. They agreed to send a delegation to Athens to procure copies of "the laws Solon gave to that city" and to make new laws for Rome based on them. They then created the all-powerful magistracy of the Decemviri, among them Appius Claudius whom Machiavelli describes as "astute [sagace] and restless [inquieto]." (We recall that, in *Discourses* 1.55.27, Machiavelli characterizes as "inquieto" the spirit of those "ambitious" men who would have to be transformed into "gentiluomini" in order to convert a republic of "great equality" into a principate.) To give the Decemviri unimpeded power to legislate, "all the other magistracies, especially the consuls and tribunes," were annulled and appeals to the people were suspended, thus making the Decemviri the collective "principe di Roma" with "autorità assoluta." The support Appius enjoyed with the plebs caused the full power of the magistracy to come into his hands. But because he had previously been viewed as a "cruel persecutor" of the plebs, his new displays of friendship toward them made it seem a wonder ("maraviglia") that he had so quickly assumed a new nature and character [una nuova natura e uno nuovo ingegno]" (*DL* 1.40.4–7). This echoes Livy's comment about Appius' "novum . . . ingenium" (3.33), but in light of what Machiavelli had written in the *Ghiribizzi* and repeated in *Prince* 25 about the fixity of each person's distinctive "ingegno," the attribution to Appius of such mutability hints at opportunism and fraudulence. This impression is reinforced when Machiavelli claims, slightly modifying Livy's account, that Appius himself was the source of opinions circulating in the city that the ten tables of the laws initially drafted by the Decemviri required two more to be complete. This, Machiavelli says, gave the people the opportunity to renew the magistracy for another year with a new election—precisely what Appius wanted. The people were happy with this, in part because it meant that the consular office would not be re-established for at least that year. All the city's nobles sought election to the new Ten, and Appius was among the most active seeking to be chosen. In the electoral bargaining he showed so much affability to the plebs that the other members of the Decemvirate began to suspect him and schemed to disqualify him by letting him name all the new Ten, which, according to tradition, ought to have prevented him from appointing himself. But Appius went ahead, "to the astonishment and displeasure of all the nobles," and selected himself together with nine others who supported him. This, Machiavelli says, awakened both the people and the nobility to the gravity of their error. Echoing Livy's phrase, he writes, in Latin, that "Appius stopped playing the part of someone he wasn't [finem fecit ferendae alienae personae] and began to manifest his innate arrogance [innata sua superbia]." Reversing their initial strategy, the Decemviri now began appeasing the nobles and treating the plebs cruelly, so much so that the latter, "having recognized their mistake, and in great distress, looked for any hope of liberty to the nobles"—Machiavelli quotes Livy—"from whom they had so greatly feared servitude that they brought the republic to its current state." The nobles were only too happy to let the plebs wallow in despair. With the two new tables of laws completed but not yet approved by the people's assemblies and hence not made public, the Decemviri used this as a pretext to remain in office: they "began to hold on to power [lo stato] with violence" and to "make the young men of the nobility their supporters"—their "satelliti" (which can also mean bodyguards or henchmen)—"by giving them the possessions of persons they convicted." Paraphrasing Livy in Latin, Machiavelli says "the youth were corrupted [corrumpebatur] by these gifts and preferred their own license to the liberty of all" (*DL* 1.40.10–22). The corrupted young nobles are akin to the "partigiani" who "fed off the riches of the prince," the "sons of Brutus."

In the midst of this constitutional crisis Rome was attacked by the Sabines and the Volsci. The Decemviri realized "the weakness of their rule [stato]": they could not fight a war without the senate but would lose much of their power if they reconvened it. "Constrained by necessity," they summoned the senators, many of whom, especially "Valerio" (Lucius Valerius Potitus) and "Orazio" (Marcus Horatius Barbatus), denounced the arrogance of the Decemviri. This, says Machiavelli, could have "completely extinguished their power [autorità]," but the senate, "not wanting to display its authority [autorità] because of its ill-will [invidia] toward the plebs," refused to force the Decemviri to relinquish their office. The senators preferred that they leave voluntarily, which, so they hoped, might forestall a restoration of the tribunes. Although the nobles hated and reviled the Decemviri, because of their even greater hatred of the plebs they let them remain in office until they stepped down of their own accord—the aim being to obstruct a revival of popular power. Machiavelli quickly summarizes the ensuing events (recounted at greater length by Livy): the war in which Rome's armies were led by members of the Decemvirate while Appius remained in power and ruled the city alone; his infatuation with and attempted rape of Virginia, whose father killed her to "liberate" her; revolts in Rome and in the army; the secession of the army and the plebs to the Mons Sacer, where they remained until the Decemviri quit their office; and, finally, the resumption of both the tribunician and consular magistracies, by which "Rome was restored to the condition of her former liberty" (*DL* 1.40.23–6). In Machiavelli's narrative these tumultuous events originate in the nobility's willingness to endure the tyranny of Appius and the Decemviri rather than suffer a revival of plebeian power.

Shifting from narrative to analysis, Machiavelli ties together the threads of the story of the Decemviri, to which he devotes unusually detailed attention, and draws some conclusions. First, "one sees from this account that the regrettable creation of this tyranny [questo inconveniente di creare questa tirannide]"—the first appearance of "tirannide" in the chapter since a brief mention at the beginning of the errors Appius committed that undermined the "tirannide" he wished to establish—"occurred in Rome for the same reasons that most tyrannies occur in cities, namely, the people's great desire to be free, and the nobles' great desire to dominate [comandare]." Machiavelli thus situates the emergence of tyranny at the interface of the conflicting aims of the people and the nobles. Tyranny results from the dysfunctional clash of the classes and from the decision of one or the other to resort to extra-constitutional remedies and an authoritarian champion to beat down its rival. "If," Machiavelli says, "they do not agree to enact a law to uphold liberty, and if either of the parties throws its support to one man, that is when tyranny suddenly springs up." He reviews the steps that led to the tyranny of Appius. "The people and nobles of Rome agreed to create the Ten" and to give them "such great power" because of each party's "desire"—the people's desire to abolish the consuls, and the nobility's desire to annul the tribunes. This "agreement" allowed each class to cancel the magistracy that protected the rival class, thus undermining the balanced antagonism that maintained Rome's liberty. The people initially supported Appius, believing he had taken their side and would persecute the nobility. To give power to someone so that he can injure those one fears or hates, Machiavelli affirms, is an error; and "if he is shrewd [savio], it always happens that he becomes tyrant of that city." Supported by the people, he will attack the nobility and "will not start oppressing the people until he has destroyed [spenta] the nobility, at which point the people will realize they have become enslaved and have no place of refuge." "This method"—playing the classes off against each other—"has been employed by all those who have founded tyrannies in republics" (*DL* 1.40.27–33). Machiavelli here reaffirms what he suggests throughout his account of the Decemvirate, namely, that tyranny in republics emerges from the choices—and errors—of the classes whose contentious co-existence determines the fate of republics.

Machiavelli does not ignore Appius' errors. If Appius had persisted in his initial tactic of befriending the people and beating back the nobles, "his tyranny would have been stronger and would not have collapsed so quickly. But he did exactly the opposite and could not have conducted himself more unwisely." Switching sides to hold on to tyrannical power, "he made himself an enemy to those who had given him the tyranny and could have preserved it for him"—namely the plebs—"and allied with those"—the nobles—"who had not helped him gain it and would not have been able to maintain it for him." Tyrants, at least those who emerge in republics, depend on the support of one or the other of the classes. No tyrant in a republic stands alone in his power. Appius "lost those who were his allies [amici] and tried to gain as allies those [the nobles] who could not be his allies." Whereas, like all tyrants, Appius could have preserved his power with the support of the people, this would not have been possible with the nobility, because "although nobles desire to tyrannize [tiranneggiare], the part of the nobility that finds itself excluded from the tyranny will always be hostile to the tyrant." To put it differently, because the nobles will always want to be, in effect, co-tyrants with the tyrant, or at least the privileged beneficiaries of his tyranny, he will never be able to win over the entire nobility "because of its overweening ambition and great greed [per l'ambizione grande e grande avarizia che è in lei]." He "cannot have such great wealth [tante ricchezze] nor so many offices [onori] to satisfy" all those who want to feed at the princely trough. Here again Machiavelli puts his finger on the craving for wealth as the core of noble ambition. Tyranny based on alliance with the nobility requires constant payoffs, direct or indirect, to those who already possess great wealth but desire still more. This is the same wealth nexus that connects the tyrant to the nobility in *Discourses* 1.16, where he adduces the desire to return to the profits enjoyed under the tyranny of the Tarquins as the motivation behind the betrayal of the republic by the sons of Brutus. Abandoning the people and cozying up to the nobility was Appius' "most glaring error." "Those tyrants who have the multitude [l'universale] as their friend and the nobles [grandi] as their enemy are more secure because their violence is sustained by greater force" than is that of tyrants "to whom the people are hostile and the nobility friendly." Enjoying the people's support, a tyrant can defend himself with forces available to him in the city, whereas one who lacks their support must look elsewhere for defense (*DL* 1.40.34–9).

Machiavelli increasingly focuses on the noble/elite class as the foundation of most tyrannies in republics. After reiterating, in *Discourses* 1.41, Appius' mistake in switching so suddenly "from having been a friend to the plebs to revealing himself as their enemy," he comments in the next chapter on how easily the young nobles Appius gathered around him—the "satelliti" as he calls them (*DL* 1.40.22)—were corrupted by monetary gain: "One sees, in the story of the Decemvirate, how easily men are corrupted," if "one considers how much the young men Appius chose" as his companions "began to be friendly [amica] to tyranny for a little profit [per uno poco di utilità] that came to them as a result." Those who write laws for republics and kingdoms, Machiavelli adds, should learn from this to "curb human desires [frenare gli appetiti umani] and deprive people of every hope of being able to go astray [errare] with impunity" (*DL* 1.42). In *Discourses* 3.3.2–4 Machiavelli reflects, again, on the necessity of "killing the sons of Brutus." Reiterating, with a nod back to 1.16, how necessary and beneficial the severity of (the first) Brutus was for Roman liberty, he offers the general rule that "after a revolution in government [mutazione di stato] from republic to tyranny or from tyranny to republic, some unforgettable action [una esecuzione memorabile] against the enemies of the new order is necessary. He who seizes a tyranny and does not kill Brutus, and he who institutes a free government and does not kill the sons of Brutus, will survive but a short time." The pairing of "republica" and "tirannide" as opposites is noteworthy. Here tyranny is a form of government (a mutilated form, to be sure), and not, or not only, the illegitimacy or cruelty of a prince. In *Discourses* 3.7.2 Machiavelli says "some may perhaps wonder why it happens that among the many changes of government [mutazioni] from a free to a tyrannical way of life [dalla vita libera alla tirannica], and vice versa, some occur with bloodshed and others without." Tyranny here is a species of "vita," a term

Machiavelli often uses to denote not only forms of government but also the socio-cultural norms underlying a polity and, in this sense, a "way of life."

If one wishes to "overthrow [alterare] a republic," says the title of *Discourses* 3.8, "one must assess its substance [suggetto]"—its people and their socio-political organization. Reminding the reader that "a wicked citizen cannot," as he wrote in *Discourses* 1.34, "do harm [male operare] to a republic that is not corrupt," Machiavelli now provides examples of two Romans who tried to "male operare" when the republic was as yet uncorrupted. The first is Spurius Cassius (consul in 485 BCE), who was "ambitious" and "eager to seize unlawful power [pigliare autorità istraordinaria]." Briefly summarizing Livy's account (2.41) of the episode, Machiavelli says Spurius sought to curry favor with the plebs by offering them half the lands seized from the Hernici. When the Senate stopped him, he announced a plan to give the plebs the proceeds from the sale of imported grain. The plebs rebuffed both offers, and Machiavelli comments that "if the plebs had been corrupt, they would not have refused" and "would have opened to [Spurius] the road to tyranny that [instead] they closed." Livy's account helps us understand why the episode struck Machiavelli as significant. Alluding to the reforms of the Gracchi centuries later, Livy calls Spurius' proposal for land redistribution the first "lex agraria," adding that "since then, the issue has never been raised without causing the greatest upheavals." Spurius also intended to distribute state property ("publicum") that he accused private citizens of possessing illegally ("possideri a privatis criminabatur"). Many senators who held such land were "terrified" by this threat to their interests. But their opposition to Spurius' plan was also motivated, Livy writes, by a "concern for the state [publica . . . sollicitudo]" and by their fear that his generosity to the plebs was giving him power that would be "dangerous to liberty." His fellow consul sided with the senators and predicted that Spurius' "largesse would be destructive, that those receiving the lands would be trapped in servitude, and that the road to kingship was being prepared [regno viam fieri]." In Livy's narrative the threat to the republic and the danger of a return to monarchy stem from the conflict between plebs and patricians over land and wealth. He acknowledges that the plebs had an "inborn mistrust of monarchy [suspicionem insitam regni]" that motivated them to reject Spurius' offer. But it is the patricians, according to Livy, who more insistently resisted his plan to redistribute land to the plebs, fearing that he was accumulating power detrimental both to liberty and to their interests. Curiously, Machiavelli omits to mention the patricians' motive of protecting their wealth and focuses instead on the people's rejection of Spurius' enticements and their suspicion that "he seemed intent on paying them the price of their liberty" or, put more simply, buying it. Machiavelli credits the uncorrupted plebs with preventing tyranny by refusing the consul's proferred gifts (*DL* 3.8.3–4).

The second example in *Discourses* 3.8 is Manlius Capitolinus, the patrician credited with saving the Capitol in 390 BCE from the invasion of the Gauls.

Machiavelli had discussed Manlius' sins against the republic in *Discourses* 1.8, where he emphasizes the rapidity with which the Senate appointed a dictator to investigate, judge, and punish his malicious accusation that private citizens were usurping state property. In that chapter Machiavelli's focus was on the need for institutional means by which republics can suppress "pernicious" calumnies and castigate slanderers. In *Discourses* 3.8 he presents Manlius as a "much greater example" of the danger represented by Spurius Cassius. Manlius' story reveals how a "dreadful lust for rule [brutta cupidità di regnare]" cancels even great "virtú d'animo e di corpo" and many "buone opere" of benefit to the patria. Manlius' envy of the honors bestowed on Camillus so "blinded his judgment" that, losing sight of the city's "modo del vivere" (its love of liberty and republican institutions), and not taking into account the "suggetto"—the people and political culture of Rome—which was "not suitable to receiving a perverse form [trista forma]," i.e. a monarchical government, he set about stirring up disturbances against the senate and the laws. Without repeating the events summarized in *Discourses* 1.8, Machiavelli comments that in this case "one sees the perfection of that city and the goodness of its people [materia], because none of the nobles, although they were fierce defenders of each other, made any move to defend him, and none of his relatives did anything to support him." Even the tribunes took the side of the nobles to "suppress a common danger [peste]." The plebs, Machiavelli adds, usually sought their own advantage and loved everything done against the nobility; however, when the tribunes indicted Manlius and remitted his case to the people, even the plebs, "having become judges where once they were defenders," unhesitatingly condemned him to death. "I think there is no better example in [Livy's] *History* with which to demonstrate the goodness of all the republic's ordini than the fact that no one in the city made any effort to defend" Manlius, despite his abundance of virtú and many laudable past deeds. Everyone, Machiavelli says, gave greater consideration to the dangers posed by his present actions than to his past merits (*DL* 3.8.5–11).

Machiavelli concludes that, "if Manlius had lived in the age of Marius and Sulla, when the people [materia] had become corrupt and he could have stamped the shape [imprimere la forma] of his ambition on them, he would have achieved the same results as Marius and Sulla and the others who later aspired to tyranny." And if Sulla and Marius had lived in Manlius' age, they, like him, would have been stopped early on. Again Machiavelli emphasizes that corruption and, therefore, tyranny are not the work of one man. "One man can indeed begin to corrupt the people of a city with his wicked methods and ways, but it is impossible that a single lifetime would suffice to corrupt it so much that he himself could thereby derive benefit." Therefore, "to seize power in a republic and introduce a perverse form," one must find its "materia disordinata"—corrupted—"and brought, little by little from generation to generation" to "disordine." This will happen, Machiavelli says, echoing *Discourses* 3.1, "unless [the republic] is frequently revitalized by good examples or returned to its beginnings with new laws" (*DL* 3.8.14–18). Machiavelli assumes his readers no longer need to be reminded that the corruption that makes tyranny possible is the private power of the wealthy and ambitious who weaken or even destroy the ordini. Citizens seeking to promote either liberty or tyranny must, therefore, take into account the "suggetto"—the nature of a city's people and institutions. What links ancient Rome and the Florence Machiavelli knew is the dilemma that all republics face: the relentless desire of elite classes to privatize power, exercise it on their own terms, establish their hegemony over the people, and make the state "their thing" instead of the "public thing." Machiavelli's last word on Manlius is that, if he had been born in a corrupt city, he would have been "uno uomo raro e memorabile" (*DL* 3.8.19–20). This is a curious characterization, and it merits a moment's reflection. Because Machiavelli has already told us that, if Manlius had lived in a corrupt city, he would have done things comparable to the damaging deeds of Sulla and Marius and the others who aspired to tyranny, these adjectives obviously do not convey favorable judgment. Their appearance here sheds light on Machiavelli's characterization of Cosimo de' Medici as a "uomo raro" in *Histories* 7.6 and, as we are about to see, on his use of the same two adjectives in the chapter on Genoa near the end of the *Florentine Histories*.

"A TRULY SINGULAR PHENOMENON: LIBERTY AND TYRANNY, CIVIC AND CORRUPT LIFE, JUSTICE AND LICENSE WITHIN THE SAME CIRCUIT OF WALLS"

The tyranny of wealthy elites appears yet again, in chapter 29 of book 8 of the *Florentine Histories* in a remarkable discussion of Genoa and its association of communal creditors known as the Banco di San Giorgio.[6] During Florence's border conflicts with Genoa, the town of Sarzana was occupied by Agostino Fregoso of the powerful Genoese family. The Florentines, says Machiavelli, thinking it shameful that a "privato gentile uomo" had snatched Sarzana from them, prepared a military operation to recover it. Unable to meet this attack with his own "private forze," Fregoso "gave [Sarzana] to San Giorgio." Machiavelli interrupts the narrative to introduce San Giorgio and its role in Genoese politics. The commune of Genoa, he explains, had borrowed large sums from its citizens to finance the "very important war" against Venice "many years ago" (the War of Chioggia in 1378–81). Because "the republic" (the Genoese commune) was unable to repay these loans, it conceded to its creditors the receipts of the "dogana" (customs duties) together with the government building where communal officials had overseen the

[6] On this chapter, see Carlo Taviani, "Machiavelli e la fortuna del Banco di San Giorgio," in *Niccolò Machiavelli*, ed. Gabriele Pedullà, *L'illuminista* (2017): 391–424.

collection and disbursement of these receipts. The creditors created "amongst themselves a form of governance [uno modo di governo]," Machiavelli says, calling it the Banco di San Giorgio, with a council of one hundred members that deliberated policy and an executive committee of eight that implemented the council's decisions. Subsequently, the commune, in need of more funds, turned again to San Giorgio, "which, being wealthy and well administered," provided the needed loans. As a pledge, or lien ("per pegno"), for the loans, the commune now gave the creditors' association entire cities and towns within the Genoese dominion—in effect, a piece-by-piece dismantling of Genoa's communal government and territorial sovereignty, ceded, indeed surrendered, to an association of its wealthiest citizens. It was, we might say, the ultimate privatization, the surrender of public finance *and* territory to private creditors. The commune's need for cash and San Giorgio's ability to provide it resulted in the transfer, Machiavelli claims, of "the majority of the cities and towns" in Genoa's territory to San Giorgio, which "administered and defended them and every year sent its own elected officials" to manage them—"without the commune being involved in any way" (*IF* 8.29.1–8). (It matters little to Machiavelli's explanation of the functions of San Giorgio that it was actually much older than he implies.)

The political consequence of this handover of governmental functions and powers from the commune to San Giorgio was, Machiavelli says, "that the citizens withdrew their affection [amore] for the commune" as a "cosa tiranneggiata"[7] and transferred it to San Giorgio, which they regarded as "an equitably and well administered *parte*" (which usually means faction in Machiavelli's lexicon and is used here presumably to indicate San Giorgio's private character). This sentence presents several puzzles. First, which citizens withdrew their "affection" from the commune? The non-noble citizens, because they saw it "tyrannized" by the powerful and wealthy creditors of San Giorgio? Possibly, because, a few sentences further on, Machiavelli says the "majority of citizens stand aside and leave the government [stato] of the commune as prey to the victors [in preda al vincitore]" in the struggles for control among the leading families. Or is it the elite/noble class that withdrew its devotion to the commune and transferred it to their own San Giorgio? Second, who was "tyrannizing" the commune? The wealthy families of San Giorgio who sought control over it? Or the Milanese and the French who frequently imposed external rule? The weakening of the devotion of citizens (whether noble or non-noble) to the commune, Machiavelli says, is the cause of "the easy and frequent overthrows of government [mutazioni dello stato]" and the reason why the Genoese sometimes "obey one of their own citizens and

[7] Machiavelli does not say the commune was "tyrannical," as some translations have it: *Florentine Histories*, tr. Laura F. Banfield and Harvey C. Mansfield (Princeton: Princeton University Press, 1988), p. 352; *Machiavelli: The Chief Works and Others*, tr. Allan Gilbert, 3 vols. (Durham, N.C.: Duke University Press, 1965), vol. 3, p. 1423. He says the commune was "tyrannized."

sometimes a foreigner, for it is the commune that changes governments [varia governo], not San Giorgio." Hence, Machiavelli says, "when the Fregoso and Adorno families fight for dominance [principato] in the commune," the non-noble "majority" of citizens are indifferent to contests over the increasingly irrelevant "stato of the commune." And "when one [faction or family]" has taken the "stato," San Giorgio does nothing more than make it take an oath to observe its own laws"—the laws of San Giorgio—"which, up to the present, have not been modified." San Giorgio has "arms, finances, and an administrative structure [governo]," and any attempt to change its laws, Machiavelli predicts, would court "the risk of a dangerous rebellion" (*IF* 8.29.9–11). Machiavelli does not say whether the rebellion would come from the wealthy creditors, who had made their lucrative and expanding parallel government possible, or from non-noble citizens, who, seeing their commune "tyrannized," might take advantage of any weakening of San Giorgio to rebel.

"Tyranny" reappears in the chapter's enigmatic and variously interpreted conclusion. Characterizing San Giorgio as a "truly exceptional instance [Esemplo veramente raro], never previously identified by philosophers among the many republics they have theorized and seen," Machiavelli defines its uniqueness in the simultaneous presence, "within the same circuit of walls and among the same citizens, of liberty and tyranny, civic and corrupt life, justice and license, because"—and this next phrase is especially puzzling—"this arrangement [ordine] alone keeps the city full of traditional and venerable customs" (*IF* 8.29.12). Do the opposing terms in each pair both refer to San Giorgio, or does one term refer to the unstable, faction-ridden commune and the other to the powerful Banco? Machiavelli certainly did not have a high opinion of Genoa's communal government, and he quite possibly associated it with the three negative conditions of tyranny, corruption, and license. He characterizes the commune as "tyrannized," and the subversion of Genoese "ordini" by the nobles (see below) was grounds for associating the commune with "corruption" and "license." But did he see "libertà," "vita civile," and "giustizia" in San Giorgio? Its exclusionary character alone would seem to foreclose any such reading. Only if one assumes that Machiavelli admired as an exemplary model of constitutional government a private association of wealthy creditors who appropriated the finances of the republic to serve their own interests and, in so doing, destroyed the institutions and territorial integrity of their republic is it possible to entertain the notion that he associated San Giorgio with "libertà," "vita civile," and "giustizia." But such an interpretation contradicts everything he wrote about wealth and power, civic life and corruption, nobles and popolo. Is it possible that, for Machiavelli, San Giorgio itself exhibited all six conditions, good and bad? In this hypothesis he might have seen San Giorgio ensuring liberty for its own members, while exercising financial tyranny over the commune; adhering to its own internal republican ("civile") constitution with its council and executive magistracy, while corroding the institutions and civic loyalties of the commune; and rendering justice with the payment of interest due to its creditors/members on shares of the debt, while leaving the commune bereft of resources and in a condition of license, or anarchy, that made it easy prey for powerful foreign states.

The chapter concludes with still another curious assertion. "And if it should happen—as, with time, it must—that San Giorgio swallows up [occupasse] the entire city, it would be a republic more *memorabile* than the Venetian [republic]" (*IF* 8.29.12). Could Machiavelli have viewed with favor the eventual disappearance of the weak and unstable Genoese commune and its replacement by the well-managed Banco di San Giorgio? It is true that San Giorgio changed but little, while the commune—the republic—wavered and weakened in the midst of factional struggles and often fell under the control of Milan or France. But there are obvious problems with this interpretation. First, Machiavelli did not admire the Venetian republic. Second, the prospect of the Genoese republic becoming more "memorabile" than Venice's republic by its complete absorption into San Giorgio raises the question of what he means by "memorabile," and here we may recall Machiavelli saying (*DL* 3.8.19) that Manlius Capitolinus would have been a "uomo raro e memorabile" if he had lived in a corrupt city and become a destructive tyrant. If Genoa, swallowed whole by San Giorgio, were judged similarly "memorabile," the word must have negative as well as positive connotations. However successful Genoa's elite was in accumulating and protecting wealth, the Genoese republic is the most glaring instance in fifteenth-century Italy of a failed state. Interpreted in the light of Machiavelli's concerns about why republics fail, the "exceptionality" ("esemplo veramente raro") of San Giorgio is that it carried to the extreme the destructive effects of private power and wealth. Like most republican tyrants, San Giorgio neutered constitutional government. As an association of wealthy creditors on whom the commune depended for loans, San Giorgio served and protected the interests of its members. It took control, first, of the commune's fiscal apparatus, thus guaranteeing the payment of interest, and then of much of the Genoese territorial dominion as collateral for loans to the commune. In appropriating communal revenues and arrogating to itself the jurisdiction and management of territories nominally under the dominion of the Genoese republic, San Giorgio rendered Genoa's communal government largely irrelevant, a dubious prize hardly worth fighting for. When he asserts that the citizens transferred allegiance from the commune to San Giorgio because of its efficient administration, he does not say whether they reflected on the fact that San Giorgio served the interests of a small group of wealthy families. Machiavelli probably knew that over time the great majority of shares in the Banco accumulated ever more steadily in the hands of wealthy merchants and nobles.[8]

[8] Steven A. Epstein, *Genoa and the Genoese, 958–1528* (Chapel Hill: University of North Carolina Press, 1996), pp. 260–1, 277–81; on this point, p. 280.

Earlier in the *Histories* (5.6), Machiavelli had already pointed to the damage Genoa's wealthy elite inflicted on the republic, asserting that the city's numerous "noble families are so powerful that they are loath to respect the authority of the [communal] magistrates." Two of the most powerful families, the Fregoso and the Adorno, he says, create the city's "divisions" and cause its "republican institutions [ordini civili] to be broken [si guastono]." These families battle for supremacy "with arms, not with laws [civilmente], and, consequently, it always happens that one family is in command and the other tormented. Sometimes, those out of power and deprived of political offices have recourse to foreign arms and subject the patria they cannot govern to the rule of foreigners" (*IF* 5.6.3–4). In Machiavelli's persistent critique of the malfeasance of Italy's noble/elite classes these are the central articles of indictment: privatization of power, factional division and violence, subversion of the ordini, and recourse to foreign arms to defeat domestic rivals. The families that contended for power in these ways, with such deleterious consequences for the Genoese republic, were those that created, and profited from, the Banco di San Giorgio, which Machiavelli sees as a continuation by other means of the dismantling of the republic and its ordini that originated in the struggles for domination among the same leading families.

Placed strategically near the end of the *Florentine Histories* and a few chapters before the hints of Lorenzo de' Medici's manipulation of Florentine public finances, the chapter on Genoa and San Giorgio serves as a validation of Machiavelli's insight that tyranny in republics is imposed by wealthy elites, with or without a prince/tyrant. In the introductory chapter of book 4, theorizing class tyranny he asserts that cities not "bene ordinate"—lacking sturdy and resilient ordini—are incapable of liberty and are therefore reduced to the alternatives of "servitú" inflicted by the "nobili" and "licenzia" fostered by the "popolari." Equating servitú under the "nobili" with tyranny, he says that "republics lacking strong ordini can only vary between tyrannical regimes [stato tirannico] and licentious regimes" (*IF* 4.1.1–4). The tyranny of the Genoese financial elite that created San Giorgio and destroyed the Genoese republic serves as the culminating example—and caveat—of the corruption to which the ambition, arrogance, and avarice of the "noble" classes subjected Italy.

Index

For the benefit of digital users, indexed terms that span two pages (e.g., 52–53) may, on occasion, appear on only one of those pages.